THE CONCEPTION OF

STRATEGIC
BOMBING

GUERNICA
CHONGQING
HIROSHIMA

TETSUO MAEDA
Translated by Akiko Takemoto

BIKOH

THE CONCEPTION OF
STRATEGIC BOMBING

—GUERNICA · CHONGQING · HIROSHIMA

THE CONCEPTION OF STRATEGIC BOMBING
—GUERNICA·CHONGQING·HIROSHIMA
Tetsuo Maeda
Translated by Akiko Takemoto

All the photographs in this book come from the original book, 戦略爆撃の思想 (*The Conception of Strategic Bombing*) by Tetsuo Maeda, first published in 2006 by Gaifu-sha Company in Tokyo, Japan, excepting the two photographs on P.508 from 二つの祖国の狭間に生きる (*I Live In Between the Two Lands of My Ancestors*) authored by Akiko Hasegawa, published in 2012 by Dojidai-sha Company in Tokyo, Japan.

This Edition Published by BIKOH Publishing, Takamatsu, Kagawa, Japan.

Printed in Japan, 2016

First Edition: December 2015
ISBN978-4-86387-068-0

THE CONCEPTION OF STRATEGIC BOMBING
—GUERNICA CHONGQING HIROSHIMA
戦略爆撃の思想—ゲルニカ、重慶、広島【英文版】

ISBN 978-4-86387-068-0
2015年12月20日　初版第1刷
2016年 6月11日　初版第2刷

著　者：前田　哲男
翻訳者：武本　明子
発行所：株式会社　美巧社
　　　　〒760-0063 香川県高松市多賀町1-8-10
　　　　〈電話〉087-833-5811

CONTENTS

—— THE INTRODUCTION ——
THE WAR PERFORMED WITHOUT GIVING ANY VISUAL CHECK

—— CHAPTER I ——
WHAT HAD LED TO THE AIR RAIDS UPON CHONGQING (1931-37)

The Birth of the Anti-Japanese Capital

How the Strategic Bombardment Came into Being

—— Chapter II ——
The Indiscriminate Bombings Started (1939)

—— CHAPTER Ⅲ ——
NO.101 OPERATIONS (1940)
—THE STRATEGIC & POLITICAL
BOMBINGS WERE PUT INTO PRACTICE—

The Japanese Navy Air Corps

The Unfolding of No.101 Operations

A Nightmare of the U.S. Gunboat *Panay's* Case

America's Warning to Japan

── CHAPTER IV ──
THE WAY TO PEARL HARBOR (1941)

—— CHAPTER V ——
ZHOU ENLAI & HIS COMRADES UNDER THE AIR RAIDS

——— Chapter VI———
From Chongqing to Hiroshima

Then There Came the Atomic Bombing upon Hiroshima

—— THE FINAL CHAPTER ——
THE MASSACRES FROM THE AIR STILL GO ON

THE ANNOTATIONS

INTRODUCTION

THE WAR PERFORMED WITHOUT GIVING ANY VISUAL CHECK

● **Goya Lucientes & Guo Moruo**

In a series of copperplate prints created by Goya (1746-1829), entitled *Desastres de la Guerre* (*Disasters of the War*), we see a series of scenes of carnages performed by Napoleon's Army that had invaded Spain, as if it were a catalogue of cruelties and miseries: The soldiers who were about to be shot or gashed or hanged to death; those people behind the front lines, having been deprived of their possessions and raped only to remain helplessly standing in starvation. To each of these eighty-two works of his, Goya gave a pithy epigraph, such as:

> *A Sad Foreboding of Something to Come*
> > *(Tristes presentimientos de lo que ha de acontecer)*
> *When Reason Falls Asleep, Monster will Appear*
> > *(El sueno de la razon produce monstruos)*
> *Then, like Beasts* (*Y son fieras*)
> *Get them Buried, and Make them Hold their Tongue!*
> > *(Enterrar y callar!)*
> *What for?* (*Por que?*)

His monumental oil painting entitled *On May 3, 1808* (*El tres de mayo de 1808 en Madrid*) is also famous as a masterpiece he created on the basis of what he had actually seen that day: On the hill of Principe Pio in Madrid, Goya—having caught sight of that frozen expression of a guerrilla standing in

1

May 3, 1808 by Francisco Goya

front of a French firing squad about to shoot him to death the next moment—
put it on his canvas, thus to give an eternal life to the *Desastres de la Guerre*.

In producing this work, which is regarded as one of the best war-paintings
in the world, Goya went out to see with his own eyes what sort of cruelties
were being committed by the French Army. His old servant Isidoro's testimony,
which still remains, goes as follows:

That morning, my master, on seeing *that*, got as furious as if he had gone
mad, and he thought of putting that horrible scene into his painting. In his right
hand, he held a gun; in his left hand an old-fashioned musket. And from this
window, he was watching that volley of fire given on that hill. (omission)

"Master, what makes you produce a painting of such a cruel scene?" I asked
him. Then he answered:

"I'd like to enjoy the pleasure of leaving my eternal message to human
beings: "Stop such a barbarity as this!"

—From Goya authored by Shikiba Ryuzaburo (A Japanese
psychiatrist: 1898-1965)

The city of Chongqing being attacked by the Japanese bombers (1939)

The same kind of impulse that had driven Goya into that action on that occasion was to bring us another masterpiece that also denounces war— *Guernica*—by Picaso (1881-1973), another Spanish artist. And then, more than a century later than Goya's days—but on the same date of "May 3" by a strange coincidence—a Chinese poet, Guo Moruo (1892-1978), was to witness the ravages of war and expressed his emotion in a traditional style of Chinese poetry. He created it in 1939. Almost two years had passed since the Sino-Japanese War broke out. The scene took place at Chongqing in Sichuan Province, China. And those who had acted that barbarity were the Japanese Navy Air Corps. His poem—*The Sight of the Miseries Makes me Groan*—goes as follows:

On May 3 and 4,
The enemy planes came again,
Intending to devastate Chongqing,
Causing the dead to be piled up like mountains.
Among them I saw a mother and her two children:

One lying under her abdomen, the other in her bosom.
Their bones and flesh had turned into coke, but
They remained inseparably stuck together.
Ah, the mother's love for her children can
Never be turned into ashes forever!

As Goya did, Guo Moruo also went out to see the terrible scenes in the town of Chongqing where the embers were still smoldering. In his irresistible anger, those scenes of carnage were being carved into his memory. In the introductory note for this poem he wrote about a week later (May 12) under the title of *The Sight of the Miseries Makes me Groan*, he wrote: "The dead are piled up like mountains; their flesh and bones have been scorched into ashes." (*Chaoxi-ji* or *Collection of Tides*)

Japan—where Guo Moruo spent many years, firstly as a student, then as a resident—had now turned into his enemy country. But, even though he was a poet of remarkable intuition, he would not have been able to imagine how those scenes in Chongqing would be turned into something to befall to many cities in Japan, too, five or six years later, as if by a boomerang effect.

But when we look back later, the scene Guo Moruo had depicted in his poem that day was to turn out merely the result of "the first volley of fire" brought about by the Japanese Army and Navy Air Corps. Because their indiscriminate bombings upon Chongqing or the then *Capital for Fighting Against Japan*—especially aiming at its citizens there in order to "conquer their fighting spirit"—were to last as long as more than three years since then. The victims of "5 · 3 & 5 · 4 air raids" alone numbered as many as 4,091, something unprecedented in history so far. But at that point, those living in Chongqing had not known that they would have to spend three more summers—hot and humid as if in a steam bath—in the caves as their air-raid shelters. Neither Guo Moruo nor the citizens of Chongqing could simply perceive their fate to suffer those atrocities brought about by the world's first strategic bombardment.

● **The Missing Link in the Evolution of War**

As for the aerial bombardments upon Chongqing, which had been planned and performed by Japan's powerful aviation capability, their full-length pictures have not yet been made clear, excepting for partial or fragmental accounts or recollections, even though many decades have passed since then. So it is usually impossible to find the name of "Chongqing" in the history of indiscriminate bombings. The reason for that would be explained: because Japan had failed to conquer, submit and occupy that city as the seat for the China's National United Front Against Japan,—and because Japan was defeated in World War II —the Japanese military were practically unable to tell what had become of what they themselves called "strategic and political bombardment."

On the other hand, if seen from the Chinese side, it can be guessed that: even though both the military and general public in Chongqing were heroic in fighting and going through many trials, considering that Chongqing was a wartime capital of Jiang Jieshi—"White District" against "Red District" ruled by the Communist Party—and that they were soon to engage in the civil war— applying a positive light upon "Chongqing for their admirable resistance against Japan" would not have been an attractive theme especially from the period immediately after the Revolution through the age of the Great Cultural Revolution. Anyway, all that had happened in Chongqing during those years of air raids and their evaluation still remain largely blank in the history of the war. But, if seen from the point of the 20th century's war history, this aerial tactics that lasted for more than three years will be found to have kept in it an especially grave significance in the thesis of "the evolution of war." It was to develop into *Hiroshima* and finally into "the terrors from the sky" as performed by ICBM (intercontinental ballistic missile) or more frequently by MRBM (medium range ballistic missile). I shall not be exaggerating the fact even if I assert that: one of the "missing links" in the history of the development of wars lies in what Chongqing witnessed in those days.

● **The Plan of the First Strategic Bombardment in the History of Wars**
Firstly, Japan's bombardment upon Chongqing was the first of the intentional, systematic and continual air raids performed under the formal name of "the strategic & political bombing." This occurred about a year later than the bombing upon Guernica by the German Air Force, but unlike their one-day attack upon their target, Japan's bombardment upon Chongqing lasted for three years, recording 218 attacks upon the same target. According to the total computed by the Chinese side, the number of those who were killed directly by the air raids alone amounts to 11,885. According to the latest study by the

Investigation Committee in the Chongqing Administration, 36,202 (the dead and injured within the urban area alone) is considered fundamentally reliable. Even before the German Air Force launched the attacks named "Adler-Tag (Hawk-Day)" against the British Isles and started "the Battle of Britain (the air battles over the British Isles and air raids upon London)," Chongqing had already experienced two "summers of air raids," and it was reported by the Japanese airmen that its urban area had already been "made flat." "The 5・3 and 5・4 Air Raids" upon Chongqing had been performed fifteen months earlier than the air raid upon Berlin by the British Air Force. In other words, Chongqing was to be remembered in the world history as the first city that had suffered the greatest number of strategic bombings for the longest period of time.

In that sense, "the air raids upon Chongqing" became a precedent for an indiscriminate bombardment upon a city prior to the air raid upon Tokyo, and even though no nuclear warhead had been employed, as long as its conception was concerned, it was unmistakably a manifestation of the aggressive will that had brought about "a *Hiroshima* before Hiroshima."

When we think about the reality in which "the conception of strategic bombing" that came into being during the World War II was to move into nuclear strategy, making Hiroshima and Nagasaki a turning point, before it jumped from aerial attack to "an attack by way of the space" by ballistic missiles, thus weighing heavily upon the earth and human beings, the process of "Guernica → Chongqing → Hiroshima" can be said to have formed the original pattern of what might be called an extermination war that leads to the extinction of humanity.

In addition to that, if we turn our eyes to another stream that started also from Chongqing—"from incendiary bombs to napalm bombs"—we shall be able to witness another bloody flow of flame attacks—from the air raid on Tokyo to the Korean War, the Vietnam War and the Persian Gulf War・the Iraq War. This is not unrelated to "the negative legacy of Chongqing," either.

● The War Lacking in a Visual Check

Secondly, the tactics of indiscriminate regional bombings adopted by those Japanese bombers in attacking Chongqing had immediately changed our ways of concerning ourselves in warfare. This change occurred not only in such aspects as massive deaths inevitably caused by indiscriminate bombings and "the vanishing of boundary between battle lines and home front" but also in somewhere much deeper to change the relationship between the war and humanity.

That was a war which had totally lacked a visual check. Not even a single person in Chongqing had ever witnessed Japanese airmen about to deprive him of his life. This was always so throughout the period of that warfare. From the first air raid performed as if tentatively upon the airport in Chongqing on February 18, 1938—by the seven middle-sized attack planes that had taken off at the air base of Nanjing—to the last one in August, 1943, not a single combatant presented himself on the ground of Chongqing. Simply bombing from high above was the only way for the Japanese airmen to have something to do with the citizens of Chongqing.

In the painting by Goya—*On May 3 in 1808*—the guns held by the executioners were so close as to touch the chest of the man about to be shot. In the copperplate prints of the *Disasters of the War*, the distance between the killers and the ones about to be killed was even closer, making their relationship even more intense. Their gazes being entangled, the killers would never be able to forget the victims' expressions at their last moment.

On the other hand, *On May 3* in Chongqing, not a single figure of their murderers could be seen. Only the buzzing and the sight of the airplanes high in the sky were approaching, followed by the sounds of falling bombs slashing the air and their explosions on the ground to make all the hells break loose all over the city.... There was neither physical crash nor eye contact that revealed their relationship; that was a world of massacre unilateral and mechanized. The people were simply killed without having any opportunity to witness what those invaders looked like.

As for those in the air, they were even more deprived of their awareness of what they were doing—a homicide. Neither faces distorted in pain nor voices for seeking for help nor smell of burnt flesh were known to those flying high above. That was a warfare that totally prevented the combatants from employing their sense perception; that was a world of massacre, where there was a tremendous gap between one's action and the result it brought about. The world seen through the bombsight—that was expected to bring about a new technique in the wars to be performed in the years to come. One year and a half before, at Nanjing, which was also in the basin of the Yangzi, the

Japanese Army had committed the barbarities that could be called "the cruelest massacre performed during the agricultural period in the world history"; now at Chongqing, the Japanese Air Corps took the initiative in the tactics of what might be called "a slaughter in the industrial period" in the world history. By and by, the same kind of nightmares was to befall to the residents of the major cities in Japan, such as Tokyo, Osaka, Nagoya and so on.

What accompanies the attacks from the air—the airmen's having never seen the scenes and having never had the sense of having done something—easily deprives them of the opportunity for undergoing something like religious conversion. Those soldiers engaged in the holocausts in Nanjing around December in 1937—even those who happened to remain free from any sense of guilt—must be burdened with "*the scenes*" left in their eyes or "*the touch*" left in their palms, from which they will never be able to escape as long as they live.

On the other hand, what was left to the pilots who had been engaged in the bombings on Chongqing would be only "a touch left in their palm" in operating the device for dropping the bombs and a visual impression of the burst of flames caused by the bombings. Just like the pilots of the B29s who had been engaged in the air raids on the cities of Japan and Colonel Paul Tibbets who had dropped the atomic bomb on Hiroshima, the Japanese pilots who had brought about the massive deaths in Chongqing also remained estranged from what their actions had brought about. For that very reason, what happened in Chongqing has not been recounted in the same way as what the holocaust at Nanjing meant has been asked about. Among the former Japanese soldiers, some did visit Nanjing and confess what crimes they had committed there, but none of the former Japanese pilots have ever done anything like that. No Japanese, therefore, are qualified to laugh at Colonel Tibbets who "has never got converted," even after the war was over, consistently asserting their righteousness in having dropped the atomic bomb.

● "Another Pearl Harbor"

Thirdly, the Japanese Air Corps' having bombed upon Chongqing—though it has undoubtedly played a great part for the Chinese people to form their feeling toward Japan—has also exerted a serious effect on the Americans' view of Japan. That *not only* became a primary factor for bringing about a catastrophe in the history of the U.S.-Japan relationship at that time *but also* still drags something like a shadow of "the roots of unfair Japan," which is still referred to every time an opportunity arises.

Such journalists as Edgar Snow, Agnes Smedley and others, who, staying in bomb-bound Chongqing, kept sending a large number of reports to American readers. Not only *Time* but also *Life*—a photographic magazine which had just started—had sent to Chongqing their special correspondents, such as Theodore White and John Harshey, along with cameramen, including Carl Mydans, to keep publishing their reports and photographs from Chongqing.

White, who happened to be at that very scene of "the 5·3 and 5·4 air raids," said later: "Talking of the Japanese, I still bristle with anger," and wrote in *In Search of History:*

> What was important about this carnage was their purpose of terror. Nanking and Shanghai had already been bombed; Those, however, were military bombings. There was no military target within the old walls of Chungking. Yet the Japanese had chosen, deliberately, to burn it to the ground, and all the people within it, to break some spirit they could not understand, to break the resistance of the government that had taken refuge somewhere in Chungking's suburbs. I never thereafter felt any guilt when we came to bomb the Japanese, (omission) The senseless terror bombings upon Chungking had a result immediate and fundamental in my thinking on politics.
>
> *Nanking = Nanjing *Chungking = Chongqing (their snellings are not uniform)

In Search of History was a memoir written in 1978. The author White, who had led an active life as a journalist for as long as half a century until his death in May, 1986, wrote his last essay, *The Crisis from Japan*—for *New York Times Magazine* (issued on July 28, 1985)—while emphasizing the melody of "unfair Japan" by fitting Japan in the 1930s on top of Japan as a major economic power at that time. What was crossing his mind then would have been the images of Chungking being drowned in the fires and the black shadows of the Japanese planes flying proudly above the inferno they had created.

The following was the gist of what White told at the TV interview he received just before his death, and that was televised by NHK (Japan

Broadcasting Corporation) on April 26, 1986, as a special program under the title of *An Admonition from America**:

> I still hate those Japanese who were engaged in the war. So the Japanese now may have no need to take my statement so seriously or so straightforwardly. But the Japanese in those days had given us attacks when we had *not* given any attack on them. And, they were cruel in treating their captives and the Chinese people. So....
>
> But if I bring these things now, after such a long time has passed, the Japanese may say I should forget all these things. Certainly it might be better for the people now to have forgotten them all.
>
> But I still think it better to have the Japanese know that: *some* people have still kept in their mind what the Japanese were doing *then* and *there*.

The bombardments upon Chongqing have still retained such significance and influence as might be called "another *Pearl Habor*" in the history of Japan-U.S. relationship, as if they were aftereffects of residual radiation. That would have been handed down also to the successive U.S. Administrations that would not admit "the crime they have committed at Hiroshima."

● **In the Capital Thrown into the Swirl of Conspiracies**
                                   of the Nationalist-Communist Collaboration

In Chongqing suffering from the air raids, there were various individuals and groups of people. The unoccupied area of Sichuan Province—which was turned into the seat of the headquarters of the National United Front Against Japan or "the Great Rear Area"—was what was called "the White Area" and an emergency capital, where conspiracies and terrorism were flourishing, while being ruled by Jiang Jieshi and the four families (the Jiangs, the Songs, the Kongs and the Chens) standing against "the Red Area" in Yan-an ruled by Mao Zedong. An unusually large number of people—including those from the diplomatic establishments to the universities and museums from all over the mainland China, and even those first-class restaurants from Beijing (Peking) and from Shanghai—were also coming up to Chongqing along the Yangzi together with their public articles and personal possessions.

Zhou Enlai, who was later to be the Prime Minister of the State Council of the New China, had also been sent there by the Communist Party as the representative of *"Balujun* (the Eighth Route Army) Control Office," to stay with Jiang Jieshi. The citizens of Chongqing listened to Zhou Enlai at the ruins of the war fire when he talked to them, analyzing the international state of affairs. (Chapter III)

Guo Moruo completed *Qu Yuan*, a drama on a patriotic poet-statesman, Qu Yuan (ca.343BC—ca.277BC), and presented it on the stage there for the first time. Thus "the Art Festival in the Foggy Season"—when no bombers came over because of the thick fog covering them all—became a cherished event for the citizens of Chongqing. (Chapter V)

Chongqing, featuring such specific backgrounds and conditions in those days, had been found unusually attractive to the Japanese bombers.

Chongqing under the Air Raid, Painted by Chen Kezhi

CHAPTER I

WHAT HAD LED TO THE AIR RAIDS UPON CHONGQING (1931-37)

The Birth of the Anti-Japanese Capital

● **Another Long March**

"Let's go to Chongqing, to our Great Rear Base!"

The year 1938 was coming to an end. The Chinese people had been in the second winter since the full-scaled Sino-Japanese War broke out on July 7, in 1937, with the sounds of gunfire at Lukouqiao in Beijing, and the Chinese people's intention to keep fighting against Japan seemed to be charged into this slogan.

Shanghai and Nanjing had already passed into the possession of the enemy, and even within the walls of Beijing Castle City, Japanese soldiers could be seen. The sovereignty over most of the major cities along the eastern coasts of the Chinese Continent having already been deprived of by the enemy, all they could do then if they were to keep fighting was to retreat along the Yangzi River to the hinterland.

Now going up the Yangzi, avoiding the air attacks from the enemy, the endless flow of people and articles on board a variety of boats of all sizes were leaving the three abandoned anti-Japanese bases—Wuhan, Hankou and Hanyang—to reach Chongqing as the new anti-Japanese capital now under construction. Those who had chosen to take an overland route were also making a long march, looking like as many ants, along the ancient precarious paths around the lofty peaks that overlooked Sichuan Basin.

They were all heading for Sichuan Province, which had long been known as the Land of Shu admired as "the Nature's Treasure-House," which used to be governed by Liu Bei (161-223) and Zhuge Kongming (181-234). That had also been known for its "difficulty" in approaching, as the poet Li Po (701-762) had once groaned in his poem:

> Ah, how dangerous! How high!
> Following the path to Shu is
> Harder than rising to the azure!

But the people, who were not going to give up their protest against the enemy, were heading for Chongqing as their next strong foothold, while loudly singing a protest song against Japan.

That was also an epical, heroic attempt, which could be called another Long March. During this period—from the fall of Wuhan to the foundation of their new base at Chongqing—it is estimated that nearly ten million people moved from the coastal areas to the southwestern or northwestern districts of China, driven by the wartime fires or burning with the anti-Japanese passion. The seven millions of them entered Sichuan Province, and those who settled in or around Chongqing as the second largest city in the Province reached more than one million. This caused this ancient city on the mountain, which used to be the capital under various names such as "Ba" during the Chunqiu (Spring & Autumn) period (403BC-221BC), "Badu (Ba Capital)" during the Qin period (221BC-206BC), "Yuzhou" from Sui period to Tang period (581-618 / 618-907) and the name of "Chongqing"—meaning "repeated congratulations"—had started at the opening of the Song period (in 960). But now, that ancient city which had long been known as a commercially prosperous city was to vanish unexpectedly because of its new obligation and situation that had suddenly been given to it. That was, it was expected to offer resistance to the Japanese military, while glaring over the whole land of China. This racial migration toward the Great Hinterland could be compared with "the Long March"—12,500km—performed by Mao Zedong's Red Army several years before. Even in the world history, there have never been so many cases in which so many men and women, political parties and business corporations, brought themselves together and moved under the same consciousness of saving their own country. Thus their battles of the National United Front against Japan were to be fought by making "those fatherly men of virtue"—who had moved to the Great Rear Base from Beijing, Tianjin, Shanghai, Guangzhou and many other cities and towns in the coastal area—an essence of China.

● **The Final Stronghold for That Great Retreating Strategy**

On the other hand, when seen from the standpoint of the passage of the war, this war had been strategically staged on and along the Yangzi, inviting the Japan's ground army farther and farther into the hinterland of China, thus gradually depriving them of their maneuverability and powers of concentration by the time they were induced into the final fortress. After Lukouqiao Incident* at Beijing (July 7, 1937), the Japanese Army failed in giving what they called "an attack of punishment" on North China and this led them to give up their "non-expansion policy" and mainly to move along the Yangzi, chasing the main force of Jiang Jieshi's Army that was simply running away. Japan had succeeded in sweeping the great seaside city of Shanghai (November, 1937) after the three months' fierce battles; then Japan made a triumphal entry into the then capital of China, Nanjing, 392km upstream from Shanghai (December, 1937), then after going farther upstream by way of Anqing and Jiujiang, they captured the three towns of Wuhan, Hankou and Hanyang (October, 1938) about 1,125km from Shanghai, as if they had been pulled up by the water belt of the Yangzi until they were gulped up by that greatest river in China. From that city of Wuhan the Japanese Army had taken by storm, the fog-bound capital of Chongqing on the mountain lay 1,370km beyond along the River, though 780km in a straight line.

Now at that city, a couple of anti-Japanese powers—the Nationalist Government led by Jiang Jieshi and Balujun (the Eighth Route Army) Control Office of the Chinese Communist Party led by Zhou Enlai—entrenched themselves and began to give commands to all over the country. So "the Battle on the Yangzi" was now brought as far upstream as 2,500km from Shanghai, and whether Chongqing would be captured or guarded to the very end had become the deviding line between victory and defeat.

For the Japanese Army that was good at an intensive surprise attack, Jiang Jieshi's way of carrying out the war—"to gain the time at the cost of the space"—appeared pointless and irritating, but for the Chinese side, too, it was something totally unexpected to make use of the Yangzi in such a retreating strategy. The traditional strategy for the national defense the Chinese had adopted so far was to retreat from north to south, because their enemy usually came from north, making bulwarks of the three large rivers running from west to east—as were known by their nicknames: Defensive River (the Yellow River), Defensive Huai (the Huai River) and Defensive Jiang (the Yangzi River). When they lost the first line of defense, the Emperor's Army retreated as far as the next river while trying to repulse their enemies, and this used to be called "*yi-quan nandu*" or "officials' moving southward." Enticing the invaders farther and farther south until they were exhausted to collapse by their ceaseless combat actions—this had been traditional strategy cleverly adopted by the successive generations of Chinese leaders, but the Japanese invaders now presented themselves not only in North China but also in Middle China and now they were coming up even along the Yangzi. All the main force of the Nationalist Army could do then was to adopt "*yi-quan xi-jin*" or "officials' moving westward"—something the Chinese had never experienced before.

The Japanese Army moved up along the basin of the Yangzi, while the Chinese sailed up along the same river farther and farther. After the battles of attack and defense at Nanjin and at Wuhan, "the transference of the capital to Chongqing" was put into practice, and it was after the middle of 1938 that a fixed state of things came to be seen in their positions. The Japanese Army stopped marching onward after having advanced as far as Wuhan. They had no longer had any stratagem for moving onward. They might manage to emerge as far as Xuanchang in Hubei Province, situated 270km west of Wuhan, but it seemed totally impossible for their regular army to cover the whole distance by crossing the rugged mountains, which were connected by "the plank roads of Shu (Sichuan)." This meant that: the Army's strategy had come to an end at Xuanchang. On the other hand, the Japanese Navy had also been well aware of their limitation: the canyon area beyond Xuangchang—known as "the Three Gorges of the Long River (Chang Jiang or Yangzi)"—where the river flows down in a frenzied manner—was simply the last place for the regular navy to try their ability. The Navy, which had also built their base at Wuhan, now glared toward Chongqing. The greatest reason why the two cities—Wuhan and Chongqing, connected by the Yangzi and separated by Tapa-shan Mountains— were soon made inseparable in the Japanese military's performance of terrors from the sky (strategic bombing), had exclusively come from such geographical circumstances as these.

● The Dragon's Head or the Peninsula Lying between the Yangzi and
the Jialing

The shape of Chongqing seen on the map may allow us to imagine a dinosaur drinking water by extending its neck toward the lake. Because the pointed head of that peninsula washed by a couple of large rivers leads us to associate a dinosaur's nape on such an occasion. In fact, this neighborhood of Sichuan Basin is known to the world as one of the places where a large number of dinosaurs' fossils have been unearthed, and several dinosaurs have been restored, as we see them at the Municipal Museum of Chongqing. Seen from the angle of place-names, we are easily able to find several names as have apparently been associated with such huge dragons as *Long-men-hao* (Dragon-gate lake), *Hua-long-qiao* (Dragon-turned bridge), *Bau-long-men* (Viewing-Dragon gate), *Long-qiao-zhen* (Dragon-bridge town) and so on. Throughout the Chinese territory, 499 place names are said to have "*long*" (dragon) in them and more than forty rivers include "long" in their names, and Chongqing and its neighborhood are unmistakably among the greatest ones in such statistics.

The urban area of Chongqing has developed itself, looking like the dragon's head thickly covered with its scales. Actually, the whole of that peninsula consists of a huge, rocky mountain, whose highest ridge is 370m with the average height of 240m. Those who look up at that high cliff on board the ship sailing up the Yangzi cannot help receiving a strong impression from that rocky mountain standing immovably against the reddish flows gashing at the confluence of the Yangzi and the Jialing. It is quite understandable why that city has been endearingly nicknamed "Mountain Castle, Chongqing" by those traveling by boat. To those who had finally arrived there after a long voyage, the sight of that city on top of the mountain was none other than that of *Shangri-la* they had long been anxious to visit.

In 1892, Isabella Byrd, a professional woman traveler, visited here and wrote in her book, *THE YANGTZE VALLEY AND BEYOND:* "Chongqing situated at 1,050 feet above sea level is quite an impressive city whether one may approach it from upstream or from downstream. It is really surprising that: this greatest commercial center in western China—one of the most prominent commercial cities in the Great Empire of Qing (1644-1911)—is situated 1,500 miles away

The Castle Walls & Gate Tower of Chongqing
(from *Unbeaten Tracks in China* by Isabella Byrd)

from the sea."

The landing place is called *Chaotian-men* (the Gate to the Imperial Castle), and that was none other than the gate to that ancient castle. Leaving the ship, one found oneself at the foot of a long flight of stone steps that seem to lead to the heaven, and it was only after one climbed to the top of it that one finally found oneself on a street of that city. Those stone steps that connect *Chaotian-men* and the urban area of Chongqing were what might be called a symbol of Chongqing and they were often referred to by those from abroad during the period when the Chinese were engaged in the National United Front Against Japan. One of the witnesses of Japan's strategic bombings upon Chongqing, Han Suyin, a writer, counted the number of the stone steps and found it was 478. Joseph Needham, an English historian on science, who had arrived there as a scientist-adviser to the British ambassador, found it 480 steps. Lieutenant General Albert Wedemeyer who had visited there as the Commander of the U.S. Army toward the end of the War found it was 366 steps. For those who disliked giving their legs so much toil, a palanquin was available. At present it is replaced by the cable car and the escalator.

The history of this mountain castle dates back to 314 B.C., when Zhang Yi (?—309B.C.) built a castle upon this peninsula on the rivers in obedience to King Hui of Qin. At that time, that mountain castle was called Ba Du (the Metropolis of Ba); During the Sui and the Tang eras (581-618 & 618-907), it was called Yuzhou; then at the start of the Song era (960), it began to be called Chongqing-*fu*, as it is still called so by letting it retain its former status of the capital with the suffix of "-*fu*." Situated at the important position for water transport, controlling the route to Wuhan and to Shanghai, it had kept remaining a leading city in the southwestern inland area throughout the long history. Especially from November, 1937 to April, 1946—for more than eight years— it had accepted the capital of Nationalist China, thus to perform the important role as the headquarters of the National United Front Against Japan. In fact, no other period in history had ever seen her so active and spirited as that period. Even though the stench of the dead was hanging in the air, the people had kept their will to stay alive all right. Even though they had been thrown into the worst degree of destruction, they finally kept bearing it. The Japanese military opened up "the new route for their bombers" and tried to conquer their fighting spirit by dropping the incendiary bombs upon the city below, but those who relied on the natural fortress and water transport that had remained dependable since the age of Zhang Yi (a strategist during the Warring States period: 770BC—221BC), finally succeeded in enduring the hardship. The dragons healed their wounds for themselves, and in the end, crashed those invaders with their sturdy tails of resistance empowered by their "Land of Natural Resources" or Sichuan Province. For those who happened to be in Chongqing to see that day when China got victorious over Japan, Chongqing—重慶 meaning "Piled-up Congratulations"—was literally the place of overflowing joy, having finally got released from the cruel era of invasion and colonialism.

But looking back on those days in 1938 when Wuhan fell and Chongqing in the hinterland began to be called "Anti-Japanese Capital," attracting the attention from all over the country, the citizens of Chongqing were simply unable to tell what was going to happen to them and no preparations for warfare had been made. The ancient castle town on the mountain was firstly disturbed by a large number of military personnel and officialdom from other parts of China, and then was turned up by the enemy's air raids. But since both North

China and Shanghai from which the war had started seemed virtually foreign lands to those living in that southwestern highland whose climate is almost that of a subtropical zone, what sort of miseries were going to befall to them was something they could not even imagine. Chongqing at the early stage of the Sino-Japanese War could be compared to a creature sleeping like a log, even though its flank was being kicked out.

Around Shizhong Ward or the former central area of that castle city—only 9.3 square kilometers—Chongqing then (in 1936) had a population of 339,204 living in 74,398 houses. All the streets in that ward, running along the contour lines of the rugged mountains, were far from straight, and they were all connected with a variety of winding lanes or side streets. On both sides of the mountain ridge whose average height above sea level is 240m, one could see numberless houses of great variety from the mountaintop to the riversides. And everyone had to move around by means of stone steps whose numbers were varied—from dozens to three hundred. So the life there might be said to be regulated by the curve, the undulation and the overpopulation. For the travelers crossing Sichuan Basin from Chengdu, their eyes, according to the sense of perspective, had got accustomed to seeing the vast expanse of the landscape, but on entering Chongqing, they had to give their eyes a vertical motion, to their pleasant surprise. A German journalist, Collin Ross, who had visited Chongqing in 1939 when it was suffering from the air raids, described that city, as follows:

> Rome is built on the seven hills. Chongqing is built on seven times as many hills as Rome is. Or on many more hills? In the new section of the city—outside the castle walls—each of the houses appears as if built on a different hill. My friend Gunther's house is only several hundred meters away from the (German) Representative Office. But if we walk there, we have to walk much longer, because we have to walk up and down again and again.

Beside that central ward or Shizhong Ward on the peninsula, Chongqing-*fu* or the metropolice at that time consisted of two more wards—Nangan (South Shore) Ward and Jiangbei (North Side of the River) Ward. Nangan Ward was to the south of the Yangzi which, at the flooded season, became about one kilometer wide; Jiangbei Ward was on the northern shore of the Jialing which is a little less wide than the Yangzi. Both Nan-an Ward and Jiangbei Ward had several ports for ferries, and the crowded boats used to cross the river, adeptly avoiding the cargo boats or junks sailing up or down the Yangzi or the Jialing. Upon the Yangzi, one could see a gunboat *Tutuila* with the Stars and Stripes raised above it in order to protect the U.S.' rights and interests, but most of the citizens had never imagined that their daily life peacefully going on on that peninsula between the Rivers might be disturbed by the rain of bombs and the huge columns of water that rose on the Rivers. But even to such a provincial city as this, the Sino-Japanese War was relentlessly coming rushing; and Jiang Jieshi began to call that city "the capital to offer resistance to Japan," even though that must have sounded to be the greatest challenge to the Japanese military. As the wartime fire moved from Shanghai to Nanjing, and then to Wuhan, the ancient townscape and the atmosphere of Chongqing were rapidly changing.

● **The Japanese Settlement was Abandoned**

The first that had gone out of sight from that old city of Chongqing was naturally the Japanese people and the Japanese concession. The Japanese settlement was closed three weeks after the outbreak of the Sino-Japanese War—on August 1, 1937—and the twenty-nine Japanese residents left Chongqing under the escort of the gunboat *Hira*. Along with Shashi—a city also on the shore of the Yangzi—Chongqing was the first where the Japanese concession was discarded.

It was when Japan won the Sino-Japanese War (1894-5)* that Japan started its concession here. Under the Treaty of Shimonoseki (1895), Chongqing-*fu* in Sichuan Province, along with such cities as Shashi in Hubei Province and Suzhou in Jiangsu Province, was expected to "open the city and its port so that Japanese nationals might live and engage in commercial, industrial and manufacturing activities there." The same treaty had also mentioned Japan's right to "sail along the Yangzi, including the route between Xuanchang in Fubei Province and Chongqing in Sichuan Province." This was how Chongqing and Japan came in contact with each other. The air route between "Xuanchang in Hubei Province to Chongqing in Situan Province" was later made the regular route for the zero fighters of the Japanese Navy, as is mentioned later, but toward the end of the 19th century, none had naturally been able to look ahead into such a matter in the future.

In February, 1896, Chinda Sutemi, Consul-General at Shanghai (who was later to be the Ambassador to the United States, and then a Privy Councilor and concurrently the Grand Chamberlain), visited Chongqing to notify the city authority of Japan's wish to have its concession there. The bureaucracy of the Qing Dynasty (1616-1912) gave a variety of reasons for postponing that matter but in vain, and in May the Japanese consulate at Chongqing was opened with Kato Yoshizo as the first consul. In 1901, "the treaty of the concession exclusively for Japanese merchants in Chongqing" was signed by the fourth consulate, Yamasaki Katsura. At the beginning of that treaty, it was promised that "Wangjiatuo on the south shore outside Chaotian-men Gate of Chongqing-*fu* shall be the site for the Japanese concession." No other nation but Japan had ever had a concession in Chongqing, and it was decided that "the right for the police" and "the right for the administration of the roads" and all the rights for the administrative management within the concession should "be placed under the jurisdiction of the Japanese Consulate." The branch office for the consulate and the meeting place for the Navy were brought into being. Thus Japan made itself the only nation to have her leased ground in Situan Province.

Thus the Japanese concession was established at Wangjiatuo—143,080 *tsubo* (ca.47,2km squares)—to be opened to the Japanese engaged in commerce. Ten corporations, including Osaka Kisen, Nisshin Kisen (steamship companies), Osaka Yoko Company, Dairi Yōkō Campany and Yulin Match Company, came to edge into a new field, and it was not long before they came to take pride in the second largest trading area that ranked next to the U.K.'s. Dairi Yoko was a company for washing the pigs' bristles and making their sizes uniform; Yulin Match Company managed to stay among the six local match companies and sold their products at Guizhou. At a spinning mill, most of whose stocks and techniques in production control were dependent on the Japanese enterprise, four hundreds of boys and girls had been working until it was closed because of the outbreak of anti-Japanese campaign. According to *Chongqing Kaibu-shi* (*A History on the Opening of Chongqing as Port Town*) authored by Wei Yingtao and Zhou Yong (published in 1983, by Chongqing Publishing Co.), "The Imperialist Japan was the first to open its concession in Shichuan Province, and it brought about another Japan at Wangjiatuo in Chongqing, so that they could exercise their absolute authority there."

It is not hard to imagine how greatly shocked the Japanese in Chongqing were to hear of the outbreak of the Sino-Japanese War.* Unlike those in such a large concession as in Shanghai or in Tianjin, they could not expect any protection given by the Japanese military. So their apprehension was serious. The Japanese government in Tokyo had assigned the gunboat *Hira*, which had been honored with the shining "Imperial Chrysanthemum Crest", to the task of guarding the people over there, but it was impossible for such a small warship whose displacement was only 305 tons to protect that settlement, and apparently all they could do then was to pull out of Chongqing.

In July, 1937, when the Lukowkiao Incident* broke out, there were twenty-nine Japanese in Chongqing, including the Consul Kasuya. Immediately after the outbreak of that incident, the local newspapers' tone of anti-Japanese argument began to be intensified, and anyone could perceive the changes of the Chinese feelings toward Japan. A week later—on July 14—His Majesty's portrait at the Consulate was moved into the gunboat *Hira* just in case. That was the first step to their evacuation. As of July 25, a telegram had been sent—"We are feeling slightly uneasy"—by the captain of *Hira*, Cmdr. Doi Shinji, to the chief of the Bureau of Military Affairs in the Naval Department, On July 28, the center of the Ministry of Foreign Affairs sent Consul Kasuya an official instruction that: the Japanese residents should leave there before it was too late, and this led the consul to give them instructions that: they should take their possessions on board the Giyo, the company ship of *Nisshin* Steamship Company. Since that day, the local people's feeling toward Japan had rapidly been growing worse. Some set off firecrackers to celebrate the Chinese Army's victory over the Japanese Army; the shopkeepers were prohibited to sell things made by the Japanese under the declaration that those who violated this rule would severely be punished, thus to turn the atmosphere of the town into confusion. No longer could any Chinese people be seen in the factories in the Japanese concession.

Under such situations as these, early on the morning of August 1, the Japanese who had been in Chongqing left the Japanese concession in the Giyo that had been anchored at the Jialing and sailed down to Hankou by way of Xuanchang, while being guarded by the Hira. That was a runaway voyage made against the stream of the Japanese Army that came marching on and on. Talking only of the situation in which they were running away to a safe distance, they resembled the Chinese who were soon to rush into Chongqing from their hometown that had been burnt and occupied by the Japanese Army, but those Japanese settlers had been forsaken by the future, too. So all they could do then was to hurry away as fugitives who would never be allowed to come back. Those factory buildings and houses they had left behind were soon withdrawn by the Nationalist Government of China, and in one or two years they were to be nullified by the bombs dropped by the Japanese planes.

Thus Chongqing, where no Japanese were seen, gradually began to be equipped with the function and the atmosphere as the wartime capital. In October, 1938, when Wuhan fell and Chongqing as "the Great Rear Area" became the seat for the hope held by the whole of China, more and more people and things kept flowing into it, and it was to be known all over the world—not as "Ba Prefecture in the Land of Shu"—but as "the Capital of Free China."

● **The Glory and the Misery of "Jiang Jieshi's Capital"**

If we were to describe Chongqing then as the new capital of China, no other would be more appropriate than "Jiang Jieshi's capital." Both of the Chinese Nationalist Party and the Nationalist Government had actually been embodied by Jiang Jieshi himself. If one were to take a glance at the powerful position he had been occupying at that time, one would easily be able to understand that strong trinity of "the Capital, the Government and the private person." The list of the titles of his positions, including the temporary ones, went as follows:

The President of the Chinese Nationalist Party, the Chairman of the Party's Executive Committee, the Chairman of the Supreme Committee of National Security, the Chairman of Military Affairs Committee, the Commander-in-Chief of the Army & the Navy, the Chairman of the Nationalist Government, the Chairman of the Executive Council, the Chairman of the Conference for the National Mobilization, the Leader of the Youth Association of the Three Principles of the People—Nationalism, Democracy and Livelihood—the Chairman of Sichuan Province and the Chairman of the Office of the Union of the Four Major Banks (the Organization to Control the Four National Banks) ....

From the head of the Party, the armed forces and the administration to the president of the youth association of the Three Principles of the People (a Chinese version of Hitler-Jugend) and even to the president of the China's Boy Scouts—all the powers had been in the hands of Jiang Jieshi. From among so many titles of his positions, his official status was usually expressed as "Chairman" or "Generalissimo." (This was officially so, but among the Communists in their private gatherings, he was satirically called "the supreme" or something like that.

It was in October, 1938, after the fall of Wuhan, that Jiang Jieshi entered Chongqing for the first time. Since then, for more than eight years, Jiang had reigned over the incomparably powerful trinity until he transferred the capital from Chongqing to Nanjing once again, while the state of things after Japan had surrendered was inevitably moving toward the civil war. His determined, untiring encouragement given to the fighting soldiers did lead him into both the limelight as an international leader of the Anti-Fascist Union and the glory as the victor of the National United Front Against Japan, but at the same time, he was to be dismissed eternally from the seat of the founder of the United China, because of the terrorism, the corruption and what had been accumulated by the administration kept within his own family while flourishing their powers in Chongqing. The fruit of the victory over Japan was to be something unattainable to Jiang, because he lost the Chinese Civil War that was to break out soon after "the Chongqing Negotiation" (October in 1945) was broken off. Looking upon it from a historical bird's eye view, Chongqing under the rule of Jiang Jieshi was a melting pot of glory and misery, and what had heated that giant melting pot of the anti-Japanese war and the revolutionary war was incendiary bombs dropped by the Japanese bombers. In Chongqing as the provisional city offering resistance to Japan, both glory and misery had been clearly illuminated with the bright red shadings brought about by those indiscriminate bombardments.

● **Transferring the Capital from Nanjing to Chongqing to Make it a Base for the National United Front Against Japan**

As for the idea of a protracted war by making Chongqing a base for the National United Front Against Japan, it seemed to have been formed in Jiang Jieshi's mind from the early stage of the National United Front Against Japan. That can be judged to have been his basic plan on the resistance to Japan as well as the core of his political strategy and the open battle strategy even before May, 1938, when Mao Zedong gave a series of lectures entitled "On a Protracted War" at a study meeting of the resistance to Japan. Both of them had seen through the progress of the anti-Japanese war from the same viewpoint.

Mao Zedong, in that series of lectures, raised a question why the National United Front Against Japan would be protracted, and pointed out: "The Sino-Japanese War is none other than a life-and-death war fought between half-colonized, half-feudalistic China and Imperialist Japan in the thirties of the 20th century. This is where all the roots of the problem exist." Then he said, presenting the three stages of that protracted war, as follows:

> The first stage is for the enemy to give strategic advance upon us; for us to give strategic defense. The second stage is for the enemy to keep strategic maintenance; for us to prepare for the counterattack. The third stage is for our strategic counterattack against the enemy's strategic withdrawal. As to how these three stages would turn out, I cannot predict any concrete situations of these three stages, but seeing what is happening at present, I am able to point out something like the outline of what will become of this war. As to how the objective realities would turn out, it would be so abundant in twists and turns that no one would be able to produce any "book of fortune-telling" of the Sino-Japanese War. But, having drawn some outline of what would become of the war is something necessary for us to take a strategic leadership of the war…. Looking at it in this way, it is apparent that: the war will be prolonged with an inevitable result that it would come to assume the nature of cruelty. It is impossible for the enemy to annex the whole of China, but they might be able to occupy a large number of districts for a considerable period of time. We Chinese would not be able to drive them away so soon, so quickly, but most of the land would remain ours. In the end, the enemy will go down and we shall win the war, but until then, we must follow the path of sufferings.
>
> *—A Selection of Mao Zedong's Military Essays*

This was the outline of Mao Zedong's theory of the protracted war, and this was transferred by Zhou Enlai to Bai Chongxi, the Vice-Chief of the General Staff of the Nationalist Army, thus to be agreed upon by Jiang Jieshi himself.

But even though Jiang Jieshi had not produced any such work on war as Mao Zedong did, he had already taken the initiative in leading the actual fighting, while putting into practice what Mao Zedong had thought "necessary in performing a strategic guidance from the points of holding out, keeping defense and winning the victory." Through the entries in his diary, his words of admonition and his lectures, we are able to read how Jiang Jieshi came to make up that great strategy by turning Sichuan Province and Chongqing into a base of operations for the resistance to Japan.

On April 12, 1933, when the Japanese Military intending to invade China were pointing to Shanhaiguan, a strategic point of North China, Jiang Jieshi, who held a military readjustment conference at Nanchang, gave an admonitory speech, as follows:

All we should do now to deal with Japan is to give it a long, persistent resistance. If Japan broke our first line of defense, we shall recruit in the second and third line. Even if Japan breaks through our first position, we shall go on resisting at the second, and then at the third position.... Such a long-term resistance would turn out more and more advantageous to us, if only we do not give it up. If we are able to keep resisting for three years, four years or five years, we shall see totally a new development in the international situation, too, and there will surely be some new changes in the enemy's side, too.

—*Jiang Jieshi's Secret Memoir 9, the Manchurian Incident*

Also on March 4, 1935, before the Sino-Japanese War turned into a full-scaled one, Jiang Jieshi flew to Chongqing from Wuhan and gave an address, which included: "Sichuan Province is important not only as a place in performing the revolution, but also as the base upon which we, the Chinese people, will founded our nation." Considering that: at that time a full-scale war against Japan had already become hard to avoid, this speech might have been made, keeping that fact in his mind. In July in the same year, he gave a speech of the same purport in military terms:

"Against Japan, the Yangzi and southward and Beijing-Hankou line and westward shall be made the mainstay of China. Sichuan, Guizhou and Shanxi Provinces shall be the core, with Kan-Su District as the rear area."

The way Jiang Jieshi had adopted in dealing with this war was: to press the enemy force to engage in a long, all-out war; as for themselves, not to fall into a trap of "an intensive surprise attack" in short-term limited warfare. This could be confirmed in another article he published by using another person's name:

Suppose that Japan will make war with China for some reason or other. China's force of arms cannot be compared with Japan's and we are bound to make a great sacrifice, as we, the Chinese, admit. But this is also the point where Japan's difficulties lie..... In a war fought between the two nations, it is considered important to occupy the enemy's political center, but in the case of the war waged upon China, it is impossible for our enemy to seal the fate of us Chinese, even if they might occupy our capital. All that Japan could occupy would be a number of cities convenient for transportation along with some important harbors. It is simply impossible for them to occupy the whole of this great land of 45,000,000 square *ri.** It is true that if all the important cities and harbors were to be occupied by them, we shall certainly get stuck and be obliged to make a great sacrifice. But, Japan will still remain unable to send the presence of China to total extinction.
*ri = ca. 3.92km

—*Jiang Jieshi's Secret Memoir 10*

Here we see that Jiang Jieshi's "theory on a protracted war" was presented earlier than Mao Zedong's.

Also on October 6, he said in the address he made in Chengdu, the capital of Sichuan Province: "Sichuan Province is blessed with mild climate and fertile soil and it has excelled in the field of culture, too. So, as the leader of all the provinces in China, this province can present the most suitable base for the restoration of our race."

These lead us to judge that: even before the war broke out, Jiang Jieshi had kept Sichuan Province and Chongqing in his mind as "the base upon which the nation is founded," while planning to build a base there for fighting against Japan by letting its armed forces advance only to be checked *there*. True Jiang Jieshi did not write any full-scale thesis on this war, but his plan for strategic actions and instructions for fighting could be called a practical version of Mao Zedong's theory on position warfare. Jiang Jieshi, avoiding "the line from north to south" Japanese army had adopted, chose "the east-west line" so that he might "earn time by means of space."

In October, 1937, when the Japanese army's fast heading for Nanjing began to endanger the capital of the Nationalist Government of China, Jiang Jieshi summoned the Conference for the Supreme Council for the National Security (the predecessor of the Highest Council for the National Security) and gave an address entitled: "The National Government's Move to Chongqing and the Prospects of the Warfare," thus proposing the moving of the capital (on 29). On November 20, its transfer was formally declared. The declaration went as follows:

> (The enemy wants us to "come to terms with them at the gate of our castle,"*) but how could they know what we have in our mind? Since that day when we decided we should offer resistance to Japan, we have borne in mind that: this should be *the last door to death*, while thinking that: we have admitted no submission for the sake of our people's life, our people's personality, our international faith, and the world peace. For anyone with proper vigor, he will rather choose to die in honor than remain alive in dishonor. Now our Nationalist Government of China is going to move to Chongqing so that we may better adjust ourselves to the state of the war, and we may gain a wider-view in performing a larger-scaled long-term resistance to our enemy.
>
> *Traditionally, that has been considered the least honorable thing to do.

> —*A Study on the Chinese Nationalist Government* edited
> by the Association for the Study of Modern Chinese History

Still Jiang and his military and diplomatic organs, instead of going straight to Chongqing, moved to Wuhan situated half way between Nanjing and Chongqing and fought "the Battle to Guard the Great Wuhan," thus to demand more time and more bloodshed of the Japanese army; but as for the Nationalist Government organs, they had begun to move to Chongqing as soon as Nanjing fell. It was at this point those ceaseless parades of people started to move to "the Great Interior of Situan Province" from all parts of the Chinese Continent according to the slogan: "To Chongqing, to our Great Rear Base!"

Those eleven months—from their evacuation from Nanjing to their retreat to

Chongqing by way of "the Battle to Guard Wuhan"—were the maximum length of time available to equip that hinterland of Sichuan Province with the functions needed as *the Capital for Offering Resistance to Japan*. The Chinese having grappled with this project with an amazing concentration and perseverance, they, instead of having merely exiled themselves there, succeeded in that difficult task of removing their counteroffensive base.

Immediately after he extricated himself from Wuhan (on October 31), Jiang Jieshi gave his *Statement to All the People on his Abandonment of Wuhan:*

> Our enemy may have occupied Wuhan for a while, but that was only after they had spent eleven months while sacrificing as many as several hundreds of thousands of their soldiers. What is worse for our enemy, what they have obtained was nothing but scorched earth and an empty city. They have failed to achieve their important purpose of exterminating our main-force units by winning a short-term operation at Wuhan. From now on, we shall put up all-out resistance. The movement of our army, whether it is retreat or advance, will be free from being restricted. The leadership will remain with us. On the other hand, our enemy will not gain anything at all. Our enemy will be sinking deeper into the swamp only to encounter more difficulties until at last they go to ruin.
>
> —*Jiang Jieshi* authored by Dong Xianguang

This prediction made by Jiang Jieshi was to come exactly true, but China also had to experience purgatorial sufferings for years to come, with Chongqing placed under the disastrous conflagrations beyond description.

● **The Relocations of the Factories Turned out to be the Hardest Work to Do**

Among the institutions and commodities moved into Chongqing, nothing was harder than the relocation of factories. Above all, spinning mills and factories to produce machinery and arms were indispensable to the industrial base for keeping resistance to Japan, but since these were nonexistent in Sichuan Province seated on the agricultural area, all they could do was to bring them all from Shanghai, Nanjing and other industrially advanced areas in the Eastern Coasts or in the Riverside Areas. According to the rallying cries of "the Removal of Factories," spinning mills and textile factories were moved from Shanghai, Taiyuan and Jinan; from Nanjing, arms factories were moved into the suburbs of Chongqing. In August, 1938, when the Japanese Army was approaching Wuhan Castle, more than one hundred and seventy factories that had been moved to Wuhan for safety and about one hundred and fifty factories that had originally been there began to move westward as far as Sichuan Province by the Yangzi. During that half year, about 200,000 tons of machine parts and materials were carried out of Wuhan. It is estimated that the 60 percent of them entered Sichuan Province, and one-third of the whole is presumed to have been relocated to Chongqing and its outskirts.

It was extremely hard for them to disassemble all those heavy machines into parts to send them all on board the ships that sailed up the River. Those operations were done while avoiding the attacks from the enemy planes. Ahead of them, the famous Sanxia—the Three Gorges of Chang Jiang (the Yangzi) —were waiting for them, keeping "their fangs" bare. Along that canyon whose total length was 189km—which the poet Li Po (701-762) had once sailed down happily, as he wrote: "Monkeys on both shores are ceaselessly crying to please my ears, while my boat is lightly passing through the thickly-folded mountains"—those heavy loads were being carried up in the ships with their waterline unusually lowered. All these loads were collected at Xuanchang at the entrance to Sanxia as their transit port, from which cargoes were transshipped on to smaller ships. What was carried up here by more than two hundred ships were to be reloaded into eight hundred and fifty small ships—including wooden ones—before they sailed up the Three Gorges. It is recorded that 1,200 tons of those cargoes had been lost when the ships were gulped by the swift currents or broken by sunken rocks.

In the same year—1938—when the fight to guard the Great Wuhan was being fought with a watchword of "Wuhan shall be a Madrid of the East!" acting in union with the antifascist civil war being fought in Spain, at that immediate upstream of the Yangzi, this strategy of sending such a large amount of things of great variety had been going on against the Yangzi, whose powerfulness could be comparable with that of the Japanese forces. In fact, it was unprecedented even in the Chinese history that so many goods were carried up along the Yangzi in such a short period of time. So far the people of Chongqing used to call anything new carried up from Shunghai by way of the

Yangzi with the prefix of "Western"—Western oil, Western cloth, a Western lamp and so on—since many were from the Western world by way of Shanghai, but this time everything was simply puzzling to them, because it was a strange combination of the Chinese and the Western, and above all, it was beyond their imagination in every point. This was how "the only one comprehensive industrial area in the rear area" was brought into being in Chongqing and its neighborhood—to produce arms, steel, machines, ships, cotton and chemicals in that one and only industrial zone in the rear base, acting as "an industrial lifeline during the wartime." Liu Jingkun, the author of *Chongqing and its Eight-Year Resistance*, describes it as follows:

> Each of those factories was situated along the River within 20 to 25 kilometers away from the city of Chongqing—among the mountains or huge rocks so that they might hardly be found out. All those cotton mills at Yufeng and Yuhua, and Daxin Machine Manufacturing Plants, and iron works at Ziyu and Zishu were all brought into being after burying the valleys or by clearing the forests in the mountains. As for the arms factories constructed at Ciqikou, Xiangkousi and Tangjiatuo, we were especially so careful as to build their workshops in the tunnels—by constructing their production lines within them. The techniques were progressive ones (all those blueprints had already been purchased from Germany before the war started) and as long as we were staying there, we were kept safe without being exposed to any bombardment from the Japanese bombers. Those zones along the Chang Jiang (the Yangzi) were far from dark even at night and the machines were always roaring vigorously. There still remain some traces of what they used to be.

It was through this opportunity that the framework of what is now called "Da (Great) Chongqing," whose population is 31,300,000, was brought into being.

● **The Appearance of a Miniature of the Chinese Society**

Naturally, it was not only those parts of machines that were carried up by means of the Yangzi. The 20,000 boxes of cultural properties that had been kept in storage at the Palace Museum (*Gugong Bowuyuan*) in Beijing had been moved to Nanjing—after what the Japanese called "the Manchurian Incident"[*]

which started in 1931 later to develop into the Sino-Japanese War—according to the directions given by Jiang Jieshi, but because of the wartime fire coming after them, they were divided into three at Nanjing, and one of them was carried into Chongqing by way of Wuhan. Later it was to be hidden at a village in Leshan at the foot of Mt. Emei-shan.

Universities and colleges were also coming up to Chongqing. At that time when the Sino-Japanese War broke out (1937), there were 108 universities and colleges in China with students more than forty thousands, and fifty-two of those universities and colleges moved to those rear districts including Sichuan Province, and nineteen of them moved to Chongqing. Considering that Sichuan Province so far had had only two such institutions—Chongqing University and Sichuan Province Educational Institute—this was something really amazing. Besides non-specialist universities such as Zhongyang (Central) University (from Nanjing), Futong University (from Shanghai) and Jiaotong University (also from Shanghai), special course schools such as National Academy of Music (from Nanjing), National School for Special Courses of Arts (from Hangzhou), National Medical Academy in Jiangsu (from Zhenjiang)—Military Staff College and Military Engineering School also moved to Chongqing to start their series of lectures. Those universities and other educational institutes seated themselves mainly in Shaci District in the city and in Baisha-zhen town in the suburbs, and they began to be called "the two major cultural areas," even though the former was soon to suffer saturation bombings by the Japanese bombers. Nankai Middle School, where Zhou Enlai as a boy used to attend, had also moved from Tianjin. Zhou Enlai, who had been in Chongqing as the representative of Balujun (the Eighth Route Army), was pleased at his unexpected reunion with the principal, Zhang Baling; and he never failed to visit him to offer his words of congratulations on the anniversary of the foundation of that school as well as on Zhang Baling's birthday.

In the field of publishing newspapers and other publications, too, Chongqing must make herself the eyes and ears of the whole of China.

The leading newspapers based in Chongqing during this period of resistance to Japan were as many as ten morning papers and three evening papers, and their news agency was represented by Zhongyang Tongxun-she (Central Communication Company) placed under the control of the Nationalist Party, but the leading newspapers were all those new comers, such as *Dai Gong Bao* (the Great Official News) from Shanghai, *Zhongyang Ri Bao* (the Central Daily) from Nanjing and *Saodang Bao* (the Cleanup News) from Wuhan. Among them, there was *Xin Hua Ri Bao* (the New China Daily), which was the only daily paper the Chinese Communist Party published in the district of the Nationalist Party. This newspaper, which had been launched on January 11, 1938, at Wuhan, was moved up to Chongqing on October 25 in the same year to keep publishing it until it was forced to stop publishing by the Nationalist Government on February 28, 1947. By that time, they had kept publishing it for nine years, one month and eighteen days, mostly at Chongqing, till the final issue of No. 3,231. The one who led this newspaper *Xin Hua Ri Bao* was Zhou Enlai, whose official status in Chongqing was "the representative of Balujin (the Eighth Route Army)," though his secret status was "the secretary of the Central Southern Bureau of the Chinese Communist Party." Zhou Enlai, who in Yan-an had been occupying the seat of the Vice Chairman of the Political Bureau and also the seat of the Vice Chairman of the Revolution Military Committee—both under the Chairman Mao Zedong—is known for having often written a leading article as chief editor, severely criticizing Jiang Jieshi's Anti-Communist policy, and for having protested against Jiang Jieshi when the Communist paper was prohibited, as is mentioned later.

All these newspaper companies had their main office in Shizhong Ward or the city's central area within the walls that stood around what used to be the castle area, and many of them having had their factory burnt down by the first full-scale air raids on May 3 & 4, in 1939, they had to unite themselves in issuing a one-page paper for a while.

Beside these newspaper companies, several publishing companies, such as Shangwu-yiu-shu-guan (Commercial Business Book Store), Zhonghua-shuju (Great China Book Store), Shenghuo Shudian (Life Book Shop) had also moved their base to Chongqing so that they could continue their business there. All the paper they could obtain was inferior in quality, while the censorship under the Jiang Jieshi's administration was growing more and more oppressive, but the publishers remained high-spirited. Zou Taofen, who in Shanghai had been setting forth his argument for an anti-Japanese campaign to save their country, came to settle in Chongqing by way of Wuhan, and while publishing a weekly magazine *Quanmin Kangzhan* (The whole People's Resistance to Japan), he scaled up the network of his Shenghuo Shudian (Life Bookstore) all over China till their number became more than fifty, thus keeping standing at the front line of the progressive verbal activity, while fighting against the oppression of the Nationalist Party.

Thus in Chongqing, which had turned into the wartime capital, one could see a great variety of miniaturized Chinese societies, and the most interesting of them all were none other than the people themselves who had come up here all the way. What one could see here was not a monolithic group of people purified by the same ideology as was seen in Yan-an but the two groups of people—the Nationalist Party and the Communist Party—both supported by their sympathizers and the ordinary people that numbered several dozens of times larger than those political-minded. Unlike Yan-an, which had simply been linked directly with the days to come in the future, Chongqing had been going along with the actual international situations, thus daily breathing the air of the Anti-Japanese War and the Great World War. That was also the sphere where underhand designs and bargaining were exercising greater influence than the ideal and ideology. The new and the old, the left and the right, the poverty and the wealth, the Western and the Chinese, oppression and resistance, and many other elements were being mixed, struggling against or smashing into each other, thus bringing about peculiar aspects of human life.

A half-Chinese, Han Suyin, whose husband was a commissioned officer of the Nationalist Government of China, Edgar Snow, the author of *Red Star Over China*, which made Mao Zedong known to the world, and Theodore White and other special correspondents of *Time-Life Books*, and several others from abroad who had brought themselves close to the contemporary life of the Chinese being thrown into an unusual commotion in the modern history—wrote down the vivid pictures of what had been happening there by bringing themselves into that human dramaturgy. Through that journalism they had embodied, the calamities which had suddenly been brought down from the sky upon this city in the middle of the 20th century were written down—along with the struggles going on between the Nationalists and the Communists—to be turned into an indelible history.

● The Secret Duty for Zhou Enlai to Perform

Jiang Jieshi's arrival at Chongqing could be taken as a transfer of the capital under the rule of "the Song Dynasty" headed by Jiang and his wife Song

Meiling from the Song family. This meant that: a fashionable society, which could be comparable to the Imperial Court, was brought into being in that provincial city in Sichuan Province. It was by no means rare that the common people were driven from their houses, and a magnificent edifice for those nobles was newly built where the twenty houses used to stand. All the people could do when they lost their old house suddenly was to build a shanty—"with forty-five pieces of scrap lumber on the site as wide as four mahjong tables," and this was soon to become standard living quarters for the common people or refugees or displaced persons.

On the other hand, skilled cooks were indispensable in the fashionable society, and famous restaurants were also arriving from various parts of the continent, along with their customers of high-ranking officials or millionaires. "Quansheng-yuan" from Guangdong, "Qiuerguan" from Beijing, "Lugaosun" from Suzhou, "Sixiangcun" from Hubei and others opened their establishments in Chongqing and provided those from the class that was privileged to visit them with a variety of tastes.

There was a night life, too, activated by singers and string musicians in the new capital under the blackout. As is mentioned later, the writer Mao Dun described such an aspect of life in his novel *Fushi* (*Corrosion*) with disgust but in a lively style. That was another side of "the Song Dynasty" which was to lead Jiang Jieshi to downfall.

Another group of people who had entered Chongqing along with the Nationalist Party was represented by Zhou Enlai. His official status was the vice-director of the Department of Politics in the Military Committee or the Supreme Committee of the State Security (the director was Chen Cheng, a trusted retainer of Jiang Jieshi, who was later to be the Chief of the Executive Council and the Vice-President of Taiwan). Another of his official status was "the representative of the office of *Balujun* in Chongqing." In other words, he could be called a military official leading *Balujun* (the Eighth Route Army called so under the unit number of the Nationalist Army).

In other words, Zhou Enlai was officially placed "under Jiang Jieshi," but the most important duty he was expected to perform at Chongqing was "to be the representative of Yan-an or the center of the Chinese Communist Party" or "to be the Secretary of the Central Southern Bureau of the Chinese Communist Party," even though this must be kept strictly secret.

The Central Southern Bureau established in January, 1939, elected Zhou as Secretary and six others, including Dong Biwu and Ye Jianying, as members of the standing committee. Mrs. Zhou, Deng Yingchao, was the head of the women's party in the Southern Bureau. They all, depending on their public status that could be compared to their identification card—such as Dong Biwu and Deng Yingchao who were both members of the National Participation Assembly, and Ye Jianying as the head of the Control Office of the *Balujun* ("the Eighth Route Army")—were maneuvering the people in general under "the law of the restriction of performing the activities for different parties"— while endangering themselves as if walking upon the blade of a sword. They were also making efforts to impress on the consul officials from other countries and on the special correspondents from abroad that: the legitimate successors to the revolution performed by Sun Wen[*] were none other than themselves. That was such a dangerous task to perform as to fight for food with a lion in the same cage.

[*]Sun Wen (1866-1925): In the turning point of the Chinese history toward the end of the Qing Dynasty (1644-1911), he lived an active life, firstly as a student while traveling around the world, to establish himself as a physician and an active thinker to lead modern China under the banner of the *Three Principles of the People—Nationalism, Democracy and Livelihood.* He founded the Nationalist Party (1919) to make the first collaboration with the Communist Party (1924). He was and still is endearingly called the Father of the Nation.

—*Heibon-Sha's World Encyclopedia*

In the suburbs of Chongqing, there were such establishments known as "*Bai-Gongquan* (White Diplomatic Establishment), *Zhazi-dong* (Dregs Cave) and the like—the blood-curdling establishments for torturing and execution— keeping active, while the Special Service Agency run by Dai Li and the Chen brothers, Guofu and Lifu, who were being whispered as "fears of Chongqing," were keeping their watchful eyes upon Communists. This meant that Zhou was living in a situation where he might be caught by terrorists at any moment.

Zhou Enlai once told one of his comrades:

"Our comrade Liu, patience alone will lead us to our destination. In order to perform this revolution, we must persevere in everything: If our chagrin had caused our clenched teeth to crumble to pieces, we must swallow them down together with the blood. For the sake of our revolution, we must make ourselves concubines. If necessary, we must make ourselves prostitutes."

—*A Critical Biography of Zhou Enlai* by Sima Changfeng

As is known by this, the Communists' life in the capital under the rule of the Nationalist Party was of false obedience even though they were pretending to have compromised with their rival party. Zhou Enlai, a man of amazing coolness and self-control as well as unshakable confidence toward future, was to perform his duty as a diplomat at "Jiang Jieshi's Capital." At the same time, these were the days when their fatal rivalry reached its climax, since it started under the Representative Sun Wen in 1920s when China's first military academy—Huangbu Military Academy—was established with Jiang Jieshi and Zhou Enlai as "the Principal" and "the Chief of the Political Department" respectively. As for this, part of the Fifth Chapter is to be spared.

Among the institutions under the direct control of Zhou as the vice director of the Department of Politics, there was "the Third Agency of the Political Department" and the poet-historian, Guo Moruo, came to take office as the person in charge of it. Tian Han, a writer, too, came to take office as the person in charge of its advertising activities. There were some Japanese names left in the list of the Third Agency of the Political Department. They, like the married couple of Kaji Wataru and Ikeda Sachiko, were the members of "*the Union of the Japanese People Staying in China, Supporting the Anti-War Revolution.*" They belonged to the Department of the Propaganda for the Enemy, and wrote advertising handouts to distribute among the Japanese soldiers in the front line, which said: "Soldiers are human bullets; Decorations are given to generals; The people will starve; The millionaires will earn more." They presented an anti-war play, *The Three Brothers*, too, in "the Art Festivl during the Foggy Season," as will be mentioned later. There was a Japanese woman, Hasegawa Teru, known to the Chinese by her pen name of Luchuan Yingzi (Green-River Bright-one)—along with her Esperantist name of "Verdant May (Green May)"—was also living in Chongqing with her husband Liu Ren, thus to witness the indiscriminate bombings performed by those from her own country. Those

Japanese were also to make themselves the recorders and denouncers of those air raids performed by their compatriots.

It was also about this time when Theodore White came flying to Chongqing in a light-hearted manner, as he happened to find, while traveling around Hong Kong, there was a job he might engage in at the "Chinese Information Committee" of the Nationalist Government over there. The young man, twenty-three years old, who had learned the Chinese history at Harvard University and had received 1,200 dollars as a researcher from Yanjing Research Institute there, was then simply wondering which way he should take—return to Boston to follow an academic life or start following a path as a journalist. It was on April 10, 1939—three weeks before those terrible air raids. It was also about this time that Han Suyin, who was later to be a writer, was looking up at those soaring cliffs upon which Chongqing lay—while sailing up the king of the rivers, the Yangzi, together with her husband, a young commissioned officer in the Nationalist Army under Jiang Jieshi. To the capital under the reign of Jiang Jieshi, another trinity—a union of time and place and situation in the horror of the air raid—was about to steal upon it moment by moment, even though that cruel trial remained unknown to anyone there.

How the Strategic Bombing Came into Being

● The Bombshells have Gained the Wings

Before I give a chronicle of the indiscriminate bombings upon Chongqing performed by the Japanese Air Force for as long as three successive years, I should like to follow "the way to Chongqing" by reviewing the history of the aerial attacks. When on earth and in whose thoughts was this strategy of sending "a terror from the air" brought into being? Following the way to Chongqing does connect with the research on the origin of what is known as "strategic bombings."

As everyone knows, the modern method of attacking the enemy from the air started with the arrival of the 20th century when the cannonball got wings, or "the artillerymen were sent high up in the sky" by the appearance of the air craft, and "the cities became something to be looked down over from high above."

The news of the Wright brothers who had made a successful flight in 1903 was taken—irrelevant to the Brothers' aim and intention—as an appearance of a shockingly new weapon of war, thus inevitably bringing forth an effect of changing the men's views of war. This could be compared to Magellan's circumnavigation round the globe, which brought about a revolution on our geographic awareness of the world to open up the Age of Discovery. Likewise, in the field of warfare, the aircraft—irrelevant to the purpose and intention of the inventors—was taken as an appearance of a shockingly new weapon and caused to change our view of warfare. Since then until today, war and aircraft have kept themselves inseparably close together, training each other to grow stronger and fatter.

As early as 1914, when World War I broke out, the aircraft were adopted as part of the army's equipment soon to be made much of. At first, this newly-introduced weapon was made use of in reconnoitering the movement of the enemy force or in observing the range of guns or cannons, but it was not long before these new arms had become identified as "flying gunners" or "flying cavalrymen." Before long, a new type of "fighters" who had been trained to send bombs to somewhere as far as several hundreds kilometers away began to present themselves in the skies of the cities which had turned out to be "roofless fortresses." This led Winston Churchill (1874-1965), who had experienced several battles in the 19th century as a cavalryman, to write in a deplorable tone in his autobiography, *My Early Life:* "War, which used to be cruel and magnificent, has now become cruel and squalid. ....It is a shame that we should turn instead to chemists in spectacles and chauffeurs pulling levers of aeroplanes or machin guns." But he himself, as World War II broke out, turned out to be a fervent supporter of the air force until he came to take the side of promoting the indiscriminate bombing upon German cities, saying: "Our military aim is the people's fighting spirit." (Chapter 6) In the United Kingdom, as early as 1918, the Air Force had been made separate from and independent of the Army and the Navy, thus preparing for the new era to come. So it was only fifteen years from the first flight of the Wright Brothers to the birth of the U.K. Air Force.

The first sight of "the artillerymen on the wing" taking part in an action was seen in Europe during World War I. Each nation at war having been striving to be the foremost in improving the capacity of the plane and in finding a new usage of it, it was not long before they began to see bombs being dropped upon the cities. In the war history of Europe, we see many examples of a long-term siege of a city, thus to give it gradual pressure. But the new strategy that appeared during World War I could be called its three-dimensional development, or "a perpendicular & three-dimensional seize of a city." By employing the aircraft that bring the rainfall of bombs directly upon the inhabitants, it led to the arrival of a new era that enlarged the existing tactics and battlefields.

The airships and bombers of the German Air Force performed nineteen air raids on London and forty-four air raids on Paris throughout the period of war, inflicting 510 deaths and 1,540 wounds on the former and 255 deaths and 593 wounds on the latter. (*The History of the Development of the Aviation in the World* authored by Kuwana Takuo, published in Japan in 1943) On the other hand, the Allied Nations, mainly making somewhere in France a base, dispatched their bombers to the German industrial belts in such districts as Ruhr, Saar and Rhein-land, and the number of the missions they flew is said to have reached 614 times from 1915 to 18. (*The History of the Aerial War* authored by Suemori Yoshimitsu, published in 1943, in Japan) By the end of the War, the Royal Air Force had come to work on a design for a super-heavy bomber or a four-motor bomber whose bomb-carrying capacity had become as heavy as three tons.

Be that as it might, even if a portion of bombing upon cities might have been glimpsed, it still remained, strictly speaking, in a germinal stage and had not gone beyond something demonstrative. It had lacked a guarantee of its capacity and productivity, and above all, those aircraft had been sent out to the battlefield without any background of firm conception of its operation. As was rightly summarized in *The First World War* by B. H. Riddell-Hart, a British historian on military affairs, the air force at that time still remained "more in the expectation of performance than in any actual performance."

So, if the twenty years from the end of the First World War to the following World War were seen from the standpoint of the history of the airplanes, it would be called a period necessary for the experiments or for the trials and errors before they could reach the stage of even greater massacres, and at the same time it would also be called a period needed in hatching out the conception that would lead to the strategic bombing and making it stand alone.

Just as the theory of a total war was brought about—after the Napolenic War—by Jomini Antoine Henri (1779-1869: a French and (later) a Russian military researcher) and Clausewitz (Karl von. 1780-1831, a general of Prussia and a military researcher), in the world after the Treaty of Versailles (1919), there appeared several Clausewitzes advocating some new theories on the omnipotence of the air force, thus anticipating the arrival of the new era in which the aircraft would be made main forces.

● **A New Military Theory of Attacking the Private Citizens**

There were, indeed, some people who, like General Foch (1851-1929) in France, simply disregarded the plane, saying: "Certainly it makes a good sport, but to us in the army, it's simply worthless." Seen from the viewpoint of the strategic planners or the military administrators, most of their contemporaries still remained as conservative as Foch. This naturally led those proposers of the new theories built on the great function of the airplanes to be performed in the next war to remain contented with their standpoint as prophets who had to find it hard to keep staying at home, and not a few of them—like General Billy Mitchell—kept following the thorny path till he came to the end of his career. This is one of the reasons why the tone of those early theorists of strategic bombings sounded unusually outright even to a cruel extent:

"If we wish to exterminate birds, it's not enough to shoot the flying ones. Their eggs in the nests must be cleared, too." This was the assertion made by Giulio Douhet, an Italian major general. In *The Supremacy in the Air* authored by Douhet in 1921, he presented a new strategic theory: "the air force shall be the attackers; the ground army shall be defenders." According to him, the enemy force in the battlefield is nothing but a false aim; what they should regard as their true aims shall be the enemy's cities, industries, railroads and bridges. In his book mentioned above, he wrote:

The concept of fighters and non-fighters has gone out of date. Today, those engaged in war are not only the military but all the people in the countries concerned. All of the private citizens are fighters, thus all are exposed to the dangers of war.

Inevitably the enemy's attacks are directed toward them.

In order to win the victory, we must crush their foundations upon which both their physical life and spiritual life are dependent on; we must expose them to endless, dreadful changes here and there and everywhere, until their social organization is brought to the final collapse. In this kind of war, private citizens shall be made the objects for decisive blows, and since they are the least able to bear such blows, bringing them to an end as early as possible will be the mercy we shall be able to offer them.

This was the theory Douhet presented. Just as the French Revolution had brought about a war made by all the people, instead of the war made only by the nobles, Douhet insisted on the importance of the aircraft whose military capability would be so revolutionary that it would upset the old order of war. It would not be wrong if I make a different version of Douhet's theory— by making another version of aphorism given by a military historian John Fuller: "The musket has brought about infantry; the infantry has brought about democracy,"—"The aircraft brought about the bombing upon the urban areas; the bombing upon the urban areas gave an advance notice of the era of frontless war." Anyway, this new conception on warfare registered in history by an Italian soldier has promptly been directed "from prediction to realization" in keeping pace with the on-coming age of industry and mass production.

● **General Mitchell and his Following**
Another person who had contributed to founding the theory on strategic bombing would be a U.S. General Billy Mitchell. His name sounds important to the Japanese in two ways: one was his being a prophet of bombing upon cities, just as Douhet was; the other was his having his subordinates who came to have a high regard for the theory taught by their chief came up to the mainstay of the air force of the U.S. Army and came to direct the strategic bombings on Japan. Among them were Henry Arnold, Karl Spaatz, Ira Eaker. .... In 1944 and 45, when B29 bombers that had taken off from the airports in the suburbs of Chongqing or from those on the Mariana Islands came flying to perform the air raids upon the urban areas of Japan, those who had been leading those bombing squadrons were the generals known as "Mitchell boys," and the one who had performed his responsibility of performing the atomic bombings on the cities of Japan was Curtis LeMay who was also among Mitchell's following.

What Mitchell advocated concerning the logic on the air force as the mainstay of the military forces was not so different from the one retained by Douhet. The two who had served as commissioned officers in the army one in the U.S. and the other in Italy—were to create a similar theory based on what they had learned on the battlefield of World War Ⅰ. But if we were to find any difference between them, it could be said that the attitude adopted by Douhet remained more or less academic, while Mitchell, who had been exerting an influence upon those around him by his fiery temperament and fighting spirit, was thoroughly eager to listen to any opinion brought about from the scenes of the actual battles. As a result, Douhet was to be known as a theorist, while Mitchell was to leave capable persons behind him.

Mitchell had joined World War Ⅰ as an airman, and as soon as he was promoted after coming home to the post of the Vice Director of the Army Air Force, he became known as a theorist who gave absolute priority to the aviation for its military capability. He, who argued that the main purpose of the air battle was not in the combat with the enemy unit but in "attacking the nerve center of the enemy at the very moment when the battle started, so that we may paralyze their nerve center as much as possible." Thus he made a prediction of a totally new phase of war, saying: "We are to regard—I mean, we must regard the whole nation of the enemy as a fighting union," as was also mentioned in his book, *Winged Defense*, published in 1925. Thus while predicting a totally new phase of the war, he asserted that their Air Force should be made independent, and he never hesitated to shower abuse upon the military leaders who would not listen to him, calling them "the incompetent."

In order to prove how true his opinion was, General Mitchel often performed his experimental bombardment upon a warship in order to prove how effective the aerial attack could be, but all he could receive from these demonstrations was the sanctions against the harsh criticism he had made against the higher-ups and their military administrations—a legal decision made by martial law. That military tribunal given to Mitchell seemed to be a sort of the Inquisition to judge his military theory, and even though those commissioned officers— Arnold, Sparts, Eaker and others who had been brought up by General Mitchell—made themselves witnesses or assistants to the defense council so that they could support their master by demonstrating the validity of his opinion, but in vain. Mitchell, who had been sentenced to five years' suspension of his status and its appending duties, chose to retire in 1926. One of the judges that attended that court was Major General Douglas MacArthur, who was the only person that had been against that judgment of "guilty," as he recalled in his *Memoir*. To the Japanese, this might be called one of the curious turns of fate. One of Mitchell's statements had predicted America's war against Japan: "Any attack against Japan must be performed under the cover of our Air Force." Later on, MacArthur, who later became the commander for offensive operations toward Japan, was to proceed to Tokyo from Melbourne on the wing of North American B25 bomber, whose code name was "Mitchell."

Among the commanders of the Air Force who had opened the way to Tokyo for MacArthur, there was a person named Curtis LeMay. He was General Arnold's favorite disciple or Mitchell's second-generation pupil, and the way he followed did show the history of strategic bombings. This youthful colonel who had become known—for having achieved the plan of the aircraft operations as the commander of those carpet bombings upon Berlin and Hamburg—was promoted to general for his distinguished services. In 1944, LeMay presented himself at the headquarters of the U.S. Air Force at Chongqing, which had been made full of holes by Japanese bombers, and from the suburbs of Chengdu or the capital of Sichuan Province, which had also often suffered aerial attacks— he participated in the early stage of the strategic bombings upon Japan, performed by the long-range bombers known as B29. His having sunk Hankou (present-day Wuhan, which had been made the base for the Japanese Army and Navy Air Force while they were attacking Chongqing) into the sea of flames by incendiary bombs of an advanced type (napalm bombs) on December 18, 1944, turned out to be a preliminary drill for his bombing upon the mainland of Japan. The air raid on Omura in Nagasaki Prefecture in southern Japan— from whose air base Japan had sent its bombers to Nanjing in the early stage of the Sino-Japanese War (on August 15, 1937)—was also led by "LeMay in Chongqing" on October 25, 1944. After that, General LeMay who had moved his headquarters to the Mariana Base, was to make himself a leading figure in a strategy to burn down Tokyo and other cities of Japan by combining an even greater formation of B29s with napalm bombs.

Thus the birth of the theory of strategic bombings and its unfolding in the U.S.—carried out by Mitchell first, followed by Arnold and then by LeMay— were exactly on the same track of the U.S. Air Force's strategy against Japan.

Looking back in this way, the conception of strategic bombing had connected Japan and Chongqing with an unseen thread since its birth in 1920s.

● Hitler, Mussolini and Franco

The world in 1936, wrapped in a turbid air with disgusting odor from the haze caused by gasoline, had been left uneasy with a tinderbox waiting to explode. Those who were sharp-eared had already been hearing some clear sounds produced from several fuses that had already been lighted only to go on and on, giving some sparks, till they burst into a catastrophe several years later. Certainly the air of the time was suffocating enough to the contemporaries, but for those who were anxious to try and see the military capability of the newly-born air force by putting the conception of strategic bombing into practice as soon as possible, no other time could offer them a better situation than this. It was not long before the sound of the approaching aircrafts and the wailing of sirens became part of the daily life of the people.

In March, 1936, the German Army under Hitler advanced into Rheinland and reoccupied it even though it had been prescribed as a demilitarized zone under the Terms of the Treaty of Versailles and the Locarno Treaty. These were his willful actions followed by his declarations of the breach of the Treaty of Versailles and of Germany's rearmament, which did demonstrate his insatiable desire for building up "das Dritte Reich (the Third Empire: 1933-45) to extend their lebensraum (area for existence).

In May, the Italian Army under Mussolini entered Addis Abeba, the capital of Ethiopia, and declared it should be annexed to Italy. By this march onward performed by "the New Roman Corpse" that dreamt of a revival of the ancient Roman Empire, the only state that had remained independent in the African Continent, was made to collapse, and Ethiopia, along with Somaliland and Eritrea, was incorporated into "the East African Federation as Italian territory."

In July, a civil war broke out in Spain. To the Government of the People's Front that had come into being by the general election in February, the military came to respond with rebellion. Since the war-making capacity on the Anti-Communist Nationalist Army under the leadership of General Franco was limited and, since they were ready to depend on the assistance from Germany and Italy, they soon allowed the scale and strength of their warfare to be decided by those two nations—with the result that: the civil war in Spain came to assume a plausible-sounding reason for fighting a fight between the fascists and the democrats, thus allowing the warfare to assume an international character, while bringing the fascists a golden opportunity for trying their new weapons and new strategy.

In February in the same year, Japan had also experienced a rebellion by the militarists. Even if that Army's rebellion known as "the incident on February 26" was immediately suppressed, Japan's despotic tendency in the domestic politics as well as its territorial ambition became even more distinguished, and it helped to impress Japan as "a nation with extremely powerful defenses," well comparable with those nations of Nazism or Fascism. Already four years before—1932—Japan had founded "Manchoukuo*" through Manchurian Incident* at a corner of the northeastern China and, after having withdrawn from the League of Nations (1933), it was following its own way all by itself.

In the international society in the 1930s, no other nation but these three had been made to follow the common fate. In politics, they all believed in totalitarianism: as belated colonialist nations, they claimed a share for a lion, showed only a slight concern about the international partnership, and were quite ready to break away from the League of Nations when accused of their undesirable behaviors as its members. It was also in 1936 when the rapid approch of those three nations of Japan, Germany and Italy attracted the attention of the world. The movement that had started when Ciano, the foreign minister of Italy, visited Berlin (in June), went on toward Germany's and Italy's approval of Franco's administration (in November) and toward the conclusion of the Anti-Comintern Pact between Germany and Japan (in November). In the following year, Italy came to join them to conclude "the Anti-Comintern Pact," thus to bring about "the Berlin-Rome-Tokyo Axis" that was to shut up the world in even thicker mist of the combustible.

Japan, Germany and Italy were also common in having noticed the military capability of the aircraft even from the early stage of its development. It was these three nations only that had performed large-scaled aeronautical strategies during the two World Wars, and those who had written the first chapter of the bloody history of strategic bombings were their flying corps. Even though they were later forced to pay for what they had done at colossal interest, nothing can be more obvious that the first step toward the responsibility for having invented this new terror from the sky—now known as strategic bombing—lies in these three nations. Japan committed in China, Germany in Spain, Itary in Etheopia

Guernica after the air raid

and in Spain what Churchill called in *The Second World War* "the experimental atrocities upon the defenseless cities," thus opening up a new era of massacres by warfare.

● **The German Air Force Attacked Guernica from the Air**

The horror attack performed by the German Air Force's Condor Corps upon Guernica as the sacred town in the Basque Country in Spain has elaborately been made to revive by several documents. It has also become widely known through that great work, *Guernica*, produced by Picasso. Picasso, who had been staying in Paris at that time, started to work on *The Holocaust at Guernica* five days after he heard of what had happened in Guernica, and while leaving a large number of preliminary sketches for that work, he finished it into a mural painting (12.54m by 7.7m) that consisted of many symbols. Thus Picasso, like Goya, who had produced *The Ravages of War* and *May 5 in 1808*, was to bring himself among "those recorders of war to be remembered throughout the history."

The initial report on the air raid on Guernica was sent to the world from the actual place by George Stier, a special correspondent of *The Times*. The date of the attack was April 26, 1937; the time was 4:30 p.m., when this town with a historic background was still enjoying the atmosphere of a market day.

Guernica, the oldest town in the Basque Country and the center of its cultural tradition, was thoroughly destroyed yesterday afternoon by the air raid unit of the rebel army. They spent exactly three hours and fifteen minutes in destroying this open city lying far behind the front; the powerful formation, consisting of three kinds of German air planes—Junkers' type and Heinkel's type of bombers and Heinkel's type of fighters—kept dropping bombs that weighed 450kg or more and (according to our calculation) about 3,000 one-kg aluminum bombs upon that town. On the other hand, the fighter planes entered the skies of the central part of the town from a low altitude so that they could strafe the inhabitants who had taken refuge somewhere out of doors.

The German airplanes that took part in that bombardment were: twenty-three bombers of Junkers' Ju 52 type, twenty fighters of Heinkel's He 51 type (also carrying bombs) and six fighters of Messershumitt's Bf109 type. The attack was given by going through three stages, and it was considered extremely "logical," according to the article given in *The Times*. That was, the first group gave a strafing raid from a low altitude, thus causing a panic on the crowded streets on a market day. The square had soon turned into a pool of blood. Thus after having driven the people into the buildings or basements, the second wave of the formation of high-altitude horizontal bombers, sent the rain of bombs all over the town. The stone buildings collapsed, making the basements burried in clouds of dust. Then came the third waves of destruction, accompanied by the hell of flames from the incendiary bombs. The electron incendiaries, mainly consisting of thermit composed of powdered aluminum and iron oxide, were ignited by the shock of impact, kept burning intensely for more than ten minutes, blowing up incandescent flames of nearly 3,000 degrees. Fires broke out everywhere in the town and they mercilessly drove and killed those who had managed to get out of the heaps of wreckage.

By these three waves of attacks ceaselessly given upon the town, 1,654 people were killed and 889 injured. Considering the fact that the total of deaths caused by the German air raids on London throughout the whole period of World War I was 510, the meaning of what happened at Guernica during that single day will be realized even more keenly. The people in Guernica that day were fated to see before their eyes how a new Mars who had flown from the sky flourished his incandescent whips around himself, bringing about atrocities upon their families and streets.

The Mars who came flying with the Condor Air Corps was not only lightning-like and "logical" in his way of attack but also "creative" in selecting his target. That was, those they attacked were none other than civilians or those who lived in an open city left in a defenseless state. What they had intended to do was to spread horrors and make them grow among those who supported the government of the people's front. That could be called a faithful way to put "Douhet's theory" into practice. "The notion of separating the fighters from non-fighters is out of date. All the private citizens are fighters; and they are all exposed to the danger of war."…..

The authentic bombs that had been dropped on the town of Guernica on April 26, 1937, was none other than *this*. Since then, even to this day, all the people in every part of the world are to be injured and distressed by this "theory that has been put into practice" in various forms of disturbances and wars. The plague bacilli named "strategic bombings" that had been sown at Guernica were to wrap up—from the air—the condition of human existence in an amazing rapidity.

As was expected, "that trinity" possessed by that new Mars—the conceptions, the powers and the scars brought by him—had not been publicized around the world so openly so soon. For the government of any state, it had coolly been recognized that: acknowledging *it* would be a dangerous departure from the international law. The German armed forces with Goring as the Supreme Commander of the Air Force did show their satisfaction with the outcome of their attack, but they remained careful in recognizing the child of horror they themselves had brought into being.

Three days after that bombing, Franco's army that had occupied Guernica declared that: the city had been destroyed by the incendiarism committed by the people's front. The Nationalist newspapers devoted a large space, asserting that Guernica had been burnt by "the red" making a retreat.

Because of the victory won by the faction of Franco, this explanation had long been regarded as authentic in Spain. Thus *Guernica* by Picaso had also become a political symbol to oppose such a covering up as this. It was not until 1981 after the disintegration of the Franco administration that the history was finally corrected by the *Guernica's* return to Madrid—in accordance with Picaso's will: "This painting shall remain here till Spain regains democracy."

In April, 1997, President Herzog sent a letter to "The Ceremony held at Guernica for the 60th Anniversary to Memorialize the Bombardment upon Guernica," thus to admit the crime committed by Nazi Germany, begging for reconciliation with the survivors and the bereaved families, saying: "I clearly admit the German soldiers' guilty concern in it. I should like to extend my hands to beg for reconciliation with all the people who are still enduring under the weight of our crime we have once committed." In response to this, Mayor Baleo of Guernica said: "That confession made by President Herzog was none other than what we had long been awaiting."

But these sixty years needed before "Guernica" had finally restored its honor—if seen from a different angle—could be taken as a period in which the scales, the number of times and the targets of the strategic bombings were growing both in number and in intensity in a terrifying rapidity.

Today if we were to make a list of bomb-blasted cities, it would be doubtful whether or not we can see the name of Guernica within the first hundred entries in that list. This does mean how inconspicuous "the vertical invasion into other countries" has become, while being adopted in the warfare during the 20th Century.

● The Italian Air Force's Bombardments upon Ethiopia

The Italian Air Force's aerial bombardment upon Ethiopia should also be mentioned as a milestone of the early "massacres from the sky." Benito Mussolini, who organized his Fascisti in 1919, assumed the reins of government (1922) and started his dictatorship in "the ideology, the nation and the party," took aim at obtaining a colony in North Africa, and started invading Ethiopia in 1935 (the third Italy-Ethiopia War).

This invasion and annexation performed by Italy were going more or less along with Japan's "Manchurian Incident"* and its escalation. Italy's invasion into Ethiopia in order to annex it was the first step to realize "a revival of the Roman Empire," which was Mussolini's dearest wish. His expedition to North Africa was something that would be more properly called hunting out or subjugation rather than warfare, in which aircraft as fighting power went on the rampage as much as they liked.

In October, 1935, when the Italian army started their invasion into Ethiopia, the League of Nations at once branded it as "invasion." But that was of no use in stopping the Leader's Army. "It's not our army alone that is marching onward. All the population of Italy or forty millions of Italians are also marching along with us. We are all going to seize the place in the sun," said Mussolini, simply disregarding the resolution of criticism from Geneva. The League of Nations took action to punish Italy, but it was far from being called sanctions: the navigation along the Suez Canal, which was literally the lifeline in moving the army, had not been included in the forbidden clause; Among the articles under an embargo, there was nothing like petroleum or steel indispensable in performing war; instead metallic aluminum, the only article Italy had retained surplus power to export, was added to them. These were the steps that could not be called sanctions. Thus Mussolini dispatched the strength of troops that exceeded 500,000 to Ethiopia, along with a powerful air force and new weaponry.

In 1922, the power of the Italian Air Force had been entering a period of great soaring, taking advantage of Mussolini's coming into power. Douhet who had written a doctrine of the theory of strategic bombing had to stand court-martial before he was transferred to the reserve—as Mitchell in America had to—though he made a comeback, and after he retired from service, he made himself a military commentator to advocate supremacy in the air. Mussolini advocated the air force, saying: "The air force is the national arms young and brave and passionate; in other words, they are befitting fascists," and he paid special attention to the improvement and extension of the air force. In 1925, the air force was made independent, following the example of the Royal Air Force, the first to be made independent. And now Ethiopia was made a battlefield to give it a try.

The aircraft sent to the African front reached as many as three hundred and fifty. Fiat RC32 fighters, SM79 medium-sized bombers and CA101·111 bombers were the representative ones. Even though they were poorly armed as was known by their being called "colony-bombers," the Etheopean Army led by the Emperor Haile Selassie I had no fighters of any kind and their antiaircraft capacity was perfunctory. To the men of Italian Air Force, flying a mission was as good as a sort of refreshing sport.

A son of Mussolini's, Vittorio, nineteen years old, was also serving as an airman. Later he was to write in his memoir about how it was like when the bomb he had dropped hit the mark: "The bomb dropped in the middle of a cavalry squadron. The way they flew off in all directions appeared as if the bud of a rose had burst into flower." Nothing but gravity prevented the airmen, and this allowed them to engage in their one-way action of beating out their enemy. The bear-footed Ethiopian soldiers whose only arms were spears were easily killed on their march.

It is also known that the Italian Air Force had performed large-scaled droppings of poison gas upon the enemy forces on the run. Using poison gas upon the enemy had been made among the prohibited items in 1925 in the Geneva Protocol, but that had simply no effect on the colonialist dictator engaging in the war. Thus Italy became the first to violate the Geneva Protocol. The mustard-chemical, which causes loss of eyesight and skin erosion, was charged into bombs, and more than five hundred tons of chemicals were dropped from the bombers from 1935 through 39.

This had long been denied by the Italian government until 1995, when that fact was confirmed through a disclosure of information performed by the Defense Minister. According to the record of the Defense Ministry of Italy, the Air Force dropped 972 bombs charged with yperit or mustard gas (C500 T type) in the northern front by sixty-five series of attacks. In other fronts, too, chemical weapons were used in large numbers and all the chemicals dropped amounted to about 500 tons.

These attacks had been made even on the institutions hanging out the mark of Red Cross. To the League of Nations in Geneve, many reproaches were brought from Ethiopia, but it simply remained useless, since the Italian Government released the statement that always denied the facts. On May 5, 1936, the Italian Army captured Addis Abeba, and in July the League of Nations lifted sanctions which had remained rather ineffective on Italy.

The aerial strategy adopted by Italy in its war against Ethiopia was not like what was seen in Guernica that had indiscriminately been attacked by the German Army. Instead of seeing it in the lineage of strategic bombings, it would be more understandable if seen from the standpoint of tactical development in settling the colonies. Even if so, it is undeniable that the Italian Air Force did take a part in enlarging the potentiality of the newly-born air force in a rush. And as if responding to "the Guernica-type of bombing on cities" developing itself on to what was to be seen in Chongqing, Hamburg, Tokyo and Hiroshima, "the Ethiopian-type of bombing for subjugation" was also forming an uninterrupted stream of bloodshed in atypical warfare, now in sight and now out of sight in the history of modern times—in the American Army in Vietnam, in the Soviet Union's Army in Afganistan, in the Israeli's Army facing Palestinian refugees, and the American Army against those in Afghanistan and Iraq. In many of these strategies for intervention or for suppression, the usages of chemical weapons are commonly talked about. In that sense, too, the Italian Army's invasion upon Ethiopia cannot be removed from the genealogy of the terrors from the sky.

While Italy and Germany were opening up a new era of the war that would bring about indiscriminate mass murders—the former in Ethiopia, the latter in Guernica—Japan was also groping for a new way of utilizing the military capability of aircrafts in moving forward its policy of aggression into China.

It was not long before the Japanese military's strategic bombardment upon many cities in China were to far surpass what was performed in Guernica in both scale and intensity, and that with such tenacity as would outshine those air raids upon Ethiopea.

The Bombardment on Jinzhou Performed by Ishiwara Kanji

● **Flying a Mission with Bombs Hung with Braids**

On July 7, 1937—ten weeks after the air raid upon Guernica—the gunfire was exchanged between the Japanese and the Chinese Armies with Lukouqiao Bridge in between in the suburbs of Beijing. And this led the Japanese Empire to go on seeking even greater rights and interests than it had already secured by the occupation of Manchuria* in northeastern China through the Manchurian Incident—by going along the Huang He (Yellow River) and then the Yangzi Jiang (Long River).

That was an impulse held by the Imperialist Japan, which was to be

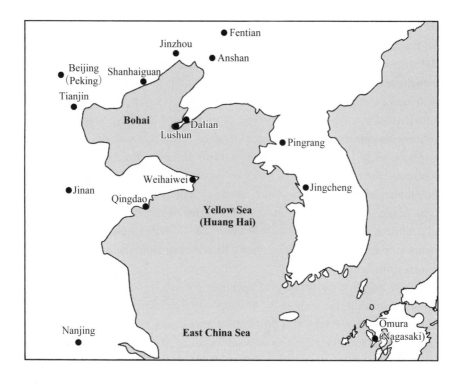

expressed by the term of "*Dai Tōa Kyoeiken* (Greater East Asia Co-Prosperity Sphere)," even though that was Japan's impulse for obtaining a larger "living sphere" and also a decisive step on to the process to destruction through fighting against the world. That could be compared with what Hitler called the Third Reich and what Musolini called the New Roman Empire.

Thus concerning the characteristics of what was called "China Incident" and its solution strategy, the discord and cracks caused between Japan and the U.S. grew so large that they could no longer be mended but must crash into what was called "the Greater East Asia War."

The behavior pattern repeatedly adopted by the Japanese military in dealing with Chinese issues was: arbitrarily bringing about "a situation in which no withdrawal was possible," and by making it an excuse, they pressed the government and military authorities to ratify it in a form of "the government policy" or "the guidelines in dealing with China issues." The Cabinet remained unable to hold ground against the military's prerogative of supreme command;

on the other hand the mainstay of the military remained unable to grasp what their expeditionary army was doing overseas, while the overseas Japanese military was impetuously hungry for fame, and this caused what situations brought about abroad to overrule the non-expansion policy at home, thus every time minor victories were brought about by an intensive surprise attack or with lightening-fast operations, the government had to lose a large footing in the field of diplomacy. In a vicious circle of the military's arbitrary actions, their international isolation growing deeper and their new disturbing actions, Japan's diplomacy ceased to exist and its policy toward China had simply come to mean its military tactics.

What was it that had created "the situation in which no withdrawal was possible"? Everyone would mention the aviation power and its usage. As a matter of fact, the newly-formed air force played a conspicuous part in all the phases of the actual front—from the arbitrary actions on their own authority to their intensive surprise attacks. This was especially so in the early stage of the war, when the Chinese air force still remained perfunctory, Japan's Army and Navy—like the Italian Army in Ethiopia—made a thorough use of the superiority of their aviation, easily clearing the legal framework of the central government both geographically and physically, thus readily expanding their battle line. As was expected, the indiscriminate bombings upon the cities, which were later called "strategic-political bombings," were naturally among their important tactics.

On September 18, 1931—five years earlier than the air raids on Guernica and on Addis Abeba—Japan's Guandong Army[*] attacked a Chinese Army in the suburbs of Fengtian (present-day Shenyang), thus to start "the Fifteen-Year-War between Japan and China" that was to last till Japan was defeated in 1945. In that military action, which became called "the Manchurian Incident,"[*] the air force of the Guandong Army went into action for an air raid on Jinzhou, thus playing a part in the escalation of the disturbances of war. For this reason, if we try to seek the origin of strategic bombings in the history of Japan's military affairs, we cannot overlook Japan's aerial bombing on Jinzhou. This was not only Japan's first aerial bombing on the city but also the first aerial attack on the city after World War I, thus internationally inviting a severe and concentrated criticism to what Japan's air planes had done.

The plan for seizing Manchuria[*] was worked out by Lieutenant Colonel

Ishiwara Kanji, the chief of the strategy staff of the Guandong Army, and was put into practice arbitrarily on the authority of the Japanese Army there. At midnight on September 18, 1931, the Japanese Army known as Guandong Army deliberately blasted the railroad of the Manchurian Railway, and by attributing it to the subversive activities by the Chinese side, they at once started attacking the Chinese barracks nearby and by making their headquarters emerge from Lushun to Fengtian, they formed a camp, intending to expel the Northeastern Frontier Defense Forces dictated by Zhang Xueliang—who was later to be a central figure in "Xian Incident" (February, 1936) in which he kept Jiang Jieshi in custody in order to realize the National United Front Against Japan. Zhang Xueliang then had been receiving medical treatment in Beijing, but no sooner had he been informed that Fengtian and Changchun were occupied by the Guandong Army's blitz tactics than he moved his local government office of the Northeastern Frontier Defense Forces to Jinzhou in Liaoning Province, and ordered the unit under his knee to assemble there so they might rebuild the base for counteroffensive. Zhang Xueliang, who had had his father Zhang Zuolin burst to death by an underground intrigue of Japan's Guandong Army (1928), had kept this humiliation as something totally unforgettable. Numerically, the Northeastern Frontier Defense Forces under him had held priority.

The air raid on Jinzhou, planned by Lieutenant Colonel Ishiwara, and performed mainly by the 10th squadron of the independent flight in Guandong Army, was carried out in such a situation. Such a long-distance movement to the enemy's seat of administration—something totally impossible for the ground army to perform—had kept in it a double aim for giving a shock to Zhang Xueliang's Army and for thrusting "a situation in which Japan will never be able to back out of it" to the Central Government and the Military's Center in Tokyo—thus simultaneously to smash Japan's "week-kneed diplomacy" led by the foreign minister Shidehara Kijuro trying to check the incident. On the afternoon of October 8, the air raid was performed by a formation of eleven planes—six of which were Model 88 scout planes and five were light bombers of Pothier Type 25 produced in France, which he had confiscated from Zhang Xueliang. The staff officer Ishihara in a passenger plane accompanied the formation so that he could fully observe what their bombers were performing. Since the Chinese side had not owned even a single fighter plane, they had no worry to be attacked in the air.

Those Model 88-type scout planes having had neither bomb-sighting device nor bomb-hanging installation, each of them had had four 25kg bombs hung outside the plane with some braids so that they could be cut down when they judged the planes had arrived above their target. The number of the bombs dropped on Jinzhou that day was seventy-five and its power was worth the 1.8 tons of TNT gunpowder, according to *The Aviation Strategy of the Army in the Manzhou Region* in *Japan's Defense Agency's Library on the Military History of Japan*. As for the scale of "the strategic & political bombings," which were soon to get into full gear, this might be regarded as very simple and far from efficient. But when judged from the strategic purpose of causing a panic on the Chinese side, and from the political purpose for forcing the Tokyo Government to change its non-expansion policy by making it face "the situation in which it could no longer remain half-hearted," the seventy-five bombs released from the braids, each of which weighed 25kg, could be said to have perfectly succeeded in hitting the mark.

At noon on October 8, the planes took off at Fengtian Airport; at 1:40 they reached in the sky of Jinzhou 270km away, and at an altitude of 1,300m they dropped the bombs on Jiaotong University (a non-specialist university) or what was presumed to be the seat of Zhang Xueliang's military administration (in the northwestern part of the city) and on the barrack of the 28th Army Division (in the eastern part of the city). At Northeastern Jiaotong University, Zhang Xueliang had his Headquarters for the Army to Guard the Northeastern China. As for the effectiveness of their bombing, as was observed from the air, ten bombs were reported to have hit Jiaotong University and twenty-two bombs to have hit the barracks respectively. (*The Defense Agency's Library of the Military History of Japan*)

As was expected from the non-pinpoint bombings, more than half had missed the mark even by the judgment made by the Japanese side. The bombs that had been dropped near Jinzhou Railroad Station caused some casualties. That was the first air raid upon the city the Chinese people had ever experienced. The Department of Foreign Affairs of China announced that: the bombardment and strafing from the air killed one Russian professor, one soldier and fourteen citizens, while injuring more than twenty citizens.

According to the report made by the Lytton Commission sent from the League of Nations in the year that followed (1932), many of the bombs were dropped here and there in the town, and some hit the buildings of the hospitals and the universities. Japan had asserted their bombings were restricted ones, but this was considered open to question; their having bombed the government office (of military administration)—apart from the barracks—could not be justified. Thus the Lytton Report suggested Japan's having performed an indiscriminate bombing upon that Chinese city.

When this was adopted by the margin of 42 : 1 at the general meeting of the League of Nations in March, 1933, Japan was to withdraw from the League of Nations.

● **Ishiwara's Testimony at the Tokyo Trial**

Ishiwara on board the airplane had been observing the whole of the air bombing on Jinzhou. The man who had written the script of the Manchurian Incident was also the first Japanese who had performed the aerial bombing on the urban area, and had looked at it with his own eyes from high above. In the affidavit presented at the International Military Tribunal for the Far East, Ishiwara testified to the fact that they had committed accidental bombings:

> As for the aerial bombing on the Jinzhou region, I was then making my men reconnoiter what was happening in the Northeastern Army occupying Jinzhou at that time, employing six spotters of 88 type and five Pothier Type planes we had confiscated; then we invited some return shots, and this led me to protect ourselves by dropping only 75 bombs on Jiaotong University as the seat for the Military Administration and the barracks of the 28th Army Division along with Zhang Zouxiang's private residence. As it was, these bombs were as large as mountain guns seven centimeters in diameter, but our planes had not had any installation to release these balls, and we had to throw them with our own hands. This certainly might have made the balls drop somewhere we had not expected. But comparing this with what the German Air Force had done at "the air raids upon London" during the European War or what was done by the U.S. bombers B29 in the bombardments on the Japanese cities or those ravages brought about to Hiroshima and Nagasaki in the latest World War, what I did then and there was something rather insignificant, I believe."

Ishiwara on board the plane would have been intensely watching the scene similar to what was to be witnessed over Guernica by the airmen of the Nazi Air Force five years and a half later. Later (in 1940) Ishiwara was to write *On the Final War*, in which he delivered his prophecy: "(In case of fighting a decisive battle in the final war) the weakest people and the most important facilities of the nation will be made attack targets. The industrial cities and the center of politics will be thoroughly destroyed. This means that: men and women of all ages, all the nature including mountains and rivers and all lives there, even pigs and chickens, will be caught in the same net of fire. Thus the war will be turned into a really unrelenting extermination performed by the air force. The people must train their mind so that they may keep up with these miserable situations."

This was to turn out to be a sort of prophesy, but Ishiwara himself then would have never dreamed that the bombardment he performed at Jinzhou would turn into a long switching bridge that would lead everyone, including himself, to "the start toward the end"—by way of Chongqing.

On the other hand, the air raid upon the urban area of Jinzhou at once invited an international chorus of criticism. The news of "the air raid upon Jinzhou" sent the people in big cities in China into a panic. In Nanjing, the VIPs started to take refuge; the Army set their field artilleries toward the sky in case of the air raid, while these commotions were being reported to the world by telegram. From many of the European countries, which had recalled what air raids were like during World War I, there rose a chorus of criticism against Japan.

In America, the Secretary of State, Henry Stimson, had his trust on Japan begin to shake. This led him to say to the Japanese Ambassador in the U.S., Debuchi Katsuji: "So far I have placed confidence in the statement released by the Japanese Government, while paying no attention to the attacks given to it by some people in the U.S. Government." Then he went on, mentioning Japan's aerial bombing upon Jinzhou in a tone of nervous tension: "That was something really amazing, and frankly speaking, I cannot help doubting whether or not the Japanese Government's policy has been thoroughly understood by the Japanese military overseas." Then Stimson entered a protest with Japan's Foreign Minister Shidehara through Edwin Nevil, the U.S. Acting Ambassador in Tokyo, warning that: dropping bombs upon an open city without giving any warning is the worst type of military action that cannot be approved of even in time of war. This led Stimson to write in his diary: "I wonder if the time has come when America can not help taking a firm attitude and an offensive stance toward Japan."

● **The League of Nations' Decision on Making Japan Withdraw their Troops from China and the Occurrence of the First "Shanghai Incident"**

On October 10—two days after Japan's bombardment upon Jinzhou—each of the U.K., the U.S., French, Italian and Spanish ambassadors resident in Tokyo, filed a protest with the Japanese Government against the air raid had performed on Jinzhou. Responding to the motion from China, the League of the Nations also summoned the board of directors and submitted this subject for debate. Immediately after this incident occurred, the League of Nations had adopted a resolution (September 29) that: the Japanese Military should withdraw as soon as possible. In fact, what Japan had done in Jinzhou—having been regarded as the sign of her intention to spread the wartime fire all over China without making any discrimination—could be stimulating enough to all those members of the League of Nations.

The Board of Directors, after having spent one day in the statements and reciprocations given by the representatives of China and Japan, proposed the matter as to whether they should allow America to join this deliberation as an observer, because it was interested in this matter. Japan asserted that America's participation in that deliberation was illegal and unnecessary, but all of the thirteen voting members, excepting Japan, having admitted America, America was allowed to join them at the board of directors from the following meeting onward. It was from this point that Japan was to have a huge shadow of America in performing its future policy on China. Thus the base of America's policy on Japan was to be founded upon the series of indiscriminate bombings Japan came to engage in with the first one in Jinzhou.

The deliberation of the League of Nations proceeded with the U.S. representative as a new member, and thirteen of them, excepting Japan, agreed in adopting a bill that: Japan should withdraw its troops from China by a certain date. They also decided that: "the Lytton Commission" should be sent to the site of that incident to inquire into the Sino-Japanese Dispute. In the meantime, however, *that* war fire leapt as far as Shanghai in the south to become what was called "(the first) Shanghai Incident."[*] In January, 1932, the planes of the Japan's Navy Air Force made their first appearance in the scenes of Japan's indiscriminate bombings upon the urban areas in China.

The Shanghai Incident—which had started with the anti-Japanese movement performed by the Chinese who had been deeply resentful at Japan's Guandong Army's having blown up the Manchurian Railroad—was put in motion by the Japanese military who wished to check *it* as soon as possible. Here again, its priming was the trick and provacation brought about by the Japanese military staying at Shanghai. Since Shanghai had been included in the area for the Japanese Navy to keep watch over, the Navy was to be active in the battle scenes this time, and that was why the airplanes based on such aircraft carriers as *Kaga* and *Hōshō*, and the seaplane carrier *Notoro* were to engage in the bombings upon that international city, Shanghai, from the beginning.

On the day that followed when the war became serious—on January 29, 1932—a scout water plane (15 type) from the *Notoro* bombed on North Railway Station and strafed the Malu Main Street. This air raid having destroyed the Printing Office of Commercial Documents and the Oriental Library as an annex to the Printing Office, a large number of precious documents from the ancient times of China were reduced to ashes.

In February, the carrier-based aircraft from a couple of aircraft carriers that had emerged at sea 30 kilometers off Shanghai came to join the indiscriminate bombings in concert with the strategy made by the ground army. The numbers of the bombers and fighters on board the two aircraft carriers were 41 and 26 respectively. Both the 13-type attack planes and the 3-type fighter planes were biplanes and slow in motion and frail in strength, but as for the command of the air they could remain unrivaled and their power was overwhelming. That was the world's first attack by the planes from the aircraft carriers—something unheard of before. On February 5, the unit of fighters of the carrier Hōshō performed an air battle against the three enemy fighters in the sky of Zhenru, the first air battle in the history of the Japanese Navy Air Force.

Edgar Snow, an American journalist, who was to devote himself to reporting what China was and how China achieved her revolution—was then following the final process of his journey to awaken himself to what China was—through witnessing that war fire in Shanghai. Snow, who had been following the trail of the Japanese Military's invasion into China—from Manchou[*] to Shanghai— was to witness a large number of dead bodies of civilians killed in the air raids and the Japanese planes proudly flying around the sky above. The following is what he described in his first work—*the Far Eastern Front* (1934):

On another side of me lay a young English officer, a bank clerk in normal times, now learning that his member-ship in the Volunteer Corps was more than an entrée to Shanghai society. His face was blanched. He uttered an exclamation, and pointed skyward. Some giant seaplanes, whose motors droned above the rapid terrestrial fire, hovered almost directly above us. Suddenly two of them dipped low, so that you could see clearly the Rising Sun painted red on their silver wings.

"Good God ! They're going to bomb them !" The Englishman gasped. I saw the planes nose upward them, and leave two white missiles streaking earthward. The ground under me shook and timbers flew high in the air. Then a column of smoke rose slowly from beyond the Station, and soon a burst of scarlet flame.

Other planes joined in the deadly circus. Tons of explosives were dropped into the Station, and scattered over the surrounding area. I kept tally for 36 explosions, some of them very near. The young English officer looked at me grimly. "There are nearly half a million innocent people trapped out there ... I wonder how many will never come through alive ?"

The air raid continued for nearly an hour, the planes releasing their cargo of four or six bombs, then repeatedly returning to re-load. Incendiary bombs, carrying 50 to 100 pounds of sulphur were dropped, along with high-explosive torpedoes, and detonated over districts densely populated with Chinese civilians. Unwarned of the attack, they had no chance to escape; scores now were blown to bits, or incinerated in the rapidly spreading fires.

The Commercial Press, largest publishing house in the world, China's greatest, most modern cultural enterprise, early became the target for repeated bombing. It shot up in flames shortly before one o'clock in the afternoon, to burn for days afterward. Greater than the complete loss suffered by chinese woners of the $10,000,000 publishing plant was the later destruction of the celebrated Oriental Library, where priceless, irreplaceable manuscripts from Sung Dynasty, more than 1,000 years old, had been carefully preserved for years. Many Chinese might have forgiven the murder of civilians, but after the bombing they became convinced that the Japanese were barbarians.

The Commercial Press, according to Snow, kept burning for several days on end. From then on, Snow was to keep witnessing what atrocities the Japanese military had done at Nanjing, Wuhan and Chongqing.

Thus, not only in Jinzhou but also in Shanghai, and not only by the Army but also by the Navy, Japan's Air Force came to steep both of their hands into the pool of blood. In 1937, when the war fire spread all over the Continent of China, the Japanese Army and Navy never hesitated to perform even a greater scale of indiscriminate bombings upon the cities.

The Transoceanic Bombings upon Nanjing

● **The Japanese Government Abandoned its Non-Expansion Policy**

It was 1937. Several months had passed since the gunfires were exchanged between the Japanese Army and the Chinese Army with the Lukouchiao Bridge in between, and Japan's military action in China had come to assume the generality and the international nature that never seemed to come to an end in the mere "incidents." From within those imbroglios, there arose a conception of strategic bombings or attacking a city itself indiscriminately— a conception which reminds us of Alexander the Great, who cut "the Gordian knot" in two with a single stroke of his sword, when he was presented that riddle as something for someone to be the King of Asia to solve. While going up the Yangzi by way of Shanghai, Nanjing and Wuhan, the outline of this conception—"cutting the knot in two with a single stroke of the sword"— became gradually clearer until at last its whole image came to reveal itself at Chongqing.

On August 15, 1937, the Konoe cabinet of Japan released the statement to give a warning to Jiang Jieshi's Nanjing Administration: "As for our Imperial Empire, its patience has reached the limits of endurance, and this has inevitably led us to take a drastic action to chastise the Chinese Army for their atrocities so that we may urge the Nanjing Administration to reconsider this matter." Two days later—on August 17—the cabinet session decided on making a complete change in their policy on China by discarding the non-expansion policy they had adopted so far:

1) We shall abandon the non-expansion policy we have adopted so far,

and we shall take all measures necessary in establishing a wartime organization.

2) As for the expenditure for the expanded situation, an extraordinary session of the Diet will be summoned around the third of the coming month of September.

Because of this decision made by the Cabinet, that abnormal relationship between the government and the military, in which the military abroad acted arbitrarily and created one fait accompli after another only to be confirmed by the government to be made into national policies, was brought to an end, though formally. But this never meant the Government had recovered its disciplinary power over the military, but rather it was none other than a government administrated by the military so that powerful military policies might be carried out. Another element that strengthened this tendency was the oncoming of the Navy that had so far remained critical toward the Army's policy on the Continent. The Minister of the Navy, Yonai Mitsumasa, and other leaders in that ministry simply discarded their play-it-safe strategy and came to undertake positive actions in what they had regarded as their own beat—the basin of the Yangzi and southward. Now the Naval flags were also seen to sail up the Yangzi to Wuhan by way of Shanghai and Nanjing. Ishiwara Kanji—a major general— who had been made to leave his post as the head director of the General Staff Office, because he, after the Lukouqiao Incident, regarded Japan's making war upon Soviet Union as something more important than its keeping going farther into the inland area of China, was railing at how opportunistic the leaders of the Navy were, saying: "If the Army is a robber, the Navy shall be called a pickpocket," but nothing or nobody could stop their momentum any longer. The Navy, which would never have any battle line on the ground—especially after having had the air corps join it—was to exert a decisive influence upon the unfolding of Japan's strategy.

On the day that followed the Lukouqiao Incident, Jiang Jieshi wrote in his diary (dated on July 8): "Now that Japan has come to challenge us, we should make up our mind to fight back." And on July 17, he was to give what he called *"the speech made at the death's door"* at a conference held at Lushan in Jiangsu Province:

Even if we might be a weak nation, if we were to "stand at death's door", all we can do will be to seek the way for the existence of our nation even if we all have to give our lives for it. On such an occasion, a half-hearted compromise should not be allowed to make; and we should keep in mind that: such a half-hearted compromise would turn into the conditions of the surrender and downfall of us all. All the nation should do now is to be clearly aware of what "the final door to death" really means.

Now "the nation's unanimity" to fight against Japan was steadily being brought into being. On the day when that speech of "the final door to death" was given at the conference for national security held at Lushan by the name of Jiang Jieshi, Zhou Enlai had also been invited as the representative of the Chinese Communist Party. Here the legal status of the Chinese Communist Party was confirmed. In response to this, on August 22, the Red Army consisting of 45,000 soldiers with the northwestern part of China as their base of operation was incorporated into the order of battle of the Nationalist Army with Jiang Jieshi at its head, and the Eighth Route Army of the Nationalist Revolutionary Army was decided upon—consisting of three army divisions with Zhu De as Army Chief, Peng Dehuai as Deputy Army Chief, and three division leaders were Lin Biao, He Long and Liu Bocheng—and this led them to receive supplies of ammunition and a fund from the Nationalist Government. In September, there came from the center of the Chinese Communist Party "The Declaration for Resistance against the Enemy in their Harmonious Cooperation and Sincere Devotion," and when that was accepted by Jiang Jieshi, as he announced it the following day, the Second Collaboration between the Nationalists and the Communists formally started. Thus Zhou Enlai and Zhu De were invited to be among the members of the Supreme Council for National Security, whose chairman was Jiang Jieshi. China in those days was in a state of civil war, but when they faced the common crisis of being invaded by the Japanese, the Communists "canceled the policies of insurgency and red activities" (as they mentioned in *The Declaration of the Resistance against the Enemy*), while the Nationalist Government temporarily ceased to be "anti-Communist" so that they might fight together against Japan. To the Japanese military who had been holding the divided China down since the Manchurian Incident* by means of threat and stratagem, this new state of things meant that they were to face a new situation totally different from what they had been

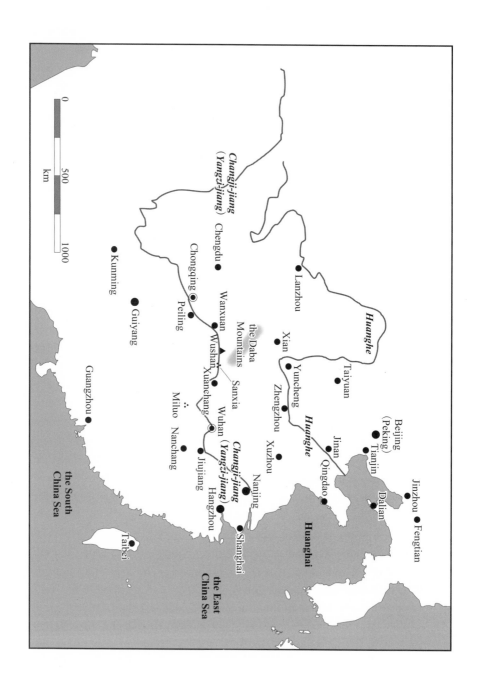

acquainted with so far. But, to the bloodshot eyes of the militalist Japanese who had gone raging mad, this change remained unseen.

● **"The Greatest Air Raid in the World History of the Aerial Battles"**

Under such circumstances as these, the air corps of the Japanese Army and Navy had kept their air raid operations. It was since this period that the original form of systematic and intentional indiscriminate bombing on the city came into being. The airplanes that belonged to the Army or the Navy had been engaging in the bombing on the battlefield or in helping the Army going on in their battle, but on the other hand, they had kept carrying out what the Naval Department announced as "an unprecedented air raid in the world history" on Nanjing where the Jiang Jieshi's government had confined themselves, and on Wuhan, and on Shanghai and Guangdong (Guangzhou) which had been regarded as the entrances for commodities. These series of strategies could certainly be regarded as "the greatest air raids that had ever been performed in the world" from whichever aspect they might be seen—in the number of planes, in the quantity of explosives and in the distance they had covered before they achieved their intent. Only six years had passed since they performed "the aerial bombing on Jinzhou" during the Manchurian Incident (1931), but as for the bombs dangled on braids, they had already been turned into something to be remembered only in talking about "old times."

August 15, 1937. This was the day when the Japanese Government announced: "We shall send a punitive expedition to China." This was also the day when in China "an order for the mobilization of the entire nation in order to fight against Japan" was issued. This was also the day when "the transoceanic bombardment" was performed upon Nanjing as the seat of Jiang Jieshi's Administration. On that day, despite the atmospheric depression, twenty newly-produced 96-type land-attack bombers (whose abbreviation was middle-sized bombers) took off at Omura Base in Nagasaki Prefecture, Japan, flew 960km, including 600km overseas, as far as the skies of Nanjing— spending four hours—and each plane released the twelve 60-kg land-bombs on their targets or a couple of airports and their neighborhood. On the same day, another transoceanic bombing had been performed on Nanchan in Jiangxi Province by the same type of land-attack bombers that had taken off at the base in Taipei. Excepting the German military planes that had flown across the

English Channel (34km across) to make an air raid on London during World War I , these could be called the first transoceanic bombings in the world. And these 96-type land attack bombers of the Navy Air Force were to retain the capital position throughout the period in which "strategic-political bombings" were being performed on the Chinese cities. This success in the transoceanic bombing upon Nanjing was to provide them with a new vista in their advancing operations, especially in the strategic bombings to be performed by the air force as an independent power.

It had been made public by the Navy Department that: during the sixteen months from July 7, 1937, when Lukouqiao Incident[*] took place, to October 27 in the following year when the occupation of Wuhan Sanzhen (Three Wuhan Cities: Wuchang, Hanyang & Hankou) took place, the number of planes that joined the bombardments amounted to the total number of about 10,000 from Navy Air Force alone; the bombs used were about 35,000 in number, about 3,000 tons in weight, and about 320,000 bullets were consumed in strafing attacks. During a single month from September to October in 1937, when the severest attack had been made, the Navy's air raid unit dropped 4,950 bombs. Most of them were 60kg, 80kg or 120kg bombs to be used on land (3,937 bombs in total), incendiary bombs having not yet been brought into use on a full scale. Captain Onishi Takijiro, the then director of the Department of Education at the Headquarters of the Navvy Air Force, is recorded to have said:

"Talking of the air raids performed at Nanjing, the number of air raids was 36; the total number of air planes engaged in them was 600; the bombs dropped amounted to about 300 tons. As for Guangdong, the total number of planes was 360; the bombs dropped were about 101 tons." (The shorthand notes of the speech he made at the Economists' Club on November 15, 1937). According to another material, he talked of the battle in capturing Guangdong: "During the period of only a little more than half a month, a total number of 2,000 Navy planes were active; the bombs dropped numbered 6,900, weighing 560 tons," introducing these figures as something "amazing." These had been published as "the attacks made on the military targets," but in many cases, such targets as the institutions of military administration and government offices being located at the central area of the city, the borderline between "the military targets" and "the urban area" was rapidly becoming ambiguous. As if proving this situation, Vice-Admiral Hasegawa Kiyoshi, the Commander-in-Chief of the Third Fleet which had been appointed to be the Navy's unit to put the strategy into action, offered his opinion to the Naval General Staff on July 16, when ten days had passed since the start of the war:

If we were to break down the status quo of the relations between Japan and China by dint of armed force, all we should do will be to make the central power of present China surrender to us. If we were to take a strategy of restricting our action within the limits, we shall only have the war prolonged, helping the enemy's power concentrated, thus bringing about a danger of preventing our strategy from being performed properly. ..... For these reasons, as to how our operations should be guided, it is necessary that we should delete our first purpose of "subjugating China's 29th Troops," so that the second purpose of "subjugating China" should be adopted as the one and only purpose of our strategy.

This was how the enlargement was requested in the recognition of the enemy and in the sphere of the combat. Here it was suggested that they should break away from "the principle of sticking to a military target." Those at the battle field had wished to give a full-scale attack on the enemy country rather than the extermination of the enemy force before their eyes. This opinion was to be adopted in the unfolding of the strategy thereafter in a concrete expression. On September 19, a written directive (dated 14) to give an air raid on Nanjing went as follows: "The work team.... shall perform the air raid upon all the institutions of military affairs, politics and economics under the command of the air." The attacks not on the military but on its maintenance bases had clearly been mentioned from the stage of setting up its purpose. That was a moment of a leap of serious significance. As a matter of course, the attack could not help becoming an indiscriminate bombing on the urban area. Among the details of operations, there was a description as follows:

5. It is not necessarily expected to give a direct hit on the aim, because the main purpose of this strategy is to give horror to the public mind. Accordingly, considering the enemy's defensive gunfire, the bombs should be dropped at the altitude of about 2,000 to 3,000 meters and all the bombardment should be finished during a single transit across the city.

This, however, was something very difficult to perform, considering the capacity of the 90-type bombsight produced in Japan by improving the one produced in Germany. On the day that followed the air raid on September 19, the Commander-in-Chief Hasegawa gave an announcement, by way of Consul-General at Shanghai, that: all the Chinese non-combatants should leave the urban area of Shanghai, but this was as good as the announcement that Japan would perform an indiscriminate bombing there. The series of eleven air raids that lasted till September 25 having been performed under this declaration, they were to bring about tremendous damages upon the lives of the citizens and non-military facilities.

● **The Large-Scaled Air Raids Comparable with the Holocaust at Nanjing**

The Japanese Terror In China, Death From The Air authored by Timperley, a reporter of *the Manchester Guardian*, is well-known as a fundamental material on the holocaust at Nanjing, and it does offer the vivid descriptions of the hell caused by the air raids there.

The civilian casualties resulting from the air raid on Nanking, Sept. 25, amounted to 600 persons killed and wounded. About 500 bombs were dropped by the raiders, which made a rapid succession of five attacks on the capital city between 9.30 a.m. and 4.30 p.m. The Central Hospital and the National Health Administration which are situated on the same compound were the targets of two Japanese raids in the afternoon. Fifteen bombs exploded in the compound, though none of them scored a direct hit.

Two raids previous to those above described were carried out by Japanese airmen on Sept. 22. An armada of over fifty planes participated in the attack, which lasted from 10:35 a.m. until noon; fifteen machines took part in the second raid, which was very brief.

An average of two or three bombs were dropped over three hundred different places, including the South City, and the new residential area as the seat for the American, Italian and German Embassies and for the residences of most of those from abroad, two or three bombs were dropped every day. According to the report by the Reuter's, during the second air raid, the Refugee Reception Center at Xiaguan was bombed, killing or injuring more than one hundred; according to the observers, many dead bodies were lying here and there while straw-thatched huts were burning.

These scenes were commonly seen not only in Nanjing but also in Shanghai and Guangdong (Guangzhou). In the air raid on the city of Guangzhou performed with "an amazing number of 6,900 bombs, whose total weight was 560 tons." According to the document issued from the Navy Department, most of the slums in the vicinity of Dongshan were crashed, and "it was unbearable to see the limbless bodies looking like flies on the flying papers," as Timpalee wrote in his report for the Reuter's News Agency.

The realities of these air raids, being reported to the world through such news agencies as AP's, UP's and Reuter's, were to be widely known to the world, excepting the Japanese. It was exactly during this period when Picaso's mural painting "*Guernica*" was completed and exhibited at the Hall of the Republic of Spain at the World Fair being held in Paris, attracting the visitors' attention.

It was the United States of America that had sharply reacted to what was happening to China, showing its great sympathy to China. In *Ten Years in Japan*—a diary of Joseph Grew, the U.S. ambassador to Japan till the start of the U.S.-Japanese war—we can see frequent references to the air raids performed by the Japanese air force since July, 1937. Reflecting the strong attitudes of President Roosevelt in Washington and the Secretary of State Cordell Hull, who came after Stimson, Ambassador Grew retained a severe attitude toward Japan's bombing upon the cities. In September when Japan declared the air-bombing on Nanjing, he wrote in his diary: "I've come to find I must protest at once against their plan." (On September 20, 1937) Grew did not take time in asking the Foreign Minister Hirota Koki to come and meet him, as he wrote in his diary:

> I saw the Minister at 6 and talked to him in much stronger terms than I had yet employed, feeling that the time had come for the most emphatic language. In the course of my remarks, I said that we must not forget history; that neither the American Government nor the American people had wanted war with Spain in 1898, but when the *Maine* was blown up nothing could prevent war. The American people are the most pacific and patient people in the world; we lead the world in matters of international peace

and disarmament and the maintenance of the sanctity of treaties. But under provocation we can become the most inflammable people in the world. It is well not to forget history.

——*Ten Years in Japan*

This was the warning Grew gave to Hirota. Grew then urged upon the foreign minister the fact that Japan had now been causing disbelief, suspect and antipathy among the people in the world, because of the direction of its action, and the foreign minister Hirota was now responsible for stopping what the Japanese Army and Navy were doing in China. This led Hirota to promise Grew to do his best so that the Chinese civilians might not be affected, but it could not be realized, to the U.S. ambassador's disappointment.

Grew also wrote back as follows, refuting to a Japanese who had critically asserted that "the indiscriminate bombings performed by the Japanese" were none other than mere stories made up by the news media abroad:

Thirdly, on page 19, you mention only one instance of Japanese bombing (in Canton) in which the non-combatants (a very small number, you say) were killed through an accident. We have a great deal of absolutely reliable evidence, based on the direct observation of neutral observers, of many instances of Japanese bombing of undefended cities, towns, hospitals, missionaries, educational establishments, in which great masses of bombs were dropped by Japanese planes many miles from any Chinese military establishments, and therefore not accidental, and in which a very large number of non-combatant civilians were killed. Very few, if any, of these bombings were reported in the Japanese press. They were reported, on the basis of absolutely reliable neutral observation, in the American press, and these reports are largely responsible for the waves of indignation which swept over my country from coast to coast. I enclose, for your own personal and *confidential* information, a list of some of these incidents of which we are officially aware.

——*Ten Years in Japan*

The ambassador Grew closed his letter, saying: "I am sure you will appreciate from all this that quite apart from propaganda there has been a great deal of ground to explain and to justify the feelings against Japan which has arisen in my country." But the Japanese government had kept denying their having committed indiscriminate bombings and having killed civilians abroad—not only to their own people but also to the people abroad.

According to *The Actions Taken by the Imperial Navy in the Sino-Japanese Incident*, issued in January, 1938, from the Naval Department of Japan, the following "information" was given as "a report sent by a reporter from a third power": "The air raids performed by the Japanese Air Force never fail to miss the target of military facilities, and this keeps the private houses safe, allowing the general public to keep engaging in their daily occupation as usual," along with a talk by a foreign aviator that went: "The Japanese airmen are so brave and so excellent that they are incomparable to any other airmen in the world," thus trying to prove the authenticity of their statement.

But apart from the Japanese people in general who had been left totally ignorant of what was happening abroad, such false information as mentioned above simply remained far from persuasive to the rest of the world. They had already known how a Japanese plane had given strafing attack at the car with the British ambassador Hugensen in China in it to give him injury or how the U.S. gunboat *Panee* to be mentioned later (in Chapter Ⅲ) was attacked by another Japanese plane, and the B.K. warship *Ladybird* had been shot to sink by yet another Japanese plane, and how in Zhunzhou a missionary hospital had been bombed, and for each of these illegal attacks they had officially received the appologies and compensations from the Japanese government. In consequence, therefore, the Japanese government's false explanations to their own people simply helped to widen the information gap between the Japanese nation and the other nations concerned.

● **The League of Nation's Resolution of Criticism against Japan and Roosevelt's Speech Criticizing Japan**

By that time, Japan had already withdrawn from the League of Nations, but what Japan's having been dropping bombs upon the cities in China had been taken up at the general meeting of the League of Nations, and on September 28, 1937, *The Resolution of Criticizing Japan* was unanimously adopted by the Advisory Committee consisting of twenty-three nations. The whole statement went as follows:

A.56.1937.VII.

Geneva, September 28th, 1937.

Communicated to the
Assembly, Council and
Members of the League.

RESOLUTION ADOPTED ON SEPTEMBER 27th, 1937,
BY THE ADVISORY COMMITTEE SET UP UNDER A RESOLUTION ADOPTED
BY THE ASSEMBLY ON FEBRUARY 24th, 1933.

"The Advisory Committee,

"Taking into urgent consideration the question of
the aerial bombardment of open towns in China, by
Japanese aircraft,

"Expresses its profound distress at the loss of
life caused to innocent civilians, including great
numbers of women and children, as a result of such
bombardments,

"Declares that no excuse can be made for such acts
which have aroused horror and indignation throughout the
world,

"And solemnly condemns them".

On the day before that decision was made, the Japanese Government had announced the informal opinion delivered by the chief of the Public Information Division in the Ministry of Foreign Affairs who appeared for an interview with a press corps from abroad. A part of his speech went as follows:

We have never done such things as to make any civilians our military target. .... In both Nanjing and Guangdong, the military installations and other buildings concerned with military affairs—in other words, the buildings and institutions of inimical quality are not located in places clearly separated from the living quarters of the general citizens or those engaged in business activities—that is, they are mixed together. The representatives of certain nations are not fully aware of this fact, simply assuming that all the military facilities are located only outside the city limits, and this wrong idea has led them to believe that the Japanese military are intentionally aiming at the civilians, thus criticizing us, as if we were doing something wrong.

By way of a feint, he also expressed his indignation, saying: "Just recall what those from Great Britain and France said at the Conference on the Aerial Strategy at The Hague. Haven't you insisted that: everything recognizable as of military purpose shall be air-bombed?" But his speech was not effective.

A week later, the U.S. President Roosevelt delivered a speech in Chicago—known as "A Speech for Isolation." (October 5)

The overwhelming majority of the peoples and nations of the world today want to live in peace. They seek the removal of barriers against trade. They want to exert themselves in industry, in agriculture and in business, that they may increase their wealth through the production of goods rather than striving to produce military planes and bombs and machine guns and cannons for the destruction of human lives and useful property. ... I am compelled and you are compelled, nevertheless, to look ahead. The peace and freedom and the security of 90 percent of the population of the world is being jeopardized by the remaining 10 percent, who are threatening a breakdown of all international order and law. ....

The situation is definitely of universal concern. The questions involved relate not merely to violations of specific provisions of particular treaties;

they are questions of war and peace, of international law and especially of principle of humanity.

President Roosevelt compared this global injustice to "a spread of an epidemic" and said: "When an epidemic of physical disease starts to spread, the community approves and joins in a quarantine of the patients in order to protect the health of the community against the spread of the disease," thus making his attitude clear in this matter, which could be taken as his appeal for communal sanctions against this international outlaw. Though he had not mentioned who that outlaw was, it was apparent that he meant Japan. The U.S. newspapers that reported this speech the President had made at Chicago commented that: this was a sign that the foreign policy of the U.S. was being changed from isolation into international collaboration. Both the League of Nations' resolution of criticizing Japan and Roosevelt's speech on his policy of keeping the epidemic in isolation had proved the fact that Japan's air raids being performed in China had attracted the world's attention, causing the voices of indignation to rise and spread, but those voices from abroad never exerted any influence either upon the public opinion or upon the policy of Japan, and its attacks upon the Chinese cities from the sky were to become even more intensified, as its battle line was moving from Nanjing to Wuhan.

The Battle for Keeping & Guarding the Great Wuhan

● **"Let's Turn Wuhan into a Madrid in the East!"**
On December 17, 1937, General Matsui Iwane, the Theater Commander of the Central China Region, entered Nanjing, the capital of China—which was still filled with the smell of blood because of the holocaust that had recently occurred there—by way of Zhongshan-men Gate, leading his unit. At that same hour, Vice Admiral Hasegawa Kiyoshi, the theater commander of his fleet, also entered the city, followed by his naval landing party by way of Yijiang-men Gate. In accordance with that ceremony for that triumphant entry into the city, there was a flypast of the Air Corps of the Army and the Navy. The city of Nanjing, which had totally been damaged by ultimately more than fifty air raids by Japan's Navy Air Corps, was now appearing as good as dead. This was the

same with the inhabitants who had managed to survive the hells. These scenes, which were soon to be commonly seen both in Europe and in Japan, were unmistakably of a new type of *Disasters of the War* brought about by the air raids.

For the Japanese military and government, what they called "China Incident" was expected to be brought to an end then and there. The Japanese Army at the site of that Incident had confidently declared to the High Command that: Jiang Jieshi would surely surrender when he lost Nanjing as his capital. As it turned out, Jiang Jieshi now strongly urged the people to keep a long-term resistance to Japan, as if he were laughing at Japan's easy expectation for his choosing a short-term operation, and he, who had declared to transfer the capital to Chongqing even before the fall of Nanjing, had already been in Wuhan, thus encouraging the people to keep resistance to Japan. Mao Zedong at Yan-an was also completing his mobile forces' tactics of "luring the enemy into farther position." It was half a year after the fall of Nanjing that a couple of his works—*A Discourse on Position Warfare* in which he criticized opinions on national ruin and on prompt victory and *On the Strategic Problems in an Anti-Japanese Guerrilla Warfare*—were made public from the cave of Yan-an. Both Jiang Jieshi and Mao Zedong at that time had already been collaborating with each other, setting their sights on their top-priority issue of fighting out the National United Front Against Japan. Then all that Japan could do was to go on and on, following them. On January 16 in the following year (1938), the Konoe cabinet of Japan released a statement:

> Our Imperial Government, after our capture of Nanjing, has been waiting until today, so that we may give the Nationalist Government of China a final opportunity for their self-examination. Unfortunately, however, they have failed to grasp our real intention and now they are recklessly working out a plot for keeping fighting against us, disregarding their people being left in great misery, without making any effort to achieve peace for the whole aspect of the Great East Asia. For this reason, we, the Imperial Government has decided that: we should not keep company with the Nationalist Government of China from now on, but we should expect to have a newly-risen Chinese administration which will really be worth cooperating with us so that both of us may regulate the diplomatic relations with each other and

may cooperate in founding a newly-rectified China. (The rest is omitted)

This statement known as "Konoe's Statement" had been made for breaking off his relations with Jiang Jieshi. Thus the Japanese Government might have simply intended "not to keep company with the Nationalist Government of China," but the Japanese Armed Forces could not accept it so soon, so easily; their elective was either to withdraw their troops from China or to perform a farther invasion upon China.

Thus the war for invading Hankou (Wuhan) was to break out. By way of the military operations in Xuzhou, they succeeded in charging the Three Towns of Wuhan at the end of October in 1938, but their march was to go on until what seemed to be "the final" victory went vanishing beyond the upper part of the Yangzi. Here, too, the military capacity of the air force was employed not only in the bombings on the battlefield or in the cooperation with a ground operation but also as a new power only the air force was able to employ—by making use of its mobile power—totally independent of the ground forces' operating area.

The Japanese military called that usage of the air force "an attack on the strategic point" or "a strategic-political attack" and regarded it as an important part of the aerial strategy.

By July 11, 1937—four days after the outbreak of Lukouchiao Incident*— the center of the Navy Department had finished a new version of the Specially-Constituted Air Force Unit in preparation for the all-out war that would break out in the near future. On the same day, the President of the Naval General Staff, Prince Fushimi-no-Miya Hiroyasu, an Admiral of the Fleet, visited the Emperor at an Imperial villa at Hayama to report that new scheme and how to actualize it, and it was readily sanctioned. From this time onward, this Air Force Unit was to be the main force of operations from the first attack on Shanghai to the drive of Wuhan by way of the command of the skies of Nanjing.

That especially-organized Air Force Unit consisted of four corps:

1) "the 1st United Air Corps" that consisted of Kisarazu Air Corps and Kanoya Air Corps (96-type land-attack planes = 42 middle-sized planes and 12 carrier-based planes of 95-type)

2) "the Second United Air Corps" that consisted of Saeki Air Corps and Omura Air Corps (67 planes = 94-type carrier-based bombers and 92-type carrier-based attack planes)

3) "the 21st Air Corps" from Kure, consisting of 6 scout planes

4) "the 22nd Air Corps" from Sasebo

They were placed under the commander-in-chief of the Third Fleet. Each air corps emerged from its home unit to Omura, Saishuto Island or Taipei, and according as the war situations changed, they extended their base of operations as far as the central southern area of the Chinese Continent. Those middle-sized attack planes were expected to fly a mission mainly for ground attack and warship attack, and their total number was eighty-four. The Navy having no front on the ground, all of their military capacity could be used for bombing on the cities.

On the other hand, the Army had finished organizing "the Headquarters of the Air Corps" by August, 1936. Since then, the Army air force left the leadership of the divisional commander of the Ground Army to be placed under the command of the Chief of the Air Corps.

The Chief of the Air Corps was expected "to be a close adviser to a general or a lieutenant general, and to be placed under the direct control of the Emperor, while directing all the flying corps placed under him" (as was stipulated in Article 1 of the Air Corps). The person who was appointed by the Emperor to be the first Chief of the Air Corps was Tokugawa Yoshitoshi, a lieutenant general, who was known to be "the first aviator in Japan" when he was still a captain. In August, 1938, the Air Corps was made to move under the Expeditionary Force in the Mid-China; and placing the first, the second and the fourth air divisions under his command, its military force consisted of eighteen companies (three reconnoitering companies, five combat companies, six light bombers' companies and four heavy bombers' companies), with the seventy-eight bombers as its usual number.

Making these military forces as its mainstay, Japan's advancing operations into China by air had been driven forward, but in the aviation strategy adopted to gain Wuhan, which had become the final barrier to the way to Chongqing, Japan was to face an unexpected resistance. In response to the Spanish Civil War, which had been going on against Franco's Army about this time, the Chinese called Wuhan "a Madrid in the East," so that they might play a part in that anti-fascist united front. Especially the Chinese Communist Party insisted on fighting "a fight to guard the Great Wuhan," so that they might timely check the Japanese military whose front had already become too far to go on. At the office of the Eighth Route Army in Wuhan, Zhou Enlai, Ye Jianying, Dong Biwu, Deng Yingchao and so on were permanently staying, while calling out their opinion to the citizens. Guo Moruo was also among them. He had once sought refuge in Japan, but he was no longer a historian as he used to be, but a fighter for "the save-the-nation movement" at the United Front. The journalists from abroad were now writing their reports, comparing Wuhan with Madrid.

● *The Poetry Reciting Day* Started with Guo Moruo's Appeal

By the middle of 1938, when the Japanese military's marching onward along the Yangzi was approaching Wuhan, Madrid of Spain had been besieged by Franco and his Army for a little more than a year. The government of the Republic of Spain had already moved to Barcelona about the time Nanjing had fallen, but the popular front of the volunteer corps and the citizens kept enduring a hard life in the city seized by the enemy with their slogan of "No pasaran (Don't pass them)." The bombers sent by Mussolini and Hitler, who had secretly participated in the war, dropped the bombs at random on their city, trying to make them lose their will to keep fighting. The Army of the Republic of Spain produced posters out of the photographs of the children who had been killed by their indiscriminate bombings and appealed to the public: "Look at these pictures! Who won't take arms to exterminate their fascism?" All of these were amazingly similar to what was happening in China. These points in common were accelerated when Japan went so far as to import as many as 72 Fiat BR20s— the main bombers that had been mobilized at the air raids on Madrid—and Japan employed them, calling them "Italian-style heavy bombers" in its early bombardment upon China. In December, 1937, the Japanese government had recognized Franco's Nationalista Administration as the legal one in Spain. And this had certainly brought the two cities under the same fate.

The Chinese people at Wuhan had intended to share a sense of solidarity with the Spanish Civil War. That had kept substance more than a mere slogan. "The Great Wuhan as the Eastern Madrid" was to hold out more than four months—one month longer than Shanghai—instead of falling in several days as Nanjing and Guangzhou did. It was during this warfare that the Chinese Communist Party started publishing their only newspaper *Xin Hua Ri Bao* (New China's Daily News) on January 11, 1938, to keep publishing throughout the area under the control of the Nationalist Party, and *Quan Min Kang Zhan*

(All the People's Resistance) edited by Zou Taofen was also republished. It was also in Wuhan that a Theatrical Company consisting of nine groups and an Advertising Company for Protesting the Enemy consisting of four groups were also brought into being. These did enliven Wuhan—though only for a while—as if it had returned to the days when Sun Wen inspired the people with the *San-Min-Chui* (p.34). Before the collection boxes placed at the five points in the three towns of Wuhan Sanzhen (Wuchung, Hankou and Hanyang) in memory of the first anniversary of the National United Front Against Japan, there was a long stream of citizens and more than a million *yuan* and a variety of commodities were offered.

Guo Moruo, who had just returned from Japan where he had taken refuge, had already been appointed to be the chief of the Third Office of the Administration Department in the National United Front Against Japan. The following passage in his speech did carry the atmosphere of Wuhan at that time. Certainly the people must have been feeling a spiritual uplift while living in the town that could rightly be called "Madrid in the East."

On April 8 in 1938—on "The Day for Singing & Reciting"—Guo Moruo called out to the great crowd of people who had assembled at the Overseas Chinese' Racecourse—even though in a year or so this very place was to be turned into what was called "W Base (Wuhan Base)" from which the Japanese airmen were to fly a mission to Chongqing:

Zhangliang, a strategist of the Founder of the Han Dynasty (206B.C.-8), did make use of the power of singing-songs and succeeded in making the enemy soldiers under the King of Chu break up. Even though the King of Chu had been as brave as to pull out a mountain and cover the earth (as brave and Strong as Achilles or Hercules), he could not override the power of poetry-reciting and singing.

Now, however atrocious our enemies may be, and however large the number of enemy planes may be, we are quite ready to smash them by the power of poetry-reciting and singing. Zhangliang had given the King of *Chu the Song of Chu*, and we, the modern Chinese, will give the Imperialist Japan our version of *Songs of Chu.**

By dint of our poetry-reciting, we must make our propaganda reach farther and farther. By dint of our singing, we must celebrate our oncoming victory."

—My Memoirs on the National United Front Against Japan

*When the King of Chu, Xiang Yu (? -189B.C.), had his castle at Gaixia surrounded by the army of Lieubang, who was to be the founder of the Han Dynasty, the latter made his men sing the songs of Chu, so that the King might be mistakenly think his folk had already fallen.

In fact, no Japanese song was sung on that occasion, but they did produce some new Chinese songs and marches such as *The Volunteer Army March* and *The Long Sword March*, thus to awaken the mind of the Chinese people and to produce some creators of new music, as Guo Moruo recalled in later years.

● **Some Volunteer Aviators Came from the U.S. and the U.S.S.R.**

The power of songs and music turned out to be of great help, and now even more direct help began to be offered from abroad. Though a little different in character from "the International Brigade" in the Spanish Front, Wuhan also was to have some volunteer aviators from the U.S. and from the U.S.S.R. to join the air battles. Claire Chennault, a former U.S. Air Force officer, who had made himself an advisor to Jiang Jieshi's Air Force, was then organizing an international squadron that was to become known as "Flying Tigers." Among those foreign aviators, whose monthly pay was 600 dollars plus a special pay of 500 dollars every time they succeeded in shooting down a Japanese plane, there was someone like Jim Marison who had fought in Spain for the Republic Army. At the start of the U.S.-Japanese War, the Flying Tigers were incorporated into the 14th Flying Corps led by Claire Chennaut who had been made to return to his active service, and his Flying Corps based in Kunming and Yunnan were to annoy Japanese planes in later years.

But those who stood most conspicuous among those volunteer aviators who had come to help guard Wuhan were those from the Soviet Union, known as "Swords of Justice." Through the four air battles fought in 1938 along with Chinese aviators, which the Chinese have still kept in their memory as "2.18 Air Battle," "4.29 Air Battle," "5.31 Air Battle" and "8.3 Air Battle," they became the objects of admiration of all the citizens of Wuhan.

This aviation corps from the Soviet Union had been sent there according to the Non-Aggression Pact that had been concluded at Nanjing between China and the Soviet Union. It consisted of two squadrons of bombers and four squadrons of fighters and those that fought against the Japanese planes were fighter I15s and fighter I16s (イ 15 and イ 16 or E15 and E16 according to the Japanese way of writing). What was more, four hundred airplanes produced in the Soviet Union were also sold off to China to compose the main force in the early stage of the Chinese Air Force.

Then the first thing for the Japanese planes to do was to win command of the air, and attacking the strategic point was left as something to do next. That was something they had never experienced either in Shanghai or in Nanjing. Concerning "the 4.29 Air Battle," the greatest one since the Sino-Japanese War broke out, the Chinese side announced that: they had brought down 21 Japanese planes, thus to "give massive losses to the crazy invaders." (According to the record of the Japanese side, it was four planes that were lost.) At the air raid on August 3, too, the Chinese side announced: "eleven planes were shot down," while the Japanese side mentioned "three."

● The Fall of Wuhan Leads to the Relocation of the Capital to Chongqing

Certainly Japan was made to have hard times at Wuhan, but the damages Wuhan suffered were much greater. According to the record on air raids they suffered in August, 1938, the number of bombs dropped on the three towns of Wuhan was 1,715, causing 829 deaths, 2,283 injured seriously or slightly, 2,298 houses or buildings burnt down, 35 private vessels were lost, and one cow and sixteen horses were burnt to death. Fifteen airmen from the Soviet Union were also killed during their interception to be cordially buried as "the Heroes of the Air Force of the Soviet Union." The Commander and the Vice Commander of the Fourth Battalion of the Chinese Air Force, Li Guidan and Lu Jichun, also lost their lives during the air battle.

This was how Wuhan fell on October 27, 1938. Madrid was to hold out till March in the following year, but "the Battle to Keep the Great Wuhan" had reached its limits in four months. The Nationalist China's Capital for Resistance had already been made Chongqing. This was to lead both Zhou Enlai and Guo Moruo to leave for Chongqing.

At this period, Guo Moruo made a poem, entitled *The Timidest are the Cruelest*. Thus the poet had already presumed exactly what "the strategic and political bombings" essentially meant, even before they got into full gear:

"Our planes are coming!"—
This cry of my friend makes me rush up to the balcony.
My heart dances in endless joy,
Because I have just seen the three enemy planes
Flying low leisurely while dropping bombs desultorily.

Wherever they have dropped bombs,
It is always on our Chinese territory.
Those killed by bombings are all Chinese.
The enemies in the planes have no need to rack
Their brain to scout the aim of their bombardment.
Without even the slightest danger on their own side,
They are able to display their ability as "a hero."
Fortunately, "the heroes" are guarded with "bullet-proof belly band"*
And also with a charm of the *Quanyin Bodhisattva* of Compassion
                                        whose effect is margical.
This makes us learn a wise saying: "The most cowardly are the cruelest."

The sounds of anti-aircraft guns reverberate at the edges of the clouds,
The aim of their cruel strategic bombings—which started at Jinzhou
     to go on to Shanghai, Nanjing, Guangzhou and Wuhan—has now
     focused upon Chongqing in Sichuan Province as the pivot
                              of Nationalist-Communist Collaboration.
Sure enough, our planes have now come into my sight.
I turn my eyes to my watch to find it a little before 3:30 p.m.
Those three enemy planes have flown away somewhere else.

*A cotton belt with one thousandred stitches, each of which sewn by a
 different woman, to be worn by a soldier as a protective charm.

The Construction of the W Base at Hankou

● The Supply Line has been Stretched to its Limit

About the same period when the fortress of the National United Front Against Japan was being brought into being in Chongqing upon the base of the Nationalist-Communist Collaboration, the city of Wuhan in Hubei Province—780km downstream from Chongqing in a straight line—was also having the Japanese military trying to give the last finish upon their new plan of advance.

This had kept the staff busy in going to and from Tokyo to make contact with the other members of the staff till it led to an outline of their advancing operations by air force "for the purpose of gaining over the enemy in the center of their strategy and conquest." By and by, that outline came to present itself in the Emperor's Orders—"the Great Order to the Army" and "the Great Order to the Navy." Then, they came to be expressed in more clarified words in the orders of operations given by Hata Shunroku, the Commander of the Expeditionary Force to Central China, and by the Commander-in-Chief of the Third Fleet, and it was not long before it was expressed in more precise words and phrases in the order of operations given by the name of Vice Admiral Oikawa Koshiro as the Commander-in-Chief of the Fleet of the (Enlarged) China Region.

This newly-adopted offensive operation from the air could not help becoming a great turning point in three ways: firstly in the point of the aim of the war or "the disposal of the China Incident," secondly in the significance of the Navy Air Force's taking a leading part in the plan of operations, and thirdly in the flight from the traditional conception of what war was. This ambitious trial to destroy the capital of the enemy nation only by dint of the air force—a new strategy about to be adopted—was something to mark a new epoch in the military history of the world.

The materials and the personnel needed to perform that new strategy turned out to be enormous. At Hankou which lay along the Yangzi, the local headquarters was set up and supply depots which were to be turned into storehouses were brought into being one after another, while the military units that arrived one after another, and no sooner had they performed a march in celebrating the new formation, raising yellow dust behind them, than they kept themselves busy in training and in preparing for putting a strategy into action. By and by, bombers, fighters and transport planes that belonged to the Army or the Navy came flying as if from nowhere and began to spread buzzing sound day and night. The airmen in an aviation cap and in a pair of flying goggles were seen everywhere. In "the military district" which had been taken over by the Japanese military, more and more storehouses were brought into being and everything—from adjustment operation at the airfield to bringing "bordellos" into being—was carried out in a hurry. The Chinese were not allowed to live in that military district called "the special district" or "the Japanese district." They, who had been ordered to live only in the district for the refugees, were not allowed even to leave that place without carrying "a certificate." All they could do then, therefore, was to watch how their own town was being turned into a place for the planes to take off in order to perform even further slaughter of their own people.

As for what they should do after their successful capture of Wuhan, the Japanese Government, the Center of the Military and the Expeditionary Force had all agreed that it would be impossible for them to to make farther advance by land. Because before their infantry, they had a great chain of Mt. Daba; making their fleet sail upstream farther than Wuhan was also out of question. These were not all the reasons for which Japan must stop extending their front. By that time, the Army had already sent almost all the troops into action, and the only regular unit available in the mainland of Japan was the Imperial Guard Division. The supply line had come to its limit, too, and no flexibility was left to establish any new front. So all they could do then seemed to accept the idea of making Wuhan the final point for their aggression by land. It was too obvious for them to see the failure in their attempt to give "an intensive surprise attack" in land war.

On the other hand, however, it was an undeniable fact that they could not retreat from Wuhan so soon and so easily. Even though they had proudly declared something like: "We shall not listen to Jiang Jieshi," they had to follow him all the same, because they had failed to take "the final necessary step" either in Nanjing or in Wuhan, and this had turned this war into something too hard to bring to an end. Those in the actual spot had badly been seized by the opinion that they must not retreat before they made Jiang Jieshi come out with his hands up. On the other hand, the generals had misunderstood the Chinese having chosen to retreat to the hinterland as the result of their adeptness in strategy, comparing it to "the heavenly horse galloping across the sky." Thus they were so devoid of any feeling of frustration in having failed to reach any prompt solution that it made the matter even more difficult to settle.

Among *The War-Making Policies from the Autumn of the 13th Year of Showa (1938) Onward*, which had been decided by the Army Department of the Imperial Headquarters, there was a statement: "If the Chongqing Administration accepts the following conditions, we shall recognize it as their submission to us and allow ourselves to cease fire," and the first condition went: "The Chongqing Administration shall abandon the policy of resisting Japan and accepting communism, and shall make a definite promise to perform a personnel reshuffle necessary," and as for whether or not Jiang Jieshi should resign, it said, clearly demanding his resignation: "If the Chongqing Administration surrenders, we shall have talks with Jiang if it is necessary in order to realize a cease-fire, but after it is realized, Jiang shall immediately leave that post of responsibility."

Major Horiba Kazuo, one of the war leaders in the General Staff Office, wrote in his memoirs, *A History on How the Chinese Incident was Guided along its Course:* "The arrogance of the Ministry of War was such that the words of "submission," "tolerance" and the like were indispensable if we were to make anything pass through the conference." Not only in the Army in the battlefield abroad but also among the Military Executives at home, an arrogant mood had helplessly been prevailing.

It could be said totally impossible that Jiang Jieshi should accept such arrogant and megalomaniac cease-fire terms. Eleven days before—on October 28—at the People's Participation Party (at the second meeting in the first term), he had stressed the need of their do-or-die resistance, and he had taken pride in their advantage, as was expressed in his speech—"In abandoning Wuhan, I proclaim to all of the government officials and the people" (given on 31):

Our fighting base now is not in a small area on the coast of the Yangzi or the sea but in the interior vast and profound. What the *Battles for Keeping and Guarding Wuhan* meant was to make the enemy's marching west stop there, while making the enemy's power exhaust there, while we were preparing for the traffic at the rear base so that we could transport necessary arms, while making our industry in the southeastern area and the central area move to the interior, so that we may promote the development of the transportation and economy in the northwestern and southwestern China. Now, the changed situation of war and the necessity of a long-termed policy have led us to abandon Wuhan. But you must not be led to regard it as a retreating tide of battle or as a back down. Seen from a military point of view, this is a turning point from the defensive to the offensive.

● A Plan of the Bombardment upon Chongqing has Arisen

Even if the circumstances might have thrown them together, now that the Nationalist-Communist Collaboration was realized, it was totally unthinkable for Jiang Jieshi to bend his knees or to yield to the enemy. For Jiang Jieshi, the fall of Wuhan was nothing but a transition from the stage of defense to the stage of rivalry. Now both the frontal battlefield and the rear base for resistance were formed. It was under such circumstances as this that Japan's plan for conducting airstrikes upon Chongqing was brought into being as a means of recovery from the brink of defeat. As for the characteristic of the strategy adopted by Japan at that time, the following conspectus is given in *The History of the Navy Air Force (4)* in *The Library of Military History* edited by Japan's Defense Agency:

> Since the strategy taken by the land army was such that the only military force available in performing positive blows to bring this Incident to an early end was none but the air force, and this inevitably led the air force to be entrusted with most of the positive strategies to defeat the enemy. Thus it turned out that almost all the strategies taken by the ground army since then were to promote the air bases so that they could obtain greater sphere of aerial attack. This was how both of the Army and Navy Air Corps came to cooperate with each other in achieving their common aim of defeating the enemy.

Then in the same data, we can see the *War Guidance* as follows:
1) In bringing up the enemy's *new* administration by subduing Jian's Administration, it is necessary to bring an occupation zone into being, while maintaining the public order and mopping up resistance, while receiving the air force's cooperation.

2) In making Jian's Administration surrender by attacking their political and strategic points in the hinterland, thus crashing their fighting spirit, while intercepting their supply of strategic materials and cutting off ground supply by intercepting the transport routes, while performing a naval blockade.

3) As for the aerial strategy, the aviators should cooperate in the mopping-up operations mentioned above, while performing the attacks on the points of strategic importance in the hinterland as well as the import routes there. Local transportation shall be intercepted. The aviators shall also cooperate in the strategy for enforcing a naval blockade.

It was under this recognition of the state of affairs that on December 2, 1938, the Supreme Direction by the name of the Emperor or *The Great Order No. 241* was issued by the General Chief of the Staff, Field Marshal *Kan·in-no-miya* Kotohito to be reverently received by the theater commanders (Sugiyama Hajime in Northern China, Hata Shunroku in Central China and Ando Rikichi of the 21st Army). Here at this point, "strategic and political bombings" were turned into a rigid mission to be performed by them according to the supreme order, whose basic purpose was stipulated in its first clause, as follows:

The Imperial Headquarters' intention is: to secure the territory under occupation, while promoting its stability under the firm, long-term seizure and striving for suppressing the anti-Japanese power still existing until it is brought to fall.

Then in the fifth clause, it was revealed that: their intention was to destroy the enemy's strategic and political center by performing their aerial advancing operations:

The commander of the expeditionary force in Mid-China shall attend mainly on the advancing operations by employing aerial strategy, placing its aims in destroying and disturbing the enemy's strategic and political center, while making efforts in crushing the enemy's air force. Close cooperation with the Navy will be necessary.

According to this *Great Order No. 241*, the direction of operations—the *Great Guidance No. 345* under the name of General Staff, Imperial Prince Kotohito—was given on the same day to the three theater commanders in the field headquarters. Here, the directions concerning the advancing operations by air had been placed at the beginning:

According to the *Great Order No. 241*, the following shall be directed:
1) The central agreement between the Army and the Navy in performing the aerial operations all over China shall be given in the separate volume.

   In attacking the enemy's strategic and political nucleus, our military capacity shall be concentrated by seizing a proper opportunity so that the enemy's organs for their supreme command and for their supreme politics might be caught and exterminated.

As was expressly stated here, the strategic and political operations they were expected to engage in had made it a rule to be performed as their joint operations according to the central agreement made by the Army and the Navy, even though that was something extremely exceptional in the strategy to be performed by the Japanese military. Both of the high commands of the Army and the Navy had been well aware that: employing a great deal of concentrated military force was the secret of success in strategic bombings.

Another remarkable direction that should not be overlooked was included in the section 6) of the *Great Guidance No. 345:*

6) Each corps staying in China is allowed to use special smokes (red tubes, red balls, green tubes), but in using them, one must be careful not to use them in urban areas, especially in the residential areas of those from abroad. In using them, one must mix them with smoke so that one's having used them may not be revealed, while taking care not to leave behind any sign of one's having used them.

"Special smokes" meant poison gas, and red tubes and red balls meant arsenic diphenyl cyanic zirsin; green tubes meant tear gas. The facts of the Japanese military's having used poison gasses during the Sino-Japanese War had already been made clear by many materials, and that action had been performed under the orders of the Chief of the General Staff, and it was not long before the citizens of Chongqing became nervous about the gas attack or the poisoned tobacco dropped from the Japanese airplanes. Just like the Italians in the front of Ethiopia, the Japanese in China, despite their having signed in the Geneva Protocol, did not seem to have any intention to be bound by it. *The Great Guidance No.345* was thus demonstrating Japan's resolution to disregard the two international laws—"a protocol of prohibiting to use poison gasses and the like" and "a rule of the air battle" (especially Article 22 that "prohibits bombing the civilians and the like.")

● **A Honeymoon of the Army and the Navy with the Aircraft between Them**
"The Central Agreement between the Army and the Navy in performing the aerial strategy all over China," which was given "in the separate volume"— as was mentioned in *the Great Guidance No. 345*—was made as follows in December of the same year (1938):

Ⅰ. The Strategic Policy:
　1) The Army Air Force and the Navy Air Force shall cooperate with each other in performing strategic and political air battles in the main regions of the Chinese territory so that we may frustrate the enemy's willingness to go on fighting.
　2) As for the direct operations either on land or on water, both of the air forces shall take the mission upon themselves.
Ⅱ. The Main Points in Strategy:
　1) The Strategic and Political Operations by the Air Force
　　① The Army Air Corps shall perform the strategic & political operations mainly upon the important areas in Central and Northern China
　　② The Navy Air Corps shall perform the strategic & political operations mainly upon the important areas in Central and Southern China.

Sichuan Province where Chongqing lies is situated in "Central China." This Central Agreement led both the Army Air Force and the Navy Air Force to clearly aim at cooperating in starting their strategic-and-political operations in such main points as Chongqing and Chengdu situated in what the Japanese military called "the Hinterland" in Sichuan Province. Their aim to pursue was "to frustrate the enemy's morale to go on fighting" or the conquest of their fighting spirit. "The indiscriminate bombings upon the urban areas" had not been written down overtly, but *the* way of expression could easily lead them to interpret it as something like that.

As for the strength of the air force to be employed in "Central China" at that stage, it was stipulated as follows:

Army:
    Flight Squadron No.59 (20 fighter planes)
    Flight Squadron No.12 (15 heavy bombers)
    Aviation Corps
    The First Flight Group (18 scout planes, 12 fighters, 30 heavy bombers)
    The Third Flight Group (9 scout planes, 24 fighters, 45 light bombers)
Navy:
    The First Combined Air Corps (24 middle-sized attack planes)
    The Second Combined Air Corps (54 carrier-based planes, 24 warship-attack planes, 12 warship-bombers, 26 middle-sized attack planes)
    The Third Flying Corpse (24 water scout planes)

Later there were some changes in the names of these units and in their force of arms, but this turned out to be the first virtual air force Japan had ever had, and its sole mission was to perform strategic bombings. Under this central convention, a large number of "local conventions" were to be made at the local headquarters situated in China—with detailed rules to be applied to those headquarters of various levels of importance.

All these units of the Army and of the Navy dispatched to China did maintain a very good relationship with each other as long as the making of the operations was concerned throughout the whole period of them. This could be regarded as really amazing, viewed from their home agencies, which remained simply antagonistic to each other. The reasons would be that: they were both tied with the common system of aviation technique, and that: the aircraft capability itself was something new and kept them comparatively free from any particular tradition or what might be called a territorial instinct. Comparing this with that civil-war-like conflict between the Army and the Navy in 1943—concerning which would be "the first to make an armed entry into northern French Indochina"—their having kept themselves in such a close co-operative relationship in Wuhan could be regarded as something amazing and exceptional.

At the seat of the officer in command in Wuhan, such men of great individuality as Tokugawa Yoshitoshi and Endo Saburo in the Army and Inoue Shigeyoshi, Yamaguchi Tamon and Onishi Takijiro in the Navy were to be seen according to the changes of the war situations, and their powers of leadership were to be directed not in a low-level fame or territorial dispute but rather in the integration and concentration of their offensive strength. This would also be counted as one of the primary factors that had kept their relationship a friendly one.

On the other hand, however, their having strengthened such an attitude toward their co-operative strategy was readily reflected in enhancing their ability to perform the air raids, and this was something horrifying to those to be attacked. Among the three great operations—"Operation No. 100" (1939), "Operation No. 101" (1940) and "Operation No.102" (1941)—the last two operations were to reduce to ashes all of what traditional Chongqing used to be. The enemy planes that kept coming again and again had simply kept the people in their air-raid shelters until they began to call "Operation No.102" "the Fatigue Bombings." It was not until the autumn of 1941—when Japan-U.S. War was about to break out—that the people in Chongqing were finally released from *the* fatigue they had long been suffering.

● **"The W Base" for "The Regular Flight to Chongqing"**

Wuhan, which was made into the base for those Japanese bombers, consisted of three districts—Hankou, Wuchung and Hanyang—and it was in an area of Hankou district near the Yangzi that the flight base was brought into being. The occupation forces of Japan took over a couple of racecourses—the World (Wan Guo) Racecourse and the Overseas Chinese (Hua Shang) Racecourse—and leveled the ground to bring a spacious airport into being. The hastily-prepared Hankow Air Base, which was called W Base for concealment, was spacious enough to accommodate more than two hundred planes of the Army and the Navy: the Army's First and Third Flight Groups and the Navy's First and Second Combined Flying Corps. The stands of the racecourse were converted into the headquarters and barracks, followed by other installations for supply and support, including aerial arsenals, storehouses for bombs and a transmitting station, before the base was opened. But the pair of runways, simply made up by leveling the ground of the Racecourse, naturally remained unpaved and, as the planes were moving out of their lines into the taxiways and then into the runways, the air around simply turned into clouds of yellow dust, to the distress of the pilots. After the plane before their planes took off, the pilots needed to employ "an instrument take off" before they left the runway. If the shift of wind caused the changes of directions for a takeoff, there was a danger of causing a collision of planes in the thick clouds of sand. Still in December, 1938, such a hastily-built air base was considered to have been prepared to perform the strategic-political bombing upon the hinterland of Sichuan Province, and the deployment of the attacking units—consisting mainly of the Navy's Model 96 middle-sized attack planes and the Army's Model 97 heavy bombers—was reported to have been finished. For "the regular bombings upon Chongqing," which were to be performed for as long as three full years, this base—Hankou W Base—was to serve as the largest base for their sorties.

The bomber fleets of the Army and the Navy that came over to Hankou Base were also of the same nature as the racecourse-turned air port, since they were formed so hastily that they could not help remaining imperfect. Including those Zero Fighters that later came to join them as escort fighters for the Navy's middle-sized bombers, all the aviation put into the Chinese front about this time used to be sent out to the front line as soon as they went through the trial stage and were officially named, without going through any proper training to obtain ample experience. The Navy's middle-sized bombers had exceptionally had one year before they were officially named, but the Army's 97-heavy bombers were made to succeed to the seat of the main bombers as soon as they were officially named in December in 1937. As for the Zero Fighters, they were pressed so much as to receive both their finishing touch and attack training at the same time. Minor adjustments or conversions might be done at the aerial arsenal at the Wuhan Base, but as for the improvements concerning their structure such as the improvements in defensive power or the counter measure to the fire caused by being shot, they had simply no time nor energy to spare, since the priority had been placed on the schedule for performing their strategy. This inevitably led them to go on fighting, leaving the weak points of the newly-produced airplanes unattended, until several years later they were to encounter the strong aviation power kept by the U.S. Air Force. When they were clearly made aware of what they were lacking in, everything was too late to mend.

The Navy's land attack planes, such as middle-sized attack planes, had originally been developed as an auxiliary capability for the capital ship in fighting a decisive battle against the U.S.' on the Pacific. What had started Japan to develop such middle-sized attack planes was also based on the idea of developing twine-engined, land-based planes capable of being active at the ocean for the purpose of countervailing the inferiority Japan had suffered by having had her capital ship's tonage reduced to the sixty percent of the U.S.' by the Disarmament Treaty of Washington (1921-22). This led Japan to intend to set off a merit against a demerit by attacking the main force of the enemy from the sky before the fleets of both parties encountered at sea by removing a part of it from the scene of their decisive battle. This was none other than the forte of the Japanese Navy's landing party.

Considering that such was the mission of those middle-sized bombers which had originally been produced to fly fast across the Pacific Ocean to give the U.S. fleet horizontal bombings or torpede hits, employing those bombers for the bombing upon the cities in the Chinese Continent could be called a departure from the normal tactics. But since the war fire came to spread to the south of the Yangzi, the Navy had become attracted to the Chinese Continent almost as much as the Army, and their rational thinking and sense of equilibrium were as good as nonexistent. For three years since then, the Japanese Navy was to move its core to the Riverside in order to perform their attack into the depth of the continent, even if they appeared far from reasonable when seen from every point of their major strategy, tactics and the battlefields they had assumed, only to drain their energy in vain. Seeing the fact that Inoue Shigeyoshi (the Chief of Staff of the Fleet of China Region), known as "a resourceful general," was the most enthusiastic in promoting this scheme, I cannot help feeling some irony in it.

● **The Strategic Bombings were Brought into Being by the Japanese**

The Navy now was going to take the initiative in "the strategy of the aerial bombings upon the Continent" by employing the newly-produced airplanes now being sent directly from the factories to the battlefield without being given any opportunities for improvement. This was how "the strategic and political bombing" was being performed everyday by sending their planes from the race-course-turned runway to Chongqing as faraway as 1,000km.... This meant 2,000km's commuting.

At first, the air raids upon Chongqing remained inexperienced and awkward, still staying at the stage of trial and error, despite the brave words and phrases written in *the Great Order No. 241* and the Central Agreement between the Army and the Navy. But considering that it was still in 1930s or in the early stage in the history of the strategic bombing, this was something that would naturally occur.

This was where the history of the strategic bombing dawned.

In Europe, there had already been some examples of aerial attack, but they were all short-termed, temporary and short-distanced ones. None of the aerial strategy over there had been performed with "the intention to frustrate the enemy's will to go on fighting." Thus the Japanese military in the battle line in China was to develop the techinique of "strategic bombing," while providing a precedent of it for the world to come.

On the other hand, the conception that had brought the strategic bombing into being was closely connected with the Japanese cognizance of Asia and their view of the Chinese. In China, the Japanese had failed to adopt such a notion as to draw a sharp line between the combatants and non-combatants or between the frontline and the civilian front. It was certain that the strategy taken by the Chinese side—in which they avoided fighting a decisive battle, while trying to induce the Japanese into illegal places of battle—did strengthen this tendency, but the Japanese military had faced all the Chinese, regarding them as their latent enemies, as long as they would not swear to cooperate with them. For those attacking from the sky, this was a very convenient view to adopt. All they should do was to defend themselves, saying: "In China, there is no dividing line between the military facilities and the living quarters for the people in general,"—just as the chief of the information bureau talked on the air raid upon Nanjing the Japanese military had inflicted. This was how easily the conception of "strategic bombing"— bombing upon the city itself along with all its residents—was spontaneously brought into being to be kept on as something quite natural. The aerial capacity toward the end of the 1930's could not be called so powerful, but that was what we could say according to our hindsight.

Toward the end of 1930s when the airplane itself was something new, the newest aerial strategy performed by the strongest military forces in Asia did not come off without bringing tremendous fears and carnages to the Chinese cities and their inhabitants.

On the same line, the history on the air raids upon the Chinese cities performed by the Japanese military did reach a peak at Chongqing, but if we trace back to its origin, we can go as far back as the Manchurian Incident* (1931), thus revealing the fact that: that was a traditional method Japan had maintained. The history of Japan's invasion into China can be called "the history of the development of air raids" in the world history of wars, and the aerial capacity and tactics kept by the Japanese Army and Navy Air Forces could be said to have been maintained and developed through the experiences they had in China. The Civil War in Spain (1936) had turned out to be a testing ground for the German Air Force, while Mussolini's invasion into Ethiopia (1935) allowed the Air Force he had developed to have a try, and now the wartime fires Japan had brought to China did help the Japanese Air Force to establish their own strategy. And both of the Manchurian Incident* that started in 1931 and the Shanghai Incident* that followed it (1932) were to give Japan the opportunities for establishing the strategic-political bombing much earlier than the Civil War in Spain and the Italia's Invasion into Ethiopia. So it was inevitable that the method of "the invasion from the sky" would assume a style peculiar to the Japanese Air Force.

The First Air Raid upon Chongqing

● **The Points in Common in What Happened in Chongqing and in Guernica**

It was at 5 p.m. on December 25 in 1938. At Hankou Air Base (W Base), an order was issued from Terakura Shozo, a major general, the chief of the Army's First Air Division:

The main force of our Air Division shall attack the urban area of Chongqing in order to shock the high and the low of Jiang's Administration. The date and time shall be tomorrow, the 26th—1 p.m..

For Major General Terakura Shozo, who had been transferred from Shimoshizu Flying School to take the post of the chief of the First Air Division here, taking a decisive action by performing the air raid upon Chongqing was the mission he had been most impatiently waiting for. To the airmen whose main duty so far had been assumed to help the Army in their ground operation since the outbreak of the China Incident or the Sino-Japanese war the order to perform a genuinely aerial operation was finally given. Since the strategy planned by the Imperial Headquarters was decided to be an aerial advancement into the depth of China—into the strategic points of Sichuan Province—it had been expected that the first to perform this feat would be the Army' First Air Division with its headquarters at Hankou, consisting of three squadrons of heavy bombers. Terakura—even before *The Great Order No. 241* prescribed that the strategic-political attack should be turned into the central strategy—had been ordered by Lieutenant General Ebashi Eijiro (the successor to Lieutenant General Tokugawa Yoshitoshi) to spend five weeks in training to perform the exterminating air battle to be made *after* the long-distance flight and *before* attacking the strategic points, so that everything might be completed in seven weeks, and this had kept his corps extremely busy in training in bombing, shooting and navigation.

It was apparent that "this exterminating air battle fought after a long-distance flight" meant the aerial advancing operations to be performed upon Chongqing and upon some other cities in Sichuan Province. The five weeks having already passed by December 24, 1938, they were quite ready to receive an order to fly a mission. Because of the bad weather, they could not spend as much time as they had expected in brushing up the heavy bombers' teamwork, but the morale of each squadron was kept high and there was no element for them to think twice about executing their plan. On the day that followed—on December 25 (at 5 p.m.) —Major General Terakura collected the leaders of the flight members at the command post and made their aim clear, saying: "The city of Chongqing shall be attacked so we may shock the enemy's administration from top to bottom." The leaders were of the bomber fleets from the 60th and the 98th flying corps, of the combat forces with command of the air from the 59th flying corps and the 10th squadron of the independent flight, and of the 18th squadron of the independent flight to assume the aerial reconnaissance of the Chongqing area. As for the bombers, there were twelve heavy bombers of 97-type and ten heavy bombers of Italian type. Now Terakura explained to each of the leaders which quarter would be the aim of their first attack upon Chongqing.

It was impossible that Terakura should have been well acquainted with the air raid upon Guernica performed a year and a half before by the Air Force of Nazi Germany. By that time, Japan and Germany had regarded each other as a sworn friend, but Hitler, being afraid of receiving a concentrated accusation from abroad, had firmly denied his having been engaged in the indiscriminate bombing upon Guernica, while in Spain General Franco had been repeating his statement that Gernica's having gone up in flames was caused by the army of the Basques, who had set the town on fire.

Captain Nishiura Susumu, a member of the Bureau of Military Affairs in the Ministry of War, who happened to be studying in France at that time, had once entered the front line with great difficulty to fight for Franco's Army and brought back a report on the war situation there to Japan's General Staff Office, but since this had happened before the bombardment on Guernica, no report on that indiscriminate bombing upon that city had been included in it. So, the tragedy that happened in that ancient capital of Basque had not yet been known to Japan, just as those works by Picasso had not.

But comparing the orders given by Terakura and by Wolfram von Richthofen as the chief of staff of "the Condor Corps," we can find many points in common; as is easily imagined, the greatest point in common was that conception: "there is no need to give any consideration to people in general." There was simply no demarcation between combatants and non-combatants, or between the battle lines and the home front. According to *The Diary* kept by Wing Commander Rchthofen Wolfram, the order of the bombardment upon Guernica went as follows:

Fly the mission at once. A 88 and J 88 (middle-sized bomber fleets) shall attack the roads within the districts of Marquina, Guernica and Cuerkais. K88, VB88 and Italian Air Force shall destroy the roads and bridges just east of Guernica (including its suburbs). The districts concerned must be blockaded so that we may finally win the fruits of the battle in terms of the number of people and materiel.

——*The Birth of Picasso's Guernica* by A. Brandt[*]

Pilot Officer Hans Asmus, an aide to a strategist-officer of the Third Squadron of Bombers, did remember the chief of staff Richthofen saying: "We must regard everything moving along the roads and bridges as our enemies to be destroyed." (*Guernica* by G. Thomas & M. Witz*) What they meant by "winning the fruits of the battle in terms of the number of people and materials" was none other than another expression of performing an indiscriminate bombing. That was as close as a Siamese twin to what Terakura, the chief of the Army's First Air Division, told his men about their aim to achieve: "The urban area of Chongqing shall be attacked so we may shock the enemy's Administration from top to bottom." Looking back upon them from the viewpoint of the long history of warfare, the two strategies performed upon the same conception had occurred at an interval which can be regarded as the same time—one in Europe, the other in Asia.

If the Nazi's bombing upon Guernica was an experiment for their arms and tactics, Japan's air raids upon Chongqing could be called its overall finish of "the accumulated air raids" upon the Chinese cities that had already lasted for seven years.

● **"The Central Park," the Public Square, shall be the Target**
Terakura's order had referred to further information about their attack targets and a practical method to be adopted on the basis of the information gathered by a scout plane, Model 97, (which belonged to the Headquarters), as was recorded in *The Army Air Force's Operations in China* in Japan's Defense Agency's *Library of the War History of Japan:*

7) The 60th flight squadron and the 98th flight squadron shall be prepared for the cooperative attack on the urban area of Chongqing at 13 o'clock tomorrow—on the 26th.

The first aim for both of the squadrons shall be the Central Park and Metropolitan Military Government Office … the district where the office buildings for the Public Safety Commission and for the Prefectural Government stand side by side; the second aim shall be Chongqing Airbase. The bombs employed shall be more than 100kg.

The Central Park, which was made the target spot, was situated at the center of Shizong (Mid-City) Ward. It was located at the joint of the upper half and the lower half of that castle city and the Park itself had also many slopes and stone steps in it. But since it was impossible to expect so much space for the public park in that city which had been developed as if upon a dragon's nape, the scanty space of that park had efficiently been made use of as a recreation center equipped with teahouses, restaurants, tennis courts and so on, thus offering the citizens a moderate place for recreation and relaxation. Since it also provided a green zone, when seen from above, it ought to have been easily recognizable. Around the park, there were a large number of shops and houses closely connected by irregularly complicated lanes and stone steps. Among them there certainly existed some Provisional Offices for the Military Committee and the like, but it was totally impossible to find in and around the neighborhood any such military targets as army posts for military units or armories. Still it had been made a standard impact area for the 100kg bombs. It was simply apparent that it could not help causing tremendous damages in and around that area.

Still having made their bombing a regional one by employing the bombs which weighed 100kg or more, and having set the time at 1 p.m. had come from "our study to gain the greatest effect in frustrating the enemy's will to go on fighting," as was commented in *The Army's Aerial Strategy in China* in the Defense Agency's Library of the War History. By displaying Japan's military power by trampling upon the enemy's capital in the broad daylight, they had aimed at discrediting Jiang Jieshi's dignity, thus to make the citizens get weary of war. Precisely at that period, Wang Zhaoming, a powerful political figure next to Jiang—the deputy Chairman of the Chinese Nationalist Party—rebelled against the Party by Japan's political maneuvering, and escaped to Hanoi (on December 20). This also helped the Japanese side to judge: this would be a good opportunity for them to take advantage of the enemy's agitation both in their administration and in public mind. This was how the senior staff of the headquarters judged that: there arose the conditions that would enable them to destroy their enemy nation's will to go on fighting.

As it happened, however, despite that meticulously-prepared project to attack the enemy, that first attempt turned out to be a total failure. The First Air Division failed to achieve any such result as the Condors that had attacked Guernica did. What caused this failure was none other than the clouds and fog that were to keep preventing the Japanese airmen from being successful throughout the period of their operations upon Chongqing. The German Air Force was able to reach Guernica in twenty minutes, and in an hour and half they could be ready to go into action again. On the other hand, the Japanese flying corps took three or even four hours before arriving at the sky of Chongqing. Naturally, the misjudging or the sudden changes of weather were to weigh heavily upon the whole operations of that day. The success or failure of the operations cannot be measured without assuming their risk bearing. Thus the Japanese Army's first aerial attack upon Chongqing turned out to be a failure.

● **The First Mission by the Army's 22 Planes Failed to Achieve their Purpose**

At 8 a.m. on December 26, at Hankou Air Base (in Wuhan), Major General Terakura entered the command post for the First Air Division. At 8:30, the two chiefs of the squadrons—Colonel Tanaka Michitomo of the 60th squadron and Colonel Hattori Takeshi of the 98th squadron—arrived there with their troop commanders and received the orders. Major General Terakura told them the decision he had made, after considering the weather forecast brought by the scout plane: "The volume of the clouds is large but seems to move away by the time our planes reach the skies of Chongqing. So I believe you will be able to attack the designated targets from the height of 5,000 meters."

That was the first time for the army planes to make such a long-distance flight to perform such a long-range bombardment. The airmen, intently listening to their chief, were extremely eager to perform their duty, and after folding their aerial map, they held it in their left hand, and after raising their right hand in salute to the chief, they all made for their own plane.

The bombers that had been arranged in lines at Hankou Air Base were twenty-two in all: twelve Model 97 heavy bombers (for the 60th squadron) and ten Italian-style heavy bombers (for the 98th squadron). The former was new and powerful, but its production had just started and its number was still far from enough and that was why the Italian-made Fiat BR20 bombers were adopted to make up for the shortage. Naturally this fact had not been mentioned in the announcement of the achievements performed by the Army Air Force admiringly called "Eagles," but that was an unmistakable fact.

The Army, which had been stimulated by the Navy's brilliant transoceanic bombings upon Nanjing, was too impatient to wait for the completion of their

Model 97 heavy bombers, and as a makeshift measure they planned to purchase some from abroad and sent a negotiation committee to have direct negotiations with Mussolini and succeeded in purchasing 72 planes known as BR20. The planes of this type had already been thrown into the Spanish front along with the Italian Air Unit to engage in the bombardments on the battlefields and cities along with Junkers' Ju52 of the Condor Corps, and this led Japan to judge that its capacity needed in action had already been proved. The Fiat BR20 bombers, which were to be known as "the Italian-style heavy bombers" in Japan, had been carried from the factory at Torino to Livorno Naval Port situated in the south of Pisa to be directly transported by sea to Dalian Port in China, and after having been assembled there and having made the pilots learn how to manage it there, they were assigned to the flying corps of the Japanese Army. The 98th squadron was among the recepients of the Fiat BR20. If it were to carry 500kg of bombs, its action radius would be reduced to 750km, and this would prevent it from going to and from Chongqing, so its carrying capacity had to be reduced to 300kg, and still "the Italian-style heavy bombers" that came to join the 98th squadron were to remain as something meaningful in the world history of aviation—because from that day onward, the Fiat BR20 bombers that had been developed by Mussolini's Air Force were to be the first to perform the air raids upon a couple of capitals in the world—Chongqing in Asia and Madrid in Europe.

Before entering their plane, the aviators took off their cap with a pair of windbreak glasses fixed upon it and bowed toward far-off Japan. The sun had risen at 8:16. Only two hours had passed since then, and this caused a long shadow behind each of those who were making a profound bow. Even though Wuhan was situated in a warm area, the winter solstice had already been over and this caused their expiration to appear white.

Then the twelve 97-type heavy bombers began to move toward the taxiway one by one. Bathing in clouds of sand that caused the planes to be occasionally invisible, they moved on to the takeoff point and began to take off at 10:30. High up in the air, they flew into formation before they turned their nose westward. At 10:50, the ten Italian-style Fiat BR20 bombers also disappeared into the same sky. There were twenty-two planes in total. This was about the same military potential as the twenty-three bombers of Junkers Ju 52 which had joined in the bombardment upon Guernica. But the latter had been accompanied by the same number of fighter planes, while the former had none, because in those days, there were not yet any such fighter planes in the world as would be able to accompany such a long-distance bombing action as this, so the number of the planes themselves was about the half of that of the Condor Corps. If they were to meet the interceptor fighters sent by the Chinese Army, they would have to engage in the bombardment while fighting against them by means of the five machine guns with the muzzle of 7.7mm.

Ahead of the heavy bomber fleet that had flown into the open air, the thick layer of clouds looking like walls was awaiting them. Setting their course along the Yangzi, they were coming into the skies of Xuanchang which lay a little before a halfway point, but all they could see before them were nothing but thick layers of clouds. At 1:35 p.m. they were supposed to have been in the skies of Chongqing, but they could see no rift in the thick clouds about 3.000m in altitude.

As is commonly said: "The dogs in Shu (Sichan Province) bark at the sun," that was nothing but a common phenomenon in the foggy season in the southern part of Sichan Province, but for the airmen who made it a rule to aim at something they had caught by visual inspection, nothing could be done but returning home, carrying their bombs along with them. That was what happened to the 60th squadron. Twenty minutes later, the 98th squadron of the Italian-style Fiat BR20 bombers arrived in the skies of what seemed to be the urban area of Chongqing, and from among the clouds they managed to have a glimpse of what seemed to be the eastside district of Chongqing, and this led them to drop some bombs upon it but they could not see how effective they were.

As for these attacks that day, no entry could be found in the records kept by the Chinese side: *The Statistical Chart of the Damages Caused by the Air Raids in Various Parts of Sichuan Province—in the 27th year of the Republic of China*. Then the bombs might have been dropped either in the mountain or in the Yangzi. Thus the first air raid upon Chongqing turned out something far from their original intention to "shock the upper and the lower of the Jian Administration."

But Japan's bombardment upon Chongqing had just started. Even if their first plan had been frustrated, it could not have affected in their fundamental plan of action to perform the strategic and political bombings upon Chongqing to make the Jiang Administration surrender, nor Japan had had any other electives to perform. The Army Air Force kept making efforts, intending to set their "regular bombings upon Chongqing" on their way with their mixed formations of the Model 97 heavy bombers and the Italian-style heavy bombers. On the other hand, the Navy, which had largely reorganized its air force in the China Region when the Battle for Capturing Wuhan was over, was now building up the war potential even larger than before at "the W Base" in Wuhan. The Order issued by Terakura was by no means an unexploded shell but a bomb with a late-time fuse, because it was soon to burst out like thunderbolts in the midst of the citizens of Chongqing.

● **The First Air Battle against the Chinese Fighter Planes**

The second mission to the urban area of Chongqing was performed twelve days later—on January 7, 1939—by those same two flying corps and the Twelfth Corps (consisting of nine Italian-style heavy bombers). In total, there were thirty-one (twelve 97-type heavy bombers & nineteen Italian-style heavy bombers). As for the bombs, each of the former was equipped with a couple of 250kg bombs (24 bombs in all); each of the latter with three bombs of 100kg (57 bombs in all). On that day, too, the skies of Chongqing were filled with thick clouds about 2,500m in height, but the Italian-style heavy bombers of the 12th Corps flying ahead caught sight of the summit of Mt. Jinfu (2,200m above sea level) in the southeast and making this a reference point, they bombed upon what seemed to be the urban area. The two other corps that followed also did the same thing from the altitude of 4,200m. According to the record kept by the Chinese side, they had nineteen enemy planes that day, and 74 bombs they dropped caused five deaths and seven injuries, and five houses were destroyed. But since the impact areas were far and wide, the urban area was saved from being seized with panic.

On January 10, Japan gave the third attack; on January 15, the fourth attack. On the 10th, they had sent three squadrons with 30 planes (a dozen of 97-type heavy bombers & 18 Italian-style heavy bombers). From between the broken clouds, they were able to confirm where they were, and this led them to drop their bombs on the urban area from an altitude of 4,500m; most of the bombs seemed to have hit the marks, and the squadron chief was finally able to give a satisfying report to the headquarters. In that report, there was a reference to the four Chinese fighter planes that had taken off, but no air battle took place nor they received any anti-aircraft fire, and this led the squadron chief to report that Chongqing's air-raid preparations still remained insufficient. According to

A Brief History on the 60th Squadron, they "saw Chongqing for the first time from afar" and they "took an opportunity to perform pinpoint bombings," but the brief description found in *The Statistical Table concerning the Damages Brought by the Air Raids in All Parts of Sichuan Province during the 28th Fiscal Year of the Republic of China (1939)* simply goes as follows, suggesting the scanty achievement on the Japanese side:

> January 10: In Chongqing, 27 enemy planes appeared in three waves and dropped 10 bombs.

On January 15, Japan made the fourth mission. It was then that they fought their first air battle. From the scout plane flying ahead, they had received the information: "the skies of Chongqing are clear" and "the twelve fighter planes are seen in the sky." Thus against the twenty-nine Japanese bombers about to invade the skies of Chongqing, a dozen of Chinese fighters came to bar their way. From the ground, there came anti-aircraft fire, too. The Chinese fighter planes concentrated their attacks upon a couple of squadrons of the Italian Fiat BR20 bombers, which were rather slow in motion, and more and more Fiats got shot but kept remaining in the air. On the other hand, many of the anti-aircraft fires burst at the wake of the formations, thus keeping the planes from being damaged.

In the meantime, the twenty-nine bombers dropped their bombs in the urban area to wrap up the vicinity of their aims in flames. This led the Reuter's News Agency in Chongqing to give its first report from the actual place of Chongqing: "By the aerial bombings performed by more than twenty Japanese airplanes, several places on both banks of the Jialing were bombed, causing many people to be killed or injured." UPI (United Press International) gave more precise information* on what the air raid was like:

> The main targets of the Japanese military's air raid had included the suburbs of Chongqing and the quay at the tip of the peninsula between the Yangzi and the Jialing. The quay having been totally blown up, the storehouses there were sent to collapse. Five junks on the Yangzi were capsized. On the 15th, the citizens of Chongqing were forced to hear the loud reverberations of huge bombs' explosion far and near; in midair the anti-

aircraft shells burst violently while the rattling sounds of machine guns' shots came falling from the planes being engaged in the battle. All of these unprecedented experiences having deprived them of their peaceful dream, the citizens were forced to taste a real sadness.

According to *The Statistical Chart on the Damages & Casualties Caused by the Air Raids in Various Parts of Sichuan Province in the 28ᵗʰ Year of the Republic of China*, there were 34 deaths and 55 injuries that day. But no damage had been given on "the line that runs from the Metropolitan Military Government Office.... to the Prefectural Government Office in the vicinity of Central Park."

Thus in the four expeditions made by the Army's Heavy Bomber Fleet, five hundred and twenty-one 100kg bombs, twenty-two 250kg bombs—57.6 tons of bombs in total—were dropped and 2,692 balls were released from machine guns during the strafing attacks. Even if the fruits of the battle were far from what they had expected, but through that series of bombardments, they found that the enemy's air force was lacking in fighting spirit and that their air defense setup had not yet been properly provided, and this led the headquarters at Hankou to intensify their confidence in performing a day-time fierce attack on the capital only by the squadron of heavy bombers.

On January 22, the Domei News Agency[*] in Shanghai reported: "Among the people in Chongqing, there has arisen a rumor that the Japanese airplanes will come to exterminate all the cities in China, and after Wang Zhaoming got away from Chongqing, that fearful rumor has spread uncontrollably too far." On the day that followed—23ʳᵈ, Reuter's News Agency also reported: "The citizens of Chongqing are rushing out of the city day after day, and the number has reached as large as 30,000 a day. Those evacuees are crossing the Jialing to go on along its northern bank." Thus it also made reference to the psychological effect of the indiscriminate bombings exerted upon the citizens. Either of the reports was regarded by those who were engaged in the bombardments as an encouragement to keep on "their strategic-political assaults."

[*]The Japanese News Agency (1936-45), which had been active with its branch office in several cities in China and other cities in the Southeast Asia.

At the Wuhan Base at Hankou, the Navy Air Force, while investigating what sort of attacks the Army Air Force had been making, thus extracting some lessons from them, was picking the timing of their own turn. At the Base, the 96-type attack bombers (the middle-sized attack bombers whose flying range and carrying capacity of bombs were superior to those of the Army's) had been brought together, and in and around the noisy airbase, they were being kept busy all day long, because of the training given to the flight crew and the maintenance given to the air frames. The kinds of bombs kept at the storehouse of military supplies were increasing in number, and along with the 97-type No.6 land bombs (60kg bombs), the 98-type No.7-6 bombs (incendiary bombs) became conspicuous in number. The fact that the incendiary bombs were the most effective in bombing the city had already been demonstrated in other cities in China. In December, 1938, the Headquarters of the Navy Air Force instructed that: the standard supply of No.7-6 bombs (incendiary bombs) should be 300 to each flying corps, and in April in the following year, the same Headquarters issued the order to the Aerial Arsenal to produce 3,000 bombs of this kind.

According to the report on "the stock of bombs and aerial fuel" sent by Hankou Supply Office of Munitions to the Headquarters of the Navy Air Force, their stocks on April 10, 1939 were as follows: (*The Daily Record on China Incidents kept by the Headquarters of the Navy Air Force*)

No.25 land bombs (250kg bombs) 584
The once-improved version of the above 150
No.6 land bombs (60kg bombs) 2,494
97-type No.6 land bombs (60kg bombs) 8,559
98-type No.7-6 bombs (incendiary bombs) 419

It was in May, 1939, when the Navy Air Force's series of aerial bombardment upon Chongqing—which had declared to be the Anti-Japanese Capital—started for the purpose of reducing the Jiang Jieshi's Administration to submission. Counted from the day when the first air raid was performed in February the year before—after the bombers had taken off at the base of Nanjing—Chongqing was to have been placed under the fear of Japan's aerial bombing for as long as five years and a half, and the most exacting days for the citizens there were those of the two years and a half—starting in May, 1939.

The U.S. Gunboat *Tutuila* at anchor on the Yangzi, seen from Chongqing（see P.20）

The Japanese Gunboat *Hira*（see P.20）

The 88-type scout plane employed by Ishiwara Kanji（see P.56）

The 96-type land-attack bombers（see P.67）

The U.K. gunboat *Ladybird*（the central one）was sent to the bottom by the Japanese planes trying to capture Nanjing （1937）（see P.73）

An Italian-style heavy bomber （Fiat BR20）（see P.80）

I15 and I16 fighters from the Soviet Union Air Corps (see P.83)

A 96-type attack plane and the aircraft carrier *Kaga* during the operations in China. (see P.78)

The world's first aircraft carrier, *Hōshō*, built as su from the stage of its design (see.P.61)

What seemed to be Wuhan Base seen from the air (1941) (see P.85)

Zaotain-men (Emperor's Gate) to Chongqing (left) & the private houses along t Jialing (right) in summer, 1938 (from a graphic magazine, *Liang You*)

In 1911, Captain Tokugawa Yoshitoshi piloted the plane (above) brought out by Henri Farman (1874-1958) (see P.79)

CHAPTER II

THE INDISCRIMINATE BOMBING STARTED (1939)

The New Capital in May

● The People Anxious to Bathe in the Sunshine of May

Nothing is more welcome than the sunshine of May for those who live in the southern part of Sichuan Province. The curtain of fog that had been immovably hanging for as long as half a year since November of the previous year—keeping the people feeling as if suffering from migraine—was now vanishing slowly but steadily, and they were allowed to bathe in the sun after a really long wait. That was the arrival of the radiant month of May, for which everyone would really like to express one's welcome to it.

The winter of this mountain castle city, which is also called by the name of "the foggy capital," is especially characterized by the unusual thickness of fog, and it is by no means an exaggeration even if one may say: "Here in Chongqing, we are separated from the rest of the world for as long as six months in a year." In fact, the number of foggy days in a year reaches as many as 150 days or even 180 days; As for the hours of sunshine, its yearly mean is only 1,188 hours; and in December and January, the very foggy days last for as many as 25 to 28 days a month, and the hours of solar radiation are less than 30 hours a month—barely an hour a day. So it is quite understandable why that popular saying—"the dogs in Shu (Sichuan Province) bark at the sun"—was brought into being. No wonder how anxiously the people in Chongqing are (and were) waiting for the arrival of that blessed season of sunshine.

Guo Moruo, who had been living in Chongqing throughout the period of the Anti-Japanese War, wrote about the fog there—partly cursing it and partly feeling nostalgic for it—in the 13th volume of his anthology: *The Heaven is Black; The Earth is Yellow:*

> Six full years had passed since I began to live in Chongqing. Almost every day I had been cursing what Chongqing is. This was the case with my neighbors, too. But when I was about to leave here, I found I had come to love it so much that I could not bring myself to leave it so soon and so easily. (omission)
>
> We have cursed the fog of Chongqing. Here we cannot enjoy sunshine for as long as half a year; we cannot be blessed with ultraviolet rays for so many months. Indeed, this is none other than a fatal defect of this city. But, sometimes, this fog of Chongqing can be admirable. Throughout the periods of the air raids we suffered, the fog had kept us safe, performing its responsibility for protecting us. Now I recommend you to look at those noted mountains and rivers through the veils of fog. You will find them indescribably beautiful. They are none other than what Chongqing really is—something unable to find in any other region either in Jiangnan (South of the Yangtze) or in the Northern China.

Those who had come from the coastal areas such as Shanghai or Beijing, just as Guo had done, must have entertained themselves with almost the same kind of emotion as Guo did.

In 1939, too, the people in Chongqing had been expecting much of the arrival of May in which they would finally let the fog go and enjoy the arrival of the beloved season of sunshine. No one had ever dreamed—what would be sent from the heaven would be the light and heat of the terrifying bombs.

Naturally, since the capital was moved up there, the leaders of the Nationalist Party had fully been aware that: the air raids upon it would be inevitable sooner or later. They had also grasped even to the details of how much preparations were being made by the Japanese Army and Navy Air Force at Wuhan—their having built what they called W Base while collecting their bombers there. Now that the fog was lifted and the dividing point of the Yangzi and the Jialing became easily recognizable, the urban area of Chongqing was as good as defenseless. Naturally the relevant authorities had taken measures to meet the situation in both ways of positive air-raid precautions (interceptor fighter planes and anti-aircraft guns) and of passive air-raid precautions (air-raid caves and evacuation measures), but as was usually the case with the side placed under pressure, they remained unmistakably forestalled, compared with the operation readiness made by the Japanese Military. The Government had failed to inform the people of the air raids to come before long; they had also failed to give the air-raid instructions and the evacuation drills to the people, partly because the recent assaults given by the Japanese Air Force during the winter had come off without giving them much damage. This had naturally led the people to remain unprepared against the air raid they might suffer at any moment. Among the rumors the people in town had shared through the newspaper report, there was such a one as "the Japanese planes are planning to destroy all the cities in China," as Japan's Domei News Agency (1936-45) at Shanghai had once reported, but the public opinion in Chongqing had still remained rather optimistic, saying: "The Japanese military may be cruel, but they won't go so far as to drop bombs on the urban area."

The sudden increase in population and an unusual rise in price having made their life harder and harder, the people had tended not to accept any more bad news. The fog having gone, the people—both the locals living there generation after generation and those who had unexpectedly been made to move up there— had simply wished not to hear any more bad news but to meet the days when they would be able to enjoy more and more sunshine as the days went by.

This was how the new capital came to expose herself in the long-awaited sunshine of May. As for what Chongqing used to look like about this period, a German journalist, Lily Abegg, had recorded it in *CHONGQING* she later published. As a Far East special correspondent of Frankfurter Zeitung, she had frequently been coming and going between Japan and China. It was after the fall of Wuhan when she entered Chongqing, following the Jiang Administration.

In this work of hers, one can see the remarkable reflections of the times from the Anti-Comintern Pact between Germany, Italy and Japan (1939) to the Tripartite Pact (1940). (*The Preface* to its Japanese version was written by a Japanese Army Officer, Colonel Yoshino Hiroyuki.) What was described in it was what Chongqing used to be, that dear old mountain-castle city, which was soon to be destroyed never to be restored:

Chongqing, the new capital of China, is one of the most beautiful capitals in the world. That is situated in Sichuan Province, whose soil is the richest in China. Before the war, if one took a boat at Shanghai, one could reach there in a dozen days or so by the Yangzi, but today since this voyage is cut off by the Japanese Navy, one must reach there either by land or by air. The scenic beauty in and around Chongqing is such that one may feel as if one were in a park wherever one may go, and this easily makes us forget its climatic inconvenience or discomfort. The terraced paddy fields on the slopes of the high grounds, bamboo groves, Chinese windmill palms and navel oranges make us feel as if we were in a subtropical region. This fertile plain in the valley is surrounded by the mountains with a romantic atmosphere caused by the ample pine trees whose branches are curiously curved and by the unusually-shaped huge cliffs or fantastic precipices. It is only after one visits Sichuan Province that one is finally able to understand why the Chinese painters and artists have been able to produce such fantastic works as those we have seen so far.

As to what the city looked like and what its residents were, Lily Abegg was rather vitriolic, but as a whole she seemed to have come to like it very much and wrote: the summer is hot, but the winter is mild, and this makes the Westerners feel as if they were staying in a greenhouse.

● The City whose Scenery Gives Kaleidoscopic Changes

To another woman, Han Suyin, who had also entered this city in the midst of confusion, the same scenery apeared rather different from what was admiringly taken by Lily Abegg. Unlike Abegg who was able to identify herself as a special correspondent, Han Suyin had entered this city as the wife of a Chinese officer of the Nationalist Army then retreating as far as Chongqing. Suyin, then twenty-one years old, had never imagined that she would be a writer in the years to come to produce a huge autobiographic modern history of China, which included *Birdless Summer* often quoted in this book. Han Suyin at that time, however, was nobody but a Chinese woman, who was born between Chinese father and Belgian mother. Han Suyin then was doing all she could in the wild waves of that era, while being annoyed by the widening crack between her husband and herself. Her life at Chongqing under air raid after air raid could be called a household version of the Chinese Civil War then being fought between the Nationalists and the Communists. But it was through none other than that struggle that she herself was also able to reach a turning point which was to lead her to a victory in her own life.

Han Suyin's impression of the new capital of China was dark and fierce, as she had depicted in one of her works, *Birdless Summer:*

> Chungking was a phantasmagoria, a monster, brusque chimera, an unreal and thorough freak; a fortress where trees could not grow on the inch-thin soil covering the rock. A city of squalor and filth, and with one of the most impossible climates on earth; a furnace in summer, in winter swallowed by unrelenting fog; and yet, for all its squalor, its rats, its misery, its desolation, its impossible cruelties, it was also magnificently, raucously alive, palpitating with the storid triumph of its million people, whose sufferings seemed endless, whose courage, determination and forbearance towards gross injustice was the cindery mask over the flame that would one day devour all this structure of evil.

The two women ought to have seen the same things in the same landscape, but the impressions they received had become sharply different from each other because of the difference in their situations and political viewpoints. Abegg's impression of the inhabitants there was a detached one, which led her to say: "Generally speaking, the inhabitants in Chungking are idle, as is known by the fact that: they frequent at the eating-and-drinking places whose number is greater than that in any other cities in China, and while drinking and smoking, they are talking all day long." On the other hand, Suyin had an ear sharp enough to catch "the phlegmatic war cries given by one million inhabitants there" in the depth of their way of life, because she had been placed in such a place as would enable her to hear those cries.

As Suyin had seen, the landscapes kept changing as rapidly as if they were those of a revolving lantern. In May, the population of Chongqing was announced to have reached 700,000. Since the population of the whole city in 1936 was 339,204, it had grown about twice in three years. Still, more people were flowing in. Shizhong (Mid-City) Ward was overcrowded with newcomers and new institutions. It was easy to tell whether one was a local or a newcomer.

Hearing one speak was one of the ways to find it, but a mere sight of one enabled anyone to tell it, because the new comers were in Western clothes or in the uniform of the Chinese Nationalist Party or in military uniform, while the locals were in traditional clothes and a hemispheric cap. But it was not long before the influx of population was such that the locals began to appear rather conspicuous among the crowds.

All the vacant lots in Shizhong (Mid-City) Ward became thickly occupied with dwellings—from palace-like houses to shanties—and this was to send the coolies and beggars into the streets or parks. The urban area was rapidly expanding to the west of Shizhong (Mid-City) Ward and to Nan-An (South Shore) Ward that lay beyond the Yangzi and to Jian-Bei (North of the River) Ward beyond the Jialing, and still they could barely accept such a growing population. When some guests of honor arrived, the police blocked the traffic of the streets and drove all the beggars away from them, as was observed by Suyin. The capital of the Free China was often visited by "the Mission for Assisting Jiang" from the United States, the United Kingdom, the Soviet Union and so on, and every time one of those Missions arrived, those simple huts of the wandering people—each of them was "as wide as four mahjong-tables"—were pulled down only to be rebuilt overnight.

Suyin herself, even if being on the fortunate side as the wife of a high-ranking officer, had to spend the first two weeks at a flophouse-like hotel, where "at night, herds of rats ran noisily around the staircases, and during the daytime the prostitutes, also in groups, paid a regular visit there." On both sides of the two rivers, innumerable junks of all sizes, whose sails were unanimously patchy, had tied themselves together so that they might not be washed away by the powerful flows of the Rivers, thus forming the large communities there, too.

For Zhang Xiluo, a reporter for *Xin Min Bao* (*The New Information for the People*), this sort of active life in the new capital was a series of stimulating experiences. In later years—after having spent half a century as a journalist—he became a member of the Chinese People's Political Consultative Conference, while occupying the post of vice-chief editor of *The Report on the People's Political Entente Conference*. But Zhang at that time, a fledgling news reporter still in the first half of his twenties, was simply enjoying going out here and there by *rickshaw* to collect news materials.

Chongqing had been known for its cliffs and stone steps, and not until only ten years or so before, even a single automobile could be seen. Several years before, they had come to have a motorway that made a circuit of the Shizhong (Mid-City) Ward, and this was to lead to the advent of rickshaws along with the passenger cars and buses. As a means of traffic, palanquins still remained rather common, and this did cause the young reporter to feel rather proud of employing a *rickshaw* in his outing to gather information.

Xin Min Bao (*The New Information for the People*) for which Zhang worked had been established at Nanjing in 1929, and since May in 1938, when its headquarters was moved to Chongqing, it had kept publishing the same paper. The compact lineup consisted of fifteen reporters and eleven editors under the chief editor, and along with its branch offices in Nanjing, Shanghai, Beijing and Chengdu (the Capital of Sichuan Province), it printed 15,000 copies of its morning paper. As for the rotary presses, they were bought in 1931 from the *Asahi* Newspaper Publishing Company in Japan, and after the fall of Nanjing, they had been carried up here with great difficulty. According to the memory kept by Zhang Xiluo, they had kept only three rotary presses at that newspaper company in Chongqing at that time.

● **Those who were Working at Zhou Enlai's Office**

The publisher of *Xin Min Bao* (*the New Information for the People*) could not have obtained the permission to publish his paper without professing himself to be pro-*Kuomintang* (Chinese Nationalist Party), but since he had originally been among the newly-arrived entrepreneurs called democratic capitalists, also having a close relationship with some important members of the militarist clique of Sichuan Province, he had maintained an attitude to report without sticking too close to the Establishment but from a standpoint comparatively free from the Nationalist Party's regime. Still the authorities' censorship was so strict that a certain article was all deleted, and he could not help issuing a paper some of whose space remained blank. Such a blank was called "a skylight window," and how that blank made in the first printing could be filled in the next printing was considered to be a chance for a copy editor to show his ability. Zhang, a fledgling reporter, who remained politically independent, had once written a report of an interview with a member of Communist Perticipators in Politics— Wu Yuzhang (whose secret position was a standing committee of the Central Southern Bureau of the Chinese Communist Party)—without knowing what he was and caused the chief editor to feel a chill (even though this article did not make "a skylight window").

In his information gathering , Zhang occasionally came across a reporter of *Xin Hua Ri Bao* (New China Daily News). That newspaper, the Chinese Communist bulletin in Chongqing, had exceptionally been allowed to publish in "the capital of Jiang Jieshi." But few were the institutions that would readily accept the reporters of that newspaper whose virtual chief editor was Zhou Enlai. For the reporters of *Xin Hua Ri Bao,* whose having shown their visiting card simply led to being declined to meet someone they wanted to meet. This often led Zhang to cooperatively provide the unfortunate reporter with the information he had obtained. He had gradually come to pay respect to those who kept collecting news materials even under such tough conditions.

For *Xin Hua Ri Bao* at that time, Qiao Quanhua, who was later to be the foreign minister, Huang Hua who also was to the foreign minister after having been the first ambassador to the united Nations, and Mrs. Qiao or Gong Peng who was also a news reporter, were working, while employing a variety of identities openly or not openly, thus helping Zhou Enlai, the chief editor, who had always been kept busy. As was expected, the frequency of their having "a skylight window" in their paper, *Xin Hua Ri Bao,* was much greater than *Xin Min Bao*, and its frequency became a scale with which to measure the stability or the tension in the Nationalist-Communist collaboration. At one time, Zhou himself wrote the editorial; at other times, he—as the vice director of the Department of Politics in the Military Committee or as the representative of the office of "Balujun (the Eighth Route Army)" at Chongqing—argued with Jiang and his administrative organ.

"Zhou's Office" at No. 50 in Zengjia-an of Shizhong (City's Central) Ward was the office of Zhou Enlai as the representative of Balujun (the Eighth Route Army), and Zhang Xiluo often visited there, and among the reporters from abroad, he ought to have seen Edgar Snow and Theodre White who, after having entered Chongqing, chose to be a special correspondent of *Time* or the U.S. news weekly. White, who came to call himself "a reporter on Asia," had made himself a constant visitor to "that old house which might fall at any moment." As he later wrote in his book—*In Search of History*—he was to "meet many interesting characters at this parlor during the five years that followed." Among them were Dong Biwu, one of the legendary founders of the Chinese

Communist Party, Ye Jianying, a pleasantly light-hearted person, and Lin Biao who appeared hard to please. White called Qiao Quanhua, a reporter of *Xin Hua Ri Bao,* "a journalist both passionate and revolutionary"; as for Gong Peng, he offered such a great admiration as "the most beautiful Chinese woman I have ever met" and "a speaker of good English, not only correct but also fluent, even though she used to be active as an anti-Japanese guerrilla in northern China— an authentic heroine carrying a pistol—before she was nominated to come up to Chongqing."

Zhang Xiluo himself, while frequenting Zengjia-an, had come to receive a strong impression from Zhou Enlai and his comrades not only for their political view but also for their charm as human beings.

Zhang Xiluo as a reporter of *Xin Min Bao* (The New Report for the People), who had been allowed to approach the military information and facilities to a certain extent, was well aware of the fact that: this new capital would be extremely weak in the attack from the air. Upon each of the four hills surrounding Shizong (City's Central) Ward, an anti-aircraft battery position was brought into being, equipped with six anti-aircraft guns. But when Zhang visited one of them, the troop commander expressed his frustration that: the effective range of these guns was only from 1,500m to 2,000m in altitude, and so they would simply remain ineffective to the invasion of Japanese airplanes. To Zhang's immense worry and frustration, the Chinese Air Force had still remained insubstantial, too; to make the matter worse, neither full-scale air-raid drill had ever been given to the inhabitants nor proper amount of information had ever been provided for them.

● The Air Defense Setup still Remained as Good as Nonexistent

Wen Shayang, the chief of the Department of Medical Examination at Renji Hospital—the general hospital at the heart of the City of Chongqing—was second to none in worrying about the late implementation of measures to meet the expected air raid. As a doctor, his concern was mainly in the arrangement of relief activities, but to his eye, things remained simply far from adequate. Dr. Wen had been appointed as "a company commander for the relief activities in the Central District," but to his dismay, he was simply left ignorant of what to do." Afraid that the air raid might occur any day or any night, he was feeling enraged at the lack of any necessary information.

In March or April, 1939, Wen was invited to dinner by Wang Meibai, an old friend of his. Wang was a bacteriologist who had once learned in France. While dining, Wang told his friend that he had been appointed to be the Chief of the Relief Corps of Chongqing, and this led him to divide Shizhong Ward (Central Ward) into several sections so that each of the local hospitals might become the medical center, and that he would like his friend Wen to be the chief of the relief corps of the Central Section. Wen at once accepted it. Several days later, four jute bags with a label of the Red Cross upon them were sent to him, but he had not yet received any official announcement of appointment. In the jute bags, he found some gauze and bandages, but no medicine nor medical instruments. Apparently they were far from helpful in giving any proper treatment to those who had fallen victims to the air raid. This lack of practicality made him rather uneasy, but all he could do then was to return to his busy life at his consultation room.

Seen from a general point of view, too, the precautions against the air raid remained neglected and far from effective. Formally, the Headquarters of Chongqing's Aerial Defense had started on September 1, 1937—immediately after the Sino-Japanese War broke out: Li Guangkun or Chongqing Security Commander was made Commander, and Mayor of Chongqing, Li Guangkun, was appointed to be Vice Commander. At an emergency situation, they were expected to command all the Army Air Force and the Amphibious Police Corps, and the following preparations were expected to be made at once:

A : To make all the anti-air-craft artillerymen get ready
B : (omission)
C : To establish the air-raid wardens' stations
D : To introduce sound detectors
E : To carry out a restriction on lighting
F : To make positive effort to keep the fire-fighting equipments
in good condition
G : To start a team to collect information on aerial attacks

One year and eight months had passed since then, but everything still remained in the process of outfitting and by May, 1939, none of the items had come to the level to be judged as passable. Fire fighting had largely depended

on what was called *Long-tu-shui* (Water-Disgorging-Dragons) which needed
a party of eight men in shooting out the water kept in a wooden box. As for
the air-raid caves, the digging of the Large Tunnels had just started, and the
explosive sounds in breaking through the rocks—which made one feel as if
one's stomach was being pushed up—were being heard all day long, but they
still remained far from useful in time of need.

In a photograph taken by Carl Mydans to be sent to *LIFE*, we see several
men in fire-fighting costume standing against the fire-fighting equipment that
seems to have been used in the medieval ages. Certainly the fierce looks they
wore do appear impressive, but it seems fairly questionable how effective those
primitive devices were for the fires brought about by the incendiary bombs.
True the modern fire-fighting equipments were being installed, but their number
still remained small to a desperate extent.

As for the air defense setup, the same things could be said. After Wuhan
was abandoned, the anti-aircraft artillery of the Nationalist Revolutionary
Army was said to have been moved to their new places of duty in the vicinity
of Chongqing according to the changes of the war situations. (*A Brief History
of the Resistance War* published by the Defense Department of the Taiwan
Government), but as for the realities, its level still remained extremely
unreliable, as Zhang Xiluo had observed. The interceptor fighters, which
should be placed at the head of their active air-raid precautions, had not yet
been provided sufficiently. The four airports had been built, as if surrounding
Shizhong (City's Central) Ward upon the peninsula—Shanhu-ba Dam (on a
sandbar of the Yangzi), Baifu Station (in the west), Guangyang-ba Dam (in
the northeast) and Jiulong-ba Dam (in the south)—and fighter interceptors
had been distributed, with the priority given to Guangyang-ba Dam, the
closest to the enemy planes' advancing route, and Baifu Station, the closest to
the urban area of Chongqing. But their main force being biplanes known as
E15 & E16 made in the Soviet Union and biplanes known as Cartis Hawk P6
made in the U.S.—both of which had been active one generation before—they
were simply inadequate in both quality and quantity in preventing the enemy
planes' invasion into their sky, even if the Japanese bomber fleet's inability to
accompany their escort fighters was estimated to be of the maximum advantage.
To make the matter worse, the chronicle shortage of spare parts and aviation
fuel had kept them even from hoping to perform any intercepting activities.

In the eyes of the Japanese Navy Air Corps making steady preparations at the Wuhan Air Base, the Chinese air defense ability could not help being judged as good as nothing. The same sort of comment had been given by the Japanese Army Air Force that had once made a tryout attack upon Chongqing. This had kept the Japanese airmen's morale as high as high could be. The skies of Chongqing after the foggy season, having been left unattended even by "the natural air-defense setup," remained simply bare and defenseless toward Hankou 780km away to the east.

On May 3—when Japan's Navy's Air Corps was expecting to give its first attack upon Chongqing, the hapless city had been gleaming in the sunshine sent to her for the first time in half a year.

The Middle-Sized Bombers' Takeoff

● **Chongqing's Aerial Defense Headquarters after the Foggy Season**

On May 3, 1939, Chongqing had daybreak at 7:13. As the sun rose, the fog that had covered the urban area was rapidly disappearing. The blue sky, though remaining a little foggy, was shining all over. It certainly seemed to be the start of the day when anyone would finally be able to realize the end of the foggy season characterized by its duskiness and dampness.

At the Aerial Defense Headquarters at Zuoguan-jie Street in Chongqing, a resident cook, Qin Zhixuan, had already been working on the large pans at the kitchen. Even in the new capital, where everything still remained lacking in a feeling of tension, this Headquarters alone had been kept busy day and night, and this had led even the cooks to have no time to feel at ease. What was more, the workers at the Headquarters, including the cooks, had strictly been ordered not to leave their place of duty until they heard "an emergency warning" to inform them of the enemy planes' arrival in the skies.

For that matter, however, the air-raid cave for the staff was so close to the Headquarters, there was no need to feel uneasy. Qin Zhixuan, 27 years old and single, had always been saying to himself thankfully that he was lucky enough to have a place of work that had kept him safe at Chongqing where refugees were everywhere and joblessness and beggary had become part of their daily life.

There were three kinds of menus. The number of plates and the items on them were different. For the table of the commander Li and other leading members, the menu consisted of two dishes of appetizers, four dishes accompanying the boiled rice and a bowl of soup. For the ordinary staff members, two dishes of appetizers, two dishes accompanying the boiled rice. There was another group of people to receive their meal—a boiled rice and a bowl of soup with no ingredients in it. They were criminals suspected and detained for various reasons at the prison cells that shared the ground with the Air Defense Headquarters. Among those detained, there were political prisoners—the majority of whom were regarded as communists and their sympathizers. When the interrogation was over, they were usually transferred somewhere, but as for where they were sent, there was no knowing to anyone like Qin.

The citizens' material life had already become serious. Though living in Sichuan Province known as "Tianfu (Heaven's Warehouse)," they were suffering from a sharp rise in price even of foodstuff, but the the Air Defense Headquarters having received exceptional food supply from the Government, the cooks like Qin had been spared a hard time of going out to obtain food.

That morning, the wind had died down, and the streaks of smoke from the kitchen chimneys of the Aerial Defense Headquarters had been rising straight upward, smearing the precious azure sky above them. The fuel used in this area was *meiqiu* (charcoal ball made of Sichuan charcoal) and around the mealtime in the morning and in the evening, the smoke from *meiqiu* used to cover all over the sky, filling the air of the whole town with the smell of sulfa. The foggy season was to be succeeded by what was called "*huolu* (fireplace)" or the fierce heat with no wind, and this had earned Chongqing an unwelcome nickname of "*huolu.*" In fact, Chongqing was "one of the three great *huolus* in China" along with Nanjing and Wuhan. When that season set in, those who had felt too hot to sleep in their house, took out their bamboo beds in the street so that they might get any proper sleep, even though in the morning they had to find themselves having sunken in the mat wet with their own perspiration all the same.

If Qin Zhixuan had had any opportunity to enter the operational room of the Aerial Defense Headquarters about the time he had cleared the table after their breakfast, he would have noticed the unusual atmosphere that had strained all over the room. As it was, all the sounds that had reached Qin's ears then were his colleagues' talking among themselves, instead of the buzzing of the Japanese planes heading for Chongqing. This had left Qin Zhixuan simply having a brief rest he was allowed to enjoy then and there.

Around a little past ten o'clock, the stuff began to surround the aerial defense map hung on the wall so that they could find out where their enemy planes were flying at that moment. As the time went on, more and more people came to join that throng, talking louder and more seriously. What they had eagerly been watching was a map about three meters square. With Chongqing at the center of the map, all the cities in the southern part of Sichuan Province were marked with a large circle, their distance from the capital shown by the concentric circles drawn at intervals of 50km. The broad, winding line stretching from Chongqing to the east was the Yangzi, along which there were many dots that marked the cities. At the point where the farthest concentric circle and the easternmost part of the Yangzi intersected was seen the name of Wuhan (Hankou). The distance to Chongqing in a straight line was 780km, roughly a three-hour flight. Now the two groups of enemy planes that had taken off at Hankou were flying west even after having invaded into Sichuan Province. According to the report sent from the Aircraft Spotters' Stations, the commissioned officer on duty pointed at a new transit point with his long stick. Every time a pin was stuck upon it, there rose a commotion. Presumably, the enemy planes were heading for Chongqing or for Chengdu as the Provincial Capital.

● The Navy Air Force's Desire for Fame

The air raid unit that had received an order to perform the bombardment upon the urban area of Chongqing that day was the First Air Raid Unit formed by those who had been selected from the Second United Air Corps and the Third United Air Corps of the Navy Air Corps that had steadily been preparing for that mission at Hankou W Base. That Air Raid Unit, which consisted of forty-five 96-type land attack bombers (middle-sized bombers), was composed of the Second United Air Corps and the Third United Air Corps. As for the direction of the whole strategy, the commander of the Second United Air Corps, Rear-Admiral Kuwabara Torao, was grasping it at the Combat Commanding Station at Hankou.

Rear-Admiral Kuwabara, a member of the 37th graduating class of the Naval

Academy, had firstly been selected as a member of the 4th research committee to make himself a genuine air force officer, then to successively hold various posts such as the chief of a flying corps at Kasumi-ga-ura, and the captain of the seaplane carrier, Notoro, and the captain of the aircraft carrier Ryujo. Thus Kuwabara—along with Rear-Admiral Onishi Takijiro, who was soon to succeed him—was among the pioneers of Japan's Navy Air Force.

Now he was about to engage in the first full-scale air raid upon Chongqing by the Navy Air Corps. Since the first air raid by the Army Air Corps had ended in failure, his determination to be successful had been made even greater. As for "the attack upon the interior"—a general term employed to mean the strategic bombings upon Chongqing and several other cities in Sichuan Province—the Army and the Navy were expected to achieve their cooperative adjustment by the Central Agreement that had been concluded between them, but this did not mean they had overcome their desire for the priority or for the fame they might obtain through scrambling for it. Especially the Navy, having regarded the Yangzi valley as their own teritory to go on patrol, was full of ardor to show the Army how able they were in bombing upon Chongqing as the wartime capital putting up resistance to Japan.

On May 3—at 8 a.m., on both sides of the taxiway that led to the runway of Hankou W Base, the forty-five middle-sized bombers were seen to have lined up. Because of the bombs they held, their body had been made so heavy as to come near to touch the ground even though firmly supported by their short but stout legs. Their bodies had been camouflaged by being painted green, so that their figures might be melted into the mountainous scenery through which they were to fly. On the taxiway, the final inspection was being given to each of the planes by the ground crew.

The middle-sized bombers, whose formal name was "the Navy's 96-type land attack bomber," had had its experimental version completed in 1935 at Mitsubishi Heavy Industry Co., which had been ordered to produce as an experimental plane, and at the formal public test flight, though no bomb was being carried, it flew at the fastest speed of 324km per hour and its flying range reached as long as 5,000km—something unheard of in the world so far. The twine-engined plane with a slender body, whose legs could be drawn in, featuring the tapering wings and the disappearing mounting, had fully met the requirement of its excellent speed and great durability in flight given to

Mitsubishi Heavy Industry Co. by Rear Admiral Yamamoto Isoroku, the then director of the Technology Department of the Navy Air Force Headquarters. It was able to load one 800kg bomb or a dozen of 60kg bombs. In the year that followed (1936), that was adopted as a regular type of strategic aerial force to be deployed at all the air corps with their own base, and since then it had been made the main force in the long-distance aerial attacks throughout the period of the Sino-Japanese War.

The crew members being seven in one plane, three hundred and fifteen airmen in all lined up in the open ground before the commander's office for the middle-sized bombers and received detailed directions from their attack-leader as to the judgment of the enemy's movements, the attack target for each squadron, the adjustment of the time to invade and so on, the close arrangements were made. The offense leaders that day were Lieutenant Masuda Shogo of the 13th Air Corps and Lieutenant Irisa Toshiie of the 14th Air Corps, and the former, senior to the latter, was to control the whole. Beside him stood the Commander of the Second United Aviation Corps, Rear-Admiral Kuwabara.

The crew members—after having made their final arrangements on the ground with the windbreak glasses they had pushed up on their forehead glittering in the sunshine which was beginning to glare—sent a hand salute to the Commander Kuwabara, thus to finish the ceremony before they took off. All over the green grass covering the open ground, the air was shimmering in the heat. The crew members in their red aviation shoes, stepping firmly on the earth of Hankou in May, headed for their planes arranged in lines.

The door at the nose of the airplane was pushed open, and the crew members entered the plane built of duralumin. When the whole crew manned their own station, the chief pilot, a petty officer of flight, who had seated himself at the right-hand cockpit, started the engine while confirming what to do in a loud voice: "Fire the right engine; Fire the left engine." A couple of engines—Venus Model 45 whose capacity was 1,000h.p.—gave a flash of blue exhaust gas to set the engine going and the propeller whirling. The chief pilot, who had been listening to that burring, gave a profound nod to send a signal of "all right." Seeing this, Captain Masuda in the leading plane, leaned out of the windshield and waved his hand two or three times toward the men to attend the plane on the ground, so that they might run up to it to remove the stoppers of the wheels. Thus the middle-sized bombers, while twisting their nose, brought themselves toward the starting point. This having left the blinding yellow sand behind them, the ground crew in white uniform who had been seeing them off, waving their field cap in their right hand, were immediately gone out of sight.

● The Forty-Five 96-Type Land Bombers Flew Straight for Chongqing
780km Due West of Hankou

After the forty-five planes of the Navy Air Corps soared into the wide sky, filling the airfield of Hankou W Base with yellow sand and buzzing, they formed themselves into a couple of attack formations—one consisting of twenty-one planes of the two squadrons from the 13th Flying Corps; the other of twenty-four planes of the three squadrons from the 14th Flying Corps—before they set their course almost due west. The first plane of the first formation had Lieutenant Commander Masuda in it, while the first plane of the second formation had Lieutenant Commander Irisa, who had taken part in all the main aerial advancing operations performed by the Navy, starting with the transoceanic bombing upon Nanjing, until he was known as "the supreme treasure of the Land Attack Force."

When looked up from the ground, the formation composed of three triangles, each of which was composed of nine planes, appeared to be the Chinese character "人"*—meaning "a human being"—drawn against the wide open sky. Now the couple of formations, relying upon the compass and the sight of the Yangzi, were heading straight for Chongqing.

*All the written forms of Japanese language—not only *Kanji* (the traditional type of Chinese characters having been employed long in the Chinese culture area) but also both types of *kana* (*hiragana* & *katakana*)—are of the Chinese origin. The former had been transported in earlier days by those from China by way of Korean Penninsula. Ex. 安 → あ 世 → セ

It was not long, either, before the initial report was sent to Chongqing by the Chinese observers who had been watching what was happening at Hankou Air Base. No sooner had the Japanese bombers gone out of sight than they sent their first report: "The Japanese aircraft in large numbers have taken off, heading for Sichuan Province." The Chinese people in Wuhan had been forbidden to enter "the Japanese military base," but it was impossible even for the Japanese military to hide what they were doing in the sky—such as sending their air raid troop somewhere. For the Chinese, therefore, it was easy to tell how many Japanese planes had flown toward a certain direction; that was why that information had reached Chongqing's Aerial Defense Headquarters by way of the emergency telephone network.

The middle-sized bombers covered the 780km between Wuhan and Chongqing in four hours on their way there and in three hours on their way back. Unlike those days five months before, when the Japan's Army Air Corps had given five-time attacks upon Chongqing, the weather they had that day was perfect as perfect could be. Having passed Xuanchang, they could see on the right an endless range of the Daba mountains; below their eyes, the bright brown Yangzi proudly meandering among the mountains clad in fresh green could be seen so close as if it could be touched with their own hands. The middle-sized bombers in a couple of formations, having been taking the shortest route to their destination, were flying across the River at one time, and far away from it at another time, thus repeating their meeting and parting as if playing with that meandering flow. The point where that great river was parted into two, and where the huge mass of rocks had risen out of the water—that was where they were going to attack. In such fine weather as they had that day, it was impossible to miss it.

Until the end of the 1980s, the ANTHNHB An24 of a China's domestic airline, 中国民航 (Zhong Guo Min Hang) used to be engaged in the flight of that very same route. That passenger plane with a carrying capacity of 46, only a size larger than that Japanese middle-sized air-raider, also a twin-engined propeller plane whose passenger capacity was 46, used to reach Chongqing in a couple of hours. The contrast in the colors of the mountains and the River seen below, the spectacular sight of Sanxia (Three Gorges) when overlooked from high above—something new even to the one who had once seen it while sailing up the River—those dazzlingly white clouds which grew thicker as we approached Chongqing, and the bouncing of the plane as if it were stumbling over something.... All of these must have been experienced by those on board the middle-sized bombers that day. What was it that they had in their mind while flying across this spectacular view?

Two hours after their departure, they passed over the canyon Sanxia mentioned above. They ought to have overlooked the range of mountains of

Wuxia and "the clouds over Mt. Wushan," which is said to keep those mountain ranges from receiving any sunshine. One of those who had brought about "the Incident of 5.15, 1932,"* Mikami Taku, Sub-Lieutenant First Class, once wrote the words of *A Song of the Showa Restoration* in which "the clouds over Mt. Wushan" were referred to as something symbolic of the patriotism and the public-spiritedness cherished by those youthful commissioned officers. "The Miluo" had long been known as where Quyuan, a poet-statesman in Chu (?-223BC), drowned himself to death. (cf. *Quyuan* in Chapter 5)

On the abyss of the Miluo, waves are being perturbed,
The clouds over Mt. Wushan are flying in disturbance.
　　Now we rise in the world of turbidity,
　　Our blood boils in moral indignation.

In the spring sky of the Showa Restoration*,
Men of manliness being connected by justice,
Filling their bosom with a million of soldiers,
Will fall in tens of thousands of cherry petals.

Lieutenant Fujii Hitoshi in the Navy Air Corps at Kasumigaura, who had been among the key persons* of the fascist movement in the Navy—along with Lieutenant Junior Mikami Taku (an assailant of Prime Minister Inukai) and Lieutenant Junior Koga Kiyoshi (an assailant of the Minister to Assist the Emperor, Makino Nobuaki)—was killed in February, 1932, when his plane was shot down during the First Shanghai Incident. That was the first Japanese plane shot down by the Chinese ground fire. That occurred during a series of aerial bombings upon the urban area of Shanghai performed by the Japanese airplanes, as was witnessed by Edgar Snow in the previous chapter. Neither Mikami nor Koga who had been imprisoned—to say nothing of Fujii who was no more— could join that flight that day to perform the air raid upon Chongqing. But in a sense, this route being followed by the Japanese bombers that day could be said to have been prepared by them. Though not so conspicuously been manifested as the Army was, the Navy also, since 1930 when the Navy's Disarmament Treaty was concluded in London, could not escape the influence of ultra-nationalistic ideology that had come spreading to some young commissioned officers, and especially their disdain toward China was remarkable. The feelings they had entrusted to "the clouds on Mt. Wushan" were none other than their self-complacent view of the world cherished by those tough elements of the Navy. While looking at the clouds on Mt. Wushan, the Navy's air raid unit was now flying to Chongqing. That might have been the moment when the invisible rings of cause and effect got linked together with a click.

*They were conscious of the Meiji Restoration (1867) in which the Imperial Court became the center of the new administration.

● The Enemy's Oncoming was Kept Reporting
to the Aerial Defense Headquarters in Chongqing

While the formations of the middle-sized bombers were flying west, the Headquarters of the Aerial Defense in Chongqing was being kept busy, receiving the information on the latest position of *them: "They* are now passing over Fengjie," *"They* are now over Wanxian," "The thirty-six enemy planes are now over Fuling," and so on. The Chinese people, by making use of various means of information, had set up a cobweb-like network of the aircraft spotting stations or a sort of police cordon to notify the approach of the enemy planes.

In the plain area from Wuhan to Xuanchang, which had already been placed under the control of the Japanese Army, they mainly adopted signal fires. Since there was little or no wind, the signal fire rose vertically in the sky, enabling its message to reach fairly afar. In the mountainous region beyond Xuanchang, watchmen who had disguised themselves as coolies performed their duty by making use of wireless radios or manual signals or flag signals. When the message reached Wanxuan, Fuling and farther areas, which remained unoccupied or what was called "Da-houfang (the Great Hinterland)," they could use telephones and wireless, thus quickening the speed of transmission. Hundreds of spotters' stations arranged in a radial symmetry from the vicinity of Hankou W Base to the suburbs of Chongqing—along with the secret organizations consisting of hundreds of air-raid wardens—were carrying out their duties so that all pieces of information could be collected and entered into the large map at the Headquarters of the Aerial Defense in Chongqing. Since the information was transferred through many people who employed different means of communication, its quality could not necessarily be valid; and this day, too, the forty-five planes in a pair of formations had been reported as "the thirty-six planes in two groups." Still there was no room for doubt that Chongqing was about to face the air raid performed by such a large number of bombers.

For Qin Zhixuan and the other cooks at the Aerial Defense Headquarters, preparing for lunch had already been out of the question. By a little past eleven, the information obtained from the great map in the operational room had already been going around the whole building. If things went on in this way, the enemy planes would arrive in the sky of Chongqing a little after eleven. Then what would happen? To Qin, who had been living in Sichuan Province all his life, totally ignorant of what a modern warfare was like, what was about to happen to him still remained simply vague. It was unimaginable to him that the enemy planes should indiscriminately drop their bombs all over this urban area. The one and only thing clear to him was that: he would not be able to leave this place of duty until an emergency warning was issued.

On the other hand, those who were standing before the indication board had had no illusion concerning what the Japanese were about to do. Most of them had fought the battles at Shanghai, Nanjing, Guangdong and Wuhan. Through their own experiences, they had been well acquainted with how the Japanese Air Force had wielded their power over those cities in China, and what sort of power their blanket-bombing had demonstrated. Now, Chongqing was about to have its turn. Japan must be plotting to give it an indiscriminate bombing thus to utterly destroy it.

Xuanchang, Fengjie, Wanxuan…. As the transit points of the enemy planes came nearer, Commandant Li Gengu and his staff were kept busier, while the time limit was rapidly approaching. To Jiang Jieshi as the Chairman of the Military Committee, to the headquarters of the Nationalist Party and to the Executive Council of the Nationalist Government, the report on what was happening was being sent moment by moment through their official lines. Both of the Interception Forces at Guangyangba and Baifuyi Air Stations had also received the order to be on the alert. The most convenient airbase at Shanhuba was not available then, because half of its runway had been flooded, because the Yangzi then was in its flood season. Then the interceptor fighters must take off at Guangyangba, while the defense over the capital must be done by those from Baifuyi Station. After all, it would be no more than thirty that could intercept the enemy planes..

Now they must decide on the time to issue an air-raid warning, too. It seemed certain that enemy planes were heading for Chongqing, but it might not be improbable that they were aiming at Chengdu, the capital of Sichuan Province, which was farther northwest of Chongqing. If they received a report from Beiling, there would be no room for doubt that they were heading for Chongqing. That would be their zero hour.

● The Red Lanterns to Alarm the Citizens
of "the Arrival of the Enemy Planes"

As for the means of alarming the citizens of "the arrival of the enemy planes," there were two kinds prepared: one was to sound a siren; the other was to put up "the red lantern" on the hanger built on the elevated ground. Radio broadcasting had started in 1933, but electricity was available only in the urban area, and even in Shizhong (City's Central) Ward, oil lamps were by no means rare. So, radio still remained far from being a means of mass communication. Then what was found the most effective was to raise high what was called "a red lantern" made of red paper and thin bamboo sticks. When that bright red lantern, one meter across, was raised high up on the elevated ground, the people were able to know what situation they were in: One lantern meant "warning"; two lanterns "enemy planes are coming nearer"; three lanterns "enemy planes are over the city." The two red lanterns ordered them to enter the air-raid cave to stay there till they were reduced to one. (When the attack by poison gas was estimated, a black lantern was to be raised.)

For those who lived in the places where the visibility of the lanterns was bad because of the stone-steps or the cliffs in the neighborhood, the sound of siren was to alarm them. But, on that day, many people had simply disregarded such warnings. The people in the new capital had not yet been aware of what horror the air raid would bring to them. Some even expressed their wish to go out and see the sight of the Japanese air raiders. But if they all had intended to observe the rule, they would have immediately found that the number of air-raid caves was simply far from sufficient. Many of the public air-raid caves were still under construction, and those who were not government officials or the employees of business corporations had nowhere to go to protect themselves. Thus Chongqing that day proved itself to be simply lacking in its preparedness for receiving the air raid both in the citizens' awareness and in the Government's preparedness.

At 12:40, an air-raid warning was issued all over the city. Fifteen minutes' later, it was changed into an emergency warning. On top of Mt. Bipa 370m above sea level, two "red fire balls" were raised high, and it was not long before one more was added to them. The siren began to sound noisily. Along the side streets and lanes below the cliffs whose field of vision was poor, the members of the civilian defense corps ran around, pushing the three-wheeled handcarts with a hand siren tied upon them, shouting: "Air raid! Take refuge!" The cook, Qin Zhixuan, too, entered the cave as the air-raid shelter for those working at the government office. In the sky, he could catch a glimpse of more than thirty fighter interceptors called E15 and E16 getting ready for interception, keeping themselves at an altitude of 5,000 meters.

About that time, within the middle-sized bombers in the formation, the crew members were having an early lunch, as they had expected to enter the sky of Chongqing to start bombing sometime past 1 p.m.. Because of the large windows they had not only ahead of them but also on both sides and in the ceiling, they were feeling as if in the sunroom, and having lunch in such comfort made them temporarily forget the bloody mission they were about to perform before long. Through the windows, they could see those in the other planes also having lunch in turn. The menu consisted of a box of boiled polished rice with a single pickled red plum placed in the middle of it* and a side box with as many as ten kinds of delicatessen, including broiled fish after having been sprinkled with salt, grilled meat and sugar-and-soy-flavored omelet. The crew of seven members, after having finished lunch, drank warm coffee kept in their vacuum bottle. Below their eyes, they could still see the spectacular sight of the Yangzi though it occasionally went out of sight. The sunshine was bright and dazzling; the thick clouds that might prevent their visibility had not spread as far as the skies of Chongqing.

*Because it looked like the Japanese national flag, it was called a "Rising Sun" lunch.

From the leading plane with the commander in it, there came a signal of "warning." They had passed Fuling. A little more than seven kilometers' flight would bring them in the skies of Chongqing. The captain in each bomber pressed the buzzer to order the crew to prepare for the battle: "Man your stations for lookout." At once, the atmosphere in the plane had grown tense. The observer, who had been concentrating his attention on the aeronautical map spread before him, crasped his binocular and, standing in the middle of the central passage, began to keep a lookout through the windows on both sides. The telegraph operator moved his attention from his radio to his 20mm swivel machine gun to make sure if its magazine was working properly. At the cockpit, the chief pilot, looking at the platoon commander's plane, concentrated all of his attention in forming a formation. Over that shoulder of his, the copilot's attention was kept on the dashboard. Among the directions given before the departure from Hankou, there was the one that said: "If you find an enemy plane or planes, you shall start war in the air even without any order to do so." At the turrets of the machine guns 7.7mm across, another telegraph operator and a maintenance man were at their battle station, and set their eyes fixed outside the windshield while gripping the handles. Those middle-sized attack planes were not guarded by any combat planes. Even if they were armed with one machine gun with 20mm muzzle and four machine guns with 7.7mm muzzle, they were apparently handicapped in the air battle against the combat planes capable of moving quickly. So it was considered a fundamental manner of fighting for the middle-sized attack planes to perform repulsing while breaking through the enemy's line keeping themselves in a close formation so they could support one another in breaking through their blind spots. Once they entered their bombing route, an evasive movement being likely to prevent them from capturing their aim, their cooperative concentration of defensive fire was to become even more important. When the telegraph was sent to the Commander's Office in Hankou: "We are ready to make a dash at the enemy," the crew silently pulled themselves up in fighting posture of "we won't miss the enemies to fight against."

● The Appearance of the Incendiary Bombs as a Product of the City Bombing

In the bomb bays under the wings of the middle-sized attack planes, along with No.25 land bombs (250kg bombs) and No.6 land bombs (60kg bombs), what the Navy generally called "No.6 bombs" or incendiary bombs, whose formal name was the 98-type No.7-6 bombs, had been equipped. They were the same type of electron incendiary bombs as the German Air Force had once dropped at Guernica. In the frame of electron—an alloy made from magnecium

(92%-96%) and alminium (8%-4%)—thermite consisting of iron oxide (76%) and alminium powder (24%) were filled up, before it was completed with an ignition device and the tail unit. It weighed about 20kg. By the shock it got when dropped on the ground, its ignition device caught fire, while thermite got fire by its own priming, then to set the electron in the frame on fierce fire. The heat it released reached 2,000 to 3,000 degrees and the burning lasted for ten to fifteen minutes. The white flames it gave were too fierce to extinguish. Even if oxygen was cut off, it kept burning for a while. It was considered to have power to break through the concrete roof twenty centimeters thick. No. 6 bomb, developed and adopted formally in 1938, had already been of wide use in the Chinese front.

Another kind of bomb or a grease incendiary bomb called "No. 6 bomb Type II" had also begun to be prevalent to the corps at the battlefield. In producing that new bomb, instead of thermit employed in "No.6 bomb (Type I)", 9.78kg of solid oil incendiary composed of the mixture of benzine and paraffin was packed, and when it was set on fire, it burnt in flames as tall as five meters while giving black smoke, before the melted grease went lapping all over the floor to spread the fire, thus demonstrating the characteristic of a new weapon. That could be called a precursor of the napalm bomb which was to be developed by the U. S. Armed Forces. At the stage immediately before the 5 · 3 Air Raid upon Chongqing, the supply depot at Hankou had kept 419 No.6 Bombs (Type I) and for the Second and the Third United Air Corps, it was considered the standard to keep 300 bombs of that kind. At that same period, the Headquarters of the Second and the Third United Aviation Corps at Hankou had received from the Headquarters of the Navy Air Force in Tokyo the Users' Manual on No.6 Bombs II along with the N.B. (*Nota Bene*). At this point, a weird combination of bombing upon the city and employing the incendiary bombs was clearly being brought into being.

Unlike the bombs that hurt the enemy with their blasts and scraps of iron, the fire attack of incendiary bombs was characterized by the nature of its self-expansion. In contrast to the momentary and limited destructive power of the ordinary bombs, the flames of incendiary bombs did spread their destructive range on and on, and stayed long, bringing about incomparably greater destruction and dread than the explosives of the same weight would do. Indeed, it could rightly be called a product of the air raids upon the city. Two years had passed since the air raid upon Guernica occurred, and another appalling tragedy about to be brought to Chongqing seemed to turn out unmistakably even more atrocious, when the scale of that city was taken into account.

The Bombardment on May 3

● The Thirty Chinese Attack Planes Responded to the Japanese Invaders

It was 1:17 p.m. on May 3 that the middle-sized attack bombers made an invasion into the skies of Chongqing. The forty-five attack bombers, while retaining the formation of two groups that drew the converted wedge-shape in the sky, prepared for an attack at an altitude of 4,700m, keeping the plane with Lieutenant Commander Masuda on board in the lead. The weather was good; the air was clear. Chongqing, the mountain castle, soaring on top of the peninsula being washed by a couple of large rivers—the Yangzi and the Jialing—had clearly presented its whole figure, bathing in the sunshine of May. That was also a full view of the anti-Japanese capital brought to the eyes of the Japanese airmen. Looking down from on high, the peninsula on the Rivers looked like a leaf of a tree floating in a stagnant pool.

The moment they entered the path for dropping the bombs, the China's Air Force planes, about thirty in number, which had been watching and waiting at an altitude of 5,000m, began to give a strafing attack. They appeared to be of I 15 and of I 16 produced in the Soviet Union. Both of these types of plane had once been of the main force of the Republic of Spain and had once met the planes sent to its capital, Madrid, by Hitler and Mussolini, and now—by a curious turn of fate—they were to fight against the Japanese planes in the skies of the wartime capital of China. Setting aside those dull type of biplanes known as I 15 with fixed legs, those of I 16, equipped with machine guns with the 20mm muzzle could not be made light of, because of their excellent capability in fighting. The Chinese planes flew down from upper ahead and no sooner had they crossed the formation of middle-sized bombers in a moment than they turned round and started their next attack from upper behind. Their strafing was concentrated on the third squadron of the 14th Corps. The middle-sized bombers made a desperate counterattack, but once they entered a bombing route and set the sighting device working, they were not allowed to change their course for about twenty seconds before dropping bombs. The middle-sized bombers ready for dropping bombs resembled a herd of zebras followed by lions. All they could do then was to advance in mass formation while keeping their firing lines crossed by five machine guns equipped in each plane. For the bombers lacking in the ability to fight in the air, they had to fight under the disadvantageous conditions. The second plane and the third plane were seen to have fire started near their engine and both immediately turned into the masses of bright red flames and went falling down. The formation having broken up, they were gradually being compressed into a single formation. Still when they arrived over their target, they all set the apparatus for dropping bombs going to release their bombs of 720kg—250kg bombs, 60kg bombs and No.6 incendiary bombs—before each of them started to describe its falling orbit.

To the Japanese then and there, the Chinese Air Force's sturdy resistance was something they had not expected. But to the Chinese side, this was something quite natural. The Chinese airmen had had their fighting spirit even more stirred up at their first air battle to be performed in the presence of Jiang Jieshi, the chairman of the Military Committee, and the whole citizens of Chongqing. Unlike the air raid which had been given in the thick clouds of January by the Army Air Force, the one that day was performed in the literally perfect weather.

Most of the people having never been informed of the horror of the aerial bombing on the urban area, they were simply looking up at the planes in the sky only to satisfy their curiosity to witness the aerial battles. This did motivate the Chinese airmen to fight as bravely as they could, since they knew they were being watched by Jian Jieshi, the Chairman of the Military Committee, as well as by so many people in the city. They did fight brave battles. Thus they achieved something admirable. But apparently there were limitations in their resistance—because of their limited number of planes, the capacity of the planes themselves and their skills to employ them efficiently. They had failed not only to check the enemy's advancing into their sky but also to check them in dropping bombs upon their city. The difference of the power between the attackers and the defenders was great, though not so great as was seen toward the end of the Pacific War between the U.S. B29s and Japan's interceptor fighters. Now all the bombs were dropped in the urban area of Chongqing—in the midst of the people who had been out, wishing to witness what the Chinese Air Force would achieve.

Upon the Yangzi, there floated a U.S. gunboat, Tutuila, 50 meters long, its displacement tonnage was 385. That had been built by considering the specific requirements in sailing up and down the Yangzi so that it might defend the ambassador Nelson Johnson, the embassy staff, and the U.S. citizens staying at Chongqing as the temporary capital of China. From the deck of Tutuila, the bombardment performed that day could be seen to a scrupulous extent. Kemp Tree, one of the officers on board that gunboat, who had professed himself to have experienced more than two hundred air raids at Guangdong from 1937 to 38, wrote what he had witnessed that day in the book he authored—*The Yanzi Patrol:*

The weather finally cleared enough to let the Japs through and they grabbed the opportunity to stage the greatest mass slaughter I've been privileged to witness so far in the war. Canton was nothing! We had been sitting around for half an hour or so, with the crew on deck, expecting the air alarm to be the usual false variety, when there was a roar like a million bees approaching and when we looked up, there seemed to be bombing planes in one continuous line from one horizon to the other. Forty-five of them, wingtip to wingtip. The explosions were beyond description, and the whole thing done before our eyes from start to finish. The first bombs landed on the same side of the river as Tutu's anchorage, the line of explosions crossing the river and walking up the side of the hills on which Chungking sits.

We didn't miss a thing, except possibly the few bombs that dropped while we were diving for cover down off the top of the bridge into the armored pilot house.

It was all so unexpected we didn't have the shutters down, tin hats on or anything else ready. We just gave vent to a wow! of dismay and amazement, grabbed our hats and down we went. The concussions made the ship toss like a cabbage lead, even though the bombs landed half a mile away. The whole show was over in five minutes and the Jap planes were disappearing down the Yangtze. There were three big trails of smoke through the sky where burning planes were dropping and two parachutes swaying from side to side like kids' balloons at the fair.

Enormous fires literally leaped up as soon as the smoke and litter from the bomb explosion had died down and the flames seemed to reach ten times as high as the houses that were burning. The pole of smoke was beyond belief, and made the bright blue day almost black, hiding the sun for hours.

● The Air Raid Experienced by the Citizens of Chongqing

Under such a sky as that, the cook, Qin Zhixuan, remained far from viewing an aerial performance given by the Chinese Air Force in the sky. Because his place of work, Chongqing's Headquarters of the Aerial Defense in Zuoguan-jie (Left Government Street), along with Central Park and the Military Committee's Encampment (at Kaixuan-lu or Triumphant Return Road), had been made the standard point of aerial bombing that day. Naturally, that was something unknown to Qin, but when the whole sky was filled with the buzzing of the enemy planes, he could not help feeling terrified. Central Park, Zuoquan-jie and Kaixuan-lu lay side by side at the east-southern part of Shizong (City's Central) Ward, which used to constitute the hub of the former castle of Chongqing. When the formation of the middle-sized bombers caught sight of that single patch of bright green of Central Park in the center of their sighting device, they performed blanket-bombing, thus trying to catch their aim unfailingly in the network of fire. According to the instruction they had received, the secret of success in bombing the strategic point was to do it at a scheduled time at a scheduled place to cover it with a scheduled amount of barrage. Thus hundreds of bombs released from the blue sky came falling upon where Qin was or the busiest quarters of Chongqing.

As soon as an emergency warning was given at 12:55, Qin rushed into the cave as the air-raid shelter for the staff. As was expected, there was not any such atmosphere there as to see the sight of the aerial battle about to start. That air raid shelter which had been brought into being by digging out the hill just behind the Headquarters of the Aerial Defense was certainly sturdy, but its defect was: it had only a single entrance. What if a bomb was dropped just at that entrance? More and more people came in. The political prisoners who had been detained at the lockup of the Security Department also seemed to be driven into the cave. The air there was becoming rank and sultry, when a series of concussions occurred, making Qin's body rock. A bomb must have been dropped somewhere near here. ....

Zeng Zhiwei, a store clerk, was then out in Luohan-si Street. An emergency

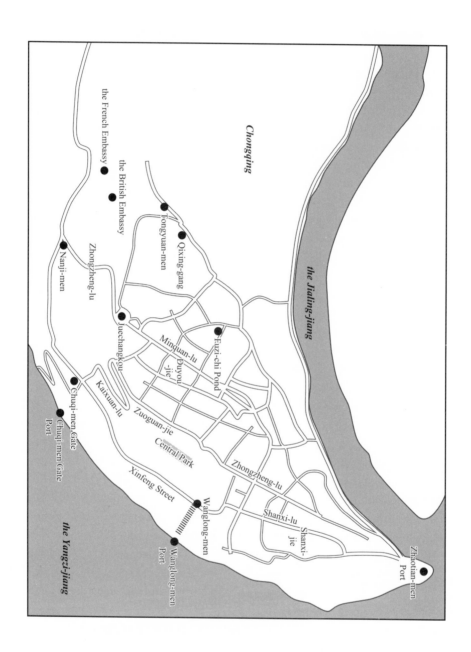

the French Embassy

the British Embassy

Chongqing

Tongyuan-men

Qixing-gang

Nanji-men

Zhongzheng-lu

Juechangkou

Minquan-lu

Duyou-jie

Fuzi-chi Pond

Kaixuan-lu

Chuqi-men Gate

Chuqi-men Gate Port

Zuoguan-jie

Central Park

Zhongzheng-lu

Xinfeng Street

Wanglong-men

Shanxi-lu

Shanxi-jie

Wanglong-men Port

the Yangzi-jiang

the Jialing-jiang

Zhaotian-men Port

warning had been issued, but he did not head for the air-raid cave, because he was a member of a civilian defense corps. As he had no time to be looking up at the enemy planes in the sky, he could not tell what it was like when the Japanese planes were shot to fall. Wearing a yellow armband with red characters of 防護団 (the Civilian Defense Corps) on it, he was eagerly crying, intending to make the people take refuge in a nearby cave. "The members of the Civilian Defense Corps must not enter the air-raid cave but must put a large number of people in order and lead them to a safer place"—That was "the order and discipline" the twenty-one-year-old Zeng Zhiwei had received and kept in his mind since it was given by the Headquarters of the Civilian Defense Corps. One of the problems he faced then was that: the number of the public air-raid caves was not large enough to accommodate all the citizens, but another problem that annoyed him was that many people liked to stay out so they might see the bombs come falling from the sky. For the natives of Sichan Province, it was simply unbelievable that someone should throw bombs, aiming at them. To their mind, the war was made only between the armies, and even if something might bother civilians, such things as they might have any bombs thrown at their living quarters were simply unthinkable. "What's more," they said: "The Japanese Army has not yet been marching toward Chongqing. Right?" Then all the twenty-one-year-old youth could do was to let them do as they liked.

Though he was on a civilian defense corps, he was not giving his full time to it, but was employed at a grocery store. Though he became a member of the civilian defense corps as he was ordered to do so by his employer, no opportunity for training or for receiving any short-term course on what he should do in time of need had been given, and he himself could not tell what would happen in the future, much less tell others what they should do. Those belonging to the civilian defense corps were all in their twenties and remained as ignorant as Zeng Zhiwei did. Now, he called people together in a loud voice, but having found the air raid cave had already been beyond capacity, he led some of them under the trees and others to the riverside. Central Park was just over there in the south, but he was told it had already been crowded with the people. Many of them would have come there to entertain themselves with something like stunt flying. The moment the deafening sound of the bombing craft filled the whole sky overhead, Zeng Zhiwei who happened to be on the road to Luohan-si Temple, hid himself in a concavity he found in the stone wall with *Luohans'* images carved on it and clang to one of them. It was not long before that part of the neighborhood known as the seat for the *Five Hundred Arahats** was wrapped up in flames.

> *Arahats (*Luohans* in Chinese) means "Disciples of Buddha, who had attained *Nirvana* (Supreme Enlightenment)."

Zheng Suqing and Zou Huaqing had been living in the same neighborhood, even though they remained strangers to each other. Suqing, thirty-two, a housewife and mother of a girl. Her husband was then out of work, and this led her to take in washing to earn some money to make up for family finances. Her address was: Zheng Yang Street 33, less than 300m away from Central Park. On the morning of May 3, too, she was busy with the laundry she had taken in.

As for Huaqing, twenty-eight years old, was earning her living as a live-in maid at the Zhangs from Shanghai, living in Zourong-lu Street. As a housemaid, she mainly engaged in laundry and subordinate work, but since she could not move around promptly because of her small feet as a result of foot-binding, she seldom went out of the house. She was always in sandals made of grass. Both Zheng Suqing and Zou Huaqing were of traditional type of Sichan Province, who had never been related to nor interested in the international circumstances or what was happening in the current war. So they were simply astonished when the air-raid warning kept them from working on their laundry. The first thing they should do, they thought, was to go somewhere safe.

For Zheng Suqing, the only place she could think of was Central Park. When an emergency warning was issued, along with a civilian defense corps' scolding voices and the screams given by those who were seeking refuge, she simply decided to hide herself under one of the trees in the park. Never had she imagined that the park should have been made the main aim of the enemy's bombardment. As for the air-raid facilities, neither of the private one nor of the public one had been provided for anyone like Zheng whose husband remained unemployed. This led Suqing to run to Central Park, holding her daughter in her arms.

When she reached there, she found it had already been overcrowded with evacuees. Considering that: that was the only public park existing in Shizong (City's Central) Ward—geographically short of flatland, but overcrowded with shops and stores—it was only natural that everyone should have headed for it.

As it was, even if called park, it was a narrow square—a hundred meters long and several dozen meters wide—divided by slopes and stone steps. The people had been squatting there, huddling themselves together. Suqing then managed to find a space for herself and her daughter below the pedestal upon which the stone statue of Sun Wen stood, and thought they must be secured as long as they were staying so close to somebody so great as Master Sun Zhongshan (Wen).

She crouched below that large stone statue, holding her child in one arm, putting the other hand on a branch of a tree nearby. Thus managing to maintain a proper posture, she was praying for their safety. Then there came an explosive sound overhead, and the shock she felt as if her body were being raised caused her to release the branch she had held. Her hearing was gone, keeping her in a silent world for a while. Looking up, she found Master Sun Zhongshan's head was gone. This led Suqing to grasp the fact that a bomb had dropped so close to them. Looking around again, she saw, to her horror, human arms and legs hanging on the trees here and there. On the ground, many more bodies were scattered. As her sense of hearing was being recovered, she could hear screaming and groaning that had filled the whole park. She felt as if she were seeing those struggling in the Pond of Blood in the Hell, as was mentioned in the Buddhist legend. She wished to leave there as soon as possible. The flames of fire were filling her sight. The survivors were running for their own lives. Among them, there ought to have been Zou Huaqing with small feet, which prevented her from walking properly. Then Zheng Suqing felt a sharp pain at her hand and found the forefinger of her right hand had gone from near its base.

● The Scenes of Horror Witnessed by a Boy Xiao

Xiao Jianxiang then was a schoolboy, whose school was situated far west of the center of the bombing performed that day, so he remained free from such damage as many citizens had to suffer on May 3. But in his mind, he still retains a vivid memory even after more than half a century has passed. The sights he was peeping out of the underground cave—the sights of the sky of fire and the sea of fire—and the sad news brought to them day after day for a week or so were unforgettable to him. But Xiao then had not imagined that: he would outlive all those years of maelstrom of the war and the civil war that followed it, to become a writer, and to revisit Chongqing he used to live as a boy, in order to write his autobiography, thus to meet and review himself as a boy.

Xiao Jianxiang became a member of the China's Writers' Association and even after he had experienced a variety of things in his life, he still believes firmly that: what the citizens of Chongqing had experienced since May 3, 1939, was much more atrocious than the atomic devastation Japan had received. The atomic bombing was done only once in Hiroshima and in Nagasaki respectively. But the bombings on Chongqing were performed again and again, year after year. Those were psychological tortures, too, so even more atrocious than what the Japanese suffered.... Even after half a century has passed, Xiao still thinks so.

Xiao was one of the refugees who had moved to "the Great Rear Area" early in that year. Xiao's family, who had lived in Suzhou near Shanghai, began to feel uneasy in living there since the Sino-Japanese War broke out on July 7, 1937, Xiao's mother, who belonged to the intellectual class known for their clear-cut patriotism, did not think it gallant to live a life of slaves in the land placed under Japanese occupation. Thus his family decided to move to the Great Rear Area or Sichuan Province. His family consisted of seven, including his mother, brothers, sisters, grandfather and grandmother. By way of Anhui Province, Jiangxi Province, Hunan Province, Guangxi Province and Guizhou Province, they reached Sichuan Province. They traveled mainly on foot with a small amount of their household goods on wheelbarrows, without taking a train or riding in a horse-drawn carriage. That was a horrible journey. At every city they passed, they suffered an air raid. The one they had at Guiyang, the capital of Guizhou, was a large-scale one. When they were fortunate enough to be able to take a train, it was made a target for gun shooting. "These made me feel as if we were being followed by enemy planes. I even suspected we might have some special connections with the bombs being carried by those enemy planes," said Xiao, looking back on those days in his boyhood. At Guizhou, he found everything was in chaos with crowds of fugitives. But their destination was just over there. His family, together with other fugitives, hired a motorcar and entered Chongqing by land. It was immediately before the air raid on May 3. Unable to find any house to rent in the central area of the city, they were brought to Lianglukou, a new city area formed outside the former castle area. Anyway, it was pleasing for the boy, Xiao, to be finally able to have their own house to live in.

On the morning of May 3, Xiao and his big sister went to school. When the number of the red fire balls raised on top of the hill called Pipa-shan became two, all the pupils were ordered to enter the cave as an air-raid shelter. There being no electric light, all they could depend on was candlelight. It was not long before the sounds of dropped bombs began to reverberate through the cave. Looking out of the entrance, he found the eastern part of the city or the former castle area had turned into the sea of fire. Then someone said Liang Lukou where the Xiao was living was burning, too. This set the boy Xiao and his sister sobbing. Both of them had learned what sort of disasters the air raid would bring to them, as they had seen so many horrible examples on their way to Chongqing. It was simply unbearable to imagine what their mother was doing amid that terrible fire, but they were not allowed to leave the cave. This made them spend the rest of the day in growing uneasiness and impatience.

● **"That Bombing was Intentionally Aimed at the Urban Area…."**

The reporter of *Xin Min Bao* (*New People's News*), Zhang Xiluo, who had been looking up at the sky from the main office of his company at Qixing-gang, jumped out of his office as soon as the Japanese planes went out of sight, so he might start collecting news material on that air raid. Qixing-gang was situated in the vicinity of Tongyuan-men Gate or the only gate that led to the road to Chengdu or the Provincial Capital situated to the west of Chongqing, when all the other sixteen gates in this city faced either the Yangzi or the Jialing. His office, therefore, was far away from Central Park which had been made the main target for the bombing that day. Zhang set off in the direction he thought it would be the right one. So far he had never done any such serious task as this. Driven by anger and excitement, he was walking on and on, simply wishing to send his report as soon as possible….

As he approached the center of the city, he was to be caught greater amazement: most of the former castle area had already been wrapped in fire. He simply could not believe in the destructive power that had turned everything to such a terrible extent in such a short time. The enemy planes had been in the sky of Chongqing from 13:17 to 13:30 or so. They, having unexpectedly met with the Chinese fighter planes before them, could not have enough time to command the air to give such a thorough bombing upon their target as they had expected. When compared with what they were to perform in the days to come, what they had done that day was rather too simple. But upon the citizens of Chongqing, who had never had any such air raid before, still remaining unprepared for any such attack, while living in such inflammable wooden houses and buildings, the Japanese attack that day had brought about a tremendous effect, as was confirmed by the newspaper reporter Zhang through what he was seeing before his eyes.

From Zhaotian-men Gate (Emperor's Gate) at the farthest end of Shizhon (City's Central) Ward, where the two Rivers joined, to the western side of Central Park, the whole length of 2km of the urban area—the busiest part of Chongqing—was now being wrapped in flames. Many of the houses and buildings were of wood, but some of the buildings—like those of Meifeng Dalou (Meifeng Bank) and Chuanyan Dalou (Sichuan Salt Industry Bank) —were so stately as to have more than eight stories. According to a Chinese woman official, Liu Manqing, who paid a short visit to Chongqing in 1927, its central street was such a stately one, as was described in her journal, *A Woman Ambassador Goes Through Tibet:*

> When I left my inn, I found myself on a shopping street or the commercial center in Chongqing. All the buildings stand in good order; though no skyscraper was seen, the short eaves and the round pillars of the buildings were of Western style. The whole city, excepting several lonely side streets, is composed of shopping districts and it is certainly worthy of the fame she has earned as the most important port town in the southwestern part of China.

Ten years later, Han Suyin, who came to turn to her uncle, Zhou Jiansan, a business leader of Chongqing, described the downtown of Chongqing just before the air raid, as follows:

> The Meifeng Bank was my Third Uncle's business address: an imposing building, eight-storied, with brass-and-glass doors, and a large and busy hall with many counters inside. Opposite it was the Szechuan* Salt Bank, also with a large facade. The Szechuan Salt Bank and the Meifeng Bank together held most of the capital of the Szechuan landed gentry, lately become businessmen and capitalists. Before 1921, the Meifeng Bank had been the America Oriental Banking Corporation, but after the uprisings of 1923 and 1925 American capital had fled, and the Szechuanese capitalists had the

bank in their own hands.

— *The Birdless Summer*

*Szechuan = Sichuan

That shopping center of the most important city in southeastern China was now burning furiously, blowing black smoke into the air, raising the fiery tongues here and there. Those overwhelming sights had almost made Zhang Xiluo forget himself. But he soon thought of those who had been caught in the fires. Had those in the theaters or movie houses managed to run away? What had become of the port below Zhaotian-men (Emperor's Gate)? What about his own home at Jiechangkou? Jiang Jieshi's Military Committee's Encampment had long been moved to the new station outside the castle walls, and since that fact had been published, it ought to have been known to the Japanese side, too. This led Zhang to think that: this bombing in the urban area must have been performed intentionally. Within the walls of the former castle, neither camps nor barracks had ever existed. Several decades later, Zhang Xiluo, who had become the vice chief editor of *Renmin Zhengxie-Bao* (The News Cooperatively Published by People & Government), happened to see a popular television drama *O-Shin* imported from Japan and the scenes of the air raid on Tokyo did remind him of that air attack upon Choungqking. The horrible scenes that had emerged from his memory were far more overwhelming than those of Japan he saw on T.V..

Zhang had intended to run to the scene of that disaster when he left his office, but soon he found it impossible to do so however reckless he might be. It was not until May 5 that Zhang, together with a reporter of *Da Gong-Bao* (The Great Official Bulletin), Fan Changjiang, entered the scene of the disaster and stepped into the Central Park. In that park where live trees were still smouldering, they had an actual close look at what that indiscriminate bombing on the city—what the Japanese military called strategic-political attack—had brought to them. Since the scenes they saw that day were so impressive that he was able to recall them clearly even after many years had passed since then.

● **The Furious Smoke had Shuttered the Sunshine of May**

Just about that time, Wen Shayang, the chief of the Department of Medical Examination at Renji Hospital, who had been appointed to be the Company

Commander of Relief of Shizong (City's Central) Ward, left his office, intending to start their relief activities, since the droning of the planes could no longer be heard. For a moment, he got stunned at the sight of the horror-driven people moving about in utter confusion. Smoke and dust having shuttered the sunshine, the air had turned dusky as far as his eyes could reach. Until some time ago, they had been enjoying the azure sky of May. The changes were simply unbelievable to him.

There was no need for Dr. Wen to wait. Because the victims of the air raid came rushing to him as soon as they saw him standing there with bags of jute with a mark of Red Cross upon them. That was how his days and nights of curing them started—without sleeping and resting.

As for that wretched spectacle which had frozen Dr. Wen Shayang, Theodre White described as "the response given or the sheer horror shown by a mediaeval city when confronted by the first cruel blow given by the modern world," and went on writing: "After having suffered that first bombardment, Chungking gave such a response as if the ancient world would have given if it had happened to face any such crises." Indeed, that could be called an insult given by the modern world toward the mediaeval city. Upon that defenseless, over-populated city made of wood and bamboo and paper, the Japanese military planes dropped bombs and released incendiary bombs indiscriminately, thus committing every conceivable form of destruction and arson. That effect was explosive as well as intensive. At the moment of explosion, the 98-type 250kg land bomb made about 10,000 pieces of bomb scatter at an angle of 15 to 20 degrees to kill those within 45m and to injure those within 200m. Around the funnel-shaped pit brought about on the ground—in case of a 250kg bomb, its diameter was as large as 8m, its depth 1.5m, even at Chongqing seated on the rocky zone—the degrees of tragedy could be witnessed in a moment. Some had their bodies scattered into nothingness even without leaving any traces of them; others had badly been injured to groan in the pools of their own blood; yet others, driven to fear, ran this way or that to make their escape.... At every point of its explosion, such scenes were being revealed.

Even Dr. Wen, who had often come in contact with the injured, could hardly bear to look at the miseries. To make the matter worse, fires followed immediately. The incendiary bombs scattered from the sky were ignited by the shock of landing to give further ignition to termit by means of termit-priming powder, then to be ignited to an electron weighing 17.8kg to cause it burn furiously, spreading showers of white sparks. Thus the wooden houses arranged on the slopes were helplessly burnt up, causing the houses below the cliffs to be burnt by the fires that came falling from above, while the houses above were also burnt down by the strong blasts of fire from downward. From between the houses, people came running out, as if swimming out. From the depths of the lanes, long shrieks were coming and remained long. The effect of the incendiary bombs was such that the fire began to rage on a full scale after the enemy planes left the sky, thus magnifying the range of flames to drown the people to death. The water mains having been blown up and contorted, they simply damped the ground in vain. The fire brigades equipped with their primitive devices for shooting water on fire or the bucket brigades were simply of no use before the cruel fires brought about by the modern world.

Dr. Wen, looking at those miseries before his eyes, started his relief activities. The greatest problem for him was the shortage of hands. Among the rubbles, bloody bodies were being left, while the injured were groaning in pain. Still doctors and those engaged in relief work were desperately small in number. While an injured person was receiving a brief treatment like stopping of bleeding, dozens of others came to form a long queue. All he could do then was to tell them to go and find some proper hospital. Wen could not suppress his irritation and anger at the shortage of hands and medicines. In 1986, Dr. Wen, who had already retired long, wrote a long essay retrospective of what he had experienced as a doctor for a bulletin published by a medical society he had belonged to. The mortification he had been feeling forty-six years before still kept lingering in his writing:

Wan Meishan was a battalion commander for a relief corps, but he was totally lacking in power to perform medical activities. So we, simply relying on our morality and friendship, invited several colleagues of doctors and appointed them to be company commanders. Each of those company commanders organized a platoon of medical workers according to the conditions of the hospital he worked at, so that they could perform the relief activities in case of air raid. None of them refused to take that duty since they were willing to work for such a good cause as defending their own country as well as their own family. All they could do then was to perform their duty, simply relying on what they had read on the injuries the soldiers received at the battlefront during World War I or what little experience they had when they joined a relief corps during the civil war between the military cliques. The citizens of Chongqing had remained rather ignorant of how dangerous the air raid could be. The authority concerned also had not taken the air raid so seriously that they had not been prepared for anything like evacuations. That was why many of the citizens had been out on the streets when they had the Great Air Raids of 5.3 and 5.4. The busy streets having been bombed, many had to fall on the pools of their own blood. Several men of the relief corps with a first-aid bag across their shoulder were only able to give such temporary treatment as arresting of bleeding or putting on a temporary bandage or helping the severely wounded to be sent to Kuanren Hospital.

What Dr. Wen could do then was nothing more than such simple treatments as checking bleeding and binding up the wound or repairing a fracture. They could not deal with burns or relief of pain. All they could do then was to give directions so that they could be sent to Renji Hospital or Kuanren Hospital. Upon the asphalted road, drops of red blood were clearly seen.

Not faraway from where those relief corps started their activities, Qin Zhixuan, a cook of Choungqing's Aerial Defense Headquarters, was thinking deeply about his great good fortune of having narrowly escaped death. When he left the air-raid cave, he was astonished to find the neighborhood having totally been changed. A bomb had hit the entrance to the cave. He then realized what had caused that unusual shake he felt in the cave. Many men, probably over one hundred, had been killed, he thought. It was impossible to count the deaths, because many of the bodies had been badly broken apart. His intuition made him say to himself: "They are political prisoners." Those political prisoners or the suspected as such who had been detained there by the Security Department were too late to be taken into the cave as the air-raid shelter or the shelter itself was too crowded for them to enter. Anyway, they must have received a direct hit while they were staying around its entrance. Though shuddering with horror, Qin felt thankful for his having been safe. After the enemy planes were gone, the first thing Qin and his companions were told to do was to clear the dead bodies away. They were collected in a spot to identify each of them, and those unable to be identified were carried in a truck to Zhaotian-men Gate so that they could be buried in the sandbar up the Yangzi.

Xiao Jianxiang, a schoolboy, remained uneasy even long after the air raid was over. The fire below his eyes had abated and night was falling, but he could not yet tell what had become of his mother. His classmates had had their family member come to take them home. Some of them, however, like Xiao himself, had been waiting for someone of their family to come and fetch them, but in vain. Their teacher encouraged them, saying the traffic seemed to have got confused to an unusual extent, but Xiao himself, having been prone to imagine something worse, remained restless. It was already at night when his grandfather came to fetch them. Then he was finally able to find all of his family being safe. Their home at Liang Lukou had been saved from the fire, since it was fairly far away from the bomb-blasted area. Those were pleasant news to him, but he was not able to express his pleasant relief, because some of his classmates still remained unable to meet anyone of their family. It was several days later that Xiao was told many of his classmates had none of their family members come to fetch them home that night.

● **"The 673 People were Killed; the 350 People were Injured"**
The area destroyed and burnt up by the air raid on May 3 was what was called "Xiahan-cheng (the Lower-Half Castle)," closer to the Yangzi in Shizhong (City's Central) Ward 9.3 square kilometers. With Central Park in the center, the area 1.5km long from northeast to southwest, 500m wide—including the 19 of the 27 main streets in the capital, featuring Taiping-men Gate and Zhuqi-men Gate—had suffered damage.

According to *The Statistical Data of the Damage caused by Air Raids on the Various Parts of Sichuan Province—for the 28th fiscal year of the Republic of China* (1939), the attack on Chongqing that day was performed by "thirty-six enemy planes that arrived in four waves. The number of bombs dropped was 166, causing 673 deaths, injuring 350 people, destroying 1,086 houses. It was the first in the history of the Sino-Japanese War that a single aerial bombardment caused more than a thousand deaths and injuries. But none had known this appalling record was to be broken on the day that followed.

About this time, when the Headquarters at Wuhan Air Base 780km away received the news of their great success, and this led Commander Kuwabara to decide to "immediately perform a successive attack tomorrow so that our military achievement may be even more perfect," Chongqing still remained in the midst of confusion.

At the Control Office of Balujun (the Eighth Route Army) at No.70 in Jifang Street, the leading members such as Dong Biwu, Bo Gu and Qian Zhiguang had already been preparing for their moving somewhere else. During the bombing that day, a 500 pound bomb (probably 250kg bomb) had fallen near Qian Zhiguang's public room. Fortunately it did not go off and no lives had been lost, but soon they were informed that the office building of *Xin Hua Ri Bao* (*New China Daily*) had been burnt down. Its factory was safe in a different place, but the editing and business departments having been annihilated, there would be little or no hope of keeping publishing their paper from then on. Thus they decided: if they were to maintain their activities ether overtly or covertly, it would be better to move their base to the place they had already selected.

● **Zhou Enlai's Return from Guilin to Chongqing**

Zhou Enlai, a person responsible for the Chinese Communist Party in the capital, who was also the representative of Balujun (the Eighth Route Army) in Chongqing and the secretary of the Chinese Communist Party's Central Southern Bureau, had then been away on a journey around the Jiannan area, expecting to spend a couple of months there, and at this period he had been staying at Guilin. Guilin, along with Chongqing, was one of the bases of "the Great Rear Area," which was then protecting many intellectuals. After having attended a reception dinner held by Xia Yan, Tian Han and others, Zhou Enlai had kept himself busy in giving lectures to a group of students who were being trained to be interpreters between Chinese and Japanese—the group placed under the control of the Administration Department of the Military Committee of the Nationalist Government with which Zhou himself had been concerned as its deputy head. In Guilin, there was a temporary depot for the Japanese soldiers who had been made prisoners of war at Funan and Guangdong areas, and partly for the purpose of giving them a proper political education, "the Anti-War Union of the Japanese Residents in China" with a Japanese named Kaji Wataru as its responsible person had been established the year before. It was also then and there that a group of Chinese students began to be trained to be interpreters between Chinese and Japanese. Zhou Enlai gave those students a lecture on "How to crash the enemy's conspiracy," and advocated the necessity of learning Japanese and the importance of giving proper education in politics to those prisoners of war, as was recorded in *The Material for the History of the Southern Bureau of the Communist Party,* published in 1986 by Chongqing Publishing Co.

It was then and there that Zhou received an urgent message: "Chongqing was badly damaged by the Japan's air raid. We beg you to return as soon as possible." It was also reported that the function of the Office of the Eighth Route Army and the New Fourth Army in the mid-city was decided to be moved to No.13 at Hongyan-cun Village in Hualong-quiao. Without waiting for Zhou Enlai's return to Chongqing, they put the papers in order and packed their things, and the first group left there that very night by way of Tongyuan-men or the only castle gate that led to the land (instead of the water) so that they could reach an orchard in what was then called Hongyanzui situated on the way to Chengdu to the west of Chongqing.

This was how the Control Office of Balujin (the Eighth Route Army) and the non-open organization of the Chinese Communist Party's Central Southern Bureau had finished moving to the suburbs and since then, "Zhou's Diplomatic Establishment" which assumed Zhou's personal office alone was left in Shizhong Ward in Chongqing to perform their duty as the Chinese Communist Party's Headquarters in the capital. Be that as it might, if all the fuses equipped in the bombs dropped from the Japanese planes that day had worked as precisely as they had been expected, some of those who had come to stand at the balcony of Tianan-men Gate at Beijing on October 1, 1949—including Dong Biwu and several others—would not have been seen there.

● Zou Taofen Fought his Verbal Battles to Save the Nation against Japan

On the Duyou-jie Street, only one block away from the Cangping-jie Street—where the office of the *Xin Hua Ri Bao* (the *New China Daily*) had been burnt down—Zou Taofen as the representative of Shenghuo (Life) Book Store had been desperately struggling to save as much stock as possible from the blazing fire. The managing office of Shenghuo Book Store and its storehouse had already caught fire. Every time the fire spread to another mountain of books, the intense fire gained more upward force and pieces of burnt paper were blown up only to fall down everywhere. Zou, standing at the head of the staff, took command in carrying what had narrowly escaped fire somewhere safe. His glasses kept falling because of gushing sweat, but the chief editor had to fight furiously, trying to make "the time limit of merciless flame" as late as possible.

Zou Taofen, born in Fujian Province, spent his student days in Shanghai, and in 1926, at the age of thirty-one, he became the chief editor of *The Weekly Life,* thus to start his career as a man of the press. He positively took up social problems by starting "the pages for the readers' letters," and by launching a new department for helping the readers by sending them books, magazines and daily necessities by mail, he succeeded in increasing the circulation of that weekly from about 2,500 copies at the time of his having taken office to 120,000 copies six years later.

Since "the Incident of 9.18" or "the Manchurian Incident"* that broke out in 1931, Zou Taofen made himself a positive advocate of an anti-Japanese campaign to save the nation, and by making use of the comments on this matter argued in *The Weekly Life*, he assembled those youths and intellectuals who were feeling unsatisfied at Jiang Jieshi's policy of non-resistance against Japan. When he had *The Weekly Life* banned, he published *The Weekly New Life* and *The Weekly Life of the Masses* one after another, thus appealing to the public for organizing all of the anti-Japanese groups in order to bring about the National United Front Against Japan in the true sense of the words.

On October 19, 1936, when they were confronted by the death of Lu Xun, Zou Taofen attended his funeral and read aloud a short message of condolence:

"It is already too late to say everything I'd like to dedicate to our Master Lu Xun, so I should like to offer a short oration to him: Many people surrender without fighting, but Master Lu Xun never surrendered in his fighting."

This speech was also a revelation of his own determination. A month later, Zou Taofen was arrested—along with the leaders of the save-the-nation movement being performed by the leaders from various walks of life in Shanghai—by the Nationalist authorities and was moved to the prison of the High Court of Justice in Suzhou. That was, he was involved in the affair to judge those who were later known as "the Seven Noble Characters of the Save-the-Nation Movement." Zou's verbal activity so far had long been beyond the tolerance of the Nationalist Party.

On July 7, 1937, the Anti-Japanese War broke out, and on July 31, Zou

Taofen and the six comrades of his were released from prison. This led him to launch *Three Days' Resistance* (according to the Authority's interference, this was changed into *Resistance* and then into *Fighting Back*). After Shanghai fell, he went to Wuhan by way of Hongkong, and he had his weekly combined with *Quan Min Zhoukan* (*All People's Weekly*) which had been edited by Li Gongpu, and by changing its name to *Quan Min Kang Zhan* (*All People's Resistance*), he came to stand in the forefront of the verbal activities of the Great Wuhan's Keep-Guard Battles. The new weekly adopted a position as a bulletin for democratic powers, which did not belong either to the Nationalist Party nor to the Communist Party. His declaration entitled *All People's Mission to Make Resistance,* which appeared in its initial number to make his own editorial policy clear, went as follows:

The first mission we should achieve is: to strengthen the unity of all the nation, to enhance our national consciousness, and to increase our knowledge concerning resistance to Japan; then we shall explain the Government's policy and transmit it to the people, while analyzing the state of things in domestic administration, military affairs, economy, culture, and the international state of things. In other words, these are something to be achieved as a mission of education and publicity.

The second mission we should achieve is: to keep conveying to the Government the people's complaints and sufferings, the state of things in mobilization and the superiority or inferiority in administration, so that the Government could properly lead the people to fight against our enemies by supplying reference materials in achieving the administration. These are the political duties for us to perform.

—*Bring a Revolution to China: Zou Taofen as A Forerunner of the Press*

Apart from the first mission, as for the second mission, the authorities of the Nationalist administration would not distinguish it from the Communists' verbal activities performed under a mask of democratic parties. Jiang Jieshi gave Zou a seat for the members of the National Government Conference, thus trying to keep him within the group of "critical co-operators" with the Nationalist Party, but while he was moving from Wuhan to Chongqing, Zou Taofen became devoted to the personality of Zhou Enlai and deepened his friendship with him, but toward the administration by Jiang Jieshi, Zou was to strengthen his phase as "a cooperative criticizer." To Zhou as a journalist, "the second mission" would have been felt even more important than "the first mission."

Zou Taofen and his Shenghuo (Life) Book Store were to live in Chongqing for two years, while being annoyed at frequent invitations to the Nationalist Party, at the incessant intervention in the editor's right through censorship, or fighting against many other pressures, including the discrimination in distributing commodities, and those great air raids performed on May 3 and May 4 were among those trials they had to face. Having had the managing office and the storehouse burnt down, Zou lost his greatest foothold as a publisher, but he led his subordinates and moved to an office he had previously decided upon. But now what had come to prevent him from performing his verbal activity was not only the Nationalist Party but the incessant air raids that forced him to spend much of his time in the air raid cave. This led him to stay and write usually at the entrance to the cave only to move into the depth of it at the arrival of the enemy planes.

When almost all the newspaper companies were lost in fire on May 3 and 4, the editorial staff of *Quan Min Kang Zhan* (*All People's Resistance*) produced the mimeographed copies of their wall newspaper and posted them on the walls all over the city. It was also the same staff, who not only criticized the insufficiency of the relief activities but also formed their own "relief party" so that they could offer any emergency care to the victims of the air raids.

● **The Fire that Scorched the Night of a Lunar Eclipse**

Even after the night fell, the fires remained unabated, scorching the sky here and there. Under such uncanny illumination, the many who had had their houses burnt up were heading for the suburbs, intending to turn to their relatives there. They were all silent, carrying nothing or only a small bundle with them. On the roadside or in the squares, the bodies that remained unclaimed were left as they were or were arranged. The sight of them was extremely gruesome, but even more horrifying was the news that the Japanese planes had dropped "poisoned cigarettes," too. Members of the civilian defense corps walked around the street, ringing a bell, warning not to pick up any cigarette lying on the road. According to the explanation given by the authority, hundreds of the poisoned cigarettes were put in boxes with "xinyue-pai (crescent mark)," and it was also said that some of them were made of cotton wool contaminated with poison, so that they might be picked up by unfortunate children out of curiosity. Those who belonged to the Civilian Defense Corps came round, giving a warning that: some children who had picked up one of them outside Jinzi-men Gate had their hands swollen; so one should be careful *not* to pick up any such things....

Those voices had reached Theodore White, too. The Publicity Bureau of the Nationalist Government he then worked for as an advisor to the Information Department had already finished evacuating from Shizhong (City's Central) Ward, and this had kept him safe from the air raid that day, but since his lodging was within the walls of the former castle, he came home in the evening, as usual. This American youth, who had just become twenty-four years old in May, had not imagined that he would come to perform such a conversion as he would later write in his autobiography: "That air raid upon Chungking which turned out to be an indiscreet terrorism was to exert a direct and fundamental influence upon my view of politics." White then was to gaze at the final night scenes of Chongqing as the ancient castle city from his room in the building of Friend Mission situated in Shanghan-Cheng (Upper Half Castle Area). In his recollection, he wrote: "That night we had a lunar eclipse. Because of the bombing we had that afternoon, the smoke was still rising, but the Buddhist priests were performing a ritual to expel the evil spirits that were supposed to have brought about that lunar eclipse."

● **The All Night Preparation for the Continuous Bombing upon the Same City**

At Hankou, too, under the same moon of a partial eclipse, the all-night maintenance work was being carried out by the ground crew. Because the Commander Kuwabara of the Second United Aviation Corps had decided to perform another attack upon Chongqing the following day, and all of those middle-sized bombers, which had just returned from the seven-hour bombing tour to and from Chongqing, had to be serviced and re-equipped.

As for the achievements that day, they were recorded as follows in *The Summary of the Battle Report No.513* given by the Central China Corps (the Third Fleet):

Taking advantage of the fine weather, the First Air Raid Unit, consisting of 45 middle-sized bombers (24 planes of 14^{th}fg; 21 planes of 13^{th}fg), gave Chongqing, the enemy's capital, the first attack of the current year. At 15:30 (as it was written), our fierce bombardment started in and around the encampment of the Chairman of the Military Committee, from the northeastern part of Central Park to Shuini-chang Height, thus to give great damage to our enemy.

Our squadron, despite the fierce defensive fire, fought against about 30 enemy planes and downed more than ten of them, (including the five that surely fell).

The two planes in the 14th flying group started fire by receiving the enemy bullets, thus to cause the crew to perform their heroic deaths.

The air battle caused almost all the planes to be bombarded: In the 13th group, two were seriously injured and two more were slightly injured. In the 14th group, one died in action; two were seriously injured; four were slightly injured.

Even though it was judged that they had given a serious damage on the Capital of Jiang's Administration, what they had suffered was also serious. Along with the fifteen excellent members of the crew, the two middle-sized bombers they had treasured were no more, while all the other planes had also been shot. These were something they had never expected. Even if they were to make another attack the following day, it was impossible for them to employ as much power as they had done that day both in the number of flight crew and in the number of bombers. But because of the repairs having been made and the maintenance work having been done throughout the night, they were able to have a prospect of making use of 27 middle-sized bombers (15 bombers from the 14th Flying Corps & 12 bombers from the 13th Flying Corps), and this made them decide that the second attack upon Chongqing should be performed by those 27 planes of the Navy Air Force. Thus each plane had its bomb rack carefully applied with No. 25 (250kg bombs) and No.6 (60kg bombs), along with *No. 6* (incendiary bombs).

It was directed that the time of performing the attack should be at twilight. The area to be bombed upon was directed as follows: "Chongqing's Aerial Defense Headquarters, the Military Committee's Chairman's Encampment, the Prefectural Government Office and the whole city area around them, or the half of the city area to the west of the north-south line that went through Central

Park.

That half of the city area called "Shanghan-cheng" or "the upper-half of the castle"—the commercial and residential area closer to the Jialing—had been left unburnt. There were none of any such institutions as armed forces' camp, their headquarters or munitions factories and the like. But something remarkable about that area was that: "the half of the city area to the west of the north-south line that goes through Central Park" did include Lingshi-xiang (Consulates' Lane) and Tianzhu-tang-jie (Cathedral Street) where Christian churches were seen here and there. That was why one of the sections of the written directive went: "In performing the bombardment, you must be careful not to damage the Third Powers' rights and interests," but toward the Chinese people, the Navy Air Force's written directive had only declared their intention to give limitless fear and panic "throughout their streets."

The Bombardment on May 4

● **The Newspapers Criticized Japan's Indiscriminate Bombings**

On May 4, 1939, the southern part of Sichuan Province was blessed with fair and clear weather again. But none of those in the city of Chongqing had been in such a frame of mind as to appreciate that sunshine of May. Even the retreat of the foggy season that had been cheering up the people so much until the morning of the day before now seemed rather deplorable. The sun had led those bombers to come over.

Naturally all the morning papers had filled their pages with all sorts of damages they had suffered from the air raid the day before. *Da Gong-Ba* (The Major Official Bulletin) gave the headline coverage that had crossed the six columns on the front page in reporting the indiscriminate bombings performed by the Japanese Air Force. It also appealed to the public: "Never forget this great regret we suffered on May 3!"

The Enemy Planes Recklessly Attacked the Urban Area of Chongqing.
This Bloodshed on 5.3 has Made Our Resentment Even More Greater!

In its editorial, the same paper pointed out that: the area upon which the enemy planes had made an aerial attack was where not even a single target for military attack had ever existed, and that: those who were sacrificed or forced to suffer damage were all general citizens without exception, and that: because incendiary bombs were employed amply especially upon the commercial areas, the enemy's intention, dirty and cruel and inhuman, was clearly revealed.

Xin Shu Bao (News Report on Shichuan Province) described the disasterous scenes the air raid had brought about under the title of "Once the Bombs Burst, the Flames Rose High, Making Flesh and Blood Shoot Side Ways," while reporting how more than a hundred women and children were burnt to death in their own houses, also describing how the center of the commercial area was turned into piles of rubbish: "that prosperous marketplace has suddenly been turned into piles of rubbish; several streets were reduced to ashes." Both *Xin Hua Ri Bao* (New China Daily) and *Xin Min Bao* (New People's News) had reported the details of the disasters. Most of the papers eagerly commented on the indiscriminate bombings performed by the Japanese Air Force, while condemning their having dropped incendiary bombs, but some papers gave their opinion that: the enemy had aimed at some military institutions but probably because of the bombardiers' having lacked experience, the residential areas had mistakenly been bombed. This comment had come *not* from their kind view of the Japanese military *but* from their total inability to believe that: such a height of inhumanity as to perform an indiscriminate bombing upon their urban area could be something intentional.

But on that day, the people had been kept too busy to have a leisurely talk about the air raid they had suffered the day before, and around noon, they had to take shelter again, as they were forced to do so by the siren and the red lanterns. It had been announced that the Japanese planes that had left Wuhan were heading for Chongqing again.... Now, no one had remained so easy-going as to have a look at an air raid, as they had done the day before. In a moment, all the population in the downtown had gone out of sight.

● The 27 Middle-Sized Bombers Presented themselves Again

As for what the Navy Air Force had achieved the day before, it was reported in Japan, too. *The Asahi* for May 4 gave it a scare headline and reported as a Reuters Report from Chongqing: "On the afternoon of May 3, the Japan's Air

Force made an air raid upon Chongqing by sending the rain of bombs upon the military facilities in the central part of the city on the northern bank of the Yangzi. The great fires caused by this brought about a tremendous loss on the Chinese side. The office building of *Da Gong-Bao* (the Great Official Bulletin) was also burnt down," and on the following day, they gave the precise report announced by the press section of the Fleet at Shanghai, under the headline: "We fought a fierce battle against the thirty enemy planes till we finally downed ten of them. How heroic! Two of ours were blown up, too," along with the portraits of Lieutenant Commanders Masuda and Irisa.

The Naval General Staff, under the name of the vice-chief Koga Mineichi, sent a telegram to Theater Commander of the Fleet of the China Region, Vice Admiral Oikawa Koshiro: "Congratulations on your having succeeded in performing a great air raid upon our enemy's capital, Chongqing, thus to bring their military center to destruction!" It is easily imaginable how encouraging such prompt praises as these were to those engaged in this attempt.

On May 4, the twenty-seven middle-sized bombers led by Lieutenant Commander Irisa Toshiie took off at Hankou Air Base. Lieutenant Commander Irisa had flown the mission the day before, too. The number of the planes that day was reduced to twenty-seven. The 14th Air Corps, which had two bombers shot down the day before, had to reduce the number from twenty-four to fifteen; the 13th Air Corps had also reduced it from twenty-one to twelve. The air battle the day before had caused almost all the planes to receive more or less damage, and it was totally impossible for all of them to be repaired and given maintenance in a single night; since the spare planes were far from ample, the number of the planes for the mission that day could not help being reduced. But these twenty-seven planes were to bring about even greater ravages upon the urban area of Chongqing.

On May 4, too, the whole area from Hankou to Chongqing was blessed with fine weather. The air raid unit flew westward, as they did the day before, overlooking the brown Yangzi meandering among the mountain ranges of fresh green. In the city of Chongqing, the air-raid warning had already been issued.

Theodre White—who had been offered a post as "an adviser to the Information Department of the Chinese Government" and had been made a member of the U. S. Advisory Group—had been staying in an air-raid cave more or less away from the castle area, together with his commrades, including the chief of the Information Department. Since the air-raid cave that had been brought into being in the earlier stage was not equipped with any ventilating facilities, it was hard to stay there long. But there was no sign for the air-raid warning to turn into an emergency warning. This led White to decide to leave the cave and go down to the shore of the Jialing to see the sunset there.

The post he had found in the Information Department of Chongqing Government was of a supervising editor for the advertising articles written in English for the American citizens. But the six Chinese reporters under him having been so competent as to have been at work at the English-language newspaper companies at Shanghai, White, just out of university, was found too impractical to stay at the post he had been offered and was soon demoted to an ordinary reporter. But soon White found he had been cut out for that work. This was how he, who had graduated at the head of the class at Yanjing Research Institute of Harvard University only to learn musty Sinology at the library as a budding scholar, made a complete change in the course of his life and began to follow the path for a journalist, thus to have something to do with China *then* and *from then on.*

White, who had just come down to the shore of the Jialing, intending to see the setting sun there, was to see the Japanese planes flying toward the sky of Chongqing, as he wrote:

Then, I saw in the spotlessly clear sky the twenty-seven Japanese bombers come flying with a whirr in a dotted line of perfect order.

The anti-aircraft shells of the Chinese Air Force were being shot through the falling dusk, while the tracer bullets gave their pink and orange mushroom-like sparkles toward the Japanese planes coming in formation. But they were flying too high for any of those counterattacks to reach them. Then there came thudding sounds from behind the roofs of the houses in the former castle area, while the Japanese planes were flying away without receiving any effective counterattack.

White, intending to see what was happening at Shizhong Ward, walked to the castle area six kilometers away. It was then and there that he clearly witnessed "the response of the Medieval city when given a cruel blow by the modern world."

The same scenes were being witnessed by those on the gunboat, Tutuila, too, as Lieutenant Kemp Tree recorded in his *Yangzi Patrol:*

The raid on the following day was even more spectacular and beautiful if possible, (if one can say such a thing about mass death) than the one the day before. They came in almost without warning, after several false alarms during the day had got the people less alert. Twenty-seven of them came over, just at sunset, brilliantly silhouetted against the bright evening sky. There was a vertical hell for about five minutes—the colossal explosions of the bombs, one after another, the crash of the antiaircraft guns, and the bursts of the shells in the air. They were shooting tracer shells and in the deepening twilight each of them looked like a rocket, flying out of a ball of flame at the gun's muzzle, then gradually slowing down and curving over like a flower stem, until the bloom, the bursting shell, the ball of black smoke appeared at the end. The same fire this time, but infinitely more terrible at night, with the whole city on fire and outlined in flames like a map lying draped across the stairstep hills. The electric lights were out, of course, and the only illumination was the red glow from the blazing city.

When White was hearing those thudding sounds of fallen bombs, Dr. Wen Shayang was just under what had caused those sounds. He, who had been engaged in relief activities without sleeping or resting since the daytime the day before, was again on the street with his Red Cross bag on his shoulder, when he heard the warning of "the enemy planes on their way." Dr. Wen later wrote:

Then I was hurrying to the park together with a member of the relief corps. Nine enemy planes came flying toward us. We threw ourselves flat on the ground. It was as if a mountain had come falling and the earth had split. I had my trunk tremble and leap on the ground, my ears filled with droning sounds of bombings, while gravel and dust were thrown against my body.

People were screaming in the fire and smoke, while the buildings that had been bombed collapsed and fell down. Bleeding pieces of flesh of human beings were blown off onto the branches and twigs of the trees, and human beings who had been alive a moment before came to fall flat into the pool of their own blood. Those still alive called their children or their mothers, the injured were groaning because of the pain they were suffering. In those uproars, only the dead were lying silent amid their own pool of blood.

While giving some medical treatment to the slightly injured, we carried those seriously injured as far as the hospital by mobilizing the people.

● **The Chinese Air Planes were Counterplotted**

In the mission that day, not a single Japanese plane got damaged. Certainly, the Chinese fighter planes waiting for them in the sky of Chongqing had been reduced in number, but it was largely because of the strategic effect for having changed their attack hours from broad daylight to evening twilight. Lieutenant Commander Irisa as the leader in the air, having judged it wiser for his downsized unit to perform a short-term operation, decided to kill time at the point just before they entered the sky of Chongqing, and it was not until their last possible hour when they could see their aims that they finally presented themselves above them.

The Chinese side, having been informed of the enemy planes' departure, kept their fighter planes waiting, but the delay of the enemy planes' arrival led them to waste their fuel in vain, and even when they finally made their appearance, the Chinese pilots, who had little experience in night flight, could not afford to make a persistent counter attack as they had done the day before. To make the matter worse, their air base having no lighting, there was no showing where the runways were. Thus the ground fire seemed to be the only dependable means to repulse the enemy, but the bombers having kept themselves as high as 5,000 meters, their small-sized high-angle guns soon proved to be simply useless. The twenty-seven middle-sized bombers in three squadrons, while leisurely flying round and round above the urban area of Chongqing, formed themselves into bomb-dropping formation to achieve their mission. Not a few fires that had started the day before still remained amply, thus readily helping the bombers to choose where to drop their bombs then.

The General Outline of the Third Fleet's Actions (*No.514*), based on the then captain or Lieutenant Commander Irisa's report, reads as follows:

The First Air Raid Unit consisting of 27 middle-sized bombers (15 from the 14th flying group; 12 from the 13th flying group) flew among clouds and mountaintops, waiting for the evening dusk to fall; around 20:30, we started attacking the enemy's capital to give destructive damage to Chongqing's Headquarters of the Aerial Defense, the Military Committee's Chairman's Encampment and the Prefectural Government Office and the whole urban area around them in the western half of the urban area to the west of north-south line that goes through Central Park. Around that area, there were several dozens of anti-aircraft guns. This was especially so in and around the western part of the urban area where not a few consulates exist. We, while repulsing the enemy's fighter planes, succeeded in returning safe without suffering any injury even if we had had our planes considerably bombarded.

Under the sky they left behind, another hell, much worse than the one they had the day before, had been brought into being.

● **The Citizens Left in the Sea of Fire Caused by the Incendiary Bombs**
During the twilight attack on May 4, the area that suffered most was Shanghan-cheng (the Upper Half of the Castle) of Shizong Ward, which lay along the Jialing—including the area known for Xiaoliangzi, Duyou-jie Street, Fuzi-chi Pond and Qixing-gang Hill. Each of them being a bustling quarter, it was totally impossible to find any kind of military establishment. In Duyou-jie Street, fifteen stores of silk fabrics were burnt down, thus losing 167,200 *pi* (one *pi* equals to make a couple of formal clothing). Jijie Street also known for long-established stores that featured *Huahua Chouduan* (gorgeous handiwork of Shu brocade) had been turned into a heap of rubble by a single bomb dropped upon it. In fact, since that street had totally been destroyed, it was renamed "5.4 Street." At Guotai Movie Theater, the three hundred audience were directly hit to be killed or injured. Most of the damages and injuries had occurred in those places. Among the thirty-seven banks in the city, fourteen were burnt down that night, as was reported by *Da Gong Bao* (the Great Official Bulletin).

Many of the bombs dropped being incendiary ones, the damage on May 4 turned out to be even greater than that of the day before. The incendiary bomb, when dropped in a street of wooden houses, easily started a gush of fire, and while causing puffs of wind for itself, it never stopped burning until it lapped up the whole area around. This was how the major fires—fourteen in number—were brought into being that night. Within the area from Zhaotian-men Emperor Gate to Qixing-gang Hill (2km from east to west) and from Central Park to the shore of the Jialing (700m from south to north), fourteen fires had started almost at the same time. Those fires started in different spots but soon got together to turn into huge swirls. Both water supply facilities and water mains having been destroyed for the most part because of the successive air raids, nothing could be done but only let them go on burning. There was no means of saving those left in the sea of fire. Screaming and calling the names of their family members, the crowd of people ran through the streets. All they could do then was to help themselves. Some were jumping down the stone steps to reach the ferry; others were walking along uphill roads, trying to head for the western suburbs by land. Everyone, according to his or her destination in mind, had been in the streams going along those narrow streets.

● **The Air Raid upon Chongqing, as was Depicted by Han Suyin**

Among those frantically going this way or that, Han Suyin was there, too. Han was a Chinese whose mother was a Belgian. Han was married to a young commissioned officer on Jiang Jieshi's staff. Han and her husband had been living in Chongqing since they arrived there at the beginning of that year. Her married life was a miserable one. Her husband wished to make himself a trusted retainer of Jiang, but she could not share his opinion either in the view of the world or in the course China would take in the future or even in the way of their family life. Her husband grew more and more violent every day, and this had led her to think of making herself independent of him, but it was none other than an impossible dream to get away from her husband as a retainer-officer of Jiang Jieshi in "His Capital" which stood isolated from the rest of the world. Han Suyin in those days had been facing all these eerie bright red flames both inwardly and outwardly.

About this time, Suyin found that her father's younger brother, Zhou Jiansan, had made himself a successful banker in this city, and this led her to come to board at his residence. Meifeng Bank used to be American East Bank, but the U. S. funds had already returned home, and that building had come to belong to the gentlemen of Sichuan Province. That eight-storied building, along with that of Sichuan Salt Industry Bank, had been a symbol of the modern phase of Chongqing. Her uncle's home on Banshi'lu Street in Shizhong Ward was also a stately mansion quite suitable to such a gentleman as he. Entering the gate, one had to pass three courtyards before one reached the residence with a drawing room in it. Suyin and her husband were allowed to use a fine room with a large bathroom and they were to be waited upon by the domestic staff. Thinking of what a miserable life they had to live while traveling from Wuhan to Chongqing—and even after having arrived at Chongqing, they had to spend several months at a flophouse to be annoyed by many rats and prostitutes—their life at that mansion was literally heavenly. But soon she was to suffer those air raids there. In her autobiography, *The Birdless Summer*, she described it, as follows:

It was late in the afternoon on May 4 that the residential area in the city was totally devastated by the vehement bombings. We had thought the all clear siren had already sounded, but the enemy planes that had appeared to have flown away reversed their course and began to bomb heavily upon the densely built-up area to cause fires everywhere. My uncle's house being hit directly, I and two employees were buried under the wreck of the shuttered house, but we managed to get out of it before long, and the fire that had started there made us run away. The enemy planes were still keeping bombing. More and more people came running out of the burning houses, and the town was thrown into a total confusion.

Han Suyin kept walking all night and managed to reach the branch office of Meifeng Bank in the suburbs.

While all the houses closely lining both sides of the street were blazing furiously, the crowds of people went along, seeking a place of refuge, until they could enter that large stone building of Meifeng Bank. The only light inside that building had come from a small oil lamp placed there, but outside we saw the sea of fire! That night, the staff of the bank, I and about one hundred people left the town and went to the branch office of the bank at Daere in the countryside. Because we heard a rumor that those Japanese planes seemed to keep bombing upon Chungking until it was turned into a huge heap of rubble. We were able to see how these huge waves of people—including ourselves—were moving toward the suburbs under the illumination of the holocausts licking up the whole town. We kept walking all night, as if being carried by the streams of people, and around dawn we crossed several hills full of pebbles and at seven a.m. Erge and I reached that bank building. Those who had accompanied us were fourteen girls and thirty-nine boys and men.

● What Theodore White had Witnessed

Unlike Han Suyin, Theodore White happened to be away from the castle area when he witnessed that air raid, but what he saw on his way back to Shizhong Ward, to find out what was happening to the building of the Friend Mission at which he had taken up his lodgings, was not so different from what Suyin had witnessed, as he wrote in *Search of History**:*

> When I walked up the hill, I saw a bright red sea of fire, in which people were frantically running around, trying to escape. Some were walking in feeble steps; others were hurrying away in a rickshaw; yet others were going by palanquin or pushing their hand cart. All were going away in their own way. When the people were flooding the road, a limousine or a military truck came running while whistling a warning. Then their parade was divided into two only to fill the road again to resume their procession to the countryside. They were carrying bedding, earthenware pots, pans, foodstuffs, a little furniture and so on. Some were carrying babies in their arms, some men carrying old women on their back. But none uttered any word. In that sheer silence, nothing but the sound of their dragging feet could be heard.

Approaching the central part of the city, White was to be immobilized by the sight of some other scenes.

> Every time the fire lapped the bamboo stuff used in the wooden houses, the joints of the bamboos gave terrible bangs. Here the noises were everywhere; women were screaming; men were roaring; babies were crying. Some were seated on the ground, singing a song with their body rocking. Screamings were heard from back alleys. Several times I saw people come rushing out of the lane on the slope onto the main road. There they were rolling about, trying to put off the fire they had caught on their clothes.

● **Many Dresses of Various Colors had Flown up in the Flaming Night Sky**

Many dresses—women had taken out in their desperate wish to carry them along soon to find them too nuisance and let them go in the hustle and bustle on their way somewhere—had been scattered on the roads. By and by, they began to rise into the night sky. Being toyed by an ascending air current and being illuminated by the heaven-scorching light, they were now swaying to and fro over the crowds of people like so many spirits of dead persons.

Lai Chunming, then a fifteen-year-old girl, was still able to recall the clear sight of those pretty cotton clothes flying away into the flames even though she was also running for her dear life. Since that scene had been accompanied by the sight of many people being scattered in all directions, her impression of it might have been intensified.

Chunming lived in Baojie-yuan of Qixing-gang. "Gang" meant a flat-topped height. Qixing-gang was a street for the common people, where shops and houses stood side by side. Being situated about the center of Shizong (City's Central) Ward, it was certainly included in what the Japanese military in Wohan called "the city area to the west of the north-south line that goes through Central Park," but it was nothing but a mere downtown more than one kilometer away from Central Park, thus remaining simply irrelevant to anything military or governmental. Her family was of six members; her father was a carpenter, but when he was unemployed, he helped her mother peddle vegetables. The bombing occurred when she was alone with her mother at home. When their neighborhood became agitated, she tried to turn on the light and found the electricity had been cut off. They crawled under the bed and clang to each other. It was not long before the explosive sounds became ceaseless. This led them to judge that staying there was dangerous and that they should leave there, carrying something precious to them. They put accessories or other small things into a china pot and wrapped their clothing into bundles to carry them on their back. The lane had already been too crowded to carry their bundles with them. Probably buffeted by blasts of fire, signboards came flying. The sky above Zhaotian-men (The Gate to the Imperial Castle) in the east had turned crimson. The neighborhood of Qixing-gang from which they had run away seemed to have been drowned into the sea of fire. It was unknown what had become of her father and brothers.

She and her mother decided to cross the Yangzi and seek refuge at the southern shore. They passed through Lingshi-xiang (Consuls' Town) and came to the rampart of Nanji-men (one of the five gates to the Yangzi), only to find it had already been crowded with those whose destination was the same as theirs. Junks of all sizes—overcrowded with passengers—were heading for the other side of the River about one kilometer ahead. It was impossible for women like themselves to edge into any one of those junks. Chunming and her mother had climbed down the ladder-like stone steps to reach the shore and tried to get onto the floating pier again and again, but in vain. This led them to give up the idea of going to the other side of the River. When they were standing there, unable to tell what to do next, they heard a terrible sound and saw a pillar of fire start near the place they had been standing until several minutes before. The floating pier they had been trying to get on had been blasted. In a moment, that floating pier went out of sight. None was seen to be swimming. What Chunming felt then was a sheer dread rather than relief. That night the mother and daughter remained sleepless at a park they had been guided to by a member of the civilian defense corps. It was a week later when they were finally able to meet the rest of their family.

Huang Suhua, a seventeen years old girl, had also been moving about in utter confusion. She had been married since the year before according to her parents' order, even though she had still been at school. Her husband, nine years older than she, was a clock-mender. In those days, many parents, who had daughters, were impatient to give them away in marriage. What the Chinese called *San-Guang* Campaign (Japan's Three Policies: "Killing All, Plunder All & Burn All) had been known to them, too, and this had led them to think it less worrying for them to have their daughters get married even to opium smokers than to be made victims of *Donyang-gui* (Oriental ogres or Japanese soldiers). One of Suhua's classmates, too, had been made to get married to a middle-aged man. All she could do then was to leave school and obey her father's order. On the nights of "5.3 & 5.4" Suhua, who had already been pregnant, ran and ran in desperation together with her husband from street to street, from lane to lane, driven by furious fires. Later she was to hear that a sister of her elder sister's husband had lost a leg in that fire. But what remained in her mind as something most unforgettable was her having lost the box in which she had kept her gala robe. Nearly half a century has passed since then, but this still recurs to her from time to time. Another thing unforgettable to her was her having to give up her dream of becoming a teacher. Had it not been for those Japanese attacks, she would not have had to leave school so soon, and instead of getting married so young to spend her youthful days only in raising children, she would have been able to live a different life. Even now—after having got nine children and twelve grandchildren—the memory of that horrible night makes her feel unusually hot in chagrin.

- **"The Killed were 3,318 and the Wounded were 1,937"**

May 4, 1939. This was the day for memorializing the 20th anniversary of "5.4 Movement." This day in 1919, students in Beijing made a demonstration march in protesting against Japan's having invaded into Shandong Peninsula, thus to enhance the national movement of "Anti-Japanese and Save-the-Nation Drive." It was only several days before that Zhou Enlai who had been at Guilin had addressed to the youths in response to the request of *Jiu Wu Ri Bao* (*The Save the Nation Daily News*) that: they should succeed to the glorious tradition of 5.4 Movement and fight positively for expediting the national liberation movement and for the sake of science and democracy. On that very memorial day for the demonstration toward Japan, the citizens of Chongqing had received an utmost revenge in the form of indiscriminate bombing upon the capital. This did cause them to feel a dual humiliation.

A writer, Lao She, was one of those who were looking up at the sky, trembling in anger. He was then dependent on the Young Christians' Association that had taken him in at the machinery room in their church in the devastated area in the center of the city. He had established his fame by *A Camel named Xiangzi*, but he remained poor all the same. Since he was practically responsible for All China's Literary Association for Protesting the Enemy as the chief of its general affairs department, he had decided to settle himself in that provisional capital, keeping himself busy both in performing his duty and in pursuing his profession. When he found the fire had come up, he took the unfinished script of his new drama—*The Fog Still Lingering*—and went out to take refuge at his friend Hu Feng's temporary abode in the suburbs. What he experienced then is recorded in *The Night of Wu Si* (*May 4*):

On May 4: Yesterday I did not stop writing even during the air raid. Today also I kept writing on and on and on. At four in the afternoon, Zhou

Wen, Zhi Di and Luo Sun came to see me. We had been talking for a while, when there was an air-raid warning! At five, another warning! We all went down to the underground air-raid shelter. I was carrying my script. A little after six, hearing the booms again and again, I was aware that they were signals of approaching death. This made me clench my teeth. At seven, the air-raid warning was called off. This led us to get out of the shelter. All the sky was brightened. Red flames were rising everywhere. This had turned the whole sky unusually red. The vehement flames were burning human fresh and bones, houses, household goods and books, till they all got burnt; even stars and the moon had turned bright red. At this moment, none could tell who were alive and who were dead. The terribly disastrous scenes were seen everywhere. Again there came the voices of warning for evacuation. I went into the garden, carrying my script and the important papers of All China's Literary Association for Protesting the Enemy. We fled through the fire. The people hurrying to the Park were unbelievably orderly—so much so that I could hardly believe: this was happening in China; they were behaving in orderliness, cooperation and bravery. That was the culture and civilization we had kept nurturing for those five thousand years, and in the midst of fires and bloodsheds, we had been demonstrating no mean power and mettle retained by us all!

This was the night of 5.4, which turned out so blazing and so bleeding! Never shall we forget *this* resentment and *this* regret forever! Never!

Even at midnight, the force of fires never showed any little sign of abating.

Hu Feng, upon whom Lao She came to depend, also wrote about the "5.3 & 5.4" in his *Memoirs*.

Hu Feng, a friend of Lu Xun, who was later to be known as a distinguished literary theoretician, after having graduated Qinghua University, came to Tokyo in 1929 when he was twenty-five. While he was striving to master Japanese language at a Japanese language school, he got acquainted with such left-wing Japanese writers as Eguchi Kan, Oya Soichi, Kobayashi Takiji and so on, and while putting his record of enrollment at the department of English literature of Keio-Gijuku University, he began to incline increasingly toward the proletarian cultural movement guided by the Japanese Communist Party. In 1930, when the League of Chinese Left-Wing Authors started, Hu Feng organized the Tokyo chapter of it along with the other Chinese students in Japan. Thus while being engaged in anti-war activities, Hu Feng was to spend the days when Japan was going on her way to invade China through the Manchurian Incident* (1931) and 5.15 Incident* (1932) and Japan's withdrawal from the League of Nations (1933). In 1933, about a month after Kobayashi Takiji (1903-1933: a man of proletarian literature) was arrested and tortured to death, Hu Feng was arrested on suspicion of his political activity in Japan to throw its government into confusion, thus to be violently examined for four months. Even if the case against him was dropped because of insufficient evidence, he was ordered to leave the university and then to leave Japan. After returning home, he joined the leftist federation's activities, and while mixing with Lu Xun, Mao Dun, Tian Han, Xia Yan and so on, he kept arguing about Japan's policy of aggression and Jiang Jieshi's policy of anti-Communism, while encouraging people to fight against Japan. In December, 1938, Hu Feng, escaping from the horrors of wartime fire, sailed up to Zhaotian-men at Chongqing and "looked up at the long flight of stone steps that led to the downtown of Chongqing seated high up on the mountain," as he wrote in his *Memoirs*. There he obtained a position at the Chinese Literature Department of Fudan University which had already moved to Beibei Ward on the other side of the Jialing. While giving lectures on creative writing and teaching Japanese language, he was engaged in literary activities, too, by starting a magazine *July* as part of his anti-Japanese activities. Then he was to encounter the ravages of "5.3 & 5.4," as he wrote:

May 3: The sky was as clear as clear could be, as it had been for several days on end. The foggy season in Chongqing had already been over, and summer had fully set in. During the morning, I did some office work, and at one in the afternoon, I took lunch. After a while, we heard an air-raid warning resound.

Hu Feng entered the air-raid shelter of Chuandong Normal School. In the darkness caused by power failure, they heard the buzzing of the enemy planes, followed by the sounds of the anti-aircraft fires and the rumblings of the bomb-dropping. At this period, the area where Chuandong Normal School was seated had not yet been made an aim of bombardment. It was not until "No. 101 Operations" started the next year that this area was made a target of bombardment. On May 4, while he was preparing for supper, he heard an emergency warning. "What a time zone for an air raid!" He said to himself. Then Lao She, who had gone through some experiences he was to write later in *The Night of May Fourth,* came to join him at his house. After the air-raid warning was called off, Hu Feng went to the printing house in Shizhong (City's Central) Ward. As he later wrote in his memoirs, "the streets were desolate and dilapidated; at Qixing-gang Hill many coffins remained unattended." That was where Lai Chunming had suffered from the air raid. Having anticipated they would have many more air raids, Hu Feng determined to move somewhere in the suburbs.

The area that had suffered most on May 4 was Shanhan-cheng (the Upper Half of the Castle) or the northern half of Chungking Castle. According to *The Statistical Chart of the Damages & Casualties Caused by the Air Raids in Various Parts of Sichuan Province in the 28th Year (1939) of the Republic of China*, the bombing raid that day was performed by the twenty-seven planes that arrived in three waves; the number of bombs dropped was 126, causing 3,318 deaths and 1,937 injuries, while destroying 3,803 houses and buildings. This had far surpassed the damages the day before: 673 deaths, 350 injuries and 1,086 houses and buildings lost. It was apparent that the fires caused by the incendiary bombs were the greatest factors. In fact, the fires had still kept burning here and there even after the following day dawned.

About this time before World War II, having had more than 5,000 people killed or injured by a single air raid was something unheard-of. It was also what the world had first experienced that a single air raid could be so destructive as this. But what was even more serious than those figures in statistics was the sorrows and regrets that had badly clung to each of the men and women who had narrowly survived "5.3 and 5.4 (Wu San and Wu Si)." They still remain with them even after the century has passed into the next one.

The Buddhist priest Haichang at Luohan-si Temple, who is now called "the old master," still remembers clearly how he was feeling at the sight of that beautiful temple, a witness of his youthful days, being reduced to ashes in a single night. Both Luohan-si Temple and the five hundred images of *Luohans** were reproduced with unusual effort, but they were shuttered again by the vandalism of the Great Cultural Revolution (1966-77), and in 1986 the second reproduction of them was performed. But what the seventy-five-year-old Haichang had still held in his memory was that great main hall of supreme magnificence—*Da Xiong Bao Dian* (Grand Hall for the Treasured Heroes)—built in the early period of the Qing Dynasty (1616-1912) to house those five hundred seated images of *Luohans* as tall as two meters. The mere entrance into that grand hall used to strike him with awe.

*Buddha's Disciples who have attained *Nirvana* or the supreme enlightenment

Luohan-si Temple at that time was the ancient temple of *Zen* Buddhism, whose fame was the greatest in Chongqing. It was founded during the Tang era (618-907) and because of the grandeur of its building, it was recorded in *Ba-Xuan-Zhi* (A Topography of Ba Prefecture) as "the best of this kind in the world." According to *Shu-Zhong Ming-Sheng-Ji* (A Record on the Spots of Fame in Shu), in 1064, Zuyue, the founder of this Buddhist sect, took part in repairing the temple, and named it Zipin-si Temple in memory of the then era name Zipin (Peaceful Government), but about the middle of the Qing era (1644-1911), Priest Longfa built the hall for the *Luohans*, and this led it to be called "Luohan-si Temple."

It is located about the borderline between Shang Han Cheng (the Upper Half of the Castle) and Xia Han Cheng (the Lower Half of the Castle) and it is not so far away as 500 meters from Central Park. Closely surrounded by a large number of houses and stores that have developed from the markets that used to surround that temple, the temple had no longer retained any such atmosphere of having been detached from the secular world as it used to be during the Tang era, but for the citizens of Chongqing, it had still remained an edifyingly solemn place of worship.

It was in 1931 (the 20th year of the Republic of China) that Haichang received the precepts of Buddhism at the age of twenty. Haichang, having been bereaved of his mother at two and his father at eight—prompted also by economical reason—began to feel like secluding himself from the secular world. This led him to take tonsure at fourteen and at twenty he was made a priest of Luohan-si Temple. At that time, this large temple had as many as one hundred priests in it.

Even when Sino-Japanese war broke out and Chongqing was made into the anti-Japanese capital, the daily life at Luohan-si temple remained unchanged.

At the bell-ringing at five, they got up, washed their face and performed the first sutra-chanting of the day. After finishing a simple breakfast in silence, they sat in meditation unless they had no Buddhist mass to perform anywhere. It took an hour for a single stick of incense to turn into smoke. When four sticks were burnt, his morning service was over. Neither the Sino-Japanese War nor the behind-the-scene battles between Jiang Jieshi and the Chinese Communist Party had ever disturbed their daily life at Luohan-si Temple.

On May 3, when they suffered the air raid, Priest Haichang had been away from the temple because he was invited by one of the patrons of the Temple to perform a Buddhist mass. A rich merchant at Mihua-jie Street had been bereaved of a member of his family and they were to hold a funeral. Ten priests, including their leader, were reading a service; Haichang as a young priest had also been behaving in a dignified manner, wearing in a religious vestment and a cap called Fangyan-kou (Flame-releasing mouth).

In the midst of the sutra-chanting, the siren went off, and after a little while, the bombs' droppings began to be heard from somewhere afar. Affected by the sound of sutra-chanting, they had mistaken the emergency warning for a mere warning, and even before they ran to the air raid cave, they had had the buzzing planes arrive overhead. The ten priests hid themselves under the long table at the drawing room. That was all Haichang had remembered. Because the ear-splitting sounds and quakes had sent him to black out. Then there dropped an incendiary bomb to start a fire on the house, it seemed.

It was not until he received medical treatment after having been dug out of the debris of the fallen building by the civilian defense corps that Haichang was brought back to his senses. He had had his left leg broken; his head and back had also been badly cut. The eight of the ten priests there had been killed. The one who had been sitting in meditation with his legs crossed under the long table was dug out as he had been. Including the attendants at that funeral, more than twenty were found dead there. Even the body in the coffin had been blown out of it because of the blast it got from the explosion. Haichang, even though seriously injured, turned out to be among the small number of those who had narrowly escaped death at that house.

● **The Buddhist Statues at Luohan-si Temple were Smiling**
upon the Wailing Capital.

Haichang was taken to the hospital, and it took six months before he was strong enough to be able to walk on crutches. The first place he visited then was where Luohan-si Temple used to be. But that temple—where he had spent his ascetic life for nine years since he was twenty—was no more without leaving even a single tile behind. On the same day when he was buried alive, Luohan-si Temple, nearly one thousand years old, had also been made to vanish in flames along with all those five hundred images of *Luohans*, and together with many of the residents in the neighborhood.

It was probably about that temple or Luohan-si that Theodre White, who had been walking around the city that night—turning himself into a walking camera—recorded the scenes he had come across that night.

White had just witnessed his room of Friend Mission having been shuttered into fragments and a dead body that could be known as a woman's only because of its uncovered breasts. Then he happened to meet Robert Martin of UPI, and this led them to walk together from street to street till four in the morning. It was then that he happened to see *the* Buddhist image:

> While walking with Martin throughout the night, I was to witness an overwhelmingly large number of changes that had been brought about in the town. Behind the street I thought I had already been well-acquainted with in these two or three weeks, I could see a slope which had been kept out of our sight so far because of the row of houses made of bamboo and mud. Now that all those houses were burnt down, there came into our view a huge bronz image of Buddha in Zen contemplation, which had been carved upon this side of the cliff. Shining brightly by reflecting the flames, the noble face of the Buddha with a mild smile upon it was gently turned toward the wailing people in the capital.

On entering the main gate to Luohan-si Temple, one sees on one's left what is called *Gufuya*, a cliff carved with about four hundred ancient Buddhist images, large and small, that dated back to the Northern Song Era (960-1127). It was in the shade of those images that Zeng Zhiwei, a member of a civilian defense corps, had thrust himself in one of the concavities he found there.

Since the images stood close in a line looking like a wall, it is sometimes called "Luohans' Wall." What White had taken as "a bronze image" would have been the darkened expression of a Luohan illuminated by the flames rising furiously from the main hall of Luohan-si Temple. About this time, Haichang also was wandering in the trench of pain and grief.

In 1981, when Haichang finally came back to the Luohan Hall rebuilt in the same place—after having outlived both the National United Front Against Japan and the liberation war, followed by the ten years' confusion of the Great Cultural Revolution—that youthful priest had already become seventy.

● **The Churches Protected by Foreign Rights & Interests also Suffered from Calamities**

In Shang Han Cheng (the Upper Half of the Castle Area), there were not only the Buddhist temples such as Luohan-si, Changan-si and so on but also several Christian churches and their facilities, and they also had to suffer from the 5・4 air raid. Since most of these Christian institutions belonged to America or France, their having suffered the air attacks was to be immediately reported to Europe and America as Japan's indiscriminate bombings upon Chongqing. Certainly in the order issued by the Japanese military, there was an item: "In performing the bombardment upon the city of Chongqing, you must be careful not to damage the third powers' rights and interests." But practically this had not meant anything. In fact, on May 4, not only the churches placed under "the third powers' rights and interests" but also the British, French and German Embassies were damaged by the air raid.

The Catholic church, which has now been known as "Chongqing City's Christian Patriotic Association," used to be called "French Church," and was operated by Paris' Oversea Missionary Church, and Father Bourget, whose Chinese name was Yang Muhua, and a Chinese father used to be engaged in their missionary work. They had their church on Qixing-gang (Seven Stars Hill) and seven chapels at seven spots in the city. By the air raid on May 4, their church on Qixing-gang was burnt down. Only the clock tower, 36 meters tall, and the bell brought all the way from France have remained to this day to impress the visitors there. Father Bourget, having been furious at that outrageous attack upon that divine territory, took a large number of photographs and sent them to France so that they might help to advertise the atrocities being performed by the Japanese military. There seemed to have been some negotiations for compensation through the French Embassy, but since it was concerning a foreign property, what had become of it could not be known to Bishop Liu Zongyu, a Chinese, who belonged to the Christian Patriots' Association. The following was also what he told me:

In the air raids in 1939, this neighborhood was burnt up, and more than twenty people concerned with this church were killed, I hear. St. Teresa Church in Jiangbei (the Northern Shore of the Jialing) and the chapel at Shapingba were also bombed. It was in that year when Sister Ding died. No longer have we had anyone concerned with this church who had actually seen or heard what happened here at that time.

In 1979, the Christian Patriots' Association was permitted to resume their activity. According to Bishop Liu, 800 people attend at a Sunday service; at the mass of the Four Great Masses, 1,500 devotees gather together. Bishop Liu has been a member of the standing committee of Chongqing City's People's Representatives' Convention.

There was "an American Church" of the Methodist Communion, too, which was also destroyed by the air raid in May. No one has kept a clear memory as to what sort of damage was inflicted upon what was known as Holy Communion Hall, which was later renamed Chongqing Christian Chapel. According to what Father Chen Yuanrong looked back upon, the air raids on 5.3 and 5.4 had burnt the Holy Communion Hall, the Sabbath Association Hall, the Public Play Hall and the China Christian Church—four in all.

Father Leble, an American missionary, collected those broken pieces of bombs that had been brought about by the air raids on 5.3 and 5.4, and carried them along all the way to America, and in his tour around the country, he preached that: (since America at that time had kept exporting petroleum and scrap iron to Japan) *the* bombs dropped from the Japanese planes were as good as U.S.-made; The U.S. Government, therefore, should immediately revise their policy of exporting scrap iron and petroleum to Japan.

Upon this American churchman, Jiang Jieshi himself conferred a decoration at the Grand Hall of the Wartime Capital of Chongqing, as was witnessed by Father Chen, who was still a boy then. As for what had been happening to

Chongqing, it was being known to the rest of the world through such channels of information as these, too. Just as the appalling tragedy at Guernica was gradually becoming known to the rest of the world—however hard Spain and Germany might have tried to deny and conceal it—Japan's bombardments upon Chongqing also became known to the rest of the world through a variety of routes.

That may have been a fruit brought about by Priest Leble who had carried out his own original activity.

Haga Takeshi, a Japanese, who lived in New York at that time, had a couple of identities: one was of a bank clerk at a Japanese bank known as Shokin Bank of Japan; the other was of a member of the American Communist Party. He was on friendly terms with Jack Shirai, who joined the Spanish Civil War (1936-39) to die in action, and with Ishigaki Ayako, a Japanese woman critic (under the name of Haru Matsui). The following was what Haga wrote about what the New Yorkers were feeling toward Japan at that time:

In America, a world's fair was being held from spring to summer in 1939 in a couple of sites—New York and San Francisco. Naturally Japan also took part in it. One day in August, "Japan Day" was held as one of the Fair's formal events. As was expected, the ambassador Horiuchi Kensuke came to make a speech. What was amazing on that occasion was that: Mayor of New York, La Guardia, pointed out the wrong of Japan's invasion into China. His bitter speech given in front of the Japanese ambassador was played up as something remarkable by every newspaper. The gist went as follows:

The theme of this exposition is "the World Tomorrow." What we imagine when we hear of this theme is the world where all the peoples are able to live in happiness and in harmony according to the conception brought about by scientists and artists. Whereas Japan now is being engaged in war in China. Japan may say they are making war to bring peace to China and to make the Chinese people's life a steady one. But to the rest of the world, this explanation sounds very perplexing. We do hope the Japanese government and the Japanese people will explain to the world how we should take what Japan is doing in China at present.

Haga Takeshi had once witnessed the scene, in which the Chinese people protesting against Japan's invasion into China were marching in a demonstration parade as far as Wall Street. They were carrying the placards with "A Bowl of Rice" written on them, and they were receiving shouts of encouragement from all those lining the street. He had also noticed that: women in New York began to wear stockings of lisle thread instead of the silk stockings made in Japan. When the former ambassador Saito Hiroshi—the ambassador Horiuchi's predecessor—died at his post, the U.S. Government showed such consideration as to send his remains back to Japan in a warship. But at present, anti-Japanese feelings were being on the rise in the diplomatic field, too.

● **The Embassies and the Consulates were also Damaged**

In being bombed out, the diplomatic and consular offices were not exceptions. At this period, Japan had not intended to adopt any aggressive position toward either the U.S. or the European countries. Especially, the Navy that had once accidentally bombed and sunken a U.S. gunboat Panee, while helping the Army being engaged in their ground attack in capturing Nanjing, thus to cause the strained relationship between Japan and the U.S.. So they had taken care not to damage the third powers' rights and interests, as was clearly written in the directive they had received. But it was practically impossible for them to put the third powers' right and interests—especially their diplomatic establishments—out of the range of their attack. One of their attack targets on May 4, Qixing-gang Hill, was no more than 500m away from the area where embassies and consulates stood close together. As a natural consequence, many were to be bombed or burnt down in the spreading fire.

The British Embassy and Consulate had one foreigner and twenty Chinese killed by the bombardment. The British Government on receiving the report from the Ambassador Archibolt Clark-Car, ordered the Ambassador Robert Craigie, resident in Tokyo, to make a strict protest with the Japanese Government against what they had done. The French Consulate had two bombs dropped and had one of their buildings totally destroyed. The German Consulate suffered a great damage by the spreading fires that had started from the buildings that stood around it. After Ambassador Oskar Trautmann was called back, Germany virtually stopped its embassy activities in China, but at Chongqing their business as a delegation was going on, making their consulate their base. Lily Abegg, a special correspondent of Frankfurt Zeidong in the Far East, too, had checked the fact that the German Embassy Building suffered the air raid, as she wrote in her work, *Chongqing:*

> During the fiscal year of 1938, the air raids by the Japanese Air Force were performed, keeping their aim only at the military facilities, but since 1939, their air raids began to be performed even within the city limits and this led some citizens to leave the city. The air raids performed in May, 1939, were extremely fierce and caused a considerable number of deaths. This led more and more citizens to leave the urban area.
>
> The German Embassy, where the acting ambassador was also staying, used to be on the hill just behind the urban area until May, 1939, but because of the air raids by the Japanese Air Force, we had our embassy building damaged in doors, windows, roofs and so on. This led us to move to the district where the Chongqing Government is seated, but the recent air raid has caused us to suffer some damages all the same .

The photograph taken and sent by Carl Mydans to *LIFE* shows a member of the embassy staff who had just spread an extra-large Hakenkreuz as a symbol of strength and fear in their front garden so that it might help the Japanese airmen engaging in the air raid to notice that: that was the seat for "the German representatives." That Nazi flag as a symbol of strength and fear had thus been employed as a signal for begging the Japanese bombers for mercy. This photograph taken from a somewhat ironical point of view was to inform the U.S. readers not only of what was happening to "free China" but also the close relationship which had been formed between Japan and Germany. It was more than one year later that the Tripartite Pact was brought into being by Japan, Germany and Italy, but Japan and Germany had already been recognized as allied with each other.

● **Jiang Jieshi's Advisor to his Air Force, Captain Claire Chennault**

from the U.S.

On the other hand, among foreign residents in Chongqing, there was such a person as Claire Chennault, an ex-captain of the U.S. Army, who had turned his two-day experience of being under the air raids into a rare opportunity to bring himself somewhere new. Chennault, whose duty to perform at Chongqing was to strengthen the military power of the Chinese Air Force, would not take refuge even when an air-raid warning was issued, but was studying the way how the Japanese planes were behaving, as if he were "a football coach studying a documentary film of the other team with whom his team was going to play soon," according to what Theodore White mentioned in describing him. Chennault had been invited to China to be Jiang Jieshi's advisor to his air force by Song Meiling (Jiang Jieshi's wife and the Chief Secretary of the Air Force Committee), and while starting to form an American Volunteer Group (AVG) which was later known as "Flying Tigers," he was trying hard to develop the ability of Chinese Air Force to the level high enough to cope with the Japanese planes.

Chennault was to be remembered in the history of the air force in a way different from Billy Mitchell known as the father of bombing theory. That was, Chennault had always been a supremacist for fighter planes, not for bombers. Being an excellent pilot of a fighter plane, he intended to establish a theory for operating a fighter plane unit, thus to open up the future of the Army Flying Corps. He meticulously analyzed all the air fights after World War I, made it into a text entitled *A Principle of an Interception Force*, and submitted it to the Department of the Army, expressing his wish that it would be adopted. The main point of his idea was: fighting for the command of the air must be regarded as something of great importance, and if a closely connected pair of fighters were to fight against a single enemy plane, the fighting power of that formation would be 4:1, instead of 2:1. That was why, Chennault concluded: the strong unit of fighter planes and their training were now being requested.

As Mitchell did, Chennault also tried to prove his theory through the scenes of military exercises, but in vain. To say nothing of the bureaucracy of the Department of the Army, Mitchell's theory on bombers' omnipotence had already become supported by all, and this caused his theory not to be accepted even by the job site of the Air Force led by those who had once been his favorite pupils like Hap Arnold and others, Chennault found himself left alone, his military rank barely reaching "captain," despite his twenty years' career there.

In 1937, Chennault, who had retired from the U.S. Army at forty-seven, made for Nanjing in May in the same year, having been attracted by the conditions shown by Song Meiling: "an adviser on aviation," "one thousand dollars a month," "a three-month contract" and "the Chinese warplanes are available."

A couple of months later, the Sino-Japanese War broke out. Chennault at once sent a telegram to Jiang Jieshi, expressing his wish: "I am a pilot who have dedicated my life so far at air battles by fighter plane. I shall be happy to fight against the Japanese Air Force by making use of the tactics I have long been studying." Then his employment contract was prolonged indefinitely. As a member of Jiang Jieshi's staff, he took part in various battles in Nanjing, Wuhan, Kunming and Chongqing. At Wuhan, he fought in cooperation with the Soviet Union's Volunteer Army—"Swords of Justice"—and at other times, he himself drove a fighter plane to fight against Japanese planes. Joseph Alsop, who was then Chennault's aid-de-camp and later became a famous columnist, once said: "More than forty planes were brought down by Chennault."

Training airmen for the Chinese Air Force and offering advice in building the base for the Air Force were also included in his occupation. It had also come from his suggestion to bring into being a cordon or a cobweb system of aircraft-spotting stations and a system of spying on the enemy's movements all over that vast area, so that they could grasp early what Japanese planes were going to do.

On May 4, Chennault at Chongqing left his record as follows:

> In a perfectly V-shaped formation, 27 bombers came flying. They looked like a skein of Canadian geese flying north from Louisiana in spring. When they got ready for combat, they got abreast all at once with such peerless accuracy that I could not help admiring them even if they were enemies. Bombs were dropped, and numberless incendiary bombs glittering in sliver were scattered, and this was to burn up the central part of the city and the hell fires kept burning furiously for three days and nights.
>
> —*Chennault and his Flying Tigers*

Chennault took pictures to record how the attacks were being made, while taking notes about them. As a matter of fact, he had had another far-sighted aim he wished to achieve. The following was what Owen Lattimore, an American Sinologist, who had met Chennault at Chungking, wrote in his *China Memoirs—Chiang Kaishek and the War Against Japan:*

Tactically, Chennault was perhaps the most brilliant trainer of fighter pilots of his day. His "tiger" was not, as most people still think, named after the jungle beast, but after the tiger shark. Each plane had a shark's head painted on the two sides of its nose, with gaping jaws and huge teeth.

Chennault himself was a simple-minded man. Strategically, he had a blind spot in thinking that when the war with Japan was over, it would be easy for Chiang (Jiang Jieshi) to "clean up" (that was the phrase) the Chinese Communists from the air with the air force trained in battle against the Japanese. This was the political-military line that he was trying to sell to Chiang—never with quite complete success—throughout the time that I had anything to do with such affairs. We all know that in the civil war with the Chinese Communists, Chiang Kaishek's air force, with U.S. planes available to back them up, had complete control of the air but was unable to cope with the loose, flexible Communist style of campaigning on the ground.

This proves that Chennault's strategy was not omnipotent, but through his studying on Japan's air raids upon Chongqing, he was at least able to offer a couple of suggestions to the top leaders of the U.S. Air Force. One was concerning the effectiveness of employing the incendiary bombs in air raid on the city, and he recommended that America should also promote a production of incendiary bombs in their preparation for the war against Japan. The other, which was offered later than this, was a suggestion on fighting against Zero Fighters or the newly-produced carrier-based airplanes the Japanese Navy had recently put in the Chinese front. When the Zero Fighters were being proud of their invincibility in the skies of Chungking, Jiang Jieshi's advisor to his Air Force, silent and polite, was looking up at the formation of the Zero Fighters, while trying to create what was to be called "Dog-Fight Tactics"—which was to be adopted in 1943 after the start of the Japan-U.S. War, when Grumman F6F "Hell Cat" appeared: a pair of planes' nose-driving and one fanning before hurrying up. That was air fight tactics (dog-fight tactics) or the tactics to turn the ratio of number of planes of 2:1 into the ratio of military potential of 4:1. Chennault had found that the Zero Fighter was highly mobile but inferior in power and this led him to conclude that: if his plane kept higher than a Zero fighter were to nose-dive to attack it, he would succeed in crushing it.

About the time when the confusion caused by 5.3 and 5.4 air raids came to a halt, Chennault wrote to the Chief of the General Staff, General Arnold, suggesting that: they should develop five-pound incendiary bombs to employ them for Japan. What had motivated him to do so would have been something more practical than revengeful: His having seen with his own eyes how effective the incendiary bombings were in destroying Chongqing led him to think of employing incendiary bombs in destroying Japanese cities whose constitution was of the same nature as that of Chongqing. He eagerly expressed his opinion to Theodore White, saying:

"If we were to seek for an overall victory, we need to annihilate everything of the enemy—their cities, productivity, sea routes and so on. Airplanes in Japan, as in Germany, are the tools for achieving that purpose. What can be the purpose of war, except defeating the enemy?"

—*In Search of History**

After the outbreak of the war between the U.S. and Japan, Chennault was called back to the U.S. Army to be promoted from captain to brigadier general. Then he was made Commander of the 14th Air Force based in Kunming, China; at the end of 1944, Chennault—joining forces with the young general Curtis LeMay who had burnt up Hamburg and Berlin— performed their first "concentrated incendiary bombings" upon the Hankou Base, from which the Japanese military had performed their air raids upon Chongqing. That turned out to be a dreadful revenge of fire upon the base from which the Japanese mission on 5.3 and 5.4. had taken off.

● **The Yangzi and The Jialing with Numberless Bodies Floating upon them**
   These things mentioned above, however, were to occur much later. On the night of May 4, 1939, the city of Chongqing was on the verge of death after the two-day attacks by destructive bombs and incendiary bombs. They had no electricity nor water service. Everything appeared exaggerated under the floating flames, as if having been turned into swinging shadow. Many of the dead were still left on the roads or in the park. Both of the Yangzi and the Jialing were covered with floating bodies, so much so that the masters of the junks must reach the shore by pushing them aside with a pole with a long hook upon it.

The weekly, *Qun Zhong Zhou Jian* (A Weekly for the Multitudes), published in the week that followed, had carried a report of the scenes collected by Lu Yi, a reporter. Some of the passages went as follows:

On the afternoon of "5.4", the enemy planes performed their second massacre. The urban area was wrapped up with fires caused by the bombs thrown at random. When they came falling with the sound of *hyuu*, both explosive sounds and human screams rang throughout the town. Men and women, and all of our fellow countrymen from the aged to the children, had their fresh blown off, their daily commodities broken to pieces, only to vanish into the air filled with flames and smoke. The pitch-dark smokescreen did shutter the sunshine.

At night, a large number of fire-pillars rose high and this made the both banks of the Yangzi clearly seen. The flames of fires went on lapping up the neighborhood voraciously. The people had got frantic, and carrying as much property as they could, they were all running toward the banks of the River, calling their children's names.

All the tears having already been shed, they were no longer even able to weep. All they could do now was to clench their teeth, cursing their cruel enemies. When I, the reporter, was walking down the slope from Linjiang-men (Overlooking-the-River Gate), an old woman, who appeared to have gone insane, caught me and said:

"The Japanese robbers have killed my family. Right? Then I must go and join a corps of rangers, carrying a kitchen knife with me. Yes, I must go and get revenge for my family!"

Looking up from the riverbank, I saw the fires had turned the sky crimson and I heard the cursing, crying and groaning coming from everywhere. These flames and these voices of the people will have been carved forever at the depth of their memory.

Those who Put those Bombardments on Record

● A New Form of Holocaust was Brought into Being

Even after those horrible days of 5.3 and 5.4—which seemed endlessly long—the confusion in the city was far from coming to an end. The people had to start inspecting the whole aspects of the tragedy in broad daylight in order to check them, confirm them and accept them, however heartbreaking it might be. And this caused the new voices of lamentation to be heard everywhere. Those who were red-eyed because of sleeplessness came to the parks or to the ruins of the air raids, and making their eyes even more bleary because of the smoke still lingering around, they were trying to find out the whereabouts of the missing members of their family.

The fires that had started here and there by the incendiary bombs still remained inextinguishable. The water had been cut off. As for the houses on high ground at the end of the flights of stone steps, no one could do anything but wait till they all burnt out. In some bystreets or at the depths of some alleys that had fortunately been kept safe from fire, the volunteer fire brigades were trying hard to make a firebreak belt, intending to check the spreading fire. It was in such situations as these that the citizens of Chongqing came to face once again what ravages had been brought about by 5.3 and 5.4.

Here and there in the city, the smells of blood and gunpowder still seemed to be drifting about. As for the dead bodies, they had casually been piled up at the public parks or by the roadsides. Those who were searching for their family members went up to those piles and leaned over them to gaze at the faces of those silent people who had been piled up on their stomach. Some corpses were burnt, others had their head or limbs torn off; some children had breathed their last with their nose bleeding; men and women had been stripped off their clothes probably because of the force of the explosion. Their appearances were varied, but they were all common in having been thrown into death by the bombing. They had been killed by a new usage of aerial potential named "strategic & political bombing" or "by destroying the organization of the enemy's political, economic or industrial center or by making a direct air raid upon the residents so that their fear might frustrate their fighting spirit." (*The Directions for Employing the Air Force* adjusted by their Headquarters of Japan's Army Air Force in 1937)

In performing such a massacre as these, the military force employed was no more than 45 planes on May 3 and 27 planes on May 4 with a total of 72 bombers and 504 airmen—seven airmen in each bomber. The 504 air men never stepped on to the ground of Chongqing, never shot at any Chinese nor flourished any Japanese sword to slash any Chinese, but they performed a great massacre, in which more than 8,000 people were killed or injured in a couple of days. All the airmen did in performing that massacre was to put themselves at a height of the sky—so high that they could not regard each of the people below as even a spot, nor could they tell the barracks from the dwellings—and all the energy they employed was to pull the lever for dropping the bomb, only spending as much energy as needed in putting the car into gear in performing that great massacre that had killed or injured more than 8,000 people in a couple of days. That was the beginning of a new type of holocaust which could *never* be imagined by those airmen who were relieving their fatigue at Hankou Air Base after having been released from their bombing flight. That was also a starting point toward the strategic conception, in which the exclusive employment of the air force was the point in achieving a decisive success in warfare. Those who were killed in Chongqing, therefore, could be regarded as the first victims of the strategic bombings, to be followed by those involved in many strategic bombings performed during the Second World War, which reached its climax at Dresden and at Tokyo, and then it was united with nuclear energy, as was seen in Hiroshima and Nagasaki, and further on to the nuclear threat to the whole of mankind by the driving force of intercontinental ballistic missiles during the cold war—which leads to the nuclear deterrence strategy. Already in 1939, those who were killed in Chongqing had warned us of what the future war would be like, where the battlefield would be mechanized and automated, where the relations between those who are killing and those who are being killed will get blurred till the relations between the murderers and the murdered disappear. Evidently, that could be called "the conception applied on *Hiroshima*" before Hiroshima actually suffered the atomic bombing.

Those who had found the bodies of their blood relatives from among the heaps of the dead bodies carried them in their handcart to the place for a funeral. Others, rearranging the broken pieces of bodies, were trying to find out the missing parts. Here and there were seen the scenes in which they were about to part with those who had been living together, sharing their love and life both in joys and in sorrows. So many deaths at one time prevented them from turning to any undertaker, and this led every family to do everything for themselves. Firstly, they had to find the coffins had long been sold out. Coffins of all qualities—from those of the best quality made of thick board, whose inside was painted in lacquer upon lacquer, to the simplest ones made of six boards for the common people—had been sold out in no time. Many families had wrapped the remains in rush matting and carried them to the burial ground. Through those coffins, too, one could tell their positions in society. As for the bodies no one came to claim, the soldiers and men of relief corps with their face covered with a large mask carried them by truck to the suburbs or to the sandbars of the Yangzi and buried them all in the hole they had dug there. Day after day, the same work was being done.

● Guo Moruo had Left his Wife & Children in Japan
to Join the National United Front against Japan

Guo Moruo, the chief of the Third Board of the Political Department of the Military Committee, lived at No. 4 in Tianguan-fu Street at Qixing-Gang Hill. Though it was to be burnt down by the air raid a month later, it had been left unburnt by the air raids on 5.3 & 5.4. The poet, seeing the dreadful sights of miseries every day, had been suffering from such indignation as it might cause his blood to flow backward. At the news of the 7.7 Incident (the outbreak of the Sino-Japanese Incident (1937-45), he was badly driven to restlessness and chose to return home instead of keeping living in exile in Japan. Not even a couple of years had passed since then. From Kobe, he stole a passage to Shanghai, from which he had always been kept breathlessly fighting on successive fronts—or rather retreating or running away from Hongkong, Wuhan, and Changsha before reaching Chongqing. Now, no sooner had they thought they had built a foundation there for their long-term resistance than they were to face terrible attacks from the sky.

In Japan—at Ichikawa in Chiba Prefecture—he had left his Japanese wife, Anna, and four boys and one girl of his own. The youngest boy Hongni (Koji in Japanese) was still six. Guo was afraid that his confiding in his family about his decision to go home might cause the rumor to spread; it was also too unbearable for him to see them being thrown into grief. So, he steeled himself against pity, and simply left a note behind, before slipping out of the house while they were fast asleep. On board the ship, he wrote a poem, in which he expressed his sorrow of having left his wife and children behind despite his overwhelming reluctance to do so:

> I parted with my wife, throwing our young ones.
> This was how I cut off the threads of lotus.
> I shed my tears of blood for the first time
> Since I left my land more than ten years ago.
> On board the ship, I gaze at the Sansu-jing-qi.*

> *the Three-Asterism Flag
> (the national flag of China at that time)

Now in a certain spot in the urban area of Chongqing, the poet's eyes became fixed upon the bodies of Mother and her children fixed together in their huddle even after they got carbonized. In the heart of Guo Moruo, who had parted with his wife and children, thus disengaging himself from his personal sentiment, there must have occurred the visages of those he had left behind. This was how that poem—*I groan at the sight of the misery* (introduced in *The Prelude*)—was brought into being. At the sight of that misery, the forty-eight-year-old revolutionist had returned into a loving father of his own children.

● The Liberated Area for Cultural Activities:
The Third Office of Administration Department

During this period, Guo Moruo's Third Office of Administration Department was the only liberated area for cultural activities secured for the Communist Party and the left-wing power in the capital. The chief of the Department, Chen Cheng, was a faithful right-hand person of Jiang Jieshi, but on the other hand, he gave much attention to the adjustment of their relationship with the Communist Party so that the Nationalist-Communist collaboration might be turned into a reality. The vice-chief of the Political Department, who supervised practical matters, was Zhou Enlai as the representative of the Chinese Communist Party, and this had enabled Guo to exercise his talent as much as he liked in organizing and activating the cultural battle line against Japan.

On April 9, Guo Moruo gave a lecture at the meeting for celebrating the first anniversary of All China's Literary Association for Resisting the Enemy; on the day that followed, he was present at the public performance of a dialogue-driven drama—*For One Year*—created by Xia Yan. On April 23, he attended at a large meeting of "Chongqing City's Cultural Circles' General Mobilization" which had recently been organized on the recommendation of Jiang Jieshi, and acted as a joint chair person together with Den Yingchao, the wife of Zhou Enlai and a member of National Suffrage Association (whose secret status was the chief of the Chinese Communist Party's Central Southern Bureau's Women's Group) and Zou Taofen as the representative of Shenghuo (Life) Book Store. On April 26, Guo Moruo as the chairman of the Sino-Soviet Literature Association had to host a conference concerning how they should collect the works of literature for resistance, which would be carried to and exhibited in the Soviet Union. In the meantime, he had published his essays, poems and the record of his lectures in *Xin Hua Ri Bao* (New China Daily News) and *Jiu Wu Ri Bao* (Save-the-Nation Daily News). Indeed, he was engaged in many-faceted activities.

It was in the midst of such an active life that Guo Moruo encountered the horrors of 5.3 and 5.4. His gaze given at the scorched bodies of the mother and her children did lead his thoughts upon his own wife and children he had left in Japan. His heart ought to have been swaying and torn between what Japan used to be when he was a student, a resident and a husband and father, and what Japan was at present—the land of invaders, bombardiers and slaughterers. That was the fate all the Chinese intellectuals who had been familiarized with the Japanese must face.

● Hasegawa Teru, a Japanese Woman, who Declared:
"I Don't Care being Called a Betrayer"

Though on a standpoint different from Guo Moruo's, another person in Chongqing was being made to moan by being torn between Japan as her native land and the noble cause she had chosen to cherish. Her name was Hasegawa Teru. She also had to suffer from bitter grief at the sight of the Japanese planes having performed indiscriminate bombings upon the Chinese people in general.

Born in Yamanashi Prefecture in Japan, Teru, who had literary leanings, was studying at Nara Higher Normal School for Women, when she came to approach the movement of peasants and laborers through the learning of Esperanto she had started on her own initiative. This, however, led her to be arrested and driven into leaving school. Thus Teru went up to Tokyo and at the meeting of Esperantists she attended, she came to meet a student from China—Liu Ren, who had graduated from Tokyo Higher Normal School. It was not long before they loved each other and got married without the knowledge of their parents. It was in the autumn in 1936. Four years had passed since Fengtian in Liaoning Province, from which Liu Ren came, was incorporated into a puppet nation called "Manshu"* by the Japanese. Thus their marriage turned out to be far from being agreed upon by either side of the people at home.

In April in the following year, Hasegawa Teru, twenty-five years old, sailed over to Shanghai, wishing to find a new world to live in somewhere in her husband's homeland. But what had been awaiting them was the news of the full-scale spreading of Japanese Army's invasion into China, and the outbreak of Lukouquiao Incident* on July 7, 1937. From Shanghai to Hongkong, they kept making a wedding trip, while escaping from wartime fires and the eyes of authorities of both Japan and China. On board the same ship were Guo Moruo on his way home from Japan, where he had been seeking asylum so far, and Kaji Wataru and Ikeda Sachiko, a couple who had been pursued by the Japanese authorities, just as Teru had been.

After a short stay at Guangzhou, they entered Wuhan which was soon to fall, and there Hasegawa Teru obtained a position at the department of advertisement toward Japan in the Nationalist Party's International Advertising Department. Thus she made herself an announcer to perform anti-Japanese activity. On the other hand, she wrote "*A Letter of Support for the Chinese Soldiers*" for *Xin Hua Ri Bao* (New China Daily News), thus to clarify her standpoint as an anti-war internationalist. In China, she used her pen name 緑川英子 (Luchuan Yingzi / Green-River Bright-One), while as an Esperantist, she called herself Verdant Mayo (Green May). After the fall of Wuhan, "her treason against her own country" was disclosed by *The Miyako Shinbun* (the Capital's Paper) published in Tokyo, dated August 11, 1938. Strong language had been employed in the headline:

This is the true form of a betrayer of her country:
Employing fluent Japanese in cursing at her own land,
Hasegawa Teruko has made herself a flop as a *Red*.

But no longer had she shrunk back. In the letter she wrote to a Japanese Esperantist immediately after she entered Shanghai, she had declared herself to have broken away from Japan as a militarist nation:

> I shall not mind if you may call me a traitor to our country. I shall never be afraid of it. For me it is more shameful to belong to the nation who has not only invaded the other people's land but also has brought about the hell upon the innocent refugees without feeling any pang of conscience. Authentic patriotism will never be confronted with the progress of human beings. If not, it will be exclusionism. And now, in Japan, what a large number of exclusionists have been brought into being through this war! Even those intellectuals, who have once identified themselves as conscientious, progressive, or even Marxist, are now shamelessly admiring "the Imperial Army" and "their justice," simply imitating the reactionary militarists and politicians. Seeing all these things, I cannot suppress my anger and disgust.

After three months' stay at Wuhan, Liu Ren and Hasegawa Teru joined the crowds of people heading for Chongqing and came to live in the Great Rear Area. Teru was able to go on working at the International Advertising Department, as she used to do in Wuhan. Thus their strained life started in the Anti-Japanese capital, where they had to speak in Esperanto even in quarreling. As an Esperantist, Teru had named herself Verda Mayo (Verdant May), and now the Japanese bombers had turned that verdant month of May into a bloody one. Their house facing Taitian Bay in the western suburbs had not suffered from the air raids, but her fury remained intense all the same. The poem, *At the Capital in May*, with the date of "May, 1939," was written in such a situation:

In between the couple of Rivers....
I look up at the sky, high and clear,
White is the clouds floating upon that deep azure sky.
From the level ground to the top of the highest mountains,
The fresh green glitters, streaked with gray or black castle walls
                                              Meandering on and on,
Large straw hats are moving along, some in a hurry,
                                    others in a leisurely manner.

—My beloved Capital of the Great Continent, you, Chongqing!

Thus after having addressed to her beloved capital, Teru describes another scene that came into her view so abruptly:

With the silver wings floating in the air, the devils appear in the sky.
Bang! Bang! Bang"
Under my feet, the great earth gets streaked with blood,
Above You, the sky keeps burning.
And, the people....
Ah, You are shaking Your head.
You don't seem to like me to tell of the tragedy of the tragedies
this world has ever seen.
You are weeping over thousands of the dead You have had,
and even a greater number of miserable orphans and widows,
Your broken arms and burnt feet are giving You much pain.
You've got bloodstained all over—still You remain fearless.

Hasegawa Teru then thought of the same month of May she used to know in Tokyo, and this led her to write as follows, under the title of *Tokyo in May:*

That specific beauty in downtown Tokyo in May
After the cherry blossoms have gone
still remains unforgettable to me,
because I used to spend my sensible girlhood there
until the war broke out.
Occasionally, I am caught by the inexplicable
"melancholy in the season of verdure,"
as my friends and comrades are also caught.
Oh,—in my homeland, no planes nor artilleries are rampant,
but something eerie is weighing heavily upon her.

And her poem *At the Capital in May* is closed as follows:

And, what will happen next May?

Oh, who is afraid of what will happen?
If only it must happen—
Whatever it may be, the whole of Chongqing
                                        might as well turn red.
The whole China might as well turn bright red
                                        year after year.

In due course, the time will surely come,
When everywhere on this continent,
The flowers of May will begin to smile in such freshness
                                as has never been known before.
Because the flowers have not taken our blood in vain.

Hasegawa Teru was to keep staying in Chongqing until 1945 and did witness how this anti-Japanese capital had outlived all kinds of trials it had to face. But until then—when Chongqing finally witnessed the arrival of "Verdant May (Green May)"—it had to go through several more years in which it was turned "bright red." Hasegawa Teru's collection of her work in Esperanto—*The Whispering in the Storm* (published in Chongqing in 1941)—was brought into being literally from among those bomb blasts and fires she had gone through.

● **The Newspaper Version of the Nationalist-Communist Collaboration**
The bombardments of 5.3 and 5.4 had destroyed almost all of the commercial areas of Chongqing, and the newspaper companies also could not help suffering a great deal of damage. *Da Gong Bao* (*The Great Official Bulletin*), which had moved their rotary press from Shanghai to Wuhan and then to Chongqing, *Xin Hua Ribao* (*New China Daily News*) or the Chinese Communist Party's only officially-recognized paper, and the local newspaper, *Xin Shu Bao* (*New Report on Shu Province*) had all had their head office and printing factory burnt down. *Xin Min Bao* (*The New Report for the People*) for which Zhang Xiluo was working had also had its head office on Qixing-gong Heights burnt down by the 5.4 air raid. Many other companies also seemed to be forced to stop issuing their papers.

This led the authorities of the Nationalist Party to order each of these newspaper companies to stop publishing their own papers but to publish a united version of newspaper. As everyone could see, it was very difficult for any of these newspaper companies to keep publishing their paper on their own, but that idea brought about by the authorities of the Nationalist Party was by no means easily acceptable to every other company. Because it was quite apparent that the authorities had intended to make use of this opportunity in uniting all of the newspaper companies so that they could efficiently control their freedom of speech. This was especially so in the case of *Xin Hua Ri Bao* (New China Daily News) or the party bulletin of the Chinese Communist Party, because the unity of the newspapers had essentially been concerned with the vested rights of the Nationalist-Communist collaboration.

This was the first problem Zhou Enlai had to face on returning from Guilin. Zhou Enlai now had to solve two problems without any inconsistency— the first problem was of a practical matter that: publishing their own paper independently was practically impossible; the other was that: the publishing a united version of the papers would lead to the unity of papers and to the loss of the Communists' organ of public opinion in the capital. Zhou Enlai consulted with Pan Sinian, the president of the *Xin Hua Ri Bao* (New China Daily News) and decided to express their intention that: even though they admitted that starting a united version of the papers would be inevitable under the existing circumstances but that it should be done so only for a limited period of time; otherwise they would not join the united version of the papers.

As a matter of fact, this was something dangerous for Zhou Enlai. The Nationalists had already been aware that the Communists would not be able to publish their paper by themselves; it was also clear that Mao Zedong in Yanan would find it unacceptable if he found that Zhou had announced his personal decision to the Nationalists without consulting him about it. If things had turned out wrong, Zhou Enlai might have been driven to the corner.

Zhou Enlai made a strong request to the Nationalist authorities for clarifying the limit of the period in which the unification would last, and after obtaining their pledge that one month would be the minimum and after that they could leave it any time, he indicated his intentions to join the united version of the paper from the one dated May 6. He had been fully aware of the weakness of *Xin Hua Ri Bao* (New China Daily News), but if the authority were to take advantage of it, it would be impossible to keep publishing a united version of the newspapers that included the ones of neutral lines and of ethnic lines, because, as Zhou Enlai was saying to himself, he was ready to crash *it* by making use of the influence of the Communist Party.

● **In the Criticism from Yan-an**

Still Zhou Enlai had to receive from Yan-an a severe criticism against this solution strategy he had adopted. The telegram he received on May 17 had criticized the situation in which *Xin Hua Ri Bao* had stopped publishing it on their own, only placing its name on the united version of ten newspapers, and gave directions to Zhou that he should talk with the Nationalist Party so that they could soon return to what they used to be. Though no direct reference had been made, there seemed to be some hidden displeasure toward Zhou Enlai's having made that decision according to his own view. Between the headquarters of Communist Party in Yan-an and Zhou Enlai in Chongqing, there used to be such a friction as this once in a while. Naturally, making their newspaper return to the independent publishing being the greatest concern for both the Communist Party's Southern Bureau and *Xin Hua Ri Bao* Publishing Company, they concentrated their main power of editing and carrying on business at Gaofeng-si at Ciqikou, while setting their printing division at Hualong-qiao also in the suburbs, until at last they were able to resume their independent publishing on August 13.

As for *The United Version of Chongqing Newspapers,* it started its publication on May 6 or two days after the bombardment of 5.4. This two- page paper was the only paper they had in Chongqing for a while. The ten papers that had participated in it were: *Zhong Yang Ri Bao* (Central Daily), *Da Gong Bao* (Great Official Bulletin), *Shi Shi Xin Bao* (Current Affairs News), *Xin Hua Ri Bao* (New China Daily), *Sao Dang Bao* (Clean Up Report), *Kuo Min Gong Bao* (Official Report for People), *Xin Shu Bao* (New Shu's Daily), *Xin Min Bao* (New People's Daily), *Shang Wu Ri Bao* (Business Daily) and *Xi Nan Ri Bao* (South-Western Daily). "The formal message in launching *The United Version of the Chongqing Newspapers"* went as follows:

Those might be the most miserable pages in the history of the Chinese press. Those insane bombardments performed during those two days had perfectly revealed the Japanese Military's barbarism and cruelties that had been kept demonstrated since the opening of the National United Front

Against Japan. In response to *this*, the spirit we should like to demonstrate here in this paper or the feelings we should like to demonstrate to the Japanese military most of all are: how firm our unity remains.

These words did carry the sentiment having been shared by many of the citizens of Chongqing at that period in May in 1939. Through their own experience of having been air-bombed for two successive days, they had finally come to realize acutely that: they had been standing at the forefront of the war against Japan. So far they had regarded their Sichuan Province as "the Great Rear Land" or somewhere which had nothing to do with any modern warfare, but now such vision as these had been blown off, since they had seen so many miserable scenes *here* as had already been seen in such cities as Shanghai, Guangzhou, Nanjing, Wuhan and many other cities in China. Thus the people, even though a little too late, began to make up their mind. Their having published that united version of their papers and that formal message in launching *it* could be called an expression of what the citizens of Chongqing had been feeling then, including the whole of their inner discords that did exist before reaching that outcome.

Even if it was impossible to expect any authentic union of the Nationalist Government and the Communist Party, they had still retained that principle of Nationalist-Communist collaboration—"Everything shall be done for the sake of the Resistance to Japan"—in controlling their advantages and disadvantages. Later, when the Japan-U.S. relations went straight to catastrophe, and when Jiang Jieshi became confident of the U.S. government's backing up, the Nationalist-Communist cooperative relationship based on their collaboration grew weaker and weaker until Chongqing had to see the storm of White Terrors brought about by Jiang Jieshi's special service agency. But what caused the Japan-U.S. relations to fall into such a bottomless pit was none other than the Chinese people's unity that stood upon the Nationalist-Communist collaboration. So Japan's having performed their air raids upon Chongqing turned out to be none other than the actions to polish the swords to perish themselves.

● **How Many were Killed or Injured in 5.3 and 5.4?**

It is impossible to calculate precisely how many people were killed in the air raid of 5.3 and 5.4. To say nothing of the numbers of deaths in Dresden, Tokyo, Hiroshima and Nagasaki, even the number of deaths in Guernica in 1937, whose damage was comparatively less large, took many years as well as twists and turns before they finally reached the estimated numbers of 1,654 deaths and 889 injuries. The indiscriminate massacres, characteristically brought about by strategic bombings, having combined with the mobility and anonymity in the large city, do make it difficult to give an exact number of deaths. This was especially so in Chongqing as the provisional capital, where the incessant inflows of refugees were causing confusions. So all the figures given here cannot help being approximate ones.

Today, the formal numbers of deaths caused by the air raids of "5.3 & 5.4" were about 1,000 and about 4,400 respectively; the injured of the two days were about 3,100. The two days had seen 5,400 deaths and 3,100 wounded. Such large numbers of victims caused by the air raids were something unprecedented before World War Ⅱ.

Theodore White, who had fully experienced the two days' bombardments, wrote as follows:

These bombardments have now become among forgotten landmarks in the history of Horrors from the Sky, but at that time—in the history of growing violence—these were the greatest mass murders inflicted from the sky upon the defenseless people on the ground. It was none other than the Japanese military who had done it.

As for the number of the deaths, there were more detailed figures, too, which were published by the authorities concerned immediately after the 5.3 and 5.4. According to *The Statistical Chart on the Damages & Casualties Caused by the Air Raids on Various Parts of Sichuan Province in the 28th year of the Republic of China*, on May 3, there were 673 killed and 350 injured; on May 4, there were 3,318 killed and 1,937 injured. Thus the total estimated was 3,991 deaths and 2,287 injuries. These numbers were considerably smaller than the numbers we are given at present. Even if they should be taken as valid because they were estimated by the then administrative organ, considering that the

Nationalist administration at that time had a tendency to announce their damage as not so serious (as was typically revealed in the accident in 1941 in which many were pressured to death in a cave as an air-raid shelter, as is mentioned in Chapter IV), these numbers are not acceptable just as they were. Because none other than Jiang Jieshi had admitted it, saying: "In the air raids of 5.3 and 5.4, more than 4,400 citizens were killed, and about 3,100 were injured" in the 13th volume of *Jian Jieshi's Memoir* (15 volumes, published in 1975-77 from the Publishing Bureau of the Sankei Newspaper Company, Japan).

There was another information source in those days, and numbers made public to the Reuter's News Agency by Yan Fuqing as the Assurance Executive Chief in the Chinese Nationalist Government, were: 5,000 killed and 2,000 wounded. Through *LIFE* and so on, these numbers were given to the American citizens. On the other hand, as was written by Martin Caidin in *The RAGGED, RAGGED WARRIORS:* "On the first night, 10,000 people were burnt to death." These do reflect the confusion Chongqing at that time had been thrown into. Theodore White wrote, based on another information source: "According to the official statement, a large number of people from 3,000 to 4,000 were burnt to death that night by the incendiary bombs dropped by the Japanese air forces." (*In Search of History*)

In the final analysis, it should be regarded that: on those two days in early May, about 5,000 people, mostly civilians, were killed by the air raids performed by the bombers of the Japanese Navy Air Force. In several years, this number ceased to be regarded as something amazing, but since this was the first blow of strategic bombing, and along with the air raid upon Guernica in 1937, it became a precedent of indiscriminate bombing upon a city to be recorded in the history of the aerial battles. Looking back at how the flow of the world history went along, something unbelievable had occurred: Japan and Germany, which were to fall into the worst victim of the strategic bombings, did stand on the side of the starters of the strategic bombings.

As for the toll of the victims announced by the Chinese side, there seems to be no room for the Japanese side to make any complaint. In the book entitled 防空 (*The Aerial Defense,* published in 1942 by Diamond Co., Japan.) authored by the Japanese Army's Lieutenant Colonel Namba Misoshi, who was on the staff of the General Staff Office, the following list is given under the title of *An Outline on the Air Raids on Chongqing* performed from 1939 to 1941,

giving the eleven main air raids performed there, and in the first column given
for 5.3 and 5.4, he mentions "the great fires in the urban area" along with "the
estimated number of casualties was about 10,000." The following explanation
concerning the list (given on the following page) does reveal that: what they
were performing then was none other than the indiscriminate bombings upon
the urban area.

At the first air raid on Chongqing on May 3, 1939, they had only about
ten anti-aircraft guns and the number of planes was also small. The air-raid
shelters for the people were also as good as nothing. This, therefore, caused
such severe damage as was reported that: about 10,000 were killed or injured
and not a small number of important buildings were completely or largely
destroyed, while a large number of wooden houses in the urban area easily
caught fire, and this, prompted by the shortage of fire-fighting organizations,
allowed the fire to keep burning for about twelve hours, lapping all over the
area from Shansi-jie Street to Xiubi-jie Street, as was reported by *Zhong
Hua Ri Bao* (The China Daily News).

Considering what Lieutenant Colonel Namba was doing at his office in
the Army and what his rank was, this account he had given here could be
regarded as good as Japan's official view. This book had been written to
make the Japanese realize the horror of the air raid and to make them realize
the importance of aerial defense, but it does reveal what the air raids upon
Chongqing were really like. In other words, Japan had long been informed of
what were the air raids upon Chongqing made for, and what sort of miseries had
been brought about to Chongqing. It was ironical, too, that the number of deaths
the Japanese side had given—10,000—was larger than any other numbers given
by the Chinese side.

An Outlook on the Air Raids upon Chongqing

May 3 & 4, 1939
    The area for bombardment: The buildings to accommodate military
        officials, military factories, storage places of petroleum and the like.
    The outcome: About 10,000 were killed or injured.

The buildings:

The totally-destroyed buildings included some military factories, armories and a broadcasting station.

The largely-destroyed buildings included the Headquarters of Aerial Defense, the Department of Transportation, Newspaper-publishing companies and petrol storehouses.

The downtown area was drowned into a holocaust.

Remarks for Reference: On May 3, a large formation reached there around 13:30. On May 4, a 27-plane formation arrived a little past 18:00, as was reported in a Chinese newspaper. Chongqing's Army's aerial defense has 8 aircraft guns; airplanes are small in number.

May 26-28, 1940

The area for bombardment: Chongqing's central area & its neighborhood within a 15km radius.

The outcome: Over 2,000 were killed or injured. 700 houses and buildings (including the ones of the newspaper companies) were totally destroyed; 1,000 were damaged by large formations.

N. B. May 27,

A large formation was active from noon to 14:00.

June 10, 1940

We bombarded military facilities & main factories. Because of the early warning, the numbers of deaths & injuries were small on the whole.

June 16, 1940

We bombarded military facilities. Because of the early sheltering, the numbers of deaths and injuries were small on the whole. 3,000 houses were destroyed. The time of the air raid was around 15:00.

June 24, 1940

We in a large formation arrived in the afternoon and bombed military facilities, causing about 200 deaths & destroying 1,000 houses.

June 26-28, 1940

We in a large formation bombed military facilities, inflicting a great damage.

July 4, 1940

> We bombarded the military facilities placed in the university (which is being turned into military facilities). The gasoline storage there suffered great damage.

August 19, 1940

> We bombed military facilities and transportation facilities, causing several hundred deaths and injuries. The great fires started at 38 spots, reducing the 70% of the remaining houses to ashes.

June 1 – 2, 1941

> We bombed Chongqing's central area and the northern bank of the Jialing to cause approximately 100 deaths and injuries, also inflicting considerable damage on several buildings.

June 6, 1941

> We bombed some military facilities. Several hundred people were choked to death because of our bombing upon the air raid cave to destruction.

June 15, 1941

> We bombed some military facilities, bringing about 50 deaths or injuries, while destroying a large number of houses.

● **The Navy Minister Yonai's Evasive Answer**

As for the indiscriminate bombings, the following question and answer were exchanged at the Diet deliberations the National Diet soon after the outbreak of Sino-Japanese War:

> An interpellator, a Diet member Azuma Takeshi (a member of the
> Constitutional Party of Political Friends):
> "I should like you, the Navy Minister, to tell us what you think about the British notification that: it is inhuman of the Japanese Navy Air Force to attack the noncombatants overseas."
> The answerer, the Minister of the Navy, Yonai Mitsumasa:
> "The Japanese are not such a barbaric people. In our Navy, too, such a barbarity is not included in our education."

On that same occasion, the Foreign Minister Hirota Koki also gave his answer to that same question given by Azuma: "It is a matter of course that we, the military, will never deliberately make a bombing raid upon the non-combatants whether they are the Chinese people or the people of other nations. As for this point, ample attention is being paid both by the Army and by the Navy." (the Standing Committee on Budget of the House of Representatives on September 6 in the 12th year of Showa (1937))

These answers made by the Navy Minister and by the Foreign Minister were none other than a sort of evasion even at that time. In Shanghai and Guangzhou about this time when the Sino-Japanese War broke out (1937), the indiscriminate bombings by the Navy airplanes had become an everyday occurrence. It was August 15 in the same year (1937) that the transoceanic bombings on Nanjing were performed by the middle-sized attack planes, and it was also in the same month (September) when the Navy Minister Yonai's answer was given that "the previous notice of the air raid on the urban area of Nanjin" was declared by Vice-Admiral Hasegawa Kiyoshi as the commander-in-chief of the Third Fleet dispatched to the China Region. It goes without saying that the advance notice of the air raid does not nullify its indiscriminate nature.

As is seen in *An Outlook on the Air Raids on Nanjing* in *The Aerial Defense* by Lieutenant Colonel Namba, we can see as many as four such references as was notified as "the very important part of the urban area" or "the important part of the urban area" or as "the urban area." It was apparent that what was actually happening was far from being able to say: "In our Navy, too, such a barbarity is not included in our education," and the like.

Judging from this trend and its momentum, their opinion that the air raids upon Chongqing had been restricted only to military targets could hardly be persuasive. That had obviously been aimed at the city itself and therefore it had been indiscriminate bombings preformed intentionally and systematically toward civilians, and the air raids upon Chongqing could be regarded as an action to scale up or reproduce "the road up to Nanjing" on a progressive scale—as the first step upon "the road from Chongqing." Because until the point of the air raid upon Nanjing, the air force had still remained to be of aerial assistance to the Army's advancing operations to attempt to occupy that city (therefore they had properly been acting on the international basis of "the laws and regulations of land warfare," but in bombing upon Chongqing, the air force had got over that framework and displayed a thought of different perspective by employing the ability of the air force to perform what might be called terror-bombing upon the city or destroying the enemy nation's will to fight.

Here at this point, indiscriminate bombing was converted from the "outcome" to the purpose, from "the error" to the intention. And in the following year, when Rear Admiral Inoue Shigeyoshi, was appointed to be chief of staff of the Fleet of the Chinese Theater, the strategic bombings began to be performed on an even larger scale with a nature of even more "elaborate indiscrimination." Even Admiral Yonai and Admiral Inoue, who were able to let their reason and coolness assert themselves in dealing with their policy toward the U.S. or the U.K., as far as being judged by their plan of operations toward China as was seen from the Chinese viewpoint—they could not help being regarded as good as any other member of the Japanese armed forces, who would not hide their barbarity toward the Asians.

Having suffered as many as 5,000 deaths turned out to be the greatest shock to Jiang Jieshi as the representative of "the Chongqing Administration." That was a sufficient attack "to throw all the strata of the enemy administration into a panic," just as the Japanese side had aimed at.

● **Jiang Jieshi was Watching Chongqing in the Sea of Fire**
from his Official Residence on Top of Mt. Huang Shan

On May 3, when the air raid started, Jiang Jieshi had been at work at his official residence on top of the hill named Huang Shan. There were three more official residences—one in Linyuan, another in Zengjia-an and the other in Bei Wenquan Hot Spring—and he used to stay at different places according to the different seasons or different situations. His favorite one was that upon Huan Shan, where he had a villa named "Ying Chao (Eagle's Nest)." The Military Committee's Chairman's Encampment in Shizhong (City's Central) Ward, which had been made a target by the Japanese planes, had long been left unused. Since the mountain villa was far away from the urban area, Jiang could remain safe. Until the night of May 4, Jiang had been gazing at his capital that had already been turned into the sea of fire just below his eyes. In his diary dated May 4, he wrote:

Our enemy has not minded committing atrocities and cruelties. Indeed, they are at the height of meanness and shamelessness. In my life so far, I have never seen such atrocities as these. Indeed, seeing these scenes is simply unbearable. I believe the heaven will surely send them proper punishment before long.

—*Jiang Jieshi's Secret Memoir 13*

Dong Xianguang, one of those close to Jiang as vice-director of the Central Advertisement Department of the Nationalist Government (the ambassador to Japan after the war), later wrote in his biography entitled *Jiang Jieshi*, as follows:

On May 3, 1939, there was the first vehement air raid. On the day that followed, too, the enemy planes appeared to perform even more vehement attack. These two days' attack was inflicted upon the most densely populated areas and the commercial centers. The consulates of the neutral countries and their churches and hospitals could not escape disaster, either. Those who were killed or injured reached as many as five thousands. These air raids were the enemy's direct response to the moral discipline Jiang Jieshi had recently started to raise the morale of the Chinese people. It was apparent that the Japanese leaders in military affairs had intended to make our government incompetent by turning this urban area into ruins. Without any antiaircraft facilities, only provided with some primitive places of refuge, the Government's preparations against these bombings were woefully inadequate.

Still, even though such was what we were in those days, if the enemy had thought that such bombardments as these would be effective in destroying the Chinese intention to go on fighting, they must be regarded as having been far from thoughtful. Our government business had ceaselessly been made to move onward.

In that year (1939), Jiang Jieshi, fifty-two of age, had stood at the summit of authority. On January 1, the Nationalist Party's Central Standing Committee decided upon the eternal ejection of and an arrest warrant for Wang Zhaoming, an influential person next to Jiang, who at the end of the year before, had fled from Chongqing to commit himself to the side of Japan, and decided to reorganize the political system so that the power could be concentrated on the National Defense Supreme Committee formed by uniting the National Security Supreme Conference and the Central Political Committee, and Jiang Jieshi was recommended for the chairman of the Committee. Thus all the leadership of the Nationalist Party, the Nationalist Government and the Nationalist Revolutionary Army were to come into the hands of Jiang. Backed up by this power, Jiang had the chiefs of local militarist cliques, Han Fugu and Shi Yousan, shot to death on a charge of having remained disobedient, thus trying to centralize his military authority, while building up a campaign for general mobilization of national spirit on the basis of the Three Principles of the People—nationalism, democracy and livelihood—as were advocated by Sun Wen (p.34), so that all the efforts for resistance to Japan might be united under him. The young people's association as the driving force of the Three Principle of the People was also led by Jiang Jieshi as its captain, while the shady organs that directed white terrors—Dai Li who was feared as "Chongqing's Horror" and the Chen brothers, Guofu & Lifu, who led the C. C. Group—were also grasped securely by Jiang. In other words, as far as the power structure was concerned, Jiang Jieshi's control had been made perfect.

On May 1, two days before the air raid, a large meeting for making an oath of the manifesto of general mobilization of national spirit was held and it was decided to build "a spiritual counterguard" at the flourishing area of Shizhong (City's central) Ward. The characters to be carved on the wall of that tower had been decided: 国家至上・民族至上・意志集中・力量集中・軍事第一・勝利第一 ("Our Nation is Supreme・Our Race is Supreme; Our Intention is Concentrated・Our Capacity is Concentrated; The Military shall be the Foremost・the Victory shall be the Foremost." Jiang, who had acknowledged himself to be the spiritual successor to Sun Wen,* had come to call himself Jiang Zhong Zheng after Sun Zhong Shan (Sun Wen's honorific title) since this period. This person, who had come to hold the absolute powers over "the liberated China," had eagerly wished that: his control over the people might be changed from the one controlled by fear to the one carried out by the people's spontaneous support.

The air raids on 5.3 and 5.4 performed just at this timing were undoubtedly regarded by him as something that had disgraced his established authority. Then he had to be prepared for the criticism on the imperfection of the air defense setup and for the recovery strategy given by the group that intended to make peace with Japan, following Wang Zhaoming.

● **"Turn this May of Disgrace into the May of Revenge!"**
On the night of May 4, when the bombers went out of sight from the skies of Chongqing, Jiang Jieshi left his official residence on Huang-shan and entered the city to make an inspection. Wherever he might go, all he saw was fire and smoke, and endless lines of victims coming and going. Jiang had been accompanied by his wife, Song Meiling. She also had the title of Chief Secretary of the Aviation Committee, and was responsible for bringing on the Air Force by encouraging Chennault as well as for the air-raid precautions, and this had kept her from being an idle spectator, but none of the citizens could be so courageous as to complain of anything in the presence of Jiang Jieshi and his wife. Jiang, having been astonished at the miseries brought about by the air raids, denounced the commander of the Air Force, and while trying to have every officer in command give his frank report and opinion, he had a committee of evacuations in groups start with He Yingqin as chief. The committee was allowed to have authority to require all the vehicles and vessels available, public or private, and both Jiang's private car and his wife's were to have a patch of paper of "For Refugees" on them. The entry of his diary goes as follows:

Last night (on the night of 4th) I spent all night in making a plan for rescuing the refugees, while encouraging everyone I met. Even in such miseries, people in general never complain of anything. This makes me feel even more unbearable to stay with them. Even in such sufferings, they still keep a lovable expression on their face. The sight of such innocent people does keep carrying me away. Even if confronted with such appalling, unbearable difficulties, our people are able to behave like this.—This does help me to retain greater courage and hope.

—*Jiang Jieshi's Diary* dated May 5

Day by day, I am committed to the relief of the people. This does help me to get even a little consolation. But the misery and sorrow do come to fill my heart all the same.

—*Jiang Jieshi's Diary* dated May 6

Jiang had also given directions to bring the Nationalist Army stationed around Chongqing into the city so that they could engage in transportation, relief activities, burials, cleaning and so on. Those officers and men who presented themselves the following day were carrying a shovel and a shouldering pole, wearing an army band of "Help People Party," instead of carrying any arms. This consideration had come from the fact that: to the people in general, "armed forces" had simply been associated with "enlisted men" who were to press them into service or with soldiers of military cliques as plunderers.

During the first three days—from 5 to 7—250,000 people were reported to have been moved to the suburbs of Chongqing. The evacuees, who had been in fear of the military at first, began to lower their guard while coming in contact with the soldiers working bravely among the embers still smoldering under the scorching sun. Jiang's maneuvering for appealing to public opinion turned out to be successful. The people's anger, instead of bursting forth as criticism for the Government's lack of policy, came to fruition into such a direction as Jiang could not have asked for a better one—as an indignation toward Japan's indiscriminate bombings and as their rising up for fighting against the enemy till they won their victory:

"Let this May of national disgrace turn into the May of vindication of our honor!"

On May 5, Jiang Jieshi appealed to the public. Its contents were almost the same as what he had written in his diary the day before:

> Having our Chongqing bombed like this was something most unbearable for me to see in my life. Last night I spent the whole hours giving directions to save the citizens. Even though they have suffered such miseries, they would never give even a single word of grievance. The mere sight of the people desperately enduring these difficulties did give me the confidence of our victory and the courage to obtain it. The Chinese people's sanity has always revealed itself from ancient times when a different people came to invade our country. Whatever violence they may employ, they will never be able to overpower us nor subdue us.

- **"Everything shall be Achieved through the United Front!"**

As far as the approach to the people was concerned, the Communist Party had not been outstripped by the Nationalist Party. Since they had accepted that fundamental policy: "Holding fast to the Resistance to Japan under the leadership of the Nationalist Government," they had scruples about performing any activity under the name of Communist Party, but they had been performing mass-maneuvering through the Department of Politics in the Military Committee, which was a foothold for both Zhou Enlai and Guo Moruo, and through the Communists' bulletin *Xin Hua Ri Bao* (*New China Daily News*) and other periodicals under the direction of the Communist Party such as *Qun Zhong Zhou Jian* (*A Weekly for a Maltitude*) and *Xin Zhong Fua Bao* (*New China Report*). What had made Zhou Enlai reluctant to let *Xin Hua Ri Bao* join "the United Version of Papers" was his having valued the independency in the means of advertisement as much as the independency in thought and in organization. During the period after the air raids of 5.3 & 5.4, when they had no paper of their own publishing, they formed a volunteer group to keep an activity to transmit the daily news by word of mouth, thus informing the people in general of the realities of the air raids and what that war meant.

The children's dramatic company organized under Guo Moruo's Third Office of the Administration Department having officially been recognized by the Military Committee, its activities were even more positive; when the lovely boys and girls gave skits, advocating that: that was the time for the people and the Army to help each other to win the National United Front against Japan, dozens of the old women, deeply touched by their appeal, went over to the neighboring camp so that they could be of some help in mending and washing the clothes there. The Communists would not raise a frontal attack against Jiang Jieshi's manifestos of the General Mobilization of the National Spirit, and in fact, it was the Communist Party's strong point that they were flexible enough to march at the Nationalist Rally of Making the Oath on May 1—under the name of "International Laborers' Festival (May Day)."

It happened that on May 4, the Center of the Chinese Communists at Yan-an had issued a direction as to what they should do when the secret Communist members living in the area under the Nationalist control were invited to join the Nationalist Party: "In order to guard the profit of both the National United Front Against Japan and our own Party, the Center of our Party has made a decision, as follows: As long as one does not have any special reason, one should join it uniformly, and report it to one's higher organ and ask for the recognition of it. All the members of the Communist Party who have joined the Nationalist Party should attend diligently to their duties so that they might foster their ability, thus adopting a line toward helping the progress of the Nationalist Party."

Even though it was done under the beautiful motto of "Everything shall be done through the United Front," the Nationalist Party and the Communist Party were to retain the part in which they were as incompatible as ice and charcoal, while keeping invisible fighting against each other throughout those days of air raids. But all those efforts made by both parties having been done to win the people's mind and to save their own country by winning the war against Japan, it simply remained of no use to Japan.

● **The Two Journalists from America**

Immediately after these air raids on Chongqing, two American journalists arrived there. One was John Hersey from *Time;* the other was Edgar Snow as a free-lancer. The former, though staying there only for a week, had found a kindred spirit in Theodore White, one year younger than himself, went around to see the devastated downtown area and the miserable life of the residents there, while being guided by White. To Hersey, who had been born at Tianjin, China, as a son of a missionary, what he had seen in Chongqing immediately after the air raids must have been a series of pitiable scenes, but he would not have dreamt that seven years later he himself would come to write a record of the miseries brought about by *the* indiscriminate bombing that had grown intensified to an even more terrifying extent:

At exactly fifteen ninutes past eight in the morning on August 6, 1945, Japanese time at the moment when the atomic bomb flashed above it. Miss Toshiko Sasaki, a clerk in the personnel department of the East Asia Tin Works, had just sat down at her place in the plant office and was turning her head to speak to the girl at the next desk.

This is the opening passage of *Hiroshima* (published in 1946) or the report of the greatest misery caused by "the strategic bombing = the indiscriminate mass murder," which could be traced back to Guernica that had witnessed the first instance of this kind of bombing, to be followed by Chongqing, Hamburg, Dresden and Tokyo. Neither Hersey nor White had known: "*the* manner of bombings that started at Chongqing" would lead to Hiroshima to be attacked by the nuclear bomb, but the years of World War II that started in 1939 had also prepared such a circle of cause and effect as that.

John Hersey's journey to Chongqing had been made for the purpose of picking up some talented journalists there rather than of writing any report on what was happening there. Henry R. Luce—who had been publishing such noted magazines as *Time*, *Life* and *Fortune*, thus bringing the U.S. press and publishing circles under his domination—intended to organize a powerful group of news reporters in preparation for the oncoming period of the world war, and sent to China John Hersey, his favorite reporter, twenty-five-years old, who had also been born in China as the son of a missionary, so that any talented "reporters on Asia" might be obtained there.

The photographic weekly magazine, *Life,* which had been launched on November 23, 1936, still kept growing then in 1939, even after its circulation had reached two millions. For the photographic magazine which had declared "to gaze at our life, to watch what is happening in the world and to become a living witness of any great event," no other subject could be more attractive to the readers than the war. To Henry R. Luce—born at a missionary house built of mud-brick, to grow as *Lu Shao Ni* (Little Boy Luce)—the war in Asia had been in the field he had been interested in for a long time, while his footing as pro-Jiang Jieshi had remained firm. It was not long before Luce himself made his appearance in Chongqing to publish what he found these on *Life,* reporting what the capital of "Free China" under the bombardments looked like, but what he was seeking for in 1939 was a young stringer who was able to give a series of vivid reports on the war situation in China.

Hersey talked Theodore White, who had just become twenty-four, into becoming a correspondent of *Time*. White, who had totally been fascinated by Hersey for his personality and talent, also pleased at the condition that he might keep working for the Information Department of the Nationalist Government, immediately started collecting information for *Time*. This was how Theodore White, a Pulitzer Prize winner in a later year, was found by the author of *Hiroshima* and started a life of a journalist which was to last as long as half a century.

Life issued on June 23, 1939—though the writer remains unknown because no signature was given—carried an article on "the 5.3 & 5.4" air raids along with the photographs:

> Chungking, the new capital of China, has been turned into a place to provide us with the most horrible example of what a modern warfare has brought about to a large city. Chungking seated farther up the Yangzi is usually protected SKY by the clouds hanging low over it. But on May 3 and 4, the skies had cleared up. At noon on May 3, the twenty-two Japanese bombers made their appearance and kept dropping the bombs upon the crowded commercial areas of Chungking seated on the peninsula on the Rivers. In the evening on the following day, the twenty-seven Japanese bombers released even a larger amount of bombs on the blazing downtown area.
>
> The nature unique to Chungking has caused the disaster to be of a peculiar nature to a terrible extent. Chungking, a very populous city, is seated on a bottle-shaped peninsula lying between a couple of rivers. A large population is rapidly moving toward the other sides of the rivers, but the peninsula has still remained overflowing with people. Since 1937, when the Chinese Government was moved up here, its population has been increasing so much as to reach two millions. To make the matter worse, most of the houses and buildings are made of wood and mortar. The high-yield bombs had turned the city of Chungking into an inferno like a melting furnace to burn more than 5,000 people to death....

In June, 1939, such an article as this, along with the photographs, was to be sent to several millions of Americans — through *Life*.

Another American news reporter, Edgar Snow, entered Chongqing probably in mid-June—early summer in 1939, according to his own record—and, while experiencing several air raids there, he contemplated the military significance of bombing upon Chongqing, and wondered if those strategic bombings would be able to "conquer the fighting spirit" of the enemy nation. He asked himself if it would be an achievable strategy to paralyze the enemy's important city both spiritually and technically. His conclusion was: under a certain kind of conditions, it would be achievable, but the Japanese military would never find it successful.

Edgar Snow's Advance Notice

● The Bombardments upon Chongqing, as was Witnessed by Snow

Edgar Snow, another American reporter, was thirty-four then. As a special correspondent of *London Daily Herald*, he was collecting news materials concerning China. Snow also, as Theodore White had done, had tried a penniless journey around the world after having graduated the university and at Shanghai in 1928, he was to awaken to the China issues.

In 1928, as he wrote later, he sailed for the Pacific Ocean by way of the Panama Canal, and after having spent three months in Hawaii and Japan, he sailed for Shanghai. At first, he was to stay in China for six weeks only. As it turned out, he was to keep staying there for as long as thirteen years before he returned to America, as he wrote later. Shanghai at that time consisted of foreign concessions where "the Chinese and dogs were forbidden to enter" and of the damping place of the poverty-stricken natives of China, and the view of "the united China" trying to get out of that yoke was about to be snatched by the hand of Jiang Jieshi, the President of Huangbu School for Military Officials, who had fancied himself as the successor to Son Wen (p.34), who was no more. Snow, at Shanghai, visited John Powell, the chief editor of *China Weekly Review*, and while helping him to issue its special edition, became totally fascinated by those who were struggling against China's reality while pursuing their ideal of national self-determination.

"Won't you stay here and help me with my *Review* ?" said Powell to Snow, and this led him to help him as vice-editor of the *Review*. By that time Snow had come to have some doubts about Jiang Jieshi's Anti-Communist United Line. "Before I came to the end of my journey, I found how far this country was from being united, and began to wonder if a real revolution had already started," wrote Snow in one of his earlier works, *Far Eastern Front.* Thus Snow kept staying in China for thirteen years instead of the six weeks he had first expected. This was how he had started on his own "Long March."

In 1931, no sooner had he heard of the Manchurian Incident[*] having broken out than he went up to various parts of the Northeastern Region before coming down to Shanghai, following the Japanese Army's operations performed in various parts of the Continent, and at Shanghai he actually witnessed "how the Japanese planes performed their bombardments upon the civilians in the densely-populated areas without giving any advance notice." In 1936, he smuggled himself into "Yan-an as the Capital of Red China" as the first person from abroad and this led him to write *Red Stars Over China* (published in London in 1938), through which he informed the world for the first time of what Mao Zedong and his comrades, who had so far been known only as bandits, really were. After Lukouqiao Incident* as a starting signal of the Sino-Japanese Incident (1937), White resumed his life of pursuing the wartime fires: in early summer in 1939, he took the plane at Hongkong at midnight and reached Chongqing at dawn. According to his own expression, he shared a Douglas plane for "a night guerrilla flight," and after having flown from Shanghai 1,500 miles (2,400 km) up the Yangzi, he reached the anti-Japanese capital which had recently been bombed to a terrible extent.

Snow's first impression of Chongqing is recorded as follows:

> When I visited Chungking for the first time in early summer in 1939, I found it humid and hot, unsanitary and uncannily confused. So the central government that had moved up there had been making efforts to introduce the skill for building up some order, finding some time when they had expected no air raid. Chungking was a medieval city which had spread many square miles in all directions without any city planning. In time of peace, its population was more than five hundred thousand, but now it has been reduced to about one hundred thousand. This figure was raised when they had a series of moonless nights, and it was rapidly reduced when they had the moon shine over the yellow Yangzi. The speed of traffic facilities there has been reduced to that in the rural district. There is no taxi available. As for a *yangche* (*rickshaw*)—even if one was able to persuade the man to pull it for one—it took as long as two hours in reaching another town in the same city.
> *Chungking = Chongqing

While Snow was staying there, too, the Japanese Air Force kept performing air raids upon Chongqing: After "5.3 & 5.4," they gave three air raids in May, two in June, six in July, eight in August, and six in September. (*The Performance of the Imperial Navy during the China Incident*—the Navy Ministry of Japan)

Snow wrote in another of his works, *The Battle for Asia** (published in 1941) :

The areas where there used to be many Western-style buildings had totally been destroyed in the barbaric air raids in May and in June, and more than four thousand citizens had been killed. And still, pile after pile of rubbles were brought into being week after week throughout this season of fine weather.

Now what was called "the regular flight to and from Chongqing (780km × 2) " or the bombing strategy by the middle-sized bombers was about to be the main operations for the Fleet of the China Region to perform. The military authorities of Japan were now coming around to the judgment that: since they could not practically send the land army as far as the interior of Sichuan Province, the only means available to subdue the Jiang Administration would be to proceed with the indiscriminate bombings upon the capital so that it might be led to the destruction of their administrative function and the people's intention to keep fighting against Japan. Thus Chongqing now was to become the first city that had been bedeviled by the new form of mass murder named "strategic bombing" (or "strategic & political bombing" according to the denomination of the Japanese side).

Snow went from one devastated area after another, listening to what the people had experienced, and examined what Chongqing was "after having been exposed to the bombings by the Japanese Air Force so mercilessly as not any other cities in the world had ever experienced before," until he came to a conclusion: "Under certain conditions, it will be possible to send an important city into a paralyzed state only by the attack from the sky, but those conditions are totally specific and they will not be applicable to Chungking." That was an evaluation given by the observer at the actual scene to the strategic aerial theory presented by Douhet and Mitchell, and was also a formal objection based on the practical lesson to those who believed in the omnipotence of the air force. Seeing that his publishing of *The Battle for Asia* was in 1941, Snow, after having seen Japan's bombardments upon Chongqing, had come to see through the horrors of strategic bombings and their limitations.

Edgar Snow wrote, after seeing what the Japanese military was doing upon Chongqing: Yet the bombing convinced me for the first time that the air blitzkrieg is not entirely a myth, and that under certain conditions, the mortal and technical immobilization of a key city can be accomplished in this way. These conditions are, however quite special:

First, the response of the city's defenses and precautions must be so weak as to create in the minds of the population the retaliation or salvation and that the city is doomed.

Secondly, high explosives must be framed with incendiary bombs dropped over the widest area so that fear deepens into despair, despair into panic and panic into utter demoralization and headlong flight.

Third, the invading planes must maintain this psychological depression by continuous flights over a period sufficient to harass the people into a state of physical collapses and to bring about the breakdown of normal city routine. People must be continuously robbed of sleep, food and comfort; communications, industry and city services must be paralyzed.

The continuity of the terror is the deadliest factor in the conquest of mortable, and for this purpose no great air armada is necessary. Flights of only a few planes every hour or two would be enough, if strengthened several times a day and night by heavy bombardment squadrons. A fortnight of such punishment, without any letup, would suffice to break the heart of a poorly prepared city and immobilize it as a war factor. The cost of the operation would, however, be"justified"only of the city lay near enough to the land front to enable a break—through force to occupy it after it had (presumably) been taken over first by parachutists and Fifth Columnists from within. Only if their mission is in that way"completed,"however, can air attacks designed to annihilate civilians be considered"successful."

—*Far Eastern Front*

● **"Chungking will Never Perish"**

Snow, as mentioned above, inspected the actual scenes of "the air raids of 5.3 & 5.4," and after contemplating "the conditions of strategic bombing," concluded that: there was certainly some probability of success in that blitz tactics from the sky, but it is impossible for them to destroy Chungking as the center of the Chinese politics by means of the tactics they are adopting at present. Because he thought Japan would not be able to fulfill all of those conditions indispensable for their success. According to Snow's viewpoint, the citizens did suffer from several tens of thousands pounds of high-yield bombs and incendiary bombs, but they still remained free from suffering spiritual destruction, and their willingness to keep fighting was being made even stronger, and since the air raids were intermittent or unexpectedly nonexistent as if the Japanese military had suddenly believed in their "having cleared Chungking of its inhabitants," it helped the Government to reorganize their evacuation and aerial defense; what was more, there would be no probability of Japanese military's taking possession of Chungking; therefore, the Japanese military might be able to clear away all the buildings in the traditional area of the city, but they would not be able to achieve their purpose of depriving Chungking of its function as Capital for Resisting Japan, but it must be thrown back to the invaders in a kind of boomerang effect only to cause them to suffer even greater physical fatigue....

This projection made by Snow did come true. The capital for offering resistance to Japan was not annihilated, and it was the invaders themselves that got exhausted to collapse. This axiom brought about by Snow can be said to have remained valid even to this day, when applied not only to the Sino-Japanese War but also to the strategic bombings performed during World War II and to the U.S. Air Force's attack upon North Vietnam after the War.

● **The Jiang Administration was Expected to Submit**

But about this time—in May, 1939—the Japanese military, who had formed a camp at Hankou, 780km downstream from Chongqing, had a different idea. They had firmly believed in their own ability to defeat their enemy if they went on with their air raids by their powerful air-commanding fighter planes and a large number of bombers.

It was not until September, 1941, that "an opinion on the uselessness of Chongqing bombardment" was offered to the General Staff Office by Major General Endo Saburo, the chief of the Third Air Division of the Army, pronouncing that: "…. Therefore it is absolutely impossible to make them surrender only by means of bombing raids," and prior to that, in 1940, No. 101 Operations—which was said to be equal to "the Battle of Tsushima (1905)"— and No. 102 Operations performed in the following year, which lasted for several dozens of days on end, did compel the citizens of Chongqing to suffer even greater pain and bloodshed, while the Japanese Navy itself was to dissipate all those mechanical equipments, personnel necessary and fuel they had collected the hard way in preparation for a decisive battle against the U.S.—in the place of a wrong direction. Certainly that was none other than a boomerang effect inflicted upon Japan.

In the summer of 1939, when Edgar Snow in the devastated area of Chongqing was analyzing the tactics adopted by the Japanese military at Hankou, the Navy Air Corps was being excited at the great success they had achieved at Chongqing. Unmistakably they had caused a great damage to the heart of the enemy's Administration. This led them to conclude that: if they were to intensify their air raid by making use of this opportunity, they would surely be able to expect that the anti-Jiang faction would drift away and those who wished to make a peace offer to Japan would come to the front. Thus the line of policy was clearly agreed upon both in Hankou and in Tokyo: Bombing should be kept performing, while intensifying its degree of oppression so that the Chongqing citizens' intention to go on fighting might be frustrated, thus by enhancing the public feeling of war-weariness, the Jiang's administration would be weakened, isolated and broken up until it was brought to the seat for peace talks. That was their conclusion. Thus it led to the budding of another series of air raids known as "No. 101 Operation." Such limitations of strategic bombings as was brought about by the analysis made by Snow was simply disregarded, and Hankou Flight Base had been throbbing with the boisterous laughter of those aviation supremacists, to whom their bombers seemed to have brought them a new theory of war.

At the center of the military in Tokyo, too, they were not so different from those in Hankou. They had judged that: Chongqing as the stronghold of the Anti-Japanese Administration had thoroughly been overwhelmed and the Jiang Jieshi's Administration had been beaten into the ground. They had once tried hard to capture the enemy's main force by ground force, but in vain, but now they had finally found a clue to attack them from the sky, to the immense satisfaction of the Navy. That was the same tactics as "vertical besiegement" which in later years the U.S. Armed Forces in Vietnam adopted in a stratagem for exterminating guerrillas by a heliborne operation, believing in their having been successful.

No sooner had Vice Admiral Koga Mineichi, the Vice Chief of the Naval

General Staff, received the official telegram from the actual place than he sent a telegram to Vice-Admiral Oikawa Koshiro, the Theater Commander of the China Region:

> The Vice Chief of the Naval General Staff congratulates Vice-Admiral Oikawa, the Theater Commander of the China Region, on his great success in achieving the air raid upon Chongqing, thus disintegrating the military center of our enemy's capital.

● **The Bragging Given by the Chief of the Press Section of the Navy**

The Navy's raptures went on. The chief of the Navy's Press Section of the Imperial Headquarters, Rear-Admiral Kanazawa Masao, published his informal talk on May 6, and on the presumption as if the Jiang's administration had already abandoned Chongqing, he declared to go on performing even greater bombardments and warned that the citizens would not escape being sacrificed, either.

> The great bombardments performed by our Navy Air Force in rapid succession on the 3rd and the 4th had thrown their government and the mind of the people into the utmost confusion; the capital of Chongqing, which Jiang had been relying upon as a stronghold after his loss of Wuhan, has already become impossible to continue to exist, and Jiang Jieshi's flying from the capital is again being talked about. Some say that his destination is Chengdu in Sichuan Province; it is also said that some institutions are moved to Kunming and Xushou (also called Xuanbi: about 200km upstream from Chongqing). Even if he might seek safety at Chengdu, it is only a little more than 200km away in a straight line from Chongqing. Even if they may say it is situated in a hinterland, it will be nothing but a temporary solace. If we fly straight, we can reach there just as soon as we reach Chongqing. So this removal will be useless even if they do so to avoid our air raid. Now that the ability of our Navy's bombing squadrons have come up to such a level, they will no longer be able to escape from our air raid, and however spacious their land may be with more than four hundred provinces in it, Jiang will have no place to stay at in safety.

Thus after having cut off Jiang Jieshi's retreat, Kanazawa, the chief of the Navy's Press Section, mentions the citizens of the capital:

> Now we are about to greet the summer, the best season for the air raid, and our Navy Air Force will bring the entire land of China under our wings until they come to grieve over their having no refuge under the sun, as long as Jiang's Administration exists.
>
> Be that as it may, if he were to transfer the capital so often, the people living in the city that has been turned into the capital ought to be feeling annoyed. Even if it goes without saying that our air raid is strictly made only on the military institutions, it would be natural for the citizens to be prepared for such misfortune as to suffer the momentum of violent bursting of bombs. As long as the Anti-Japanese Administration exists, those living in the city chosen as the capital will have to find it extremely annoying.

Such a pretentious speech made by the chief of the Navy's Press Section had been backed up by his pride that their strategic use of the Navy Air Force had brought about a great turning point in the evolution of the Sino-Japanese War. Now the Navy Air Force had finally achieved the long-distance-bombings, inflicting the severe blow upon the enemy capital. That was something that had remained incapable of performing either by the ground force or by the Army Air Force. So far the Navy had been playing rather a smaller part in this war, and that had kept it from being experienced or achieving anything remarkable, thus frustrating the Navy's rivalry with the Army in their struggle for the leadership. Now the leaders of the Navy were being intoxicated at the news of their having succeeded in the bombardments upon Chongqing, and its over-emotional involvement into the idea that the air force could be omnipotent in destroying the enemy was to lead finally to what they called No.101 Operations and No.102 Operations performed in 1940 and 1941 by deploying all the Navy Air Force deep into the Continent, aiming at making an invasion upon "the Peninsula on the Rivers"—even though it only came to reveal their having lacked in a broader view of the matter.

● The Navy had Half Admitted their Indiscriminate Bombing
even if it was Against the International Custom

That informal talk given by the Chief of the Navy's Press Section had revealed his having half admitted that their air raids upon Chongqing would become indiscriminate bombings, even if he adopted an indirect expression. For one thing, what had become of the urban area of Chongqing had already been known to the world by the news items and photographs sent by such correspondents on the scene as Carl Mydans of *LIFE*, Robert Martin of UPI, Tilman Dardin of *NEW YORK TIMES* and so on, and the newsreels of *The Enemy Planes Madly Sent Explosions upon Chungking* produced by the Central Movie Studio of China. No longer could the Japanese Navy deny those facts. But that was not everything. There was a warning of "terror bombings" or a threat of "terrors from the sky" named air raids. Their aim was changing from the enemy's administration to the enemy's capital. It could be compared to the strategic changes from the shooting of the foxes to the sending of fire and smoke into the hole where the foxes were hiding in oder to smoke them out. That was the very lesson the Navy had learned from their air raids of 5.3 & 5.4. Their recognition of the taboo on making the noncombatants an attack target and the consideration for the international common custom of war had backslided from the Navy Minister Yonai's answer—a resolute answer (even if it was a mere pretension) made one year and a half before: "In our Navy, too, such barbarity is not included in our education"—to "it is a matter of common knowledge for the citizens, too, to expect to fall victims to the bombardments." And that gap was to be filled with the strategy performed by the concentrated employment of middle-sized bombers and the indiscriminate droppings of incendiary bombs.

Captain Takagi Sokichi was the chief of the Investigation Section of the Naval Department. He used to serve under the Navy Minister Yonai Mitsumasa, under the Vice-Minister Yamamoto Isoroku and then under Inoue Shigeyoshi, the chief of the Bureau of Military Affairs—as a staff member of the Investigation Department, as a provisional chief of the same Department, and then as the chief of the same Department—and toward the end of the Japan-US War, he was to be busily engaged in preparing the ground for the termination of hostilities. But about this time, he had been in partial charge of the Navy's policy toward China. In his diary—*Takagi Sokichi's Diary*—he often mentioned the air raids performed on Chongqing, as follows: "On 3rd, at 15:20, the 45 middle-sized bombers of the Navy started performing air raid upon Chongqing under the direction of Lieutenant Commander Masuda. (omission) On 4th, Lieutenant-Commander Irisa led 27 planes and started air raid on Chongqing at 20:30. Four enemy planes came to attack only to be repulsed." (May 6) "Yesterday or on 25th, the middle-sized bombers led by Lieutenant-Commander Yamagami began to bomb upon Chongqing at 21:00; During the air battle against four enemy planes, one of our planes was blown up by the ground fire" (May 26). "The 27 middle-sized bombers led by Lieutenant-Commander Masuda performed the 6th air raid upon Chongqing at 21:20." (June 12)

Thus Takagi, the chief of the Investigation Department, had meticulously recorded how the air raids were being performed, and while analyzing and deciphering the encoded telegrams dispatched from the Nationalist Government and the U.S. Embassy in Chongqing, he was trying to measure how much shock they had given to the Jiang Administration. The Japanese Navy had intercepted and deciphered a fairly large amount of diplomatic telegrams of the Chinese side and this had let them know such a thing as Lady Song Meiling was their interpreter when Jiang Jieshi held a conference with the U.S. Ambassador Johnson to China, and that on July 21 Jiang Jieshi sent a telegram in code to the Chinese ambassador Guo resident in Great Britain, giving instructions that he should give representation to the U.K. Government: "The Sino-Japanese War is now becoming an issue upon which the fate of the Chinese people has depended, and that at this most critical time, all the Chinese are eager to receive some financial support form the U. K.." Such pieces of internal information on the Chongqing Administration as these had also been brought to Captain Takagi.

While observing and judging what commotions were being brought about on the enemy's side, the Navy had come to a conclusion that: if their strategic bombardments performed by their middle-sized bombers or the encircling operations from the sky were to make Chongqing stand alone to a thorough extent, they would be able to bring Jiang to the peace negotiation with its initiative taken by the Japanese side. With the air raids of 5.3 & 5.4 as a turning point, the Navy's strategy for China was to make a rapid progress in its deployment, while showing such momentum as to drag even the Army Air Force into their strategy, as if the bombardments upon Chongqing were the chance for them to stake everything on one last throw of the dice.

● **The Anti-Japanese Consciousness was Enhanced**
among the Citizens of Chongqing

The state of things, however, was not so simple. True, the air raids had brought about tremendous damages. Many lives were lost, and the air raids still being performed had sent the people to exhaustion. But physical damage does not necessarily lead directly to the spiritual collapse or to the setback of morale. The Chongqing citizens' intention to maintain their anti-Japanese sentiment, which could never be caught by any reconnaissance photograph, was rather becoming enhanced. The Japanese military had tried to lead the inhabitants' fear of air raid to a feeling of war-weariness and to the direction of surrender, but as Edgar Snow had seen, the people had chosen to determine to fight against their enemy.

As was later proved in the cities of Germany and Japan, and later in Vietnam, too, the strategic bombings turned out to be effective in enhancing the fighting spirit of the people rather than in depressing it. It leads their ingenuous anger against that unilateral, outrageous attack to be directed to those who have attacked them. This was also the case with Chongqing which had been made the first to suffer a large-scale strategic bombing. The citizens, having come to know that Japan was to continue their attack upon them, were determined to put their heart into their resistance. In other words, this was to lead what the Japanese military had expected—arousing the people's anti-government feeling, Jiang's Administration's becoming weak-kneed and the appearance of another Wang Zhaoming—to simply vanish. After "5.3 & 5.4", their efforts to assume a combat-ready stance against Japan's following offensive were to come into action all at once.

Zhou Qiansheng, living in Daluoxiang town of Shizhong (City's Central) Ward, was working for a seal maker. Since he was apprenticed at the age of fifteen, he had been engaged in carving seals for fourteen years. On the night of May 3, when Shizhong Ward was drowned in fire, he ran for his dear life and took refuge at Chenjia-qiao in the suburbs. It was on May 14 when he returned. All the city had turned into ruins, and several companies and stores that had survived the fire were mostly closed. Since the shop for which he had been working had fortunately escaped disaster and while they were preparing for the reopening of their business, a staff member of the Aerial Defense Headquarters visited them, saying: "I've had a hard time in finding out this place."

This was to help Zhou Qiansheng to remember clearly what sort of orders they had received then: forty-eight official seals for the forty-eight aerial defense companies, which were to be started soon, should be made as soon as possible, and sixty-two stamps for sixty-two acute care hospitals also should be made even sooner. Li Gengu, the Director of the Headquarters of the Aerial Defense of Chongqing, was replaced by the Mayor of Chongqing, He Guoguang, while the air-defense companies and the relief corps were being reorganized or newly organized; if they had no seal, they could not send out even a single paper, so they were all eager to get new seals as soon as possible. Thus Zhou was to receive so many unexpected orders. On the night of the air raid, he had run only for his own life without carrying anything with him, but now he was feeling as if luck had turned his way. This was how a puff of liveliness was returning to Chongqing.

The Relief of the Foggy Season

● 1939 Turned out the Year of Great Calamities for all the World

The year, 1939, turned out to be the year of great calamities not only to China but also to the rest of the world. On September 1 or four months after the air raid of 5.3 & 5.4, the German Army's advance into Poland did cause the Second World War to break out. The wartime fires that started in Europe and Asia or in the east and the west of the Eurasian Continent were now simultaneously burning fiercely, spreading one of those fires to the African Continent and the others toward the Atlantic Ocean and the Pacific Ocean.

It was during these years of unprecedented strives brought about upon the two continents and the two oceans that the aspects of battle fronts were changed into the armor strategy by concentrated use of tanks, and into the mobile troops on the aircraft carriers from the battleships, while a new dimension of fire attack performed by the combination of bombers and incendiary bombs was also to acquire an immovable position in the war history of the Twentieth Century. The indiscriminate bombings performed upon the aim of population and industries, which is termed "area attack" or "terror attack" or more often "strategic attack"—an indiscriminate bombings upon the people and the industries—not only made it possible, during the six years of World War Ⅱ, for the British Air Force to perform the strategy of "Bombers' Stream" with a thousand bombers in it but also developed a means of transportation from "aerial attack" to "attack across the air," as was realized in a Germany-built V1 (a jet propulsion cruise missile) and V2 (a rocket propulsion ballistic missile). What was more, aerial bombings were to be developed into such aerial bombs as "fragmental bomb", "incendiary bomb (napalm bomb)" and "nuclear bomb," thus bringing about "the endless progress in war," while weighing more and more heavily upon the earth and the people, thus breaking down the borderlines of the battlefields one after another. In that sense, the true nature of the bombings upon Chongqing prior to World War Ⅱ can be taken undoubtedly as an action to predict what would be brought to Hiroshima and Nagasaki or undoubtedly what was intended to be "an extermination."

In mid-September, 1939—when the German armored unit under General Guderian broke through the Polish border and made a drive, while adding the word "a blitzkrieg (a lightning war)" to the dictionary of military terminology, until they completed the regime of besiegement of Warsaw, the capital of Poland—the citizens of Chongqing had been in their last month of the first year of being besieged from the sky by the united air raid corps of the Japanese Navy. The air raids had already been made into the part of their landscape and rhythm of life—as if they had been something indispensable to that city.

It was on September 25 when Warsaw, which had been encircled heavily, began to suffer from the indiscriminate bombings upon the urban area by the united force of bombers and dive-bombers. In Europe, that was the first "fear bombardment" since they had one in Guernica. By the air raid performed around the clock, the residential areas, the power plant and water reservoirs were devastated, and many bodies were being scattered on the roads. On September 28, Warsaw Broadcasting Station, which had been playing *The Heroic Polonaise* by Choping so far, trying to appeal for resistance to the people, changed their music to the *Funeral Polonaise* soon to fall silent. This was how the Polish Army's systematic resistance was over.

On the same day, upon Chongqing 7,000km away to the southeast of it, the 28 middle-sized bombers—the First Air Raid Unit composed of Takao Flying Corps and the 13th Flying Corps—were performing a night bombing upon Guangyang-ba Air Port in the suburbs of Chongqing. That was the Navy Air Force's 23rd bombardment that year. On September 29, too, when German infantry corps entered Pilsudski Square at Warsaw, Chongqing was being exposed to another air raid. Until October 7, they were to suffer three more air raids.

● **The Arrival of the Foggy Season Blessed with the Natural Smoke Screen**
  Warsaw and Chongqing. What the two cities were facing then resembled each other, but Chongqing did not fall after all. The ground upon which the capital was seated as the base for their resistance always remained secured on the Chinese side. The primary factor that caused this difference would not be simple, but certainly it was largely due to its geography and weather conditions. In her long history so far, Chongqing had once sheltered the Emperor Juanzang (685-762) who had been driven away by An Lushan (705-757); it had also provided Liu Bei (161-223) with a refuge by means of "Shu's plank road" which prevented his large enemy force from advancing. What was more, what was called "Sanxia's Xian (the Dangers of the Three Gorges)" did prevent the invaders from entering Chongqing by the river route. Seemingly, even if Japan had had a General Guderian, he would not have found any opportunity to make use of his ability in capturing Chongqing.

  What was more, the arrival of the foggy season was to provide Chongqing with "a providential hiding place." As soon as October sets in, the capital on the mountain gets sunken to the bottom of the white fog, keeping itself from being seen from outside. In summer, especially in the moon-lit night, the Yangzi was quite likely to guide the formation of bombers by turning itself into a glittering belt. But now, the Yangzi, hiding itself in the fog and darkness, remained unseen all day, thus proving itself useless as a guide of a flying corps on "a regular flight to Chongqing." Jiang Jieshi, when he moved to this city, used to feel displeased at this fog, but after having spent a single summer there, he had completely changed his view of that fog. In the morning, when he looked down from the window on the third floor of his official residence or "Ying Chao (Eagles' Nest)" on top of Huangshan (Yellow Mountain), and found the whole city wrapped up in the fog that looked like candy floss, Jiang's expression began to get loose and relieved, because that was the most reliable sign that there would be no air raid that day. This was also the case with Guo Moruo, as was found in his grateful words he wrote in 1945, when he was about to leave this city: "The kind fog had performed its responsibility of defending our country." To all of the citizens, too, the foggy season had turned into a welcome season in which they did not need to be driven ahead by the sound of siren and bombardment. Those who had been away from Shizong (City's Central) Ward since May began to return home when the foggy season set in.

● Japan's Bombardments upon Chongqing were Performed Arbitrarily Prior to the History of the Strategic Bombings

Thus, on October 7, Japan's bombardments upon Chongqing in 1939 came to an end with the attack on Baishiyi Air Base as the final one. Even though Japan was forced to stop that series of bombardments because of the thick fog, the air raids it had performed on the urban areas and on the air bases in the suburbs during the five months since May 3 were twenty-seven, spending twenty-three days. If the three air raids performed in January by the Army Air Force were included, it became thirty.

The greatest damage was given on "5.3 and 5.4." but every air raid performed had brought about deaths and injuries. According to the *Statistical Chart on the Damages & Casualties Caused by the Air Raids in Various Parts of Sichuan Province in the 28th Year of the Republic of China*, the 20 air raids caused 4,601 deaths and 3,848 injuries. The other statistics given in *A Record of Chongqing at War* were: 34 air raids were performed by 865 airplanes; the number of bombs thrown was 1,897 to destroy 4,757 houses and buildings, to cause 5,247 deaths and 4,196 injuries. Whichever record we might take, it was certain that Chongqing that year had seen the world's largest number of sacrifices of the aerial attacks.

The wartime fire that had started in Europe had already given glimpses of indiscriminate bombings under the name of "regional bombings" soon to become uninhibited—as was seen in the German air raids upon Warsaw and Rotterdam, but England and France as the other countries concerned had made it clear to control themselves by refraining from bombings upon the regions excepting their military aims and the nearest regions of their army's strategic action. This was how they had acted in response to the request made by the U.S. President Roosevelt on the day that followed the outbreak of the War: "We should be discreet enough to refrain from making the citizens the aim of our bombings." On the third night after the start of the War, the U.K.'s ten Whitley bombers performed the air raids upon Bremen and Hamburg as the Germany's important port cities and the six other cities in the Ruhr District as the heart of industry, but what they scattered over them was 5,400,000 advertising flyers or paper bombs. On February 15, 1940, Prime Minister Chamberlain had declared* in the Lower House:

Whatever be the length to which others might go, the Government will never resort to blackguardly attacks on women and other civilians for purposes of mere terrorism.

It was in May, 1940 or after Winston Churchill took office as Prime Minister, that this policy of the U.K. was made to execute a 180-degree turn. It was true that the German Government had also allowed to perform indiscriminate bombings by performing a partial air raid upon the urban area to make their army's advance easier on the process of their strategy for capturing Walsaw and Rotterdam, but in Europe, until the British Air Force started "the regional bombings" upon the cities of Germany, they had never turned their hands to the bombing upon any city excepting when they were working together with their ground operation. So Japan's air raids upon Chongqing was to be ahead of "the history of the strategic bombings" even more than a year before the start of the Second World War.

On the other hand, the damages of the Japanese planes caused by the aerial fight and by the ground fire were also steadily growing too great to disregard. The middle-sized bombers the Navy had lost in 1939 during the operation upon the strategic point (regional bombing) amounted to twenty-six. This number included the planes lost in some strategic points other than Chongqing, but considering that the number of the planes produced during the year before was thirty-eight, that number was by far over the normal tolerance. Along with the loss of the planes, the ninety-three men, including the pilots, observers and flight-specialists, had been killed in action, thus to give a heavy blow on the Japanese side, too. Under the overwhelming sense of predominance brought about by brilliant military achievements, such a rise in a coefficient of damage and casualties was hard to be noticed, but the number of airmen who were to fall and leave their bones in the hinterland of China was steadily rising. Since the frontline of the airmen was several hundred kilometers farther ahead than that of any ground army, even if they fell into a situation in which they needed to be rescued, they were usually left as they were and their corpses, too, were left as they were.

● **A Boy Xiao Has once Seen Seven Bodies of a Japanese Flight Crew**

Xiao Jianxiang, who has become a writer, wishes to write some day about those seven bodies he has once seen with his own eyes. The scene had occurred at what is now called Baixi in Jiangjin-xuang Prefecture.

The boy Xiao Jianxiang and his elder sister, after 5.3 & 5.4, had moved for safety to Jiangjin 20km southeast of Chongqing. There he was to see the remains of a middle-sized bomber knocked out of the sky and the dead bodies of seven crew members laid out at a school yard. It was on the morning of May 27, 1939. Men and women and children had come to see them.

The plane that had been downed was that of the 13th flying corps or one of the twenty-six planes of the First Air Raid Unit. The following is what was recorded in *The Operations of the Imperial Navy in the China Incident* (edited by the Naval Department):

On the 25th (in May), the air corps led by Lieutenant-Commander Yamanoue, which was carrying out the fourth air raid upon Chongqing in full force and in high spirits, making use of the moonlight, appeared in the skies of Chongqing around 9 p.m. and dropped the rain of huge bombshells upon the Military Committee's Chairman's Encampment, thus to blow many important military facilities to smithereens, while bringing about fires in several spots.

Among the four enemy planes that came to offer a challenge, one was shot down successfully, but our planes also were to receive fierce attacks of anti-aircraft guns and large-sized machine guns from the suburbs—especially from the vicinity of the living quarters of foreign residents—and one of our planes was finally shot before they crashed itself bravely into the enemy position.

As it was, the middle-sized bomber that had been shot had not "crashed itself into an enemy position," but the pilot and the others tried hard to pick it up to the bitter end, but in vain. Probably the control system had been destroyed, and this led the plane to fly toward the upper reaches of the Yangzi—toward the opposite direction of its base in Hankou—and crashed head-on into a farm. When the Chinese military and people came and surrounded the plane, they found none had been alive in it. On the following day, the the Aerial Defense Headquarters of Chongqing sent there the chief of its First Department, Zhang Shilun, to perform a careful inspection of the scene and seized the eight maps (including those of topography of military importance, those of the routes between Chongqing and Yunnan, and those of the urban area of Chongqing) and some other papers and diaries, as was recorded in *A Record of Chongqing's Resistance to Japan.*

It was after the officials left the scene that the boy Xiao saw the dead bodies of the seven Japanese. Those in their flying suit had been placed side by side on the straw mats. They were being surrounded with the crowd of people. Xiao brought himself among them. Some spat at the dead bodies. This led Xiao to imitate them in spite of himself. His spitting was very far from reaching them, but he never thought what he had done then would leave an unpleasant feeling even after he grew up. Xiao still keeps asking himself what had made him spit at those dead bodies of the Japanese airmen. Had he hated them? Or had he simply imitated the grownups around him? As he grew older, those dead were turning to the ones of the same generation as his own sons, and this led him to think of their bereaved family, asking himself: "Had their family been told of what their final flight was like? Had they ever heard of them having been buried *here* politely?...."

● The Chinese People in General Believed in their Victory
If Only they Held out

The year 1939 was gone, after having carved a variety of things into their memory—even though most of them were tragic ones. Chongqing, the capital living up to its resistance to Japan, was now having a brief rest in the fog that offered them their hiding mantle of fog. That was certainly a blessing to them, but they had already been aware that: that was none other than the end of the first chapter of their sufferings. When the foggy season was over, the enemy would surely come back. Then they would have to try to survive that cruel trial throughout another summer. Could they be strong enough to survive it?

Throughout the winter, "the foggy capital"—which could be compared to the white night in the arctic—the people were working as hard as they could, trying to restore things to their normal state, while making new preparations for their resistance to Japan.

On the other hand, some people—though they were small in number—had already regarded the year 1939 as "the beginning to reach the end" of the Sino-Japanese War. They had survived such hideous aerial bombings as none of the other cities in the world had ever experienced before, and this had shown to the world how they had been able to retain the unity and intention of their resistance. Unlike the cases of Nanjing and of Wuhan, Chongqing had succeeded in demonstrating the enemy the base of their invincibility. The enemy also must have felt a response they had never known before. What was more, the outbreak of the Second World War seemed to work on China making a resistance in a favorable way. More and more people came to believe that: if only they held out, they would surely win the victory.

The December issue of *Liang You* (*Good Friend*)—an illustrated magazine—placed a photograph of Jiang Jieshi at the opening of the feature article of "Looking Back over the Past Year," giving the title of "Time is a Friend of China, but a Great Enemy to Japan" for his address whose gist was: "Japan will surely be defeated. The new year will reveal the unfailing victory of our resistance."

● **Mao Zedong's Words Quoted by Kiryuu Yuyu in his Personal Magazine**
　　　　　　　　　　　　　　　　　　　　　　　—A Stone from Another Mountain

About the same period of time, a Japanese journalist, Kiryū Yūyū, wrote down *Mao Zedong's Declaration*—which had been made when Mao met Edgar Snow—in Yūyū's personal magazine, *A Stone from Another Mountain,* issued on January 20, 1940.

Kiryu Yuyu, who used to be the chief editor of *The Shinano Mainichi* (a local newspaper distributed in and around Nagano Prefecture), wrote an editorial comment for August 11, entitled "I laugh at the idea of carrying out a great drill to provide for the air raid on the Kantō district," in which he severely criticized what they were doing, saying: "Having the enemy planes come flying in the skies of the Kanto district and in the skies of the Imperial Capital means none other than our armed force's being defeated," and this led him to be deprived of his post by the pressure of the military authorities. This, however, led him to keep criticizing the military through his personal magazine: *A Stone from Another Mountain* (a Chinese proverb—from China's oldest *Book of Songs*—metaphorically meaning: A mistake made by someone else can be something to learn by). In the year when Japan's aerial bombings upon Chongqing got into full gear, he wrote: "If either of the nations were to attack the capital of the other nation, the other nation will also return their attack ..... And the one who had given the first attack is more likely to be defeated in the end. (September 20, 1939) As for the Sino-Japanese War, too, he gave a severe criticism, writing: "Japan is waging war against China, still the Japanese military say: 'We are fighting against China but we do not regard it as our opponent.' This is a strange logic." *Mao Zedomg's Declaration* was probably Yuyuu's own view of the Sino-Japanese War, seeing that he had brought a long quotation from it:

> China is a country whose territory is so spacious that it would never be conquered unless all of its territory was placed under the swords of the invaders. Even though Japan had occupied the wide area populated by one or two hundred million people, we shall not yet be regarded as defeated. The Japanese must not forget the fact that the war will be carried out in China. This means that the Japanese are always surrounded by the Chinese as their enemy. The Japanese must maintain their army along all the connecting lines, and while defending their bases of operations in both Manchuria and Japan proper, they could not help providing them with food, while keeping watching over them.

Thus Kiriu Yūyū gave us Mao Zedong's words: "China would be the ultimate victor," and closed his article, as follows:

> The third spring has come since we started this war, and now is the time for us to recall *these words* mentioned by Mao Zedong so we may reflect deeply upon ourselves.

Zhou Enlai also mentioned the same thing as Mao Zedong did in a more explicit wording, as White quoted in his work, *In Search of History:*

Even if Japan were to succeed in occupying the whole land of China, they would not have armed forces large enough to maintain it. A simple calculation will reveal how true this is: In North China there are more than three hundred cities and even if the Japan's armed forces were to distribute one company to each of the cities, they would not be able to maintain all of them. Even if they were able to do so, that would turn out simply pleasing to us. Because all we should do then would be crushing it one company after another.

Zhou Enlai in Chongqing, while facing the air raids by the Japanese military, had held a prospect that: the Sino-Japanese War and other war fires that started in Europe would develop into a war between two Imperialist nations—Japan and America. For Zhou, too, the time had taken his side.

David Lilienthal—who was later to be the first chairman of the U.S. Atomic Energy Commission, and at that time the person in charge of the New Deal Policy being carried out by President Roosevelt—has also written in his *Diary* (dated November 23, 1940) about the Chinese view of war which also depended on time, mentioning a Chinese man of literature, Lin Yutang:

> Dr. Lin had just gotten back from China. He is a soft-voiced, sensitive-looking man, very domestic, very modest and retiring in appearance. The only thing he was positive about was that China was to find to win against Japan and that Japan cannot possibly win. He said that if Japanese continues to kill only four Chinese for each Japanese lost, they are bound to lose. He also told some stories that illustrate the lomg-time perspective of the Chinese.
> —*Lilienthal's Diary*

Among the people who had been entrenching themselves in Chongqing, too, such a view as this—"Time is a friend of the Chinese and the worst enemy of the Japanese"—began to be upheld, though they still remained in the minority. From their point of view, the enclosed were *not* Chongqing *but* the Japanese military themselves. Still, the arrival of their reinforcements remained ahead. Against the background of a tumultuous period of the world history, another year of the confrontation between the Chinese who relied upon the time and the Japanese who controlled the space was steadily approaching.

Chongqing before being bombed（from a grafhic magazine
Liang You）

1）Duyou-jie（one of the main streets in Chongqing）
2）The riverside
3）The city's central area when Chongqing was called "Little
Shanghai"
4）The palanquins were available in climbing the stone steps
5）The flight of stone steps beyond the Zhaotian-men Gate

Wanxian District & Wushan
xian District in those days（se
P.130）

A street in Chongqing under the air raid in May, 1939（see P.143）

wntown Chongqing suffering what was called "5.3 & ·" （see P.136）

uyou Street after the air raid in Chongqing（see P.145）

"Zhou's Office"in Zengjia-an ＝ the Office of the Eighth Route Army（the Chinese Communist Party's Central Southern Bureau）（see P.118）

The German flag spread before the German Embassy （see P.181）

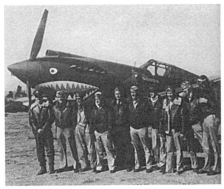

The Flying Tigers and Curtis P40（see P.184）

The Indiscriminate Bombing Started (1939)   237

A scene in Warsaw after the air raid by the German Air Force (see P.227)

The photogravure of *Liang You (Good Friends)* — *Looking Back upon This Year* — issued in December, 1939 (see P.233)

CHAPTER Ⅲ

NO.101 OPERATIONS (1940) —THE STRATEGIC & POLITICAL BOMBINGS WERE PUT INTO PRACTICE—

Drawing up a Plan for the Indiscriminate Bombings

● **The Planner of the Indiscriminate Bombings · Inoue Shigeyoshi**

Around the period when the year was changing from 1939 to 1940, (the men of great ability and the best of the aviators that had supported the air corps of the Imperial Navy began to cross the Japan Sea and went up the Yangzi to reach the battlefront in China. Inoue Shigeyoshi, Onishi Takijiro, Yamaguchi Tamon, Teraoka Kinpei and Yamamoto Chikao were among them. They were commanders and staff officers. Each of them, being a good pilot, was known as a match for a thousand. In a part of the Navy, they had firmly built up the foothold of aviation capability, and this had led them to firmly believe that the striking power from the sky would be the principal power that would take the place of battleships. Keeping this secret plan of utilizing the newly-produced airplanes under their control, they now set their feet on the Continent, letting themselves overflow with self-confidence and ambition.

The new plan of aerial operations to advance into the hinterland of China, which would largely surpass what they had performed the year before in both the scale and the number of times—the No.101 Operations—was about to be put in motion. Rear Admiral Yamaguchi (Commander of the First United Air Force), Captain Onishi (Rear Admiral during his service, Commander of the Second United Air Force), Rear-Admiral Teraoka (Commander of the Third United Air Force) and Captain Yamamoto (Commander of the 15th Flying

Corps) arrived at Hankou Air Base (Wuhan), while Rear Admiral Inoue (Vice Admiral during his service), who had been appointed Chief of the Staff of the Fleet of the China Region, arrived at *Izumo*, a maritime defense warship (9,773 tons), with its flag raised at Huanbu-jiang Bay at Shanghai. As for Commander-in-Chief, in place of Vice-Admiral Oikawa Koshiro, (who, after two years in office, was transferred in May, 1940, to be Commander-in-Chief of a Naval Station at Yokosuka), Vice Admiral Shimada Shigetaro (though called Admiral during his service) came over to take office, too, after leaving his post as Commander-in-Chief of the Second Fleet. In performing No.101 Operations, the Fleet of the China Region was to be their pivot, and the First United Air Corps and the Second United Air Corps were expected to demonstrate their powerful strength.

In the storehouses that stood along the Yangzi, a large quantity of material had been laid up, while the planes kept flying over there from the east every day. Jiang Jieshi had already been informed of these facts from Wuhan since the year before:

> Lately the enemy's supply ships have entered Wuhan with a large amount of munitions, while a hundred planes have flown to Wuhan. We humbly report these facts.
>
> *—A Collection of Letters Received by Jiang Jieshi*
> Edited by Ding Qinjie & Song Ping

Many of those outstanding Japanese that had come up to Wuhan by the Yangzi were to die dramatic deaths in the Japan-U.S. War—like Yamaguchi Tamon and Onishi Takijiro: the former, the commander of the Second Aerial Squadron at the Battle of Midway during the Japan-U.S. War, sank with the airplane carrier *Hiryu* (*Flying Dragon*); the latter, the originator of *Kamikaze* corps (suicide air corps) performed a *hara-kiri* (suicide by disembowelment) on the day that followed Japan's surrender. Their lives and deaths have now been known as the notable scenes left behind by the Second World War.

In the case of Inoue Shigeyoshi, too, who survived the war and punished himself by imposing a house arrest throughout the rest of his life—apart from the appreciation he received as "anti-war general" in and after the 1980s—it will be quite probable to leave his name in the history of the world wars for a couple of reasons, as follows:

① He was the commander of one of the conflicting fleets of air craft carriers in the decisive battle: according to the expression made by Chester Nimitz, the U. S. Commander-in-Chief, it was "the world's first naval battle fought between the two conflicting fleets, keeping each other beyond their field of vision" (in the Battle of the Coral Sea fought in May, 1942).

② He was the drafter of the indiscriminate bombings performed under the name of "No. 101 Operations" upon Chongqing as the wartime capital of China—the indiscriminate bombings performed on the same city—32 times (80 times according to the record of the Chinese side), spending 112 days.

In these two points, Inoue Shigeyoshi must be judged not just from the point of his personality and his own belief but also from what he had actually done and what sort of results were brought about by them, when viewed from the point of the world history. Inoue himself seems to have been aware of them, and that was presumably why he chose to live in total silence that seemed to others to be a sort of self-punishment.

The following was a comment on Inoue Shigeyoshi that appeared in *Tokyo Nichinichi Shimbun* (*Tokyo Daily News*) dated October 24, 1939:

He is a man of military spirit, clear-headed and self-possessed. Especially when he was the chief of the Bureau of Military Affairs under the Navy Minister Yonai, he proved himself to be razor-sharp in coping with many happenings he had to deal with in the Navy both at home and abroad, thus to be admired for his skillfulness in political savvy. So his promotional transfer this time is being regarded with great expectation in every sense of the word.

About this period of time when Inoue Shigeyoshi was transferred from the chief of the Bureau of Military Affairs in the Naval Department to the front of China, the Fleet of the China Region had changed its formation so that it could perform its own strategy independent of the Combined Fleet. Its military capability consisted of the first, the second and the third expeditionary fleets for China Region, and of the first, the second and the third united air corps, and of the corps of the special bases of operations at Hankou, Guangdong and Qingdao, and so its force was so majestic as might be called "the Second Combined Fleet." Its origin dated back to July in 1932, when it was formed as "the Third Fleet" when the first Shanghai Incident* occurred, and while it was escalating into the second Shanghai Incident* that followed Lukouqiao Incident* in July, 1937, "the Fourth Fleet" was brought in, and in February, 1938, the Fifth Fleet was also added to be developed into "the Fleet of the China Region," and three weeks after Inoue took office as the Chief of Staff (on November 15, 1940), it moved into a newly-organized fleet that stood abreast of the United Fleet.

● **The New Commander-in-Chief, Vice-Admiral Shimada Shigetaro's Enthusiasm**

Vice-Admiral Shimada Shigetaro, who was made the new director of the reformed Fleet and became Inoue's superior, used to be the chief of staff of the Third Fleet at the time of the Shanghai Incident,* and now he came to get on board the flagship *Izumo*, burning with his strong wish to put an end to the China Incident before his term expired. In October, 1941, he was to be the Minister of the Navy and to decide upon the Navy's course toward the outbreak of the Japan-U.S. War, but at this period he must not have imagined that the Sino-Japanese war he was leading would develop into the Japan-U.S. War. The Commander-in-Chief Shimada, who had supported the Air Force's advancing operations upon Chongqing and other places in the hinterland of China, often visited Hankou to encourage the unit there.

What the Chief of Staff was expected to do then was to make himself the brain of the Commander-in-Chief and to make up a plan of operations. Inoue now, in requesting the center of the Navy Department for the reinforcement of the Air Force, expressed his idea, even employing such a strong wording as "the success or failure in that offensive tactics to the strategic points in China's hinterland will be a key to the solution of the Sino-Japanese War, and for that reason it can be compared to the Battle on the Japan Sea in the Russo-Japanese War.*" And after the operations were put into motion, he made a four days' inspection on the frontline of Hankou Air Base, and expressed his ardor for the No. 101 Operations by encouraging the Commander Yamaguchi of the First Aviation Corps and the Commander Onishi of the Second Aviation Corps along with the officers and men under them. Thus the strategic bombings performed intentionally and systematically for a long period of time under this single name of "No. 101 Operations" were inseparably connected here and there with Inoue Shigeyoshi.

In a sense, what Inoue Shigeyoshi was then suffering both physically and spiritually was not dissimilar to what Robert McNamara, the U.S. Secretary of Defense, was to be suffering thirty years later in dealing with the Vietnam War. Both of them had sharp intellect with which to find something impure in carrying out the war, but in the actual process, they had to devote their fine brain and sensible ability to think in performing the war (or the operations). Both were not lacking in the courage with which to face their own setback and failure and performed their duty in digging out the essence of their failure for the benefit of their posterity, but their personality had not necessarily been so made as to seek acquaintance among their contemporaries so that they might expand their influence upon those around them. To both of them, and to both of their countries, this could be regarded as loss and tragedy. As for having been able to have such persons in the ages of such insanity, both the nations might feel some consolation and a certain kind of satisfaction. But just as the image of McNamara seen from the Vietnamese side was unfailingly that of the decider of "the indiscriminate bombings upon North Vietnam," Inoue Shigeyoshi, seen from the Chinese side, cannot escape an evaluation different from the viewpoint of "the liberalist in the Navy." What No. 101 Operations in 1940 meant to Inoue was none other than *his* version of "the indiscriminate bombings upon North Vietnam."

Without achieving the aim of the Operations—without being able to win "the Sea Battle on the Japan Sea" in the Sino-Japanese War—Inoue returned to Tokyo and sat on the chair for the director of the Air Force Headquarters. It was not long before he finished writing *A New Plan for Military Preparations*, in which he delivered an important part the planes would play in the modern warfare and after having deplored how slow Japan had been in realizing this fact, he admonished that Japan should at once grow out of being dependent on large ships equipped with huge artillery, and that the Navy should be turned into a part of the Air Force. Thus without hesitation Inoue was trying hard to get over this bitter experience he had suffered. So this idea of his, as was delivered in *A New Plan for Military Preparations,* could be read as a self-criticism on his failure in the Plan of No. 101 Operations.

Ironically, however, this document of his own creation, full of discernment and predictions, also became "a farewell note Inoue as a military man left behind." On September 27, 1940—three days before he was officially announced to be the director of the Air Force Headquarters—the Tripartite Pact between Germany, Italy and Japan, which he had kept opposing even at the risk of losing his position as the chief of the Bureau of Military Affairs, was signed at Berlin and it had been decided that Japan should be among the Axis Powers and that "a war against the U.S." should be inevitable. Now the Japanese Navy was to change their stance completely from being "an influence upon the Pacific" (deterrence to the U.S.) to being "a fighter against the U.S. in their decisive battle." To Inoue, that meant the death of the Navy he had kept in his mind. Inoue, who had returned to Japan after a year's absence, must have been feeling as if he had been estranged not only from the battlefield but also from the main stream of the Navy. *An Opinion on A New Plan for Military Preparations* was to be offered in such a situation and background, and it might be called a bitter lesson he had learned and extracted from his own direct experience of one great aerial strategy performed in the Chinese front.

About the time when Inoue, the chief of staff of the fleet of the China Region, started to draw up the plan for the operations in the flagship Izumo floating on the Huangbu-jiang River in Shanghai, the ground forces on the Chinese front had totally been bogged down. The Army had simply been kept busy in securing and maintaining the occupied regions by dint of their security battle, and as for any clues to break through that difficult situation, all they could think of was to put the enemy camps into confusion or agitation or rebellion under the name of "a stratagem." As for the initiative in a ground operation, nothing was left for the Japanese Army, and practicing such a stratagem as to move their troops on to Chongqing as the anti-Japanese capital where Jiang Jieshi had entrenched himself was simply unthinkable. Even the Army that had kept their self-confidence so far had now found it hard to do anything effective. Naturally the Army Air Force had its own bomber unit, but unlike the Navy Air Force, they had to spend much of their strength on "the strategic cooperation with the ground forces," so it was by no means possible for them to perform any strategic bombings on their own.

On the other hand, the Navy was active on both domains of sea and sky. They had no fixed battle line or the occupation zone on the ground, while the

Chinese Navy was extremely weak, and this enabled the Japanese Fleet of the China Region to take their initiative in undertaking offensive operations that would go for the enemy's weak point. Sealing off the coastal waters and aerial advancing were the two main strategies adopted by the Japanese Navy, and its central headquarters with Commander-in-Chief Shimada and the Chief of Staff Inoue in it was floating not far away from the mouth of the Yangzi in Shanghai.

● **A Strategy for Intercepting the Routes for Supporting Jiang Jieshi**

Japan's efforts to cut off supply routes by spreading the nets of naval blockade along the coasts of the Chinese Continent had constantly been made since August 25, 1937, when *The First Declaration of Blocking Traffic* was made. This meant blocking the whole of the coastline as long as more than 5,300km—from Shanhai-quan Barrier as the borderline between "Manchukuo"[*] and China to the border of Indo-China under French rule or present-day Vietnam—by forming a cordon, and performing inspection and seizure of Chinese shipping—in order to intercept "the Routes for Supporting Jiang Jieshi" by supplying him with arms, ammunitions and war materials. There were land routes, too, such as "north-west route" between the Soviet Union and Lanzhou, "Burma-Yunnan route" and "Hanoi route." Some other routes were by way of such ports as Hongkong, Guangdong, Amoy, Shantou, Haikou and so on, and in the early stage of the Sino-Japanese War, by far the larger amount of things had been brought in by sea.

To cut off these "supply routes" in order to send Jiang Jieshi to starvation does remind us of that fantastic idea in Napoleon's policy of "a continental blockade" against England, but it was totally impossible to blockade all of those coasts as long as 5,300km with numberless ports dotted upon them. What was more, many of these ports, including Tianjin, Shanghai and Hongkong, had a large number of concessions and leaseholds, where the foreigners' extraterritorial rights were guaranteed. But Japan at that time having been using armed force without declaring war even upon China—calling their military action "incidents" because they had started their use of armed forces without giving any formal declaration of war. This did prevent Japan from adopting such regulation as a war-time blockade upon all the shipping sent in. So Japan could not help overlooking the things sent in by the third countries. That led Japan to go on fighting without obtaining anything they had expected, despite their painstaking effort.

Feeling dissatisfied with such a slack method they had to adopt, more and more in the Navy began to support the means by which the Army had once enlarged their theater of war by disregarding the diplomacy, only keeping to their military logic that: they should capture the important ports so that they could cut off "the routes for supporting Jiang Jieshi." Thus they did enforce a naval blockade of Amoy, Guangdong, Xiantou and Hainan-dao Island, to be followed by landing operations and battles for invasion, thus drawing the Navy also into "the bogs" of the Chinese Continent. That was to destroy the Japanese Navy's traditional policy in two ways: Firstly, they had done something wrong when they landed and fought and remained there as occupants; Secondly, while going through the process of developing their strategy, they were to have more and more opportunities to cause frictions with or to fall out with the American, British and French rights and interests in China, especially with their settlements and assets, with the result that in the direction of unfolding any diplomatic policy, Japan had no other way but to incline towards the Tripartite Pact with Germany and Italy, and as its further reaction, the Japanese Navy was to raise not a few young officers as "pro-Axis powers" who came to loudly advocate a hardline foreign policy. Thus while going farther and farther along such a blind alley, the Navy who had enforced their blockade along the long coast of China was to form a situation in which Japan could not say "No" to the war against the U.S. and the U.K.. That fleet dispatched to China and Inoue Shigeyoshi—who had been known as "a liberalist in the Navy" who was advocating the renunciation of war against the U.S.—seem to make the least appropriate combination imaginable, but history was to arrange such a paradoxical fortune for them.

● **The Navy Trying to Promote the Aerial Operations**

Along with the blocking of the sea traffic, another mission the Navy was expected to perform was the promotion of the aerial operations. At this period, when the Japanese Army's advancing operations had come to a standstill, because of the great depth of the Chinese territory and the rugged terrain that surrounded Chongqing as the wartime capital, yet remaining unable to find any opportunity to fight a decisive battle against the main force of the enemy, even if they had wished to change the tides of war, all they could do then was whether to show the conditions for peace and withdrawal of their troops or to promote aviation's long distance maneuverability to turn the enemy's capital and other major cities into ruins so that they could make Jiang Jieshi realize all he could do then would be to surrender. The option of acknowledging the Jiang Jieshi's Administration and negotiating with it before retreating from China was the last thing the Japanese Army would accept. Then if they were to get out of this quagmire, all they could do would be to intensify their aerial advancing operations. Thus more and more expectation was to be placed on the strategic and political bombings upon the hinterland of Sichuan Province (Chongqing & Chengdu & other cities) to be performed mainly by the Fleet of the China Region placed under the command of Inoue Shigeyoshi.

The war situation in 1940 was surveyed as follows in *The History of the Navy Air Force of Japan (4)* in *The Series of War History (Japan's Defense Agency)*:

The numeral strength of the Army had already surpassed the limits of dispatch to the Continent in view of the situations both at home and abroad. And this led the Army to plan to decrease their military capability with no plan for any further positive advance, until they came to cease their advancing operations. The Jiang Administration, regarding their abandonment of Wuhan as the end of their first stage of the National United Front against Japan, rebuilt their Army and loudly advocated their counterattack, and having anticipated Japan's having no surplus power to extend a war zone, they were quick enough to take their offensive in April and in summer; then when they saw some movement for establishing the Wang Administration at home and Europe being caught in the disturbance of war, which might cause their policy of supporting Jiang to cool down, Jiang demonstrated what his fighting was like by his offensive in October and in December.

The ground forces being as they were, the only force of arms to bring the Incident to an early end would be the Air Force, and this inevitably led to the fact that: the majority of the strategies for reducing the enemy to submission would be entrusted to the Air Force to perform their strategy. This led to the fact that: most of the ground advancing operations performed as something especially necessary since then were done to promote the air bases in order to enlarge the range for our aerial attack. This was how the Army and the Navy Air Corps came to cooperate with each other to defeat the enemy.

In view of the positive obligation for the Air Force to perform during this fiscal year, the Navy had placed the great importance in overthrowing the seat of Jiang's Administration. Even though we had had an inward thought that it would be easy to destroy the city of Chongqing which is mostly made of earth and tiles, we were by no means confident of our success in achieving that purpose by our scanty force, but since we could not find any other means to subdue our enemy, we placed what little hope we had on our air force.

As was written here, the Navy was "by no means confident of our success". But there was no other means available to them. The same kind of hesitation had been shared with the side of the Army, as was seen in *The Assessment of the Situation of the Army Dispatched in the Midland of China* submitted to the Vice-Minister of the Army, Lieutenant General Yamawaki Masataka from Major General Yoshimoto Teiichi, the chief of the staff of the Expeditionary Army in Central China (July 24, 1939). He had offered what appeared to be a hard-line policy: "We shall dare to carry out a strategy toward the strategic point in the Interior of China so that it may lead both troops and people there to get weary of war and seek for peace," and still a faint feeling of apprehension was expressed, as follows:

While Jiang Jieshi's authority is kept imposed and their anti-Japanese consciousness remains solid, our bombings, especially those upon the innocent people in general may strengthen their anti-Japanese consciousness, but I firmly believe: they would gradually become aware of their disadvantages they might suffer by keeping fighting, and as their antipathy to Jiang and weariness of war grow stronger, the effect of our bombings would suddenly turn out to be greater.

Pretending to be confident and keeping high hopes for their wishful thinking—this was none other than an actual application of what Kiryuu Yuyu—mentioned at the end of the previous chapter—had pointed out, writing: "Japan is waging war against China, still the Japanese military say: "We do not regard the Chinese as our opponents. This is a strange logic."

At the same period when the Fleet of the China Region was reorganized and its top leaders were completely changed, the Imperial Headquarters' Navy Department consolidated the foundation of the Plan of Operations Against China for the first half of 1940 and presented it to their overseas agency. The section of "the strategy which is likely to be performed in the near future" in the guidance of strategy, delivered in the second section in "the opinion on how to deal with the China Incident," (issued on February 19, 1940) went as follows:

1) For the Army, there shall be no more invasion operations, but coastal blockade shall be performed while maintaining public security in the occupation zone. The air force shall be employed in attacking the enemy's air force, in cutting off the enemy's transportation routes, and in performing the attacks on the strategic points in the hinterland.

Beside this "first proposal," "the third proposal" suggested: how they should declare war (on China) or declare being in the state of war and perform wartime blockade so that they could thoroughly prevent the war materials from reaching Jiang's Administration." But this meant none other than the intervention in the inflow of commodities from the U.S., the U.K. and France that had held the foreign rights and interests in China, and considering their resistance and retaliation, this proposal was too dangerous to perform. "The third proposal," therefore, did not seem to be able to adopt, excepting when "the U.S. took a step against Japan by adopting an embargo, disabling Japan to import anything from the U.S.. After all, the high command of the Navy turned to "the second proposal," that was: "while carrying on with the first proposal in the most effective manner," the aerial strategy, especially the operations to invade into the interior, should be made to break through this situation, and this led the Navy to request the Army to seize Xuanchang so that they might have an advance air base there for their escort fighters. On the assumption that the Army would cooperate with the Navy on this matter, the framework of strategy in the first half of 1940 was brought into being.

Naturally, the following was mentioned as something necessary: "Along with the strategy mentioned in the first proposal, land strategy shall be prompted (omission). For the time being, we shall perform the strategy to occupy

Xuanchang that seems most effective at present so that we may be even more positive in performing our aerial strategy to give our enemy spiritual blow." (*The Naval Strategy Adopted in the China Region* (2))

Xuanchang was situated about a midway point between Hankou and Chongqing—722 km from Hankou along the Yangzi and 270 km by plane. It was also from that point that the navigators come to face the rapid flow of the Sanxia. This meant that even a large-sized warship managed to sail up to Xuanchang to secure their supply there with Chongqing 480km ahead in a straight line. If they had an air base there, it would be immensely useful not only as their transit port for the air raid upon Chongqing but also as a takeoff base for their escort fighters. Instead of a single mission of middle-sized bombers whose damage rate was large, having escort fighters with them had eagerly been requested so far by the field headquarters.

The Navy Department in the central government also supported this opinion and in *The Opinions Concerning How to Deal with China Incident*—dated February 19, 1940—they published their idea of "securing Xuanchang" as a strategy translatable into action, while expressing their wish "to make our aerial strategy even more aggressive if only Xuanchang was secured." Commander Onishi Takijiro had eagerly said to Imoto Kumao, a staff officer of the Army Department in the Imperial Headquarters: "Our wish to secure Xuanchang has been very intense," as was recorded in *The Army's Strategy in China Incident* (3) in *The Series of War History* (*Japan's Defense Agency*).

● **The Occupation of Xuanchang was Carried out by Gathering**
What the Emperor had Wished

On the other hand, however, the Army circles were not so enthusiastic about heading father than Wuhan into the hinterland. To them, none other than arms reduction had been recognized as a pressing problem. Certainly, the Army side had understood the Navy's request for securing Juanchang as something necessary in making a direct approach to Chongqing, but if they were to occupy Xuanchang as spacious as the Kanto district in Japan, it would require the stationary troops about as large as a couple of divisions. To the Military Affairs Department in the Ministry of War, whose preconceived plan so far had been to have the force 800.000 strong in China reduced to 400.000, this request was the last thing they could accept. But they knew they must show their intention to make a firm counterattack to the Chongqing Forces, which had taken their successive offensives in April, in summer and in winter, and this led them to perform a tentative strategy for capturing Xuanchang. "The Supreme Direction No.426" dated April 10, 1940, went as follows: "The supreme commander of the expeditionary force in China shall perform in May or June a tentative operation in the area of the Mid-Southern China, as mentioned below." But according to the commentary given in *The Army's Strategy in the China Region (3)* in the Defense Agency's *Library of the War History*, "this order means that: the Army should return to its original base as soon as the operation is over, instead of keeping staying in the newly-occupied area." This meant a limited strategy in which they may "capture *it* but not get hold of *it*." Its intention to support "the bombing upon Chongqing" was weak.

As it turned out, the situation suddenly changed into "the second plan" submitted by the Navy. The 11ᵗʰ Army (whose mainstay consisted of four divisions including the 13ᵗʰ division) had captured Xuanchang after the fierce battles under a blazing sky for six days and after having routed the enemy troops (on June 15), they, according to the order that had already been issued, were preparing for returning to their original base. But in Tokyo, the argument that Xuanchang should be occupied was becoming heated. At this point, on the European front, Italy entered the war on June 11 and the German Army occupied Paris on June 12, and these factors favorable to the Axis powers did encourage positivists, as one might well say so, but what had become a conclusive factor was the Emperor's utterance, as is recorded in the Defense Agency's *Library of the War History* mentioned before:

At 1:30 on June 15, Prince Kan-in, the Chief of the General Staff, and the (Deputy) Chief of the Naval General Staff, stood in a row and submitted to the Emperor "the matters relevant to what is concerned with the high command, which came into being accompanying the start of the negotiations on the new relationship between Japan and China." On that occasion, no sooner had it been mentioned by the Navy's side that "Xuanchang" would turn out to be an extremely useful as the transit air port for the Navy Air Corps then carrying out their bombardment upon Chongqing than the Emperor made an inquiry: "Isn't it possible for the Army to do anything about Xuanchang?"

This request of his Majesty given in a form of question immediately decided the attitude of the General Stuff Office toward securing Xuanchang. On the day that followed (the 16th), the arguments in the ministry departments reached an agreement on the same day, and this led to the issue of the order: Xuanchang should be secured for a while.

In accordance with this "Imperial decision," the 13th Division and other corps, which had already started their evacuation, reversed their course and returned to Xuanchang. Thus Xuanchang was to become secured.

As is seen here, it is apparent that the Emperor Hirohito had fully been aware of the strategic significance of the bombardment upon Chongqing and the merit of securing Xuanchang in achieving that purpose. Rear-Admiral Sawada Shigeru, the Vice Chief of the General Staff, also recorded in his *Memoirs*: "The Navy, having kept an idea that having the air base (for their combat planes) in Xuanchang would be very advantageous in performing their bombardments upon Chongqing, eagerly expressed their wish to occupy Xuanchang..... In those days, His Majesty himself having an ardent wish to capture Xuanchang for some reason unknown to me often inquired of the Chief of the Military Aide de Camp about this matter." The Emperor himself would have been greatly interested in the success or failure in "the No. 101 operations" to be performed as a subtle stratagem to break through the situation. This was how the original purpose of "the Army's operations upon Xuanchang"—of "defeating the main force of the Chinese Army soon to withdraw after having achieved that purpose"—was changed into continuing their occupation of it for the convenience' sake of the flying corps' bombardment upon Chongqing.

After these twists and turns, that aerial strategy, which had been incorporated into "the first plan" in the basic policy of the Naval Department of the Imperial Headquarters, was named "No.101 Operations." Its purpose was to subdue the enemy's administration by performing such a large-scaled series of aerial operations as to discourage their intention to keep fighting. The term for the Operations was from May onward, when Jiang Jieshi's capital, Chongqing, revealed itself from its hiding veil of fog. Thus the Operations were positively supported by the central government, while the cooperative system with the Army was also brought into being. This was how the No. 101 Operations were to be equipped with the framework of what was to be known as the world's first strategic bombings upon the capital of another country. Thus earlier than London or Berlin or Tokyo, Chongqing as the wartime capital of China was destined to receive its baptism of the strategic bombings. This attack—in the clarity and uniqueness of its intention to force the enemy to submit only by means of the air force—was something unheard of and differentiated from any other earlier bombardments performed upon such capitals as Nanjing and Warszawa.

"The Agreement between the Army and the Navy concerning the No. 101 Operations" was made on May 13, 1940, between the Army's representative, Lieutenant General Kinoshita Satoshi as the Chief of the Third Flight Group, and the Navy's representative, Rear-Admiral Yamaguchi Tamon as the director of the United Air Raid Unit.

The plan of strategic actions was stipulated as follows:

> The Army unit and the Navy unit shall closely cooperate with each other in advancing into the hinterland in order to frustrate the enemy's intention to go on fighting. What we should do first to achieve this purpose, therefore, shall be to gain ascendancy over the enemy's air force that will come into the mainstay of our strategy and invasion. Destroying their important facilities shall follow this performance.

The period for the Operation was about three months, starting in mid-May. It was divided into two periods: the first period was mainly for the attack upon Chongqing; the second period upon Chengdu, the capital of Sichuan Province. Thus their hidden aim was to destroy the capital first and then Chengdu the people would head for, seeking their refuge. This had kept in it a farsighted aim of cutting the line of retreat of Jiang's Administration.

● **The Flight Unit with 300 Planes was Rarely Seen even in the World**

The Air Force established by the agreement of the Army and the Navy went as follows:

The Strength of the Armed Forces to Join the Operations:

① the Army

　The Third Flight Group's Headquarters（Nanjing）

　　No. 60 Flight Squadron（Nanyuan）

The 97-type heavy bombers (36) Supplementary ones (18)
Independent Flight: No. 16 Squadron (Nanyuan)
　Scout planes (6) Supplementary ones (2)
No.44 Flight Squadron the First Squadron (Hankou)
　Scout planes (5) Supplementary ones (2)
Independent Flight No.10 Squadron (Taiyuan)
　The 97-type fighter planes (9) Supplementary ones (3)

No.60 Flight Squadron as the main force was placed under the direct control of Lieutenant General Kinoshita Satoshi, the chief of the Third Flight Group; Under the Squadron Chief, Colonel Ogawa Shojiro, 528 officers and men unfolded themselves at Yunchen Airbase in Shanxi Province along with the 51 planes, including reserve ones. Their flight distance to Chongqing was about 800km. Thus they were to concentrate only on the mission of bombardment on the hinterland.
② the Navy
　The First United Flying Corps (the United Air Raid Corps)
　　　　　　　　　　　　　　　　　The Headquarters: Hankou
　　Kanoya Flying Corps (18 middle-sized attack planes &
　　　　　　　　　　　　　　　6 supplementary ones)
　　Takao Flying Corps　(18 middle-sized attack planes &
　　　　　　　　　　　　　　　6 supplementary ones)
　The Second United Flying Corps　The Headquarters: Hankou
　　The 13th Flying Corps (27 middle-sized attack planes &
　　　　　　　　　　　　　　　15 supplementary ones)
　　The 15th Flying Corps (27 middle-sized attack planes &
　　　　　　　　　　　　　　　15 supplementary ones)
　　The 12th Flying Corps (27 carrier-based fighters &
　　　　　　　　　　　　　　　9 supplementary ones)
　　　　　　　　　　　(9 carrier-based bombers &
　　　　　　　　　　　　　　　3 supplementary ones)
　　　　　　　　　　　(9 carrier-based attack planes &
　　　　　　　　　　　　　　　3 supplementary ones)
　　The 14th Flying Corps (9 carrier-based fighters &
　　　　　　　　　　　　　　　3 supplementary ones)

A Contingent to Mid-China

The number of 96-type (middle-sized) attack planes as the main force of the Navy's bomber fleet was ninety in common use alone, and if probationary ones were added, it reached a great force of 132 planes. The number of the middle-sized attack planes was too large to be kept at Hankou Base alone, and surplus ones were sent to Kaogan Airport about 50km northwest. The following is what was recorded in *The Résumé of No.101 Operations* (drawn up by the Headquarters of the United Air Raid Unit):

The number of the middle-sized attack planes that had been assembled at Hankou was about 90. Beside these, there were about 70 carrier-based ones. When transport planes and army planes were added, the number reached about 300; what was more, in Kaogan, too, there were about 42 middle-sized attack planes. In case the enemy planes should assault there, this congestion of the planes would turn out to be our weak point.

The last mentioned was by no means an imaginary fear, considering the fact that they actually suffered casualties: During the daytime on October 3 the year before, Hankou Air Base suffered a surprise attack by the nine Chinese SB2 bombers (made in the Soviet Union) from the height of 6,000m, and Rear-Admiral Tsukahara Fushimi, the Commander of the First United Air Force, had his left arm blown off, while both of the vice chiefs (Commanders) of Kisarazu Flying Corps and Kanoya Flying Corps were bombed to death. In those days in 1940, such a large sortie base as this with as many as three hundred planes in it could rarely be seen in any other countries in the world. So the atmosphere of Hankou Air Base had been kept tense, while trying to establish a combat-ready stance under the deliberate guard kept by the carrier-based fighter planes. This was how things were going on at "Hankou W Base" in Wuhan half way up the Yangzi in May, 1940. when Captain Onishi Takijiro, who had also been made Bombardment Commander along with Rear Admiral Yamaguchi, arrived there as the Commander of the Second United Air Force.

The Japanese Navy Air Corps

● Onishi Takijiro's Command of the Air Corps

Onishi Takijiro had been in Tokyo for three years and a half, serving as the head of the Department of Education at the Headquarters of the Navy Air Force. Then on October 19, 1939, he received an official appointment to be the Commander of the Second United Air Force, and this led him to arrive at Hankou Air Force Base in high spirits, trembling with excitement at the important charge he was going to take as the commander of the troops at the front. Soon after that—on November 15—he was to receive the warrant of appointment to make him "take charge of Rear-Admiral." Now he had been promoted not only to the commander to perform the strategic bombings but also to the post which would lead him to be called "Admiral." One piece of good news after another would have made him, a passionate one, even more passionate. A letter he sent to an acquaintance of his in January, 1949, did reveal a part of his lively feeling of joy.

> My Dear Mr.__,
>
> I sincerely wish you a brilliant new year of the 2,600[th] year of the Imperial reign. (omission) As for myself, on October 19th last year, I received an official appointment to the post of the commander of the Second United Air Force, and this led me to arrive at Hankou on the 27th of the same month. Since then, I have been keeping myself busy, flying around central China, Sichuan Province, the Hinterland, Lanzhou, Guang-xi and so on. Since I am fit and healthy, I simply enjoy devoting myself to my task of putting the strategy into action. So please feel safe about me. By the personal reshuffle announced as of the 15th of November, I was promoted to Rear-Admiral.
>
> Sincerely Yours, Onishi Takijiro

It was in the 2,600[th] year of the Imperial reign or in the 15th year of the Showa era or in 1940. Two years had passed since Sino-Japanese War broke out, and the third year had just started. For fourteen months and a half from then on—when he was in his forty-ninth year to fiftieth—Onishi, staying at the commander's office at Hankou, while holding the command firstly of the Second United Air Force, and then of the First United Air Force, kept commanding the strategic bombing on the interior of Sichuan Province—Chongqing, Chengdu and several other cities. He himself often boarded a middle-sized bomber, trying to help Jiang Jieshi's capital to turn into ruins. No.101 Operations in 1940 turned out to be a flourish given by Onishi Takijiro with all his might. No sooner had he received the order than he braced himself up "with immense pleasure," trying to promote the strategy with all his might in order to exterminate Jiang's Administration by dint of the aerial strength. Not any other person would have been better cut out to realize Inoue Shigeyoshi's project than Onishi Takijiro.

● **No. 101 Operation Accelerated the Enlargement of the Aerial Battles in the World**

If seen along with the flow of the aerial battles that had ever been fought in the world, this No. 101 Operation could be regarded as the forerunner of those European aerial battles that came into being during the last two months of this Operation—"Adler-Tag (the Eagles' Day)" performed on August 13, 1940, or the German Air Force's full-scale offensive against the Royal Air Force, and "the Battle of Britain" or the aerial defense battle on the British Isles, and the strategic bombings upon Berlin, the German capital, which began to be performed by the British bombers according to Churchill's decision since August 25, and then the German Air Force's retaliation since September or their indiscriminate bombings upon London. Then, the No. 101 Operations could be called the first operations to be recorded in the history of the large-scaled aerial-advancing operations that had rapidly been growing in the Second World War.

As if succeeding to Onishi's No. 101 operations, Colonel Curtis LeMay, who was to be called "the Father of the Strategic Bombing" of the U.S. Air Force who was to lead the operations to exterminate Japan's main cities, flew to the skies of Asia from the skies of Berlin. LeMay flew into Sichuan Province by B-29 bomber after crossing over the Himalayas from India, and after that, he was to start a long flight of victory and promotion until he arrived at the skies of Tokyo by way of the Mariana Islands, but about this time, Rear-Admiral Onishi and Colonel LeMay remained far away from each other, and they never had any opportunity to know of each other.

For Onishi Takijiro, who was being engaged in the No. 101 Operations at his command office at Hankou W Base, it was totally impossible to foresee how these operations of setting fire to the cities in China were to be returned several years later not only to Hankou (Wuhan) he was then staying at but also even to the whole of the Japanese Islands—in a form of huge fires of retaliation that had come across the Eurasian Continent. What was more, it would have been totally unbelievable for Onishi, a firm believer in the omnipotence of the bombing craft, that the Chinese people who had been shutting themselves up in Chongqing and its neighboring "Great Rear Area"—like the British who were to fight through "the battle of Britain" in the same year—were to survive Japan's violent assaults given from the air with all the might of their Army and Navy. As it happened, the conquest of the Chinese Capital by dint of the Japanese Air Force could not be realized, and No. 101 Operations, which failed in conquering the Chinese capital, were to be remembered in history more clearly as the Chinese people's "Battle of Chongqing."

Both Onishi Takijiro, who believed in the supremacy of the aerial capability, and Inoue Shigeyoshi, the chief of the General Staff of the Fleet of the Chinese Region, who had armed himself with the European intellect, could not finally understand the Chinese volition to protest by placing their foundation upon their good earth. The flow of the war situation—as Edgar Snow had contemplated and predicted while walking around the ruins in Chongqing brought about by the war fire—was to lead the Chinese who had survived the unprecedented aerial attacks of "5.3 & 5.4" again to succeed in surviving the No.101 Operations that lasted for four months, thus to totally frustrate the efforts and calculation made by Onishi and Inoue. That was, the result was the same with that of "McNamara's bombings upon North Vietnam."

Onishi, who left Hankou in January, 1941, to get transferred to be the chief of stuff of the Eleventh Air Force Fleet to perform his new duty to draw up a plan for a surprise attack on Hawaii and a plan for the aerial strategy to be performed in the Philippine regions, must have had a heavy residue at the bottom of his heart, as Inoue had.

● **The Life of Onishi, who had Run through his Life like *Asura****

It would rightly be said that Onishi Takijiro had embodied the rise and fall— the glory and misery—of Japan's Navy Air Force. Following the course of his life as a serviceman would be following the history of the Navy Air Force in Japan, and considering the fact that: he had expressed his mourning over the death of the thirty-three-year-old Navy Air Force by performing *hara-kiri*,** it could rightly be said that he had shared his fate with the times he had lived in.

    * an evil god in the Indian mythology, who was jealous and fond of fighting
   **killing oneself by performing disembowelment as a form of honorable suicide—a Japanese custom that started among the warriors' class toward the end of the 12th century.

Onishi had intended to be a serviceman when the aircraft was still called "flying vessel," and in the year when the Navy Air Force was founded in 1912, he was appointed a naval cadet, and when he was in sub-lieutenant junior class, he was chosen to belong to the Air Force Department (on a seaplane carrier, *Wakamiya*), thus he lived to see the air force in the cradle grow into the one whose strategic bombers came to carry nuclear bombs. He was Japan's first commissioned officer who was appointed to be the commander of the Navy Airship Corps (at Yokosuka in 1921); he was also Japan's first officer that had parachuted down from the airship on the wing (1921). While living in the period when the airship developed into the biplane and then into the bomber made of metal all over, he distinguished himself as a character who advocated that: the air planes should be the mainstay of the warfare, and that: the warships should be discarded. Then he authored *A Study on the Aerial Preparations* (1937) and promoted No.101 Operations, the surprise tactics on Hawaii and the aerial-advancing operations on the Philippines, and toward the end of the Pacific War, Vice-Admiral Onishi, as Commander-in-Chief of the First Aerial Fleet, became the originator and commander of the *kamikaze* suicide attack to be made especially upon the U.S. aircraft carriers, which he himself called "the heterodoxy of leadership." Until he committed *hara-kiri*** after Japan was defeated, saying: "I, too, shall follow my dear youthful ones," Onishi Takijiro had lived a life as if he had been an incarnation of *asura*.*

When the Sino-Japanese War broke out, Captain Onishi was the chief of the Education Department at the Navy's Aerial Headquarters, but he was far from being able to keep himself desk-bound as he was expected to. No sooner had he heard that one plane after another that had taken off at the airports in Kyushu or on Cheju-do Island (the largest island of Korea, which had been occupied by the Imperialist Japan) were being brought down while being engaged in the transoceanic bombings upon Nanjing than he made himself a member of the flight crew on the pretext of an on-site inspection and experienced what the air battles and the transoceanic bombings were really like at the initial stage of the Sino-Japanese War. That action he took part in on August 21, 1937, was a wretched one in which four out of fifteen planes failed to return or made a forced landing, but Onishi was born to be so dauntless as to be able to enjoy even such a dangerous task as that. At Hankou, too, he was persistent in putting the commander at the head, openly saying: "How many captains or rear-admirals have been dead so far?" And this kind of straightforwardness he had naturally revealed led him to win the greatest confidence and popularity of those airmen in the front-line. Being exactly the opposite type of Inoue Shigeyoshi as a man of proud independence, Onishi Takijiro, a man of a big-brother type, had always been wrapped up in an atmosphere of the guru of some religious cult.

● Onishi's Opinion: the Battleships should be Abolished and the Air Force should be Made Independent

On November 15, 1937, immediately after Onishi joined the transoceanic bombardment upon Nanjing, he gave a lecture at an economists' affairs club in Tokyo under the title of "On our Navy Air Force's Activity during China Incident." In this lecture he had given to the business leaders, Captain Onishi, the Chief of the Education Department of the Navy Air Force Headquarters, indicated that: the bombardment on the cities in the interior of the Chinese Continent had been a deviation either from the Navy's primary function of "securing the maritime power and the command of the seas" or from the Army's mission of "attacking the castle" or "performing field operations," and emphasized that: adopting such strategies as these were none other than new modes of warfare. This view of his, which had been expressed two years and a half before the Plan of No. 101 Operations was put into practice, is worth reading in finding out how such a conception as strategic bombing was brought into being:

> To cope with this Incident, our Navy Air Force has performed bombing raids in the interior of the Chinese Continent. But considering that the Navy's original duty is securing the maritime power and the command of the sea, as I mentioned at the beginning, our having attacked such cities as

Hankou, Nanchang and Nanjing had nothing to do with our command of the seas. In short, we might have done something unnecessary, as we might be criticized. Then should *those* have been done by the Army? No, I don't think so, either. Because what the Army should do would be in "attacking the enemy's castle and performing field operations"—or "capturing the enemy's strategic points or invading their territory—as the Army is doing in Northern China or in and around Shanghai. These actions, I think, are none other than what the Army should do as their true mission.

On the other hand, if it gives us an advantage to attack Nanjing, Guangdong, Hankou, Nanchang and so on directly by plane in order to achieve the purpose of the war, there will naturally occur a question as to who should engage in such performance—a newly-born mode of war-making. In former days when we had nothing like airplanes, we naturally had not had any such system as to make use of them at war. Now the time has come when we must decide upon what department should engage in this sort of new job. So far the Navy has done something like this, simply because they happened to have some ability to do so. In order to perform our original purpose of attacking the enemy's warship on the Pacific, our Navy planes have been so built as to make a long-distance flight in order to attack the enemy's warships on the Pacific, and then it happened that we came to face the China Incident. We could not say "no," even though fighting against China had not been within the scope of our job. We must do everything we can to achieve the purpose of this Incident. Our planes had not been brought into being in order to do such a job as this, but now that they have turned out to be useful in achieving *this* purpose, they are now being made use of very effectively. Because the Navy planes have usually been trained in the skies of the Pacific Ocean, they are readily able to fulfill their mission.

As to what we should do in the future in dealing with such force of arms as this, we shall have to find out a proper answer, whether we should start what might be called the Air Force Ministry or we should make the Navy go on doing what they have done this time, or we should make the Army start doing it. This is what is called "the Air Force issue" or "the issue for making Air Force independent.

Onishi, widely known as a supporter for abolishing battleships, criticized the on on ongoing plan of building a new Yamato-type battleship, calling it a white elephant or a tremendous loss not to turn it into aerial preparations, thus to have frequent arguments with those supporters of the warships who had constituted the mainstream of the military society. In those days, when the Sino-Japanese war broke out and when he was feeling more keenly the necessity for a greater substantiality of aerial armaments, it was only natural for Onishi to have pictured to himself an independent air force as the unit to perform the strategic bombardment.

As for this idea of making the air force independent, several months before he had given a lecture at the economists' affairs club in Tokyo—at the stage just before the Sino-Japanese War broke out—Onishi, the chief of the Educational Department at the Aerial Headquarters, had distributed in his Department a document entitled *A Study on the Aerial Preparations*, in which he had revealed his opinion that: "It is already outdated to think that the Navy is an organ to defend the state by depending on the military force whose mainstay is warships and other vessels," adding that: "the nucleus of the Navy should be turned into a genuine form of the Air Force, or the Navy itself should turn into the Air Force." This document was regarded as a nasty anonymous letter and an order was issued from the Bureau of Military Affairs, saying: "*that* document should be withdrawn," but Onishi himself did not seem to have concerned himself about it so much, and he never stopped advocating to the business leaders how the Air Force should make itself independent of the Navy:

> This is something very important, so both Army and Navy, instead of sticking to their own standpoints, should give a careful investigation from a point of view wider than the prospect only from the Navy or from the Army—in order to find out the most efficient way and the most economical way when seen from the national point of view. As for myself, I think the most practical way to realize *this* will be to adopt what the Navy has done this time by systematizing it and regarding it as the official stance.

As is seen here, Onishi Takijiro then—in the midst of those who had not had any other idea but to entrust their future command of the sea only to the battleship *Yamato* then under construction—had cut a conspicuous figure because of his awareness of the war potential of the airplane and its usage which was to be known later as "strategic bombing."

● The Navy's Opportunism and Adventurism

At the same time, however, this had exposed the Navy's opportunistic attitude through which they had allowed themselves to intervene in the Sino-Japanese War without having any principle of its own—as was once criticized by Ishihara Kanji, saying: "If the Army is compared to a robber, the Navy will be compared to a pickpocket." Unlike the Army that had been persistent in securing any territory—as its Guandong Army* was persistent in keeping Manchuria,* the Navy that had remained free from any such obsession of territorial expansion toward the Continent, could remain a step apart from the China issue. In other words, the Navy had never conformed to the Army as far as its policy on China was concerned. For the Navy, whose basic strategy was "*not* to wage war but to make itself a weight upon the Pacific," their armed intervention, which would lead to the provocation of the U.S. and the U.K., ought to have been out of question.

But those in high authority in the Navy, including the Minister of the Navy, Yonai Mitsumasa, could not resist their sense of rivalry against the Army who—unlike the Navy—had always been in the limelight (and that was reflected in their budget), and would have been dazzled at "a new mode of war in the new age" or the long range bombardments that had been made possible by the newly-produced middle-sized attack planes. On the wings of adventurism, they could no longer resist their impulse to extend their flight to Shanghai, Nanjing, Wuhan and even as far as Chongqing. Though it appeared paradoxical, the Navy, who had made the Pacific Ocean their imaginary front to fight against the U.S. and the U.K., was now geographically moving away from it, while in the field of politics and diplomacy, they were driving Japan into an abyss by closing the distance toward "the Pacific War."

One of the legs that had supported the Navy's inclination to take advantage of opportunities and their adventurism must have been the assertion to attach the great importance to the aerial capability or "to turn the Navy into the Air Force," as was soon supported also by Inoue Shigeyoshi or the idea of "turning the Navy into the Air Force" and the appearance of the long-distance bombers to realize that idea. On the other hand, the other leg had been placed in the mud of their arrogance that had come from their ignorance of and disdain toward the national self-determination and the anti-colonialism that had been aflame all over the Chinese Continent. Ikeda Kiyoshi wrote about this in his book, *The Navy & Japan*, published in Japan:

> If it happened that the Navy's policy toward China was at first less severe and less destructive than the Army's, it had come from the difference in their approach to China, *not* from their having valued the Chinese nationalism as they should. (omission) The greatest reason why after Lukou-qiao Incident[*] the Navy had failed to check the Army's arbitrary action and their extension of the front lines was because the Navy's view of China had not essentially been different from the Army's.

In their recognition of China, the leaders of the Navy were even more superficial and arrogant than those of the Army. Rear-Admiral Onishi, as was in the case of William Westmoreland, the commander of the Expeditionary Force in Vietnam in later years, might have been keenly feeling the shortage of their military potential then, but had never had any such self-reflection as to inquire about what that war was being made for or about the fundamental weaknesses found in the Japanese Military. Since it was impossible for them to have any such self-reflection as to take a skeptical view of the war itself—even in such a form as was taken by Inoue Shigeyoshi—Onishi Takijiro's prescience and intrepid courage had been so made from the beginning as to struggle in the mud through which the wartime history was going on.

Even though the Navy's having made light of China issues was not restricted only to Inoue and Onishi, since the greatest rationalist and the ablest leader of the Navy Air Force at that time had made themselves the planner and the operator of the strategic bombings on the bank of the Yangzi, it followed that: the Sino-Japanese War, the Japanese Navy and the Japan-U.S. War were to be connected in an inextricable form. Thus the No.101 Operations upon Chongqing turned out to be a powerful glue to keep them inseparable.

● **Under the Name of "an Attack on a Strategic Point," the Conception of Strategic Bombing was Formulated**

Two years and a half had passed since Captain Onishi referred to "the new mode of war in the new age" in his lecture. By the time the new strategy was being prepared under Onishi as the Commander of the Second United Air Force, the conception of strategic bombing retained by the Japanese Navy had ceased to be so casual as it used to be at the outset of the Sino-Japanese War. In one of the fields of aerial tactics, the concepts and the terms of "strategic-political attack" and "attack upon the strategic point" had already been introduced to be explicitly written down in the books of criteria and in the drill manuals. In *The Draft of A Sequel to the Order for the Important Naval Actions (the Air Battle Division)*—which had been sent to the Commander of each fleet, the Commander-in-Chief in each of the Naval Stations and the Port Admiral in each of the Important Ports on April 10, 1940, in the name of the vice chief of the Naval General Staff—we can see that: the conception of "strategic bombing" had been formulated under the name of "the attack on a strategic point." This draft having been distributed to the Fleet of the China Region, too, it was placed on Inoue's desk and on Onishi's, too. This *Air Battle Division* or an addition to *The Order for the Important Naval Actions*—which had been brought into being just before the Russo-Japanese War* to be made a cordon of the Navy—still retained the conception of "warship first / air force next," but as was explained at the opening: "This draft is prepared, expecting to be used tentatively in line with the current situations of air battles now making rapid progress, also expecting to be revised or supplemented." Here we can see their willingness to establish the base of aerial tactics, while adopting what they had learned at the battle line of China, characteristically giving much space on attacks upon important spots and the air forces with their own base. In that *Draft*, the attack on a strategic point was defined as follows:

It means the attack from the air upon such strategic points of the enemy nation as follows: military, political and economic centers; important resources; principal traffic lines and the like.

As for the execution of the attack on the strategic points, it was to be performed as follows:

No. 74: The attack shall be given, conforming to the progress of the strategy, mainly according to the strategic demand, upon the central organs of the enemy's military, political and economic systems, so that they may no longer work, or the enemy may find it hard to go on fighting because their important resources have been destroyed, while frustrating the enemy nation's will to fight so that their strategy will no longer work properly with their force of arms being prevented from moving around or their supply of war materials from being replenished.

Here we can see clearly the hard and fast principles, which may properly be called "The Three Principles in Strategic Bombings," which have remained valid even to this day. That is, the following features were clearly given: ① It is based on the strategic demand (made independent of the ground army's advancing operations) ② The enemy's military, political and economic central organs shall be attacked (regarding the capital and other important cities themselves as their target) ③ Frustrating the enemy nation's will to go on fighting (by employing the arms effective in killing or wounding the enemy).

These were the tactics that had already been applied upon Chongqing since May the year before, but when written down in a missive like this, it sounded grave enough. Even before the (British) Royal Air Force adopted the bombardment upon the city, calling it "regional bombing," the Japanese Navy had allowed themselves to apply indiscriminate bombings upon the Chinese cities, calling it "bombing upon the strategic point." As long as the introduction of the conception of strategic bombing was concerned, Japan was apparently on the side of the originator-offender, and it was more than four years later that the U.S.—as the offender of the strategic bombings upon Japan—officially adopted that conception. *The Sequel to the Order for the Important Naval Action* had given another stipulation, succeeding to the prescription No. 74 mentioned before:

No. 76: The attack upon the strategic point shall be given by a large unit to a fierce extent, exposing the enemy to persistent assaults, day and night, if necessary. According to the aim of the strategy, a proper amount of military force shall be applied, while an appropriate method of attack shall be adopted.

The No.101 Operations applied to the interior of Sichuan Province was literally "a tentative appliance" of *The Sequal to The Order for the Important*

Naval Actions and the prescribed words and phrases were to be turned to the citizens of Chongqing "to a fierce extent" in the form of "persistent assaults."

The Unfolding of No.101 Operations

● **The Navy as the Mainstay of Flame Attack**
The bombardments upon the interior of Sichuan Province performed under the name of No.101 operations started on May 18, 1940, and lasted till September 4. That was a long series of air raids performed 72 times, spending 112 days. As for the bombardments upon Chongqing as the anti-Japanese capital, including its urban areas and its industrial areas, intending to "frustrate the enemy nation's morale," they lasted for ninety days from May 26 to August 23. In *The Navy's Strategy in China Region (2)* in *The Library of War History* edited by the Library of War History in the Defense Agency of Japan, the significance of No. 101 Operations was summarized as follows:

During the winter, the Fleet of the China Region was being trained, waiting for the season of fine weather to come round, since they had expected to perform a large-scaled aerial strategy or what was called "No. 101 Operations," eagerly supported by the central government in Tokyo, and on May 1, the 1ˢᵗ United Air Force was again sent to join the Fleet of the China Region. The Army also was to cooperate with the Navy.

For Japan, impatient to bring the China Incidents to an early settlement, this was the best concrete measure available at that time.

During May, the Navy had sent about 130 middle-sized attack bombers to the Hankou region. The bombers' capacity having been improved, remarkable progress was seen in climbing power and high-altitude flight. The Zero fighters as their secret weapons, though still remaining unfinished, came to join them from the middle of the operations to demonstrate their power. As for the personnel, the first-class members were collected, and it appeared as if all the able ones available in the Navy Air Force were brought together.

Great was the damage given to the enemy by the large-scaled operations that lasted for more than three months. But as for the crucial purpose of reducing the Chongqing Administration to submission, not even a sign of it could be seen.

Meanwhile the total number of the planes employed in attacking what the Japanese military called "military facilities in and around Chongqing City" was recorded as follows:

The Navy   1,737 planes

The Army   286 planes

As for the tonnage of bombers dropped:

The Navy   1,280.81 tons

The Army   124.85 tons

As for the kinds of bombs dropped, the Navy's was six kinds; the Army's was four kinds. The kinds and the amount of the bombs were as follows:

The Navy

No.6 (the 97-type No.6 land bombs = 60kg) 6,688 rounds

No.7 (the 98-type No.7-6 incendiary bombs) 184 rounds

No.25 (the 98-type No. 25 land bombs = 250kg) 2,474 rounds

No.30 (No.30 land bombs = 300kg) 64 rounds

No.80 (No.80 land bombs = 800kg) 278 rounds

Ka 4 balls (the Army 100-type 50kg aerial incendiary bombs)

131 rounds

The total = 9,819 rounds

The Army

50kg-bombs = 259 rounds

100kg-bombs = 664 rounds

250kg-bombs = 182 rounds

Hand grenades = 96 rounds

The total = 1,201 rounds

The total of the Army & the Navy: 11,020 rounds

(*The General Outline of the No.101 Operations*,
reported by the Headquarters of the United Air Raid Unit)

The most frequently used bombs were destructive ones of 60kg and 250kg in weight. Their outburst of bombardment by bomb-blasts and the effect of scattered shell fragments were such that they mowed down wooden houses and small buildings and killed or injured those who were within a one-hundred-meter to two-hundred-meter radius. The 800kg-bombs, which had been brought into being by modifying the principal guns—40cm across for the battleship, into the ones to be used on the land, were of the largest scale in the world at that time, and their aim was to bring a high-rise building to crumble down by the effect of earthquake caused by their hit upon it. Usually, a middle-sized bomber was able to carry twelve bombs in case they were of 60kg only; if mixed with 250kg bombs, one No.25 and six No.6 or two No.25 and three No.6 were combined, and the rest was for incendiary bombs. In case of a 800kg bomb, carrying a single bomb was all the middle-sized bomber could do

As for the incendiary bombs, two kinds—the 98-type No.7-6-1 and No.7-6-2—were adopted by the Navy; one kind—the 1,00-type 50kg—by the Army. They were mainly used by the Navy Air Force. The Army Air Force, which was much smaller both in the number of missions and in the volume of bombs to be dropped, had given greater priority to destructive bombs than to incendiary bombs.

This meant that: the flame-attacks upon Chongqing were mainly performed by the Navy. The Navy made much use of incendiary bombs in 1939, and in the following year, when they heard of the Army's having developed a new type of incendiary bomb (ka 4 bomb), they at once took it over and tried it upon Chongqing, even before the Army gave it a temporary official name.

● **A New Type of Incendiary Bomb was Brought into Being**

The 98-type No.7-6 bomb No.1 was brought into being from electron (92~96% of magnesium, 4~8% of aluminum), and thermite (made from 76% of powdered iron oxide & 24% of powdered aluminum), and No.2 of the same bomb was an improved one stuffed with solid fat and oil mixed with benzin and paraffin around the thermite, and when ignited, the fat and oil melted and spread itself on and on. The type No.1 had always been among the standard equipments of the Navy Air Force since the early stage of the Sino-Japanese War, and the Second and the Third United Air Force had usually been supplied with 300 rounds and Takao Air Force with 100 rounds, but as for the efficiency of them, they had not been rated so high. The incendiary bomb No. 7-6-1 had been so made—with 0.3 second slow-motion fuse—as to shoot through the roof of a fairly strong building, get ignited inside it and go up in flames, but in China there were not so many sturdy military landmarks, and if it fell on a wooden building, it gave neither bomb clouds nor fire, and those in the plane were quite likely to judge it a misfire. There were many that had fallen flat because the fuse failed to work because of the shortage of shock at the moment of impact.

This led the Navy Air Force Headquarters to start experiments to develop such an incendiary bomb as to be applicable to the ordinary private house, preferably with no waiting time, as was recorded on December 1, 1938 in the *Diary of China Incident* kept by the Navy Air Force Headquarters, and what they finally got in April in the following year was the 98-type No.7-6 bomb Ⅱ. This type was not only stuffed with a greasy base but also was equipped with explosive fuse (with no time to wait before it went into action). In April, 1939, the Headquarter of the Air Force sent the operating manual for using this new type of incendiary bomb—No.7-6-2—to the Navy Air Force Headquarters in China, while they ordered the Aerial Technological Factory to produce 3,000 bombs of this type, as was recorded in the *Diary* mentioned before.

In the bombardments upon Chongqing in 1939, therefore, there were two kinds of incendiary bombs employed, but in the Plan of No.101 Operations in 1940, what was commonly called *ka 4* balls (the 100-type 50kg incendiary bombs) were also added. They were large-sized bombs the Army had been developing in place of the old types of incendiary bombs (the 93-type 1kg & the 97-type 2kg), and since its iron ball had been stuffed with pieces of rubber that had absorbed a yellow phosphorus solution, when it burst violently, the pieces of rubber turned into flaming balls and scattered for 100 meters in every direction. Yellow phosphorus in the air was led to spontaneous combustion, and it caused the people to get burnt, while its offensive smell and tremendous smoking were effective to cause people to feel fear. Its flash point being high, it was considered a flaw, but when it stuck to something inflammable, it was hard to extinguish; if it got into human flesh, it kept smoldering there, keeping the unfortunate suffering from terrible pain. If this type of incendiary bomb was to be the predecessor of a napalm bomb, the *ka 4* ball might be called a prototype of white phosphorus bomb.

Since the United Air Raids Corps at Hankou had placed their aim at destroying the function of the capital, they had been fully aware of the effectiveness and necessity of the incendiary bombs, and when they heard of the Army having succeeded in producing the *ka 4* balls, they at once took them over and used it experimentally in the No. 101 Operation. Great was its effect, and this even led to the fact that: toward the end of that operation, Yamaguchi Tamon, the Commander of the United Corps for Air Raids (the Commander of the First United Air Force) sent a top secret telegram to the Headquarters of the Navy Air Force: "In carrying out this strategy successfully, we are quite anxious to obtain powerful incendiary bombs. So I hope you will thoughtfully arrange this matter so that we may be supplied with "*ka 4* bombs" or even more powerful incendiary bombs as soon as possible." This does tell us how tenacious they were in reducing the enemy's capital to ashes—in subduing the Chongqing Administration.

● **"The Hours of Being Bombed" had Become Part of their Daily Life**

Thus the No. 101 Operations—in the length of its term, in the scale of war potential put into it, and in the variety and novelty of the bombs used in it— was to open up a new scope in the history of Japan's aerial strategy. But for the citizens of Chongqing, even if they had been prepared for the resumption of the aerial attack they would suffer as soon as the foggy season was over, they had never imagined that the terrors that came falling from the skies of Chongqing would have kept them in such an ordeal for such a long period of time.

The area of the basin of the Yangzi in the southwest of Sichuan Province— where Chongqing is situated—is known for its high temperature and humidity, just as Nanjing and Wuhan are. A long series of summer days, whose average daytime temperature is 36.5℃, whose humidity is over 80% with no wind, suddenly comes to stay on and on, making a sharp contrast with the foggy season, until at last autumn sets in. People, weary of this unwelcome season, used to call it "the season even the sparrows come falling from the sky." Thus, trying to outlive this uncomfortable season, those who had kept all the doors removed from the house, used to take their bedstead into the street at night, trying to get any coolness available there. But the citizens of Chongqing *now* in that national emergency were to spend their three summers in the even more humid underground cave as their air raid shelter. It was much more sweleringly hot there than on the ground, but at least they could remain safe from being bombed, and it was easily bearable, comparing it with the terrible heat of the incendiary bombs that came falling from the sky. During those three years, the infant mortality in Chongqing was high, obviously because of the very poor quality of sanitary conditions in that half-underground life, adding to the deaths brought about by the bombardments upon the city.

Xiao Jianxiang, who grew up to be a writer, had lived in Chongqing for ten years since his eighth year to seventeenth, visited there in the summer of 1986 after a lapse of dozens of years and visited his old primary school, and had his own answer papers and a list of students' records found out only to get surprised at how badly he was doing at school. What surprised him even more was the fact that what he and his classmates were learning then was simply too elemental. As a matter of fact, they had no time to learn anything. They spent most of their school days in the cave as the air-raid shelter. By recalling what they were doing every day, he was able to convince himself of everything. Seeing that the following was one of the questions for an examination in mathematics in those days, one would easily be able to imagine what their daily life was like:

At the top of Biwa-shan Hill, a child is counting the Japanese planes. When he counted them, assuming that they were in a three-plane formation, he had two planes left over. Counting them again, assuming they were in a five-plane formation, he again had two left over. Then he assumed they were in a seven-plane formation, and he had two left over. How many Japanese planes are there?

Biwa-shan, 345m high, is the highest hill in Shizhong (City's Central) Ward, and it was practically improbable in those days for a child to climb to its top. But the teacher who prepared this examination question would have liked his pupil to be released from the cave they had always been confined to, even through this question he had made for them. As for his having brought Japanese planes here, he might have expected that his pupils would seriously tackle with this question, since the Japanese planes used to be something that had attracted the greatest concern of those living in Chongqing at that time. Anyway, the No. 101 Operations had come into every phase of the daily life of the people in Chongqing, unduly putting them under its control. Men and women and children could not help accepting it, adjusting themselves to it, while making "the bombing hours" a part of their daily life.

● **"No.101 Operations are Comparable with the Battle of the Japan Sea*"**
At the Hankou Base, as the opening of the No.101 Operations was approaching, both officers and men had their morale being lifted even more, keeping their mind pointing to the interior of Sichuan Province—especially to the Anti-Japanese Capital of Chongqing. Both the Headquarters in Tokyo and those who were going to get into the planes had shared the same view that: the strategy they were about to perform was the best way to "the early settlement of the China Incident" by reducing Jiang Jieshi's Administration to submission. The Prime Minister was Yonai Mitsumasa, who used to be the Minister of the Navy when the Sino-Japanese War broke out (1937) and remained at the same chair when they gave the air raids on 5.3. & 5.4 the year before (1939). And the Chief of Staff in the Local Department of the Supreme Direction was Inoue Shigeyoshi, who used to be the chief of the Bureau of Naval Affairs under Yonai when he was the Navy Minister. Since then, Inoue having been known as Yonai's right-hand man, there could hardly be any room for causing any difference in their recognition in circumstances and in their Plan of Operations. The Navy's Central Agency had shown even their positive attitude in assisting the Local Department by adding forty-eight more middle-sized attack bombers than the number which had been fixed by the central agreement of the Army and the Navy. As for the mechanical equipment and materials of the middle-sized attack bombers, too, the initial 21 type was replaced by the 23 type, thus the engine's output was increased, and shooting equipment was strengthened (with the gun emplacement with a streamlined windbreaker upon it), thus the bombers in the formation had been able to raise their upper limit of operating height from 5,500m to 7,000m.

In the flagship Izumo floating on the Huangbu Bay in Shanghai, there were two officers were looking forward to what the No. 101 Operations would turn out. They were Commander-in-Chief of the Fleet of the China Region, Admiral Shimada Shigetaro, and the Chief of Staff, Vice-Admiral Inoue Shigeyoshi. Their aides were the assistant chief of staff, Rear-Admiral Nakamura Toshihisa, and a senior staff officer, Commander Yamamoto Yoshio, and below them came staff officers from several sections. All the office work was being carried out by Inoue, the chief of staff, and Yamamoto, a senior staff officer. Commander-in-Chief Shimada had arrived to take up that new position of his, eagerly expressing his intention to "settle the China Incident during my term," and he was energetic in inspecting the corps in the front line to encourage the officers and men. The chief of staff Inoue was also unusually eager to carry out the operations, as was revealed in one of the inspections he had made at that time. The following is what was recorded in *A Memoir of a Navy Officer* left by Lieutenant Commander Nakayama Sadayoshi, the then administrative staff officer of the Fleet Headquarters, who had once accompanied Inoue in his business trip to Tokyo in place of his aide-de-camp:

> The Chief of Staff Inoue, who visited the Naval General Staff, met the First Chief in charge of the operations, Rear-Admiral Ugaki Matome, and stated how the Operations were going on in the Fleet of the China Region, raising several points that needed some consideration, while expressing his several requests to the Central Government. More than a dozen people from the relevant bureaus in the Navy Ministry and the Naval General Staff were also present, making a note eagerly.
>
> The Chief of Staff told how they had emphasized their strategy of attacking on the hinterland of China by the Navy Air Force, expressing his conviction that: *that* would be the key to put an end to the Sino-Japanese War, just as Admiral Togo's having won the Battle of the Japan Sea* did lead to the victory of the Russo-Japanese War.*

As for what had led Inoue Shigeyoshi to compare the 101 Operations with the Battle on the Japan Sea fought toward the end of the Russo-Japanese War (1904-5), he himself had not given any explanation. Did he wish to stress his own idea that: its success or failure would be so decisive to the outcome of the war? Or did he wish to assert that: such a decisive battle as was comparable with the Battle of the Japan Sea would never occur from then on without taking a form of such a decisive series of aerial battles as No. 101 Operations? We can take either of them, but whichever we may take, the unusual resolution he had made then remained unchanged.

Such great expectations the Central Government and the Headquarters of the Fleet had placed upon the Operations could not help being felt by those in the Field Headquarters.

Lieutenant Iwaya Fumio was a divisional officer of Kanoya Air Corps that belonged to the First United Air Corps. Since the early stage of the Sino-Japanese War, he fought on successive fronts by piloting a carrier-based attack bomber, and now on May 11, he came advancing to Hankou Air Base. Lieutenant Iwaya had recorded in his own book entitled *The Middle-Sized Attack Planes* a resolution made by Rear-Admiral Yamaguchi Tamon as the Commander of the First United Air Corps. Commander Yamaguchi now was to serve concurrently as Commander of the United Air Raid Unit and the First United Air Corps, and together with Onishi Takijiro as the Commander of the Second United Air Corps, were to stand at the front to take command in performing No. 101 Operations. Thus Commander Yamaguchi, facing Lieutenant Iwaya and other crew members who were to get on the middle-sized air-raiders, expressed his resolution to promote their aerial attack to overthrow Jiang's Administration at a single stroke and declared that: this plan of operations should be called No. 101 Operations.

- **Commander Yamaguchi's Address of Admonition: "Let them Cut our Flesh so We may Cut their Bones."**

Immediately after the First United Air Corps advanced into Hankou, Commander Yamaguchi gathered those whose ranks were above that of warrant officers from both Kanoya Air Corps and Takao Air Corps together in one place, and again declared that: Taking this opportunity when the First United Air Force's land-attack corps have advanced into Hankou, all of our air forces in China shall concentrate all of our aerial force of arms upon Chongqing so that we may send the Chinese Administration into disintegration. And in order to achieve this purpose, he said, he was prepared to adopt *that* art of swordsmanship invented by Chiba Shusaku, a distinguished Japanese swordsman in mid-19th Century: "to cut their bones by letting our flesh cut." On that evening when we heard that admonitory speech of his, the curtain of No.101 Operations was pulled open.

—*A History on the Navy Air Force (4) in the Library of War History*

In that same speech, Commander Yamaguchi also said, encouraging his airmen: "Let Chongqing go down even before Paris and London."

Onishi Takijiro and Yamaguchi Tamon were contemporaries at the

Naval Academy, but Onishi having been outdone by Yamaguchi in being commissioned to be Rear-Admiral, it is easily imaginable that the admonition he gave to his men as the chief of staff of the United Air-Raid Corps and as the Commander of the Second United Air Corps would have been even more ardent in tone. Trembling with anticipation, he ought to have been anxiously waiting for the arrival of the season of stable weather. Even if seniority was given to Yamaguchi Tamon, the Second United Air Corps placed under Onishi Takijiro had nearly twice as many middle-sized bombers as the First United Air Corps.

The United Air Raid Corps' formation and deployment of military force were as follows, as had already been decided by the agreement on May 13, 1940, between the Army and the Navy:

The First United Air Corps Headquartered at Hankou Air Base
    Kanoya Air Corps (24 middle-sized attack planes) at Hankou
    Takao Air Corps (24 middle-sized attack planes) at Hankou
The Second United Air Corps Headquarters at Hankou Air Base
    The 13th Air Corps (42 middle-sized attack planes) at Hankou
    The 15th Air Corps (42 middle-sized attack planes) at Xiaogan

For a total of 132 middle-sized attack bombers, they had only two runways at Hankou, and this led them to use Xiaogan Air Port as their second base, 50km away northwest. But since more and more land-scout planes, carrier-based fighters and carrier-based attack bombers came to join them along with army planes, the air force in Hankou had been so bloated as "the danger of piled-up eggs" was pointed out.

The Army Air Force was not able to collect so much force as the Navy Air Force, but at the flight base at Yuncheng (Shanxi Province—800km to Chongqing) they set up the Command Post for the Third Flight Group, and under the leadership of Major General Kinoshita Satoshi, they started the 60th Squadron consisting of 582 airmen under Lieutenant Colonel Ogawa Shojiro as Squadron Chief, with 54 heavy bombers of 97 type. Thus the total of the bombers of the Army and the Navy had become 186.

On May 10, an order of operations was issued from Inoue, the chief of staff at the Fleet of the China Region, to Commander Yamaguchi of the United Air Raid Corps (the telegram order No.62 from the Fleet Headquarters of the China

Region) :

(1) From the mid-May onward, the United Air Raid Corps, co-operating with the Army Air Corps, shall exterminate the enemy air force in the region of Sichuan Province, and destroy the main military facilities and political institutions in the same Province.

(2) As for how the Navy and Army Air Forces should cooperate, it shall depend on the agreement reached by the Commanders of the United Air Raid Corps and the Commander of the Third Flight Group.

(3) This strategy shall be called No.101 Operations.

According to this order issued by the Fleet of the China Region, the Headquarters at Hankou decided on a plan of operations and an implementation manual for their attack. The whole strategy was divided into two steps: the first step was to exterminate all the Chinese Air Forces' flight bases in the suburbs of Chongqing; then after having secured supremacy in the air by depriving the enemy of all of their aerial capability, the second step of a carpet bombing raid upon the urban area was to be taken. The term of operations was about three months. Then the direction was issued: "The first attack upon Chongqing shall be given on May 17.

The Plan of Operations went as follows:

(1) The first thing shall be to attack the base of their bombers in order to dispirit them.

(2) In the first stage, the enemy's fighter planes shall be wiped out of the skies of Chongqing, and after having won the command of the air, their administrative and military organizations shall be destroyed to a thorough extent.

After having achieved sufficient results in the first stage, the second stage shall be unfolded. The same strategy shall be adopted in Chengdu, too.

Judging from the information gathered by the surveillance flights and others, a little more than 100 bombers either light or heavy, which could be a menace to Hankou Air Base, were waiting at Chengdu, Lanzhou and Yibin, while the corps of 120 fighter planes that could be a menace to the bombing action of this side had been judged to be deployed at Chengdu, Chongqing, Kunming and Lanzhou. Their military capability, including some regular units that had been sent from the Soviet Union, was formidable enough, and this had led to the plan of actions in No.101 Operations mentioned above in (1) and (2). Though not mentioned overly, their plan of action had included attacking Chengdu, too, beforehand, since it was expected to be turned into the anti-Japanese capital if Chongqing had thoroughly been disrupted.

● **"The Regular Flight to Chongqing" shall be Sent Days and Nights**

In the bombardment of Chongqing as the core of No. 101 Operations, there were a couple of new offensive movements adopted: the attack shall be given every day and preferably every night, as long as weather and force of arms permitted, and these had expressly been stipulated in the agreement made by the Army and the Navy units on the spot, too, (as is seen in the Agreement, dated May 29, made between the Chief of Staff of the Third Flight Group and the Chief of Staff Officers of the United Air Raid Corps).

> During the period when this agreement is valid, both Army Air Corps and Navy Air Corps shall point to the city of Chongqing and its neighborhood (keeping away as much as possible from the third powers' rights and interests), to keep attacking as long as the force of arms and weather permit.
>
> Both Army and Navy shall do their best in performing continuous attack day and night, making use of the moonlight which is available since mid-June.

It was not long before the flight crew began to call this tactics to keep the people in the air-raid caves day and night "taking daily care of Chongqing" or "regular flight to Chongqing," while the Chinese called it "exhaustion bombing." That was a new type of strategy adopted to exhaust the people's neuron and physical strength till they admitted their defeat. If they found it too unbearable, all they could do would make themselves surrender. That was what No.101 Operations had aimed at. That was also a war of nerves fought between those on the earth and those in the sky.

How ahead of the times this strategy was would be proved by the fact that— three years later or in January, 1943, at "the Casablanca Conference" held in

North Africa—those top leaders of the U.S. and the U.K. came to decide upon their keeping their strategic bombings upon Germany on a day-and-night shift system—the nighttime regional bombings by the Royal Air Force and the daytime precise bombings by the U.S. Air Force. Ira Eaker, the proposer of this idea, the commander of the U.S. 8th Air Force—the same general that was also to leave his name in the decision of dropping the atomic bomb upon Hiroshima—expressed the merit of this idea: "If we were to chase those devils for 24 hours on end every day, we can deprive the German Army's air defense setup of their rest hours." This, having impressed Churchill, who was fond of witty remarks, led to the realization of what was called "round-the-clock bombing." Even before that, however, Japanese military had clearly worked out the same kind of tactics of chasing the innocent citizens around by their bombings day and night, even though the scale still remained less large.

● **The Start of No.101 Operations**

No.101 Operations started on May 18, one day later than expected. The first two days were spent in attacking the fighter planes at the bases of such cities as Chengdu, Yibin and Liangshan that lay around Chongqing. The middle-sized bombers, while receiving the report from the scout planes flying ahead and adjusting the timing by making use of their ability to stay in the air, entered the airspace of the airbase, and after waiting for the enemy planes in the air to make a landing after having exhausted all their fuel, rushed over the air port to perform their bombardment. During a couple of days, thirteen enemy planes were reported to have burst into flames while the airports were destroyed, as was reported by the leader of the squadron.

It was as early as on the third day when the aim of their attack was pointed to Chongqing. On the nights from May 20 to 22, after having performed a night attack upon a couple of airports of Baifuyi Station and of Guangyangba, they began to attack the urban area since the fourth attack on May 26. On the 26 and the 27, the new urban areas, Xiaolongkan and Ciqikou under the construction around Shizong (City's Central) Ward, were bombed. Such achievements as the Central Telegraph Office having been totally destroyed, the Broadcasting Station having been smashed up, the Companies of *Zhongyang Ri Bao* (Central Daily News) and *Kuoming Gong Bao* (National Official Bulletin) having been destroyed, were also brought by the Japanese military officers serving in

Shanghai as "the information derived from reliable quarters." The international city, Shanghai, being a major collection and distribution center of information concerning China, *the Information from the Chief Military Officer in Shanghai* was being entrusted as materials to judge such military achievements as follows:

1) The Central Telegraph Office was totally destroyed; the Relay Broadcasting Station was ruined; the personnel of each newspaper company was wiped out; a couple of factories for manufacturing machine-gun tractors were ruined; a power magazine was razed to the ground; the military academy was seriously damaged.

2) This air raid caused a panic on the side of Chongqing, and for fear of the truth being exposed, they took such a step as to put censorship on correspondence, thus to prevent the third powers from publishing the facts.

3) This air raid had taken the Chinese side by surprise.

4) The Chongqing side has held a view that Japan made this plan on the basis of precise information obtained from a certain foreign correspondent resident in Chongqing.

Certainly, as was mentioned in *the Information form the Chief Military Officer in Shanghai*, the newspapers published in Chongqing had not reported any such damages as these. All the articles they had carried as the news distributed from the Central News Agency placed directly under Jiang Jieshi were: "Our Air Force bravely made an attack on the enemy planes, and this led them to beat a hasty retreat." The governmental control had thoroughly been working not only on the Communists' activities but also on the information on the war situation.

After having deprived the Chinese Air Force of their command of the air, the attack target was turned to the urban area. Before noon on May 28, the citizens of Chongqing were made to shudder up at the first full-scale air raid after the foggy season was over. The 94 middle-sized attack planes of the United Air Raid Corps, which had taken off at Hankou Air Base, entered the skies of Chongqing from three directions to perform the air raids upon the three parts in the urban area. They were:

The First Attack Corps consisting of 32 planes from the 13th Corps

(led by Lieutenant-Commander Kotani Yuji)
The Second Attack Corps consisting of 26 planes from the 15th Corps
(led by Lieutenant-Commander Mihara Gen-ichi)
The Third Attack Corps consisting of 36 planes from the First United Air Corps
(led by Lieutenant-Commander Yamanoue Shotaro)

As for the Commander of them all, the chief of the 13th Flying Corps, Lieutenant Commander Awanohara Hitoshi was appointed. In the Third Attack Corps, Lieutenant Iwaya Fumio from Takao Air Corps, the author of *The Middle-Sized Attack Plane,* had joined as the leader of the Fourth Group of the nine middle-sized attack planes. It was cloudy in Hankou district. But it was judged: "No problem in performing the air raid." As for the attack targets, the third group (the 36 planes from the First United Air Corps from Takao Air Corps and Kanoya Air Corps) was to make a bombing raid upon Guangyangba Air Base lying in their way in front of the entrance to Chongqing; the second group consisting of the 26 planes was aiming at the industrial area, especially in and around Jinling Military Factory in Jiangbei (North of the Jialing) District that faced Shizong (City's Central) Ward with the Jialing in between; the first group of 32 planes was to make a bombing raid in and around Chuandong Normal School. In other words, the attacks performed that day were for wiping out the enemy's air base and for attacking a strategic point (the bombing upon an urban area) at the same time—a transitional form toward an intensive attack upon the urban area.

The three attack corps had taken off at Hankou or at Kaogan one after another from 6:30 to 7:30 and while receiving the information on the movements of the enemy from the scout planes that had flown ahead to the sky of their attack target, they flew at their intended point. As the sun rose higher and as they flew west, they found the sky clearing, and by the time they reached Zhong Prefecture a little closer to Chongqing than to Wuhan, the ceiling was improved to be 5,000m, the degree of cloudiness was recovered to 5, and the visibility became recovered up to 36km. This led the three commanders of the corps to make their final decision to attack their first aim.

● **The Difference of Casualties and Damages Caused Above or Below**
the Clouds

Among them, the First Attack Corps under Lieutenant-Commander Kotani (from the 13th corps) in their 32 planes approached Chongqing from due north by taking more or less northerly course of Hankou—Zhonxuan—Hechuan, retaining the standard flight altitude of 3,500m, rushed to the sky of Shizong (City's Central) Ward of Chongqing at zero hour of 13:10 (11:10 local time). According to the 13th corps' *Precise Report on the Attacks & Battles on Chongqing* (the 6th Attack on May 28 in the 15th year of Showa (1940)), they were "blessed with fine weather," and they "went on with their No.101 Operations," as follows:

This day, all of our middle-sized attack bombers and five land scout planes performed the 6th attack upon Chongqing.

◎ The Attack Corps (Commander-in-Chief: Lieutenant Commander

Awanohara)

The 1st Attack Corps: 13th Corps, 32 middle-sized attack planes

(led by Lieutenant Commander Kotani)

The 2nd Attack Corps: 15th Corps, 26 middle-sized attack planes

(led by Lieutenant Commander Mihara)

The 3rd Attack Corps: 1st United Corps, 36 middle-sized attack planes

(led by Lieutenant Commander Yamanoue)

Each of them left its base during the hour from 9:30 to 10:30. The 1st and 2nd Attack Corps flew to the northern sky of Chongqing, while the 3rd Attack Corps flew to the southern sky of it. They waited there.

At 13:10, having received the order to make a dash, they flew in from northwestern sky to bomb upon Chongqing Chuandong Normal School District with several military installations in it, spending all of the 128 bombs (No.25 & No.26) to burst that area to cause four fires. On our way back, one of our planes dropped some remaining bombs (No.25-1) exactly upon Laifeng Air Port.

◎Air Battle

After the bombings by the 1st Attack Corps were over, we had an air battle with seven E15 fighters and one of them was brought down (though uncertain). Four of them persistently followed us for about thirty minutes;

one of them kept following us as far as the vicinity of Laifeng.

◎Ground Fire

The 1st and the 2nd Attack Corps received heavy fire—before and after our attack—from high-angle guns and machine guns.

◎Damage

The 1st Attack Corps had six planes bombed; one of them had 26 shots. Four planes were shot by ground fire.

The 1st Attack Corps' bombing height was 6,200m. Their speed per hour was 182km. While crossing the skies of Chongqing from northwest to southwest in 160 degrees, they dropped 62 bombs of 250kg and 128 bombs of 60kg, and they left the sky of their target area, while slipping the pursuit of E15 fighters built in the Soviet Union. According to their detailed report, "the accuracy rate of our bombing was 100 percent, causing five fires." The bullets of machine-guns consumed in the air war and strafing were 10,810 balls of 7.7mm across and 690 balls of 20mm across. In average, one plane consumed 337 balls of 7.7mm across and 21 balls of 20mm across. At 3:20 p.m. all the planes returned to Hankou W Base. The other Attack Corps, too, returned to W Base or to Kaogan Base about the same time. The 3rd Attack Corps that raided Guangyangba Air Base had had seven planes damaged during their air battle, but the damages were all judged not so serious, and reparable at their own airport. None of the crew members were dead or injured.

Below the clouds, however, things were totally different. Especially the neighborhood of Chuandong Normal School in Shizhong (City's Central) Ward had to suffer a great damage by the concentrated attacks of 250kg and 60kg bombshells. The numbers of deaths and injuries were 178 and 408 respectively. (*The Statistical Chart of the Damages & Casualties Caused by the Air Raids in Various Parts of Sichuan Province in the 29th Year of the Republic of China (1940)*).

The area where Chuandong Normal School was situated was about the middle of "the Peninsula of the Rivers," and even though it was well within Shizhong Ward, it used to be outside the walls of the ancient castle. It was only after the recent completion of the new road brought into being around the peninsula that this area began to be urbanized rapidly as a part of the new capital brought about by Jiang Jieshi. Certainly in that neighborhood, there was the Nationalist Party's Headquarters—which is now turned into the People's Government of Chongqing City—and the Municipal Government and many other governmental organizations. Before the transference of the capital, this area used to be known as an educational district with Chuandong Normal School, Bashu Middle School and Bashu Elementary School, but at that time Chuandon Normal School had housed one of the two Special Service Agencies or "the Chinese Nationalist Party's Central Executive Committee's Investigation & Statistics Bureau"—known as *Zhong Tong*"—directed by the Brothers Chen Guofu and Lifu, in order to keep watch on Zhou Enlai and other Communist elements, while performing white terror. In that sense, that neighborhood might be called "a political and military center" or "a site of the government organizations," but they could not be called military facilities, and seen from a broader view, they occupied only a very small part of that area and most of the inhabitants there were either the refugees from the wartime fires or those who had arrived there only after Chongqing was turned into the anti-Japanese capital.

Among those who were killed then were seven of the staff of Fudan University, including Professor Sun Hanbing as the head of the academic affairs section. They had been hit directly by a bomb. Professor Sun, who had once studied at Washington University in the U.S., was thirty-nine years old when he was received at the law school of Fudan University, and he had come up all the way from Shanghai as the original seat of the University, after having moved here and there along the Yangzi, only to be killed *then* and *there* in the line of duty. Behind him were left Mrs. Sun and their four children, as was reported by *Xin Hua Ri Bao* (*New China Daily*).

● **A Near Hit on the U.S. Warship *Tutuila***

The first air raid on the urban area of Chongqing according to No.101 Operations had been observed through the windows of the U.S. Embassy in China. The Ambassador, Nelson Johnson, sent a telegram at 7 that night to his chief in Washington—Cordell Hull, the Secretary of the State:

> The Japanese this morning for the first time in several months bombed portions of Chungking city proper, two squadrons of planes dropping bombs in various business and residential areas. It is estimated that civilian

casualties will number several hundred. As far as the embassy can ascertain, all the Americans are safe. One bomb fell at an estimated distance of 400 yards from the US *Tutuila* while bombs fell in the vicinity of the installation of the Standard-Vacuum Oil Company.

Repeated to Peiping, Hankou, Shanghai. Shanghai please repeat to Tokyo.

Jhonson

Upon the Yangzi, which could be seen just below one's eyes in the U.S. Embassy, one could see a gunboat *Tutuila* for fluvial navigation at anchor with Lieutenant Kemp Tolley and others on board. It had been at anchor there as a symbol of the protection of the U.S.' rights and interests in China and as a proof of the U.S.' support to China. Below the line along which the Japan's first group of the air raiders had flown from northwest to southeast, *Tutuila* had been floating. According to the report of *Zhongyang Tongxun-she* (Central News Agency), many of the bombs that had been dropped that day went into the river, and it was probably one of them that had been mentioned by the ambassador in his telegram.

Ambassador Johnson sent a telegram to Washington on June 1 and 2, too, giving even more detailed information, which included the following notice:

I carefully observed Japanese bombers on May 28 and did not observe any (attempt?) on the part of those planes which flew over the city to reach military objectives. Bombs dropped within the city 500 miles from any Japanese force that might occupy it. Anti-aircraft cannon cannot by any stretch of imagination be considered offensive weapons.

On another telegram to Washington, Ambassador Johnson drew a city map and jotted down the spots where the bombs had been dropped. This led him to find that most of the bombs had fallen so close to the French Embassy and the Soviet Union's Embassy, and this led him to report that it was a sheer miracle that those embassies had escaped danger.

From this day onward, the U.S. Ambassador in Chongqing made it a rule to count the number of Japanese planes at every air raid they performed and reported to Washington what sorts of damages they had given. It was practically impossible for anyone to tell one's military aims from the urban area or from the Third Powers' rights and interests. So despite the strict orders given by the chief of staff, Inoue Shigeyoshi, it was not long before the U.S. gunboat *Tutuila* began to be threatened by columns of water caused by the near hits upon it. Thus the distance between *Tutuila* and the columns of water had come to reflect a rise of tension and confrontation in the U.S.-Japanese relations.

A Nightmare of the U.S. Gunboat *Panay*'s Case

● **Taking care not to Damage the Third Powers' Rights and Interests**

If the No.101 Operations, by dint of which the Japanese military were trying to capture the enemy's capital, were compared to the Battle on the Japan Sea in the Russo-Japanese War,* as had once been done by Inoue Shigeyoshi—Inoue, now the chief of staff of the Fleet of the China Region, would be compared to Rear-Admiral Kato Tomosaburo (who later became Prime Minister & Admiral of the Fleet) as the chief of staff under Admiral Togo Heihachiro, the Commander-in-Chief at the flagship Mikasa of that United Fleet. Though it was unknown if Inoue had thought highly of himself to such an extent as that, he ought to have had a great expectancy in his mind. This was also revealed in the action he took when the 101 Operations were at its height: He flew to Hankou Air Base on June 4 and spent four days there, encouraging the Commander Yamaguchi of the First United Flying Corps, the Commander Onishi of the Second United Flying Corps, and all the officers and men of those air corps.

If Inoue had had a tinge of uneasiness in performing the bombings upon Chongqing, trying to frustrate the general citizens' intention to go on fighting, it would have been how to protect "those third powers' rights and interests"— especially those of the U.S.'s and the U.K.'s diplomatic channels and private assets—from Japan's aerial attack. As mentioned before, Japan's military action toward China was originally "an incident" within the sphere of applying the force of arms because of their inability to suppress it with police forces, but *not* "war" that started after having declared it against each other, and this had led to Japan's inability to take any compulsory step to the third powers' rights and interests according to the wartime international law. (Since December 8, 1941, "the China Incident" began to be called "the Greater East Asia War" after Japan's declaration of war against the U.S. and the U.K., but by that time, Japan's bombardments upon Chongqing had virtually been over.)

At Chongqing as the capital to protest against Japan, diplomatic organs from abroad had already arrived, and besides them, this commercial center in the southwestern part of Sichuan Province was soon to see many corporations, churches and hospitals brought about by those from the U.S., the U.K., France and Germany. The reason why the Japanese Air Force, while actually performing the indiscriminate bombings, did continue to give a plausible reason for "attacking the military facilities in and around the city" was because, in case their air raid had given any damage on those foreign assets or properties, they needed to assume outward appearance, saying: *that* was an accidental bombing or "collateral damage" (according to the terms employed by today's U.S. Armed Forces). Especially any direct damages upon the U.S. Embassy and a U.S. warship were sure to lead to a serious diplomatic problem, so such was the last things they would like to see. This inevitably led the Japanese Fleet of the China Region to perform a sort of acrobat upon a couple of tightropes—military and diplomatic—with the result that: while giving directions for "relentless attacks" and "serial bombings" in their strategic plan of actions and in their agreement of the Army and the Navy, such indications as "*not* to damage the rights and interests of the third nations" had to be issued again and again. That could be compared to performing riotous behaviors while setting up an alibi.

In fact, had they ever shown any such consideration for the non-military facilities and civilians in Chongqing? Never. For Inoue, the chief of staff, and for Yamaguchi, the commander of the United Air Raid Corps, "the indiscriminate bombings to put the brakes on" meant such bombings as might reduce to ashes any foreign rights and interests possessed by the U.S. and the U.K. and France in the fire caught by the Chinese military or civilian facilities, but this did not mean excluding the Chinese civic life and civilian district. Since "5.3 & 5.4" in the previous year, the Chinese had already had merciless bombs thrown from above their head, and Japan's No.101 Operations that had started and developed under Inoue Shigeyoshi, Yamaguchi Tamon and Onishi Takijiro were to intensify their nature of indiscrimination.

● The Indication of the Districts to be Bombed in the Urban Area

The bombings upon the urban area of Chongqing under the name of No. 101 Operations started on May 26, even though it was after the middle of June—when Inoue, the chief of staff, made an inspection of Hankou—that they started a full-scale series of attacks. By that time, it had become common for their attack targets to be indicated by the code, such as "the western half of District B in the urban area of Chongqing." The Headquarters of the United Air Raid Units had divided the urban area into several sections of A,B,C,D.... and H, and adopted the tactics of carpet bombing raid upon each of them: A section was Jianbei Ward on the other side of the Jialing River; B section was the eastern half of the Castle (the ancient castle area); D section the western half of the Castle, and so on. Lieutenant Iwaya Fumio, who had joined No.101 Operations as a divisional officer of Kanoya Flying Corps, wrote as follows:

> Until about early June, our attack had been concentrated on the airports and military facilities, but since we found a considerable number of antiaircraft batteries in the urban area of Chongqing, too, and this had come to give us an increasing number of damages, the Operation Guidance Department determined to start thorough bombings upon the urban area. That was, the town was divided into sections of A,B,C,D and E, starting from the easternmost area, and each section was to be given carpet bombing one after another. What came to matter then was the oil tanks of Standard Oil Company and the rights and interests of those third powers that had moved up to Chongqing along with the Chinese Government. Some of those facilities of foreign rights and interests had notified their sites or locations, but in performing the bombardment while flying in formation at the altitude of more than 5,000 meters, it was practically impossible to let those specific sites or seats alone remain safe or free from any danger. Still we started our bombardment upon the urban area around the 10th of June, paying as much attention as possible to avoid those rights and interests from abroad.

This was how Chongqing on the peninsula on the Rivers was divided into several blocks of A, B, C, D.... and H to be exposed to the incessant bombings. In the action reports since then, there began to appear such titles as "A detailed report on performing an attack on H Section" (turned in by the 13th Flying

Corps on June 11). That was an introduction of a more effective and accurate method in urban bombing, and it could be called an even thorough version of probability bombing (bombing upon a region of a certain size, at a certain time, with a certain quantity of bombs). It is unknown which of the two headquarters Lieutenant Iwaya meant when he mentioned "the Operation Guidance Department" that had determined to perform the carpet bombing raids—the Headquarters of the United Air Raid Corps at Hankou or the Headquarters in the Battleship *Izumo* in the Fleet of the China Region staying at Huangbu-jiang Bay in Shanghai, but it would not be so unreasonable if we read in it a determination made by Inoue Shigeyoshi who was interested in mathematics.

● **The Double Standards Applied for Europe and for Asia**

For the rights and interests of the U.S. and the U.K., Japan showed consideration to observe the law of nations, but for the Chinese, it performed relentless air raids, making their city itself an object for bombing—that double standard was a contradiction and a weakness Inoue Shigeyoshi and the Japanese Navy had been keeping with them. How obedient Japan was in observing the law of nations when it faced the U.S. and the U.K. appeared rather comic: At the opening of the war against America—after performing the three years' indiscriminate bombardment upon Chongqing—the Japanese Navy Air Force's obsession about attacking military targets only was such that in making their bombing raid upon Hawaii, they avoided bursting even the oil tanks for military use.

On the other hand, this double standard, even though preached, could not help being left impracticable. Because it was as if they were making the pond empty in order to kill a fish named Jiang Jieshi, while trying to make certain other kinds of fish keep alive. Since they were going to empty the pond, it was naturally estimated that all fishes would be killed, and it was practically impossible, as Lieutenant Iwaya had said, for the Japanese Air Force to perform air-raiding, avoiding only spots of the third nations' rights and interests in such a city as Chongqing where the local, the political and the military were thickly mixed. That easy-going double standard the Japanese Navy had brought about was thus foretold to be a failure from the beginning, and it was not long before Japan was pushed into the War against the U.S..

Even if that had come from the nature of the Japanese Navy as a whole,

Inoue Shigeyoshi himself could not remain free from this pitfall. Inoue, at the early stage of the Sino-Japanese War, had a bitter memory of having conducted—as the chief of the Bureau of the Naval Affairs—the affair in which a Japanese bomber had accidentally attacked and sunken the U.S. gunboat Panay in the midst of capturing Nanjing, and that experience had made him stand by the side of seeking a strict application of "military target only" (as was mentioned in his Memoir), but it was none other than "the standard adopted only for the West" by which the U.S.' rights and interests were kept safe from their attack, and it never occurred to Inoue that the Chinese non-combatants and non-governmental facilities at Chongqing should be excluded from being attacked by their air raid.

The case of the U.S. gunboat Panay occurred on December 12,1937—the day before the Capture of Nanjing or before that holocaust in Nanjing started. The carrier-based airplanes led by Lieutenant Matsumoto Shigeharu, who belonged to the 13th flying corps under the Second United Flying Corps, made a bombing raid upon the U.S. gunboat Panay at anchor on the Yangzi at a point 11 nautical miles (20km) from Nanjing, until it was made to sink, because they "had mistakenly regarded it as a Chinese military ship retreating with many Chinese soldiers and sailors on board." Joseph Grew, the U.S. Ambassador in Tokyo, Japan, recorded how surprised he was when he received the news in his diary, Ten Years in Japan:

.... Indeed, at this moment, I seriously feared a breach of relations and already began to plan the details of hurried packing in case we had to leave—precisely as we began to pack in Berlin after the sinking of the Lusitania in 1915.

When a German U boat caused the sinking of the Lusitania, a British passenger ship on May 7, 1915, during World War I, in the offing of Ireland, the U.S. public opinion came to such a pitch of excitement as to make a remote cause of the U.S.' participation in the War. Calling this incident to mind, the Ambassador Grew did wonder whether or not the U.S. Government and the people would be able to bear that strain of having suffered such disdain as this.

The Ministry of the Navy at that time was known for its "Leftist Trio"—the Minister Yonai Mitsumasa, the Vice-Minister Yamamoto Isoroku and the Chief of the Bureau of Naval Affairs, Inoue Shigeyoshi. The three, who had made it the highest priority *not* to worsen Japan's relationship with the U.S., framed a plan for conducting that affair, immediately recognized that the Japanese side was at fault, cooperating with the Foreign Minister Hirota Kōki, and accepted the four conditions the U.S. side had set—immediately making an apology for it, compensating for it, preventing a recurrence of the same sort of incident, and punishing those concerned—thus they had to run about, trying to prevent the U.S.' public sentiment from getting hardened. Though not found in Grew's diary, *Ten Years in Japan*, Inoue wrote in his *Memoir:* "The Vice-Minister Yamamoto then did his best, bringing himself to the Embassy, trying to clear up the misunderstanding on the other side, making the best use of his ability in speaking such English as he had brushed up in his career as a military attaché to the Embassy in the U.S.." On December 15, the Commander of the Second United Air Force, Rear-Admiral Minami Teizo, was dismissed and punished with a reprimand, and it was not until this matter was brought to an end that the Japanese Government paid $2,210,000 (ca. ¥6,700,000) as a compensation to the U.S. Government.

This was how "the case of *Panay*, the U.S. Gunboat" was brought to an end by the rapid actions taken by Yonai, Yamamoto and Inoue, thus managing to prevent the U.S. public opinion from getting so worse as to bring a cataclysm to Japan-U.S. relations.

● **"The Nightmare" Inoue Shigeyoshi had Dreaded**
On the other hand, however, while that U.S.-Japan negotiations were going on in Washington in conformity to good faith and logic, in Nanjing—in the very city in whose offing the gunboat *Panay* had sunken—a holocaust by the same Japanese military was being carried out indiscriminately whether they were men or women, military or civilian, thus weaving into history the contrasted scenes of the double-standard Japan had adopted. Ambassador Grew—having come in contact with these contrasted attitudes adopted by the Japanese—the Japanese military who never felt ashamed of infringing the international law in the battle fields in China and the Japanese "from all walks of life, from high officials, doctors, professors, businessmen down to school children, trying to express their shame, apologies, and regrets for the action of their own Navy" who, no sooner had they heard of their plane having attacked and sunken the U.S.

gunboat *Panay* than they brought to the U.S. Embassy "their words of apology for what their Navy had done with great humility and regrets"—wrote in his diary: ".... never before has the fact that there are "two Japans" been more clearly emphasized."

But Japan at that same period of time, while showing their good faith and sincerity toward the U.S., the other side or the hidden side of Japan. had kept giving a great deal of suffering to the non-combatant Chinese in the city of Nanjing. In that context, Inoue Shigeyoshi, who, as the chief of the Bureau of Naval Affairs, represented "the rational Japan" in dealing with the Incident of the *Panay*, had come to be regarded by the citizens of Chongqing as the dreadful killer from the sky as soon as he came to take the post of the chief of staff in the Fleet of the China Region.

The Chief of Staff Inoue's inspection of the front was made eighteen days after the Operation No. 101 started. During his stay there, the 8th bombardment upon Chongqing was performed, as was described in *Inoue Shigeyoshi* (edited and published in 1982 by the group to publish this biography):

In order to bring down Jiang's Administration, a series of large-scale aerial operations was put into action. This was the No.101 Operations and the Fleet of the China Region, in cooperation with Army's Third Flying Corps, intended to blast the Chinese Air Force in the region of Sichuan Province, the political organization of Jiang's administration, its military bases and the Routes for Supporting Jiang. The period for this Plan of Operations was about four months from May 1 to September 5 in 1940. That was the only and most effective plan of operations Japan was able to carry out in line with its national policy.

The main force of this plan of operations consisted of the Second and the Third United Air Corps and the First United Air Corps that had been sent by the United Fleet to be placed under the command of the Fleet of the China Region, and the total number of the planes concentrated at the Hankou region had reached about three hundred, including land-based attack-planes, carrier-based attack planes, carrier-based bombers and carrier-based fighter planes.

On June 4, Inoue flew to Hankou and spent four days there, encouraging Rear-Admiral Yamaguchi Tamon, the Supreme Commander of the Hankou

Air Force and concurrently the Commander of the First United Flying Corps, and Rear-Admiral Onishi Takijiro, the Commander of the Second United Flying Corps, and all of those officers and men in that Air Force. Seeing that the Headquarters of the Fleet of the China Region had entrusted their operation task to each of the fleets under them, Inoue's visit there was something that rarely happened, and this did reveal how much expectation he had placed on those operations they were about to perform.

There is left nothing like any such record as might tell us what sort of words were exchanged among Inoue, Yamaguchi and Onishi, or what sort of instructions Inoue gave to those aviators he met there, but there was no doubt that he did mention *not* to bomb upon the institutions and embassies of the U.S., of the U.K. and of other nations from Europe. What if "another version of the Gunboat *Panay*'s Incident" should happen?..... That ought to have been a nightmare for Inoue who was about to engage in the series of No.101 Operations.

As mentioned before, the United Air Raid Corps that had been ordered to perform what was called No. 101 Operations by the telegraphic message No. 62 from the Fleet of the China Region (on May 10) made *the Plan of Actions* and *the Implementation Manuel for Attacks*, and in No. 4 of the latter, concerning the attacks on the enemy's military facilities, the following paragraphs could be seen: "Both of the Army and the Navy shall do their best in performing continuous attacks day and night, making use of the moonlight, when possible." and "in deciding upon the target for bombing and in performing the bombing, the greatest care should be taken *never* to cause damage to the rights and interests of any third nations, including their diplomatic institutions and their warships."

Such wordings as "the greatest care" and "*never* to cause damage…," which had not been found in the plan of actions the year before, could be taken as Inoue's determination *not* to repeat another nightmare of "the U.S. Gunboat *Panay*'s case." This policy of action was reflected also on the Agreement with the Army and Navy Air Forces in China Region and the following expression was added: "Our attack target shall be aimed at the urban area of Chongqing and its neighborhood (taking the greatest care *not* to damage the third nations' rights and interests to the best of your ability)."

These efforts, however, were to turn out nothing but "a picture of rice cakes" or "a pie in the sky." While emphasizing the importance of that warfare, even by referring to "the Battle on the Japan Sea"* and even preparing for the carpet bombing raids to be performed day and night upon the areas they had arbitrarily set up upon the urban area of Chongqing, how could they keep safe only the third nations' rights and interests—especially in the B and D sections in Shizong (City's Central) Ward? Especially when their altitude for dropping bombs tended to be higher so that they might not meet the Chinese interceptor fighters or receive the antiaircraft fires? It was simply impossible for anyone in the crew to obey such an order as to keep only the third nations' assets from their bombardment.

● **The Damages were Given to the Third Nations' Rights & Interests**

As an inevitable consequence, as No.101 Operations moved from the early stages of exterminating the aerial bases to the main stage of bombing upon the urban areas, the damages they inflicted upon the city grew greater, including those given to the third nations' rights and interests.

The 8th bombing upon Chongqing performed on June 6, while Inoue, the Chief of Stuff, was still staying at Hankou, was the first joint mission of the Army and the Navy, but their target having been Baishiyi Air Base in the suburbs, the damage inflicted was not so great. But their air raids since June 10 had all been given in and around the central part of Chongqing, and the bombs and incendiary bombs were relentlessly dropped even upon the third powers' rights and interests.

On June 11, the 10th bombardment upon Chongqing in No. 101 Operations was performed upon Division A (Jiangbei District) and Division H (Chuandong Normal School, Futukan and Hualongqiao Districts). They entered their skies at 1 P.M. —a daytime storming-bombardment.

The Army's fleet of 36 heavy bombers led by Colonel Ogawa Shojiro, which had joined the No.101 Operations since June 6, when the 8th attack was performed, did their task that day by dropping one 50kg bomb, eighty-six 100kg bombs and thirty-six 250kg bombs upon Jinling Military Arsenal and the urban area in Jiangbei District on the other side of the Jialing, which faced Shizong Ward.

On the other hand, the 79 planes—including 27 middle-sized attack bombers of the First United Flying Corps placed under the commander-in-chief Captain Kikuchi Toyokichi, 27 planes from the Navy's 13th air corps, 25 planes from the 15th air corps, 18 planes from Kanoya air corps and 9 planes from Takao air corps—attacked H Division, the area in and around Chuandong Normal School and a new town area outside the ancient castle wall, consuming 354 bombs each weighing 60kg, and 134 bombs each weighing 250kg, and reported they had "achieved great things." The report of the mission of the same air corps in *The Detailed Report on Attacking the H Division* dated *June 11 in the 15th year of Showa* (1940) went as follows: "We attacked the district around Chuandong Normal School with all our bombs (54 bombs of No.25 & 108 bombs of No.6), covering the important facilities in the center, causing four points to flame up (giving two of them tremendous damage)."

Xin Hua Ri bao (*New China Daily*) reported this under the heading of "117 planes invaded our skies at the same time to drop more than 200 fragmentation bombs and about the same number of combustion bombs to cause more than 60 killed or injured." The same article reported not only the great damage they suffered at the central area of the city but also the Soviet Union's Embassy having suffered a great deal of bombing (despite their having raised their national flag high on their roof); German National Transozean News Agency's branch office had totally been burnt up; French Havas News Agency suffered damages; the Soviet Union's Tass' Information Telegraphic Agency in China had the whole of their buildings crumbled down.

The U.S. Ambassador Johnson at once sent a telegraph (at 8 p.m. on the same day) to Washington:

More than 100 planes of four attack formations of Japanese Air Force gave a vehement air raids in and around Chungking City and Jiangbei (North of the Jialing River) District. Judging from the intensity of the bombing, it seems to have brought about a great damage upon the assets of those living in the commercial and residential areas—which were not so spacious. The number of deaths and injuries were not reported yet, but since the air-raid shelters were efficiently made use of, the casualties are not so heavy, I think. The main building of the Soviet Union's Embassy was badly damaged because the neighboring house received a direct hit of a bomb, but it seems to be no death.

The first group of the air raiders flew directly above our embassy premises and our gunboat and one bomb dropped 30 yard away from our embassy building. According to my hasty investigation, I am able to report that the citizens of the US and their assets have escaped danger.

Johnson

The air raid occurred the following day, too. 75 Navy air planes and 36 Army air planes assaulted B Division (the eastern half of the castle area) and H Division (the neighborhood of Chuandong Normal School). The written directive had received by Lieutenant Iwaya Fumio from Takao Air Corps went as follows:

The United Air Raid Corps shall take advantage of the weather that will be improved tomorrow (12th) and do your best at your simultaneous attack upon the urban area of Chongqing, and upon the military and political institutions. This attack shall be the 11th assault upon Chongqing.

Each of the planes with the platoon leader in it had carried one 800kg bomb improved from the principal gun of the battleship. The others were of 250kg and of 60kg. Each platoon leader was directed to give consideration so that No. 80 bombs (800kg bombs) might be dropped evenly with a proper distance between them. The 800kg bomb was the world's heaviest bomb to be carried by plane. (One year later, the U.K. Air Force was to use one-ton bombs in making bombing raids upon Germany).

In *The Detailed Report of the Offensive Battle* given by Takao Air Corps, there is a concise report of *The Attack Targets of B Block in the City Area of Chongqing*: "All the bombs hit the marks, causing several great fires." The deaths caused by that bombing was 222. If the deaths that had occurred the day before were added, they were 286; the injured were 635; the houses destroyed came up to 1,769. Among the burnt buildings, there were those of Fudan Middle School that had moved from Shanghai. *Xin Hua Ri Bao* (New China Daily News) reported: "The beastliness of *wukous** has been getting worse than before, and this has enlarged the stricken area, but the damages have been kept limited thanks to the efforts made by relief squads and firemen."

*the general term given by the Chinese to the Japanese pirates who, from the

14th century through the 16th century, used to raid the Korean and Chinese coasts.

Ambassador Johnson again made out a draft of the telegram to Hull, the Secretary of State in Washington:

Today the four air raid units consisting of the 110 Japanese planes dared to perform an intense indiscriminate bombing upon Chungking, concentrating their attacks mainly on the center of the commercial area. The number of casualties reached as many as several hundreds, while the damages they suffered on their properties seem to be the greatest since May 4, 1939. All the U.S. citizens have remained safe. The Church of American Methodist Mission received some damage because of the concussion caused by the near hit upon it. The Japanese military planes flew above this embassy, but no bomb came down.

Johnson

● A Note from President Roosevelt to the Secretary of State Hull

At this telegram from Chongqing, President Franklin D. Roosevelt at the White House made a sharp reaction to it. On June 13, Cordell Hull, the Secretary of State, was to receive a short note signed by the President:

Having been confronted by this most patent fact of this indiscriminate bombardment upon the city life in Chungking, unrelated to any military installation, do we need to call the Japanese government's attention to it?

F.D.R.

——The U.S. Diplomatic Telegrams (Vol.80)

This note "from the President to the Secretary of State" (The U.S. Diplomatic Telegraph File: No.80) had expected an answer of "Yes." The answer from Cordell Hull that arrived on the same day went as follows:

Even before I received that note from the President, the indiscriminate bombings being performed on the city of Chungking had attracted my attention, and this had led me to publish my statement on the local newspaper. But taking this note I have received from the President into consideration, I have decided to send a telegraph to Ambassador Grew in Tokyo so that he could bring that statement to Japan's Foreign Minister as his personal warning.

This led Ambassador Grew to face "two-faced Japan" once again.

But despite the Ambassador's strenuous efforts, the Washington's feeling toward Japan was rapidly growing worse. From Chungking, the U.S. Department of State had kept receiving the telegrams concerning the U.S. diplomat's life being kept endangered by the indiscriminate bombings performed by the Japanese Air Force, which was immediately reported to the White House, thus to form President Roosevelt's impressions of Japan. Earlier than that, at the stage of "5.3 & 5.4", there was a following note entitled *The Chinese Incident and America—giving Consideration to the Facts* written on August 2 in the 14th year of Showa (1939), by Suma Yakichiro, a counselor of the Japanese Embassy in the U.S.. This does reveal the fact that: already in the year before, the President in person had invited the Japanese Government to pay attention to what they were doing in Chongqing:

Since July set in, Japan started large-scaled bombings upon Chungking. On July 5, Mrs Peck, the wife of a counselor of the U.S. Embassy in China, witnessed the Japanese planes came into the sky while she was crossing the river on her way to a luncheon party held by Song Meiling and on her way home, their bombing started, endangering herself and Peck, her husband who had come to take her back; their embassy's boat having been occupied by the refugees, they simply managed to hang themselves on the gunwale in crossing the river. An hour after they managed to return home, they had their neighborhood bombed, making them keenly feel their lives being endangered. This led Peck to send an ardent letter to the State Department. The telegram the Ambassador Johnson sent to the State Department was also so overwhelming that the stuff member of the State Department who had received that telegraph told me that anyone who had read the letter or telegram concerning *this* could not help hating what the Japanese were doing at present. In other words, what opinion the U.S. side offered to Japan concerning their Chungking bombardment was the last thing they could deliver, and for that very reason, the President "in person" had also called the Japanese side's attention to what Japan has been doing. Generally speaking, when the Americans bring the President forehand, it means things are far from easy to deal with. This was what proposal I received on July 10.

That note written by Suma went on:

We have not received any answer from Japan even if a week has passed, and on 19th, Hamilton, the Chief of the Far East Department, told me that it was amazing the answer had not reached yet; the Secretary of the State, Hull, asked me to urge the Japanese Government to give their answer. To my relief, that day, we received a telegram from Japan, but it did not seem satisfying to the U.S. side, and now on 26th, we have come to see our Commercial Treaty discarded.

This was how the Japan-US Commercial & Navigation Treaties were annulled (in July, 1939) as the first step to the catastrophe and warfare between the U.S. and Japan. Already at Chongqing, the U.S.-Japanese War had broken out.

America's Warning to Japan

● **President Roosevelt's Address to Criticize Japan**

The Japanese government and the military had been well aware that the White House had been turning their critical eyes upon the indiscriminate air raids they had been performing upon the cities in China, even before they received the warning from President Roosevelt in person, which had been brought to them by way of the Secretary of State, Hull. Since "the bombings upon Jinzhou" performed by Lieutenant Colonel Ishiwara Kanji during "the Manchurian Incident"* (1931), the U.S. Government had often been releasing a statement to criticize Japan for their having bombed upon those cities in China from both points of "Japan's having been against the law of nations and the laws of humanity" and "Japan's having threatened the lives and assets of the U.S. citizens resident in China." Immediately after "the Lukoukiao Incident,"* (July

7, 1937) President Roosevelt himself had referred to this point in "the Isolation Speech" he made in Chicago, which went as follows. Even if he refrained from mentioning someone by name, the Japanese Government had regarded it as his criticism against Japan:

> The overwhelming majority of the peoples and nations of the world today want to live in peace. I am compelled and you are compelled, nevertheless, to look ahead. The peace, the freedom and the security of ninety percent of the population of the world is being jeopardized by the remaining ten percent, who are threating a breakdown of all international order and law. Surely the ninety percent who want to live in peace under law in accordance with moral standard that have received almost universal acceptance through the centuries, can and must find some way to make their will prevail.—The situation is definitely of universal concern. The questions involved relate not merely to violation of specific provisions of particular treaties; they are questions of war and peace, of international law and especially of principle of humanity.... thus to destroy the orders of the world, or to destroy the international law. In fact, these lawless people, without declaring war, without any righteous reasons, are killing mercilessly the non-combatants, including women and children, by performing the air raids. This is not a mere matter of breaking a certain treaty, but a global matter of violating the international law and humanitarianism, and no nations in the world can remain indifferent to it. .....

As was seen in this warning against Japan, the stance of the Roosevelt's Administration had been kept clear from the very beginning. That was why the Japanese military had adopted that "double standard" of giving the Chinese the limitless fear by performing the indiscriminate bombings whether they were military or not, so that those limitless terrors given to them might lead them to lose their fighting spirit, while trying as much as possible to keep the rights and interests of the Third Nations out of their attack target. But now that Japan had started No. 101 Operations, strengthening their bombardments more and more, they could no longer retain such a stopgap measure as had been adopted so far. This having been keenly felt after the full-scale bombardment upon Chongqing that had started after Inoue Shigeyoshi, the chief of stuff, visited Hankou Base, the Japanese Government could not help facing a strong notice of Roosevelt, which had been brought to them by way of Hull and Grew. Just like the gunboat Panay which the Japanese military must not have touched while they were capturing Nanjing, what symbolized the U.S. rights and interests this time were the U.S. Embassy that stood by the Yangzi and the U.S. gunboat Tutuila (370 tons) with a couple of chimneys floating upon the yangzi.

At this period of time, Japan had not yet come to make a resolution to start a war against the U.S.. If such a war broke out, the Navy would have to stand at the front, but they had not yet had any such recognition of the situation. Japan's indiscriminate bombings being performed in China having grown into a central point, the U.S.-Japanese relations were going from bad to worse, until at last in July, 1939, the U.S. Government gave notice of scrapping the U.S.-Japan Commerce & Navigation Treaty and since it came into effect in January, 1940, the U.S. Government was able to take steps to impose all of the economic sanctions against Japan, but Japan had still remained depending most of the petroleum it needed upon the supply from the U.S.. Ironically, Standard Oil Company in Chongqing, near which Japan's Navy Air Force kept dropping bombs, was also among the leading companies supplying petroleum to the Imperial Navy of Japan. For the Navy's Fleets and Air Force, therefore, their dependence upon the U.S. in oil supply was something vital. This was especially so for the Navy, whose oil stockpiling was so scarce as to keep only for a single year. If oil was made among the articles under an embargo, the Air Force would be as good as birds deprived of their wings. In order to avoid such a nightmare, too, preserving the integrity of the U.S.' rights and interests had now become what might be called a supreme command.

In other words, the Japanese Government and Military had entered a dead end street while going on with their bombardments upon Chongqing. All they could do then would be intensifying the air raids by propelling No.101 Operations to subdue the Jiang Administration and realize peace, if they wished to retreat from China in honor after having settled "the China issues" and to improve the relationship with America. On the other hand, the petroleum indispensable in bombardment was imported mostly from the U.S., but the Plan of No.101 Operations was quite likely to damage the U.S. rights and interests existing in Chongqing, and that could be a trigger to invite the worst retaliation of the stoppage of oil supply from the U.S.. It was the worst problem that had kept haunting to Inoue, the chief of Stuff, in the Flag Ship of Izumo in the fleet of the China Region floating in the Huangbu in Shanghai. In "the Battle of the Japan Sea" in the Russo-Japanese War Inoue had once referred to, there was not any such political dilemma, but in the No. 101 Operations he was now leading, it had already gone beyond the limits of warfare between the two groups of combatants, and non-combatants having been made a target, and even those from abroad had become included in it. Inoue Shigeyoshi, who was later to experience a decisive battle fought between the aircraft carriers on the Coral Sea, was then, too, to be the first to face the new form of warfare the 20th century had brought into being.

As Inoue had worried, the U.S. Government's economic pressure upon Japan grew stronger along with Japan's evolution of bombings upon Chongqing, and—succeeding to the U.S.' notification of the denunciation of the Japan-U.S. Commerce and Navigation Treaty made immediately after the air raids of "5.3. & 5.4."—in the process of No.101 Operations, too, one economic punishment after another was to be inflicted upon Japan. On July 2—about three weeks after Roosevelt sent his memorandum to Hull—the President signed "the Law of National Defense" and issued a presidential decree that ordered that: the following three categories should be placed on a license system:

1) All armaments, munitions and war materials
2) All materials and materiel that, include aluminum and magnesium
3) Spare parts for airplanes, installations, accessories, optical instruments and factory equipment for producing metal goods

At this point, petroleum and scrap iron were not included in the articles under an embargo, but on July 26, they were placed under a license system, and on July 31, the gasoline for the aircraft was prohibited to export to the western hemisphere. Despite the protest made by Ambassador Horiuchi resident in Washington, the relationship between the U.S. and Japan continued to get worse and worse.

After all, the confrontation and inconsistencies that had come into being between the U.S. and Japan concerning that China issue could never be solved; Japan, turning to Netherlands Indo-China (Indonesia) to obtain petroleum, changed their policies from "marching into China" to "southward advance," while the U.S. openly ventured into supporting the Jiang Administration. Thus the relationship between the U.S. and Japan was to move into another form of explosion in another place, but at this period of time in 1940, the level of danger, though rising, still remained above bursting.

The Headquarters of the Fleet of the China Region, which had been placed in a dilemma between the purpose of their own Operations and the pressure from the U.S., offered their opinion to the Foreign Ministry and the Naval General Staff in Tokyo: that they should have those diplomatic organizations and the third powers' rights and interests "moved to some other appropriate places so that they may not restrain our bombardment"—a new idea to achieve their own purpose without causing any damage to the third powers' rights and interests. That was practically a deportation order that: they should all move to Nan-an (South Shore) Ward separated from Shizhong (City's Central) Ward by the Yangzi.

● **The U.S.' Reaction to Arita's Note**

In 1940, the following note dated June 14 was sent from the Foreign Minister Arita Hachiro to the Embassies of the U.K., the U.S., Germany, France, the Soviet Union and Belgium, resident in Tokyo:

> The Air Force of our Imperial Army and Navy has been engaged in attacking our enemy's armed forces and their military installations in and around Chongqing, and this is being planned to be intensified even more from now on. But in the urban area of Chongqing, there exist not only those who have come from your country but also the rights and interests of your country, and this naturally leads us to pay unusually great efforts not to cause any damage to them. On the other hands, there is an apparent fact that the Chinese Military has deliberately brought anti-aircraft batteries and some other military facilities in the vicinity of the third powers' rights and interests, keeping us worrying about the possibility that the intense combat missions we perform might bring some by-blows to the people and the rights and interests of your country.
>
> For this reason, our Imperial Government requests that: your Government should take prompt action for your people to retreat temporarily to a safe place—on the southern shore of the Yangzi, facing Chongqing: from Danzishi to Longmenhao (not including Haitangxi)—until our Operations

to attack Chongqing is over. Then, our Imperial Armed Forces will never attack that area on the southern shore of the Yangzi, but if the officials and the people of your country should remain and suffer any accident in the areas not mentioned above, our Imperial Government will never take any responsibility for it.

As was apparent in this Note, the Foreign Minister Arita firstly gave a warning that: Japan's attack upon Chongqing would be intensified from then on, and appealed that: Japan had made unusual effort so far not to damage the third powers' rights and interests, but that: the Chinese side had deliberately brought their anti-aircraft batteries and some other military facilities in the vicinity of those third powers' rights and interests, thus endangering those sanctuaries. This had led Japan to decide to bring about a safety zone for the Third Powers and to request them to move over there.

This request would be "the last possible adjustment" Japan could take when its military was about to attack the area where those from abroad were living— and that in the situation the war had started without giving any declaration. Naturally that request, however earnestly it might be made, did not have any legal powers. Many facilities, such as churches and hospitals and news agencies would find it hard to move. Still, this proposition, offering them opportunities for evacuation, was sure to bring some effect in warding off the accusation of the international law. But, that was none other than Japan's declaration deliberately given in the form of the Foreign Minister Arita's Note that: Japan— by dividing the city of Chongqing into the two districts with the Yangzi in between—was going to give limitless attacks upon the Chinese people living on this side of the River.

The contents of Arita's Note were sent within that night to Inoue Shigeyoshi, the Chief of Stuff, and to the Commander of the United Air Raid Corps at Hankou, too. The following was the top-secret telegram—"No.735 telegram of military secret"—sent along with the Navy Minister's view:

As for our bombardment upon Chongqing, we finished notifying the U.K., the U.S., Germany, France, the Soviet and Belgium on June 14 through a diplomatic route. As for the official advice for the warships and other vessels to take refuge, you shall send a proper notice to the Navy Officer in charge of each of those nations.

It goes without saying that this notification does not justify our bombing upon the Rights and Interests of those Third Powers. So we hope you will be as discreet as ever in performing the bombardment.

The U.S.' response to Arita's Note, however, turned out to be prompt and intense. Hull, the Secretary of State, immediately sent the gist of a letter of protest to Ambassador Grew in Tokyo (*FOREIGN RELATIONS 1904, UNDECLARED WAR*), ordering him to create a formal document on the basis of the letter he sent and to hand it to the Foreign Minister, after having a personal talk with him:

1. As for the attitude and standpoint of the US Government toward such warnings as were shown by Arita's Note have already been made clear. The US Government has already refused to accept such view as to regard the whole of Chungking as a legal aim for the aerial bombing.

   Not a few US citizens and rights and interests have existed in Chungking. Our Government has retained our embassy there and has sent our gunboat Tutuila. The US citizens resident in Chungking have legally been engaged in their business activities, while the public employees, including embassy staff are engaged in official business needed to maintain the diplomatic relations between the US and China. Still Arita's Note has given us instructions that we shall remove our embassy to a certain place set up as a non-bombardment area on the southern shore of the Yangzi. According to my personal experience so far, the air raids performed by the Japanese military had always endangered the lives of the inhabitants there whatever regions they had been aiming at. Even if our government might keep urging our US citizens to leave those danger zones, they have no duty to obey us, and in several cases, their evacuations are practically impossible. For these reasons, we US Government expect the Japanese Government to refrain from such military operations as to endanger the lives and assets of the US citizens in Chungking, and the Japanese Government to take all the responsibilities if they were to give any damage to the lives and assets of the US citizens.

2. You shall give an additional protest by your spoken language to convey Mr. Arita the explicit fact that: in case the Japan's bombardment should bring deaths or injuries to the US citizens, it would lead to a deplorable result in the relations between US and Japan.

The Ambassador Grew in Tokyo did as he had been instructed to do by Hull, the Secretary of State. In his diary—*Ten Years in Japan*—Grew had recorded his having met the Foreign Minister Arita on June 10, 19, 24 and 28. But this series of meetings had not helped to close the rift between them, as Grew wrote as if he had half resigned himself to it: "My private conversations with Arita (on June 10, 19, 24, and 28) have led to no concrete results, but they have at least served to keep the door open between the two governments, which was the primary purpose of our conversations." The US-Japan relationship was now coming to the point where it was impossible to restore.

● **President Roosevelt's Order to Investigate How to Perform**
the Bombardments upon the Cities of Japan
In this way, the Plan of No.101 Operations was soon to bring about such a destructive effect upon the U.S.-Japan relationship in the future. Even though this was not the only cause that had impeded the relationship between the U.S. and Japan, Japan's perversities demonstrated day after day in the skies of Chongqing could not help appearing something extremely provocative to the U.S.. It is not hard to imagine how all those daily telegrams sent to Washington from Ambassador Johnson helped the White House to create a view of Japan. According to Cordell Hull's memoirs, it was at the conference on January 16, 1941, that President Roosevelt mentioned the bombardments upon the cities of Japan, saying: "The Navy shall consider the probability of their performing bombings upon the cities of Japan." This dated back to nearly a year before Japan-U.S. War broke out. At this period, the U.K. and Germany had already started strategic bombings toward each other's capitals, but the U.S. had not joined the World War yet. Even after the U.S. joined it, the U.S. Air Force in the European battle line kept hesitating to perform indiscriminate bombings upon cities and persisted in pinpoint bombings performed during the daytime. In the light of this fact, what had motivated Roosevelt in January, 1941, to order the conference to discuss the matter of performing aerial bombardments upon the

Japanese cities does not seem to have been irrelevant to what the Japanese Air Force had been doing upon Chongqing—from "5.3 & 5.4." in 1939 through the Plan of No.101 Operations in the year that followed. It was true that the U.S. Air Force not only dropped the atomic bombs upon Hiroshima and Nagasaki but also adopted the indiscriminate bombings upon many other cities as their main operations toward Japan, even though it refrained from doing so toward Germany. Even if the conception that lay in the base of that action was a reflection of their racial discrimination against the Asians, what had given a basis to that prejudice would have unmistakably been the Japanese Air Force's indiscriminate bombings upon the Chinese cities, especially upon Chongqing as China's wartime capital. In other words, the Japanese Navy's "double standard" in their thoughts in which they made light of the Asian peoples and the Chinese might have given a proper excuse for the U.S. authorities concerned to disdain the Asians, thus to cause them to extract "the double standards" to apply to Germany and to Japan.

Thus while spinning out another background, the Plan of No. 101 Operations was being performed day after day as if trying to make the citizens of Chongqing remember that summer of 1940 by the blood and sweat and by the bitter taste of the counsel to surrender. Commander-in-Chief Shimada Shigetaro and Chief of Staff Inoue Shigeyoshi in the flagship at Shanghai, and Commanders Yamaguchi Tamon and Onishi Takijiro at Hankou as their outpost were all encouraging the flight crew of the middle-sized bombers. From the No. 101 Operations onward, the 800kg bombs, which had been converted from the bullets for the main guns equipped in the battleship, began to be adopted, while in the method of ignition, a new device was adopted: since they got the information that the top leaders of the Nationalist party made it a rule to inspect the stricken areas, they remade some of their bombs into delayed-action-bombs or "X fuses" which was so made as to burst *not* at once but several hours later after "the all clear" was given—when the ordinary life was resumed. The method of homicides had become so complicated as to outwit the victims.

As for what Chongqing looked like in those days, it was being observed, as follows, by a flight crew member, Lieutenant Iwaya Fumio, in his *Middle-Sized Attack Bombers:*

It was since June 24 when we, the First United Attack Corps, started a high altitude bombing by our middle-sized attack planes of Type 23.

According to the initial resolution made by Commander Yamaguchi, we had concentrated our attack upon Chongqing day after day with all our forces available. Every time the reconnoitering photographs were taken, the town of Chongqing seemed to be deteriorating into miserable ruins. No wonder when we think of the fact that: the bombs that amounted from more than 50 tons to more than 100 tons have kept destroying those densely built-up areas almost every day. The town ought to have been turned into piles of rubble and sandy dust. This bombing flight, which we called "the regular flight to Chongqing," took about seven hours, including two or three hour high-altitude flight which needed two or three hours' inhalation of oxygen, while enduring the low temperature about ten degrees below zero, and—in the skies of Chongqing, several minutes' maneuvering in the bursts of the fragmentation bombs from the anti-aircraft guns, followed by the battles against the enemy's interceptors, which lasted from 15 minutes to 30 minutes. So this bombing flight was by no means easy both physically and mentally. In July, the weather having become comparatively settled, we, attack corps, raised our degree of assault, and every day we flew a mission literally with all our strength.

The following is also from the memoirs of Lieutenant Adachi Jiro of Takao Air Corps:

In early May, the First United Aviation Corps advanced into Hankou, and cooperating with the Second United Aviation Corps, we put the Operations into action. In starting the Operations, the Commander (Yamaguchi Tamon) collected those whose ranks are above the commander of the flight corps and gave a fierce address, saying: "In order to achieve the purpose of this series of Operations upon Chongqing, I dare not mind losing the whole of this United Aviation Corps." I guess he said so to express his unusual resolution he had made for what we were going to do, but it seemed rather strange to me as if we were about to fight a decisive battle between the fleets at sea. As for what we were doing in those days, a land scout plane took off around 7 at Hankou, and an hour or so later, one squadron after another took off and after having finished gathering in the air, they usually left the sky of the base around 8:30.

In fact, the Commander himself sometimes got on the Commander's plane and demonstrated his resolution to take the initiative. Until the end of the first ten days of July, for nearly two months, we devoted all our energy to the raiding upon Chongqing; sometimes we flew a double mission in the morning and in the afternoon. Thus the city of Chongqing, when seen from above, appeared to have completely turned into ruins, and still it had kept alive.

As for what damage those air raids had brought about, the observations had been made by the bomber fleet of the Army Air Force, too. The 60th Flight Squadron had moved the base of their mission from Hankou to Yuncheng, and their squadron chief had been changed from Colonel Tanaka Tomomichi to Lieutenant Colonel Ogawa Shojiro. In concert with the start of the 101 Operations, the 60th flight squadron had deployed themselves—along with fifty-one 97-type heavy bombers and 582 airmen, including commissioned officers—at Yuncheng Air Base and joined the air raiding upon Chongqing since June 6. By July, they had flown seven missions and attacked "the military installations within the castle," "Chongqing University," "groups of factories" and so on. The record of attacks in August went as follows:

August 19. An Attack on Chongqing:
For the first time, the Navy's fighter planes came to cooperate with us. Despite the enemy's heavy barrage from the anti-aircraft guns, we performed a bombing raid upon the city of Chongqing till we made sure of large fires. All the planes returned safe. The bombs dropped were 90 of 250kg-bombs and 53 of *ka* 4 bombs.

August 20. An Attack on the urban area of Chongqing:
The Navy's planes came to help us, as they did yesterday. The enemy's fighter planes were not seen but their anti-aircraft artilleries were extremely active. Our attack today proved to be the greatest in the Operations we had been engaged in so far. According to the telegram from abroad, Chongqing has completely lost its function as the capital to fight against the enemy.

In the flight to Chongqing across the chains of mountains more than 5,000m above sea level, they had to work out a countermeasure to cope with coldness and oxygen deficiency. As was mentioned by Captain Iwaya Fumio in his writing mentioned before, in the personal accounts made by military aviators about this time, "a suit with electric heating lines sown into it" and "oxygen inhalation" were often mentioned. In the bombers of both Army and Navy, the aviation suits with heating wires sown into them and the oxygen inhalers were always provided, but no sooner had the valve of an inhaler been opened than it burst or failed to work properly, causing one pilot after another to faint away. In the entry of August 30 in *The Brief History of the 60ᵗʰ Flight Squadron*, the following entry is seen: "The squadron at Yuncheng made an invasion every day as long as weather permitted; we had 61 planes available, but there being no recruitment of aircrew, our spiritual fatigue was being intensified." The crew had been exhausted, too.

The Regular Flight for Bombing upon Chongqing

● The Relocations of the Embassies and the Consulates

According to the advice given by "Arita's Note" from the Japanese Government, one diplomatic establishment after another in Shizhong (City's Central) Ward moved to Nan-an (Southern Shore) Ward. Since the Operations No. 101 started, each air raid had given a direct hit or a near hit on one embassy or consulate after another, keeping them too restless to go on working there, so the time had been ripe for them to move somewhere safe—excepting the Embassy of the U.S.S.R.. The Ambassador of the U.S.S.R., Alexandr Panuchikin, who had graduated from The Red Army University and had been dispatched there as a serviceman-ambassador, was responsible for supervising the U.S.S.R.'s "Route to Assist the Jiang Administration."

The new address of the U.S. Embassy was No.1 on Jiangye-gang Hill in Nan-an Ward. The three-storied western-style building upon the hill commanded a sweeping view of the Yangzi. As if protesting against that proud flow of reddish brown, the U.S. gunboat, Tutuila, whose side was painted white, was at anchor. Tutuila was one of the six battleships built at Shanghai Jiannan Shipyard from 1926 to 28 in order to protect the U.S.' rights and interests in

China. Its displacement tonnage was 370 tons; its length 48.7m. Its combat equipment was no more than a couple of single-mounted guns whose battery was 7.6 cm across. If attacked by the middle-sized bombers which had been developed to attack U.S. battleships, it ought to have easily been broken, but Tutuila would not comply with the advice to take refuge somewhere safer according to the advice given by the Japanese Fleet of the China Region, even though it moved its berth only a little according to the movement of the Embassy from Shizong Ward to the other side of the River, thus demonstrating the existence of America all the same barely outside the Japanese planes' line of sight.

The district where the Japanese Government had declared to avoid their bombardment was a section across the Yangzi—about 4km long—from Danzishi to Longmenhong. Danzishi adjoined Wangjiatuo where a Japanese concession used to be, and after the Japanese retreated, it had been placed under the Government control. Behind the road that led to Longmenhong along the Yangzi, there were piles of gently sloping hills that led to the summit of Mt. Huangshan (Yellow Mountain) where Jiang Jieshi had placed his favorite operational headquarters, "Ying-Chao," which the U.S. ambassador and others literally called "the Eagle's Nest." Mt. Huangshan itself had not been included in the regions for the Japanese bombers to refrain from bombing, and this was to lead to a surprise attack performed in August the following year by the 60th Flight Squadron led by Major General Endo Saburo, the leader of the Army's Third Flight Group, who had plotted the murder of Jiang Jieshi and other top leaders during their conference at Yunxiu-lou (Cloud-Summit Lookout) in that mountain villa.

But now the hilly terrain along the Yangzi was regarded as a safe zone, each of the embassies and consulates started their business there by having some Chinese residences or villas taken over. Since part of the Chinese government organization had also been moved here, that out-of-the-way area suddenly began to assume the appearance of a hastily-made-up "Official Residence Area" or what might be called "Embassy Street."

For those locals who had been living there generation after generation, it was certainly relieving that their own district had officially been guaranteed to be safe, but they had to face something unpleasant, too. Those living in Qingshuixi (Pure Water Valley), which was turned into "Ambassador & Consul District," suddenly began to see many military police officers on their way to and from Jiang Jieshi's Villa on Mt. Huangshan, causing them to feel strained whatever they might be doing. Jiang Jieshi in his loose Chinese garment made it a daily rule to go—in a palanquin carried by four men—to and from his office at the Encampment of the Military Committee in Shizong (City's Central) Ward, while his wife, Lady Song Meiling in her straw hat, was often seen taking a walk in their neighborhood. The ambassadors and consuls usually commuted on horseback, and this led to the prohibition of the villagers' going out till all those guests had passed through their village lest they should prevent them from riding safely along those narrow mountain paths. The ambassadors and consuls having left part of their business and communication facilities at their formal office in Shizong Ward, commuted almost every day, excepting a weekend, taking a ferryboat from Longmenhao to Wanglongmen Gate before they entered the city. Longmenhao (the Wide Water at Dragon Gate)—which becomes so clear and blue in the period of drought in winter—used to be admired in a poem especially for "the moon being reflected on Longmenhao" as something special. But in the summer of 1940, what was being reflected on the River "on the moonlit night" was not a refreshing sight of the moon but unfailingly a formation of bombers. As if being in grief over the ominous bloodshed caused by them, the Yangzi from early summer to autumn had turned itself reddish brown.

Seen from Shizong (City's Central) Ward, Qingshuixi (Pure Water Valley) appeared to be in another planet. Even if the enemy planes' formation might fly over them, none of them would drop their bombs upon it. Even though the inhabitants had dug some caves on the mountainsides, none had ever thought of entering them. They simply remained spectators at the formation of bombers, which, looking like a Chinese character of "人"—meaning "a human being"—intruded into the sky of Shizong Ward, and through the air where antiaircraft fires were bursting, dropped bombs which slowly came falling. To those living in Qingshuixi, who had been seeing those scenes day after day, the number of the planes that created the "人"-shaped formation seemed to have grown larger since the Embassies moved to their side of the River.

- **The Heaviest Attack in the Plan of No. 101 Operations:**
  A Series of Six-Day Bombardments upon the Urban Area

Under that new situation, in the latter half of June, Shizhong Ward was to suffer the heaviest attack in the No. 101 Operations. Many of the sorties were the joint ones of the Army and the Navy performed on the urban area on the 16th and the 17th, followed by a series of 6-day bombardments (from 24th to 29th) —10 times by the Navy and 5 times by the Army.

The Navy Air Corps did their best, wishing to make use of this opportunity in bringing that warfare to an end. While losing their temper at the enemy who never admitted their defeat, the Japanese Government and Military had simply been trying to increase the number of bombers and bombshells. That month, the Fleet of the China Region with Inoue Shigeyoshi as the chief of staff had sent a member of his staff to the Expeditionary Army in China and proposed that they should intensify the plan of operations for bombing the Hinterland of China.

In the battle line in Europe, Germany's blitz tactics had led the Netherlands and Belgium to be conquered before May was out, and France's surrender had become only a matter of time. This had led the Navy to assess the situation that: at this time when the world powers' attention toward China was shifted and their military aid toward China had diminished, the effect of their political & strategic bombardment would turn out even greater. Then why not intensify their bombardment? Thus the Navy proposed that the number of bombers available should be reinforced to 200, and that: during the three months from June to August, they should like to attack on the Chongqing region with a total of 3,000 planes (2,000 Navy planes; 1,000 Army planes) and on the Chengdu region with a total of 2,000 (1,000 Navy planes; 1,000 Army planes), and that: if one attack was made by 200 planes, the attacks by 5,000 planes would be performed by 25 sorties—15 sorties during June and July, and 10 sorties during August.

This proposal from the Fleet of the China Region, which required the Army to increase a couple of squadrons with 27 planes, was too much for the Army to realize, but this revealed how intense was the Navy's enthusiasm toward the No. 101 Operation. The Navy, having already joined forces which amounted about the double of the central agreement of the Army and the Navy, had intended to bring the China Incident to an end at that single stretch then. Thus the No.101 Operations was to be performed by the Navy that had kept taking the initiative from the beginning to the end.

The climax of the offensive in June was the six-day intensive bombardment from 24th to 29th, when the planes mainly consisting of the Navy's United Air Raid Corps assaulted the urban area of Chongqing day after day. In *The Synopsis of the Plan of No.101 Operations,* the following description was given:

3) The attack on the military installations in Chongqing

Though we had not fully suppressed the enemy's combat planes, since their fighting spirit was generally feeble, we started to attack the military facilities and political institutions in and around the city. In performing that attack, what we had paid much attention to was to keep safe the third powers' rights and interests, especially their diplomatic institutions and warships and other vessels. Thus at the early stage of our operations when the enemy's fighter planes were comparatively active in interrupting us, we chose to attack mainly upon such places in the suburban area as Beibei Xincun, Xiaolongkan, Ciqikou, Futujian, Hualongqiao and Jianbei District, and as the number of the enemy's fighter planes grew smaller and we had come to gain ample experience in attacking them, we gradually turned our aim to the urban area of Chongqing.

On the other hand, we had delivered our opinion to those diplomatic organs that they should move somewhere proper that would not restrict our combat mission, and on June 14, the Central Government of China gave advice to those third powers that they should move to "the safety zone"—the area from Danzishi to Longmenhao (not including Haifangxi) on the other side of the Yangzi that flows southeast of Chongqing—to stay there until our Operations against Chongqing were over.

Thus since June 24 or ten days after that advice of ours was given, we resumed our thorough-going bombardments upon the important facilities in the city, thus to steadily achieve brilliant results.

This does reveal how, after "the safety zone" was brought into being, the bombardment upon the urban area became even more intensified.

Thus what the flight crew called "a daily attendance to Chongqing" or "a daily care of Chongqing" was to disfigure the urban area of Chongqing to such a miserable extent as to be comparable to the face of a boxer who had received numberless punches on the ring. The buildings in the business quarters had been collapsed, leaving only some walls and their skeleton, and the slanting utility poles with dangling electric wires were looking exactly like so many *stupas* (Buddhist grave tablets). The districts that had many wooden houses in them had been blasted to be turned into spacious vacant lots and it was not long before children with a basket on their back were seen to be looking for copper lines or pieces of metal from among the heaps of rubbles.

At the start of the No.101 Operations, the whole city of Chongqing had been divided into eight sections—from A section to H section, and now that the third powers' rights and interests had regally been moved to the other side of the Yangzi, the Anti-Japanese Capital of Chongqing upon the peninsula between the Yangzi and the Jialing, the stronghold of the Jiang Administration, had now become a target of an open attack for the Japanese planes. All the citizens could do then was to keep themselves to the cave, enduring the trial with bated breath.

● **The Missions, Day in, Day out, Exhausted the Airmen**

On June 24, the first day of that series of bombing mission, their target was "the western half of Section B"—the commercial district in the central part of Chongqing. But since it had already been bombed so frequently since the major air raids in May the year before, it retained none of the traces of what it used to be, as was extolled to be the most prosperous spot in the Southwestern part of China. The tall buildings such as those of Meifeng Bank, where Han Suyin met her uncle, and Sichuan Salt Business Bank had still stood there but because of the many direct hits they received, they had been badly pitted, and their neighborhood, which used to be a busy shopping center, had been turned into a settlement of makeshift huts.

The eighty-nine middle-sized bombers and three scout planes of the United Air Raid Corps presented themselves in three groups in the clear skies of Chongqing and from the height of 6,900m, dropped the bombs of 800kg, 250kg and 60kg, and reported: "They all hit the marks." As for how successful that sortie was, it was telegraphed to the headquarters at Hankou the following day by the chief officer of Japan's Shanghai Special Service Agency (which belonged to the Army of the Expeditionary Force in Shanghai) in the form of *The News from the Chief Officer of Shanghai Special Service Agency*—a translated version of the English language newspaper published in Shanghai:

> The 126 Japanese planes dropped literally the shower of bombs along with a large number of promotional leaflets in the district where the British and French consulates and a Christian church exist. The British Embassy that faces the British Consulate had bombs dropped on its windows and ceilings but the bombs having remained unexploded, they narrowly escaped danger. The number of the killed or injured reached 200; Houses destroyed reached 100. Both British and French Consulates were burnt to ashes because of the direct hits they received, but none were killed or injured. In the downtown area, there was a large fire. Fierce attacks were being given by the high-angle guns, while the air battles were fought against the fleets of fighter planes.
>
> —*A Detailed Report of "the 14th (daytime) Attack on Chongqing"*
> *by Takao Air Corps*

Xin Hua Ri Bao (*New China Daily News*) also carried the news of the same purport along with "the talk of Mei Deyu, the counselor of the U.K. Embassy, given to the reporter, Bai Meide, of this newspaper company." As for the casualties that day, it was recorded: there were 22 deaths, 67 injuries and 82 houses destroyed.

There was a mission every day until 29th.

At Hankou W Base, the largest base for the sortie of the Navy Air Force, there was a lining up of the crew from six to seven in the morning. All the aviators of each attack corps consisting of 20 to 30 planes, each of which had a crew of seven, stood in a row before their commander, and after having confirmed the order they had received the night before, they took off. Each face had begun to assume more and more fatigue as the days went on. The crew's accommodations had been brought into being by converting what used to be the stands of Hankou Racetrack, and after their troops were reinforced, what used to be a prison was also made used of. Hankou toward the end of June had already been in the hottest season that was comparable to "a fireplace." In *The History of Japan's Navy Air Force (3)—On the System & Technology*, there is a description as follows: "The temperature remained from 37℃ to 39℃ till late at night. There was no wind. Thus their lack of sleep was considered to be one of the main reasons of their accumulated fatigue. This led us to bring a block of ice in each of their bedrooms and to provide them with air-conditioning units sent over from home with not a little difficulty. We also had given many of the crew an intra-muscular injection with glucose and vitamins in it." Here we can see the Japanese Navy's traditional attitude in which they did their best in attacking the enemy but did not pay so much attention to what had supported their activities at the very base.

Still unable to stop their attack, and since the number of crew was limited, it was always the same members that came to line up before their commander. Lieutenant Adachi Jiro of Takao Air Corps wrote in his memoirs: "Our attack was given day after day until it began to be called a daily trimming of Chongqing, and time and again, we made a double sortie—in the morning and in the afternoon."

The following was the order, received on the night of June 27 by Takao Navy Air Corps (23 middle-sized bombers), the 13th Air Corps (26 planes) and the 15th Air Corps (27 planes)—led by Captain Sado Naohiro:

The United Air Raid Unit: Command No.53
  The order received:
    1) Tomorrow (28th) the United Air Raid Unit shall perform the 18th attack upon Chongqing.
    2) Each corps shall attack according to the following:
        a) The places to attack (the map omitted)
           N.B. (A) Each platoon of the attack corps shall carry a No.80 land bomb.
           N.B. (B) The Army Planes are to bomb the western part of B Section around 14:40
        b) The point of attack shall be made according to what has been prescribed by supreme commander in the air
        c) Communication deployment shall be the 1st communication deployment
    3) The Reconnoitering Unit must send a scout plane to make a preliminary survey over Chongqing
       Time to take off: 07: 00
       The target for the bombing: B & D Sections

Bombing altitude: over 6,500m / Direction for entry: North
How to Bomb:
a) As for Bombs No.80 (800kg weighing), each flying corps shall consider so that they may be scattered evenly all over.
b) Saturation bombings are preferable to save time.

In that air raid, Kanoya Flying Corps (18 planes) was to join, and the Army's 16th Flight Squadron at Yuncheng was to join them to attack the western part of Division D. Each attack corps, after receiving the order, started the engine, immediately causing a sandstorm that prevented even the sight of the comrade planes, and after flying up, while circling round and round, divided themselves into triangular nine-plane formations, and after fixing their course to the west, they entered the flight course that commanded the view of the Yangzi. This was how "the Regular Flight for Chongqing" started in order to perform their bombing there, spending seven hours in going and coming back.

● **The School Zone & the Source of Water Supply were also Made their Attack Targets**

"The 18th Air Raid upon Chongqing" on June 28th was to be concentrated on the B and the D sections in the former castle area. The following was the report on how it was carried out. This was sent from Rear-Admiral Yamaguchi Tamon, the Commander of the United Air Raid Corps at Hankou, to Inoue Shigeyoshi, the Chief of Staff, waiting at the Fleet of the China Region:

The Attack on the Interior

We performed the 18th attack upon Chongqing and achieved brilliant results by bombing upon the political and military centers and the source of water supply.
(1) The attack corps (Commander-in-chief: Rear-Admiral Sada)
The 26 middle-sized attack planes of the 13th group in the 3rd attack unit made a bombing raid on the northwestern part of the Chuandong Normal School district (Section D), employing the 8 bombs of No.80, the 18 bombs of No.30 and the 54 bombs of No.6.
Most of them dropped on the area of the Inspection House, Baxuan

Middle School and some military establishments in the neighborhood started fires; two of them went up in flames (one of them gave blasting flames). Several bombs dropped on the area of gun-factories did give a massive damage upon them.

(2) The battles in the air

   (a) omitted

   (b) omitted

   (c) The third attack corps: Forward below, they caught sight of eight fighters, but chose not to fight. After having performed bombardment, we had one fighter plane to fight against for about 15 minutes. After having made its fuel blow out, we repulsed it (at an altitude of 6,800m).

If we follow the attack having been made by the 15th Air Corps that day according to *The Detailed Report on the Raid & Fight of the 15th Air Corps* (under the command of Lieutenant-Commander Mihara Gen-ichi), it went as follows:

11:00	Our 27 middle-sized attack planes got together at the 14th Base
11:25	We departed from high above. The altitude of the clouds near the Base was 400m. Around Tianmen we came above the clouds.
13:30	The Sichuan plains were in fine weather. In the area 20 nautical miles south of Peizhou, the weather remained fair and clear with 40 nautical miles' visibility. At Zuanjiang, we flew at the altitude of 6,700m.
13:56	We made a dash to bomb while receiving considerably heavy defensive fire.
	We turned to a charge at the course of zero degree: the 1st and the 2nd Squadrons performed their bombardment on Shanhuba Airport and on the swarms of junks on the River, while the 3rd Squadron bombed on the commercial and residential area in the southwestern part of the castle area. Our altitude was 6,800m; our course was 355 degrees; our speed was 93 knots.
14:15	The bombardment was over.
16:45	There being no air battle to fight, we all returned without difficulty.

The following was the fruit of their mission the Third Squadron reported:

"All the bombs hit the marks in the commercial and residential areas which had remained unbombed so far. Some of the bombs hit an arsenal and started a couple of fires that caused a great damage."

The time needed for this was five hours and 45 minutes in going and returning, and 19 minutes in bombing. As for the First Attack Corps of 35 middle-sized bombers (led by Rear Admiral Sada as Commander-in-Chief) that accompanied the 15th Air Corps, entered their target position at 14:32 after Mihara's squad left their area of the sky, and dropped a dozen of 800kg bombs, twenty-eight 250kg bombs and fifty-six 60kg bombs upon Zilai Source of Water Supply and caused "facilities in its neighborhood to receive concentrated impacts and one of them started a large fire, causing its neighborhood to be greatly damaged," as was reported in *The Outline of How the United Air Raid Corps Engaged in the Battles – No.43*. Thus we are able to see that: even the source of water supply had been made a target of their bombing.

On the other hand, *The News form the Chief Officer of Shanghai Special Service Agency* (a Japanese-language newspaper) brought more specific information which could not be obtained by the observation from the sky. That was a translated version of such news sources as the English-language newspapers published in Shanghai, UPI (United Press International) or a Reuters report or *Zhongyang Tongxun-she* (*China's Central News Agency*)'s Telegram. In those news sources, what the indiscriminate bombings were really like was grasped fairly precisely. Those newspapers used to be employed as the materials for the Japanese top leaders on the spot to make their overall judgment:

A little past noon on June 28, about 120 Japanese planes gave an assault on Chongqing and dropped one thousand incendiary bombs. Due to the unusual heat day in and day out as well as the drought they were suffering this year, the fires that had started here and there went on spreading furiously all over the city despite the effort of the fire fighters. Even though several hours had passed after the air raid was over, the force of fire would not abate, and this is likely to cause a tremendous damage. The U.K. Diplomatic Commissioners' Office and Consulate General's Office also caught fire and they were made totally impossible to reside there. The office of the Reuter's

News Agency also caught fire though it was narrowly brought under control.

Today's air raid upon the city and its western suburbs had turned the city into a battlefield of *asuras* (evil gods in the Indian mythology, who fight in wild frenzy) and caused the whole city to be wrapped up in flames. A large number of junks upon the Yangzi and the Jialing were made to sink, letting piles of corpses flow down the Rivers.

The Shaci Ward (the present Shapingba Ward) that had been made one of the targets for the twenty-three planes of Takao Air Corps that day had popularly been known as "the School Ward" because most of the nineteen universities that had moved from Beijing, Shanghai and Nanjing had settled there. National Zhongyang (Central) University had suffered direct hits to be badly destroyed, and the housing for the teachers and other staff was also burnt. Fortunately since it was during the summer vacation, the number of the killed or injured seemed to have been small, according to *Xin Hua Ri Bao* (*New China Daily*). The same university was bombed the next day, too, and lost both the boarding houses for male students and those for female students.

According to *The Detailed Report of the 18th* (*Daytime*) *Attack and Battle* (performed by the Takao Flying Corps on June 28, 1940), four among the twenty-two No.25 bombs (250kg) had been fitted with "the 99-type fuse" or a delayed action fuse. This type of fuse, instead of being explosive as soon as the bomb reached the ground, was so adjusted as to operate two hours to twenty-four hours later. That was, it had led the people to believe *it* to be a blind one, and *it* was so made as to explode when dug out during their restoration work. Thus the bombardments in the No. 101 Operations were beginning to assume such nature as might be called "deliberate indiscrimination."

The air raids performed in June, 1940, reached as many as a dozen times, causing 802 deaths and 1,171 injuries, and 5,873 houses and buildings were destroyed.

The following was what UPI (United Press International) reported as to what the urban area of Chongqing was like. (*The History of the Japanese Navy Air Force* in *The Library of the War History* edited by the Defense Agency of Japan) What it appeared was not different from what was observed from high above in the sky:

1. The twenty percent of the buildings in the whole urban area were totally destroyed, while the eighty percent of them were damaged, and not even a single street remained free from any damage.
2. Danzishi in Jiangbei (North of the Jialing) having received vehement bombardments, it presents really disastrous scenes.
3. At present, eighty to ninety percent of the stores and shops in Chongqing have suspended business.
4. All the government offices and the accommodation for civil servants on Shangqing-si Street having been destroyed, they all have moved to the suburbs since June 13.
5. The important buildings destroyed so far are as follows:
    (1) The administration establishments = the newly-built government establishments were blasted, including the one for the National Government's Executive Council, which had received a direct hit.
    (2) The educational facilities = Chongqing University (50 direct hits). Fudan University (the buildings were burnt down; the person in charge of educational affairs and more than twenty of his colleagues were killed or injured). Education Institute (seven people, including the principal, were bombed to death). Chuandong Normal School and Zhongyang University (destroyed). Zhongyang Techinical School (the Experimental Factory and the Laboratory were destroyed).
    (3) The shopping areas and residential areas = Approximately 2,000 houses were burnt down.
    (4) Ice Manufactories were destroyed, causing a water shortage; Gas Oil Factories and Yufeng Cotton Mill Factory were destroyed; *Zhongyang Ri Bao* (Central Daily News) had its downtown factory totally destroyed.
    (5) Public facilities = Water service pipes and electric wires were exploded and cut, interrupting water supply and electric power supply in all the urban area, excepting Jiangnan (the area south of the Yangzi).
6. Prices have risen several times higher than what they were this spring: One *tan* of rice (16 *quan*) costs 130-140 *yuan;* one *tan* of charcoal costs 18 *yuan* (when a laborer's daily pay was 3 or 4 *yuan*).
7. Because they are forced to stay in the air-raid shelters—whose

ventilation is far from good—for six and seven hours a day, more and more people are falling ill.

8. The Government's measures taken to meet the situation: The people are ordered to move somewhere for safety, while all the important establishments military, economic, educational, industrial and so on, seem to be made to move somewhere safe in the neighboring villages.

Whatever seen around simply appeared terrible, but the Nationalist Party and its Government authorities had issued the statement, declaring that: they would never leave chongqing. On June 30, the extraordinary session of Chongqing City's Counsilors adopted a resolution to criticize the violence being inflicted by the Japanese militarists, and gave a declaration as follows:

The Japanese militarists, relying upon their violence, making the most of their air force, are now attacking our city in the hinterland. During the last two months, the air raids they performed upon Chongqing have reached as many as nineteen times. A large number of innocent citizens were sacrificed, while we had our cultural institutions, schools, news media and churches suffer damages (while such embassies as British, Soviet Union, German and French—and such news agencies from abroad as Tass, Transozean and Havas—and foreign residents' lives and properties have received damages by dint of the enemy's premeditated attacks.) Our enemy's aim is obvious: they intend to crash our will to fight against them; they intend to threaten the Third Powers' diplomatic officials and residents till they give up their staying here, so that Japan may realize its illusion of reigning over the East Asia. Now, we shall tell the military clique from Japan that: that plan of yours will never be realized. Not even a single citizen of Chongqing has not got angry at the cruel violence you have inflicted upon us by making use of those planes of yours. These grudges we have been made to carve into our mind while suffering these air raids performed with utmost cruelty will never leave us even after a hundred years have passed. The seven hundred thousand citizens of Chongqing, while being bombed by the enemy planes, have firmly believed that: some day in the future the Japan's militarists will surely be made to repay those blood debts. Now we shall deliver our hope that: each of us will keep the place of our duty, while supporting our national policy of position warfare of resistance, believing in the final victory we shall win, and hoping that: we shall have those international supports directed upon us, so that we may destroy this common enemy of humanity.

——*Sichuan Province & the War against Japan*
included in *A Record of Chongqing's Resistance to Japan*

Despite the great expectation held by the chief of staff, Inoue Shigeyoshi, "the Battle of the Japan Sea"* unfolded upon the stage of Chongqing did not seem to go so successfully as was expected by the Japanese side.

The Zero Fighters' First Appearance

● **More and More Middle-Sized Attack Planes were Shot down
to Worry Inoue & Others**

It was also during the No.101 Operations—in the summer of 1940—that the carrier-based planes popularly known as "Zero fighters" made their first appearance in the battle scene. Since then, until Japan was defeated in the Pacific War, they were known as the representative arms of Japan's Navy Air Force which kept active in the immense sky, overlooking the vast hemisphere from the Aleutian Islands in the extreme north to the Coral Sea in the southern hemisphere. It was in August that year when the Zero Fighters made their first appearance as the fighter planes to guard the middle-sized air raiders being engaged in the indiscriminate bombardments upon Chongqing. The "Zero" in the official name came from "the zero" at the end of "2,600"—the figures to be remembered by the fact that: the year 1940 happened to be the 2,600th year after the accession of the First Emperor of Japan, Jimmu who, according to the official legend, ascended to the throne in the Land of Yamato (present-day Nara), as was recorded in *Nihon Shoki* (the oldest official history of Japan, compiled in thirty volumes in 720 during the Nara period (710-784)).

Because of this dramatic appearance they made and the remarkable achievements they performed, the Zero Fighters were to bring about a turning point in the history of Sino-Japanese aerial battles, but at the same time all the processes they followed from their birth to their perishing could be compared to a looking glass which was to reflect the climax and the downfall of Japan's

Navy Air Force. Here, too, Japan's bombardment upon Chongqing was to mingle with the unfolding of the history later on, while suggesting something.

Though it had already been made clear in the preceding year, what was becoming more and more annoying to the top leaders on the spot of the 101 Operations—Inoue Shigeyoshi, Yamaguchi Tamon and Onishi Takijiro— was the growing percentage of damages given to their middle-sized bombers. As the Operations were growing fiercer, that percentage was rising from a tolerable extent to an intolerable one, and unless a quick action was taken, the Operations were quite likely to taper out because of the loss and exhaustion of the mechanical equipment and materials as well as the crew members. It went without saying that the primary cause for this was the single mission of the middle-sized bombers without accompanying any escort fighter plane, and this led the corps in the front line to keep demanding the arrival of the new and powerful combat planes they had badly needed.

During the period of the Plan of No.101 Operations, the Army and the Navy Air Forces were to lose eight planes respectively, causing 111 deaths and 49 injuries—with the greatest damages in June or at the height of the Operations. In the same month, the Navy's United Air Raid Corps had their five middle-sized attack planes shot down with 43 men in them. According to the report given in the same month, 97 planes were shot in the air battle, 57 planes were shot by high-angle guns from the ground, as was recorded in *The Synopsis of the No.101 Operations*. The bomber fleet of the Army Air Force also in the same month had their 67 planes shot in the air battle and lost four 97-type heavy bombers and two scout planes. (*The Army Air Force's Aerial Operations in China Incident* (2)). Losing planes was naturally painful, but having those expert airmen killed was even more painful. The main reason why they had suffered so many losses during their bombing at the altitude as high as 6,500m was: at the earlier stage, the Chinese interceptor fighters, having had no oxygen-supply apparatus, could not perform patrolling flight at the altitude higher than 5,000m, and this had enabled the Japanese planes to cope with the enemy planes with some wider scope than the enemy's, but as the No.101 Operations went on, all of the Chinese planes began to be equipped with an oxygen-supply apparatus that enabled them to fly as high as 7,500m and to attack the Japanese planes from above. On the other hand, when the clouds were low, the Japanese planes were obliged to perform low-altitude bombings, and this led the Chinese side to employ their ground fire effectively. Having suffered damage after damage, the Japanese side could not help decreasing their number of sorties from 12 times in June to 5 times in July.

In the 9th bombing action on June 10th, the two planes, including the captain's plane, were knocked out of the sky. That day, the fifty-three middle-sized bombers of the 13th flying corps of the Second United Air Corps had all been out to perform this mission. The clouds being low with 15 km's visibility, it was unsuitable for a high-altitude bombing. At 11:52, they took off from the base. At 13:50, they were ordered to change their targets, but at 14:08, this order was recalled, and at 14:20, there came an order: "There are signs of the weather in the Chongqing region improving. So each formation shall do its best in attacking Chongqing." Thus they decided to enforce a daytime low-altitude bombing. The director in the air was Lieutenant Commander Kotani Yuji, a 53rd graduate from the Naval Academy, who had been piloting the middle-sized attack plane since he joined the transoceanic bombing upon Nanjing, and after having taken part in aerial advancing operations at the early stage of the Sino-Japanese War, he was chosen to be a Grade One conscript to enter the Naval Staff College to learn higher military technique, and in April that year he had come back to the Chinese front for the third time. Now leading twenty-seven planes in the three squadrons, he got on the first plane of the first squadron. Each plane was carrying a couple of 250kg bombs and four 60kg bombs on board.

At 14:40, the air raid corps performed their bombing in and around the H section or the Chuandong Normal School District (to finish it at 15:02). As was done by the Director's plane, the other planes had dropped all their bombs in a single passing. The lumps of 50kg and 60kg explosives wrapped in iron went falling one after another upon the urban area below their eyes. This season, early in May according to the lunar calendar, was the time when—if in the time of peace—many people came out to enjoy their "Dragon Boat Festival" by floating their boats on the Yangzi. But now, they had Japanese air planes come to intrude on their traditional festivities, and this was to lead the newspapers in Chongqing to employ such expressions as "the air raid to disturb our superb season blessed with the congratulatory sunshine."

From the Commander Kotani's plane, a telegram of their "having finished their bombardment" was sent to the Command Office at Hankou, and immediately after all the planes under his command left the sky of Chongqing behind, there arose an air battle. A dozen of Chinese fighters ("Italian-style 15" made in the Soviet Union and Curtis Hawks made in the U.S.) had suddenly descended upon them. At 15:45, there followed a telegram: "We are fighting with eight enemy planes." The slow-motioned bombers were now facing the agile fighters. To make the matter worse, the bad weather had obliged the middle-sized bombers to fly low. The enemy's attacks were concentrated on Kotani's plane leading the formation.

"Our plane with Captain ××× on board, leading the three formations, fought against Japanese planes by adopting the tactics of flickering flash of lightening."—This was the opening of the article on *Xin Hua Ri Bao* (New China Daily News) issued on the day that followed. That was what had been distributed by Zhong Yang (Central) News Agency on a Nationalist line. The name of the commander had not been mentioned probably for the reasons of military secrecy. According to that article, the Chinese planes got into "a formation of the fierce tigers trying to snatch the sheep," and dashed into the enemy's formation to cause immediate sounds of gunfire. Such expressions as "flickering flash of lightening" and "a formation of the fierce tigers to snatch the sheep" did sound like the Chinese. Two of the Japanese planes, pouring out black smoke, vanished in the direction of the peak of Mt. Shiziling in the city of Bishan, and "the rest were scattered in all directions to hide themselves" in the dense clouds.

The plane with Captain ××× on board kept a watch, while flying around the breaks of clouds. Ten minutes later it caught sight of "the enemy's chief's plane" (probably Kotani's plane) coming out of the thick clouds. The news story went on: "Our planes at once followed it at the utmost speed and surrounded it to give it a fierce attack: The rain of bullets caused the oil tank to burst and burn till the plane fell in the western suburbs of Fuling." This was how what must have been Kotani's plane came to an end. Fuling was a city 75km east of Chongqing, also seated along the Yangzi. The newspaper account did describe how the oil tank got burst and burnt the whole plane, and this weak point was to be succeeded to its successors along with its nickname of "the 1-type lighter." That was a sort of "character inheritance" which had already been known as a weak point of Japan's middle-sized attack planes. The Chinese fighters—the Italian-style 15s made in the Soviet Union and the Hawks made in the U.S.—making themselves in two or three groups, kept strafing from behind or from either side of the formation of the middle-sized attack planes desperately heading east.

On the other hand, according to *The Detailed Report on the Attacks & Actions upon Chongqing* compiled by the United Air Raid Unit—at 16:28 or forty-three minutes after the telegram of "we are fighting with eight enemy planes" was sent, a report was sent to Hankou Air Base from Lieutenant Okuyama Masaichi, the chief of the third squadron: "At 15:52, our leading plane performed a heroic crash into an enemy plane."

● **Inoue Shigeyoshi Eagerly Requested to Send Zero Fighters**
into the Air Battle

The following was *The Report of the Outline of the Battle* sent from the Commander of the United Air Raid Unit to Inoue Shigeyoshi, the Chief of Staff:

I . The Attack on the Hinterland

This day all the middle-sized attack planes and land scout planes of our corps performed the 9th attack upon Chongqing with all our might. The 13th and the 15th attack corps, though suffering from bad weather and fervent ground fire, carried out a fervent air battle against about two dozens of combat planes, before we performed a great achievement of destroying their military facilities in Chongqing..

1) The second attack corps of the 13th air corps or the 27 middle-sized attack planes (led by Lieutenant Commander Kotani) took off at 11:30. At 15:28, they bombed on the district around Chuandong Normal School, applying 54 bombs (No. 25) and 108 bombs (No.6). We also gave a tremendous damage at the base of the high-angle guns and other important facilities to the west of the castle wall.

2) The Air Battle:

After the attack mentioned above was over, a dozen of fighter planes (E15, E16 and H-type Biplane Fighters) appeared and during the vehement air battle that lasted for about thirty minutes, we shot down 6 planes (as for one of them, we could not make sure).

3) The Damage:

After the battle mentioned above was over, the Commander's plane

(Lieutenant Commander Kotani, Lieutenant Ikeda, Warrant Officer Yano and the five commissioned officers under him) received a concentrated attack on their plane until it started a fire, and at a point about 80 nautical miles east of Chongqing, they crashed their plane to perform their heroic deaths.

As for the rest, one was severely injured; 20 planes were bombarded.

Between the newspaper article on the Chinese side and this *Report on the Outline of the Battle* on the Japanese side, there was a little difference in the point where Kotani's plane had crashed, but judging from the state of things before and after that, what was reported in *Xin Hua Ri Bao* would have been correct. Under such low clouds, it was impossible for the planes to form any tight formation so that they might cope with the enemy planes by exchanging their own gunfire; thus each plane left alone was likely to be made a target to be crushed down one after another. Nevertheless, the 96-type carrier-based fighters could not be employed as escort planes because their flying range was too short to fly to and from Chongqing. This made the crew of the middle-sized bombers clench their fists and grind their teeth with vexation, saying: "If only we had any proper fighter planes to accompany us."

Thus the appearance of the Zero Fighters at this point was a welcome trump card to enhance the effect of Chongqing bombardment to the utmost extent by winning a come-from-behind victory at a single strike when the battles performed every day in the skies of Chongqing were being tended to go from bad to worse. Both Commanders Yamaguchi Tammon and Onishi Takijiro had also been impatiently wishing to have those latest model planes sent into the air battles to improve their war situation. If only their long-range flight were to be employed, their middle-sized bombers would always be directly guarded by them, while driving away the enemy fighter planes by dint of a couple of powerful 20mm machine guns—thus to surely win the command of the air above the point where their raid were being performed—according to the judgment of the air corps at the field headquarters.

At that occasion when Inoue, chief of the staff, compared the Plan of No. 101 Operations to the *Battle of the Japan Sea*[*] at his preliminary meeting with the Naval General Staff in Tokyo, too, he had requested the Zero Fighters to be sent as soon as possible to improve the war situation, and according to one of the Staff, Nakayama Sadayoshi, who had accompanied him to Tokyo, was to record in his memoirs: "It was not long before the seven Zero Fighters were added to the Fleet of the China Region."

The Zero Fighters, which presented themselves in the skies of China, were assigned to the 12th Flying Corps in the Second United Air Corps under Onishi Takijiro. So far No. 12 Flying Corps, mainly consisting of the 96-type carrier-based airplanes, had been performing their duty of defending the sky over the Wuhan district, but now that they had Zero Fighters deployed, they were expected to perform another mission of fighting for the supremacy in the skies of Chongqing, Chengdu and other cities in Sichuan Province.

The Zero fighters had still been going through a performance test under the name of "the 12 carrier-based fighters on their trial," and since July 21, the first fifteen of them began to arrive at Hankou by way of Yokosuka, Omura and Shanghai to be received by Commander Onishi and others. So far not any such planes still under experiment for practical use had ever presented themselves at the front, to be adopted as formal fighter planes (July 24) and to join the operations as early as the following month.

*The "12" comes from the 12th year of Showa era (1937), meaning that: this model was manufactured by way of trial in *that* year. When adopted formally, it was renamed "Zero Fighter" by adopting the "0" from the 2,600th year of the Imperial Reign which Japan then had adopted,

Concerning the circumstances for these occurrences, Commander Taguchi Taro as the Head Chief of the Stuff of the Second United Air Force and Lieutenant Yokoyama Tamotsu as the chief of the flying corps of Zero fighters have left their testimony in *A History of the Navy Air Force: On the Battles*—in *A Series of War History* edited by *the Department of War History* of the Defense Agency of Japan:

These 12 carrier-based fighter planes on their trial had not yet formally been adopted when they arrived at Hankou, and even after we received them, we were to find several faults in them, and it took considerable number of days before we were able to place sufficient trust in those planes themselves.

On the other hand, however, both commanders Yamaguchi and Onishi, were rather impatient to see the newly-produced airplanes fly a mission. One night, with the permission of Commander Onishi, I, using his name, invited all the airmen who were to go on board the Zero fighters to a Japanese-style luxury restaurant in Hankou and dined together. On the morning that followed, the plan for attacking Chongqing was submitted by the chief of the flying corps, Lieutenant Yokoyama Tamotsu, and this having been adopted as it was, it was to lead to their first air raid upon Chongqing on August 19.

Lieutenant Yokoyama Tamotsu, the chief of the flying corps of Zero Fighters, also gave such recollection as follows:

I was called out as many as two times by Commanders Yamaguchi and Onishi sitting in company with each other and was urged to fly a mission as soon as possible. I had thought flying a mission should occur only after I had plenty of confidence in all of their mechanism, but there were two points which had not yet fully improved: while fighting, their legs sometimes dropped in the air; their newly-added fuel tanks occasionally would not come down. But these faults being not so absolutely fatal, I finally decided to let them fly their first mission. As for the duration of their flight, we got more confidence in it, as we flew more missions. At the early stage, they had made Xuanchang their transit port on their way to Chengdu, but in the end, they became confident in their ability to perform their mission by making Hankou their base (520 nautical miles between Hankou and Chengdu). This was to become a primary cause of Takao Flying Corps in Taiwan having adopted—at the opening of the Greater East Asia War at a later date—the direct attack upon Luzon Island (Manila).

These do prove how much expectation they had placed upon the appearance of the Zero Fighters.

- **Having Secured the Command of the Air by being Escorted**
by the Zero Fighters

The Zero fighters' first mission took place on August 19. They were expected to guard the bombers on their 30th mission for the bombardment upon

Chongqing. The latest model planes, which had been called "12 carrier-based fighters on their trial" so far, were now to be entered in *The Detailed Report of the Battles* under the name of "Zero Fighters." The mission given to the United Air Raid Unit (the 15th Flying Corps, Kanoya Air Corps and the 13th Flying Corps), each with 27 planes (81 planes in total), directed by Commander Hibata Hisatoshi, went as follows:

Tomorrow, on August 19, the United Air Raid Unit shall perform an attack upon Chongqing; the enemy's fighter planes shall be caught both in the air and on the ground to be destroyed in a single action.

As for the capacity on the Chinese side, it was estimated as follows:

As for the number of the combat planes in Sichuan Province, about 50 will be at the front line, and 20 of them seem to be permanently stationed at Chongqing. While we are raiding upon Chongqing, some of those in Chengdu will fly to Chongqing to offer their assistance.

According to the *Main Point of the Attack*, the corps of middle-sized bombers was expected to take some evasive action to adjust the timing, and about 30 minutes after the battle started, they were to dash at the sky of the city.

As for "the twelve Zero Fighters" which came to acquire a position of "a combat unit" to attack Chongqing under the command of lieutenant Yokoyama Tamotsu, the points of action for them to take went as follows:

At 12:30, the combat unit shall meet the Army's scout planes in the sky of Xuanchang and shall be guided to Chongqing to attack the enemy planes. According to the situation, dare to dash at them to capture and destroy them.

Xuanchang in Hubei Province—which was now turned into the takeoff base for the Zero Fighters—was 270km from Hankou in a straight line (722km along the Yangzi). The Yangzi from there on suddenly reduces its width, before entering the canyon area featured by "Sanxia" in between the rugged ranges of the Daiba Mountains. Xuanchang was located at the entrance to that new stage of geographical scenery. In June that year, Xuanchang had been occupied by the

Army, responding to a strong demand from the Navy, as was mentioned before, and since then a flight base had been kept developing, and from that day on, it was to be used by the Zero fighters as their takeoff base and relay exchange point. Shuttling between Xuanchang and Chongqing was 960km, and since the flying range of the Zero Fighters was 3,500km, they could not only guard the middle-sized bombers while they were doing their job but also keep circling round and round the skies of Chongqing for a long time, thus preventing the enemy fighter planes from doing anything.

On July 15, Lieutenant Yokoyama, along with six Zero Fighters, advanced into Hankou; at the end of that month, he was followed by Lieutenant Shindo Saburo, who also had led six Zero Fighters, thus to equip the Hankou Air Base with a dozen of Zero Fighters. Early in the morning of August 19, they took off at Hankou, and after the refueling at Xuanchang, they headed for Chongqing. On the other hand, the middle-sized bombers that flew straight from Hankou to Chongqing, waited for about an hour, circling around the sky of Peiling, thus making a feint so that Chinese planes might take off from Guangyangba Airbase for interception, so that at the arrival of their fighter planes they could enter the sky of Chongqing from northwest to perform their air raid upon the urban area at the height of more than 6,000m. The sky was clear; the visibility was 64km; the clouds seen were altostratus of 25,000m in the north and the west; the sky of Chongqing was perfectly cloudless.

In a mission of protecting the bomber fleet, a dozen of Zero Fighters, led by a couple of scout planes, had taken off at 12:40 from the sky of Xuanchang, and now they were approaching Chongqing, expecting to meet their enemy fighters. An hour and a half later, they arrived at the airspace they had been heading for (and sent a telegraph of their arrival there) but none of the Chinese planes could be seen either in the sky or on the ground. The bomber fleet following them telegraphed to the scout plane, asking: "Has the air battle started?" But the answer given at 14:35 was: "No enemy fighters can be seen." The Chinese side, having already perceived the appearance of newly-produced fighter planes, seemed to have taken refuge. As was least expected, none of the enemy planes could be seen to take off—either from Guangyangba Airbase or from any other airbase in the suburbs of Chongqing.

From the Zero Fighter with Captain Yokoyama on board came another telegram (at 14:38): "We see no fighter planes; there will be no air battle."

This led to the order given at 14:44 from the commander in the air to each of the three groups of the middle-sized air-raiders that had been waiting in the sky to the south of Chongqing: "Start attacking the city area at once." The aims for their attack that day had been decided to be Division B and Division D in the city when there was no plane seen in their bases. The eighty-one middle-sized bombers entered that sky not from northwest, as had been scheduled, but from south to fly toward north, thus to drop 634 bombs, each of which weighed 60kg, concentrating on the urban area in the western part of the former castle area. Excepting several bombs that had dropped into the Yangzi, all had hit the marks in that area, according to the judgment of the director in the air, and this led to the telegram sent at 14:50 to the headquarters at Hankou: "Our bombardment is over; all our planes are now flying in formation." The dozen of Zero Fighters that had not had any air battle, after supporting the bombardment performed by the middle-sized attack planes, while taking a combat-ready stance, landed at Xuanchang at 16:15, thus to fulfill their mission that day. When landing at the port, one of them was turned over to be half-damaged, causing one of the crew to get slightly injured. Those were the only damage and injury the Zero Fighters had had that day.

The following day was to see a report on the achievement in "the 30th attack upon Chongqing," sent to the Director of the Fleet of the China Region by telegraph, as is seen in the 88th issue of *The General Outlines of the United Air Raid Unit:*

> Both of the Zero Fighters and the middle-sized bombers were going to do their best in seizing the enemy fighters in and around the skies of Chongqing, but just before our arrival there, they all flew away and not a single enemy plane was seen around there all the time. Thus the bombers, guarded by the fighters commanding the air, bombed some military facilities in the urban area and the air base at Shimazhou, thus to achieve great things.

In *The Detailed Report of the 13th Flying Corps*, too, there was a description such as: "Under the perfect command of the air brought about by our fighter-planes' platoon, our bombardment was efficiently performed" and it was proudly reported that: "all of our 96-type land attack planes" would be available the following day. Certainly the Zero Fighters seemed to have brought about a great change in the form of bombardment upon Chongqing.

On *the Asahi* (one of the leading newspapers in Japan) for August 20, under the headline of "The Navy & the Army had their Wings United to Wrap the Whole City of Chongqing in Raging Fires; The Sea Eagle Fighters have also Made their Debut," the news from Domei News Agency*—sent on the night of the 19th by the special correspondent, Hayashida, at ○○ Base—went as follows:

> This day, a certain number of fighters of our Navy Air Force were to carry out their first air battle against the enemy's Metropolitan Defense Air Force in the skies of Chongqing. But when our fighters arrived there, we found the enemy's Air Force, cowardly attaching to life, had already flown away, and this prevented our fighters from performing any air battle as we had expected to.

Even though the name of "Zero Fighters" had not been mentioned, since their first military achievement turned out to be a pleasing one, they seem to have released the news within that memorable day.

● The Zero Fighters "Achieved a Great Success" at their First Mission

Under the same sky of Chongqing, where the Japanese airmen had found "no enemy plane in the sky of Chongqing," a great deal of damage was being brought about. The twenty-seven planes of the First Attack Corps (the 15th Air Raid Corps) dropped 312 bombs each of which weighed 60kg upon the southern part of D Division; the twenty-seven planes of the Second Attack Corps (Kanoya Flying Corps) dropped 324 bombs, each of which weighed 60kg, aiming upon the southern part of B Division or the southeastern part of the former castle area. Though they received "several inactive anti-aircraft guns from the ground," the middle-sized bombers "performed effective bombardments," while being guarded by the Zero fighters. But to the citizens of Chongqing, this bombardment was to be among the several unforgettably poignant experiences. A portion of what it was like could be imagined by the report from the chief military officer in the Special Service Agency in Shanghai:

> Concerning the air raid performed upon Chongqing on August 19, UPI

goes as follows: The air raid performed at noon on August 19 by about 100 Japanese bombers turned out to be such a large-scaled one as has never been made before, having brought about thorough damage upon the castle area. Though the details have not yet been inquired into, the fires spread as wide as one mile square, and fifteen streets were burnt down. In addition to these, more than ten thousand houses or straw-thatched cottages were burnt down.

The area that had been stricken that day was roughly the same that had suffered the damage on "5.3. & 5.4." though in some area the damages had gone farther. Taitian Bay, where Hasegawa Teru was living, was also burnt out. The fire that started near Zhaotian-men (the Emperor's Gate) at the tip of the peninsula spread on and on, even outside the castle walls, till it reached as far as Lianglukou which had remarkably been developing. The houses built at this period were all hastily brought into being with bamboo and wood, and once they caught fire, they easily burnt up. In an article of *Xin Hua Ri Bao* (New China Daily), the fierceness of such fires was described as follows: "The sky having been overrun by the fire, fire, fire, the smoky fire, all was dusky with no sunlight reaching the ground." *Xin Min Bao* (New Report for the People), for which Zhang Xiluo worked, had its factory burnt down and this led it to stop issuing their paper from the following day onward. In *Chongqing Kangzhan Jishi* (*A Record on How Chongqing Performed her Resistance War*), the entry for August 19th goes as follows:

From 1:35 on the 19th to 14:00 on 20th, Chongqing suffered four successive bombardments, which destroyed the commercial districts in the west, the suburbs and the wide area in Jianbei (North of the River) Ward. More than thirty-eight fires damaged or destroyed more than two thousand private houses and stores. The number of deaths reached several hundreds. The urban area of Chongqing has been made it impossible to tell one street from another.

These were the first achievements the Zero Fighters had brought about. In *The List of Attacks Performed during the Plan of No.101 Operations,* one can see a note: "At the appearance of the twelve Zero Fighters, all the enemy planes had fled, leaving all the sky for us."

On the other hand, those who were under that same sky *then* were to remember and record it as follows—in *The Statistics on the Air Raid Damages at Various Parts of Sichuan Province: in the 29th Fiscal Year of the People's Republic of China*—"On August 19, Chongqing was to have a total of 135 enemy planes to drop 411 bombs, causing 181 deaths, 132 injuries and 2,194 houses and buildings destroyed."

What was happening on the earth then was totally different from such scenes as were depicted by Japanese writers in such books as were entitled *How the Zero Fighters were Brought into Being*.

But it was an undeniable fact that the appearance of the Zero Fighters had settled the matter of which side would take the command of the air in the sky of Chongqing. The first air battle took place on September 13 between the thirteen Zero Fighters and thirty Chinese planes, and the former downed the twenty-seven planes of the latter without receiving any damage—an overwhelming victory. But even before that, the Chinese planes had come to avoid fighting against the Zero Fighters.

Claire Chennault, the commander of the Flying Tigers, had recorded what the appearance of Zero Fighters meant:

Early in the fall in 1940, the Zero Fighters of the Japanese Air Force made their first appearance at a height of 27,000 feet in the sky of Chungking. That could be compared to the eagles that had flown into a chicken house. The Chinese pilots, one after another, had their planes shot down even before they could tell what was happening to them. Among those were Curtis Light's Hawk Fighters, with which I had given them training in the sky of Kunming.

Chennault at once informed the Headquarters in Washington of the appearance of this horrible type of fighters, reporting its capacity and its technical phase of how it worked, thus providing them with "an ominous warning that: if *these* planes were to be sent toward our planes, it would bring us tremendous damage."

In reaching 27,000 feet (ca. 8,200m) high, the Zero Fighters took only six or seven minutes, while the Chinese planes had to spend fifteen minutes. This difference in mobility became evident when they came to fight. This led

Chennault to contemplate a countermeasure against the Zero fighters, while looking up at them flying in formation.

Thus the natural outcome of the supremacy in the sky of Chongqing became adamantine to Japan, and the Chinese Air Force began to make a point of preserving their aerial capacity, that was, they began to take such measures as to let their planes take refuge somewhere even farther in the depth of hinterland every time the air raid warning was issued, until the people began to mockingly call it "a warning for the planes' evacuation." Such a state of things was to be retained till summer the next year when the No.102 Operation was performed by concentrating the whole power of the Navy Air Force. In that sense, the appearance of the Zero fighters could be said to have prepared a base for bringing the conditions of the perfect strategic bombings into being.

● **The Japanese Military's Invasion into China,**

as was Witnessed by Smedley

In Chongqing about this time—in June, 1940—there appeared a woman journalist from America. Agnes Smedley was her name. She was also to experience "the summer of bombardment," as Edgar Snow had done the summer before. Snow then, while observing the dilapidation brought about by the indiscriminate bombings, was contemplating the effect and limitation of the strategic bombing; Agnes Smedley, looking at the scenes of the streets and the facial expressions of the people, was pondering over China's resistance to Japan, while recalling what her friend, Jack Belden, had once said to her: "If all the names of the people and places in Tolstoy's *War and Peace* were turned into Chinese, it would be turned into a novel concerning the Sino-Japanese War." Smedley had got herself so deeply absorbed in China and its revolution then going on as to make herself confess: "I often find myself having forgotten that I am *not* Chinese." The two reports from the scenes brought about by Snow and by Smedley—*The Battle for Asia* (1941) and *Battle Hymn of China* (1943) —were none other than the contemporary histories in which the cruelties and futilities of the air raids upon Chongqing performed by the Japanese Air Force were exhaustively described.

Snow had entered Chongqing by DC3 passenger plane, thus experiencing "a nighttime guerrilla flight," while Smedley had followed the Poets' Route or "the River Thoroughfare" of Sanxia of the Yangzi before she left the ship at

Zhaotian-men or the Main Gate to the ancient castle of Yuzhou. But this place in the 20th Century had been in the atmosphere totally different from what it used to be in those days when the poet Li Po (701-762) poured out his sentiment in his poem on *Mt. Edun* (3,099m) *in the Moonlight:*

> At night I leave Qingxi for Sanxia;
> Even if I keep thinking about you,
> It doesn't lead to your appearance.
> This leads me to leave for Yuzhou.

What Agnes Smedley saw there in the mid-20th century had nothing to do with such romanticism as that. She had to write in *China's Singing Voices:** "every day I saw swollen-up bodies of men and women come bobbing down the Yangzi, and when they bumped into the junk, its master let them go with a long pole with a large, curved nail fixed at the tip."

Smedley, while staying in Xuanchang, having heard the news of the Japanese Army "putting the Chinese Army to rout as if they were striking sparks out of an anvil block in breaking through the Moshui to advance into the plain beyond" (*Battle Hymn of China*), she got on board the ship with a British flag upon it and sailed up the Yangzi. The air raid upon Xuanchang started and it fell on June 11 to be occupied by the Japanese Army. It was just before that when Smedley got away from Xuanchang in a ship crammed with refugees and the war wounded. Securing Xuanchang had come from a strong demand of the Japanese Fleet of China Region that had wished to obtain a base for the Zero Fighters to bring Chongqing's sky under their control. So it could be said that Smedley was among the first people that had been brought under the control of Zero Fighters. It was not until a couple of months later that the air base was brought into being and the Zero fighters made their appearance there. The ship Smedley had got on board sailed up the whirlpools of the canyon area of the Yangzi, while being threatened by the incessant air-raid warnings. As she wrote, "we could not tell whether or not the Union Jack painted on the deck of that ship would surely guarantee our lives." In mid-June, the ship managed to sail in the port below Zhaotian-men Gate. It was on that occasion that she was to witness the swollen-up bodies of men and women floating around.

By this year, Agnes Smedley had already been in China for a dozen of years.

In 1928, she came to China as a special correspondent of *Frankfurter Zeitung*, and mainly accompanying the Red Army, she informed the world of what China was—concerning its poverty and the progress of its revolution—along with how the Japanese armed forces were invading China. When the Sino-Japanese War broke out and the Red Army was reorganized into the Eighth Route Army under General Chu Teh, Smedley began to move along with Chu Teh's headquarters, and on foot or on horseback, she took part in various battles in her own way, thus fully observing here and there how anti-Japanese guerrilla activities were being carried out. This led her to write: "Only when I was in company with that Army clad in rags, I was able to feel the same kind of democratic satisfaction as I used to feel in the forest of Missouri or in the coal mine in Colorado." The experiences she went through in those days were to develop into the world of *The Great Road,* which opens with *The Prelude:* "This is the story of the first sixty years of the life of General Chu Teh, commander in chief of the People's Liberation Army of China."

Compared with Theodore White and Edgar Snow, the other American journalists, who also devoted themselves to China, Agnes Smedley was clearly different from White, because she had kept her political standpoint clear, and she was farther to the left than Snow, but this did not mean she was a revolutionist, for she was an out-and-out journalist, as she wrote:

> Naturally I am not nonpartisan nor have I pretended to be nonpartisan. But I have never told a lie nor distorted a fact nor given any false report. All I am doing every day is to inform the people of what I have come to know with my own eyes and through my own experiences.
> —*China Fights Back** (1938)

She was brave enough to declare like this. Even when she was branded by the rightists as "a Communist" or criticized by the Communist guerrillas in Yan-an as "an egoist" or "a bourgeois democrat," she pleased herself by calling herself "Smedleyist." Agnes Smedley in the regulation cap and the uniform of the People's Liberation Army never appeared "a Communist guerrilla," but did appear "a daughter of the earth," the heroine of her maiden work, *A Daughter of the Earth* (1929) or did retain the atmosphere as was suggested by the title of its Japanese version—"*Onna Hitori Daichi wo Yuku* (*A Brave Woman Travels*

Alone around the Great Earth)."

Smedley, who returned to America at the end of the year that followed her visit to Chongqing, published *The Battle Hymn of China,* and started to write *THE GREAT ROAD, The Life and Times of Chu Teh,* while she never stopped appealing to the Americans how and why the Chinese people were fighting against the Imperialist Japanese. But she herself never stepped upon the great earth of China again, and when the U.S. Government made an abrupt change in their policy toward China after World War Ⅱ, she left her homeland in disappointment and came to Oxford and passed away in May, 1950—half a year after the People's Republic of China was brought into being. When she visited Chongqing, she had already been forty-six years old.

● **No.101 Operations, as was Experienced by Smedley**

As soon as Smedley reached Chongqing, she was simply thrown into the reality of the No.101 Operations being performed there. Later she wrote: "When the bombers flew into the sky, I made it a rule to lie on my stomach at any ditch I found *then.*"

The Japanese planes would come over in three or four formations ofthirty to fifty bombers each. Sometimes we would stand on the south shore enjoying an illusory sense of safety and watching the bombing of the northern city. When I first arrived, as many as twenty-four Chinese fighter planes were going up to challenge the bombers, but as the days passed there were fewer and fewer of these. Once I saw one solitary Chinese fighter turn and go after a formation of bombers coming up river. At such a moment I longed for the ability to write just one deathless poem to that little plane.

Since Nan-an Ward was guaranteed as the safety zone for the third powers, Smedley and other foreigners had some opportunities to observe the air raids being performed on the other side of the River. Along with her comment on the Chinese planes whose number was growing smaller, this passage does explain how the No. 101 Operations were going on, when seen from the Chinese side. Her having mentioned "the false sense of security" did prove that she had not trusted "the declaration of safety" issued by the Japanese military.

One night, Smedley was invited to dinner by Captain Bartlet, Commander of the gunboat Tutuila. The following was what she had experienced there, as was written in *Battle Hymn of China:*

> When I was on board the gunboat as a visitor there, there came an air-raid warning. The officers and men took up their position. The captain, having supplied me with a steel helmet and a life jacket, took me to the upper deck. So far I had made it a rule to lie on my stomach in the roadside gutter when the enemy planes came into the sky, but today I had to remain standing there with nothing to hide in around. When I asked Captain if we might have any pieces of the bomb come flying around this gunboat, he said: "Yes, indeed. We've once had one piece make a hole on the deck, the other piece hit on the chief gunner's helmet. The most important thing for us is to see where the first bomb has fallen and in which direction the bombers are heading."

For Smedley living in the wartime capital, it was a long summer of horror and fatigue caused by the No. 101 Operations. The following was her report on what she had witnessed after the air raid was over:

> Sometimes the incendiaries landed in the Yangtze and sent up while clouds of fumes and obscured our view of northern city. We would hear the crackling of the fires beyond, and as soon as the "all-clear" had sounded, the people would pour from their underground havens to try to save the city. When the fires had died down, the whole city would resound with hammering and sawing as the people rebuilt their homes and shops.
>
> All day long, we were hearing the bursting sounds of bringing underground shelters into being. Soldiers were doing drill practice or singing in chorus. A variety of government organizations had brought some new societies into being in the suburbs. Groups of coolies were always hanging around the airbases so that every time they suffered an air raid they could repair them. Factories and armories were always kept noisy and busy with the machines working there. And even at the height of the enemy planes' lightning attacks, a large number of groups of boating men in festive costumes did bring themselves over the Yangzi and its tributaries in order to perform their Dragon Boat Festival, as they usually did every year.

The conclusion Agnes Smedley had come to reach while staying in Chongqing was: "Japan would be defeated after all." That was exactly the case with Edgar Snow.

Signs of the Start of the Japan-U.S.War

● **A Fuse to Lead to Pearl Harbor**

On October 25, 1940, Rear-Admiral Onishi Takijiro, the Commander of the Second United Air Force, wrote a letter to one of his former teachers in his middle school days, as is seen in his biography, *Onishi Takijiro:*

> My dear Mr. ○ ○,
>
> I appreciate your kindness of having sent me a letter of congratulations. I am pleased to find you are as healthy as ever. I am also in good health, devoting myself to carrying out the plan of operations. As for the attack on the hinterland of China, since the weather is now becoming unfavorable, we think we must bring it to an end this year. By the personal changes on November 1st, I was transferred to the Commander of a certain unit, and after returning home for a while, I shall be going somewhere overseas again in December, I think. ….

On the day when this letter was written, the 45th bombardment upon Chongqing was being performed, and the final one to be performed the following day was to put an end to all the strategic and political bombings that year (1940).

The foggy season had already set in, and the aimed points had often been hidden deep in the white thick blanket of fog. Gone were the days they called "fire places," and the crew of those middle-sized bombers had been in what was called "radiator suit," as they flew as high as more than 7,000m where the temperature outside had already dropped to nearly 20 degrees below zero. At that height, the oxygen inhaler was also indispensable.

At 10 a.m. on October 25, the 27 middle-sized bombers, led by Lieutenant Commander Suzuki Shoichi, took off at Hankou Air Base, while being seen off by Commander Onishi. At 12:10, the escort fighters took off. Their aim was the military establishment that still remained in B Division (the eastern half of the former castle area of Chongqing). Under the body of each of the bombers, the bombs of 250kg, 60kg and incendiary bombs had been equipped. It might have been while waiting for those bombers to return to the base that Onishi wrote that letter to his former teacher. Onishi's telegraph sent to Commander-in-Chief Shimada went as follows:

Because of the bad weather since the 18th, we had stopped attacking the hinterland. But now the weather having improved since the afternoon of the 24th or yesterday, we are going to perform the 45th attack upon Chongqing.

Under the calm, clear sky they had for the first time after a week of unfavorable weather, the bombers led by Suzuki entered the sky of Chongqing from northwest and on their way to southeast at the speed of 180km per hour, they released their bombs at a height of 6,800m.

—at 13:19, we bombed some establishments still remaining in the eastern part of the city. The impact area being in the vicinity of Shanxi Street, a couple of fires that started there turned out to be very effective.
                                        —the Detailed Report of the Battle

The reports given by *Xin Hua Ri Bao* (New China Daily Paper) had revealed something even more serious:

Many incendiary bombs were dropped upon the people's houses and some upon the vicinity of the U.S. Embassy in the Nan-an (Southern Shore) Ward.

The same paper also reported that "the U.S. Gun Boat *Tutuila*" had got quite a near hit and the Turkish steam ships named *Wan Xiang* and *Wan Liu* also had some bombs fallen near them.

Johnson, the U.S. ambassador to China, sent an official telegram (at 6 p.m. on October 25) to Cordell Hull, the Secretary of State:

Today, Japanese military planes again bombed upon Chungking. Twenty-six heavy bombers came flying in formation from northwest to southwest, while dropping bombs firstly on Jiang-bei (North of the Jialing) District, then on Shizhong (City's Central) Ward between the Yangzi and the Jialing, and then on the Southern Coast of the Yangzi. The time then was 11:15 a.m.. Then at least eight light bombers attacked the western side of Shizhong Ward and the western suburbs of the city. Damages concentrated on the shops and living quarters of the poor seem serious. About one hundred were injured in the Shizhong Ward and Jianbei Ward. In the southern shore, at least twenty-five were dead and thirty-two were seriously injured.

Those heavy bombers had fixed their course right above the precincts of our Embassy and our U.S. gunboat Tutuila and dropped the bombs in the west, north and east of those aims; the closest-falling bombs were 300 yards north of our Embassy and Tutuila. Eleven bombs in all had hit the marks within the Southern Coast of the Yangzi (within the area that has been declared safe by the Japanese authorities).

On May 28 at the early stage of Japan's No.101 Operations, the telegram sent by the same ambassador was: "A bomb had fallen at a point 400 yards away from Tutuila." Then "the distance to the war" between Japan and the U.S. had been shortened 100 yards that day.

What had caused this was the freezing of the machinery. *The Detailed Report on the Battles* contains the following account:

Because of the sudden fall of the temperature since the day before, it had become 20 degrees below zero around the height of 7,000m, and this had caused almost all the machinery to get frozen, preventing bombs from falling at the right time at the right place.... causing several bombs to fall on the suburban area of Longmenhao on the other side of the River.

The B Division of the urban area, Tutuila, Longmenhao and the U.S. Embassy having roughly been placed on the same straight line, the formation of those bombers that had entered from northwest was to fly right above them. Because of their failure to draw the gear at the right moment, some of the bombs to be dropped upon the urban area went dropping somewhere farther on, or the vicinity of Tutuila and the U.S. Embassy. Beside the drawing of the impact areas in *The Detailed Report on the Battles*, there was an entry: "Six bombs fell into the River." Judging from the description given in that *Report*, it was certain that these bombings had not been intentional, but what was even more apparent was that: the U.S. side had not taken them as such. Japan's challenge to the U.S. or Japan's coercion to make the U.S. withdraw from the China issue—the freezing of the apparatus for dropping bombs was to send a totally different message to the U.S.. The Americans in Chongqing began to smell out Japan's enmity toward their own country in those indiscriminate bombings unfolded before their eyes. On July 30, the following year—when Japan's No.102 Operations were going on—four months after the bomb-drop had caused a water pillar eight yard behind the gunboat Tutuila—the Japan-U.S. War was to break out.

In that sense, Japan's bombardment upon Chongqing could be called a lighted fuse to lead to "the path to Pearl Harbor." In other words, both Japan and the U.S.—long before they came to declare war upon each other—had been raising their hatred and amplifying their anger upon that stage of the narrow peninsula on the Rivers. Thus the Sino-Japanese War was to develop into a triangular struggle with the U.S. joining them.

For the time being, however, the arrival of the foggy season was to put an end to the air raid season in 1940. It was a long summer heated with uninvited fires—46 air raids from the middle of May toward the end of October. Until September 4, both Army and Navy cooperated with each other under what they called No. 101 Operations—bombing Chongqing 32 times; after that, the Navy's Second United Air Corps was to carry it out only by themselves.

● **The General Statistics of No. 101 Operations**

The general statistics of No.101 Operations went as follows: (*The General Outline of No. 101 Operations*)

1) The total in the advances into the Hinterland

The number of days: the Navy = 50 days (54 times)

the Army = 21 days

The number of planes: middle-sized bombers = 3,627

97-type heavy bombers = 727

scout planes 177

Zero Fighters 24

The number of bombs used: 27,107 (2,957 tons)

2) Attack on the military establishments within the city of Chongqing
(excepting the air bases)

The number of days: the Navy = 29 days; the Army = 8 days

The total number of planes: the Navy = 1,737; the Army = 286

The bombs used: 10,021 bombs 1,405 tons

3) The statistics concerning battles

The total number of planes that engaged in battles:
607 (Navy: 478; Army: 129)

The number of enemy planes brought down:
Navy: 71 (12 are uncertain); Army:46 (2 are uncertain)

The number of blasts on the earth: Navy = 63 Army = 2

4) The Damages we Suffered

Combat fatalities: Navy = 54 Army = 35

The missing: Navy = 16 Army = 6

The wounded: Navy = 29 Army = 20

The number of bombed planes: Navy = 312 Army = 75

The number of suicide planes: Navy = 8 Army = 8

Either to the Army Air Force or to the Navy Air Force, or when seen from the point of their having performed co-operative operations, that was the largest-scaled one in the history of Japan's air battles, and even though it soon ceased to be so because of World War II that followed, it was something to open up a new direction in making use of the capability of the air force. It was by no means an exaggeration when Inoue Shigeyoshi, the chief of staff, declared it as "something that could be compared to the Battle of Tsushima* (1905)." Japan's Air Force made a ferocious attack upon the enemy's capital by keeping performing indiscriminate carpet bombing raids, thus to open up a new type of warfare in which they pursued their strategic and political aim of "frustrating the enemy's will to keep fighting on." If there were any point inferior to the conception of strategic bombing which was soon to be established by the U.S. & U.K. armed forces, it was only in the number of bombers and the tonnage of bombs. In its intention, in its method, and above all in its thoroughness in performing indiscriminate bombings that took away the borderline between the battle lines and the civilian front, No. 101 Operations led by Inoue Shigeyoshi,

Yamaguchi Tamon and Onishi Takijiro had been far removed from any other aerial operations that had been adopted so far. That could be called *the* moment when the strategic bombings had come into being.

If we were told of the fact that Chongqing's Shizhong (City's Central) Ward, which had absorbed most of the bombs dropped on that city, was 9.3 km squares, we should easily be able to imagine how fierce those attacks were to those who were living under that sky. Comparing this size with that of somewhere in Tokyo, it was smaller than Chiyoda Ward (11.52km square) or Chuo (Central) Ward (10.05km square) and it was about the same with that of Taito Ward (10.00km square) among the eight downtown wards that were to be exposed to the air raids by the U.S.' B29s five years later. It was upon that provisional capital 9.3 km squares, with a population of 700,000, which had rapidly increased around the ancient castle area that Japan's air raids were performed day after day. That narrow, densely-inhabited peninsula, whose three sides were bordered by the Rivers, had characteristically been made to suffer from the repetitive, long-termed air-raids. The Chinese called it "fatigue bombing." No other naming would have been more expressive of the local people's feeling of disgust.

According to *A Chronicle of Chongqing's Resistance to Japan*, what they suffered from the air raids in 1940 went as follows:

The number of the air raids: 80 times with 4,722 planes

The number of bombs dropped: 10,587

The number of deaths: 4,149

The number of the injured: 5,411

The houses destroyed: 6,952

There was no such massive deaths as those in "5.3 & 5.4" the year before, but the total of the damages they suffered during the whole summer that year almost came up to what they had suffered the year before. The following was a reminiscence of that summer, included in *Jiang Jieshi* written by Dong Xianquang, the then vice-director of the Central Publicity Department of the Nationalist Party:

Throughout the summer (of 1939), we had been suffering sporadic air raids and, when the foggy season of winter arrived, the whole of Chongqing was finally able to feel relieved. But when the spring came round in 1940, we were to suffer again from more intensive air raids. Chongqing had already brought the places of refuge into being, but throughout the spring and summer that year, the government officials had to cope with double torments—of being threatened to be killed in the daytime and of suffering from sleeplessness in the air-raid shelter. The war of nerves the Japanese were good at was performed in the moonlit night. On such occasions, the air raid often lasted as long as three hours at a stretch. All Chongqing could do then was to endure it.

Jiang Jieshi, whenever he had any opportunity to do so, called out to the citizens for their resistance. Since these air raids performed by the Japanese military were apparently aiming at "conquering the enemy's fighting spirit," he must have judged that his keeping in touch with the people in general was especially important.

—In the third anniversary of our Resistance to Japan, I have something to tell all the comrades of the Nationalist Party. (*Xin Hua Ri Bao,* July 8)

—The Nationalist Party at the Seventh National Convention has Adopted the Declaration to Carry Through the National United Front Against Japan. (*Xin Hua Ri Bao,* July 10)

—He (Jiang Jieshi) published the letter he wrote to the compatriots being left at places occupied by the Japanese Army; He also granted 50,000 *yuan* to the Headquarters of Air Raid Precautions, wishing for the safety of the citizens of Chongqing. (*Xin Hua Ri Bao,* dated August 13)

Such news items as these concerning Chairman Jiang's daily actions were being carried even in the Communist Party's bulletin *Xin Hua Ri Bao.* Just like the British Prime Minister Churchill, Jiang had compared himself to a symbol of China who kept fighting in perseverance. World War II, which broke out the year before, had moved its phase into the indiscriminate daytime bombings upon London since September that year, and to the eyes of the Chinese, what the two cities were suffering then seemed to be of the same nature. A graphic magazine, *Liang You* (Good Friends) prepared a special number under the title of "*Chongquing—London*"—featuring the photographic *Tales of the Two Cities* under the headline that went: *We have encountered the Similar Hardship, both bearing the Contemporary Trials.* Jiang Jieshi in those pages had been made to appear Churchill himself making an impassionate speech toward the people of Chongqing. The U.S. magazine *LIFE* also prepared a feature article of nine pages (the July 8, 1940), and in the article that reported how Chongqing alounded in heroic citizens, as London did. Even though they remained unknown. In the new capital of liberalist China, which was surrounded with wide cemeteries, and where the number of the dead were said to be larger than the alive, the people were smiling as the Londoners did, keeping themselves cheerful, cracking jokes cheerfully: "Business as usual," despite the bombardment they were suffering. Here, too, "Encountering the same difficulties; Sharing the contemporary difficulties" were being emphasized.

● **The Generals & Admirals were Promoted, while Inoue Suffered a Setback**
On the side of Japan, too, "heroes" had been brought into being. After the Operations were over, the United Air Raid Corps was presented with a scroll of appreciation by Admiral Shimada Shigetaro, the Commander of the Fleet of the China Region:

> For a long period of time from mid-May to early September in the 15th year of Showa (1940), you took part in the No.101 Operations, and by concentrating the great striking power, you dared to fly long to perform those magnificent attacks upon the Hinterland of Sichuan province as many as 40 times, thus to make the greatest military achievements.
>
> All this while, the attacking corps, conquering the difficulties brought about by the changes of weather and climate, while accepting the skilful cooperation of the corps of land scout planes, did succeed in destroying the large part of the front line of the enemy air force, the military facilities and the important political institutions in the city until it has been deprived of most of the functions as the capital. Thus having suffered a tremendous blow both physically and mentally, Chongqing is now about to be annihilated.
>
> Thus this operation has turned out to be an unprecedented grand project, and your meritorious service has extremely been outstanding.
>
> Now, I hope you will feel honored to receive this letter of appreciation gratefully offered to you.

Each of the leaders of the Operations was promoted to a higher rank. Yamaguchi Tamon, who had commanded the United Air Raid Unit while taking the office as the commander of the First United Air Force, was appointed to be Commander of the Second Air Squadron, and that was soon to lead him to be director of the mobile fleet that was to bring him soon to the offing of the Midway Islands. After him, Onishi Takijiro came to occupy the post of the commander of the First United Air Force. Inoue Shigeyoshi, the chief of stuff, who had been controlling the whole of the operations at the Headquarters in Shanghai, returned to Tokyo, having been appointed to be Director-General of Naval Air Force. These were treatments quite suitable to those who had "performed that grand scheme unprecedented in the military history of the Empire," and as long as judged by the Japanese side, the Capital of China had already been turned into ruins and the Chongqing Administration seemed to be on the verge of collapse. This led the Japanese military to break up their camps, loosen their uniform a little and moved into the season of distribution of honors. Those air corps that had belonged to the First United Air Corps and the Third United Air Corps returned to their former unit, and this soon made Hankou Air Base free from noise and the smell of carbon black.

In this congratulatory atmosphere, Inoue, who had returned to Tokyo to take office as Director General of the Air Force, had to suffer a feeling of profound frustration. It was true that deep in his heart, he held a bitter feeling that he had failed to realize what he had expected of the Operation No. 101, but in addition, the air he felt in Tokyo—especially in the Naval Department and in the Naval General Staff—that: the warfare between Japan and the U.S. would be inevitable. This did hurt Inoue's pride.*

*In *A Navy Officer's Memoir*, authored by Nakayama Sadayoshi, Inoue said to Rear Admiral Ugaki Matome: "According to what I've heard, in the Central Government, there is a movement to carry out a war against a third nation along with the Great Operations we are now engaged in on the Chinese Continent. If that is true, it will be something very horrible. Now we have had a large number of problems to solve in carrying out only the China Incident; as a matter of fact, we still remain unable to tell how things will turn out. So stirring up a trouble against the Great Power as a third nation is totally out of question. This is our view retained by the Headquarters of the

Fleet of the China Region."

Inoue, who had failed to fulfill what he had expected as the chief of stuff of the Fleet of the China Region, now had to see the breaking down of what he had done before as the chief of the Bureau of Naval Affairs even at the risk of his life—the checking of the Tripartite Pact before it was confirmed and his policy of retaining the renunciation of war against the U.S. and the U.K. These must have made him feel as if all of his existence in the Navy had been denied.

That deploring of his could not help being made even greater when he came to know that: that change of the Navy's policy or the approach to the war against the U.S. and the U.K. was being carried out according to "the military program that had been made during the Meiji and the Taisho eras (1868-1912 / 1912-1926). As a matter of fact, Japan, had failed to subdue China even by the spearhead of the strategic use of the air force, but the young staff of the Naval Department and of the Naval General Staff still remained in the dream of big-ship & big-gun, advocating in the naval warfare against the U.S. on the Pacific, and this had made them remain in high spirits and talk big. It was four months later that Inoue, as Director General of the Air Force, sounded an alarm bell by producing *A Theory on the Program for New Military Preparations*. It was then and there that he made a strong assertion on the upgrading of the air force, especially on the reinforcement of aerial capacity in the base, which he had learned through the failure in achieving the purpose of No. 101 Operations. But this proposal of his was not accepted by the mainstay of the Navy. By and by, this turned out *not* a mere opinion *but* a foretelling, and when the judgement was given by the facts, everything had turned out to be too late.

● Zhou Enlai's Speech: *"The International Situation & China's Resistance to Japan"*

The official announcement of Inoue Shigeyoshi's transference to his new post in Tokyo was issued on October 1, 1940. It was a couple of days before— on September 29—that Zhou Enlai in Chongqing had addressed a large number of people about the international situation and a probable form of the U.S.-Japanese War, thus to call forth a large reaction among them. Zhou Enlai had been resident at Chongqing as the representative of Balujun (the Eighth Route Army) and also as the person in charge of the Chinese Communist Party's underground organization—"Chinese Communist Center's Southern Bureau." In the very same place that had been recognized by the Japanese military that had been engaged in the No. 101 Operations as "having been deprived of its functions as the capital," Zhou had declared the occurrence of the U.S.-Japanese War in which Japan would inevitably be defeated. Unlike Inoue's crying toward the wasteland, Zhou Enlai's prediction and analysis were accepted by the audience who wrapped him up with their overwhelming sympathy and a loud singing of a patriotic song.

About the same period of time when those who had been engaged in the United Air Raid Corps at Hankou were being presented with a scroll of appreciation, there appeared in a street of Chongqing a single notice that went: "On Sunday next, on September 29, a lecture will be given by Zhou Enlai, the Representative of Ba-lujin (the Eighth Route Army) at the Experimental Large Theater." This announcement was being carried on and on like rippling waves. The title of the lecture was "The International Situation & the China's Resistance," sponsored by China's Vocational Education Company. What would become of Chongqing? Which direction was China taking? Anyone interested in the current situation in China had been anxious to get any answer given by Zhou Enlai, who, as the representative of Baljun, had been taking part in the Chongqing Administration.

That day, many people rushed to the Theater and this led to the changes of the place for his lecture—to the playground of Bashu Elementary School outside the castle area. Bashu Elementary School was situated in H Division— according to the Japanese Air Force—or in the District in and around Chuandong Normal School. The frequent bombardments that summer had turned that district into a wide stretch of burnt ruins. According to *Xin Hua Ri Bao*—dated September 30—3,000 people moved on foot to that outdoor hall outside the castle wall. The same paper made a quick report on "A Lecture Given by our Comrade Zhou Enlai" by summing it up in a broad space brought into being by removing partitions between the five columns in the lower part of the front page. That analysis of the state of things still remains appropriate and readable as something fresh even if more than half a century had passed since then. For Zhou Enlai, forty-two years old, that year 1940 could not be called so fortunate. In July the year before, while staying in Yan-an, he fell off his horse and had his right arm broken, and this made him go as far as Moscow to have it treated. In February, 1940, he returned to Chongqing by way of Yan-an and soon after he went to Guilin, he received the news of Chongqing having suffered the air raid. The air raid upon Chongqing was certainly a terrible experience to him, but what had annoyed him even more was Jiang Jieshi's increasing pressure upon the Communists. The Nationalist Party's interference with and pressure upon the New Fourth Army (Xin Si Jun)—a Communist-line Army as Balujun (the Eighth Route Army) was—was going from bad to worse day after day, and in the same month of September, a drastic change was brought about at the Military Affairs Committee's Administration Department, which had been the main stage of the Nationalist-Communist Collaboration, causing Zhou Enlai as the vice-chief of the Administration Department to be dismissed, while the Third Office, which had been maneuvering the united front under Zhou, was broken up, and the chief there, Guo Moruo, was brought down to be the person in charge of the largely scaled-down Committee of Cultural Activities. The other Communist organizations within the districts under the control of the Nationalist Party were also being broken up one after another. For the Communists, bombs were thrown not only from above but also from the side or from behind. Chongqing, unlike Yan-an as "a liberated area" where Mao Zedong stayed, was "the White Area" controlled by the Nationalist Party, and the Communists living there had to be prepared that the political instability was always endangering them.

But Zhou Enlai, who presented himself at the school ground of Bashu Elementary School, did not reveal any such sign of hardship he and his comrades were suffering. Displaying his merits in his adversity was what had made him what he was. His appearance also revealed his being cool, calm and collected. While he was in a long march, he was a hairy-faced member of the political committee; while he was leading the battle to guard Great Wuhan, he had his hair close-cropped; he, now a representative of the Chinese Communist Party, resident in Chongqing as capital of Free China, wore his hair long, had a Nationalist Uniform on, had held back his emotions behind his clear-cut features in a calm expression. For Zhou Enlai, this ought to have been the very opportunity for making a counterattack to the Nationalist Party.

Han Suyin was among the audience. She, a half-European, whose husband was a commissioned officer close to Jiang Jieshi, had already been aware that there would be no way of closing the rift they had had between them. As for the difference in their political views, which had partly caused their discord, Han Suyin's was rapidly approaching Communism. Her first impression of Zhou Enlai was written as follows:

The place chosen was a small hollow between two hillocks. On either side had been dug air-raid shelters. It was crowded with people two hours before Chou (Zhou) appeared, some of them climbing on poles, or erecting platforms of tables and chairs they brought out of their homes, to see him.

This was the first time I had seen Chou Enlai. A slim, thin-faced man with an abundance of black hair, very calm, very handsome, all his gestures supple, he is perhaps the most intelligent statesman living today, with the greatest capacity for self-abnegation, with subtlety, patience and vision. What one felt on seeing him was an almost physical impact of sureness, of self-control and intelligence. When he stood on a table so that he could be seen by the crowd, his eyes went calmly from face to face; all of us were caught, waiting for his words. He spoke for almost four hours, and we listened, untired. He could have gone on forever. It was one of the simplest, least complicated, most unrhetorical, almost painstakingly basic speeches one could have heard. But each word counted.

—*Birdless Summer*

● **"On Imperialism"—a Speech made by Zhou Enlai**

According to *Xin Hua Ri Bao* dated the following day, his speech lasted for three hours and a half, including brief break time. In his speech entitled The *International Situation & China's Resistance to Japan,* Zhou analyzed the matter by answering the following questions, thus clarifying China's communist opinion about them:

1. Which way is the world going?
2. Which way is China going?
3. How are the European fronts likely to develop?
4. Which way will the U.S.-Japanese relations develop?
5. What sort of position will the Soviet Union keep?
6. What sort of position will China take?
7. Will Japan be able to cope with the China issues?

8. Is China now facing a crisis of accepting a compromise and surrender?
9. How will China make her National United Front Against Japan go ahead?

Zhou Enlai, who had mounted the platform, gave a slight cough and expressed his thanks to his audience before him, letting his lips slightly tremble, before he entered into the main subject:

> Today, none of us will be able to avoid the problems rising from the present international situations and China's resistance to Japan. Today I should like to give my own opinion concerning the nine questions you must have been asking to yourselves.

Then after giving the list of those nine questions mentioned above, he began to give each of them his own answer, while analyzing the matter. As for the first question, Zhou Enlai answered as follows. That was an analysis of the situation he had made in September in 1940 or 14 months before the start of the US-Japanese War.

> The warfare now going on in the world in such an extensive scale has consisted of three different systems and frames. The first is a war system to scramble for the domination of the world by dint of the imperialism. The war between Germany and the united front of the UK and France has developed into the confrontation between Germany-Italy-Japan and the UK-France. This shows how the imperialism is gradually declining in a process of tapering away.
> The second is a liberation war as a revolutionary movement performed by the oppressed race. The representative of this case is China's fighting against Japan.
> The third is the Socialist Soviet Union, which holds fast to the policy of peace, keeping themselves out of any warfare. Their power has steadily been growing so much so that it may defeat imperialism, while increasing their power to assist a national liberation movement.

This was a survey of the world Zhou Enlai had made in the middle stage of

1940, or ten months before the war between Germany and the Soviet Union broke out. Then he moved on to his analysis of situation concerning each case:

Let me give my opinion about the second matter. The main aim for which China is fighting at the present situation remains unchanged. That is, it is Japan's Imperialism. While corresponding to the world situation which has largely been changing, we must hold fast to our own footing of independence. That footing will liberate ourselves in not so faraway future, and it will lead the oppressed peoples or more than half of the population in the world to follow this same road of liberation. That is none other than following the instructions given by Chairman Jiang: "Work out our salvation by our own efforts, while offering our all-out resistance."

Then he went on talking about the wars in Europe being escalated and their extension to Asia:

When France surrendered to Germany, and Japan brought the Konoe cabinet into being, the U.S. began to support the U.K. in a positive manner. Since Germany began to check the actions of the U.S. and the U.K. in the Far East by making use of Japan, the U.S. and U.K. felt it necessary to make their unity even stronger. That was how the confrontation between the two major imperialist camps or the camp of Germany-Italy-Japan and the camp of the U.K. and the U.S. came into being. These facts show us that: the imperialist war never fails to escalate, inflicting greater and greater damages upon the people in the world, thus unfailingly bringing about greater damages upon the human civilization.

● **His Clear Assertion: A War will Break out between Japan and the U.S.**
and Japan's Setback will be Inevitable

Under such recognition as mentioned above, Zhou Enlai saw through what would become of the relationship between the U.S. and Japan, as follows:

Japan now, after having been thrown into confusion in China, has found that all they could do now would only be to go down to the south to relieve themselves of their self-contradiction in their own country and to seek after resources for the defense of their own country. On the other hand, Germany, too, came to conclude the Tripartite Pact of Japan, Germany & Italy in view of the current situation. By taking Japan out on to the South Seas to meet the U.S. there, they had thought they could check the U.S. by keeping them too busy to come and fight against them in the West. The contradiction existing between Japan and the U.S. will be sharpened and the sudden changes in the situation will soon lead them to a great crash against each other. At the end of this kind of contradictory development, there is no other choice but to crash against each other.

Zhou Enlai, though pointing out the inevitability of the U.S.-Japanese War, told his audience that it would be wrong for them to cherish any illusion in the state of affairs, though it would be recommendable to make use of the U.S.-Japan crash, while maintaining the attitude of "working out our own salvation by our own efforts" and "do-or-die resistance as were recommended by our supreme leader (meaning Jiang Jieshi)—in that sense, we should not refrain from making ourselves "the tools for the imperialistic war." That was how Zhou Enlai made it clear where the Chinese should stand, thus ostensibly recommending the people to bring themselves together under the leadership of Jiang Jieshi:

"The assistance we are receiving from the U.K. and the U.S. has never let us eat to our full, but has not led us to starve to death."

Thus after having led his audience to roar with laughter, he gave "the supreme leader" a warning by reminding him of the mottoes he himself had once given: "Work out our salvation by our own effort" and "Make all-out resistance," and then he asked the audience whether or not Japan would be able to put an end to the war it was making in China. That was the seventh question he had given at the opening of his speech.

According to my analysis, it is impossible for Japan to do so. Certainly since the Konoe's cabinet started, Japan's intention is: to put the China Incident to an end and to advance southward. What Japan is planning is: firstly, to make southward advance as soon as we surrender to them;

secondly, to make up the force of arms for their southward advance by increasing the difficulties in attacking the hinterland in our southwestern district; thirdly, even if these two conditions I've mentioned may turn out impossible, if pressed in time, Japan will make southward advance without taking any notice of what they are doing. This means: if only we retain our footing of resistance and persist in making them take time, it will finally make Japan too impatient to remain as they are, and they will go ahead without thinking about what will become of them.

Thus Zhou Enlai—after having guaranteed that: it would be improbable for them to surrender to Japan as long as they were staying under the intelligent leadership of their supreme commander—concluded his speech by giving his prospect of their National United Front against Japan:

This protest of ours against Japan's imperialism will be none other than increasing and promoting the basic power we need in making our own progress. Recruiting the strength of troops, making plans for storing provisions, and making adjustment in financing—these schemes for our progress will come to face a crucial juncture from now on.

Maintaining resistance to Japan is none other than solving these problems and making them go ahead. Some may think our progress is very slow. But the progress of the Sino-Japanese War has primarily been very slow. There is no reason for us to be in a hurry. Sometimes, in facing sufferings, we may moan while tearing our hair out, but it must be on such occasions, when we must be able to find out who have been our true friends.... (hand clapping). So let's face our enemy, bracing our spirits. As long as we are united, we shall have no problem before us. Victory will unfailingly be upon our side!"

● A Loud Singing of *Our Volunteer Army March*

When his speech, which lasted for three hours and a half, was over, there was a long clapping of hands which would not cease for a long time, throbbing the air of that burnt-out neighborhood. The people, sympathetically responding to Zhou Enlai's view, were being intoxicated by his encouragement. Even if he had been removed from his post of vice-director of the Administration Department, he still remained the top-ranking leader of the United Front. The address he had given that day did reveal that fact. There was a brief break—before he gave an answer for the question 7—and what was spontaneously brought on the lips of his huge audience was a singing of what was later made the Chinese national anthem or *Our Volunteer Army March*—an anti-Japanese version of *La Marseillaise*—(words by Tian Han, music by Nie Reng):

Rise to your feet! If you do not want to be enslaved!
Let's build a new Great Walls with our flesh & blood !
We are facing the greatest crisis we have ever met!
This is when each of us shall give our final war cry!
Rise to your feet! Rise to your feet! Rise to your feet!

More than three weeks had passed since what the Japanese military called No.101 Operations was over with the presentation of their report that declared: "It is judged that the capital of our enemy has almost come to cease its function."

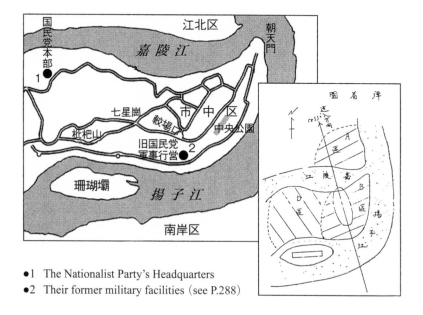

- ●1 The Nationalist Party's Headquarters
- ●2 Their former military facilities (see P.288)

tis Hawk Ⅲ of the China Air Force（see P.327）

SB2 bombers made in the Soviet Union（see P.255）

The Japanese middle-sized attack planes flying in formation over the mountainous area in China（see P.265）

96-type or middle-sized land attack planes arranged what seemed to be the Wuhan Base

A formaition of middle-sized attack planes during their bombing upon Chongqing（see P.282）

The Route for Supporting Jian Jieshi, built among the mountains（see P.245）

Chongqing wrapped up in flames and smoke（1940）（see P.298）

A Zero fighter（the type 11）of the 12th Flying Corps（see P.324）

The firefighters at work on the burni[
houses

The scenes of the urban area of
Chongqing after the air raids
（1940）

Japan's 97-type heavy bomber being attacked above Chengdu by China's I15 (in the circle) (see P.325)

Under the air-raid, another air-raid cave was being built (see P.342)

"Business as usual" even in the devastated area (see P.342)

CHAPTER IV

THE WAY TO PEARL HARBOR (1941)

What the Japan-Soviet Neutrality Pact Meant to China

● A Large Number of Air-Raid Caves still Remain

Chongqing seen from afar is often compared to a multi-humped camel's back. If one climbs gaspingly along the winding stone steps up to the top of the largest hump of Biba-shan Hill—345m above sea level—one is able to overlook a view of the whole peninsula that divides the rivers—the Yangzi and the Jialing. If you are lucky enough to be there when no fog is around, you will be able to command a bird's-eye-view of a leaf-shaped cityscape of Shizhong (City's Central) Ward with Zhaotian-men (the Imperial Gate) at its tip. It might look like a fallen leaf helplessly floating between the two rivers. Once upon a time, a poet in the boat, looking up at the majestic rocky mountain, compared Chongqing to "a mountain fortress," but the same poet, seeing the same thing from the top of the Hill, called it "a helpless leaf barely floating on the water." It is interesting to see how even the same thing might bring about totally different impressions according to where it is looked upon.

As a matter of fact, Chongqing during that period of her resistance to Japan had embodied both an indomitable mountain castle and a helpless leaf floating on the water. It had to be standing there firmly as a mountain-castle of China resisting the Imperialist Japan, while those living there had to be rolling about like fallen leaves before wind for fully two years and a half.

"The Battle of Chongqing" was recorded both in the history of China's resistance to Japan and in the history of the air battles in the world, while the miseries brought about by the air raids are still being told about among the families and relatives as something unforgettable by those who had suffered them, and even after they were faded away like dried leaves placed in between the pages of an old diary, they still keep telling us something.

What soon caught one's eyes while walking around the city of Chongqing (in 1980s) was a large number of caves that used to be the air-raid shelters. On the cliffs along the road, on one side of the road cut through hilly terrain, on the flight of stairs that led to the underground shopping streets…. wherever one might go, one could face the dark entrance to what used to be a cave as an air-raid shelter. That was what might be called an underground fortress or a cave as an air-raid shelter in a true sense of the word. Those sturdy structures had been brought into being by boring huge holes into the rock. In their scale and durability, there was almost nothing in common with what the Japanese called air-raid shelter, which was brought into being only by digging out the earth. In those days when the anti-Japanese war was going on, Chongqing had already brought into being such an underground network of living space as this.

Some of them still remain useful in the daily life of the locals. Most commonly, they are used as warehouses. But at shopping streets, we often see the space of the entrance to such a shelter have been turned into a grocery store, a general store, a meat shop and so on. There is a restaurant featuring a local specialty, "*huoguo*"—meat, viscera, fish meat and vegetables in hot water are eaten after dipping into marinade with ample mustard. When eaten in a former air-raid cave, dusky and stuffy, it turns out to be a great diaphoretic.

There are some air raid caves which still have a sign of "人民防空 (People's Aerial Defense)," but they cannot be a relic from the days of the Anti-Japanese War. Then they must be what have been converted into hiding places in case of need in the nuclear age. Judging from what has been left there, they seem to have been made use of once again in 1960's when they were suffering from an imaginary nuclear war against the U.S.S.R., for which they were expected "to dig the air raid shelter deep and store food staff there if a nuclear war should break out." It might be said that: the old layer of ruins has had another layer upon it.

● A Former Air Raid Cave has been Turned into a Place of Pleasure

There is an example of what used to be an air-raid cave having been turned into something totally different: a huge underground shopping mall, proudly named "Jinzhu-Gong (Golden Bamboo Palace)," was of a new type of reutilization that symbolized the open-door policy in 1980's, and the discotheque at its corner is used *neither* to avoid the air raid *nor* to store the food, *but* to release the young people's energy. If you are in Shanxi-jie Street near Zhaotian-men Gate—which used to be called "B Division" by the Japanese airmen in their bombers—you will find the downward stone steps beside, what used to be Sichuan Salt Industry Bank at the busiest part of the street; and if you walk down 91 stone steps to the underground 27m deep, you will find yourself in "a pleasure center" 865m long and 3,500m square. There are four entrances there, and both sides of more than twenty tunnels are fringed with shops and stores including wholesale stores, restaurants Chinese and Western, shops and stores to sell craft products and artworks. They say that huge underground commercial area is capable of accommodating 4,000 visitors.

At the end of the radial roads, there is a plaza as a big draw at that underground pleasure place; that is the very place the young people aim at. Both sides of the walls are covered with the ceramic maps of Chongqing and the Yangzi from Mt. Emei to Xuanchang; at the farthest end, a band of musicians are seen, while the young men and women are dancing happily, kicking the floor there. That is a liberated area open to the public from 8:30 p.m. to 10:30 p.m. and one can enter it by paying an admittance fee of three *yuan*. It is hard to believe: half a century before, this used to be a shelter for those who were being frightened at the indiscriminate bombings performed day and night. How could this hall, now illuminated by lights of various colors and resounding with music, be a dusky place with water always dripping from the ceiling and none could remain there without any rainwear? At present, this hall simply appears none other than a modern underground shopping mall, from whichever angle it may be seen.

Still, this place, now called "*Jinshu-gong* (Golden Bamboo Palace)'" was unmistakably the central part of the underground cave as an air raid shelter which used to be called "Chongqing Great Tunnel." The generation of those whose sons and daughters frequent this disco used to spend several years of their boyhood or girlhood at this same underground space, struggling against the infinite uneasiness they had to suffer. Everyone ought to have taken that facility as something farthest from any kind of "pleasure." All the sounds they used to hear there were crying of the fretful babies and ominous sounds of the bombs that had been dropped somewhere afar but never failed to make them shiver all the same. What was left behind was stifling silence, dripping sweat and the hands of the clock that seemed to have stuck upon its face—the rock surface of that cave still seems to retain such miserable memories of those who used to frequent there.

That was not everything. Those underground shelters or huge tunnels have firmly been connected with the dark, sad memory of their having been turned into a huge catacomb. That case remembered as "the Great Tragedy at the Air-Raid Tunnels of Chongqing"—the case in which a large number of people in the air raid cave were choked to death at night on June 5, 1941, when it got over-crowded with those who had rushed into it to escape from the air raid performed by the Japanese planes that had brought the skies of Chongqing under their control. Along with the air raids on 5.3 & 5.4, this extremely disastrous incident has never been removed from the memory of the people: During a single night, several thousands of citizens, pressed into the dark space of the air-raid tunnel, were brought to death—some by being pressed down, others by oxygen starvation. They had not been directly bombarded to death, but they could be regarded as victims of the indiscriminate bombings they were usually suffering.

● **The Completion of the Air Raid Caves to Accommodate 445,000 People**

The plan of building a large-scaled underground shelter had already been proposed in 1937, when Chongqing was appointed to be Provisional Capital. The Japan's armed forces, which had been coming up along the Yangzi, having made it a main strategy to make "an aerial attack on the strategic point" by their Navy Air Force, it had been judged that Chongqing would soon be exposed to the air raid.

As was suggested by the title of a novel—*The Scaret Rocks*—whose stage was set at Chongqing, authored by Luo Guangwu & Yan Yiyan, Chongqing's ground consisting of brown soft layer of sandstone, they could bring any kind of underground fortress into being if they were to invest a proper amount of time and money in it. Since Jiang Jieshi's arrival there, the construction of the air-raid caves began to be accelerated so that they could accommodate all those governmental organizations in those caves. As the Anti-Japanese War went on and they came to suffer even more intense bombardments, the factories and hospitals had all gone underground. Some of the underground factories built in the suburbs of Chongqing by boring huge holes on the hillside are said to be still used as munitions factories, and I was told by someone that: a certain former underground factory for repairing damaged planes had now been provided with even a runway to accommodate the planes.

What had been made the mainstays of the air-raid caves for the local residents were the seven-sectioned large tunnels as the air-raid shelter. Each of them had more than three gateways and many branch tunnels, and the fixed capacity of them was decided to be 17,299 (actually 50 percent more used to be accommodated). Most of the seven tunnels having been built upon the bedrock nearly 70m below the surface of the earth, it was impossible for them to be crashed by any bombardment.

At the air raids of "5.3 & 5.4" in 1939, these shelters had not yet been completed. At that time, all the capacities of the air-raid caves, including those caves prepared by the individuals, by those responsible for their enterprises, and by the public organizations, were only for 70,000 people. Even though the citizens were to meet a surprise attack, the inefficiency of the air defense facilities was one of the reasuns for having made the casualties so fatal. Those "terrible disasters" of "5.3 & 5.4." had prompted their building of air raid caves.

In 1940, just before the No. 101 Operations were to bring about rains of bombs day after day, the Great Tunnels had been completed. Beside them, each district had brought about their own shelters of various sizes, while some individuals and companies were also eager to have their own, and by the end of 1940 the total of those shelters became reportedly as many as 1,865 to accommodate 444,988 people. There were underground shops and stores and shelters for automobiles, too. That year, the citizens were to suffer more than fifty fierce air raids during the six months, including those of the No.101 Operations, concentrated on the area as wide as about a single ward of Taito-ku (ward) in Tokyo, still their casualty remained smaller than that of the year before. The greatest reason for this had undoubtedly been attributed to their having established the measures to take refuge in their shelters. In this way, the citizens of Chongqing had obtained the means to protect themselves against those unilateral attacks from the sky, even if they might be called passive measures.

Along with the building of the air-raid caves, a couple of systems for protecting the citizens' daily life from the air raids also came into being.

One was "the Interim Capital's General Unit to Cope with the Air Raid."

This was based upon the urgently-established organizations immediately after "5.3 & 5.4." by collecting the leading members of the Nationalist Party, government officials, intellectuals and so on, and under "the Interim Capital's United Office to Deal with Emergency Measures," they dealt with a broad field from evacuations, creating slogans for air-raid precautions and paying visits to burnt areas for a propaganda to traffic control before and after the air raid and supply of food and drink and daily necessaries when people had to keep staying in the air raid cave for a long time. As a part of it, there were also some volunteer groups of medical workers, school teachers and patriots.

The other was a civilian defense corps incorporated into the city administration and was expected to work for each of the districts in the city. As for its origin, it went back to the start of the building of the Great Tunnels of Chongqing, but until the first half of 1939, it had not done anything substantial. But now it was to be braced up to stand in the forefront of "anti-air-raid campaign" under the name of volunteer corps to fight against the air raid. In 1940, its membership became as large as 40,000 and eight regional self-defense corps and independent self-defense corps such as engineering battalions, fire-fighting battalions, relief battalions and headquarter-guard battalions were being active. Their mission was in controlling restriction lighting, maintaining the order and the traffic, guiding the people to shelters, communications, fire fighting, disinfection, relief activities and the like.

As Zeng Zhiwei, a member of the civilian defense corps, had experienced at the air raid of "5.3 & 5.4," their rate of being exposed to danger was the same as that of the soldiers in the front line, and in fact, many of the members of this corps were to die at their post of duty. When informed of the deaths of them, the people used to collect some money they could afford, to hold a funeral to mourn for their local heroes by setting off some crackers, striking the gongs and beating the drums.

● A Horrible Tragedy Occurred at the Depths of the Cave

This was how the local people in Chongqing were making a rapid progress both in their readiness for developing their air-raid caves and in their preparedness for keeping their daily life. This had led everyone to think that: they would no longer have any such miseries as they had on "5.3. & 5.4."

As a matter of fact, the number of deaths caused by the air raids seemed to be growing smaller, as the air raid caves were growing larger in number. Not a single citizen had ever imagined that another tragedy was awaiting them. It was not until the accident had happened that people knew that such an accident was predictable. In fact, no one had ever warned against anything like that until the night of June 5, 1941, when approximately as many as several thousand men and women and children were lying one on top of another, breathing no more, forming an immense heap, starting from one of the three entrances to the Large Tunnel, or from Shiba Entrance to the depths of the cave. Even today, the local people talk of this tragedy of "a great disaster in the summer of 1941"— along with "the summer of 5.3. & 5.4." (1939) and "the summer of exhaustion bombings" (1940)—thus to hand them down to their posterity as the most unforgettable things during the wartime.

In 1941—Japan's Navy & Army Air Forces were about to enter the third season for their air raids upon the Hinterland of Sichuan Province. Even if there was an interruption of the foggy season, such concentrated attacks as the Japanese Air Forces had performed upon the same region and upon the same city with such persistent intensity year after year were something unheard of even in the world history of aerial wars, even if Berlin and London have seen something of this line. The period of the U.S. Air Force's air raids upon the Japanese cities was less than a year, and most of them were temporary ones, so they cannot be compared with what Chongqing experienced year after year. Only the U.S.' bombardment upon Hanoi and Haiphong during the Vietnam War will be comparable with this in terms of its period and scale.

● **No. 102 Operations Performed by the Larger Corps**
with the Newly-Produced Bombers

In 1941, the world had become clearly divided into two camps—the Axis Powers of Japan, Italy and Germany and the Allied Powers of the U.S., the U.K., Holland and China—and the Two Powers were being engaged in fierce hostilities in the east and the west of the Eurasian Continent. The U.S., though not yet taken part in it, was clearly taking an attitude of assisting China, while intensifying its pressure upon Japan. In order to save this situation, the Japanese Government early in this year (1941) promoted Admiral Nomura Kichisaburo to the ambassador to the U.S. and tried to bring out "a plan for the mutual understanding between the two nations," but without success. By and by, the U.S.

was to do lend-lease to the U.K. in Europe and to Jiang Jieshi in Asia.

Under such circumstances, Shimada Shigetato, the Commander-in-Chief of the Fleet of the China Region, had sent his opinion to the Naval General Staff, after the No.101 Operation was over, since he had felt worried about the fact that: even the No. 101 Operations had not succeeded in reducing Chongqing Administration to submission, while he had heard: "among the Navy officers whose ranks are Commander or below, some are boastfully saying they should solve the problem in the South at a single stroke," making him feel afraid that the central stuff might lose their ardor on the Operations they had retained so far:

> Now that Europe is in a disturbance, we do feel like building a firm base in the South, but for the time being I think it better to concentrate our strength in solving the Sino-Japanese Incident, thus waiting for a while until we foster our national strength.
>
> The Sino-Japanese Incident now in the final stage of the last five minutes needs to be brought to an end as soon as possible by intensifying our attack. In order to achieve this purpose, I think it necessary to offer as much attack as possible by preferably strengthening our power around April by adding to our aerial force (preferably one aerial fleet) from CF (the Combined Fleet).
>
> The enemy's strained circumstances are becoming from bad to worse as the days go by and their voices of lamentation are growing louder. So capturing Chongqing will be most effective, but since the Army has regarded it as something most difficult to achieve, all we need to do now will be to adopt as many blockades and surprise attacks as possible, while giving serious damages by our air force upon Chongqing and other cities in the Hinterlands such as Sichuan and Yunnan Provinces.

To this opinion, the Commander of the Combined Fleet, Yamamoto Isoroku, gave him his answer: "I quite agree with you." This was how the Operation No.102 came floating to the surface.

Certainly, the camp of Chongqing also had been standing on the edge of a difficult situation, as follows:

> During the period from the successive falls of Wuhan and Guangzhou

to the end of the 30s (1941), our Air Force had to experience the hardest period of time. The U.K. and the U.S. at that time, having been afraid of being dragged into the turmoil of the battlefields, they had adopted a stopgap policy toward Japan. This caused all the arms and mechanical equipments and materials to be imported to our country to come to a standstill, and since we had lost all of our harbors available, we had no means to import anything. The U.S.S.R. had offered us a little help but because of the difficulties they faced in transportation, all of their supplementation was being delayed. By and by, Hitler came to attack the Soviet Union. This having kept the Soviet Union too busy in defending themselves, the assistance they had offered to us so far grew smaller and smaller until we could not expect anything from them. At this point, the aircrafts our air force had kept were no more than two hundred.

> —*A Concise History* in *The Published War History*
> *of the Republic of China*

Commander-in-Chief Shimada Shigetaro, having taken advantage of these difficulties Jiang Jieshi was facing then, requested the center of the Navy to risk everything on one last throw of the dice.

In *Chapter 4* in *The Navy's Operations in the China Region* (2) in the Japan's Defense Force's *Library of the War History,* their attacks in 1941 that followed No. 101 Operations were summarized, as follows:

The 22nd aerial squadron started their attack on Chongqing on May 3 and performed 22 attacks till mid-July. Then, the Central Headquarters and the Fleet of China Region started their operations for thoroughly subduing the resistance force in the region of Chongqing by sending an even greater air force. This was what was called "No. 102 Operations," and its purpose was to keep us free from any worry about China while we were still able to do so, considering the present state of things when the diplomatic relations between Japan and the U.S. were going from bad to worse. Thus most of the force of arms of No.11th aerial fleet (about 180 land-attack planes) advanced into Hankou and Xiaogan bases to be placed under the command of the Fleet of the China Region and performed their thorough aerial attacks—from July 27 to August 31—mainly upon Chongqing, Chengdu and several other strategic points in Sichuan Province.

In those Operations, the Army's bomber fleet also acted in cooperation. Aerial attacks were performed almost every day. In place of the 96-type land bombers, the newly-produced land attackers called "the 1-type land attackers" also came to join the Operation for the first time. Since almost all of the land attack planes of the Navy Air Force were mobilized for the Operation, its effect was extremely great and the third nations' news agencies were kept busy in reporting what great damages Chongqing was suffering.

In April that year, "the Neutrality Pact between Japan and the U.S.S.R." was concluded. Thus Japan kept the U.S.S.R. from giving China any military aid. The broad view kept by the mainstay of the Japanese military was that: now that they had checked one of "the routes for assisting the Jiang's Administration," they should use pressure on the Chongqing Administration straight away so that they could obtain an advantageous position in their negotiation with the U.S.. So far the negotiations between Japan and the U.S. had got bogged down because of Japan's policy in "managing the China Incident," especially in Japan's reluctance to withdraw from China. The Japanese military had thought: if they succeeded in reducing the Chongqing Administration to submission, the terms of negotiations with the U.S. would completely be changed. Even if they should fail both in their Operations in China and in their negotiation with the U.S., their large-scaled deployment in the Operations of Attacking the Hinterland of China would not be of no use if it was considered to be a preparation or a training for promoting the aerial strategy—in case they should start a war against the U.S.. Such was a secret calculation they had made. Their having sent the large corps and the newly-produced air planes to the front were also their preparations for that.

The unit for performing the attack was "the Aerial Fleet No.11," a newly-organized one according as the revision of the commanding system. Based upon "the Shimada's view" mentioned before, a new aerial formation of corps was brought into being in place of the United Air Raid Corps (the First United Air Raid Corps, the Second United Air Raid Corps and the Third United Air Raid Corps) that had engaged themselves in the No. 101 Operations. The Aerial Fleet No.11 had been formed by collecting the main units of planes whose bases were on the ground—unlike the air corps that belonged to the airplane carriers—and it had four aerial squadrons under it: No. 21, No. 22, No. 23 and No. 24 aerial squadrons. The other flying corps named after their base as they used to be were placed under them. Each new corps having 45 bombers (middle-sized ones), the total was 135. Each of them were fortified by 18 fighters to command the air—the 96-type fighters and Zero fighters. As is recorded in *A History of the Naval Air Force (4)*, such concentration of middle-sized bombers as to outnumber 100 had never occurred before.

No. 11 Aerial Fleet
    No. 21 Aerial Squadron—Kanoya Naval Air Corps
                                 Higashi Minato Navy Air Corps
                                 The First Air Corps
    No. 22 Aerial Squadron—Bihoro Navy Air Corps
                                 Motoyama Navy Air Corps
    No. 23 Aerial Squadron—Takao Navy Air Corps
                                 The Third Air Corps
    No. 24 Aerial Squadron—Chitose Navy Air Corps
                                 Yokohama Navy Air Corps

The Aerial Fleet No.11 had originally been subordinate to the Combined Fleet, but in order to perform the Operation No.102, it was temporarily moved under the Fleet of the China Regions. That was a measure taken to carry out a large-scaled plan of operations.

The Headquarters concentrated all the air forces with their own base in the important front, retaining its nature as the movable headquarters so that they could lead the operations. At first, the headquarters were placed at Kanoya in Kagoshima Prefecture, but when the Operation No.102 started in July, 1941, they moved to Hankou as the sortie base.

The first director was Vice Admiral Katagiri Hidekichi; the Chief of Stuff was Rear Admiral Onishi Takijiro. To Onishi, Hankou was where he served firstly as the commander of the Second United Air Force, secondly as the commander of the First United Air Force, and now he was there for the third time, on a mission of performing No.102 Operation that followed No.101 Operation. About this time, Onishi had secretly been ordered, by the

Commander-in-Chief of the Combined Fleet, Yamamoto Isoroku, to study on the possibility of performing surprise tactics upon Hawaii, and this was to make him sail up the Yangzi, feeling a premonition that the war to come next would occur on the great ocean of the Pacific.

On the other hand, the Army sent to Hankou Major General Endo Saburo as the leader of the Third Air Division. Unlike Onishi, he had turned his course from the artillery to the air force just before he was promoted to a general officer, and this had led him to call himself "a fledgling leader of the air division," but Endo, who had something in common with Onishi in their peculiarity, repeatedly accompanied his men on their flight for bombing so that he could properly lead those airmen from the start, until he came to have doubts about what they were doing or bombing upon Chongqing. This led him to offer his opinion: *An Opinion on the Advancing Operation on the Hinterland* (dated September 3, 1941), in which he advocated "the uselessness of the bombings upon Chongqing," but unfortunately it was rather too late or untimely. The situation had already come up to a point where war between Japan and the U.S. was inevitable, and even if Endo had not offered his opinion, Japan's pullback from China and discontinuation of the bombardment upon Chongqing had already been in sight, while "the terrible disaster in the excavation at Chongqing" had already occurred.

The Great Tragedy in the Air Raid Cave

● The Tragic Incident on June 5, 1941

Among the seven blocks of the Great Excavations in Chongqing, there was a huge air-raid cave called Juechangkou Excavation. Juechangkou was a bustling place, situated about at the center of the Shizhong (City's Central) Ward about 9.3km squares—also at the center of the downtown called "Xia-Bancheng (the Lower Half of the Castle)" against "Shang-Bancheng (the Upper Half of the Castle)" in the vicinity of Zhaotian-men Gate (the Emperor's Gate).

On both sides of the complicated stone steps and alleys, there were shops and cottages of those who were engaged in household industries such as furniture, carpentry, lithography, food manufacturing and so on, and many other people like rickshaw pullers, candy-sellers, herbal medicine sellers, and those who were called "*bang-bang* crew" because they were able to carry anything or anybody by means of a wooden pole (*bang*), had settled themselves there. Including those who were engaged in some dubious businesses, people of every possible occupation and of all classes came to hang out, walking along the narrow lanes, with their shoulders rubbing or yelling at each other—in a sense, it could be called a major "slum" that had come into being at what might be called the backdoor to Chongqing as the capital. Even today, this area with Minquan-lu and Minzu-lu—which lead from Juechangkou to northeast—is the busiest part of this city, and if we regard Shansi-jie Street as the base of economic activities, this area, concentrated with restaurants, souvenir shops and many other kinds of shops and other functions for consumption and entertainment—including the descendants of "*bang-bang* crew"—have formed an arena of hustle and bustle all day long.

It was true that the air raids performed by the Japanese Air Force did burn out all those small and frail houses in this neighborhood, but those living a simple life with their own body as their only property to depend on were able to resume their business by hastily building a standard shanty "as wide as four mah-jongg tables" as soon as they left the air-raid cave after an air-raid warning was lifted, so they could start their trade in a few hours. Most of their occupations being something like lubricating oil to keep the urban life going on, they had never been forced to move into the suburbs according to "the law of compulsory removal to be performed in the important cities in Sichuan Province," and this explained why the city still remained so populous even after the whole of the city area was made the target of the indiscriminate bombings.

The closest air-raid shelter for such people was the Juechangkou Excavation. This shelter, the whole length of which was as long as 2km and a half, and its capacity was usually 4,384, and 6,555 in time of need (though much more people were often pushed in), thus boasting of being the largest among the seven air-raid caves in the city. As soon as the enemy planes' approach was informed of by the sirens or by the number of red lanterns raised on the heights, all the people in the neighborhood hurried into the cave, carrying their necessities of life and tools of their trade—some had brought in even such furniture as a chest of drawers and the like—to stay there for several hours or even several days on end in the later period. The inside of the public caves was high enough for even the grown-ups to be able to walk without bending themselves, and spacious enough to place stone or wooden benches on both sides, and the lighting was provided by electric lamps or kerosene lamps.

As for the entrances to that cave, there were three of them—around Juechangkou Square—Ciqikou in the east, Shihuifu in the northwest and Shibati in the south. Among them, the last mentioned was to see that tragedy. The date was June 5, 1941, but if this was to be mentioned by those who had survived that calamity, the same date will be given as "May 1st in the 30th year of the People's Republic of China." Because they used to adopt the era name of the Republic of China and the lunar calendar, they had retained that unforgettable date as such. Their survival from that cave of death had left them such an intense impression as this.

In the summer of 1941, the sky of Chongqing had been brought totally under the Japanese Air Force. The Zero fighters that had made their appearance the year before had driven away all the planes of the Chinese Air Force from the skies of Chongqing. The result was that: the middle-sized bombers had "no planes to come against them," while their having obtained a transit air port at Xuanchang, about 300km closer to Chongqing than from Hankou, enabled them to stay in the skies of Chongqing remarkably longer than before. As the natural consequence, those living under such a dangerous sky must stay longer in the air-raid cave, bating their breath. Such were the air raids brought about by the Japanese, which were called "fatigue bombings" by the Chinese for the obvious reason.

The following was the description found in what Dong Xanguang had written in his work, *Jiang Jieshi:*

We were then in the third summer of terrible air raids. In a sense, the bombardments we suffered in 1941 were of the most atrocious ones. Their two years' experiences had taught the Japanese airmen how to give attacks of infinite variety and how to bring about the greatest effect in human nerves. Japan had mistakenly believed that their bombings upon Chongqing would lead the Chinese Administration to surrender to Japan. But in the third year, they had finally come to notice that they had estimated the Chinese power of patience unbelievably so low. In a certain period of this year, they performed an almost ceaseless bombardment day and night throughout seven days. During that period, the longest cease of bombing was five hours, the shortest an hour and a half. This led the government officials to spend ten to fifteen hours in the daily mean in the air-raid cave. For this blitz tactics, Japan had sent to us more than one thousand planes to keep their attack for 150 hours on end. But Chongqing had endured this suffering in an undaunted attitude.

It appeared as if all the functions of this anti-Japanese capital had moved into the underground. All of their productive activities and other activities had gone into the air raid cave. When the Japanese planes were in the skies, Chongqing appeared to have completely turned into an uninhabited city.

The high-ranking officials could be considered fortunate since they were able to stay at the cave for their exclusive use. More than 1,800 air raid caves within the urban area of Chongqing were of three kinds or ranks, and people were expected to enter one of them according to their social ranks or status or occupations. This meant one cannot always enter the nearest cave. The first-ranking ones were the private ones owned by high-ranking officials of the government or the Nationalist Party or by business leaders; the second-ranking ones were for the workers of the government offices or of business facilities; in the case of the caves for the general public, their interior conditions and environment tended to be far from good. Many of such caves as were possessed by individuals or by business facilities had been brought into being not so much for the owners' refuge but rather for the purpose of speculation, and active were the selling and buying of the cave-entrance cards, so those caves were naturally beyond the reach of the plebeian who had to feel thankful for having obtained the card that permitted their entrance into the public cave. This was especially so when they recalled how they obtained that single card for their own family: when the cave was being brought into being, they all had to lend their hands before they received a certificate of having offered volunteer labor in order to receive a single card for their own family.

● The Unusual Heat in the Cave Affected the Infant and the Invalid

Han Suyin, who had had many opportunities to enter the public cave wrote down what she had experienced there in *Birdless Summer*. Since she was in distress about the discord with her husband, Pao, a commissioned officer of the Nationalist Party, she had come to wish to be independent of him, and this had led her to spend her days as a maternity nurse and as a writer:

No sooner had the fog of winter season gone than the bombers presented themselves to keep bombing throughout summer and even to late autumn, and this had led us to feel as if that was part of our life. That was how our daily life had become regulated by that prospect of ours. People got up early. When the air-raid warning was issued, they carried their things— including kettles and iron pans—into the cave to spend the whole day there. Sometimes we had a bomb dropped very close to us, and this made us hear that peculiar whistling it gave when it came falling. At other times, we heard far-off buzzing followed by the faint sound of violent bursting of bombs. Sometimes we had a bomber fleet appear five or six times a day; at the worst time as many as twenty times a day. At one time in 1941, they kept bombing for seven days and nights on end without receiving any interception, causing many to be bombed, and at an air-raid cave, many, especially the infants, were brought to death, affected by the unusual heat and fatigue and diarrhea.

Inside the cave, it was usually cool, but when packed with hundreds of people or thousands of people, the heat in the cave became unbearable. Including the facilities for relieving themselves, the cave was quite likely to become even more unsanitary. The air was filled with an offensive odor, and the food they had brought in was attracting flies. The rise in the death rate of the infant and the invalid was a natural consequence.

It was from late July to mid-August that the bombardments of the No.102 Operations reached its climax, when middle-sized bombers numbering one hundred to one hundred and thirty were covering the skies of Chongqing. Especially the one that lasted from August 8 to 14 turned out to be ceaseless from dawn to night. Thus the citizens of Chongqing had to be exposed to such long-termed, continuous mass bombardments as had never been experienced by any other city in the world.

Also from the U.S. Embassy, which had moved to the southern shore upon which Japan had promised to avoid bombing, this long-term bombardment was telegraphed to the Government at home as something that deserved special mention. The following was the telegram sent by the then ambassador to China, Clarence Gauss, who had taken Nelson Johnson's place:

Chungking August 13,1941—1 p.m.

From August 8, 2 p.m. to the hour of this message, Chungking has sustained a total of over 30 successive raids by Japanese navy bombers. Eight of these raids have occurred at night. Total number of bombers involved over 500 by personal observation; official count would probably be larger. All planes fly high beyond anti-aircraft fire at approximately 20 to 25 thousand feet. Each raid apparently has had definite objective, including industrial areas along both banks of the Yangtze River above and below Chungking and both banks of the Chialing River. The area of the old walled city, that is, the area immediately opposite the Embassy and the paddock has not been bombed and there has been no bombing in the so-called the safety zone on the southern bank, but the city area to the west of the officially walled city has been included repeatedly among objectives.

Spacing of the raids has been such as practically to immobilize all activity in and around Chungking since Friday afternoon. Embassy radio station can operate only during brief all clear intervals thus delaying receipt and dispatch of all messages as well as code messages of the Navy. Details as the damage and casualties cannot be obtained at this time because of disruption of communication. So far only damage to American property is brief report just received that American Methodist Mission at Dzenkiangai in area west of the old city was damaged during raid at 1 o'clock on the morning of the 11th. Send to the Department. Repeated to Peiping. Shanghai repeat to Tokyo.

Gauss

The same ambassador sent another report dated 14 or the following day, reporting that: Chungking was still being kept under the air raid.

● A Hell on Earth was Brought about in the Air-Raid Cave

On one of these summer days of air raids that started in May—though it was before the Operation 102 started—in the midst of the air raids that started in May, there occurred a terrible disaster at Shibatikou Entrance to Juechangkou Tunnel.

It was on the evening of June 5. Drizzling rain appeared to keep falling and there was no sign of the rising moon. By this day, Chongqing had already had six air raids. The first one in 1941 was on May 3—on the same date of two years before when the Navy Air Force of Japan had performed the first attack upon Chongqing, and by that air raid, "Zhou's Office" or Zhou Enlai's residence-cum-office at No. 50 at Zengjia-an was damaged. But all those six air raids having been performed in the daytime and no air raid at night had been done since the autumn the year before.

The people in Chongqing, who had already been well accustomed to the air raid, used to come back from the suburbs to the castle area toward the evening. Those families who had been in their place of refuge in the Jiangbei (North of the River) or the Nan-an (South-shore) Districts, or the husbands who had been living in those Districts apart from their family for the sake of their job were now coming back in ferry boats for a brief reunion or for shopping or for going on an errand. The water of the those large rivers and those bedrocks of this Mountain Castle, which had amply absorbed the heat of daylight so far, ought to begin to release their heat slowly but steadily, when no wind stirred anything. Once again, the season of "*huolu* (fire place)" had come round, and the streets were crowded with those who had come out partly for seeking some coolness of the evening.

At 7 p.m., an air-raid warning sounded abruptly. The two red balloons raised upon the heights soon became three (indicating the changes from "the enemy planes are approaching" to "they are over our city.") The Headquarters of the Aerial Defense also seemed to have been caught off their guard. The crowd of people in the streets had immensely been thrown into confusion.

Since the enemy's appearance was so abrupt that those who had come back from the Jiangbei (North of the River) or the Nan-an (South Shore) could not afford to have even fifteen to twenty minutes to go back to the ferry boats. The old people carrying heavy loads, the mothers accompanied by many children— such groups of people who had become rarely seen in Shizhong (City's Central) Ward in those days—ran toward the nearest air raid cave that seemed available. Naturally the private caves or corporative caves were not available to them, while the small caves brought into being by each administrative section had been soon filled with those living in the neighborhood; then all they could do was just to press themselves into "the large tunnel." This was why Shibati-kou Entrance to Juechangkou Excavation—close to the Landings of the

Yangzi—got crowded with such people. The couple of landings—Ran-matou and Jiazi-matou—were connected to Shibati Street by the stone steps three meters wide, and those who had realized that they were too late to get on board the ferry just ran up the stone steps as if they had suddenly recalled that saying: "First come, first served."

After that accident, the Nationalist Government issued *The Report on the Accident in the Large Tunnel where Many were Choked to Death*, in which we can see a passage that went as follows:

> On that occasion, an unusually large number of people came to seek refuge at this tunnel. Especially, the number of women and children was larger than usual, and they were characteristically carrying a large number of bags with them.

The maximum capacity of that cave was 6,555, but it seems that at least twice that number of refugees had been accommodated that night. As was expected, the interior of the cave became badly jammed. At the depths of the cave, those old familiar people from Shibati (Eighteen Ladders) Street, Caoyao (Harbal Medicine) Street, Muhuo (Wooden Article) Street, Zouma (Running Horses) Street and so on were taking up their usual position. That was what was usually happening. But when they had an unexpectedly large number of newcomers come rushing to join them, angry voices and crying and whining naturally came up here and there. There were electric lamps and kerosene lamps hanging from the ceilings, but it still remained dusky inside. To make the matter worse, because of the mud that had been piled up at the entrance having been brought in by sticking to the soles of so many shoes and sandals, the floor had grown so unusually slippery that it was rather hard for anyone to keep standing firm.

What had turned out even fatal was the breakdown of the ventilators, which was to work with the electricity produced by the independent power generators provided in the same tunnel. The ventilators were expected to keep working properly. But they failed to. Could that be genuinely an accidental misfortune? Or an unavoidable accident caused by the officials in charge having admitted to adopt such equipment as had not come up to standard, as was often the case in those days? There is no other way but to imagine, but what was crucial was the fact that: no fresh air could be sent into the cave filled with so many evacuees, whose number was estimated to be ten thousands or even twenty thousands. Even after an emergency warning was issued, the ventilators that had stopped working remained as useless as ever, and there was no telephone equipped in the cave to find out what was happening there.

● More than Ten Thousand People Struggling in the Cave of Unusual Heat.

About the time when the inside of the cave had already become unbearably hot and stuffy, those who had stood near the entrance of the cave, being frightened both at the bombings by the bombers and at the strafing by the Zero fighters, had no other thought than going farther and farther into the cave. The entrance was firmly closed with the wooden stockade, and outside the stockade, the members of the civilian defense corps were on the lookout, saying: "The enemy planes are still over us. You must not come out yet." Fallen bombs did give bursting sounds, proving the defense corps' warning to be true.

Then even more terrifying information came to frighten those near the entrance: "Poison gas has been dropped!" By the time this reached the depth of the cave, it had been highly embellished. Those near the entrance firmly closed by the wooden fences were impelled to bring themselves farther into the cave as far as possible. That was to inflict more and more pain upon those who were inside, but those near the entrance could not simply think of it. This did increase the tightness inside.

It is impossible to find out any record to prove that the Japanese military used poison gas in attacking Chongqing. Even though it has widely been known that the Japanese Army in field operations used poison gas, there is no evidence that it was used also in urban bombings. But the Japanese Navy also "prepared a considerable number of chemical weapons called "No. 7 bombs (60kg)," as was recorded in *A History of Japanese Navy Air Force (3) System & Technology*. But the Chinese people in Chongqing had firmly believed in the Japanese military's planning to use poison gas upon them. In fact, on the occasion of air raids of "5.3 & 5.4" in 1939, the government authorities warned against "poisoned tobacco" that had been dropped around the city, as Theodore White had heard, and in the civilian defense corps, "a unit for preventing people from being poisoned" had also been brought into being. The following is from *A Record of Chongqing's Aerial Defense for These 7 Years,* which appeared in the January Issue (1944) of *The Chinese Air Force:*

The means adopted by the Japanese Militarists turned out to be extremely cruel. After having failed in their military adventure, they employed poison gas and made their campaign a temporarily successful one. Chongqing being a wartime capital, the enemy planes were quite likely to release poison gas upon us. .... (In 1940) the public organizations, in their effort to keep off poison gas, stretched a curtain at their entrance, and the order was issued from the authorities: One must carry one's own gas mask or gas helmet when one enters the air-raid cave. This led to cause a boom for keeping one's own mask or helmet, and a great variety of masks and helmets were brought into being to be put on sale.

This does explain why what might have been a mere imagination that had occurred to someone in the cave quickly went spreading as a reliable piece of information. Among those being pressed farther and farther into the depths of the cave one or even two kilometers away from the entrance, in the temperature steadily rising, breathing the air which was growing thinner, while their endurance was coming to its limit, this information of the poison gas could not help adding to their confusion. People, seeking for fresh air and coolness, began to move toward the entrance in such impatience as if the poison gas had already been wrapping them. But at the entrance, the civilian defense Corps were controlling them, shouting in hoarse voices: "Not yet! The planes are still over us!" The wooden fence had been firmly kept locked. Those near the entrance were bracing their legs, trying to resist the pressure from the interior. Here and there, bursts of screaming of people and crying of children rose all at once. This was how "the Great Tragedy at the Air Raid Cave" started. The time when the suffocation started is recorded to have been about from 7:40 p.m. to 8.00 p.m.. It was less than an hour after the air-raid warning was issued.

Among those people—more than ten thousand in number—struggling in that over-heated cave, there were Chen Chengan, Bai Sufang, Xiang Caiqun and Tang Zhengcheng, who were living in Caoyao-jie (Herb Street).

The Screaming in the Underground Hell

● "They've Dropped Poison Gas!"

(Chen Chengan's experience)

Cheng Chengan, 29 years old, was apprenticed to a blacksmith. He was living and working on the premises at a shop selling kitchen utensils at No.5 in Caoyao-jie Street. Before the air raid started in 1939, large iron pans and kettles his master had produced used to be hung compactly at the narrow frontage on to the street, but since 1940, metals had become treated as valuables, and this had kept him from having ample opportunities to improve his skill. But he had no intention to return to his birthplace where his parents were living. On that day, Chen as a young man entered that cave by the entrance at the end of Shibati Street together with his master's wife and two young men as his fellow apprentices. It was only several minutes for them to run there.

The inside of the cave was unusually crowded, and it was impossible for them to be seated on the benches placed in it. All the people remained patient, their sweating bodies inevitably pressed against one another. Because of the unusual heat or foul air, Chen was having a bad headache. Then there came a voice: "Poison gas has dropped!" The voice went spreading in no time, and this caused the people who had remained still so far to struggle to move on toward the entrance. About an hour had passed since they entered the cave, according to Chen Chengan's memory.

Chen himself moved toward the entrance, making himself part of the crowd. The floor was muddy and slippery; they made almost no progress. In the meantime, there started some signs that some people were falling. He felt something hard at his toe.

"Save me, please!" "Ouch!" Such voices resounded in the cave.

"Maama! Maama!" Children's voices sounded particularly loud, but even their cries were soon to be drowned in the screams in that underground hell.

Chen Chengan had long been separated from his master's wife and his colleagues. The lamps hanging from the ceiling went out one after another. The air seemed to have been getting rarefied. In the darkness, he found himself breathing hard, but unable to tell what to do to save himself from this difficulty, he just kept standing still, pressing himself against the rock wall he had happened to stand by, since he knew: if he were to move on, he would be clung by those lying on the floor, saying: "Help me go out." Having felt as if some air were coming along the rock surface, he kept his lips on the wall with the mouth wide open.

How long had he been there? When he came to himself, he found everything remained still. No sound could be heard. He felt as if he were "in the castle of "*gui* (the souls of the dead)." Around his feet, he saw many lying dead one on top of another; many had got their clothes taken off. Had they been struggling against one another? Or had they found it too hot to remain in their clothes?

Chen Chengan crawled over those who were no more. He kept saying to himself: "I'm alive; I want to be alive; I must get out of here while I'm alive." On breathing in the open air, he fainted, and nothing remained in his memory. It was only after he had come to himself that he was told of the deaths of his master's wife and his colleagues.

(Bai Sufang's Experience)

Bai Sufang then was twenty-six. She was a housewife living in No.35 Caoyao-jie Street. Her husband was a furniture maker. They were living an active life in a partitioned two-storied tenement-house of 40m squares, making its upstairs their living space and its downstairs a workshop. In later years, she was to have seven children, but in those days she had only one girl baby, still nine months old. Naturally, *that* day, too, she had always pressed her baby to her bosom.

Bai Sufang, as soon as she heard an emergency warning, she ran to Shibati-kou Entrance to the Tunnel. The street being so familiar to her, her feet were easily carrying her and her baby. Once they entered the cave, everything and everyone was all right, she believed. That tunnel having been brought into being by piercing through the rocky hill, its inside ought to have remained unaffected whatever explosion might occur upon it.

The inside of it had been crowded to an unusual extent. By and by, there came voices: "Poison gas has dropped!" A young man began to cry toward the entrance: "Let me go out!" Bai Sufang joined his crying but stopped soon, because this had made her too hard to breathe. If she died here, she thought, her daughter would also die. This led her to go desperately on and on. The floor had already been covered with dead bodies. It was impossible to go on without stepping upon them. Then she had one of her cloth shoes gripped by the person she had thought no more. This did make her scream.

The waves of the people rushing to the entrance were pushed back again and again to their lamentation, which was growing less and less loud. The third wave was the last one Bai Sufang had remembered well. In the meantime, it had become so quiet that she was able to hear even the water dripping from the rock ceiling. Holding her baby in her arms, she lay in the drain ditch, waiting for any helping hand to come, but in vain. There came nothing like any such sign. Far ahead, she could see a little light. This led her to crawl or rather climb up the heap of the dead bodies as far as the entrance. Near the entrance the heap had become much higher. She managed to climb up to the top of it and cried for help, but none answered her. This led her to crawl out of the cave for herself and lost consciousness then and there. It had already been five in the morning.

● **"Let me Go Out! It's Killing me!"**
(Xiang Caiqun's Experience)

Xiang Caiqun married at sixteen and gave birth to thirteen children, but when she suffered that tragic incident at that air-raid cave, she was twenty and had not yet been blessed with any baby, because her baby had always been born dead. Her husband was a joiner, who manufactured small furniture and boxes. Since the air raid started, his business had been far from going well, and he had found it rather hard to pay for the house he had rented at No. 10 in Caoyao-jie Street. As they had already found it too inefficient to close the shop every time they heard an air-raid warning, they made it a rule to keep their shop open till an emergency warning (the enemy planes above the city) was issued, and when the moment of danger did arrive, they used to run literally for life to the nearest cave without minding even if their cloth shoes might slip off on their way.

So even before they entered the cave, they had heard people talking about the poison gas. Her husband, who had run there with her, chose to stay out. She stopped him from doing so, saying he would die all the same if he were involved in the bombardment there. Still he chose to remain in the open air, even if he had to die.

It was too late when she regretted having chosen to enter the cave, which soon got into confusion. "We'll die soon. Help us out!" "Le me go out! I'm dying!" Those voices were filling the cave. She tried to go out, but wall after wall of people simply kept her from doing so. Fortunately she came across one of her neighbors, Shang Zhengzheng's mother and she was relieved of the uneasiness she ought to have suffered if she had not had any acquaintance with her. This led her to choose to come out to the central part of the passage instead of the wall side where many had piled themselves to death. And having found a wooden bench there, they were lying there.

Long time had passed before she had an idea: "If Shibati Entrance was not available, how about another entrance—Shihuifu?" This led them to walk slowly toward it, taking the direction opposite to Shibati-Kou Entrance from which they had entered. On their way, they saw dead bodies everywhere; many of them had taken their clothes off in their agony. She now realizes that: her having accompanied Shang Zhengzheng's mother enabled her to bear that painful series of scenes through which she had to walk on. The moment she finally reached Shihuifu Entrance and met her husband who had come to save her there, she felt she had finally come to life again to her immense happiness.

● **"Master, Save me, Please!"**
(Shang Zhengzheng's experience)

Shang Zhengzheng was also living in Caoyao-jie Street, and was a would-be furniture maker, a seventeen-year-old boy, who was still in training with two other apprentices to his father who had his workshop of 70m squares at No. 24 Caoyao-jie Street. In the situation at that time, however, it could be said that he was half loafing around the house. It was only less than 200m from his house to Shibati-kou Entrance; this having allowed him to sit around at home till the last moment, all he could do when he arrived there was to push himself just inside the entrance. He was alone then; his mother, sisters and colleagues had accompanied their neighbor, Xiang Caiqun.

When the temperature in the cave had grown unbearably high, making people hard even to breathe, members of the civilian defense corps came in and distributed *jinlingdan*—a Chinese medicine—which was said to refresh the takers, but its effect was so ephemeral and he were to suffer even greater sickness. He tried to get out of the cave two times by throwing himself into the maelstrom of the people, but without success, and when he tried once again, he ran out of breath and passed out.

About an hour later, he felt as if he had been brought to fresh air and came to regain consciousness. He found himself lying among the piles of dead bodies.

Since the dead no longer needed any air, some remaining air might have helped him to revive. Several dozens meters ahead, he saw a light. It was moving up and down. He found it was an electric torch.

After having got out of the cave, the boy Shang entered the cave again. He wanted to find out what had become of his mother and sisters. The seventeen-year-old boy, after having been in the open air for a while, was feeling as if he had been all right. But soon it turned out to be a reckless attempt. As he was going into the depth of the cave, he was to be astonished at having been held on to by many hands stretched from what he had thought a heap of dead bodies. "Master, please help me out...." came a voice from a pile of dead bodies, and he had his thigh in his trousers gripped. "Stop it!" he cried, but he had grown too weak to keep standing, and when he tried to get up, his trousers whose belt had been loosened got dropped to be brought over to that stranger's hand.

It was totally impossible to find out someone in that cave: the lamp light was gone, and the sporadic electric lamps were too feeble to tell one face from another. This made Shang Zhengzheng return to the entrance and had himself get out of the cave by gripping the bamboo pole brought in by the members of the civilian defense corps. Probably affected also by the fear he had felt in the cave, he fell in a faint the moment he got out of the cave, and was carried home while receiving oxygen inhalation. His mother and sisters he had been concerned about were saved by his father, who, before the daybreak, entered the cave by Shihuifu Entrance and found them accompanying Xiang Caiqun, but the two apprentices remained missing and even their bodies could not be found after all.

*　　*　　*

These were the experiences of the four persons from Caoyao-jie Street, who had fortunately survived that terrible accident. Even though half a century had passed since then, their memories still remained vivid and their speeches were graphic as if that incident had happened only yesterday. Xiang Caiqun was amply revealing her pleasure in her smile so broad as to disfigure all of her features, when she told me how happy she had been to find her husband have come to save her out of that dark cave she had been confined to. On the other hand, Shang Zhengzheng did show me how he did it, when he tried to make himself free from the grip of the hands that had been extended from the piles of the dead bodies. These four people alone could give the thirty-seven names of their neighbors in the same street who had died in that accident. Some families had none left alive. This was known when their houses remained closed since the day of that accident. There were many such families in the streets near the Juechang-kou Square—Muhuo-jie, Lao-jie, Yusikou-jie and Dingxin-jie streets.

- ● **Dead Bodies Piled Up were Tied Together and Drawn Out**

There were such persons as Zhou Furian who had a narrow escape because he happened to have entered another cave that day.

He was a fifteen-year-old apprentice for printing. His place of work was Jiangzhou Print Shop at Tiangzhu-jie Street, and he used to travel back and forth every day from No. 25 in Wushiye-xiang Alley, where his parents lived. His parents were peddlers of vegetables, carrying their offerings on a pole. An apprentice could not receive any salary and all he received for his labor was three meals a day, and the charges for a haircut and for straw sandals. If he became a printer, he was to receive a salary of twenty *yuan* which was worth 45kg of rice. This had made him wish to be a full-fledged printer as soon as possible.

So far he had always entered the cave at Shibati-kou, but somehow that was the only day when he felt worried about his parents and this had led him to head for the cave near his own home. Thus he escaped that terrible disaster and his parents were also safe. But his mother's younger brother's family were included in that tragedy and his cousins, ten-years-old and seven-years-old, were no more. His aunt, her clothes badly broken, was as good as naked when she finally got away from that cave. She, who had got separated from her children, was half insane. When he was asked to go to Shibati-kou Entrance and reached there, he found the Army had been mobilized to engage in a rescue operation. At the entrance, those concerned about what had become of their family members had thronged; all were weeping or crying in an unusual uproar. Every time the bodies of the unfortunate were brought out of the cave by the rescue corps, their voices of lamentation got intensified. Those bodies bound with straw rope were dragged out of the cave, and this was how the young cousins of Zhou Futian's were brought out of the cave. Those remains, instead of being handed over to their family, were carried in a truck as far as Zhaotian-men Gate to be transferred into sampans, which sailed up the Yangzi as far as Heishizi on the other side of the River before they were buried there. So they had no graves of their own.

Jiang Pengcheng lost his elder brother and his two-year-old nephew. In years to come, Jiang Pengcheng became counted as one of the leading experts in Sichuan cooking, and even after he left *Weiyuan*—a restaurant enjoying the greatest fame in Chongqing—at retirement age, he was invited to *Lao Sichuan* in an advisory capacity. But at that time during the Anti-Japanese War, he was still a fledgling cook who had just finished the course of vegetable-washing. His elder brother, Jiang Lianlin, having finished a period of apprenticeship, became a cook at the Shu's New Food Agency and was living at No.34, Mizi-xiang. Pengcheng himself was developing his skills at another restaurant. He had just become twenty.

Pengcheng himself had not entered Shibati-kou, but his elder brother and his family living in Mizi-xiang used to take refuge at that cave nearest to them. As soon as he heard of what happened at Shibati-kou, Pengcheng called at his brother's home and then stood at the entrance to that cave. Several hours later, his elder-sister-in-law alone crawled out by herself. She said she had fainted but a flow of water that happened to come into her mouth brought her around. His elder brother was carried out as a dead body. As for his nephew, even his corpse could not be found.

Piteous was their mother, who had lived on the money sent by his elder brother. Having small feet as a result of foot-binding, she had no means of livelihood if that allowance sent to her were to be stopped. Informing her of her son's death was too cruel to do. So Jianlin, consulting with his sister-in-law, cooked up a story that he, Jianlin, had been away from Chongqing, and kept sending her two *yuans* a month. It was not until eight months later that he went to see her mother in the country and told her of his brother's death. In due time, his sister-in-law got married, and his brother's family became no more.

The boy, Xiao Jianxiang, had got a toothache that day, and this led him not to enter *that* cave, thus to escape danger. His family, who had come up to Chongqing from Suzhou, had temporarily moved to the suburbs after the air raids on "5.3 & 5.4," but about that time they had returned to Shizhoug (City's Central) Ward. The Shibati Cave had become their usual cave and the day before the fatal day, too, they had entered it in the morning. On entering it, one was to face a steep slope that went farther on, and the main line and branch lines were connected in a complicated manner and even if the main line led to the other exits, the branch lines were all blind alleys; and this had made that cave a sort of maze for those who were not accustomed to entering it, as he still remembers.

On June 5, the boy Xiao was suffering from a vehement toothache. The tooth he had treated several days before seemed to have been badly infected. This decided his mother to take him to the dentist in the suburbs, and this led her to specify another cave near the castle wall for his sister and their grandfather in case they had an air raid during their absence so that they could meet there. That was how all of his family had been saved. But in his memory, that fierce toothache he had that morning still remains even more vividly than their good luck of having escaped deaths.

Zheng Guobin, being a member of the Civilian Defense Corps, was to be a witness of that tragedy. Living at No. 17 in Shibati-jie Street, he rushed to the air raid cave on hearing the warning, and at the entrance to the cave, he engaged himself in guiding the people into it, while keeping the order around. As for the information about the poison gas, it had certainly reached his ears, too, but none of his colleagues had ever been informed of the ventilation device having gone wrong.

The near hits around the cave did shake the neighborhood and those who were jostling around the entrance wanted to go farther and farther into the cave. The Civilian Defense Corps were also helping them go farther into the cave. As long as the enemy planes were in the sky, keeping the people inside was a natural measure for them to take, while the enemy planes were persistent in presenting themselves one wave after another. Removing the wooden fences was the last thing they would do. It was more than an hour later when what was happening inside was finally brought to the knowledge of the Defense Corps.

It was impossible for Zheng Guobin to give even a rough number of the dead bodies he had to see during the several days that followed. All he could say was: he had seen horrible scenes. Just inside the wooden fences, there were dead bodies in complicated layers as high as the ceilings. Legs entangled other legs, heads popped up from under arms, feet coming up from among heads, looking like the horns; all of these had formed pyramids of the dead. Still some did crawl out of such mountains of the dead. Zheng's younger brother was also among those who had crawled out of the mountains of the dead. The members of the Civilian Defense Corps stood facing such mountains and pulled out of it those who were still alive. This was how they engaged themselves in that work until they cleared away all the corpses.

More than fifty years have passed, but to Zheng Guobin, the sight of those pyramids of the dead—piled up at the entrance to that tunnel—still remains clearly branded on his memory. Among the dead, there were eighteen members of the civilian defense corps included, too. This makes that incident totally unforgettable to him, because he himself might have shared their fate, if only anything had gone wrong with him.

Guo Moruo's Wrath

● **The Toll of Victims still Remains Uncertain**

On the night of June 5, 1941, many people were sent to death in the darkness of the air raid cave deeply excavated into the bedrock of the mountain castle of Chongqing. But even today, none can give even an approximate figure of them. All we have are a variety of opinions that give different numbers—from several hundred to more than ten thousand.

The Investigation Committee at the authorities concerned gave the number of 992 deaths, but this figure was not accepted as valid even at that time. *LIFE*, which informed this disaster along with the photographs taken by Carl Mydans—in which men and women and children were fallen over one another on the stone steps of the Shibati-kou Entrance to the Air Raid Cave—had given the number of victims in the headline: "4,000 Chungking citizens in the Air Raid Cave were choked to death during the air raid." On the other hand, Han Suyin who used to live in Chongqing at that time wrote down: "About twelve thousand people were choked to death in the air-raid cave for the general public (though some give a different number—twenty thousand)"—as she wrote in *The Birdless Summer*. One of the citizens who experienced it, Guo Weibo, testified: "About ten thousand citizens were choked or pressed to death in a single night." (*A Chronicle of Chongqing's Resistance to Japan*) But in the same *Chronicle,* there is a statement that goes: "That night, a terrible disaster occurred at the Juechang-kou entrance to the Great Tunnel, causing several thousand deaths," and the number given by the person on the scene has not adopted as it was. Among other reports, "30,000 deaths" were given, but this is not acceptable, considering the capacity of that air-raid cave. Then it might be said that the truth is still left in the dark.

What was it that had made different people give different numbers? It was partly because the confusion caused by the successive air raids—June 5, 7, 11, 14, 15 and 16—prevented the relevant authorities from investigating the fact, but what was even closer to the fact would be that: the political situation in Chongqing at that time was rather negative in disclosing the facts plainly and was likely to have prevented any such efforts from being made, with the result that: the truth was lost forever in the dark, only causing a variety of opinions to have remained widely different from one another.

The terrible disaster occurred in the midst of the persistent air raids given in three waves at night, and in that sense it is by no means wrong to seek the foundation of that cause in the indiscriminate bombings upon the urban area. But at the same time, and even more clearly, it appeared to the eyes of many citizens of Chongqing that: if it had not been for the negligence and inaptitude in the facilities and the management on the side of the authorities concerned, it would not have led to such a calamity as that, even if they suffered the air raids as they did. In other words, that was "a man-made disaster" as well as "war damage."

Partly for that reason, the Nationalist Government's censorship organization had always placed the information concerning this occurrence under its powerful control. The news articles concerning this accident—most of which had been distributed from Zhongyang Tongxunshe (the Central News Agency) of the Nationalist line—were always treated as something inconspicuous, obviously unexpected from such a great disaster as that. The government authorities must have been extremely afraid of the situation in which all that had happened might be exposed to the public eye and the people's anger might be turned into the criticism against them. The first report given by *Xin Hua Ri Bao* (*Zhongyang Tongxun-she*) made a quick report on it under the headlines: "The three waves of enemy planes made air raids," "Chongqing was attacked last night," "Fires at several spots in Shizhong Ward" and "An appalling tragedy at a certain air-raid cave," but as for what happened at "a certain air-raid cave," only a brief report was given, simply referring to the occurrence of a case of suffocation with a result of having caused some deaths and injuries. On that very day, they might not be able to offer a proper amount of news because of the deadline for the manuscript, but in the newspapers published from the 7th onward, there ought to have been more detailed news reported. As it was, the news concerning the details, especially concerning the number of deaths and the injuries, or the articles concerning the inquiry into its cause were rarely reported. There were only some follow-up reports on "all quarters taking a serious view of the situation" or on "the Chairman Jiang's visit to the disaster-stricken area." Seeing that: that was what was happening to the largest non-government paper—the Communist Party's bulletin—we can easily imagine how the authorities concerned were trying hard to wrap up that incident in the haze. The number of deaths given in the formal announcement was at first "five hundred to six hundred," but after its underestimation was criticized, the newly-founded Accident Investigation Committee gave on July 2 a revised version: the numbers of deaths and serious injuries as 992 and 151 respectively. By that time, however, the citizens, having had it with such officially-made numbers as those, began to try to find out their own numbers by means of their own information networks. Since then, those numbers came to be established to be carried over to this day.

● **Jiang Jieshi's "Self-Confidence" had Left his Responsibility**
for the Accident Ambiguous

When the air raids of "5.3 & 5.4" occurred, too, the late implementation of their air defense setup had caused such large damages as they suffered, but Jiang Jieshi then would not hide the damages but rather made use of them, appealing to the citizens, saying: "You shall turn this May of Humiliation into the May of Vindication," thus successfully leading the people to unite themselves in engaging in the National United Front Against Japan. In the following year, 1940, when they were placed under the fierce attack of No. 101 Operations, too, he adopted an outgoing attitude, associating Chongqing with London, and comparing himself to a Churchill in China, thus giving vent to the dissatisfaction likely to be felt by the people under the unfavorable war situation. But now, the same Government of Jiang Jieshi took a different attitude: instead of accepting that tragic incident as it was, he tried to keep the people away from the facts, while making every effort to impress them that: *that* was not anything so serious after all. That might have been made so because that had largely been a man-made disaster, but even if that was taken into account, that was an incomprehensible manner of dealing with the information and of facing the people.

What was it that had made such a high-handed political measure as this come to the front? It seems that it was not irrelevant to Jiang Jieshi's growing confidence in retaining his power.

June in 1941 was when many people had lost sight of their future in the darkness of their air raid cave, but this was not the case with Jiang Zhongsheng (Jieshi), for that was exactly the time when he—the President of the Nationalist Party and the Chairman of its Central Executive Committee & its Supreme Committee of State Security—was able to aware that: his destiny, having corresponded to the flow of the world history, was now coming to meet it. The one, who had grasped the post of the successor to Sun Wen's Revolution by sheer talent, the former principal of Huangbu School for Military Officers, who had been reigning over the powerful governmental organization, was now in the spotlight as one of the leaders of the world-front against fascism and also as the top leader of Free China. His present situation was certainly at the depth of misfortune, but his future was bright and shining. No longer he was what he used to be in 1937, when he brought the National United Front Against Japan into being by making an unwilling compromise with the Communist Party. No longer it was 1938 and 39 when he was not only being distressed by having had one of the party leaders, Wang Zhaoming, betray him, but also suffering from international isolation. Jiang at present was able to look ahead into the future with confidence. The Nationalist Party had been grasped by him, and now his Nationalist Government was about to have many international supports extended by the U.S. and the U.K. and others. No wonder if such a military person as he—who was only accustomed to giving orders to others—came to regard the Communist Party and the common people as troublesome nuisance. He was now seeking for the people who would be always ready to obey him.

In January, 1941, the U.S. President Roosevelt, who had revealed his prospect: "America would be ready to become an armory for democracy" in his *Fireside Talk* on the radio at the end of the year before, presented "the law for lend-lease of arms" to Congress (to be signed on March 11). The lend-lease was mainly intended for the U.K. but for China, too, the U.S. decided to offer some munitions of free gift, since it was engaged in a war against Japan.

Now Jiang Jieshi's new source of power was in the U.S. The following is from The First Chapter on *The U.S.-China Relations for the Past One Century* in *the China White Paper* as the document of the Department of State (1949):

On March 15, 1941, four days after the passage of the Lend-Lease Act, President Rosevelt made an address in which he said: china, likewise, expresses the magnificent will of millions of plain people to resist the dismonkerment of their Nation. China, through the Generalissimo, Chiang Kai-shek, ask our help. America has said that China shall haveour help.

After a lend-lease program to meet the emergency needs of China had been developed, following consultations between Chinese and American officials, the President, on May 6, 1941, in accordance with the provisions of the Act, declared the defense of China to be vital to the defense of the U.S. A Master Lend-Lease Agreement with China was not signed, however, until June 2, 1942.

Lend Lease aid to China was begun on 1941, and was aimed particularly at improving transport over the Burma Road, the only artery through wich goods could could flow into the unoccupied China. The firstblend-lease shipments consisted primarily of trucks, spare parts, motor fuel and lubricants for use on the Burma Road and make recommendations for increasing traffic over it. On the base of these recommendations for Chinese Government undertook a number of measures to improve the administration of the road. Additional spare parts and repair equipments were furnished to China under lend-lease, and a number of American motor-traffic techinicians were recruited in the U.S., and sent to China at lend-lease expense. .... As a result of these efforts and of the arrival of large number of American trucks, the tonnage arrived over the Burma Road by November, 1941, was almost 4 times greater than it had been during the early months of 1941.

Early in 1941, this Government approved a plan which permitted American fighter planes piloted by volunteer American airmen and serviced by American ground crews to fight against Japan in the service of China. The American Volunteer Group ("the Flying Tiger"), under the command of Major General Claire L. Chennault, was formally constituted as a Unit of China's armed forces by an order issued by Generalissimo Chiang Kaishek on August 1, 1941. During the time that it was in existence the American

Volunteer Group provided an effective air defense for southwest China and rendered invaluable assistance to hard-pressed Chinese and other forces in Burma. In May, 1941, an American Air Mission headed by General Clagett was sent to China to survey the situation. Among other things, the report of the Air Mission recommended that a program to train Chinese pilots and mechanics be developed in as much as China did not have enough men trained to fly or maintain the planes that were needed to defend China from Japanese air attacks.

In addition to that lend-lease materials from the U.S., China was also to receive gratuitous financial assistance from the U.S. In April 1, 1941, the both governments concluded the aid-agreement of fifty million dollars. The year before, Zhou Enlai had said in his speech: "The assistance we receive from the U.K. and the U.S. has not fed us to the full but has kept us from starving to death,"—and this turned out to be what was actually happening then. Naturally that assistance was far from relieving them from starvation, but in line with the footing of Jiang Jieshi, that effect was tremendous.

The tragic accident at that air raid cave had occurred as if in keeping pace with this period when the system of Nationalist-Communist Collaboration was crumbling away, while the Nationalists were gradually changing their attitude from compromising with the Communists to oppressing them harder in order to establish the monopoly of the Nationalist Party. Jiang, having seen through the start of the assistance from the U.S. and the U.K., was trying to liquidate the National United Front Against Japan through such cases as attacking the New Forth Army composed of the Communists, or as breaking up the Third Office of the Administration Department (whose chief was Guo Moruo), or as inaugurating a new literary policy—no literature that had deviated from Sun Wen's *Three Principles of the People* (p.34) should be published even in the name of the resistance to Japan. Then, there occurred that tragic incident at Juechangkou Tunnel at that finishing stage of "the high tide of Anti-Communism." In that sense, this case caused by the air raid by the Japanese military could be taken as a symbolical event to bring the end to the cooperative relationship between the Nationalists and the Communists, and it could be said that the assistance from the U.S. and the U.K. and the establishment of the Nationalist dictatorship had helped that accident to be treated in such an evasive manner.

● Guo Moruo's Condemnation of "the Jiang Dynasty"

To the poet Guo Moruo, who had been made chairman of the Culture-Maneuvering Committee—after the Third office of the Military Affairs Committee's Administration Department was broken up—this accident seemed to be a kind of crime committed by the authority. From its cause to its disposal of the matter, it had given a smell of decay and doubt. On the 17th in the same month, he created a poem entitled *A Pyramid of Crimes* and published it in September in *Poetry Creation* published in Guilin. The eyes of the angry poet moaning over the massive deaths of his compatriots had apparently become different from those in the days when he wrote *On Seeing the Misery* after having witnessed that disastrous conflagration on 5·3 & 5·4,; they had sharply been turned not only to the invaders but also to the Nationalist Government trying to hide it from the people. In the note he had given to it, he wrote: "The three waves of the night air raids given by the Japanese planes caused more than ten thousand deaths. But the number of the deaths the authorities concerned gave was only three hundred-odd." This does reveal what led Guo Moruo to write as follows:

Half of my heart has been sprung out—
Do you know?—
What I feel now is not sorrow, but fury.
Not water, but fire.
Both Yangzi and Jialing had turned into the flows of flames,
Those flames—
Why were they not able to burn away all those pyramids
          built of the ashlars of crimes and sins?

The foggy season has gone.
Look! The sun of the summer season is
burning above those castle walls.
Aqueous rocks are glaring, baring their eyes
          in their incandescent dreams,
They seem to be looking back on the seashore where they were created

several hundreds of millions years ago.

The foggy season has gone, but
How thick this fog is! It's as thick as if it were likely to choke us.
I have seen with my own eyes—
Several thousands of holes, several tens of thousands of holes
                    come out of the fog.
Several thousands of hands, several tens of thousands of black hands
                    come out to cover their own eyes.

Could this be a vision?
No. This is a reality I see in the mid-day in the mid-summer.
That pyramid, the pyramid built by piling one ashlar of crimes
after another, is soaring so clearly, as we see there with our own eyes.

By making use of the fog of Chongqing metaphorically, Guo Moruo released
an arrow of criticism into the fog wrapping up Jiang Jieshi's capital. He
condemned the Jiang's dynasty as a soaring pyramid of sins and crimes. Guo
Moruo had clearly pointed out the fact that: what the Chinese were facing then
was not only Japan's imperialism as an international injustice but also the vice
and injustice having been accumulated in the interior of China herself fighting
against Japan.

This conception of his was to be taken over by *The Tangdi Flowers*, a
historical drama he finished writing to be premiered at the end of that year and
Qu Yuan he wrote the following year also to be premiered in Chongqing, thus to
leave distinct traces in his literary career.

About this time, Mao Dun and some other prominent writers left for
Shanghai or Hong Kong, having disliked their work being intervened in or their
daily life being watched over, while Zou Taofen, who had been active in his
speech at Shenghuo (Life) Book Store as his base, lost that base in Chongqing
when all the branch stores of Shenghuo Book Store were ordered to close
and *Quan Min Kan Zhen* (*All People's Resistance*) it had been publishing
was ordered to stop, and he could not help leaving for Hong Kong. Guo
Moruo, together with Zhou Enlai, kept staying at the Anti-Japanese Capital of
Chongqing, but from this period on, "the National United Front Against Japan"

was to be placed literally on the verge of collapse.

Doctor Wen Shayang was among those who had been exasperated at the authorities concerned having covered up the facts. Doctor Wen, the chief of the Department of Medical Examination at Renji Hospital, had never been at the actual spot concerning this case, but in his memoir he was to record what he had experienced: Several days after that accident occurred, he attended a party held by the Red Cross Society. Everyone was talking about that accident. Tang Yi, the chief of the Police Bureau, was there, too. Then someone asked him how many people died at that accident at Juechangkou Tunnel:

"As the paper said, it would be about six hundred," said he. According to the information I had got, or judging from the number of the trucks that had carried the dead, the number ought to have been over three thousand. So I could see very well that: *that* was the very way they were always adopting: deceiving those below them; flattering those above them.

What was more, they made money by crooked means in the midst of that disaster. While carrying the dead bodies, they took the wrist watches from their wrists, took the money out of their pockets—so much so that what they had misappropriated became some basketfuls. What deplorable things to do!

This was what was recorded by Wen Shayang, concerning how eager the officials were to protect themselves and how immoral they could be.

● "The Town of Death," as was Witnessed by Kang Daichuan

Kang Daichuan at that time belonged to the Committee of Cultural Maneuvering under the leadership of Guo Moruo, and in its third group for "studying the movements of the enemy," he was working together with Hasegawa Teru (Midorikawa Eiko) and her husband Liu Ren. Kang Daichuan had also heard of the thefts having been committed at the cave by those sent from the government. Even the gold rings pulled out of the fingers of the dead alone had amounted so much as to fill a couple of bamboo baskets for storing rice, but no one could tell what had become of them. Probably the officials concerned had divided them among themselves....

Kang Daichuan, born in Taiwan, had come to Tokyo about the time when the Incident of May 15, 1932[*] occurred there, and after having studied at Kinjo

Middle School and at Kensu (Mathematics) Academy, he entered Waseda University to study at the department of commerce. While he was a student there, the Lukou-qiao Incident* occurred. Since Taiwan at that time was under Japanese rule, all the Taiwanese had to go to Meiji Shrine (where the Emperor Meiji (reign: 1867-1912) and his consort were enshrined) to pray for an unfailing victory of Japan. Kang, who had determined to join the National United Front Against Japan, sailed in secrecy to Shanghai together with five of his friends and obtained a post at Wuhan as a member of the political committee of the 60th Division in the 19thRoute Army. His ability in speaking Japanese had helped him to obtain that post, but as for where he came from, he entered his birthplace not as Taiwan but as Fujian Province on the Continent so that he might not invite any unnecessary doubt about his authenticity.

It was also his ability in Japanese language that helped him to come up to Chongqing. The 19th Route Army was more anti-communism than anti-Japan, and even when they were on the front line, they did not fight so much against the Japanese Army. Even if called by the same name of Anti-Japanese Army, some lived up to its name, while others did not. Kang as a young man was also beginning to understand what was happening to the Chinese mainland. After having retreated from Wuhan, it was decided that they should have a Japanese language school under the Third Office of the Administration Department of the Military Committee for the purpose of making propaganda against the enemy, and this led Kang Daichuan with the title of First Lieutenant to join "the Training Team for Simple Japanese Language and Speech" which had started in Guilin. The Third Office of the Administration Department was the stronghold of the Communists—represented by Zhou Enlai and Guo Moruo—supporting the National United Front Against Japan, and Kang, who had come to know of the Communists' activities there for the first time, decided to take his direction from the 19th Route Army to the Cultural Maneuvering Committee in the Third Office of the Administration Department.

What Kang Daichuan was expected to do in Chongqing was mainly to assist the activities of "the Anti-War Alliance of the Japanese Residents in China" formed and supported by Kaji Wataru and other Japanese, and to read the Japanese newspapers so that they could publish anti-war pamphlets or produce a radio program for Japanese listeners. Their broadcasting was given once a week in Japanese, Korean and Taiwanese at the broadcasting station at Shangqingsi in Shizhong (City's Central) Ward, and this led him to go there once a week, leaving Laijiaqiao in the suburbs as the seat of the Committee of Cultural Maneuvering in the morning. Hasegawa Teru was one of the announcers there. On the day that followed that terrible disaster at Shibati-kou (or was it two days after that?), Kang came to Shangqingsi, and after having finished his work there, he entered the downtown for lunch.

To his dismay, the town itself seemed to have ceased to be alive. Not a single human being was seen around. Doors to the houses and shops were open but not a single figure was seen. It was as if the time had stopped while the people had just gone somewhere on an errand. Street after street he walked along, but things were the same. He came to a wide street; not a single car was seen; an occasional bus that came into his view had no passenger in it. Kang Daichuan, who had seen such a strange scene, was to hear of the gold rings at a later date. For Kang, who became the editor of the Japanese version of the magazine *Renmin Zhongguo* (*The People's China*) after the Liberation, that tragic disaster at that air-raid tunnel was to remain as something unforgettable he had experienced in Chongqing.

As for finding out who had been responsible for that disaster, it was left simply vague. The dismissals of the Commander and the Vice Commander of Chongqing's Air Defense—Liu Zhi and Hu Bohan—were announced, but Liu Zhi, being among the five leaders of the Army along with Cheng Cheng and He Yingqin, remained as important as ever even if he was deprived of a small post among the many of his concurrent posts. Xie Yuanmo, the vice chief of the Construction Site, was notified of being relieved of his post on a charge of neglect of his duty. That turned out the heaviest punishment, and that was the end of the cleaning up after that incident.

After a while, Jiang Jieshi's wife, Song Meiling, had an opportunity for making an on-site inspection of the interior of the cave of Shibati-kou. Entering it, she confirmed the fact that the ventilation and draining were far from good and lighting facilities were insufficient. She was easily able to perceive the reason why the people staying there long were sent to breathlessness. This led Song Meiling to reprimand those officials in charge of the aerial defense, who were then following her:

"You are all fortunate, because the one who has visited and here to inspect this cave is *not* the Chairman (Jiang). If he had seen all these things, everyone of you would be subjected to trial by court-martial."

—*Before and After the Great Tragedy in Chungking* by Li Wanling

This was how "the Great Tragedy in the Air Raid Cave"—whose mouth having swallowed up not only the tears of the numberless victims but also a cross section of the Nationalist Party's Administration—was folded into the pages of the history of the Anti-Japanese War.

Jiang Jieshi had Narrowly Escaped Death

● **A Challenge Made by Admiral Shimada**

The summer of 1941—the year when "The Great Disaster in the Air-Raid Cave" occurred—was the season for the No.102 Operation for Japan's Navy Air Corps. The Army Air Corps also joining it, even a greater number of bombers had been thrown into it and they were to stake everything on this last throw of the dice. The Navy's latest model planes or the 1-type land bombers and the Army's 97-type heavy bombers II did bring the skies of Chongqing under their control with the help of the Zero fighters that had cleared the enemy's attack.

Admiral Shimada, the Commander-in-Chief of the Fleet of the China Region, who held his wish to finish the Sino-Japanese Incident while he was holding that post, now having Okochi Denshichi as the chief of staff in place of Inoue Shigeyoshi who had planned and controlled the No. 101 Operations, had been preparing for the 102 Operations, while expressing his request to the central office even while Chongqing was still in the thick fog: "In attacking the hinterland, we need more force; the more, the better." according to his recognition the Sino-Japanese War "had already come to the stage of the final five minutes" and this was the very time to give fierce attack in a positive manner. To Shimada, overlooking it from Shanghai, the center of the Navy seemed to be losing their enthusiasm for settling this war.

If we were to put an end to the Sino-Japanese Incident,* we need to give thorough blows to the enemy by adopting a strategy as positive as possible, thus to bring them to submission.

Our enemy's distress is growing day by day; their voices of lamentation are growing larger.

For this reason, capturing Chongqing will be most effective.

* This war had been called "Incident", because it had started without giving any declaration of it, as was usually done at this start of a war.

Accepting this prospect and request of Shimada, the central government moved the newly-organized No.11 Aerial Fleet (Commander: Vice-Admiral Katagiri Hidekichi; the Chief of Staff: Rear-Admiral Onishi Takijiro) under the command of the Fleet of the China Region, and sent to their bases of Hankou and Kaogan almost all the bombers the Navy had held—the 135 planes—new and powerful 1-type and 96-type for land attack. The Director Shimada himself made an on-site inspection of the front in April and in August, and saw off the airmen take off, intending to destroy Jiang Jieshi's capital. The news movie at that time—*Japan News*—showed the Director firstly in blue No.1-type uniform and then in white linen, thus incidentally visualizing the fact of the prolonged Operations No.102, but in the end, it was impossible for them to achieve their purpose of capturing Jiang Jieshi's stronghold even by their fierce attack from the sky.

Shimada Shigetaro, who decided to discontinue the Operation No. 102 and witnessed the Navy Air Force's entire pullback from China, was appointed to be the Minister of the Navy one month later thus to play a part of confirming "the Navy's determination to start a war against the U.S." He, who in Shanghai had been watching over the Navy's changes of course with concern, was now to play a part of giving a steering order as the Minister of the Navy. That must have been the last thing he had ever imagined. That enthusiasm with which he had placed a bet on "putting an end to the Sino-Japanese Incident" did nothing but releasing the Navy Air Force's theater of operations from the basin of the Yangzi to the Pacific Ocean—including the part he was to take in it.

In *Shimada Shigetaro's Memorandum*, the total achievements of the No. 102 Operations were recorded as follows. But prior to the Operations (July 27 - August 31), Chongqing had already suffered 22 bombardments, and this makes the total number of bombardments 36:

The planes used (excepting patrol planes)
Land attack planes = 2,050
Carrier-based attack planes & bombers = 201
Carrier-based fighters = 99
Land scout planes = 39
Total = 2,389
The number of attacks = 20 times (14 times at Chongqing)
The bombs consumed:
No.80 = 94   No.25 (for land) = 2,906   the others = 11,148
Total= 15,036

The number of the days spent on the operations was thirty-six, about one third of that in the No. 101 Operation, but the number of the bombs used—15,036—was nearly 60% larger than 9,819 dropped by the Navy Air Corps during the No.101 Operation. The Zero fighters' appearance having made the hours for the Japanese bombers' staying in the sky incomparably longer than in the year before, the distress the citizens of Chongqing had to suffer ought to have been greater than imagined. Those were the miserable days exposed to the cruel, persistent air raids. It was in such situations as this that a large number of people fell down to be pressed or choked to death in that air raid tunnel.

● **No.102 Operation Turned into the Springboard to the War**
against the U.S. and the U.K.
On the other hand, No.102 Operation had amply revealed its nature as a preparation for the Pacific War, which was to break out three months after its conclusion. Casting a sidelong glance at the great difficulties with which the U.S.-Japan negotiations were going on, the commanders in the battlefront had secretly come to make attacks upon Chongqing and other cities in Sichuan Province, assuming the place and the form of their aerial operations in case the war zone should be expanded all over the Asia. That was a similar case in which the unit of blitz tactics, expecting to attack Pearl Harbor, chose the skies of Kagoshima City geographically similar to Pearl Harbor as the place of their simulation exercise and repeatedly flew low over it, thus conducting exercises of shooting torpedoes, though here in Sichuan Province, it was not a mere simulation exercise but actual warfare. Unlike the citizens of Kagoshima,

what the citizens of Chongqing actually suffered was varied, including the Zero fighters' night sorties and dawn surprise attacks, which were later to be made "the basis of the first-attack strategy in performing the air raids on Philippines," as was commented in *The Strategy Adopted by the Navy in the China Region (2)* in *The Library of the War History edited by the Defense Agency of Japan*, as follows:

The Japan-U.S. relationship having gone from bad to worse, the No.102 Operations was largely shortened: with the 20th aerial attack on August 30 as the final one, all was hastily made to return to their home unit. The Operations having been the largest one so far, it was made a model case in the aerial operations in the early period of the Greater East Asia War.

Not only the Navy but also the Army had been expecting "the next war" to come up, as was mentioned in *The Operations Performed by the Army Air Force in the China Region* in *The Library of the War History:*

The purpose of performing the Operations No.102 was: strengthening the pressure upon the Jiang Administration as part of the position warfare against China, but because of the sudden changes of the situation, it began to assume even a greater motivation of giving us preparatory training for proceeding to the South. In August, or at the climax of this Plan of Operations, Japan had suffered a complete cessation of oil importation, and this led the Imperial Headquarters to aspire for the southward operations. The unit to carry out *the* operations was the one expected to perform the Malay Operations, and their having experienced the actual fighting did contribute to the Southward Operations.

In other words, the No.102 Operation had turned into a springboard to the war against the U.S. and the U.K. That was exactly what Zhou Enlai had predicted in September the year before in the address he made at the school ground in the fire-devastated area.

As for what sort of military action Japan would take, Zhou Enlai had given three probabilities: 1) The most desirable to the Japanese would be: after submitting China, they would immediately head southward. 2) The second best would be: after having isolated China's southwestern part, including Chongqing, from the rest of China, thus making it hard to offer any resistance to Japan, they would send half of their forces southward. 3) The most absurd would be: they would become too desperate to stop and think, and simply go on and on.

As it turned out, the Operation No.102 had aimed at 2), but gradually lapsed into 3). Viewing it from the military standpoint, just as the air raid upon Guernica had become the model of the Nazi Air Force's blitz tactics in Europe, the No.102 Operations were to turn out a preparation for the Japanese military to fight against the U.S. Air Force over the Pacific.

● Jiang Jieshi's Villa on Mt. Huangshan Overlooking Chongqing

Still in the third summer of the air raids on Chongqing in 1941, besides that terrible disaster in the air-raid cave, two more unforgettable incidents had to be recorded in the chronicle of Chongqing's Anti-Japanese War: One was the Japan's Army Air Corps having attacked upon Jiang Jieshi's Operational Headquarters known as "Huang Shan Official Residence"; the other was a sensation caused by the Japanese Navy Air Corps' challenging bombardment upon the U.S. Gunboat Tutuila.

Through these two incidents, the people came to realize that: Chongqing's resistance to Japan had got linked with the framework in which the Allied Powers and the Axis Powers came to fight against each other in World War II. That was exactly what Zhou Enlai had predicted: Japan, after having been thrown into confusion in China, would inevitably come to encounter America.

It was on the afternoon of August 30 that Jiang Jieshi's mountain villa on Huang-shan (Yellow Mountain), which was known as "the Eagle's Nest" to the diplomats resident in Chongqing, was suddenly descended upon by the Japanese bomber fleet directly led by Major General Endo Saburo, the chief of the third Army Air Corps. That mountain villa, a favorite place of Jiang Jieshi, built on top of Mt. Huang-shan, 600 meters above sea level, was surrounded with the dense forests that darkened the whole area even in the daytime, though not so much as Hitler's "Wolf's Nest" was. The former acting ambassador to China, Willy Peck, who had once visited here, described it as follows:

In China, the most important person who is controlling 450,000,000 people, while deciding upon the war and peace in Asia, is living in the mountain. In front of his residence, we can see a gentle slope that stretches as far as several miles downward, thus turning that residence into a virtual throne. The quietude there is such that we are likely to forget the fact that China is now at war. People in general remain almost ignorant of the fact that this quiet mountainous region has been turned into the base of such an important matter as the command of the resistance to Japan.

—*Jiang Jieshi* by Dong Xianguang

Keeping himself away from the air raids and "*huolu* (fireplace-like heat)" inside the walls that surrounded the former castle area, Jiang was usually staying here. This official residence of Jiang was a three-storied building named Yunxiu-Lou (Cloud Summit Lookout), and his room was at the right-hand corner on the third floor, which commanded the whole of Shizong (City's Central) Ward of Chongqing beyond the Yangzi flowing below his eyes. A little below from there, one could see "Song Ting (Pine Office)" where Lady Jiang, Song Meiling, resided, and "Yunfeng-lou (Cloud Summit Belvedere)" as a summer house for Song Qingling, the wife of the late Sun Wen, though she had left Chongqing by that time. Among the forests and valley, there was "Liangquing-Lou (Lotus-Blue Belvedere)," too. That had once accommodated General George Marshall as the U.S. President's special envoy, who, in December, 1945, was sent to Chongqing as the mediator of "the Negotiation" held between the Nationalist Jiang Jieshi and the Communist Mao Zedong.

After the Liberation, they were turned into ordinary private houses, or a sanatorium for the aged executives, as Song Meiling's "Song Ting" was. At present, they are preserved as the memorial halls for Jiang Jieshi and his wife, and anyone can visit them. But in those days, this area of Mt. Huangshan used to be an off-limits area, and Jiang Jieshi's attending his duties here was a sort of information forbidden to the ordinary citizens. In between Yunxiu-Lou and Song Ting, there was their private air-raid cave brought into being so that they could come and go to each other.

● **Major General Endo Made a Surprise Attack**
on Jiang Jieshi's Mountain Villa

That day—on August 30—Jiang Jieshi had called a military conference at Yunxiu-lou as his official residence on Mt. Huangshan. From each theater of war, generals and staff officers were to come to meet there. That information happened to reach Major General Endo at Hankou.

Endo, who had been appointed chief of the Third Air Division in August the year before, had already had doubts about the effect of making air raids on Chongqing. In one of the passages of his memoir, *The Sino-Japanese War that Lasted Fifteen Years & I,* he wrote:

> I myself, joining the crew of a heavy bomber, had flown to Chongqing to perform the aerial raid several times on end. Seen from high above, the city of Chongqing situated on the peninsula between the two rivers has already been badly destroyed, but the areas beyond the rivers, especially the one on the right-hand side is being developed on and on, far and wide, and it was simply impossible for us to tell how we can make our bombings fatal to them.

Just as Endo observed, the central area of the city of Chongqing had already gone underground, while the industrial area and the living quarters along the Yangzi and the Jialing were growing larger and larger every day. That was how that original city of Chongqing with the ancient fortress at its center—which used to be 9.3 kilometers square until 1930's—had been growing into the largest city in China—8,2000 kilometers squares with a population of 31,300,000. The rapidity of the city's growth had been much greater than the increase of Japanese bombers.

Endo—though he was among the leaders of the strategic bombing corps—had been skeptical about the plan to capture Chongqing only by aerial capability, totally unlike Inoue Shigeyoshi, Onishi Takijiro, and Yamaguchi Tamon. But *now* Endo happened to receive a piece of information concerning the whereabouts of Jiang Jieshi: "on August 30, at Huangshan-Shanzhuang (his mountain villa) there would be a military conference" along with the word: "a successful attack upon it can be fatal to *him*."

Already had Endo obtained the information concerning the location of that mountain villa and even the color of the roof of that building through his personal talk with the Italian ambassador to China who was on his way home from Chongqing. To Endo this seemed to be a rare opportunity. Immediately the plan was made for the bombardment upon that mountain villa. The squadron to perform it was decided upon the 60th squadron of the Army Air Force (Colonel Ogawa Shōjiro as its chief) that had always been performing the advancing operations into the Hinterland from the begining.

According to *The Army Air Force's Aerial Strategy in the China Region* in *A Series of the War Histories Edited by Japan's Self-Defense Agency*, the attack performed that day was recorded as follows:

> Endo, the chief of the flying corps, urged Ogawa, the chief of the squadron, to go into action, and he himself boarding the plane for the squadron leader, Beppu, took off at Wuchang at 11:00. Till they came to Shayangzhen, they flew 200 meters below clouds, but for the rest of their flight, they were blessed with fine weather. At 15:00, at the altitude of 5,500m, they bombed upon the residence of the leading figure of China on the eastern shore of the Yangzi. Though enclosed by anti-aircraft shells, we all suffered no damage and all returned safe.

Probably trying to hide their failure, they mentioned their aim as "the residence of a leading figure of China on the eastern shore of the Yangzi."

In his *Memoir*, Endo Saburo wrote as follows:

> We advanced so that we might blast his official residence while Jiang Jieshi was staying there. There was no interceptor, but the anti-aircraft shells being fierce and correct, the blasts of near hits often sent us such bomb blasts as to have our bottoms lifted out of our seats. It seemed totally impossible to perform precise bombings at low altitude, while horizontal bombings from high altitude would have surely made us waste our bombs.

This failure in his blitz tactics that day also helped him to strengthen his conviction: "keeping our bombardment upon Chongqing would be of no use."

● One of the Bombs Hit the Mark and Endangered Jiang Jieshi

It was certainly nothing but a wishful thinking to let a bomb released at the altitude of 5,500m hit upon a single house in the mountain. Two days later, the Japanese at Hankou were to hear Jiang Jieshi making a speech on the radio, celebrating the memorial week for Sun Wen[*], thus to find that Jiang had remained safe and sound, and that their bombing upon his residence had been unsuccessful. As it was, even though Endo himself could not find out the fact, one of the bombs they had dropped actually hit his residence, Yunxiu-lou, and even if Jiang Jieshi himself narrowly escaped death, the hall where the military council was being held was not free from bloodshed. In fact, Jiang had simply been fortunate.

In both of *Sichuan Province & the Resistance to Japan* published in Taiwan and *A Record of Chongqing's Resistance to Japan* as a material of the Chinese side, this occurrence was mentioned.

About the hour when Ogawa's squadron of twenty-seven planes invaded into the sky above the Official Residence on Mt. Huangshan, they were in the midst of a conference presided over by the Chairman Jiang. Partly because the squadron's approach was made from the extreme height of the sky, and partly because the anti-aircraft airtillerymen were too late to judge that the enemy's aim was not in the urban area but the mountain villa itself, they had allowed the enemy planes to enter the course for dropping bombs. Before the antiaircraft fire was released, the bombs had been dropped in a mode of "one salvo in one passing," and while the bombs were falling around the Official Residence, one of them happened to hit a part of that aimed building. Those who had been in conference, without hearing any buzzing of the planes, were suddenly thrown into the urgent warning voices followed by the violent explosion. If the hit had shifted a little, Jiang Jieshi and many other generals would have lost their lives.

It was near the entrance to the air-raid cave at the west edge of the Residence that the bomb exploded. The two guardsmen on duty were killed on the spot and four were seriously injured, with fresh blood spreading all over the place. Stepping upon that pool of blood, those who had been in conference took refuge in the air-raid cave in case they might suffer the second attack, but no more attack occurred, thus the master of "the Eagle's Nest" narrowly escaped death. In his radio speech in the memorial week for Sun Wen[*], he expressed his thoughts and feelings then:

In the room, I felt strong vibrations and found we were being attacked. That night, we had rain. I remained sleepless almost all night. This experience did help me to realize what sort of pain my fellow countrymen in Chongqing have been suffering. The pain they are suffering is not a temporary one. Theirs has been lasting for as long as four years!

On the day of that attack, Endo Saburo in the sky and Jiang Jieshi on the earth had 5,500m between them, and this distance was possibly the shortest distance the Japanese military was able to bring themselves closest to "The Chongqing Administration." This also turned out to be the final opportunity for the Japanese military to have had any opportunity to endanger Jiang Jieshi himself. Never again did they have any such opportunity as this. As Japan's theater of war was expanded, including even the Pacific Ocean, while the Jiang Jieshi's Chorqging Administration was enhancing its reputation among the Allied Nations, both Chongqing and Jiang Jieshi were growing further and further from the consciousness of the Japanese military. The next opportunity in which the Japanese officers and men in China were to receive a strong impression of what Jiang Jieshi was through his broadcasting—after Japan had received her unconditional surrender—to all over China from Chongqing or from that Broadcasting Station at Shangqingsi: "Do not expose Japan's past misdeeds, but requite a wrong with a kindness."

Endo Saburo, after having returned to Hankou, made up his mind to make a direct appeal to Captain Hattori Takushiro, the chief of the Strategy Section of the General Staff Office in the military center. It was on September 3 when he finished writing *An Opinion concerning the Advance into the Hinterland.*

The Japan - U.S. Relations were Growing Worse

● **Major General Endo Saburo Presents his Opinion: "The Bombardment upon Chongqing will be of No Use"**
Endo—who had found his trial to bomb upon Jiang Jieshi's mountain villa a total failure and another sortie he joined the following day also far from successful—decided that: that was the time for him to express his opinion of "the uselessness of the bombardment upon Chongqing."

Taking part in No. 102 Operation, I have been engaged in advancing to the hinterland of China, and looking back upon what we have achieved so far from the point of disposing of the China Incident, I have come to recognize that we now need to give some reappraisal upon this kind of operations; even if we are still on our way to its completion, I should like to give my own opinion before it is too late, while offering a report on the potentiality of this air division of ours.

Endo, who started to give his opinion in this way, was to raise an out-and-out doubt about "the effect of the strategic and political bombings" advocated by the aviation supremacists.

The effect of the aerial bombings we have performed so far has been rather overestimated by the reporters. It is greatly mistaken, therefore, to think that Chongqing has already been turned into ruins. According to my humble observation, there are even some signs that Chongqing is rather expanding over the surrounding areas.

Endo, then, while referring to the national character of the Chinese people and their thoroughness in the way of taking measures against the air raids, went on saying: "Therefore, it is definitely impossible for us to submit them by dint of bombardment only," and clinched that argument by giving an example, as follows:

Upon London—that civilized metropolice holding more than one tenth of the population of the United Kingdom, seemingly representing the power of the British Empire—German Air Force has been performing air raids for more than a year, sending several thousand bombers across the narrow strip of water. Still it remains unable to submit the U.K.. This fact can be said to have amply proved the dubious effect of performing the air raids.

The German bombers' indiscriminate bombings upon London had started in September, 1940 or the year after Endo Saburo arrived at Hankou as the chief of the Third Flying Corps. Endo, paying attention to the progress of that battle overseas, must have been observing it, comparing it with what was happening to Chongqing. The German air-raids upon London had come to an end in mid-May, 1941, without achieving any decisive results, and much of the German

Air Force had already been away from England in order to join the war against the Soviet Union—about the time when Japan was preparing for No.102 Operations against Chongqing. Based upon this fact and "according to my (his) observations," Endo had created his own opinion, as follows:

The military installations in Sichuan Province are all small in scale and sporadically placed. So blasting this or that of them, as we have done so, does not seem effective enough to endanger the fate of Jiang's Administration. Then, keeping performing this kind of Operations in such a desultory manner as we have done so far is profoundly disturbing to me, considering the shortage of our aerial power and especially the shortage of the fuel. For these reasons, I do wish our superior officers would reexamine these matters I have sincerely mentioned above.

This was how he concluded his proposal. In later years, he was to record in his autobiography—*The Sino-Japanese Fifteen Years War and I*—as follows: "Fortunately, the opinion I had offered was accepted, and I was delivered from the task to perform the air raid upon Chongqing." Certainly, on September 7— three days after he offered his opinion, the expeditionary force in the China Region, according to the order from the Central Headquarters, conveyed an order to the flying corps that the operations of attacking the hinterland should be stopped. This does fit in with Endo's offering of his opinion to the Central Headquarters. But what had actually led the Central Headquarters to decide to give up that Operation should be taken as a part of preparation for the war against the U.S. and the U.K.. The cabinet meeting held in the Imperial presence on September 6 had decided upon "the Ministry's Official Guidelines for Performing the Imperial Policy of the State," and Japan—"under the resolution of *not* minding starting a war against the U.S. and the U.K. in order to fulfill our duty to perform our motto of Existence on Our Own while Guarding Ourselves,"—had been making a dash for the start of the war by the end of that year.

Endo Saburo, the chief of an air division, had set forth his opinion to the General Staff Office—by passing his immediate upper headquarters or the Third Flying Corps and the Expeditionary Force in China—but as it happened, *the* opportunity had already been lost, and the time had been growing ripe to open fire in a different form. Endo himself, in November that year, was ordered to move from Hankou to Hanoi, thus to begin his breathlessly busy career in the skies of Asia, taking part in various battles from the Landing Operations at the Malay Peninsula to the Capture of Singapore, and then to the Operations of Dashing Forward to Balembang on Sumatra Island.

● The *Tutuila* Incident

During the Operation No. 102 in the summer of 1941—along with their assault upon Jiang Jieshi's Villa upon Mt. Huangshan—they brought about another incident of having dropped bombs upon the U.S. gunboat, Tutuila, with the Stars and Stripes raised high above it. This might be regarded as a symbolical action of the final desperate effort made by Japan's Navy Air Force. This was also to turn into another main cause to bring the U.S.—which had remained an enemy behind the scene of the Sino-Japanese War, since "Panay Incident" which occurred while Japan was trying to capture Nanjing—on to the central stage of the struggle. This could be said a natural consequence brought about by the inconsistent rule established by the Japanese Fleet of the China Region, and there could be seen a secret intention on the U.S. side to make use of that inconsistent setting up of the basic rule, and still, these cases of accidental bombings upon the U.S. gunboats could be taken as blunders to disgrace the Japanese Navy Air Corps' morale and morality.

In that sense, "the way to Pearl Harbor" could be said to have amply been smoothed during the period between the Panay Incident (Dec.12, 1937) and the Tutuila Incident (July 30, 1941). Thus the Japanese Navy in China not only allowed themselves to be dragged by the Japanese Army but also brought about a cause of the war by themselves.

The plane which made a near hit on the U.S. gunboat Tutuila this time was one of the twenty-six middle-sized attack planes that belonged to Kanoya Air Corps of the 21st Air Squadron which belonged to the 11th Aerial Fleet. On the morning of July 30, while being engaged in the air raid upon the urban area of Chongqing, one of their bombs dropped at a point eight yards away from the stern of the Gunboat Tutuila at anchor near the southern shore.

"All present and correct. One ship-borne motorboat got badly broken. One motor-sampan got out of mooring gear and got lost."—This was how the damage was reported immediately after the accident happened by Ambassador

Gauss to the Secretary of State Hull. The U.S. Ambassador then had requested that this should be sent to Ambassador Grew in Tokyo.

This was the third time that Tutuila had received a near hit. On May 28, the year before, one bomb had dropped 400 yards away: On October 25 in the same year, one was observed to drop into the river water 300 yards north of the gunboat. For the third time, fell as near as 8 yards from the stern of Tutuila. Ambassador Grew in Tokyo who received the news by way of Washington wrote in his diary *Ten Years' in Japan:* "Japan has done what seems to me the most foolish of all."

By the grace of heaven the bomb missed the *Tutuila* by about eight yards, although the ship was damaged and another bomb again came dangerously near our Embassy. Fatalities were escaped only by a miracle, It seems to me utterly inconceivable that the incident was accidental: three American officials saw the thing from a hill immediately overlooking the ship; the weather was ideal; and the bomber on approaching the city at an altitude of about 15,000 feet, dropped out of formation and changed its course to a line directly over the *Tutuila* and the Embassy. It was the unanimous opinion of the American officials that the bombing was a deliberate attack on the Embassy area and the *Tutuila,* which missed its targets only by the fraction of a second.

● **The Japanese Ambassador Nomura in the U.S. had a Talk with Welles, an Undersecretary of State**

At Washington, Sumner Welles, an Undersecretary of State (a Deputy Secretary of State) was facing Nomura Kichisaburo, an ambassador to the United States. Ambassador Nomura, a member of the Naval Academy's 26th graduating class, and Admiral as a reserve officer, had been in Washington since February that year, engaging in negotiations with the U.S.. Nomura had been amazed that Sumner Wells, who had been acting in place of Cordell Hull while he was away, had taken the state of things very seriously. This led Nomura say to him, trying to make things appear something not to be taken so seriously, as he wrote in his memoir *As an Ambassador in the United States:* "These things are quite likely to happen in any battlefield. Unless we stopped bombing upon Chongqing, or unless your Embassy and gunboat were moved somewhere else, it would be impossible to prevent these accidents from happening."

Nomura Kichisaburo had long been concerned with China, and it dated back as far as the first Shanghai Incident (1931).*

This admiral-ambassador's multiple career had included in it: "In February, 1932, he was made the Commander-in-Chief of the Third Fleet by the Imperial appointment." This meant that: he had joined "the Shanghai Incident"* that followed "the Manzhou Incident,"* since the Third Fleet was hastely organized at the outbreak of "the Shanghai Incident." The Third Fleet was later reorganized into the Fleet of the China Region, but the flagship remained "Izumo," and the then chief of staff was Shimada Shigetaro, who, as the director of No. 102 Operations, was now to be the very person responsible for that incident of the gunboat Tutuila.

The then Vice Admiral Nomura in the room for the Commander-in-Chief in the period of Shanghai Incident* had once received the report that: On February 5, 1932, a flying corps of the airplane carrier Hosho had performed the first aerial battle against the three Chinese fighter planes in the skies of Shanghai Zhenru—the first of this kind in the history of Japan's Navy Air Force. Not long after that—on February 22—the fighter planes and attack planes that belonged to the aircraft-carrier Kaga fought against Chinese fighter planes, Boeing 218, in the skies of Suzhou till they brought the enemy planes down. The Chinese planes had borne the mark of "the sun in the blue sky" (the flag of the China's Nationalist Party), but the pilot was a private U.S. citizen named Robert M. Short, and he was to be remembered as the first American brought to death by the war between China and Japan. In April, Nomura himself was wounded and lost his right eye. Later (after Nomura had left that post) in August, 1937, also in Shanghai, a sailor Fredy J. Fargot on board the flagship Augusta of the U.S. Fleet of the Asia Region was killed by the accidental bombing by a Chinese military plane and he was to be "the first U.S. soldier who died in his uniform"; then in December in the same year, "the Incident of the Panee" occurred at Nanjing to be followed by the frequent water columns caused around Tutuila. Nomura Kichisaburo and Sumner Welles were facing each other at Washington, with all these things—personal destinies and international discords—behind themselves.

Welles, Undersecretary of State, according to the directions given by President Roosevelt, requested Ambassador Nomura to visit him at 11:45 on

July 30. The Memorandum of Conversation left by Welles, the Acting Secretary of State, goes as follows (FOREIGN RELATIONS, 1941, VOLUME V):

The Japanese Ambassador called to see me this morning at my request. I told the ambassador that I had just received a message from the American Embassy in Chungking and that by direction of the President, I was giving him a copy of message for his information.

The Ambassador read the message aloud.

Then he had concluded I said to the Ambassador that by direction of the President I desired to inquire through him of the Japanese Government whether any responsible officials of the Japanese Government had authorized the bombing which had so nearly destroyed American lives and which was so clearly, from the accounts rendered by American observers, deliberately undertaken. I said that I felt I must make this inquiry in view of the official assurances given this Government by the Government of Japan after the Panay incident that every necessary order would be issued by the Japanese Government to prevent any recurrence of such an attack.

I stated further that I desired to inquire of the Japanese Government what measures, concrete and detailed, the Japanese Government proposed to take in order to prevent a further incident of this character.

● **The Japanese Government's Declaration to Cease Bombing upon Chongqing was not Accepted as Trustworthy by the U. S.**

Wells' attitude toward this matter was unyielding, and he never seemed to treat it so lightly as Nomura had expected. This led Ambassador Nomura to give the home government a request for some instructions on what he should do. On the following day, Sumner Wells, the Under Secretary of State, again met and talked with the Japanese Ambassador at the State Department. Ambassador Nomura, as soon as he entered the room, took a piece of paper out of his pocket and began to read the statement aloud, as was recorded in Wells' memorandum of their conversation:

I have received an order from the Japanese Government that: I should deliver to the U.S. President a profound regret concerning the fact that the U.S. Gunboat Tutuila was bombed at Chungking. As for the fact that this case was none other than a genuine accident, the Japanese Government has guaranteed it. For the purpose of nullifying any more such unforeseen incident, the Japanese Government has decided to cease all the operations of bombardment upon the urban area of Chungking. As for the damages we have given to the U.S. assets, the Japanese Government proposes here to pay the indemnities as soon as the necessary investigation is made.

The statement given by Nomura, as was in the case of the gun boat Panay, had fully recognized that the Japanese side was at fault. What was more, Japan had let it include even taking such a step as to "cease all the operations of bombardment upon the urban areas of Chungking." If Japan had intended to put all these things into practice, it could have been her last trump card to break the deadlock in her relationship with America. The U.S. Government's opposition to Japan's indiscriminate bombings upon various cities in China had long been one of the main reasons for the U. S. to criticize Japan. Since October, 1931, when the then Secretary of State, Stimson, blamed Japan for the bombardment of Jinzhou performed in October, 1931, under the leadership of Lieutenant Colonel Ishiwara Kanji, it had remained the basis of the general voices that denounced "Japan that neglects the law of nations." And now, Japan did officially express its intention to discontinue it for the first time. So this decision of Japan to stop bombings upon Chongqing ought to have been a good opportunity to bring about a turning point for both of the Sino-Japanese and the U.S.-Japanese relationships that had gone to their worst level.

But the U.S. Government, though having accepted Japan's official apology, would not believe in its declaration to stop bombardment upon Chongqing, partly because they had received from Ambassador Grew in Tokyo an extremely skeptical estimation of it. They had simply regarded it as "a makeshift" or "Stopgap measures" often adopted by the Japanese side. And in fact, things were to move on, as had been predicted by the U.S. Government.

The day before Nomura gave Japan's proposal at Washington (On July 31 in Japan), at 8 p.m. Admiral Shimada Shigetaro, the Commander of the Fleet of the China Region, received on board Izumo at Shanghai, a top secret telegram from the Chief of the Bureau of Military Affairs in the Navy Ministry:

Because of a diplomatic talk on the case of the attack on Tutuila .... the air raid on Chongqing is to be suspended for a while, as is to be informed to the Ambassador in the U.S. So please keep this in mind.

Japan's declaration to cease bombing upon Chongqing was none other than a gesture neaded "for the diplomatic talk." And since that declaration to cease air-raiding was nothing but a gesture needed for "diplomatic negotiation," it was conveyed to the commander-in-chief in the China Region not as an order to stop the bombardment but as something just "to keep in mind." What was more, those engaged in the operations had not admitted their having sent any near hit upon Tutuila. In his memorandum, Admiral Shimada had recorded the fact that: four bombs had gone into the River and on the other side of the River, but wrote: "According to our detailed examination on the photos of the impact area, there was not any such close-falling bomb around Tutuila. At least, 350m away from Tutuila," thus denying the fact given by the U.S..

To those in the China Region, therefore, such a telegram as was sent by the Navy Ministry could not exert any influence upon their Operation. Ambassador Nomura, now a reserve Admiral in Washington, had once been presiding over the Warship Izumo, raising his flag as commander-in-chief, but now, Admiral Shimada, the then chief of staff, had become the master of Izumo, reducing Nomura only to someone playing the part of a poor clown.

● **The Declaration of Cease-fire was Disregarded by the Field Headquarters**
The declaration of ceasefire was arrogantly disregarded by the Field Headquarters. The declaration of cease-fire had been observed only for a week. Since August 8 or a week later, the longest series of bombardments in No. 102 Operation was to be resumed. To the U.S.' side, therefore, that simply appeared to have been a preparatory period for the largest attack the Japanese side would soon make rather than their temporary halt. Following was the official telegram sent on August 11 by Ambassador Gauss to his home government:

Since the 4th, Chungking has been exposed to the air raids unexpectedly fierce and long. Both urban area and suburbs are repeatedly being bombed. But our Embassy and the city area that directly faces our gunboat remain unbombed.

This bombardment performed despite that declaration of cease-fire they had made was soon to develop into what Jiang Jieshi called "the most atrocious bombardment" or "the almost ceaseless bombardment that lasted for seven days and nights." Ambassador Grew in Tokyo wrote in his *Diary* on July 31, 1941: "Ambassador Nomura told Sumner Wells confidentially that in order to avoid such incidents in the future, the Japanese would cease from attacking Chungking from the air, and the incident was called closed," adding a curt note in a margin: "Further attacks on Chungking were nevertheless made within a few days."

Thus the relations between the U.S. and Japan had totally lost the force to restore their trust. And it was apparent that not only "the Army's perversity in having their own way" but also "the Navy's strategic failure in this Operation" had greatly helped to form that cause. Even the high officials in the General Staff of the Naval Department in Tokyo—who had been advocating the renunciation of war against the U.S., while rebuking the Army for their despotism—had not shown any sign of restraint as far as China and air-raiding upon the Chinese were concerned, and never felt ashamed of engaging in frightening the people from the sky in their lowly trial to deprive them of everything. It was such accumulation of their arrogance and miscalculation that formed the main cause to open up the way to the Navy's "agreement to start a war" by crashing their principle of "no fighting against the U.S.". What the Navy called "the War on the River" also turned into a primary factor to lead Japan to the War on the Pacific.

While being engaged in the incessant air raids with the No. 102 Operation in between, Japan was being involved into even a greater swirl of war. On June 22, 1941, Germany and the Soviet Union commenced hostilities. As the German Army's irresistible advance was being informed of, there came into being a couple of opinions as to which of the two directions the Japanese military should take—to the south or to the north. The former was supported by those who wished to establish Japan's self-sufficient preparedness; the latter thought it wiser to seize an opportunity of their having been released from the heavy pressure of the Soviet Union's Far East Area and "to go north and remove what has always been annoying us."

The Army started early in June "the Guangdong Army's* specific exercise" or the operations against the Soviet Union—by mobilizing 500,000 soldiers and a large amount of munitions to Manchuria and Korea. On the other hand, on July 28—two days before the *Tutuila* Incident occurred—the 25ᵗʰ Army guarded by the war-ships of the Second Fleet of the China Region landed at Natolan in French Indo-China and on 30 they advanced into Saigon. This was Japan's entry into southern French Indochina after having entered northern French Indochina.

The U.S. Government stood against Japan by taking retaliatory measures of freezing the Japanese assets in the U.S. and a total prohibition of the oil export to Japan, thus the U.S.-Japan relationship turned the final corner to lead to the catastrophe.

For the people of Chongqing then, it was the third year of the air raids— to be remembered by that terrible disaster in the air-raid tunnel, the Tutuila incident and the bombardment upon the Official Residence on Mt. Huangshan— and toward the end of that year, when they were dozing under the cover of merciful fog, they were to hear of the war having broken out between the U.S. and Japan—on December 8, 1941.

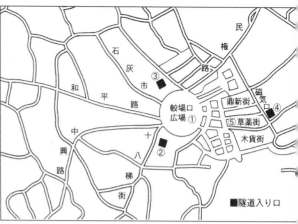

The Citizens of Chongqing entering the
Great Tunnel（see P.376）

■ the entrance to the cave（see P.376）
① Juechang-kou square
② Shibati Entrance
③ Shihuifu Entrance
④ Ciqikou Entrance
⑤ Caoyaojie Street

The dead being laid after having been carried out of the cave（in
June, 1941）（see P.390）

Many had fallen to death after struggli
out of the cave（see P.392）

CHAPTER V

ZHOU ENLAI AND HIS COMRADES UNDER THE AIR RAIDS

"Jiang Jieshi's Capital"

● **The Struggles between the Nationalists and the Communists under the Air Raids**

The spirit of the indefatigable resistance performed by those living in the wartime capital of Chongqing throughout the years of the anti-Japanese War which lasted for as long as eight years is recognized as the quintessence of the Chinese spirit not only by the Communist Party but also by the Nationalist Government which was to fly to Taiwan to seek safety there.

For the Communists at that time, their real capital was none other than Yan-an, and Chongqing as "the white area" was nothing but "Jiang Jieshi's capital." On the other hand, the Nationalist Government had to see the fame of "their Capital of Free China" began to crumble at the moment their victory of resistance to Japan was achieved and it turned into a place name which could not be called to mind without feeling the bitterness they had to taste "on their way to Taiwan." Both sides of them, therefore, have their own distorted feelings. But as for the days of "the Battle of Chongqing" when they both must helplessly endure the fierce attacks from the sky, they have never been tired of offering their maximum admirations to each other.

The following is what Liu Jingkun wrote in the first passage of *Chongqing and the Eight-Year Resistance*, which was placed at the beginning of *A Chronicle of Chongqing's Resistance*, edited by the Chinese People's Political Consultative Conference.

The eight years of our Resistance War Against Japan was the most tumultuous period in the history of the Chinese people's development. And Chongqing at this special period was to leave the most heroic and glorious records in our history. On hearing the name of Chongqing, the people never fail to recall their resistance to Japan; on hearing "the eight-year-resistance," they naturally recall those hardships they had to suffer. Most men and women over fifty this year (1985 when this chronicle was published) have something to do with Chongqing at that time. The victory of that eight-year war against Japan has been the glory of us Chinese people and the honor of those who were living in Chongqing in those years.

Sichuan Province & *the Resistance War against Japan*, compiled by the Nationalist Government, also contains the following paragraph in Chapter 6: *The Chongqing Spirit Displayed during the Bombardments by the Japanese Bombers:*

Since the Nationalist Government of China was moved to Chongqing, this city had been made the Wartime Capital or the Control Tower for Resistance to Japan. The Japan's militarists, trying to destroy this base of resistance to Japan, chose Chongqing as the target for their indiscriminate bombings, intending to blow up our nerve center. But the citizens of Chongqing under the fierce bombardments that lasted for several years fought it out indefatigably, getting over the dead bodies of those who had been running before them, thus amply revealing their spirit of all-out resistance. Seeing this, none of the respectable in the world failed to admire "their Chongqing spirit." This very spirit was to turn out to be a symbol of the resistant spirit of the whole of the Chinese people. What had made that resistance finally achieve that victory was the outcome of their having retained this Chongqing spirit.

After everything was turned into a historical event, "the Chongqing spirit" was to be shared by both Nationalists and Communists, but while Chongqing still remained in the melting pot of that indiscriminate bombing, they had not yet attained at this noble common ground to share. Under the sky where the Japanese planes were domineering, another confrontation that could be compared to another exchange of bombings—the Nationalist Party's "strategic offensive" to scale up their leadership and the Chinese Communists' underground activities in their effort to enlarge "the people's air-raid cave"— was being unfolded incessantly as if they were ruthlessly competing with each other. Jiang Jieshi, who was keeping one of his eyes busy in leading the resistance to Japan, never let his other eye off from the Communists and their sympathizers so that he might annihilate them if only he had any opportunity to do so.

While the Sino-Japanese War was largely changing its framework into World War Ⅱ, Chongqing began to assume not only the nature of anti-fascism but also the nature as the first front of international Anti-Communism.

In the depth of that mountain castle as the wartime capital, Zhou Enlai and his comrades sent from Yan-an were offering themselves in their trial to realize their "Chongqing Spirit" coolly and calmly, hiding their passion that had defied even the danger of their lives, thus enduring both the Japan's bombings from high above which could never be resisted physically and another power and oppression which were being intensified every day by the leader of "Free China." They had also made "keeping resistance to the end" their slogan, but the method they adopted was different from what was adopted by Jiang Jieshi. That was, theirs was to build a sort of "air-raid caves for offering resistance" all over the country—instead of accepting the Army "equipped in the U.S. way" and the Air Bases for B29 bombers, as Jian Jieshi did.

If Jiang Jieshi had felt the existence of his enemy before him, Zhou Enlai had to recognize one enemy in the sky and the other before his eyes—both trying to crush him down. The Nationalist Party was trying to find a way out of the difficulty in the international solidarity of "Anti-Axis powers—as pro-UK & US," while the Communist Party had it in mind "to unify the national consciousness which had been in a state of anarchy, while clearing away the ground for breeding injustice and inequality, so that they might perform a long-protracted war of resistance that would lead to liberation."

Both Jiang Jieshi and Zhou Enlai had come from the same barracks of Sun Wen, the Father of the Xinhai Revolution (1911: when the final Dynasty of China was brought to an end), but these soldierly statesmen in that period— from 1938 when they moved to Chongqing to 1946 when the capital was transferred to Nanjing—were to bring about a variety of fabrics of human relationships while struggling or compromising again and again, retaining their own Chongqing spirit in that foggy mountain-castle of Chongqing.

The bombardments, therefore, had set fire in the melting furnaces of national revolution that had been brought together in Chongqing, and the more heated they were, the more purified and strengthened their spirit of resistance became—whichever camp they might belong to. It could be said, therefore,: that was "the greatest outcome" brought about by the strategic bombings performed by the Japanese Navy Air Force, however unexpected it might have sounded to them.

● **Chongqing was Turned into an Extremely-Overpopulated City**

When Chongqing, an ordinary city of Sichuan Province in the southwestern part of China, was made to assume the function as the State Capital, the first change that occurred was a population explosion. Partly because all the cities facing the Sea or the Rivers had been occupied by the Japanese military, ceaseless flows of large numbers of people entered the Sichuan Province by way of the Yangzi or by land. That being "the hinterland" far from approachable by the Japanese ground force, it was to provide the Chinese with a base of their protest or what they called "the Great Rear." As mentioned before, the population that flowed in then was about ten million, and seven million of them settled in Sichuan Province, and more than one million settled in and around Chongqing. The flatland being scarce, that mountain castle city naturally became overpopulated.

According to the population statistics announced in March, 1936, by the Public Safety Bureau in Chongqing City, the number of households was 74,398 with 339,204 people in them. Even though being the largest city in the southwestern part of China, Chongqing, before the Anti-Japanese War broke out, was a mere provincial city. Around August in 1938 when Wuhan's withdrawal started, Chongqing and its neighborhood suddenly became busy and restless. On August 4, all the Nationalist Government's administrative organizations in Wuhan, which had been made Capital (1926-7), finished moving to Chongqing. In October in the same year, the Three Towns of Wuhan—Wuchang, Hankou and Hanyang—were occupied by the Japanese Army.

The Office of Balujun (the Eighth Route Army), led by Zhou Enlai, was also established at No.70 at Jifang-jie Street within the castle area, while Zhou's Diplomatic Office started at No.50 at Zengjia-an in Shizhong (City's Central) Ward. When *Xin Hua Ri Bao* (New China Daily News) began to be published, presided over by Pan Zinian, with Hua Gang as chief editor of the first generation (Zhang Hanfu as the second generation), with Zhou Enlai as virtual chief editor, other papers followed it: the Nationalist Party's Army Bulletin *Sao Dang Bao* (Mopping-up Report), the Government-owned newspaper *Zhong Yang Ri Bao* (Central Daily News), *Da Gong Bao* (Major Official Report) which had fled from Shanghai, and it was not long before they had ten morning papers and three evening papers in Chongqing.

Keeping pace with them, 245 business corporations of steel, machinery, electric machinery, cotton spinning, food products and so on had also come up from Shanghai, Hankou, Nanjing, Hangzhou and so on within the same year (1938). Thus the Japanese Armed Forces' lightning-like attacks performed to expand their territory were to be reflected exactly as Chongqing's unusual congestion.

In April, 1939, when Han Suyin arrived at the new capital of Chongqing together with a multitude of refugees, Chongqing's population had already reached 700,000. Considering that most of them were living in Shizhong Ward (City's Central Ward; 9.3km square), it was simply surprising how overpopulated it was. It was those people who were to encounter "the 5.3 & 5.4 air raids." In 1943, the population had grown even larger with 885,480 people in 155,549 families. This proves that even those fierce series of aerial attacks repeated during the three successive years, which caused 11,889 deaths, and several thousand deaths from suffocation in "the tragic accident in the air raid cave," remained incapable of preventing the expansion of the central foothold of the great hinterland. *LIFE* once wrote in the news item concerning Japan's Operation No. 101: In Chungking where graveyards are being increasing, the dead outnumber the living. As it was, the living were apparently larger in number, and they kept growing larger and larger.

Japan's "political and strategic bombings" remained totally useless in destroying the base of the Chinese resistance to Japan; Chongqing in time of war voraciously absorbed large populations, whose pressure and heated atmosphere did expand the city area from old times—Shizhong Ward (City's Central ward: the former castle area)—toward its hinterland as far as the depths on the other shores of the Yangzi and the Jialing, thus bringing Shaci Ward, Beibei and Daidukou into being,—to bring about a new urban area of Chongqing. That was exactly like what was reported by Endo Saburo, the chief of the Army Air Force's 3rd Air Division (mentioned in the previous chapter): "…. It is greatly mistaken to think that Chongqing has already been turned into ruins. According to my observation, there are some signs that Chongqing has been rather developing itself into its surrounding areas." The three concentric circles that show what present Chongqing is—① Shizhong Ward on the peninsula (population: 500,000), including those of Jiang-bei (North of the Jialing) and Nan-an (South of the Yangzi), ② Da-Chongqing or Great Chongqing (whose area is 73km squares and whose population is 3,000,000, including those of Shaci Ward (now called Shapingba), Beibei and Daidukou, ③ "The City under the Direct Control of Chongqing: 820,000km squares (population: 31,300,000). The origin of this enlargement does date back to the days of their resistance to Japan.

From this wartime capital and from that Great Rear of Sichuan Province, 3,000,000 men were conscripted and took part in various battles in various parts of the Continent. "The soldiers from *Shu* (Sichuan Province)" numbered as many as one fifths of all the soldiers that had been at the National United Front Against Japan, and more than 260,000 of them were recorded to have died in action. (*A Record on Chongqing's Resistance*)

On the other hand, the foodstuffs the farmers in Sichuan Province known as "Nature's Treasure-house" made obligatory supply from 1941 to 45 amounted to more than 4,220,000 tons—one third of the total amount from the whole of China. Indeed, Chongqing and its hinterland turned out to be a great strategic base for the Anti-Japanese War, and as the war went on, this tendency grew more and more extinctive and strengthened, and even if the Japanese Air Force tried its best to obtain *Shu* or "Sichuan Province as another gain of higher quality," it simply turned out to be another example of "vain effort" in obtaining Shu.*

  *Emperor Guangwu (reign: 25-57), the First Emperor of Later Han (25-220), once subjugated the Land of Long, and seizing that opportunity, he tried to invade the capital of Shu, but in vain, as is recorded in *The History of the Later Han*.

● Wicked Officials & Wicked Merchants Gained Power to Send the People to Destitution

In that over-populated provisional capital of Chongqing, what annoyed the people most of all—along with the air raids—until they felt as if they were suffering from natural enemies was none other than the hardships of life brought about by scarcity of goods and sharply rising prices. Since power plants and water mains were often broken by bombardments, power failures and suspensions of the water supply were daily occurrences, keeping housewives busy in obtaining water for daily life, which meant that: they must carry up the water they had got from one of the two rivers by climbing up those endless stone steps, and if they found it too much for them to do, they had to buy water by the pail. On the other hand, even though they lived in "the Nature's Treasures House," and they were told of "a bumper rice crop" every year, the price of rice kept rising. In 1940, the price of rice began to soar, and what had been 11 *yuan* for one *dan* (50kg) in October the year before became 37 *yuan* in June, 57 *yuan* in August, and more than 1,00 *yuan* in October. It was simply too apparent that landlords and gentlemen farmers were concealing rice, because they were unwilling to sell, while juggling with the figures in making obligatory supply of rice to the Government.

In September, 1940, Jiang Jieshi issued "his announcement to the people of Sichuan Province concerning the Administration on Provisions," thus warning not to "stockpile rice, waiting for the rise in price" or "Tunji-Juqi" and demonstrated his drastic measures by shooting 80 people, including Mayor of Chengdu, Yang Quanyu, but without achieving any remarkable results. None other than the bureaucracy of the Nationalist Government having been deeply concerned in speculation in foodstuffs by making use of its position, it was totally impossible to eradicate that evil. An article in *Da Gong Bao* (The Large Official Bulletin) criticized it, as follows: "The evil officials, making use of their positions, do stockpiling and hold off selling in such a large scale as incomparable with what is done by any dishonest merchants; thus the root cause of the steep rise in rice price lies in those evil officials."

These treacherous officials and merchants, together with house under-leasers and black marketers, were called "war-made millionaires," and lived a prosperous life, but these wrongs were to make the ordinary people's lives even harder.

The following was what had actually been witnessed by Han Suyin, as she wrote in *Birdless Summer:*

> By the end of 1940, inflation was so bad that it was difficult to get meat in the Chungking markets, and some men went out with their wives to shop; They carried choppers, hacked off portions of meat themselves at the stall, and carried them away, for there was no orderly queuing and people clawed at the food, knowing that as the counters emptied, the prices went up.

In another paragraph in the same book, she also wrote: "Now a meal at a restaurant costs 150 *yuan*, though it was 75 *yuan* three month ago." For a cup of coffee, which was none other than "red sugared water," one had to pay as much as 2 *yuan*. This meant it was worth 1kg of rice. About this period, Troelden, a special correspondent of a German News Agency Transozean stopped at Taiwan on his way home, and he had a talk with Japanese servicemen at the Headquarters of the Taiwan Forces. In one of his passages he wrote: "High prices of commodities in Chungking are surprising: a bottle of whisky costs 250 dollars (yuan): Since both whisky and beer could be sent only by "the Route for Supporting Jiang," those prices would be natural." But the reporter Troelden also pointed out the fact, as follows:

> The morale of the people in Chungking is still very high. Since they are accustomed to the air raid, they have come not to mind it so much. As for the air-raid warning, the preliminary one is issued at the same time when the Japanese planes take off at Hankou or its neighborhood; then there comes the first warning followed by the second, and by the time the planes arrive at Chungking, none but policemen are seen on the roads or streets. Bombardments have given great damage, but such important munition factories as arsenals had not received any direct hit. The air-raid facilities at Chungking are the best in the world. The larger ones are as long as one mile and a half, and they are bent in the interior. The citizens' training has reached a high level, and it is impossible for any bombardment to frustrate their fighting consciousness. Jiang Jieshi's resistance consciousness remains firm.
>
> ——*A Series of War History in the Defense Agency's Library:*

Excepting the talk of high prices of commodities, all the information he gave was something to crash the wishful thinking the Japanese side had held so far.

● **Even the Air-Raid Caves were made a Target for Speculation**

But those Japanese military in the Headquarters of the Taiwan Forces would have been amazed if they had heard that: the air-raid facilities which had been certified as "the best in the world" were being made an object for speculation by those who had got rich quick by taking advantage of those national afflictions.

Zong Zhiwei, a member of a civilian defense corps, who—at the time of the air raids of "5.3 & 5.4"—had narrowly escaped death at a concavity of a stone Buddhist image at Luohan-si Temple, later changed his place of work to an influential commercial company named Chongde Jinchu Gongsi (Noble Virtue Advance Company). What had embarrassed him then and there was that: the certificate for the company's air-raid cave was valid for a single year and cost as expensive as 2,000 *yuan*. Certainly, compared with the public air-raid cave, that private one was incomparably better than the public one both in location and in interior facilities; what was more, it was guaranteed that they would never be crammed there as in the Air-Raid Tunnel at Juechangkou. Still, it was something unthinkable for a plebeian to pay 2,000 *yuan* per year for that single certificate. The owner of that air-raid cave, which Zong had qualified himself to enter, had made it his occupation to build an air-raid cave and sell or buy the certificates for the entrance to the cave, and he had several other caves. "The fixed capacity is small, and this keeps the air clean"—this was his marketing slogan, and prices were changing from one cave to another, according to the change of seasons. Certainly that air-raid business was bizarre and laughable, but it was far from laughable, because it had been brought about by none other than the Japanese military's bombardments.

Zeng Zhiwei had a monthly salary of 30 *yuan* paid in silver coins called "*da-yan.*" Converted into "*fabi*" (legal paper currency introduced in 1935), one *yuan* in silver equaled one hundred *yuan*. In other words, in obtaining a right to make use of the company's air-raid cave for one year, Zeng had to pay two thirds of his monthly pay, but an excessive issue of these bank notes led to the depreciation of currency, thus to give a further attack on the people's livelihood.

The U.S. and U.K. governments often offered financial help for China to achieve currency stability and concluded a foreign exchange convention to buy legal paper currency with dollars in order to lower its currency limit to the level where endorsement with gold was possible, but in vain, because the dollars flown in were seldom used for the proper purpose. Most of them had been used for the luxury and money-grubbing for "the Four Major Families"— whose heads were Jiang Jieshi, Kong Xiangxi (the Head of the Department of Finances during the Anti-Japanese War), Song Ziwen and the Chen Brothers of Guofu and Lifu.

In such situations as these, Chongqing was to push herself forward as the stage for a couple of enterprises of global significance: "a Battle of Chongqing" and "the Liberation of China."

The White Terrors Performed under the Air Raids

● **The Miserable Scenes Witnessed by Mao Dun, a writer**
Toward the end of November, 1940, Mao Dun, a writer, having received a telegram from Zhou Enlai as the representative of the Office of Balujun or the Eighth Route Army in Chongqing, left Yan-an he had been staying at and entered Chongqing. It was immediately after Japan's Operation No. 101 was over.

Mao Dun then was forty-five years old. He, who came from Zhejiang Province in the coastal area, had been driven from home by the wartime fire, and for more than three years, he had to remain a traveler wherever he might be.

What had greeted him at Chongqing was the disastrous scenes of the capital as the former mountain castle, now thoroughly devastated and turned into the mountains of wreckage. The foggy season had already set in, and the fog rising from the two rivers had wrapped the city all day long, and it came even into the room to cling to his body. This led him to write: "The fog is tremendous. It makes me feel as if I had mold grown all over my body."

In such fogginess in Chongqing, another war was being made. Since that was being performed between the two camps of the Chinese themselves, it could never be interrupted by the fog, but lasted in latent manners and with fierce intensity. That was a Communist struggle against "the white terrors" performed by Jiang Jieshi's special service agencies.

Mao Dun, who had established his position as a writer by his full-length novel *Ziye* (*The Midnight*) published in 1932, had shown interest in documentary literature (reportage) while concerning himself deeply in the leftist literary movement, and in March, 1930, he joined in organizing "the Chinese Leftist Writers' League" along with Lu Xun, Guo Moruo, Xia Yan, Tian Han and so on, thus to keep positive activities in the cultural front line of battles against the Nationalist Party.

One of his activities at this period—one of the fruits from the unity of documentary literature and the cultural battle line—was "*One Day in China— May 21ˢᵗ, 1936*," for which Mao Dun collected all the contributions available from all the provinces and cities of China, excepting Tibet and Mongolia, by means of newspapers—and by editing all those happenings, events and entries in personal diaries that occurred *that* day, he informed "all the Chinese who are able to read Chinese and who have been concerned about what will become of this land of their ancestors, and are anxious to know what China is as a whole at this period of her crises of being invaded by the Japanese military on all fronts." There, one could see what China was really like—including what sort of life they were leading and what sort of opinions they were holding—in a kaleidoscopic variety. In 1937, when the Lukoukyao Incident* occurred, Mao Dun who was in Shanghai joined in starting "Shanghai City's Society to Save the Cultural Circles," and while joining in editing *Jiu Wu Ri Bao* (Relief Daily Newspaper), he started a magazine *Ne Xian* (Deliver Battle Cries) together with Ba Jin, thus bringing himself into the line of anti-Japanese literary activity. When Shanghai fell after the battle of eighty-odd days, he went to Wuhan by way of Hongkong, and after having been a witness to organize "The Chinese Writers' Resistance Association," he became the chief editor of its bulletin *Literature for Resistance*, but having been driven from Wuhan, too, by the Japanese Army, he came to Yan-an to stay and teach at Lu Xun Art Academy (named after Lu Xun*) there, when he received a telegram of invitation from Zhou Enlai.

At this period, the communists at Chongqing had been in a critical situation since the Third Office (led by Guo Moruo) of the Military Affairs Committee's Administration Department was largely scaled down to "the Committee of Cultural Activities" as the result of the Anti-Communist policy of the Nationalist Party. Now Mao Dun who had arrived at Chongqing was requested to join the Committee of Cultural Activities together with Tian Han, Hu Feng and others with the title of a standing committeeman so that he might plan and promote cultural activities from the standpoint of all the factions of democratic parties.

On his way to Chongqing, Mao Dun was recording what he saw and heard. The chapter of *Chongqing in the Fog* in *A Record of my Experiences in the Northwestern China* begins as follows:

In 1940, when I arrived at Chongqing, I had been in time for the foggy season. Unexpectedly, however, I was to bathe in the sunshine for a few days. According to the locals, that was something rare. When they talked of the air raids they had experienced the year before, their memory alone did send them not a little panicky. I myself had not experienced such an air raid, but the sight of so many pools (the holes made by the bombs dropped at the spots) and of all those buildings whose walls were unanimously damaged—these two facts alone did tell me everything of what was happening there. So, the sight of so many downtowns having been completely wiped out led me to imagine how much more terrifying those air raids had been than they were told about.

But "Chongqing in the fog" was more active than I had imagined, and there was something I was not able to identify. It is said that "Chongqing in the fog" presents "a kind of beauty of haziness." Behind that haziness, it is unavoidable to have something far from beautiful. But all I can do here would be to pick up tidbits of news.

What he wrote as "something" he "was not able to identify" was none other than the stuffy air of deterioration and terrorism in "the capital of Jiang Jieshi" that impressed Mao Dun even more deeply than the thick fog of Chongqing. The writer was at once impelled to describe the very things far from beautiful in the haze, but it was impossible to approach the real nature of things beyond the thick fog in the method of "reportage." Then what Mao Dun adopted was: writing a novel in the method of reportage. In his novel entitled *Corrosion*, which began to be serialized in the monthly magazine *The Life of the General*

Public edited by Zou Taofen in Hong Kong, Mao Dun was to depict with fury the intrigue and white terrorism whirling around the daily life of the Anti-Japanese Capital under the air raids—through the diary kept by a former female student, Zhao Huiming, who happened to fall into the hands of the Special Service Agency of the Nationalist Party and began to work as a secret agent, though unwillingly.

● **The Terrorism for Hunting Communists was Prevalent**
even in the Broad Daylight

The following are the entries of that diary kept by Zhao Huiming:

January 11

Yesterday I went to "the castle area." I felt the air there had something peculiar in its smell. That nasty odor always comes from anything going rotten, and now it smells of blood, too. If I were to give it a proper name, I think it must be "a stench of dead bodies." I don't think this is my illusion. Or have I become too sensitive?

Before the storm comes, it is unfailingly sultry. All kinds of poisonous insects, bluebottle flies covered with bacteria, spiders on the webs built at any shady corners and wall lizards usually hidden at the corners of the room, all come out to fly noisily or crawl busily around, giving some twittering, thus to engage in their own action. The world is theirs now.

January 15

A rumor is going around: a serious upheaval occurred in Wannan (the southern part of Anhui Province). The smell I was made to smell in "the castle area" four or five days ago has come over here, too, to fill the air.

While Mao Dun was staying in Chongqing, the Nationalist Army led by the Chief of the General Staff, He Yingqin, made an enveloping attack on the New Fourth Army or the Communist Army that ranked with the Eighth Route Army (in January, 1941). This incident known as "Wannan Incident" marked the start of what was called "the Second High Tide of Anti-Communism." In the capital of Chongqing, too, the terrorism for hunting the Communists began to be performed by the Special Service Agency in the broad daylight, and this led

Mao Dun, a progressive intellectual, to take refuge in the suburbs for a while. Everyone smelt a putrid smell and felt terrified at the terrors given by the state organ. According to the circumstances, Chongqing then easily turned from the anti-Japanese capital into a concentration camp for communists.

Han Suyin had once witnessed something of what the Special Service Agency used to do, as she wrote in *Birdless Summer:*

> (on an empty road in broad daylight under the air-raid warning)
> I saw a man, hands bound, face covered by a black cloth, with two slits for eyes, being marched off by three soldiers. Behind them came a plainclothes man holding a revolver loosely, muzzle down. The prisoner would probably be excuted in a small private shelter, shot through the back of the neck, and why I did not know. This was another method devised by the secret police for getting rid of "communists." The executioner usually took the victim's shoes, after death, to prevent the dead man's ghost running after him.

What was taken as "a putrid smell" by Mao Dun had been exposed in such scenes as they witnessed in their daily lives. Those intensive impressions Mao Dun had received were expressed in the form of a woman's diary; he was also careful enough not to make a frontal attack so he could pass censorship; while in describing "the structure of corrosion," he was careful enough to make the hero a member of the Special Service Agency within the regime. These techniques he adopted then also suggested the limitations of "the freedom of expressions" under Jiang Jieshi's Administration. Even though no Japanese appears in that novel, *Fushi* (*Corrosion*), the siren of the air-raid warning and red balloons (as a signal of the ememy planes' approach) do tell the readers how those inhabitants of Chongqing were being bound by the two kinds of terrors—one from the sky as the indiscriminate bombings, the other from the Nationalist Party that performed white terrors.

The air raid never occurred in the foggy season, but "the terrorism in the White Zone" having been permeated in every hour in every place, it did tear the people's daily life and their nerve to a terrible extent. To the members of the Communist Party and their sympathizers and supporters, the Nationalist Party's Special Service Agency and their secret police remained a source of immense terror. Certainly Nationalist-Communist Collaboration had been achieved, but this never meant that the Communists' political activities were recognized as legal, but only meant that "the delegation of the Chinese Communists" were permitted to reside in Chongqing and that "the Eighth Route Army" and "the New Fourth Army" were recognized as a wing of the Nationalist Army. This was also known by the fact that: Zhou Enlai in Chongqing was "the representative of the Eighth Route Army (and the New Fourth Army)" and that: his status as "the Chinese Communist Center's Secretary in the Southern Bureau" was made a secret status valid only in the underground organization. Under the powerful authority of Jiang jieshi, there still remained a law that was capable of sending anyone to death simply because one was a communist. It was under such circumstances that Zhou Enlai and his comrades were being engaged in their activities at "the White zone."

● **The Two Special Service Agencies: Jun-tong and Zhong-tong**

The special service agencies that had supported the Nationalist reign of terror consisted of two special agencies. One was *Jun-tong* known by another name of "*Lanyi-she* Company"; the other was *Zhong-tong* with another name of "C.C Group." The former was led by Dai Li, also known as "the Terror of Chongqing"; the latter by the Chen Brothers, Guofu and Lifu.

The former was founded on the Army; the latter had grown in the mainstay of the Nationalist Party. Propped up by these organizations, which half appeared secret societies, Jiang Jieshi's autocratic regime soared high and exercised their power.

Owen Lattimore, an American Sinologist, who used to be a political advisor to Jiang Jieshi, wrote as follows, concerning those two special service agencies in his *China Memoirs:*

> Like perhaps all dictators or would-be directors, Chiangkai-shek (Jiang Jieshi) relied very heavily on secret intelligence. Also, as in all such situations, he kept several intelligence services going in rivalry with one another in order to avoid becoming captive of his own intelligence services. They would leak information on one another and in that way he would get to know what they were really up to.

Jun-tong's formal name was "the Bureau of Investigation and Statistics in the Military Committee." This used to be known as "Lanyi (Blue Shirt)-sha Company," but formally that was Zhonghua-Fuxing-sha (China Reconstruction Association), a fascist secret society of the rightist military personnel who had graduated from Huangbu Military Officers' School. Since early in the 1920s when within that school there started a struggle for the leadership against the leftists that included Zhou Enlai as the chief of the Political Department, they banded together under Principal Jiang Jieshi and while supporting Jiang as their only leader, they aimed to convert China into a powerful centrally-governed state. Dai Li, one of "the thirteen *taibaos* (aides)" since the foundation of Zhonghua-Fuxing-sha, had been on a special mission of Jiang Jieshi to take charge of that specially commissioned department.

During the latter half of 1938, the Nationalist Center Party's and the Nationalist Government moved from Wuhan to Chongqing. When the National United Front Against Japan was formed, Zhonghua-fuxing-sha had pretended to have broken up; as it was, they sought to enlarge their organization in the newly-established Young People's Association of *San Min Zhuyi* (the Principles of Nationalism, Democracy & Livelihood)* and in the Military Committee, while Dai Li's Fuxing-sha's Party for Special Duty had properly been moved into the Bureau of Investigation & Statistics in the Military Committee (B.I.S.M.C.). This Bureau had moved its function to Chongqing even before Wuhan fell, and tried establishing the base for their activities. When Jiang Jieshi arrived in Chongqing, the B.I.S.M.C. had already opened its headquarters at Luojia Wan at Shizhong Ward, while providing several secret strong points in the city, and at the foot of Mt. Gele in the suburbs, they had finished bringing into being the concentration camp, which was later developed into a Chinese-American Cooperative Workshop, thus to provide the setting for the novel *Hong Yan (Scarlet Rock)*. Externally, that was known as "Military Committee's Branch Office at Xiangxia."

On the other hand, *Zhong-tong*, as was known by its formal name of Nationalist Party's Central Department's Investigation & Statistics Bureau, was an organization on special duty, backed up by the party's authority. The two Cs—Chen Guofu (a Standing Supreme Committeeman of State Security) and Chen Lifu (the Head of the Education Department and a Standing Manager of *San Min Zhuyi**—were among "the Four Great Families" along with the Jiangs, the Kongs and the Songs, and their power was so great as to be said: "the Jiangs rule over the Land; the Chens rule over the Parties," and their power had come from their having completely grasped the Nationalist Party's Central Executive Committee through *Zhong-tong*. The aim of *Zhong-tong* or C.C. Group was to realize the regime of the single party to govern the whole land, that was, to establish Jiang Jieshi's dictatorship, and in achieving this purpose, they made no scruple to adopt any such illegal means as assassination, destruction and information maneuvering.

Zhong-tong also, as soon as Chongqing was sure to be made into the capital, sent a couple of advance parties—one along the Yangzhi, the other by way of Guizhou—thus to act as a herald of bringing into being "the Jiangs' reign all over the land." Their headquarters was set up at Chuandong Normal School in Shizong Ward. This spot was always made an important target of bombardment by the Japanese air raiders throughout their Operations No. 101 and No. 102, but they kept staying there until they moved to Nanjing after the War against Japan was over—thus producing another type of horrors in the capital under the air raids. The buildings of the Normal School were destroyed by the air raids, but the headquarters of *Zhong-tong*, having been seated underground, remained safe.

● **The Communist VIPs were being Kept under Strict Surveillance**

Both *Jun-tong* and *Zhong-tong* as the Nationalist Special Agencies had kept their main activities of observation and maneuvering toward the Communist Party. The heroine of *Corrosion*, Zhao Huiming—the former student activist who had fallen from grace—ought to have been working for either of the two agencies. Her obligation is depicted as follows:

Yesterday (9.18) was the Memorial Day (for the Manchurian Incident*), and I was sent to E Section, according to the order I received in the morning. I was expected to appear there, assuming a certain kind of attitude. The three special duties for me to perform were: to keep watching what the most active person was doing; what was their relationship like; which one I should choose to hunt.

Such wording as "assuming a certain kind of attitude" and "choose to hunt" leads us to imagine what her maneuvering was like—in approaching a male communist by making use of her womanhood. On the other hand, the heroine often goes patrolling around "C-S Society" (probably meaning China-Soviet Society Guo Moruo was in charge of. That must have been a very common activity to be performed almost every day.

The VIPs in the Communist Party had naturally been placed under the strict supervision of those two institutions. "The Nationalist-Communist Co-operative United Front Against Japan" was none other than a nominal slogan and those Nationalist Special Service Agencies had never hidden their attitude of mortal enmity even for a moment.

In those days, the Anti-Japanese Save-the-Nation Movement was being promoted by various groups, and since the Communists had their underground organizations in the local schools, factories and industrial groups, the secret agents used to bring themselves around them. Chongqing's Young People's Association had a Boys' Club in it, and through its reading circle or chorus group, anti-Japanese advertisements were being carried out, and these having been regarded by the secret agents of the Zhong-tong as the Communist activities to scale up their strength, their personnel matters and activities were being watched over. The China-Soviet Cultural Society's "Cultural Salon," which had provided progressive men of culture with a place of their lecture, also attracted their attention and every time they held a meeting, the secret agents slipped in among the audience for intelligence gathering.

The following is a part of the essay written by Liu Jielu, which is included in *A Chronicle of Chongqing's Resistance to Japan:*

> The Third Office of the Military Affairs Committee's Administration Department and its largely scaled-down version known as the Cultural Maneuvering Committee—both led by Guo Moruo—used to be a main target for *Zhong-tong's* intelligence gathering. Guo Moruo's speeches and activities were all that *Zhong-tong* was seeking for. A variety of activities performed by a popular theatrical company, Nuhao-jushe (Angry Roar Theatrical Company), were also something for *Zhong-tong* to keep watch upon. This led *Zhong-tong* even to have a secret agent join that company so he might collect information about that company as well as about what that progressive actor Zhang Ruifang was doing. But the agent was never able

to notice Zhang Ruifang had already been an underground member of the Chinese Communist Party.

In the same *Chronicle*, Chen Wenrong's essay—*Jun Tong's Activities*—goes as follows:

Guo Moruo's activity in the Cultural Maneuvering Committee had also been kept watched by the *Zhong-tong*, who had regarded it as worth aiming at. They chose two persons—Wang Sizhong, a publisher of an illustrated magazine *Comic Train*, and the owner of Wen Feng Book Store in front of the gate to the China-Soviet Cultural Society—and asked them to mix with those progressive renowned persons so that they could find out what they really were. In short, their main activities were in keeping watch on the Chinese Communist Party and any other progressive groups and individuals.

These maneuvering agencies in Chongqing were called "*Yu* (Chongqing)'s Special Group" by Jun Tong, and "Experiment Group" by Zhong-tong, and both were regarded as something most indispensable to the Nationalist Government, because it was also judged that: this remote hinterland, far away from the battlefront, even if placed under the rule of the Nationalist Party, might allow the Communist power to grow too powerful to be ignored.

When the prolonged war began to bring about the industrial areas in and around Chongqing in Sichuan Province, the Communist influence began to permeate not only among the students but also among factory workers, inevitably causing those special service agencies, Jun-tong and Zhong-tong, to be driven into even more atrocious activities.

Jun-tong had five attack targets:

1) Information concerning Japanese military.
2) Pro-Japanese factions
3) Chinese Communists
4) Suspected Communists
5) Progressive men or women of literature

As for 1) and 2), their main stages were in the battlefields and the occupied areas, so "*Yu* (Chongqing) Special Group" was expected to concentrate their attention on 3), 4) and 5) by keeping watch upon them, prosecuting them and cracking down upon them.

In order to find out who were communists or their sympathizers, censorship of mail, wire-tapping, following up and monitoring meetings were openly carried out. Around the Office of the Eighth Route Army (*Balujun*) at Hongan-cun Village, Zhou's Office at Zengjia-an in Shizhong Ward, and the office of the Committee of Cultural Maneuvering at Zhisheng-gong, a fixed observation station was brought into being, and all those communists of importance— Zhou Enlai, Dong Biwu, Bo Gu (whose real name was Tai Bangxian) and Ye Jianying—were doing were kept reported to Dai Li, the Chief of the Special Service Agency.

The execution on the street, as was witnessed by Han Suyin, would have been their way of putting "*Ganxian* (one who had disturbed the order)" to death by taking advantage of the confusion caused by the air raid warning. If they saw anyone they had kept an eye on wipe his sweat on the face with a handkerchief in sweltering heat, they deliberately decided that: he had sent a signal to the enemy planes as to where to drop bombs, and he was executed at once. That was a new method of communist-hunting invented by Jun Tong. On the other hand, during the night bombings, they themselves sent a signal to the enemy planes by switching their lights on and off around the Communist-line institutions, thus to induce the enemy to drop bombs *there*. So after 1940, it became dangerous to use a white handkerchief to wipe one's sweat during the air raids, because one might be caught and executed as "spies" having signaled to the enemy planes, as Han Suyin wrote in *Birdless Summer*.

● **The Tortures & Secret Slaughters Performed at the Concentration Camp**
Such were their activities, so it was simply natural that the concentration camp—Military Committee's Branch Office at Xiangxia—run by Jun Tong at the foot of Mt. Gale in the suburbs was always full. The camp that had a couple of prisons—"Bai (White) Office" and "Zhaizi (Residue) Cave"—were situated upon the rugged mountain surface encircled with the barbed wire fences, and in that environment totally isolated from the outside world, there had always been extremely gruesome tortures and secret slaughters inflicted upon not only communists but also suspected communists and even those who had kept in touch with the communists—throughout the period of the Anti-Japanese War.

In 1942, the leader of Jun-tong, Dai Li, concluded "an Agreement with the

U.S. Government in cooperating in Specific Technique," and under "Sino-America Cooperation Organization = SACO, with Dai Li as Manager," invited the U.S. Navy's Brigadier General Milton Miles as Vice Manager, so that those Americans collected from the FBI and other secret services would be able to help them learn how to perform torture and assassination, thus scaling up their technique of white terror. The number of Americans working at SACO reached nearly 3,000, and their having linked up with that notorious Dai Li had invited criticism from the U.S. Ambassador Gauss and others, but their activities having been placed outside the Ambassador's authority, he could not do anything with it. Today, that place is preserved and open to the public as "The Exhibition Hall of Crimes Committed by America and Jiang." Several hundreds of people were tortured to death in various ways here or at what was called "the China-America Cooperative Place of Homicide." General Yang Hucheng, who, along with Zhang Xueliang, had been among those who had been the perpetrators of the Xian Incident to be mentioned (in the second section of the following division) met his fate here along with his family by the underlings of Dai Li. The history of this secret prison did not come to an end even after the National United Front Against Japan was over (1945), but lasted till the final period of the Chinese Civil War between the Nationalists and the Communists (1949).

The writer Mao Dun, having been placed in such an atmosphere in Chongqing, had unconsciously smelt "a putrid smell" in it. Not only the indiscriminate bombings from the sky but also the murders and deaths that could be felt stagnant on the earth by means of rumors and the sense of smell—these kinds of fears and anger and disgust about them were none other than what had driven him to write the novel, *The Corrosion*. The writer wanted to bring his readers the atmosphere of the contemporary time in a more direct form, but in order not to be caught in the network of censorship—also prepared by Zhong-tong—he had decided to write it in a form of a diary. The opening reads as follows:

This diary, an incomplete one, having been written intermittently, happened to be found in a community air-raid cave in Chongqing. No one can tell who wrote it or whether the person who wrote this is still alive or no more. Anyway, this was found in a hole, about 30cm deep, at the farthest end of that cave. It is unknown whether the writer deliberately put it there or she happened to leave it there—or she has already fallen into a trap of misfortune. None of these questions can be answered. The reason why I decided to make this diary public like this was because I should like to provide those who are interested in the happiness of the young people with the facts how the young people today are suffering not only from the difficulty in making a living and the hunger of knowledge but also from such unspeakable pains as were written here, so that you, the readers, might be even more careful about what you are doing and what you are going to do.

Mao Dun himself would have entered the public cave several times to save himself from the air raid and while breathing in that stuffy air there, he would have worked out the concept of his new novel. As to whether the heroine, Zhao Huiming, was killed in her trial to get away from the Special Service Agency, or she was bombed to death during the air raid performed by the Japanese planes, or she was fortunate enough to get away from the Agency and left Chongqing, the author wrote nothing about them. In the first case and in the second case, the probability of death would have been the same. And whichever death she might have died, the regret and unhappiness she felt then would have been the same. And even if she had succeeded in getting away from the capital, the difficulties she had to face in keeping herself alive would have remained totally unchanged. What Huiming was feeling while writing under the violent pressure of the times was poured out, in a passage, as follows:

> My hands are covered with the blood of those who were pure and innocent. Even if I myself am a victim, I don't feel like forgiving myself for that reason. I wish I could wash off the bloodstains on my hands with the black blood of the guilty. I may be able to do so. I may not be able to do so. But, I believe in being able to do so, if only I were allowed to fulfill the faint hope I have retained so far.

During the same period when Zhao Huiming was living in Chongqing, Zhou Enlai, whose secret title was "the Secretary of the Southern Bureau of the Chinese Communist Center," was also living in the same city, while being engaged in his underground activities under the surveillance of Dai Li or "the Horror of Chongqing."

The Man with Three Faces

● **Zhou Enlai as "the Champion in Maneuvering the National United Front Against Japan"**

Another beam of light that had lent a touch of color to the capital under the air raid was: the confrontation and concession along with the Machiavellianism and the struggles performed between the Nationalist Jiang Jieshi and the Communist Zhou Enlai—seen from a latter-day viewpoint—might appear something like a modern version of struggles as we read in *Sanguo-zhi* (*History of the Three Kingdoms*).* But to those who had been then and there, in the midst of that progress in history, it had not been recognized as anything so clear-cut in shape.

*One of the twenty-four histories of China. The Three Kingdoms were: Wei (220-265), Wu (222-280) and Shu (221-263)

Certainly Jiang Jieshi was unmistakably a person holding the reins of Government and known to everyone at that time; as for Zhou Enlai, sent from Yan-an, remained almost unknown not only to the citizens of Chongqing but also to many of the Nationalist party members—excepting progressive men of culture, students and intellectuals.

Though he came up to Chongqing as the representative of the Communist Party, Zhou's formal title of social position was no more than the representative of the 8th Route Army among the many task armies under the banner of Jiang Jieshi, and in the organization of the administration of the Nationalist-Communist Collaboration, the only post he had occupied was that of the vice-director of the Department of Politics in the Military Affairs Committee in the Supreme Committee of State Security (After it was reorganized, he was made vice-director of the Party Politics Committee at the Front). Even though Zhou was known among students and intellectuals, the powers possessed by Jiang and by Zhou had been too different in size and weight for any struggle to be performed in such a wide stage of politics as would be witnessed by all the people in the country.

Still, or for that very reason, Zhou Enlai's unusual ability and preeminent capacity did stand out even more. He was nobody but a diplomat-soldier representing still a powerless party and a minor army in his enemy territory, but without hesitating even a little, Zhou, making use of a magic of the National United Front Against Japan, rallied the forces comparable with Jiang Jieshi's giant power, proved himself a match, and made preparations for conditions of a reversal of the situation, while looking out over a wider expanse after the victory of the anti-Japanese War. It seems that Zhou Enlai had never racked his brains so hard as in those eight years at "Jiang Jieshi's Capital," but at least to outside observers, he seemed to have performed that difficult task with apparent ease, thus creating a bridge to lead Sun Wen's revolution to the socialist revolution.

Sima Changfeng, who wrote Zhou Enlai's biography at Hongkong appreciates Zhou at this period of his life, as follows:

> Mao Zedong said: "The victory of our liberation war was brought about by the three treasures we have had: The first was the Party; the second was the Liberation Army; the third was the United Front." It was mainly by means of Zhou Enlai's talent that the United Front proved itself to be miraculously effective. In all ages in history and in all places in the world, Zhou Enlai should be called a sovereign in maneuvering a united front. He is ingenious not only in gathering sympathizers and producing sympathizers but also in turning his enemies into his friends, thus to make those who remain his enemies stand alone.

Those who became captivated by Zhou Enlai to be his sympathizers were not necessarily his compatriots. About the same period when Jiang Jieshi was winning fame as the leader of "Free China," Zhou Enlai in Chongqing had been devoting himself to obtaining the international support for the Chinese Communist Party, which was different from the Comintern's internationalism. Not only such "progressive" journalists as Edgar Snow and Agnes Smedley but also Owen Lattimore as a political advisor to Jiang Jieshi and Theodore White, a reporter of *Time* as a pro-Jiang magazine and John Service and John Davis as the U.S. Diplomats who had a promising future before them, made themselves supporters of this "fascinating radical element." White, who had been saying till later in his life: "I have still kept an uncontrollable affection for Zhou Enlai," wrote as follows in his work, *In Search of History*:

To me, he was a perfect human being, instead of being a person whose picture would be placed in my business album for well-known personalities. Now I have grown old and wise, and this has made me rather cautious about the friendship offered by those great figures, just as a drunkard who has abstained from drinking becomes cautious about alcohol. But Zhou Enlai, along with Joseph Stilwell and John F. Kennedy, was among those whom we can never offer any distrust or wayward evaluation. If I were brought to the presence of these three persons now, I should never be behaving as I used to be, and this would be especially so in case of Zhou Enlai.

Zhou Enlai was a man of intelligence, hard-heartedness and perfect courage. He was also equipped with such ability as to fascinate others, to invite trust from others and to share it with others, according to the memory White had retained. Considering his political standpoint, Zhou Enlai was indeed "a character rarely found in history."

Owen Latimore also wrote in his memoire *China and I:* "He was a sympathizer with me in a sense of what the French call *sympathetique*."

Certainly such dispositions as sagacity, hard-heartedness, courageousness or decisiveness had been shared by other Communist leaders in his days, too. But seen from the point of human appeals—consideration for others, propriety and sociability—none could exceed Zhou Enlai. These were none other than what he was able to depend upon—along with his hard-hearted decisiveness—in the capital of Jiang Jieshi, and they did turn out to be indispensable arms to build up that United Front. With their arms powerful but their bullets kept fixed, with their united front large in number but remaining irrelevant to any power, Zhou Enlai in Chongqing stood facing the dazzling height of Jiang Jieshi's authority and offered a challenge to it. Even in the years of those struggles they had kept performing for more than twenty years from their youth to their prime of life, no other period can be more interesting than this period when they were being engaged in the anti-Japanese war, because of the cooperation and confrontation they offered to each other in Chongqing.

- **Zhou and Jiang were Fated to Share their Relationship**

The relationship between Jiang and Zhou dated far back early in their lives and lasted long. It was abundant in commotions and complications. At first, they were companions under the banner of Sun Wen*; then they became the worst enemies to each other, one being a nationalist, the other a communist; then they came to join hands for their great purpose of fighting out the National United Front Against Japan. They were now comrades-in-arms, mortal enemies and negotiating partners. Their relationship changed rapidly in the Chinese Revolution and in the National United Front Against Japan. Jiang once offered a prize for anyone who could behead Zhou, but Zhou, on hearing Jiang's having been confined in Xian,* entered there by himself and delivered him from captivity. Four years later, when Jiang met Zhou again in Chongqing, Jiang expressed his gratitude by inviting Zhou to his Christmas dinner, but immediately after that, Jiang issued an order that Zhou's Army he himself had brought up—the New Fourth Army—should be attacked to ruin. Zhou, staying at Jiang's stronghold, simply kept himself in "determined perseverance," hiding himself at the sanctuary of the National United Front Against Japan, until he defeated his old rival at their final struggle. Their chronological records— sometimes going together, at other times getting inter-twined—do supply us with a source of absorbing interest.

*Xian Incident: In December, 1936, Zhang Xueliang leading the Northeastern Army and Yang Hucheng leading the Northwestern Army arrested and imprisoned Jiang Jieshi who had come to Xian to encourage them to go on attacking the Communist Army staying in northern Shanxi Province, but since both of them, having already been under the influence of the Communist Party, assaulted Jiang at dawn on December 12 and imprisoned him until 25. The Communist Party made efforts to solve this problem in peace, and this led Jiang Jieshi to venture into forming the United Front Against Japan with the Communist Party.

At the Museum of Revolution and Military Affairs in Beijing, we are able to see the materials that show the Nationalist-Communist relationship from Sun Wen's Revolution* to the Anti-Japanese War, and those were none other than their roads to Chongqing.

In June, 1924, at Huangbu in Guangzhou City, China's first modern military school—China's Nationalist Party's Army Officers' School (more simply:

Huangbu Military School) was established. The president of the school was Sun Wen; the principal was Jiang Jieshi, 37 years old. The representative of the school's party was Liao Zhongkai (Liao Chengzhi's father), the representative of the teachers was He Yingqin, the Director of the Government Department was Zhou Enlai, the vice-chief of the Instruction Department was Ye Jiangying, and the Instructors in the Military was Chen Cheng and others. All of them were to come into the nucleus, governmental or military either in Beijing or in Taipei in later years.

Before long, they were to be divided into the right and the left, but now— immediately after Russia brought the Socialist Soviet Union into being by bringing down Imperial Russia—they were in the midst of the period of "keeping company with the Soviet Union by tolerating her Communism." In establishing Huangbu Military School, Sun Wen received full cooperation from the Soviet Union's Red Army, and this led their curriculum to follow what Trotsky had adopted at the Red Army, and the corps of teachers from the Soviet Union led by General Gallen began to teach and train the five hundred students who had entered that school after having been selected from 3,000 applicants. The first lesson they received was to learn how to stage a march without bending their knees. Lin Biao and Luo Ruiqing were among them.

Zhou Enlai, who had just returned from France was still twenty-six, but in this honeymoon of the Nationalist and the Communist, he was appointed to be the Vice-Director of the Political Department soon to be promoted to the Director of the same department. The reason was: because he was the chief of the Military Department of the Communist Party's Guangdong District. This started Zhou Enlai's relationship with the military forces, but his interest had always remained in politics, and the aim of his maneuvering was to make the communism spread and penetrate into the students of that military school. This was how his lifelong confrontation against Jiang Jieshi had started.

While Principal Jiang had held real power in the field of the military drill, Zhou, Director of the Political Department, got hold of political maneuvering under the Communist Party, and together with Ye Jianying, the vice-chief of the Faculty Department, also a member of the Communist Party, was busily engaged in spreading Maxism among the cadets. Under Director Zhou, a communist organ named "the Association of Military Youths" was brought into being, and their bulletin *The Chinese Soldiers* began to be published. This led the Rightest to found "The Academy of Son Wen's Principle," and as the time went on, the relationship of the two parties got worsened to an inextricable extent.

And still, in the early stage when the National Revolutionary Army was still coming into being, Jiang and Zhou unmistakably remained "comrades-in-arms." In January 30, 1925, when the expeditionary force to subdue the local military cliques were sent with Son Wen as Commander-in-Chief, it was recorded in the order of battle of the right wing army that: the Chief of Staff was Jiang Jieshi and the Chief of Administration Department was Zhou Enlai. The Right Wing of the Military Expedition to the East was the First Army consisting of the Training Group of the Military School and the Guangdong Army, and the unit that included Jiang's and Zhou's fought on successive fronts of Pinghu, Shantou and Chaozhou in less than a single month and occupied them all.

In September in the same year, in the order of battle of the National revolutionary Army's Second Military Expedition to Subjugate the East, Jiang was promoted to the Commander-in-Chief, and Zhou to the Chief of the General Administration Department. But in the following order of battle, Zhou's name was no longer found. In the meantime, Son Wen, the Father of Revolution of China, died in March in Beijing and the Chinese Revolution had lost its pioneer and leader. There remains a photograph in which Jiang and Zhou looking sorrowful were present at the ceremony held in Sun Wen's memory. Zhou was holding a letter of condolence with both hands just above eye level to offer it to Sun Wen. When Sun Wen was no more, the days were over when Jiang and Zhou could remain "comrades-in-arms," and with "the Incident of Zhongshan-jian Warship"* as a turning point, the Nationalist Party and the Communist Party ceased to remain together, and Jiang Jieshi and Zhou Enlai left each other, each intending to realize in his own way what Sun Wen had commissioned them to perform, saying: "the revolution still remains unfinished."

*Jiang's warship was ordered to return to Huangbu, which Jiang regarded as part of the Communists' coup d'etat, and all the members of the Communist Party and the advisors from the Soviet Union were dismissed.

In March, 1927, when Zhou Enlai, the former Director of the Government Department of Huangbu Military School, led the general strike performed by the 800,000 laborers in Shanghai, standing at the head of an armed uprising,

Jiang Jieshi, the former principal of Huangbu Military School, who had now become the leader of the Nationalist Party, responded it with an anti-Communist coup d'etat and a purge of the Communist Party, and this led Zhou Enlai—having been defeated and got a price on his head—to flee to Wuhan to take refuge there.

● **The Xian Incident, in which Zhou and Jiang Met each other Again after Ten Years' Separation**

Nearly ten years had passed when they met each other again—in December, 1936—in Xian where Jiang had been placed in a desperate situation. The two generals, Zhang Xueliang and Yang Hucheng, who had been demanding the cease-fire of the civil war and their unity in fighting against Japan, had caught and imprisoned Jiang Jieshi in what later became known as "Xian Incident." Zhou Enlai then came over to Xian for the purpose of releasing Jiang Jieshi who would never open his mouth to speak. Zhou, on entering the room where Jiang had been imprisoned, stood stiffly to attention and saluted him, and addressed him as "Principal," as he used to do when he was teaching at the same school. This led Jiang Jieshi to behave as he used to do, too, thus opening the way for their union to fight against Japan.

Taking this opportunity, they—the Nationalist and the Communist Parties—took a large step toward the ceasefire and, at the outbreak of the Sino-Japanese War on July 7 in the year that followed (1937), they achieved the second Nationalist-Communist Collaboration on July 17, when Zhou Enlai rushed to Mt. Lushan in Jiangsi Province to meet Jiang Jieshi and urged him to decide upon the formation of the United Front against Japan. This was how Zhou Enlai, having finally set himself free from the pursuit of Jiang Jieshi's secret agents and his army that had kept pursuing him since he left Shanghai, made himself an ally of Jiang Jieshi as he used to be at Huangbu, even though superficially.

Early in December, 1938, Zhou Enlai, accompanied by Ye Jiangying, entered Chongqing by way of Guilin. Even if his appeal of "Let's make Wuhan into a Madrid in the East!" had turned out to be in vain, he had not been disappointed, since the three major plans of action in resisting Japan—protracted resistance, all the people's resistance and all-out resistance—had already been established. Once again, the season of Nationalist-Communist collaboration had come round. Jiang Jieshi also arrived at the new capital before long. Jiang and Zhou, who had been left hostile to each other in the rapidly changing situations after Sun Wen's death—Jiang's anti-Communist coup d'etat (1926), Zhou's uprising at Nanchang (1927), Jiang's taking both offices as the Commander-in-Chief of the National Revolutionary Army and as the Head of the Military Committee (1926), and Zhou's taking both offices as the Head of the Chinese Communist Organization and as the Head of the Military Department (1928), and Jiang's exercising his authority in starting the fifth besiegement to subjugate the Communist Army, and Zhou's starting on "the Long March" (1935)—brought everything to a halt for a while and joined hands again. And their former relationship as the Principal and the Director of the Government Department of Huangbu Military School was to be brought into being here in Chongqing once again—as the chief of the Nationalist Party's Military Committee and the vice-chief of the Government Department of that Committee. Zhou Enlai now had become a subordinate of Jiang Jieshi in Chongqing as well as a subordinate of Mao Zedong in Yan-an. This was how his eight years in the wartime capital had started.

● Zhou Enlai as a Subordinate of Jiang Jieshi

This had caused Zhou Enlai in Chongqing to have several different faces to be used in different places. They were of two different types. The first type was for public use or for the open obligation, usually performed in the daytime; the second type was for secret maneuvering, usually done at night. Zhou, bringing himself among those varied duties, appeared in unexpected places at unexpected moments to leave there without leaving any traces behind.

His first face was that of "Jiang's subordinate." He was resident in Chongqing as the representative of the Eighth Route Army and the New Fourth Army. Also as the vice director of the Administration Department of the Military Affairs Committee, he was naturally expected to receive Jiang's orders and perform them. This standpoint of his did work as his official passport, but this was to bring about such unbearable pains as he was not allowed to do or say anything even if the New Fourth Army he himself had carefully raised were besieged and exterminated. The reason was because the one with the prerogative of supreme command of that Army was Jiang Jieshi himself as the chairman of the Military Committee. If it was explained as "a matter of military discipline," Zhou could not say anything. Zhou, the vice director of the Administration Department of the Military Committee, had patiently been enduring this difficult situation he was placed in.

When Guo Moruo, who was in charge of maneuvering the United Front as the chief of the Third Office of the Administration Department, expressed his wish to resign that post, having been disgusted at the endless internal discords he had to face there, Zhou gave a fierce look at Guo and scolded him, saying: "If we were to gain anything good through this revolution, we need to bear anything. Do you know the humiliations *we* are suffering are much more unbearable?" That was the first and the last scolding Guo had received from Zhou, and that led Gou to write in his *Memoir of the Anti-Japanese War:* "That was the first and the last scolding I had received from Zhou, and this caused me to fail to perform my sabotage." Sticking it out, waiting for *the* time, and being sure of the arrival of *the* awaited time—these were the mottoes Zhou Enlai had kept throughout his life.

● Zhou Enlai as a Subordinate of Mao Zedong

Zhou Enlai's second face was what he had kept as "a subordinate of Mao Zedong." Zhou himself often traveled to and from Yan-an, and he had to obey the instructions sent by a telegram in code from the center of the Party represented by Mao Zedong. Since the Communists' open activities in the capital had been prohibited, the activities of this field were performed mostly through secret communication. "Zhou's Office" at Zengjia-an No.50 had also housed in it "the Chinese Communist Central Southern Bureau" that was expected to direct the Party's activities in southwestern China, but this being a perfect underground organization, none of their activities must be known to outsiders. The more active the Southern Bureau became, the more communication they had with Yan-an, and this led them to set up a secret wireless station—with a generating capacity of 5kw—on the third floor of the Eighth Route Army's Control Office at Hongan.

Zhou, just as he had done while he was teaching at Huangbu Military Officers' Training School under Principal Jiang, sent his secret agents to each organ and each class of the Nationalist Party so that the Party's cell members might grow up there. Those secret agents whose identity was found out or suspected as communists were executed on the streets or sent to Bai Gong-guan (White Office), but Zhou had remained simply incapable of doing anything to save them out. Still it was something unthinkable that those political maneuverings would be discontinued. Many people having flown into the capital, it was not hard to find out capable persons. It was from these underground activities that not a few characters were to be produced to take the Chinese diplomacy upon themselves in the years to come—such as Huang Hua and Qiao Guanhua (both were to be foreign ministers).

The only place where Zhou Enlai was allowed to act as the representative of the Communist Party was his standpoint as the chief editor of the party bulletin *Xin Hua Ri Bao* (New China Daily News), and he, having attached great importance to it, wrote the leading article or the essay for the Anti-Japanese Anniversary. However wide apart Chairman Jiang was from Vice-Director Zhou, if he were to take a standpoint of a man of the press, he was at least able to secure a condition of being able to argue on an equal footing with the Nationalist Party. The first editorial he wrote soon after he arrived at Chongqing was "On the Enemy's Movement from Now on" for December 18, 1938, followed by the ones signed by Zhou Enlai for such memorable days as July 7 (the Sino-Japanese war broke out in 1937), September 18 (the Manchurian Incident* occurred in 1931) and May 4 (the Student Movement in 1919). These were among the fifty-eight articles and eleven short essays Zhou Enlai wrote for *Xin Fua Ri Bao*. His pseudonyms were many, including Guzhu Yeren (A Solitary-Bamboo Countryman), Fei (Flight), Guan Sheng (A Crowned One or A Man who has Come of Age), Shao Shan (A Young Mountain) and so on. Certainly these writings of his were subject to strict censorship according to the regulations against Communism, which had secretly been laid down and instructed by such anti-Communist regulations as *The Law for Restricting Other Political Parties* and *The Law for Managing the Matters Concerning the Other Political Parties*, and this often caused "*Xiao Deng* (Deletion)" or "*Mian Deng* (Total Ban)." The latter being printed with the blank space as it was, the paper often had what was called "skylight window" upon it, but this did not make Zhou stop writing an article signed by the writer himself.

● **Zhou Enlai as an Organizer of the National United Front Against Japan**
   The third face Zhou Enlai had was that of "the organizer of the National United Front Against Japan" and here Zhou was able to exhibit his natural characteristics—warm consideration for others, affluent humanity, "silky

manners" (according to Theodore White)—as much as he liked, thus strengthening the battle line of his own side. Much later than those years, the Cambodian King Sihanouk was to refer to Zhou Enlai, giving a really right comment on what he was:

> Some people cannot understand why I, non-communist, have made friends with Zhou Enlai. My answer to them is: "As you see, he is much more princely than I am, isn't he?"

What if any other person but Zhou Enlai had been sent from Yan-an? As for the first face and the second face he was keeping in Chongqing, some other persons might have equaled him. But as for his third face, no other person would have been so able as to take his place. In other words, he was the only person who was capable of retaining what Mao Zedong called "three treasures"—the Party, the Liberation Army and the United Front—in the capital of their enemy, thus to open up the way to the victory of the liberation war.

Undoubtedly, he was "the King of the United Front." He presented himself at every meeting, met anyone in a friendly manner, thus giving a strong impression upon anyone he met—from newspaper boys selling *Xin Hua Ri Bao* in the streets to the ambassadors from abroad.

Following was what Zhou Enlai had brought forward as a proposition concerning "what the United Front should be like," in August, 1938, when the Conference of the Chinese Communists' Central Government was held at Yan-an:

1) In our fighting, we should keep our own footing, but do not mind fame, position or formality. We should hold fast to our principle, but as for which method we might adopt, it should be chosen according to the situations. We should not miss timing, but be careful not to be so impatient as to be excessively impetuous.

2) In our organization, we should refrain from disclosure, intimidation and stimulation, thus aiming at practical growth, while taking care not to enter a dead end street nor to let ourselves fall into a pit.

3) In our activities, competition, cooperation and concession shall be combined; competition shall not lead to damaging others; if you were to cooperate with others while suppressing yourselves, you must not go so

far as to sacrifice yourselves only by considering the benefit of others; and even if you were to make a concession, you must not give any damage to your main force.

4) As for formalities, you must not neglect the procedure, while placing a premium on the way things are, giving a report unstintingly, keeping good faith with each other, and making it a rule to be punctual. In this way, you shall expand your influence, thus to administer to your convenience in our maneuvering.

The role he was to bear in Chongqing and his having performed what he was expected to do there would have brought him such "philosophy of the United Front" as this.

Theodore White looked back on what had happened at the banquet Zhou Enlai had held for him: In front of White, a Judaist, an unmistakable little pig roasted whole in golden brown was placed. "Qing, qing (Please, take it)," said Zhou Enlai as his host. White in perplexity explained to him that he, a Judaist, was not allowed to eat any pig. All present there, having found their guest being treated in a wrong way, dropped their head in perplexity.

Then Zhou Enlai livened up the party; he pointed at the little pig with his chopsticks and said, giving his repeated "Qing, qing (Please, take it)" with a smile on his face:

"Teddy, you are now in China. Well, please look at it once again, will you? Give a good look at it. You may take it as a pig. But in China, this is *not* a pig.—This is a duck, you see."

This led White to take his chopsticks and break the crisp thing covering it, and ate for the first time in his life the flesh of "the pig given his word for it" by Zhou. Such was what Zhou was. He was able to make his friend take a pig as a duck. According to White, this was because anyone wanted to believe in him, and also because he had understood and respected other people's society and their customs.

No doubt Zhou was a born diplomat, a mass maneuverer, a guerrilla to harass the rear, and even after having accepted all those roles into his single person, he did not shrink back even a little. Thus the mountain-castle city of Chongqing which had suddenly been turned into the temporary capital, accepting those flows of people of all sorts and in all conditions, was to be the front line for Zhou Enlai to keep himself free and active in all directions.

Meanwhile, all those air raids by the Japanese bombers had been performed ceaselessly excepting the foggy season. All of the three offices Zhou Enlai had kept at Chongqing had suffered the air raid at least once. The one that had been bombed first was the office of the Eighth Route Army at No. 70 in Jifang-jie Street. That was a direct hit from a bomb (though it turned out a misfire) dropped during the air raids of "5.3 & 5.4." Zhou himself happened to be away from Chongqing, but they took this opportunity to move that office to No.13 in Hongyan-cun Village. That office in that village also suffered from the bombing of No.101 Operations. Wu Zhijian, Zhou's bodyguard, while trying to shoot his rifle at the enemy plane, let it go off to kill himself. With the dilapidated building behind them, Zhou had a photograph of himself and his wife, Deng Yingchao, taken, so he could inform the people of their remaining safe. In the summer of 1941, Zhou's Office as his headquarters in Shizhong Ward was also bombed during No. 102 Operations. What had been threatening his life was not only the secret agent sent by the Nationalist Party but also the attacks from the sky.

Those were the days when he could not feel relaxed even for a moment, but even such air raids could be something to talk about in his efforts to maneuver the general public. At the tea party held once a month by those who were working for Shenghuo (Life) Book Store, Zhou made it a rule to make his appearance and talk to them and their families, who were also present there, about the political circumstances, and when it happened to be after the air raid, he took an opportunity to make the people laugh and learn something new:

"The Nationalist Party says to us: "It is no good for you to believe in Marxism. In the first place, Marx is a foreigner to us; Marxism is something from abroad, and it does not suit the conditions of China." This makes me answer them: "It's true that we have believed in Marxism. Those who do not believe in Marxism cannot be regarded as Communists. But how wrong it is to say that Marx, being a foreigner, does not suit the way things are in China! Now Japanese planes are dropping bombs from the sky, while on the earth old women, hearing the buzzing of the planes, are reciting: "*Nanwu Amitabha* (Save us, the Merciful *Amitabha* Buddha!)" All of them—"planes," "bombs" and "*Amitabha*"—have come from abroad, but no one says they do not suit the way things are in China, as you all know."

—*Bring Revolution to China* by Mu Xin

This was how Zhou Enlai was maneuvering the people in general. Thus while laughing away even the bombings by the Japanese air force, he was informing the people in Chongqing of how bigoted those leaders of the Nationalist Party could be.

The Covering-Up of the Wannan Incident

● Zhou Enlai & Guo Moruo in Combination

Zhou Enlai in Chongqing had divided his daily activities into three parts according to the three obligations he was expected to perform: One was the time to spend as a government staff of Jiang Jieshi, another was the time to spend as the chief editor of *Xin Fua Ri Bao* (New China Daily News), and the other was the time to engage in the secret obligation as the Secretary of the Southern Bureau of the Chinese Communist Party. Each of them was to be performed in the morning, in the afternoon and midnight respectively. Even if these were more or less disturbed by the air raids, this schedule of his had meticulously been maintained throughout the years he lived in Chongqing.

His midnight office hours and important conferences were to be maintained even when he was made Prime Minister of the State Council in the years to come. Zhou Enlai, now in the first half of his forties, had been dedicating himself to his duties in "the White Area" with affluent vitality and a sense of mission.

His first face as the vice-president of the Administration Department was employed when he engaged in his "open work" in Chongqing. When he presented himself in the uniform of the Nationalist Party he had clad in an attractive manner at the Headquarters of the Military Committee in the flat land inside Zhuqi-men Gate—one of the several gates to the former Chongqing Castle—the Nationalist guards gave him a brisk salute to receive the member of the Chairman Jiang Jieshi's staff. Here Zhou Enlai, making himself the right hand of Chen Cheng, the Director of the Department of Politics, demonstrated his ability in maneuvering the military which was the greatest purpose of Nationalist-Communist collaboration. In ranking, he was "among Jiang Jieshi's subordinates" as was registered in the staff list, but Zhou Enlai himself had not had even the slightest awareness of it, but placed himself among his enemies in the same way as he used to do and feel when he was implanting the power of Communism in the Nationalist Army in those days when he was teaching at Huangbu Commissioned Officers' Training School placed under Principal Jiang.

The system of the Department of Politics in the Military Committee had been introduced in the days when Sun Wen was engaged in the Northern Expedition, after the fashion of the military system of the Soviet Union's Red Army, and since December, 1938, when a military conference held at Nanyu adopted the manifesto that declared: "the Administration is more powerful than the Military," it had confirmed its position even more. It consisted of three offices—the First Office, the Second Office and the Third Office—each in charge of training the political secret agents, of maneuvering the people in general and of engineering the advertisement.

As for the aims to be achieved by the Department of Politics, there were four of them:

1) Advertising the resistance to Japan and heightening the morale
2) Prompting the collaboration of the military and the civilian thus to promote the latter's assistance to the former.
3) Arming the people in a theater of war to make them go ahead of the flying column.
4) Keeping watch upon the Communists' activity within the Armed Forces.

As for 4), it was impossible to be performed as was expected, as long as Zhou Enlai was the Vice-President of the Administration Department, and Guo Moruo was the chief of the Third Office of it, and that was made use of in the direction totally different from what had originally been expected.

Zhou Fuhai—who, immediately after the Nationalist Government entered Chongqing, fled from Chongqing together with Wang Zhaoming and participated in "the New Central Government" under the protection of the Japanese Military—used to be the deputy chief of the Nationalist Party's Advertising Department before he fled, and later he recollected the activities of the Administration Department while they were still at Wuhan, as follows:

What I found most painful at that time was the three kinds of meetings held every week. (omission) Those who were present were: Chen Cheng as the Chief of the Administration Department, Zhou Enlai as the Vice Chief, Guo Moluo as the Chief of the Third Office, and I and Dong Xianguang and Su Tongzi from the Central Advertisement Department. At every theme taken up at that meeting, we were made to hear Chen Cheng's superficial knowledge on political theory only to make me give a wry smile on it. At the reports given by Zhou Enlai and Guo Moruo, who had fabricated facts to deceive the people, I was made to grind my teeth and feel my heart ache. But I, whose position was so modest, remained simply unable to say anything against them.

—*Zhou Fuhai's Diary* edited by Cai Dejin

Probably Zhou and Guo, in combination with each other, would have made much use of their post and power in such meetings as those mentioned above for the benefit of their Communist Army and for their maneuvering of the people. Naturally, all these things having been reported to Jiang Jieshi, the two were driven from their post toward the end of 1940 when the Military Committee was reorganized. But since Zhou Enlai was still staying at the post of the vice-chief of the Battlefront Party's Government Committee, while Guo Moruo staying at the post of the chairman of the Cultural Maneuvering Committee, it never occurred that the Communist Party was deprived of their means of army-maneuvering and people-maneuvering. There remains a record of the lecture Zhou Enlai gave as the vice-director of the Department of Politics to the commissioned officers, high-ranking government officials and political maneuvering members, and we can see how confident he was in talking about the Communist Party's awareness of the situation China at that time was facing:

We are no longer able to say that: the whole of North China is under the rule of the United China's Government. Many of the areas have been occupied by the Japanese Army and they have fallen into the hands of so many Chinese evil-doers or co-operators with the Japanese. They have set up a puppet regime called "self-government." We need to penetrate into these areas and mobilize the population there so that we can retrieve the local government's control to the hands of the local people in order to achieve a real self-government of ours. North China's local government, which should naturally belong to China's Nationalist Government, must establish a democratic regime by assembling all the people intending to perform the National United Front Against Japan, whatever political party or military group they might belong to. All those people should naturally be given an equal opportunity and equal obligation to take part in the War Against Japan. Talking about what sort of strategy we should take, I should say it must be the one thoroughly and exclusively based upon "the anti-Japanese sentiment." This is none other than the strategy the Chinese Communist Party has brought into being. If we were to intend to survive as the Chinese people on this land of ours, we must adopt this strategy as the very base of all the political and military activities.

—Zhou Enlai by Xu Jieyu

The Communists in the audience did send him applause, but the Nationalists being engaged in political maneuvering were exchanging their puzzled looks, as was witnessed by Xu Jieyu. That was because the local governments and landholders were none other than *Jincheng* &*Tangchi* (*the castle built of metal with a hot-water moat surrounding it*) for the Nationalist Party. Zhou Enlai, though in the military uniform of Jiang Jieshi's Army, did remain a member of the Chinese Communist Central Political Bureau and the vice-chairman of the Revolutionary Army's Military Committee—an unmistakable subordinate to Mao Zedong.

● The Wannan Incident was a Trial which Zhou Enlai must Go through

The second face Zhou Enlai had retained was that of the chief editor of *Xin Hua Ri Bao* (New China Daily), which had a circulation of 30,000, employing two hundred people in editing, printing and selling it. That was the one and only daily newspaper the Chinese Communist Party had published during the anti-Japanese war in the district under the Nationalist rule. That was launched at Wuhan on January 11, 1938. Then it was moved to Chongqing to resume publishing it on October 25, and it was to come up to 3,231 in the aggregate, before it was forced to stop publishing on February 28, 1947 by the Nationalist Party.

At Chongqing, the first chief editor was Hua Gang, followed by Zhang Hanfu, who was later to be the deputy director of the Ministry of Foreign Affairs, but the virtual director was Zhou Enlai. According to *The Eleven Years*

I Spent in Following Vice-Chairman Zhou by Long Feihu who used to be one of Zhou's bodyguards, Zhou, besides writing his own article on politics, often touched up a variety of literary works created by his colleagues and friends. On such occasions, he used to sit in his chair with a new cup of tea beside him and dictated his version to his secretary. Zhou paid attention to every word and every phrase of each sentence, and used to admonish the reporters, saying: "You must not make even a single mistake in your writing. You must clearly recognize the weight of each word and each phrase you are writing, because it might be concerned with the benefit of the people that number 450,000,000."

For the paper on an important day such as the anniversary of the Anti-Japanese War, Zhou Enlai took up his pen to write its editorial, and even on the ordinary days, any such articles as important as the editorial were to be written after having been consulted with Zhou. The writer, Xia Yan, who used to work at the editorial bureau in those days wrote in his autobiography—*The Pen & The War*—as follows: "As for the important articles, we had them all read over by our comrade Zhou Enlai, and he was always engaged in that work in a very strict manner. He was very meticulous in perusing the manuscript, too; on one occasion, he had already touched up *the* article, but having still remained unsatisfied with it, he ordered us to write it once again."

The greatest concern to the chief editor, Zhou Enlai, was to keep reminding Jiang Jieshi of the fact that the Government in Chongqing was a coalition government consisting of Nationalist Party, Communist Party and several Democratic Parties, thus simultaneously enlarging the circle of the united front among the people in general. The existence of *Xin Hua Ri Bao* (*New China Daily*) itself was none other than the product of the united front, and for this very reason, keeping thrusting "this symbol of their United Front" to Jiang Jieshi who had kept strengthening his power of dictatorship every day was something that must be performed, no matter how difficult it might be.

Zhou repeatedly wrote in the editorial: "Jiang Jieshi is the only and legitimate person who is able to lead the whole people of us Chinese to our victory," thus showing "the fruit of our collaboration," while seeking to retain and develop the United Front even further. But as the pressure toward the Communists' existence and activities were becoming strengthened, the censorship put on *Xin Fua Ri Bao* (*New China Daily*) grew stricter, and the pages of the paper came to have more "skylight windows" or blank spaces caused by deletion. According to Xia Yan's memoir, *The Pen and The War:* the newspaper carried almost every day one or two lines of "an announcement respectfully offered by the editor":

> The study by Mr.××, which was planned to appear *here* was deleted according to the decision made by the Newspaper Examination Agency. Here we express our regret to the author.

The Wannan Incident or the armed attack that occurred in January, 1941, turned out to be a serious trial to Zhou Enlai not only as the military representative of the Chinese Communist Party at the anti-Japanese capital but also as a figure of the press.

On January 11, all the staff was celebrating the third anniversary of their having launched *Xin Hua Ri Bao* at the lecture hall. Zhou Enlai, Ye Jianying and others on a standing committee of the Southern Bureau were also there, and Zhou had delivered a congratulatory address. Then a man jumped into the hall. He who was among those in charge of top secrecy at the Southern Bureau had brought an emergency telegram from Yan-an, which said: The 10,000 soldiers in the following corps—consisting of the Headquarters, the field hospital and the supply corps and others of the New Fourth Army of 100,000 soldiers—were now having a tough game, enveloped by the huge army of 80,000 led by Gu Zhutong, the Commander of the Third Sector of the Nationalist Revolutionary Army. The New Fourth Army had been placed in order and reorganized by Zhou Enlai himself with great difficulty, when that Red Army unit were made scattered after having failed in "a revolt at Nanchang" (1927), and after the Sino-Japanese War broke out (1937), Zhou had unified it into a regular unit with Ye Shan as the Chief of the Army and Xiang Ying as the Vice Chief of it. Now, that very Army was being attacked, to make his shock even greater.

Zhou Enlai, who had received that telegram while he was making a speech of congratulation, cried in a strong tone of voice as if he had forgot himself: "The New Fourth Army in Wannan on their way north, according to the order of the Center of the Communist Party, was suddenly surrounded and attacked by the Nationalist Army. That bigoted sect of Nationalist party must have done it!" Then, all of a sudden, the electric lights went out, drowning the hall in the pitch dark. After a while, the light was on again. And by that time, Zhou Enlai had regained his usual self. "Darkness is temporary; Light will surely come to help us again," he said. Then, as if encouraging everyone, including himself, too, he resumed his speech:

Anyone who has ever experienced a revolutionary struggle ought to have known how we exert ourselves whether we are in the light or in the darkness. It is important *not* to brag in a favorable wind, and what is even more important is: we must *not* be disappointed even in the dark. If we all keep confident, and keep going without being disheartened by any difficulties, struggling, and demonstrating our courage and fighting spirit even in darkness, we shall surely be able to see our victory. The darkness will surely come to an end.

It's true, as we have been informed of *it*, the New Fourth Army on their way to the north is being surrounded by row upon row of the Nationalist Army. But our warriors will surely be able to break through that envelopment and the darkness, because they have kept their faith in certain victory as well as the great intention to achieve their aim.

After the ceremony was over, Zhou Enlai immediately held an emergency conference of the Southern Bureau, sent a telegram of protest to He Yingqin and Gu Zhutong, the Nationalist leaders, demanding they should at once raise the siege of the New Fourth Army, and wrote a letter to Jiang Jieshi, requesting that the Nationalist Armies should retreat and make way for the New Fourth Army. On the other hand, the secret agents in each department of the Southern Bureau, according to the direction given by Zhou Enlai, began to inform a variety of lines—such as the resistance sect and the elders' sect in the Nationalist Party, which had been comparatively sympathetic toward the Communist Party, the various minor political parties, various cultural societies, diplomatic channels, newspaper companies and so on—of this reckless action performed by that bigoted sect of the Nationalist Party.

On the day that followed, Jiang Jieshi was to receive a letter (dated January 12th, 1941) in the joint names of Song Qingling (Late Sun Wen's consort) and three other personalities:

.... Today, our greatest enemy comes from outside. Since our interior has already achieved the unity, you need not be so particular about the form that would develop the contents; what is most important now is not to be particular about trivial details, even though the whole must be kept under control. If the one who possesses power, unable to use it against those from outside, were forced to employ it toward those inside, trying to keep himself alive, it will lead us to our isolation, while our guidance would be regarded as *not* legal by others. That is particularly far from the original intention our party members have shared among us.

　　　　　　　　　　　—*The Collection of Letters to Jian Jieshi*

But, Jiang Jieshi, despite the frequent requests or demands to terminate the besiegement, would not do anything, only giving evasive excuses. On January 14, a report arrived from the site of the incident: both provisions and ammunition finally ran out, causing the deaths of all the soldiers excepting only one thousand who had managed to break through besieging enemy lines. Xiang Ying, the vice chief of the Army, was killed in battle; Ye Shan, the chief of the Army, got wounded and was taken prisoner. That was a unilateral massacre which might better be called a holocaust rather than the deaths in a battle or a combat. This was how that large-scaled crash between the Nationalist Army and the Communist Army—the process of the manifest corruption of the Nationalist-Communist Collaboration—had started.

After the battle was over, Jiang Jieshi announced that: the attacks on the New Fourth Army were a disciplinary measure taken because they did not obey his order to move, and that: the New Fourth Army should be removed from the combat hierarchy and be broken up, while Ye Shan should stand court-martial. (Ye was held in custody at "Chinese-American Collaborative Workshop" in the suburbs of Chongqing till the end of the Anti-Japanese War.)

After the New Fourth Army was pronounced to be broken up, Jiang, who had an interview with Theodore White from *TIME*, treated that incident with a single comment: "The Japanese military suffers skin disease; the Communist Army suffers mental disorder."

For Jiang Jieshi, whose view of the world stood poles apart from Zhou Enlai's, the Communist Army was none other than his true enemy.

● **A Last Resort against News Censorship**

This incident had thrown Zhou Enlai into great indignation. But he had no trump card of doing anything effective. His post in the Military Committee simply showed the fact that he was none other than someone below Jiang, while there was not any room left for him to make use of his secret status— the Secretary of the Southern Bureau of the China's Communist Party's Headquarters. His rage made him tremble all over, but instead of letting his anger lead him to abandoning himself to despair, he made up his mind to let the people at large know of that incident by means of *Xin Hua Ri Bao*, thus to condemn what had broken up that united front. The Headquarters at Yan-an, having been afraid that things might spread as far as Chongqing, demanded that: Zhou Enlai, Ye Jianying, Dong Biwu, Deng Yingchao and their office and the leading members of the Newspaper Publishing Company should leave Chongqing as soon as possible, but Zhou Enlai had made up his mind to stay there as long as he could. He had thought he would be able to prove himself a match at least in the sphere of the press.

But the Nationalist Newspaper Inspection Office would not allow them to give any information of what had become of Wannan Incident. All that happened in that Incident having been regarded as the matters of military discipline, therefore, as military secrets, the news items were returned with the stamps of "*Shandeng* (deletion)" or "*Miandeng* (dismiss)." The announcement of the authorities had been limited to the line: "The New Fourth Army rose in revolt in the southern part of Anhui Province; the Government ordered they should be dissolved." The articles in which the Communist side reported the details were made to rewrite again and again, while the negotiations repeated again and again turned out to be of no use, and this was to cause their paper to have "a skylight window" as large as half a page.

At midnight, when the deadline for the manuscript was approaching, Zhou Enlai took up his writing brush and wrote down the following almost at a single breath—upon the skylight window on the first page:

For those who fell in Jiangnan as martyrs in the national crisis,

I offer my heartfelt moan.

— on the night of January 17th in the 30th year of Republic of China

Zhou Enlai (his seal)

Then for the skylight window on the second page, he placed a piece of poetry he had just improvised:

A false charge unheard of in our millennia
Has fallen upon a single leaf* in Jiangnan.
What had made the room-mates take arms
Just as beans were roasted with their stalk?

"A single leaf in Wannan" suggests the tragedy in which the New Fourth Army led by Ye (meaning "a leaf") Ting had suffered in Anhui Province in Wannan. The third line mentions the quarrel between brothers, suggesting the struggle between the Nationalists and the Communists. The final line was quoted from a very famous poem in China—*The Poem of Seven Steps* by Cao Zhi (192-232)—to criticize "the folly of making a quarrel between the blood brothers." No concrete fact was mentioned here, but Zhou Enlai did criticize Jiang Jieshi only by means of these literary suggestions.

That epigraph and the poetry written by Zhou's own hand were immediately made into a couple of stereotype wooden boards so that they could fill the skylight windows. Even the censor could not find any excuse to prohibit these. By the time the papers were finished printing, further interference had been prepared: "Printing is permitted but selling is not." Despite this interference, however, the delivery boys, hiding their papers in a bamboo basket or a portmanteau distributed them to each of the subscribers. When Zhou Enlai heard that the dispatch of the paper was being checked in a certain place, he brought himself there and retrieved the papers by negotiating the authorities concerned, and he walked along the street, carrying a large number of papers under his arm to sell the papers in the cold wind for more than two hours, crying: "This is *Xin Hua Ri Bao*. Today we have a specialty to offer. That's why we are selling it like this in the street."

This kind of paper bomb did burst effectively in the hearts of the citizens of Chongqing. The authorities concerned were kept busy for several days on end in confiscating the papers which were being passed from one person to another. The conversation between the secret agent F and "I" that appeared in the novel *Fushi* (*Corrosion*) would have been based on the conversation Mao Dun had actually picked up in the town of Chongqing:

"That *red* paper not only has refused to carry the order given by the Military Committee but also has been so daring as to carry out an outrageous thing against the regulations. I mean—*that* four-line poem."

"Really! Then you are going to give it a ban on publication, aren't you?" I asked him deliberately and gave a glance at his bedside.

"No. Not necessarily. But, we've been kept unusually busy. All day long, we've been capturing people all over the town—depriving them of *the* papers, capturing *the* readers, tearing *the* papers, and what not. Still someone had stuck a bill on an electric pole by the bus stop at Qixing-gong Hill: "Today's paper wanted. Ten *yuan* shall be offered...."

The behavior Zhou Enlai took that day, though not out of desperation, must have been a fairly adventurous one. He, who stood on the street with a bundle of newspapers under his arm, must have been filled with the passion which would never be quenched by any other mode of action. There was something like this sort of passion in his character. Sima Changfeng wrote about it in *A Critical Biography of Zhou Enlai:*

When he was still twenty-eight, he led the insurrection of Nanchang and made a Southern March, leading such a large army as 30,000. This single instance does tell us how daring he was. Many people from abroad, having been dazzled by his witty character and pleasant eloquence, are likely to regard him as a typical person of modern intelligence, but to my mind, they have badly failed to grasp what he really was.

On February 1—two weeks after the Wannan Incident was over—Zhou accepted Theodore White who had come to interview him. By that time, he had already had his rage subsided and was able to give that special correspondent of *TIME* a cool analysis of that Incident. In explaining the development of that case and its background, he had been careful enough not to get two things mixed—his personal anger at that massacre and his objective evaluation of Jiang Jieshi. It was certain that Jiang had not instructed that massacre nor ordered to perform it. But, Jiang must have suggested that he would not mind at all even if the officer in command at the front might have driven the communists off on his own initiative.... "It is hard to get along without any support from the Government. But we shall see *this* all the way through. We shall ask the people for help."—This was what White had written down as what Zhou Enlai had told him after the Wannan Incident.

● "Zhou's Office" as the Secret Headquarters

Zhou's third face to be applied for his work as the Secretary of the Southern Bureau of the Chinese Communist Center—where a variety of decisions were secretly made and issued at midnight—was to lead him to what was even more dangerous and difficult to perform. A single step in a wrong direction might easily take him to an entirely unexpected destination, just as Ye Shan and Xiang Ying were forced to take.

"Zhou's Office" at No.50 of Zengjia-an—which is now preserved as a branch hall of the Revolution Memorial Hall at Hongan—used to be one of the secret headquarters of the Chinese Communist Party. It is a three-storied compact building, overlooking the Jialing. Entering it, and going upstairs by a sharp flight of stairs, narrow and squeaking, one comes to a dusky corridor, which flanks what used to be Zhou's public room. It is about 4.5 meters square. There are chairs for his guests, the bookshelves made of bamboo, a bed, and a couple of office desks, upon which his ink-stone and writing brushes are neatly arranged. This was where he used to prepare many papers, including his reports to be sent to Mao Zedong in Yan-an and some secret directions from the Southern Bureau.

The room next to this was for the use of Dong Biwu, endearingly called "Old Dong"—a senior member who had seen the foundation of the Chinese Communist Party but was still active as a standing committee member of the Southern Bureau and as the chief of Propaganda Department, while engaging in what his open status—a member of the League of National Participation in Politics—required him to do.

The room next to that was for Deng Yingchao or Mrs. Zhou Enlai, who was the chief of the women's party of the Southern Bureau and also a member of the League of National Participation in Politics. Her open, big-sisterly disposition having been found so dependable, she used to be called "Big Sister Deng." Zhou and Deng were known as an affectionate couple, but while the husband was politely called "Comrade Zhou," as he should be, his wife Deng was so energetic as to keep speaking for a couple of hours on end once she came to give a public speech at Juechangkou Square, and this had led her to earn the nickname of "*the* machine gun," which sounded quite right for her. The third floor was an attic, one third of which had been lost by the slanting roof. That small space with no window was for Ye Jianying, who was also on a standing committee of the Southern Bureau and chief of the Military Group. His status open to the public was the chief of staff of the Eighth Route Army. Ye, keeping in close contact with Zhu De, the Supreme Commander in Yanan, and after having received the result of the effort in military maneuvering made by Zhou Enlai as the vice-director of the Department of Politics, was leading the activities for permeation into each grade of the units in the National Revolutionary Army.

At a corner of the inner garden surrounded with the buildings, there was an air-raid cave for private use, and this saved them running as far as the public cave. The whole area in and around Zenjia-an received concentrated attacks by Japan's Operation No. 101, and Zhou's Office had suffered from the air raid several times; on such occasions, Zhou used to stay at his own room and it was not until the second alarm was raised that he ran down the stairs to hide himself in that cave.

When he was at his Office during the daytime, he used to meet many visitors there, including news reporters, special correspondents, ambassadors from abroad, and so on. Thus Zhou's Office, along with the Office of the Eighth Route Army in Hongan Village and the buildings of the publishing company of *Xin Hua Ri Bao*, had formed "a Little Yan-an in the White District" or "the Liaison Section of the Chinese Communist Party," and this caused the Nationalist Party's supervision extremely strict. About fifty meters away from Zhou's Public Office, there was a mansion of white-brick walls, whose resident was the chief of Jun Tong or Dai Li who had been feared as "the terror of Chongqing," and from the spotting station on its third floor, all that Zhou was doing in his room could be thoroughly watched over. What was more, on the second floor of Zhou's Office, there lived a Nationalist official, too, while the reception counter on the first floor was also attended by the Nationalist guards so that it could meticulously be checked what sort of persons were coming in or going out of it.

In the neighborhood of Zhou's Office, there were several teahouses haunted by secret agents, while Dai Li's underlings were often seen, pretending to be tobacco venders. Long Feihu, who had served Zhou as his bodyguard for many years, wrote in his memoir, *The Eleven Years I Spent in Following Vice-Chairman Zhou:*

> After the Wannan Incident, the secret agents' activities were even more strengthened. Around Zhou's Office in Zengjia-an, more than fifty full-time secret agents were being stationed. If anyone left the Office, he was always followed by a couple of secret agents. When the Vice-Chairman's car started, it never failed that a secret agents' car immediately followed it.

This led his guards, trying to give the shadowing agents the slip, to drive along the winding and sloping road in full speed, occasionally changing cars on his way, or employing many other clever ways they had invented to send Zhou Enlai to his destination safe and sound.

In later years—in 1945—assassins began to be sent, and it occurred that Li Shaoshi, an editorial staff member of the *Jin Fua Li Bao*, was shot to death in a car on his way home from a dinner party he had attended in place of Zhou. No doubt, Chongqing was literally a battle field for Zhou Enlai.

● **The Reconstruction of the New Fourth Army**

Zhou, who, as a man of the press, had carved his criticism of the Wannan Incident in history, soon regained his identity as a military leader and set about the reconstruction of the New Fourth Army. It was unbearable for him to leave this combat unit as precious as the Eighth Route Army in a state of devastation. Zhou now—in place of Ye Shan, the then Chief of the Army, now placed in bonds, and Xiang Ying, the Vice Chief, who was no more—appointed Chen Yi, who had been a commander of the first branch corps, one of a few survived leading members (who was to be Foreign Minister in the years to come) to be a deputy chief of the Army and trusted him with the reconstruction of the New Fourth Army. Chen Yi and Zhou Enlai had been friends since they both were studying in France, and they could talk of anything frankly with each other. As for the member of the Political Committee, Zhou sent another reliable comrade Liu Shaoqi (who was to be the President later and died in prison at the Great Cultural Revolution). Thus Zhou devoted himself, trying to bring up the New Fourth Army into even a greater power. The New Fourth Army, which was later called the Third Field Army of the People's Liberation Army, under the leadership of Chen Yi, was to defeat the Nationalist Army in the midst of the Chinese Civil War in the very same place of Jiangnan, thus to perform the retaliation of the Wannan Incident.

When a certain period of time passed after that Incident, Zhou Enlai had an opportunity to tell the facts of the Incident to a group of students and news reporters, as was written in *A Critical Biography of Zhou Enlai* by Sima Changfeng:

After having minutely commented on the circumstances of that Incident, Zhou Enlai said:

"My dear students, this is our land. In order to conquer "the foolishness of our having made a quarrel between our blood brothers," we must forgive and forget everything that has brought about this tragedy. From now on, we must turn our eyes to the future."

After saying so, Zhou cast down his eyes and said that: his mother's tomb was in Zhejiang Province under Japanese occupation, and closed his speech, as follows:

"How happy I shall be if I were able to return there and pull out the weeds around her tomb! That would be the minimum thing I shall be able to do for her—as a libertine, who has devoted his life to the revolution and the homeland...."

In the middle of the 1950s after the Liberation, Zhou Enlai, on his way home from Southeast Asia by way of Yunnan Province—as Prime Minister and concurrently Minister of Foreign Affairs of the People's Republic of China— stopped at Chongqing. His accommodation was at the seat of the Communist Party's Committee, which was situated within a stone's throw from what used to be Zhou's Office at Zengjia-an.

The next morning, the Prime Minister went out for a walk but was very late in coming back. This led his aides—who had felt worried—to go and look for him to find him at what used to be his own room on the second floor of what used to be called "Zhou's Office." He, seated himself in the old chair, seemed to be lost in deep thought.

"Here I used to have a very hard time...."

Zhou Enlai said to his aids who had come in and found him there. Those were the days under the air raids upon Chongqing; That was where his struggles and compromises with Jiang Jieshi—upon which he had spent half of his lifetime—had reached their climax; the humiliation in the Wannan Incident and many other things he had experienced during the eight years in that Anti-Japanese Capital would have been coming and going in his mind.

Literature in Full Bloom in the Save-the-Nation Movement Against Japan

● **The Artists Keeping Active during the Foggy Season in Chongqing**

It was not only Zhou Enlai and his fellow communists in the capital who had been groping for their future in the stoic perseverance at the violent assaults of Japan's Operations No.101 and No.102.

Those writers, journalists, scholars, artists, musicians and so on—under the banners of "the minor democratic parties"—had been unfolding their own anti-Japanese literary movement that was to bring about a remarkable period in the history of the Chinese literature, thus facing against "the conception of strategic bombing," while fostering something new for the period to come.

Even though being annoyed by the two nuisances of air raids and censorship, they—accepting the new circumstances and the new stimulations from their life in exile, while being assisted by the relaxation in the restrictions of traditions and authorities—went on and on, cutting their way through the new spheres of resistance literature. A large number of works that were to win their places in history came into being; especially in the theatrical circles, they were to bring about what was later commented as "the golden period of the China's theatrical activities" in that provisional capital exposed to the air raids.

Since nineteen universities and thirteen companies to publish morning and evening newspapers had moved into that mountain castle in the hinterland, scholars and men of the press were naturally swarming about, while many artists were arriving at Chongqing because they disliked their life being bounded in the occupied areas such as Shanghai, Hongkong, Beijing and so on. Mao Dun, Hu Feng, Tian Han, Xia Yan, Lao She and Ba Jin were among those writers; Chuan Haoshi and Xu Beihong were among the painters; Sha Mei and Xian Xinghai were among the musical composers. Then there came what had popularly been known as "*Wu Zhong* (The Five Largest Theatrical Companies)"—*Zhong Hua Yuyi-she* (Chinese Dramatic Art Company), *Zhong Dian Jujuan* (Chinese Electric Acting Troupe), *Zhong Guo Wan Sui Jujuan* (China's Ten-Thousand-Year-Old Acting Troupe), *Zhong Guo Qing Nian Ju Juan* (China's Youths' Dramatic Company) and *Zhong Guo Yishu Ju She* (China's Artistic Theatrical Company) — along with their stars such as Jin Shan, Bai Yang, Zhang Ruifang and Qin Yi. These men and women of culture and their groups, though facing a number of difficulties in various ways did everything they could under the Government of the National United Front Against Japan.

It was only in the foggy season from late October to April—when the Japanese air raiders were being kept from being active—that their artistic performances were offered to the citizens. It was not long before the people began to associate this long-awaited season with what they called "the Performance in the Foggy Season" or "the Art Season in the Fog."

The writer Mao Dun stayed in Chongqing during the period between the No.101 and No.102 Operations. The scenes of the air raids and of the air-raid caves that often appeared in his novel *Fushi* (Corrosion) were based on his own experiences in Chongqing. The heroine of that novel, Zhao Huiming, asks herself as follows:

"Is this really September 15? The weather is so fine, but there comes no alarm...."

For her it was unbelievable to have no alarm in such fine weather. In September, 1940, or even four years before Japan was to suffer the first air raid, those living in Chongqing had been looking up at the sky, saying such a thing to themselves. They knew they had to wait for more than a month before the arrival of the foggy season. So Zhao Huiming soon had to write:

It was around 1 p.m. when the air-raid warning was called off. I had been in the cave for full two hours. The wavering candle lights had been lighting the sweaty faces, bleary eyes and all those idle talks of anything that happened to come up to their lips....

On another day –

There came an air-raid warning several minutes past ten and it was around one when it was finally called off. I had not eaten anything all this while. Having been confined in the cave so long, with nothing in my stomach, I felt simply miserable. My eyes having been bleary, I was feeling too miserable to say anything to anyone. To my dismay, the moment I managed to have a rest, I had a summons....

And at last, there came round a long-awaited season:

Has the foggy season set in? Yesterday, while walking along the main street, I found many shops—more than a dozen of them—preparing for starting their business; some were newly-opened, others being repaired in haste, either of them with huge advertising posters upon the unfinished establishments, declaring to open on a certain date.

But the suspension of bombings did not necessarily mean a temporary halt of bloodshed:

The foggy season has set in. The enemy planes will not come into our sky. But the bloodiness has been growing more distinct despite "this peaceful appearance of this cityscape."…..

The curtain of fog could provide a cover for political violence. Under the grayish sky, the white terrors performed by the Nationalist Party were growing more and more atrocious year after year. It was while being exposed to such an eerie atmosphere that the artists were writing or painting or singing or acting.

As for the origin of that Art Festival, it had nothing to do with the foggy season of Chongqing. Its origin dated back to the end of 1937 when All China Theatrical Circles' Anti-Enemy's Association was established in Wuhan and it was decided that: their Festival should be annually held on October 10th.

In the year that followed, the Association called out to all the theatrical groups in China to hold their First Theatrical Festival. As it happened, all the main figures in the theatrical world had already been in the new capital, and the Festival that had been held at Chongqing turned out to be of the largest scale— since 2,000 actors and actresses, including the members of the local amateur theatrical groups, took part in it, and lasted for three weeks. From then on, since they began to suffer from continuous air raids from mid-spring through late summer, "the foggy season," "non-bombardment period" and "the Theatre Festival" began to assume an inseparable relationship, and it became established as a large event that included even some other fields of artistic activities.

● Tian Han as the Leader of the Left-Wing Drama Movement

After the Wannan Incident that occurred in January, 1941, the capital also was washed by "an unusually high tide of anti-Communism," and this caused many men of culture to leave for Yan-an or Hongkong. Zhou Enlai, though he was helping Mao Dun and others by organizing their maneuvering for their getting away from the capital, he presented a plan of action for extending the artistic activities during the foggy season from October to May the following year, thus trying to turn Chongqing into a foothold of the cultural united front against the Nationalists' one-party dictatorship.

Now Zhou pointed out the fact that: the mountain castle of Chongqing had turned into "a castle of death." He went on: "We must try our best in breaking down the prohibition and blockades brought about by the Nationalist Party. Among the various forms of art and literature, *the New Drama*, which is likely to link up with the subject of struggles actually going on at present, will exert a great influence upon the people. Then why not turn our new drama into the means of breaking through the situations?"

It was in that same year that Guo Moruo's historical drama of *Tangdi Flowers* and *Qu Yuan* were premiered, and the choral piece of *The Great Chorus of the Huang Ho* (the Yellow River), created by the poet Guang Weiran and the composer Xian Xinghai, were to appeal to the audience not only for their resistance to Japan for the sake of their patriotism but also for their criticism against the Nationalist Party's dictatorship.

The Nationalist authorities' supervision and censorship were also strict in this direction, and this led to deletion of a portion of the script, to forced revision and to prohibition on presentation, and even to such harassment as to impose a heavy tax on the admission charge. On the other hand, they prohibited the people from holding a meeting or a debate.

In order to get the better of such authorities, Zhou Enlai's side or the Communist Party's Southern Bureau devised a method of holding someone's birthday celebration or someone's memorial gathering—such as "For Celebrating the Twenty-Fifth Anniversary of Master Guo Moruo's Creative Activity" or "For Celebrating the Sixtieth Anniversary of Master Lu Xun's Birth" or "For Celebrating Master Hon Shen's Fiftieth Birthday"—these were rather hard for anyone to make any complaint—so that they could guard the front line of the National United Front Against Japan.

The one who stood as the leader of these activities was Guo Moruo— who was at first the Chief of the Third Office of the Military Committee's Administration Department, and now was brought down to the chief of the Committee of Cultural Maneuvering. He administered all of these "front activities" of the Communist Party, keeping a close contact with Zhou Enlai.

The Committee of Cultural Maneuvering had a dramatist Tian Han, Mao Dun and Hong Shen on the standing committee. Tian Han, a poet who wrote *The Volunteer Army March*, which was later made the Chinese national anthem, was also a leader of the leftist dramatists. He was loved by everyone for his boldness and big heartedness. He spent most of his days at Guilin during the National United Front Against Japan, but from May in 1940 to March in the following year, he was staying at that war-time capital under Japan's No. 101 Operations, which was followed by the Wannan Incident. It was on May 20, when the No.101 Operations started, and Tian Han's arrival at Chongqing was May 23, and this was to make him lead a life in which he could not find even a moment of restfulness while moving from one air raid cave after another, but his spirit remained incorruptible and high, and he started his activities with a lecture he gave at Bashu Elementary School. His audience was mainly those in the theatrical or movie circles, and he spoke under such titles as "The Resistance to Japan and the Art Concerning It" or "Let's Confirm our Faith in our Unfailing Victory!" thus calling out to the various democratic parties for uniting themselves. His unique way of laughing that sounded "Haa! Haa! Haa!" is said to have brightened the hearts of the people around him.

On October 19 in the same year, at the meeting for "The Fourth Anniversary of Lu Xun's Demise," Tian Han and Guo Moruo gave a lecture. They had a large audience of more than six hundred, including such prominent figures as Zhou Enlai, Hu Feng and Chen Junru. The one to preside over the meeting was Feng Yuxiang, known as "Christian General," a deputy chairman of the Military Affairs Committee under Chairman Jiang Jieshi. Feng was a survivor of a military clique that had established influence in Yingyuan of China (present-day Inner Mongolia Autonomous Region) since 1920's, and now at the Chongqing Administration, he was known as one of the few people who criticized Jiang Jieshi's anti-Communist despotism—along with Sun Ke or Sun Wen's eldest son and Li Dequan or Mrs. Feng. If a memorial gathering for Lu Xun were to be presided over by General Feng, even the authorities concerned could not interfere with it.

The following was what Tian Han delivered on that occasion in admiration of Lu Xun:

What is of the greatest value in Master Lu Xun's achievements would be his thoroughgoing hatred he demonstrated toward the old-fashioned system of society and the old-fashioned custom. Our own criticism toward them usually remains far from being so acute and quite likely to make a compromise with the old-fashioned custom. In this direction, Master Lu Xun presents himself as a good teacher to us. Especially his having firmly retained his way of life, upholding his fighting spirit of non-compromise and disobedience till the end of his life, would be the greatest point we should learn from him. Our old society—like a narcotic—does provide us with power of absorbing poisons. Because we have kept much contact with the old society and have been made to get accustomed to it, we are quite likely to forget fighting, while compromising with the old society again and again. This is something least recommendable. Now is the time for us to strengthen our power of criticism, so we may not easily choose the way of compromise and submission.

—A Chronicle of Chongqing's Resistance to Japan

What Tian Han was then appealing to the audience while reviewing the life of Lu Xun was the need to assemble their powers of criticizing the Nationalist Party's dictatorship. Tian Han now expressed his protest and anger against the current that was trying to disturb—as much as that wicked power that dropped the bombs from the sky—the National United Front Against Japan by turning their noble fight for "saving the nation and their land" into a narrow-minded battle for "keeping the Nationalist Party."

After the Wannan Incident, Tian Han was also among those who left Chongqing behind, but considering his speech and conduct, it was natural for him to take refuge somewhere else. For those artists and intellectuals, who had not had any such status open to the public as "a membership of the Society of Participating National Politics" or "the representative of the Eighth Route Army" — there was nothing to protect themselves in "the white area". if the government situations had changed or they were regarded as "undesirable persons" by the Nationalist Special Service Agency.

● An Anti-Japanese Dramas, *Sishi Tang Tang*, had Begun to be Written by Lao She

The writer, Lao She, though not so active as Tian Han, was also in Chongqing, hearing the daily explosions of bombs, while working out a plan of writing a grand novel that would be passed down to the generations to come. It was in the suburbs of Chongqing that he started on the first volume of *Si Shi Tong Tang* (The Four Generations in the Same Hall). Lao She, who was to die a tragic death in the midst of the Great Cultural Revolution, was still in his earliest forties or in the prime of manhood.

Lao She, who had already made himself a writer of established fame by *Mr. Ma and His Sons, Luotuo Xiangzi* (A Camel named Xiangzi) and so on, discarded his life of teaching and writing in Shandong Province in July, 1937, when Japan's invasion into China began to show the signs of spreading all over the Continent, and went by himself over to Wuhan as the strongpoint of Anti-Japanese movement, and together with Ba Jin, Mao Dun and others, participated in organizing the China's Literary Circles' Association for Resisting the Enemy and took on the task as the chief of its general affairs department. After the fall of Wuhan, he moved to Chongqing along with that Association, and even though moving from place to place because of the air raids he suffered there, he kept staying in Chongqing till the end of the war against Japan. At the air raids of "5.3. & 5.4." which led him to write *The Night of 5.4.*, he lost his abode. By and by, the meeting place of that Association was also burnt down during No.

101 Operation.

While he was in Wuhan and then in Chongqing, he wrote many play scripts and novels; for the Theater Festival in the Foggy Season, too, he wrote *Can Wu* (The Remaining Fog) and *Mianzi Wenti* (A Matter of Honor). On the other hand, Lao She had kept a wish to write a full-length novel on the Anti-Japanese War. What he had been reading about how they were fighting against Japan in various parts of China, as was being reported in the daily newspapers published in Chongqing—the air raids and the burning streets and the people being killed in them—did stimulate Lao She as a writer, but to him, who had been born and brought up in Beijing, the climate and language in Sichuan Province seemed to be somehow or other not suitable as a setting for a novel he had held in mind. The first novel he wrote in Chongqing—*Huo Zang* (The Cremation)—had turned out to be far from satisfactory even to himself.

Still he had not run out of luck. In the autumn, 1942, his wife, Hu Jieqing, and their three children came to join him in Chongqing. They, after having taken care of Lao She's mother until she passed away in Beijing under the occupation of the Japanese Army, had left there to come up to Chongqing. Every day he was voraciously listening to what his wife told him—about how Beijing was changed, what the Japanese Army was doing there and what the life of the people in the occupied area was like. By and by, Lao She found an outline of a full-length novel about the fates of the Beijinese left in the land under the occupation coming to form itself. Now Lao She said to his wife: "How thankful I am! By getting out of Beijing after a narrow escape from death, you have brought me a full-length novel—the longest one in my life."

That was how he started to write that novel—*Si Shi Tong Tang* (Four Generations in the Same Hall). That was a story of those living in Beijing during the wartime. But it was also a saga he produced while "clenching his fists and grinding his teeth with vexation" at the rampancy of the Japanese bombers that kept annoying those living in Chongqing. The hero, Master Qian, sounds as if he were throwing his words to the Japanese bombers in the sky:

"Someday, the Japanese will ask me from above my head: "Was it your sons who had killed us?" Then I shall say, sticking out my chest before their guns: "Certainly you are right!" Then I will say to them: "We have many more youths like my sons. Even if you may arrive here in large mounted troops, we shall be ready to chop each of you into small pieces!"

In August, 1966, Lao Shi, who had a plate with a label of "Counter-Revolutionary Element" hung from his neck by the Red Guards and was subjected to a harsh kangaroo court, chose to sink himself to death at Lake Taiping in Beijing. A gatekeeper of the park had noticed an old man who had been standing by the pond all day long since early in the morning. At midnight, he drowned himself to death. No one can tell what Lao Shi was thinking about while looking at the water in the pond all day long. But it would be certain that: he had let his days in Chongqing—the days he spent as a writer and a fighter—come and go, come and go, in a kaleidoscopic manner in the final recollections of his life. Those were the brilliant days when he was fighting along with the united front of "various minor democratic factions"; those were the memories of flame and blood that led him to write *The Night of 5.4.*,—and he must have been recalling those charming expressions on the youthful face of Zhou Enlai....

● ***The Great Chorus of the Huanghe* was Premiered—the Starting Point of *Save the Nation by Fighting Against Japan***

It was also in the foggy season of Chongqing that *The Great Chorus of the Huanghe* (the Yellow River)—a piece for a mixed chorus—was introduced to the public for the first time.

Our Friends! Have you ever seen the Huanghe?

This is how this long chorus starts. The paean to the Huanghe as the Mother River for the Chinese takes a form of a dialogue with the Huanghe, an expression of their love of Her. It was also an expression of their patriotism under the pretext of their love of Huanghe, an explosion of their hatred for their enemy, the muttering of their grievance; all of these being included in this single chorus, this did remind the whole people of China of the starting point of *Save the Nation Against Japan*. It was immediately after the Wannan Incident that occurred early in 1941, when *The Great Chorus of the Huanghe* was premiered under the sponsorship of the Chinese Branch of the International Movement Against Anti-Invasion.

The First Part: *The Song of the Boatmen on the Huanghe*, the Second Part: *An Eulogy on the Huanghe*, the Third Part: *The Water of the Huanghe Comes from the Heavens*, the Fourth, the Fifth, the Sixth, the Seventh and the Eighth went on with male and female solos, recitations and choruses to reach its climax at the Eighth Part in which her anger, howling and struggling are poured out:

> We, the four hundred and fifty million people,
> have completed our harmonious co-operation.
> With no fear of death, let us defend our Land!
> Listen! Listen! Listen!
> The Songhua's calling.
> The Heilong is calling.
> The Zhu-liang is giving a heroic cry.
> On the Yangzi, there rises and rises
> The beacon of the United Front against Japan!
> Ah, Huang Ho! Give Your Angry roars!
>   Angry roars! Angry roars!

This chorus—the words created by Guang Weiran, the music by Xian Xinghai—was staged by the conductor Ming Min and filled the hearts of the audience with heated emotion. It was during the foggy season between Japan's Operations No.101 and No.102.. Those living in Chongqing—who had to bear the hardships throughout the summer of bombings, the summer of fatigue, the summer of sorrow, only to be relieved by the winter that brought about a muffler of fog and the artistic performance—were to get prepared for the end of the foggy season, so that they could face bravely at the following season to come round.

Guo Moruo's *Qu Yuan* was Premiered

● **The Determination to Perform the White Terror**
It was also during the foggy season from the autumn of 1941 to the year that followed that Guo Moruo's *Tangdi Flowers* and *Qu Yuan* were premiered. The presentations of these plays were to pierce the people with such a great shock

as might be called an event. It turned out to be another kind of bombardment performed by Guo Moruo as a playwright against the bombs released from Japanese planes and against the hand grenades thrown by white terrorists from behind the curtain of fog. The chorus repeatedly sung in *Tangdi Flowers*—the song dedicated by the big sister to her younger brother about to go on a journey to perform his aim of assassinating the King—does sound like a paean of revolutionary terrorism:

> If this is the last resort
> we shall be able to make,
> You shall go, my Brother.
> You shall go, my Brother.
> I do hope your crimson blood will
> spurt to bloom into flowers of freedom
> till they fill this ancestral land of ours,
> till they fill this ancestral land of ours.
> Then you shall go, my dearest brother.
>
> What this ancestral land seeks is liberty.
> What this ancestral land seeks is liberty.
> While our enemies like so many wolves are
> about to devour this land of our ancestors,
> Woe to the nobles, they are simply busy in
> Their personal strife, forgetting their duty.
>
> You are the one we have been seeking for.
> You are the one we have been seeking for.
> Break off the chains enslaving us like this.
> Why not declare we ourselves are masters?
> Now, come on and let's march arm in arm
> Raise our flags high, the flags of liberation!

At the end of the stage directions in the playbook, Guo Moruo wrote as follows:

——The curtain falls while the chorus is still going on. According to the situation, it may be repeated more than three times. ——

Guo had written this drama upon the bases of a historical fact in the Spring and Autumn and Warring States Periods (770BC-221BC), firmly intending to offer a challenge to Jiang Jieshi's Administration. What he wrote at the end of the stage directions could be taken: "If the inspector does not stop, the chorus can be repeated as many times as you like."

I do hope
your crimson blood
will spurt and bloom into
flowers of freedom
till
they
Fill this land of our ancestors!

Guo Moruo, triumphantly declaring like this, gave his answer and resolution on the side of the United Front against the terrorism given by the Nationalist Party. *Tangdi Flowers*, having been received with such enthusiasm that it was presented as many as twenty-four times during the period of the first performance in November, 1941.

To the audience, it was readily understandable what the author wanted to ask them: Who could really be the King and the Prime Minister of the Land of Han who were put to death by the brother and sister, Zhe Zheng and Zhe Ei? What did the hero's selfless spirit and self-sacrifice mean—when it came to such a terrible extent as Zhe Zheng, after having performed his aim of assassinating the wicked two, scraped off his eye-lids, lips, nose and even his ears with his long sword, thus turning himself into a sort of monster before he fell on his own sword, so that he could not be identified, thus to keep his sister safe? It was a historical play, but it could be recognized as a sort of criticism toward what was actually happening then in their daily life in the capital.

Xiao Jianxiang then was still eleven or twelve years old, but he could still remember very well how much he was moved by *The Tangdi Flowers* at its first performance in Chongqing. In order to obtain the ticket, he had been staying overnight in front of the ticket office. He still remembers very well how eagerly he was staring at what was happening on the stage; he trembled at each word delivered by Zhe Zheng; at the militant chorus at the denouement, he found himself joining it before he noticed it. It happened long ago, but to him the memory has still remained fresh. Xiao Jianxiang had not intended to be a writer at that time, but even today he thinks the world he was awakened to through those dramatic works of *Tangdi Flowers* and *Qu Yuan* was really wide and profound. That was what had happened not only to Xiao but also to many other youths living at that wartime capital.

Zhou Enlai, who had a good understanding of Guo Moruo, remaining always together throughout the eight years of the Anti-Japanese War, commented on him in 1941—in memory of Guo's 25th year as a writer—comparing him with Lu Xun:

Lu Xun was the originator of the New Cultural Movement, while Guo Moruo is a fighter for the New Cultural Movement. Lu Xun, a pioneer, created a road where there was nothing like that, while Guo Moruo has made that road smooth so that many people may go ahead.

● **"I Wrote, Loved, and Offered Myself to the Revolution"**

Guo Moruo was a man of versatility and sensitivity. A lyric poet, a revolutionist and a historian as he was, he made an achievement also as a statesman. He had thrown himself into a revolutionary movement led by Sun Wen about the same period as Zhou Enlai and Mao Zedong did, but he did not put himself into the framework of politics. During the nine years from July in 1937 to May in 1946, Guo Moruo engaged himself in daily activities as an excellent organizer, an instigator and a secret agent, while creating 301 poems, seven dramas, six novels, thirty-seven historical articles, twenty-four essays, forty theories on literary art, 114 critical essays and thirty-nine sketches of characters.

No sooner had he returned home with great reluctance—leaving his wife and five children in Japan where he had sought asylum—than he was to devote himself to his new sweet heart, Yu Liqun. In other words, Guo Moruo was an exceptional man of literature, a statesman of unusual ability, and above all, a man of passion—produced by China during her age of upheavals. "I wrote, loved and offered myself to the revolution," said he. No other comment would be more appropriate than this in describing his life.

While he was in Chongqing, his open status as his lifeline was the chairman of the Third Office of the Administration Department in the Military Affairs Committee of the Supreme Committee for the National Defense, that was, the war-directing organization of the Nationalist Government. As mentioned before, the Third Office was scaled down on October 1, 1940—by releasing a large number of leftist men of culture—to the Culture Maneuvering Committee in the Administration Department of the Military Affairs Committee, but Guo Moruo remained chief of that Committee. To turn this fruit or the sanctuary of Nationalist-Communist Collaboration that had clung to the center of the Nationalist authority into "the Trojan Wooden Horse" of the Communist Party was the mission for Guo Moruo to perform. If Zhou Enlai as the representative of the Control Office of the Eighth Route Army were to be the director at the backstage, Guo Moruo as the chairman of the Culture Maneuvering Committee could be compared to the actor on the stage. Thus Zhou and Guo, getting along with each other, kept producing from "the Wooden Horse" of the Third Office one fresh troop after another, thus to keep defending the Communist foothold at the capital of Jiang Jieshi.

"Chongqing's Horrors"—the Juntong's secret agents under the command of Dai Li and the Zhongtong's secret agents working for "the Two Chens"—were even more persistent in keeping their eyes on Guo Moruo and on those who were associated with him than on Zhou Enlai, but Guo could easily beat them, because he had gone through many more ups and downs in his life than any of them since he joined the Army in the Northern Expedition (1926) led by Jiang Jieshi to see the revolt at Nanchang (1927) which had brought the Red Army into being, to take refuge in Japan (1927) to return home immediately after the Lukouqiao Incident* (1937) to fight against Japan. What was more, he had kept an unapproachable amulet that declared him to be a Nationalist since he was following Sun Wen.

Beside his official position, he had kept many honorary posts numbering thirteen. The Honorary Director of the Chongqing Branch of the Young Reporters' Society, the Director of the Sino-Soviet Cultural Society, the Secretary of the Resistance Association of the United Movie Circles of China, and the Standing Secretary of All the Anti-Civil-War Associations in Chongqing were the main posts among the many, and his activities, versatile and kaleidoscopic, were to be guarded by the walls of those "various democratic parties," but his central strong foothold always remained at the Cultural Maneuvering Committee. Even after the Third Office of the Administration Department was reorganized into the Cultural Maneuvering Committee, he kept holding two offices—one in Shizhon (City's Central) Ward (at No. 7 Tianguanfu); the other in the suburbs (at Laijiaquao, Quanjia-yuanzi)—and more than one hundred members in the personnel list were being embraced with "the fund from the Nationalist Party."

The Cultural Maneuvering Committee, whose chief was Guo Moruo, had three vice chiefs—Yang Hansheng, a well-known playwright, and two others; as for the standing committees, there were Chen Yanbing whose pen name was Mao Dun, Tian Han, Hu Feng and Hong Shen. They all having already established themselves as a novelist or a dramatist or a director, they were quite suitable for their activities for Cultural Maneuvering. Their daily routine consisted of three fields: the first group was for the researches into international complications (the chief: Zhang Tiesheng); the second group was for the study on literary art (the chief: Tian Han); the third group was for the study on the movements of the enemy (the chief: Feng Aichao). Among the members of the third group were Midorikawa Eiko (Hasegawa Teru) and her husband, Liu Ren. This group, beside its formal aim of studying the enemy's movements, had another organization of analyzing the information concerning "the Second Hongan" (the Chinese Communist Center in the Southern Bureau) buried into it, and this was perfectly covered up as "the secret room in the Castle area" or "the secret room in the suburbs."

In other words, the Committee of Cultural Maneuvering was substantially the stronghold of the United Front directed by the Chinese Communist Southern Bureau, and it could be called "a culturally liberated area" in the White Area. But, however obstructive and dangerous it might have appeared to the Nationalist Party, it stood on the base which could not be destroyed so easily as long as the Nationalist-Communist Collaboration was existent. If that was thoughtlessly touched, the Government was to lose both of its internationally guaranteed fame of "Free China" and the banner of "the National United Front Against Japan." It was not until 1945 that Jiang Jieshi took the decision to break up the Culture-Maneuvering Committee, and that was none other than signal of the outbreak of the Chinese Civil War between the Nationalists and the Communists.

● **The Libretto of *Qu Yuan* was Written in only Ten Days**

It was under such circumstances in such a period of time as this that *Qu Yuan*, a historical drama, which was to be a representative work of Guo Moruo, was brought into his mind.

After the Wannan Incident, the Anti-Communist Policy was being even more intensified. And this had been affecting the activities of the Cultural Maneuvering Committee. Those who had been at the front of cultural activities—Tian Han, Guang Weiran, Xia Yan, Mao Dun, Hu feng and Zou Taofen—could not help leaving Chongqing if they were to consider their own safety. Then there came round the summer of 1941—the days and nights of fatigue and fear brought about by the series of air raids in Operation No. 102, which was made unforgettable by "the terrible disaster at the air raid tunnel."

These led Guo Moruo to criticize Jiang Jieshi's Administration under the disguise of his poem, *The Pyramid of Crimes and Sins*, but that was far from effective to relieve his indignation.

There was also a practical need for him to create that drama. Zhou Enlai had brought forward a proposition that: the art performance during the foggy season should be prolonged in a drastic scale—from October to May in the following year—to call back that enthusiasm for retaining the United Front. But the scripts of the greatest importance had to suffer a short supply, because many men of literature to produce any such scripts had already left Chongqing. All Guo Moruo could do then was to produce a play script by himself and for himself. This was how *The Tangdi Flowers*, his first work in the Series of the Warring States Period (770BC—221BC), was brought into being. What was boiling in his heart then would have made him closer to *the* terrorist he had compared himself to than a mere supporter of the National United Front Against Japan. After seeing the great success of *The Tangdi Flowers*, he at once started on his second work *Qu Yuan*.* Here, again, his fury against what was happening in Chongqing then led him to revive the ancient age in which Qu Yuan lived, giving speeches so vigorous as to gush out of the stage.

*Qu Yuan (a patriotic man of literature from the Royal Family of the Land of Chu (343?B.C.-277B.C.)) was trying hard to retrieve the power of his land, but his slanderers expelled him and led him to such despair as to throw himself into the Miluo.

The script of that five-act historical drama was finished in ten days or so. There was not a single moment of stagnancy, as if realizing that line written by Han Yu: "a gush of water goes a thousand miles in a few moments." What Guo Moruo was seeking then was not the details of historical facts but inspiring the spirit of modern times into the tragedy Qu Yuan had suffered, while calling back Qu Yuan's fighting spirit to the present day. So it was not necessary for him to do any strict checking of historical artifacts. What was more, having written about Qu Yuan in his treatises again and again from youth onward, he had already established his image of Qu Yuan. It was completed on January 11, 1942. As for that memorable moment, it was recorded as follows by Nikolai Fedlenko, a member of the Russian Embassy in Chongqing, who had been known as a scholar on the Chinese literature. He was to be the ambassador to Japan after World War Ⅱ.

One day, I was consulting a dictionary at Guo Moruo's library. The poet himself was working at his study. Then I heard him draw his chair, followed by his hurried steps. On seeing me, he said, showing me his broken pen:

"Wow! I can't tell what I should do. My pen has got broken! If I were to believe in the superstition, I should think this is a bad omen."

I just took out my fountain pen and said:

"Don't mind. Please use this."

The poet, receiving it, hurriedly went back. To me he then seemed to have had no other notion but putting on the paper *the* conception that had caught him *then* and *there*.

Exactly one minute later, the poet made his appearance again. Now his face was brightened with joy. The radiant smile upon his face, as was seen upon the face of a young man, appeared especially beautiful. He said, holding out that fountain pen toward me:

"Thanks to this pen, I have just finished *Qu Yuan*."

It could be said: none other than *the* author himself of *Qu Yuan* was the first to have been blessed with the spiritual abreaction by *it*.

● **Zhou Enlai's Support Helped to Bring about a Great Success**

in the Premiere

It was Zhou Enlai who made preparations for the presentation of that script on the stage. Zhou had been known for his love of dramatic performance; when he was still a student of Nankai Middle School in Tianjin, he appeared on the stage in a female role at the school festival; At the Eighth Route Army's Control Office at Hongyan Village, too, he used to take an opportunity of dancing with the workers there at a brief time for rest; in the downtown of Chongqing, too, he used to make time to enjoy visiting this theater or that. The actresses endearingly called him Hu Gong (by one of his aliases, meaning Prince Hu or Prince Someone from Abroad), and before the curtain was raised, they used to lift the foot of it a little, trying to find out whether or not if he was among the audience, and his presence there strained them or excited them. After the curtain fell, too, they enjoyed listening to him as a theater critic.

Now Zhou, who had read the play script of *Qu Yuan*, was moved so much that he decided on his plan of action: "The presentation of this play shall be supported by all the hands available; The advertisement shall be strengthened to back up the presentation." The substantial supreme command was to be taken by Zhou Enlai, probably because that was considered not merely the matter of a hobby or relaxation but an indication of the will to go on fighting shown by the Communist Party and the Democratic Parties to those citizens who had been beaten up by the air raids while being frightened by the white terrors.

Zhou Enlai collected the stars, disregarding the frameworks of dramatic companies. Qu Yuan was to be acted by Jin Shan, who had just arrived here from Hong Kong; a lady attendant Chan Juan by Zhang Rifang from Nuhou Drama Company; Nan Hou, the favorite mistress of the King who was to drive Qu Yuan into a corner was Bai Yang from Zhong Dian Theatrical Company. Those popular actors and actresses were chosen through the interview by Zhou Enlai. As for the director, he invited Chen Liting, who was teaching at the National Professional School for Dramaturgy, while directing the Chinese Drama Company. As for the music to accompany Qu Yuan's monologue of "*Lei Dian Song* (an Eulogy for Thunder and Lightning)," Liu Xuean, a composer, was requested to create. Thus a lineup unprecedented in history was to come into being to demonstrate their abilities on the stage.

What baffled them most was the fact that: they could rarely find any place for their stage rehearsal. Many of the theaters having suffered damage from the air raids, it was impossible for any theater to be used for stage rehearsal. This problem, however, was also solved by Zhou Enlai. He had a heap of rubbles— just next to *Guotai Juyuan* (National Peace Theater: the place for their public performance)—cleaned to bring into being a space as wide as a real stage. In that open-air stage—surrounded piles of burnt bricks and timber, wrapped up by the fog so thick that they could hardly see the expression of those they were talking to—their preparations for *Qu Yuan* were made. The fog having covered the whole of Chongqing, they were free from any worry of suffering an air raid. Zhou Enlai found his time to visit here, too.

That historical drama *Qu Yuan* in five acts, premiered in March, 1942, at the theater, *Guotai Juyuan*—which had often been made a target for the bombing— turned out to be a marvelous success. All the audience was fascinated at the stage, sharing their anger and enthusiasm, while sending their heartfelt clapping on to the stage.

When Qu Yuan acted by Jin Shan called out to the body of Chan Juan who had drunk a poisoned cup dry, substituting herself for him: "Oh, my Chan Juan, my child, my disciple, my benefactress, you are now burning into flames!" waves of sobbing went spreading all over the auditorium.

"Even I (Zhang Ruifang) who ought to "have died" by acting as Chan Juan could not suppress my tears; the author and his work had melted into one in my heart; I felt as if I had touched Chan Juan's soul; To me as an actress, that was the happiest time in my life," said Zhang Ruifang in later years.

As Zhou and Guo had expected, the people of Chongqing—instead of taking Qu Yuan's sad fate as something that had happened in the far-off days of King Huai of Chu who had to confront the tremendous power of Qin—replaced it into the conspiracies, persecutions and horrors swirling in the war-time capital being invaded by Japan, and took it as something now going on at present under "the Jiang Dynasty."

In the first performance, it was staged twenty-one times, and each time they had a full house. Students, having come from the university town in Shaci Ward, had no means of transportation on their way back, and this led them to walk back for four hours. What was recited by them on such an occasion was

Qu Yuan's monologue in *Lei Dian Song* (A Song in Praise of Thunder and Lightning) at the denouement. Jin Shan acting as Qu Yuan sang in a resonant voice to the orchestral accompaniment. That monologue, as was commented by Zhou Enlai, was "what Guo Moruo expressed his own resentment through the speech of Qu Yuan, a patriotic poet in the ancient times":

> You, Storm, howl and roar! Howl and roar! Howl and roar as much as you can! In this deadly darkness, when all is asleep, all is sunken into dreaming and all is gone dead, you'll find your time of howling has finally arrived! (an omission)
>
> Oh, the flashes of lightning, you, the sharpest swords in the universe— I have been deprived of my sword created by Lu Li. Even if my tangible sward might be deprived, none would be able to deprive me of the sward intangible!—You, a flash of lightning, you are a sword of the universe. And also the sword of my spirit. Burst! Burst! Burst! Burst this darkness harder than iron!
>
> But I shall remain tearless. The universe also has stood tearless. What is the use of tears? What I've kept with me is a thunderbolt. A thunderbolt! A Storm! We don't have anything like rain that splashes back the mud. This is my will. The will of the universe. Roar, the storm! Howl, the thunder! Flash, the lightning! Burn up everything asleep in this dead by darkness! Do burn up everything!

The students on their way back to their boarding houses used to walk along the street, thus spreading Qu Yuan's indignation all over the streets of Chongqing. In that year, when the new spirit of resistance was thus being laid up in that foggy capital on the mountain, the Sino-Japanese War had already been in its sixth year.

The Anti-War Union of the Japanese Residents in China

● **A Determination Made by Hasegawa Teru who had Married a Chinese**
Though small in number, there were several Japanese people, too, in Chongqing. While running away from the bombings brought about by their

compatriots, they were living up to their own patriotic faith that: Japan must not invade China, and that: they should admonish the Japanese soldiers in China against holding guns. Hasegawa Teru, Kaji Wataru and Ikeda Sachiko were among those Japanese.

In November 27, 1937, a French ship set sail from Port Huangbu of Shanghai for Hongkong. Only four months had passed since Lukouquao Incident* occurred. Among those who were in the passenger boat, there were Guo Moruo and Hasegawa Teru, too. The former had just returned home from Japan where he had been seeking refuge. The latter had just entered China after having left her native land, Japan, for good. The two were total strangers to each other then, but according as the war situations were changing, both of them were led to Chongqing by way of Wuhan to be united by the same mission.

Upon the Huangbu River, Izumo, the flagship of the Third Fleet of Japan, which was to be renamed Fleet of the China Region a month later, had anchored. Nomura Kichisaburo had once raised his flag of admiralty upon it, and two years later Inoue Shigeyoshi was to get on board the same ship.

When Guo Moruo was looking at it from his French ship, a water plane came up from about Izumo and flew around three times above his ship at low altitude before it flew away. What that unpleasant demonstration meant was unknown, but all the people on board that French ship, though remaining silent, had shown their fury on their face, as Guo Moruo wrote in his *Memoirs on the Anti-Japanese War*. Guo Moruo entered the cabin, as he was urged to do so by the sailors who assured the passengers of their safety once they left Wosongkou. To his surprise, he saw there many leading figures of the Nationalist Party getting out of Shanghai. Among them, he saw Zou Taofen who had kept *Shenghuo* (Life) Book Store at Shanghai. This led Guo Moruo to say to himself: "For that Japanese plane, this ship was worth   bombing, though it didn't."

As for Hasegawa Teru, having managed to find a small space on a shelf board as wide as a single bed in a room that seemed to be usually used as a private room for the odd jobbers, she was lying on it, suffering from seasickness. In Shanghai, she saw for the first time the Japanese planes drop bombs. Hasegawa Teru, a Japanese woman, who had married a Chinese, could not remain cool. She felt her words of appealing to the Japanese soldiers near by—in the sky of Shanghai and on the Huangbu River—coming up to her throat: "You are also victims of fascists." (It was nine months later that Teru's broadcasting as a pacifist announcer began to reach the front.) What was annoying her then was not only the seasickness but also the uneasy feeling toward the unknown land and uncertain future she was about to face from then on. In fact, never again was she able to step on her ancestral land of Japan.

Guo Moruo, who entered Wuhan by way of Hongkong, went to the Control Office of the Eighth Route Army, which used to be a Japanese concession, to enjoy a happy reunion with Zhou Enlai and his wife, Deng Yingchaos, Dong Biwu and some other old friends of his for the first time in ten years, and it was on that occasion that he was eagerly requested directly by Chen Cheng, the chief of the Military Affairs Committee's Administration Department, that he should lead its Third Office that was to take charge of advertisement. As for the vice chief of the Administration Department, Zhou Enlai had already been decided upon, though not formally yet. It was during the time when the Nationalist-Communist Collaboration was being put into practice with fervor and substance. While making preparations for personnel matters and projects, Guo recommended his old friends Kaji Wataru and his wife Ikeda Sachiko as the persons in charge of one of the tasks of the Third Office—the advertisement to the enemy. Guo had happened to hear that: the couple at that time, having been driven from Shanghai by the wartime fire, was hiding themselves in Hongkong, but seeking for help from the poverty they were suffering there. Guo, having felt that none would be more appropriate than Kaji in performing the advertisement to the enemy, asked Chen Cheng to employ Kaji, earnestly saying:

> "Kaji is a pacifist writer. He graduated from Tokyo Imperial University, a contemporary with Feng Naichao. Kaji was persecuted at home and this led him to take refuge in Hongkong. If we call him, I'm sure he will come and help us to a great extent."
>
> —*My Memoir* by Guo Moruo

Chen Cheng agreed to Guo Mouro's proposal and immediately sent a telegram to Hongkong and arranged for their safe arrival to Wuhan. At Hongkong, Xia Yan, a writer and the chief editor of *Jiu Wu Ri Bao* (Relief Daily Paper), made himself a messenger and went around till he finally found out Kaji's hideout. Kaji, who was invited to Wuhan a week later, was made an adviser (with the status of Major General) to the seventh group of the Third Office of the Administration Department. This was how a post was prepared for the Japanese at a corner of that Anti-Japanese Administration. By and by, Hasegawa Teru was also called to Wuhan through the kind offices of Guo Moruo, Tian Han and others, and was to engage in broadcasting against the war Japan had started—at the group of broadcasting to Japan in the International Advertisement Section of the Nationalist Party's Central Advertisement Department.

● To the Chinese Soldiers and the Japanese Soldiers at the Front Line

Hasegawa Teru's life at Wuhan lasted only for three months or so, because the fall of the Three Towns of Wuhan in October, 1938, led her to move to Chongqing. But her life in Wuhan was to be looked back upon by her with such a deep emotion as she later wrote in one of her works—*In China at War*: ".... But what an exciting, active and tense period of life we were leading then!" She was then experiencing the days when the passion brought about by the unity of the nation, the government and the military had reached its climax, and the Nationalist-Communist collaboration had been perfectly realized. While taking part in the Battle to Guard the Great Wuhan, Hasegawa Teru had grown into a new personality with a new sensibility through her own experiences of seeing, hearing and feeling what she had never come across in the narrow sphere of her life so far. Hasegawa Teru who had named herself 緑川英子 (Luchuan Yinzi: Green-River Bright-One) had her letter—"To the Chinese soldiers in the front line"—published in *Xin Hua Ri Bao* (New China Daily), dated August 20:

I have always wished I could go and fight at the front line to knock down the invaders, as you are doing, but I still remain unable to do so, because I am afraid of being killed by you. At least, you will have hard feelings against me and shout at me, because I have come from the land of your enemies.

I know it is the Japanese militarists that have driven you into such suffering and tribulation. They have killed many of your brothers and assaulted many of your sisters. We have done totally wrong, and unpardonable.

If I had one hundred bodies, I'd like to go up to the Japanese military and appeal to them *not* to kill their brothers in China, *not* to kill those farmers in China. And if I were able to obtain one hundred hands, I'd be running around the battlefields to give the injured medical treatment and do washing for them.

My dear brothers in the front line, let me tell you that: all that the Japanese military depend upon is nothing but excellent arms, and those arms do not come up to your courage nor to your capacity for union, because the Japanese military have simply kept fighting without any proper reason for fighting.

I do hope you will do your best in perseverance. I myself am going to do everything I can in supporting this Anti-Japanese war.

Now Hasegawa Teru, who had changed her name to Luchuan Yingzi (Green-River Bright-One), was to start her own fighting against Japan as an announcer, releasing her "vocal bullets" to attack Japan's invasion upon China to the Japanese in the front line by means of the mobile loudspeaker, or toward various places in Asia from the broadcasting tower in Chongqing.

● **The Anti-War Leaflets Prepared by Kaji Wataru were Airdropped on Japan Proper**

Kaji Wataru, having been received into the Military Committee, also started his activities. Kaji, who had entered Wuhan on March 23, 1938, met Chen Cheng, with Guo Moruo accompanying him, and received an official announcement of being appointed to "a committee member for planning in the Military Committee of the Nationalist Government." On the day that followed, Kaji presented himself at the inauguration ceremony for "the Chinese Literary Circle's Association for Resisting the Enemy," and was received with a seething applause.

Mao Dun, Lao She, Ba Jin and many other prominent men of literature were there when Kaji was introduced as a prominent literary critic in Japan who used to be the chief secretary of Japan's Proletarian Cultural Confederation, but because of his having engaged in an anti-war movement, he had to be sent to prison; after having been released from prison, he entered China; he was also a close friend of Master Lu Xun's, and this had led him to translate several works of his into Japanese; recently he had arrived in Wuhan, intending to raise an objection to the Imperialist Japan's war of aggression into China.

On the day that followed—March 24—Kaji made a speech at his reception held by a variety of groups staying at Wuhan. Just on that occasion, Wuchang Railroad Station happened to be bombed by the Japanese airplanes, and in that roaring sound, Kaji gave his passionate speech: "Take a stand against that Imperialism! Defend this Revolution being performed in China!"

Kaji Wataru at Wuhan wasted no time in engaging in propaganda maneuvering toward Japan. Jiang Jieshi, who had come to know of their having Kaji and other Japanese who had come to engage in their anti-Japanese War, proposed that: the Chinese planes should be sent to the skies of Japan proper and scatter the bills for appealing for the China's justice in protesting against the Japanese invasion and for the promotion of the friendship between the two nations. The draft of the bills was to be created by the Third Office led by Guo Moruo. Thus this turned out the first task for Kaji Wataru to take up at his new place of work. The operations to scatter the bills with six kinds of appeals "to Japan's Commercial and Industrial People," "to Japan's Workingmen," "to Japan's Farmers" and so on were named by Jiang Jieshi "the Humanistic Expedition to the East," and on May 19, the planes to perform that mission were seen off at Hankou Air Port by many people, including Chairman Jiang himself.

The B10 bombers that had been sent by the U.S., piloted by four Chinese with several millions of bills on board, reached the skies of Kyushu by way of the airports in southern China, taking the reverse route of Japan's transoceanic bombings upon Nanjing performed exactly ten months before. The paper bullets thrown from the bombers fluttered down to the wide area in southern Kyushu. The following report is seen in *The Strategy for the Aerial Defense of Japan Proper* in *A Series of the War History* (edited by the Editorial Office of the Defense Agency of Japan) :

> Around 4 a.m. on May 20, there appeared in the skies of Kumamoto Prefecture and Miyazaki Prefecture a plane whose nationality was unknown and disappeared in the sky of the Pacific. In the areas that corresponded to its contrail, bills were distributed, intensely appealing for the antiwar sentiment: "We appeal to the Japanese laborers….".

According to *The Naval Strategy against the China Region (2)* in the same series, "The Army's West Region's Defense Headquarters kept all the areas under air-raid warning for about four hours." This bill-spreading flight made by the Chinese planes turned out to be the first example for the Japanese to have had any Chinese planes in their sky. It was also probably for the first time when "an authentic air-raid alarm" was issued in Japan proper, excepting for the air-raid drill.

The four pilots who flew back to Wuhan were showered with a shout of joy of the welcome-home party represented by Kong Xiangxi of the Nationalist Party. At the airport, people of every walk of life had thronged. As the representative of the Communist Party, Zhou Enlai had also come to meet them and presented to them from Wuhan Office of the Eighth Route Army a banner with the following message embroidered upon it:

我空軍日本初遠征記念
気呑三島　威震九州

In memory of our Air Force having performed
the First Expeditionary Flight to Japan
To send the three islands aghast
While Kyushu felt menaced
to trembling

Apart from its practical effect, making a retaliation by their "paper bombs" was something delightful for the Chinese people who had been unilaterally bombarded so far.

● **The Start of "the Anti-War Union of the Japanese Residents in China"**

When Wuhan fell, Hasegawa Teru and her husband Liu Ren, along with Kaji Wataru and his wife Ikeda Sachiko, intended to go to Chongqing that was to be their next base. Hasegawa Teru was to engage in speaking to the Japanese soldiers over the radio as a member of the International Advertisement Department. But Kaji, instead of going directly to Chongqing, was to start at Guilin "the Anti-War League of the Japanese Residents in China." The Japanese soldiers who had been made captives at Funan or Guangdon region had begun to be sent to a provisional prison brought into being at Guilin, and

Kaji was expected to give those prisoners an appropriate education. Those prisoners, including the airmen whose planes had made an emergency landing at a point far away from the battlefield, were more than fifty in number. Giving them a proper education to turn them into advocators of anti-aggression was a mission kaji was expected to perform. On the other hand, "a Basic Japanese Language Class" for the Chinese was also set up, and Kaji was willing to give his cooperation to it, too. It was in such circumstances that the Antiwar Union of the Japanese Residents in China—Southwestern Branch—was brought into being on December 25, 1938, at Guilin. That was three months earlier than the establishment of the headquarters of the Antiwar Union in Chongqing. The following was "the Declaration made at the Grand Meeting for Starting the Union."

Here we declare the start of the Southwestern Branch of The Antiwar Union of the Japanese Residents in China. This is a prelude to the Unity of the Revolutionary Antiwar Union of All the Japanese Residents in China. This is the branch in China's Southwestern Theater of War.

The aggressive war in East Asia brought about by the Imperialist Japan has been prolonged because of the Chinese people's unyielding resistance; on the other hand, there is a growing danger of another imperialist war which might occur between Japan and those countries which had suffered disasters by Japan's invasions. Already nearly a million Japanese have suffered bloodshed, while tens of millions of Chinese people are being thrown into war fires, slaughters and hanger and coldness. And still even larger-scaled ominous clouds of war are hanging low in the Far East.—Then, overturning the foothold upon which the war-provocative are standing, thus preventing the calamities from growing larger and binding them together to discard will belong to the glorious responsibility for us, the Japanese, to perform.

You, our compatriots! Our dear Chinese friends! And all of our friends all over the world, who are against that adventurous policy of the Japanese militarists and their government that promote their invasions! We now inform you of our having established this oversea detachment of the Antiwar Union of the Japanese people.

The rudimentary purposes of our activities are as follows:

No.1 The immediate cessation of this aggressive war to be followed by the immediate withdrawal of the contingent troops.

No.2 The overthrow of the bureaucratic government that has been enslaved by the military capitalists and military adventurers.

No.3 The establishment of the perfect civil rights by achieving the freedom of speech, the freedom of association, the freedom of assembly, the freedom of culture and the freedom of education.

Kaji Wataru, who signed his name in this declaration as "the Representative of the Headquarters," immediately equipped the maneuvering party consisting of six members with the loudspeakers and sent them off to the battlefield of Kunlunquan. On December 29, from the top of a hill of Kunlunquan, where the smell of blood was still hanging over, they started their first appeal to the Japanese Army who had retreated to the level ground. The following was what Kaji wrote in his work, *The Antiwar Movement by the Japanese Soldiers:*

The Japanese Army in front was of an elite troop of the Fifth Division who had been especially trained for landing operations. Since Lukouqiao Incident,* they had ceaselessly been dragged about in the front line from North China to Middle China, then finally to Nomonhan to use up all their energy, thus recruiting after recruiting had turned the original troop into an almost different one. Now the maneuvering party revealed their identity. Thus the military authorities' purpose of war was exposed, and what sort of agonies the people of both nations had been forced to suffer while officers and men were forced to sacrifice themselves with no prospects before them, while recounting the war record of the Fifth Division so far.

(several paragraphs omitted)

At first, the Japanese Army, having been astonished, gave a warning shot of a machine gun, but it was soon overpowered by their voices. In that moonlit mountain, the voices appealing for peace did gain supremacy.

● **The Anti-War Play was Performed by the Japanese Prisoners of War**

Besides these "firing line maneuverings," the Antiwar Union made a plan of giving a public performance of a play so that they might propagate their own anti-war movement to the Chinese military and non-military. Kaji wrote a script for a three-act play—*The Three Brothers*—as the principal feature for the Chinese audience. All the cast and stagehands were Japanese captives, but partly because of such novelty as was played by the anti-war Japanese, the first performance given at *Xin Hua Da Juyuan* (New China Large Theater) in Guilin turned out to be a great success, thus giving them confidence. By and by, they—more than twenty in number—were to enter Chongqing, while keeping their performance on their way there.

On June 5, 1940, *Xin Hua Ri Bao* (New China Daily) carried an article concerning them:

> The anti-war Japanese have arrived in Yu (Chongqing) to perform
> *The Three Brothers.*
> They are on the Southwestern Branch of the Antiwar Union
> of the Japanese Residents in China.
> Guotai (National Peace) Grand Theater,
> Directed by Master Kaji Wataru,
> A writer advocating anti-invasion
> The admission fee: 1 yuan, 3 yuans, 5 yuans and 10 yuans

The maneuvering members had already been in Chongqing, while receiving a very warm reception both by the Government and the people. When the troupe arrived by boat at Zhaotian-men, they were surrounded by a large crowd of people who had been waiting for them at the landing place, even before they headed for their reception. After having received the words of appreciation from Guo Moruo as the chief of the Third Office of the Administration Department, Kaji Wataru, the chief of the troupe, returned his words of thanks, standing at the loading platform of the truck, and then they marched along Zhong-zheng-lu (the Central Formal Thoroughfare) and entered their accommodation. Upon the banner held by the two Chinese soldiers in their green-grass-colored uniform of the Chinese Army, the Chinese characters: 日本人民反戦革命同盟会西南支部工作団　軍事委員会政治部 (The Japanese People's Antiwar-Revolution Union: Southwestern Branch Maneuvering Party—Military Affairs Committee's Administration Department) had been left undyed on the field, thus demonstrating to the people lining the street that: this social entertainment was officially guaranteed by Jiang Jieshi as the Chief of the Military Committee.

Now in early summer in 1940, in the capital, upon which the Japanese military's Operation No. 101 had just started, more than twenty Japanese had arrived. Three years before, the Japanese who had been at the Japanese concession in Chongqing had all left there on board the Japanese gunboat Hira that sailed down the Yangzi. But now, many Japanese did come up to "step on the land here." Agnes Smedley, who had been staying there then, was also among those who came to encourage Kaji.

On July 4, the day before the premier of *The Three Brothers*, Vice-Admiral Inoue Shigeyoshi, the chief of staff of the Fleet of the China Region, had presented himself at Hankou Base, 780km east of Chongqing. He had intended to encourage the Operation No.101 which had started at the end of the previous month. Staying there as the base for those missions for four days, he kept encouraging the couple of commanders—Yamaguchi Tamon and Onishi Takijiro—and the airmen in that united air-raid corps.

In less than a week, Chongqing was to be caught in the fire net of the indiscriminate bombings. At Wuhan, the Japanese military were taking up their position, intending to discourage the Chinese military and civilian in the capital from keeping fighting against Japan; at Chongqing, another type of Japanese were encouraging the military and the civilian there, intending to "cooperate in China's glorious resistance against those invaders."—That was an extraordinary warp and waft of human relationship. It was in such a situation that the public performance of *The Three Brothers* started.

● The Public Performance was Put on Hold because of the Conflict
Between the Nationalist Party and the Communist Party

The performance itself turned out to be a success. But ironically, that success was to cause it to be brought to an end before the closing day. Behind it, there was a rift between the Nationalists and the Communists. As was suggested by the title, *The Three Brothers* had depicted the three Japanese brothers with different viewpoints and attitudes toward this Sino-Japanese War. Since the theme was simple, it was easily understandable to anyone. In other words, that was well made as a propaganda drama. But the anti-Communist faction having detected in it something like propaganda not only for "the National United Front Against Japan" but also for "Communism." So it was far from pleasing for the Nationalists to see this drama helping the Communists to earn a good reputation. According to Agnes Smedley, the following was what was happening then and there:

> One June night I attended a play given by Japanese captives organized in the "Japanese anti-Imperialist League". About twenty young Japanese soldier captives under the leadership of the Japanese revolutionary writer Kadji wrote their own plays, published their own magazine, and put on plays for the Chinese population and or war prisoners. The day after the play was given, the theater was suppressed by Mr. Chen Li-fu, Minister of Education. The plays were considered revolutionary because they showed the effects of war upon the poor people of Japan!

Chen Lifu is better known as the chief of Zhong Tong. His word was a law. The public performance had been expected to be given for five days, but it was made to discontinue in two days. So what Smedley saw would have been the one given on the second day.

According to Kaji's own memoir, *The Anti-War Movement Performed by the Japanese Soldiers*, the order had been given by He Yingqin, the chief of the Military Administration Department and concurrently the Chief of the General Staff. The reason was "because it exerts a bad influence upon the morale of the Chinese officers and men." At the premiere of that play, Tian Han, Hong Shen and many other people in the theatrical circles had come to make that opening a splendid one, but it turned out to be over too soon. Kaji and his comrades had already been involved into and trifled within the swirl of discord coming into being in the anti-Japanese administration in the capital.

After that, the Antiwar Union, under the situation which was growing harder and harder, kept its front-line-maneuvering and publishing its bulletin, while moving its base to Yan-an or some other areas under the Eighth Route Army, but in August in the following year (1941), it was given notice of breaking up by the chief of the Administration Department, Zhang Zhizhong, and its members were sent to a prison camp in Guizhou. But Kaji Wataru, having escaped being banished from Chongqing, maintained his own research room at a corner of the Administration Department, and while publishing a monthly newsletter, he kept engaging in his anti-war activities till the end of the war (1945). Thus, the Anti-War League's frontline maneuvering and its systematic activities were now being maintained only at the Yan-an Branch in Yan-an where Communism was legal, and a Japanese Communist there, Okano Susumu (later known as Nosaka Sanzo: 1892-1993) was to take care of them under "the Liberation League for the Japanese People."

● Hasegawa Teru's "Death in Battle"

As Kaji Wataru did, Hasegawa Teru also held her ground to the end in Chongqing, and enduring the restless life in which she had to move from place to place because of the air raids, she lived up to the internationalism as a true Esperantist she had made herself.

Upon her, too, the conflicts between the Nationalists and the Communists had exerted direct influences. Since the place of her work was the International Advertisement Office under the Nationalist Party, her activities in the 1940s had no longer been allowed to remain what they used to be in Wuhan where the Nationalist-Communist relationship still remained that of their honeymoon. Then Guo Moruo's Third Office of the Administration Department was scaled down to the Committee of Cultural Maneuvering, and this led Teru and her husband Liu Ren to move to the Third Group for Studying the Movements of the Enemy. In October, 1941, they had their eldest son, Xing (Star). Having contracted tuberculosis, she had to lead a rather inactive life, though not bed-bound, but her appetite for writing remained vigorous, and this led her to write and publish *The Whispering Voices fromWithin the Storm* and *In China at War*. She also tried publishing her Esperanto version of *The Living Soldiers* authored by a Japanese novelist Ishikawa Tatsuzo (1905-1985).

At the postscript to *In China at War*, she wrote about her life in Chongqing, as follows:

> Our life here started in winter in 1938. I cannot tell when this era of the war will come to an end. Throughout the winter, the thick fog had wrapped up the whole city of Chongqing. To one of the locals living in my neighborhood, I once said just as a joke: "Don't we have the sun in Chongqing?" That good-natured person, seemingly rather displeased, said to me: "What makes you say *that*? We have the sun all right, even though the fog is just hiding it."

Certainly, the fog of war was to clear away in 1945, and the sun came to shine in the blue sky, but her crumbling health did not allow her to enjoy those sunny days. Still they were blessed with their daughter—Xiao Lan (Dawn Orchid)—on April 14, 1946.

In January, 1947, Teru finally arrived at her husband's home at Jiamusi in northeastern China or what the Japanese used to call Manzhoukuo* which had just been liberated. But it was not long before she closed her thirty-four-year life there.

For ten years from 1937 to 47, Hasegawa Teru's life in China was similar to many Japanese soldiers' life there—a harsh traveling around the battlefields without any date of "repatriation." Hasegawa Teru, a pacifist, also died on the great earth of China.*

*The following is the latter half of the epitaph carved on the double grave— erected decades later by the People's Government of Jiamusi on the height overlooking a lake in the suburbs of Jiamusi or the land of their final repose:

Midorikawa Eiko, who had chosen to come and live in our country, spent the rest of her life here—though it turned out only eight years— passionately admiring the heroic achievements of anti-Japanese activities performed both by the Chinese Armed Forces and the people in general.

On the other hand, she made it clear what sort of invasions and criminal offenses had been committed by the Japanese military so that the Japanese soldiers might be awakened to the virtue of pacifism, while appealing to all the progressive powers in the international society, thus trying to invite many helping hands for the Chinese in their anti-Japanese campaign.

After the victory of our anti-Japanese war, she made an important contribution to promote the friendship between China and Japan and the cultural exchanges with various countries in the world.

Comrade Liu Ren made a contribution in retrieving the Northeastern China (Manchukuo*), in winning the victory of the Anti-Japanese War, and in contributing to our achievement of national liberation.

Now we dedicate to the honored couple a shared grave with the approval of the Chinese Communist Party's Central Secretary, while conferring on Midorikawa Eiko the honorary title of *A Champion of Internationalism.*

The People's Government of Jiamusi erected this on July 11, 1983

*   *   *

The above was translated into Japanese by Tetsuko Matsushita, one of the present-day Japanese admirers of Hasegawa Teru.

In Autumn, 1936, when they got married.

Their double grave erected by the People's Government of Jiamusi.
These photographs come from 二つの祖国の狭間に生きる（*I Live In Between The Two Lands of My Ancestors*）by Akiko Hasegawa, their daughter.

Zhou Enlai's room (also bedroom) in his office in Hongan Village (see P.459)

The long stone steps to connect the Upper-Half and the Lower-Half of Chongqing were bordered by the bomb-stricken houses and buildinigs. (from *Liang You*, issued in August, 1941)

The B10 bomber, Martin 139w (reformed type to be exported) (see P.499)

CHAPTER VI

FROM CHONGQING TO HIROSHIMA

A New Form of World War was Brought into Being

● The Combination of Airplanes and Flame Arms

The Japanese Air Force's advancing operations against Chongqing or China's anti-Japanese wartime capital, which lasted from February, 1938, to the autumn of 1941, was to record a new type of attack called "strategic bombings" in the history of world wars. That was a moment of serious leap in the evolution of wars. This type of murder which was brought into being in the midst of the First World War, whose fortune had been foretold by such prophets as Mitchell and Douhet, did reveal its horrible nature in April, 1937, at Guernica in Spain during its civil war. That assault from the sky, performed by the combination of airplanes and flame-arms, got established by the Japanese Navy Air Force that had been performing "its strategic bombings" upon Chongqing—until it took roots as systematic, repetitive and continuous tactics. Since the ancient times, "battles" and "flames" have characteristically remained inseparable, and now in the middle of the 20th century, in the hinterland of China, in the cubic structure of "from the air to the ground," it was enlarged into the sphere of aerial bombardments, making the horrors and tragic nature of war even greater. By and by, that conception had its cruel nature trained and strengthened in "the European Aerial War" until it was turned into the devouring flames that rushed to Tokyo in March, 1945, to Hiroshima and to Nagasaki in August in the same year.

"That advancing operations from the sky" was also a new type of "invisible invasion" into all over China; the bombings upon the urban areas were a performance of mechanized holocaust, and the combination of airplanes and flame-throwing arms began to work as "an automatic device for massacre." Into such places as too faraway or too precipitous for any ground forces to approach or into metropolitan areas with a high degree of population density, the Japanese airplanes approached by breaking through the frail resistance of the Chinese side and dropped as many bombs as they liked while giving strafing attacks—though in a method different from what the Japanese Army had adopted at "the Nanjing Incident," it could not do without bringing about indiscriminate massacres almost of the same nature in its intention and result.

● **"The Aerial Invasion" in which Japan's Navy Air Force Took the Lead**

In the map given in *The Outline of the Process of the Navy's Strategy in the 14ᵗʰ year of Showa (1939)* placed in *The Actions of the Imperial Navy during the China Incident*, published, edited by the Navy Military Propagation Department of the Navy Ministry (published in 1940), there are as many as 318 points whose place names were encircled in red, indicating "the main points to have given bombing raids."

The Navy with no ground force of arms had no need to think of marching or occupation. So their strategy on China simply meant their "aerial invasion," which started at Shanghai, followed by Nanjing, Anqing, Wuhan, Xuanchang and Chongqing—making their way along the Yangzi farther into the Continent. In that sense, the Japanese Navy in China was just as bloody-handed as the Army was. The Navy's way of massacre—unlike the Army's usage of guns and swords with which inrushes, occupations and cleanups were performed—was to suddenly invade from the sky, to bring deaths to the region under their control by means of sighting devices—without employing any human eyesight. As soon as their job was over, they simply left there without letting themselves be seen and without leaving any traces of their existence, while their lethal weapons were so made as to crash and scatter and disappear that it was impossible for them to be traced, and still the Japanese Navy in China would not be able to escape from being denounced for having been in the vanguard of Japan's invasion and having performed indiscriminate mass murder there, either.

The difference of the Japanese Navy and the Japanese Army, as were shown in the mirror of the Sino-Japanese War—even when the notions and actions taken by all those individuals who had belonged either to the Army or to the Navy were compared for evaluation—was not so conspicuous, just as the difference of "pest and cholera" was not.

On July 6, 1987—the day before the 50th memorial day of the Lukouqiao Incident*—Peking Broadcasting reported that there was an unveiling ceremony of "The Monument to the Memory of the Japanese Invaders' Bombings upon Chungking." (U.P.I.)

> During the Anti-Japanese War, Chungking as the Provisional Capital for the Nationalist Party was made the main target for the air raids performed by the Japanese military: From October, 1938, to August, 1943, a total of 9,500 bombers came flying a mission to drop 21,500 bombs and killed or injured 26,000 citizens there.
> *Chungking = Chongqing

This number of citizens killed or injured—26,000—would have come from *Chongqing Kangzhan Jishi—1937-1945—(The Record on Chongqing's Resistance to Japan)*, which the author often turned to in writing this book. In *The Record*, we see many more details such as: the number of the air raids performed was 218; a total of 9,513 planes flew over to make their raids; the number of bombs dropped were 21,593; the houses burnt down were 17,608; the number of deaths was 11,889; the number of the injured was 14,100: the total was 25,989. The sum of the direct damage the commercial and industrial areas suffered was five million U.S. dollars (of those days). Though not mentioned here, "several thousand deaths at the air-raid tunnel" in June, 1941, should be added to the number of deaths by the air raids. Those numbers given in *The Record on Chongqing's Resistance to Japan* were based on the statistics announced by the Nationalist Government, and *not* the ones investigated by the government of the New China. Considering the fact that: the numbers of damages in the formal announcement during the wartime tended to be made smaller than those which actually were—as was typically seen in the case of the tragic incident at the air-raid tunnel—these figures are dependable as long as we take them as something that could not be smaller than these. But when the number of times of the air raids and the number of planes sent into action, as were seen in the detailed report on the Japanese side, were compared to those of Chinese side, the numbers given by the latter seem a little larger than the former, but this is a natural consequence because the Japanese side gave the number of the planes and their missions while the Chinese side gave the number of the times of planes' appearance in the sky of Chongqing and the number of planes in each appearance. If a certain formation, not having finished dropping bombs at a single sortie, came back, the side to be attacked would take it as another formation's arrival.

According to the Chinese view, the Japanese air raid started on October 4, 1938, and the last one was on August 23, 1943. This means it was strictly for five years and a half that Chongqing had been exposed to the bombardments by the Japanese planes. But it was from 1939 to 41 that most of the air raids (195 out of 218 air raids) were performed, causing most of the victims (11,844 out of 11,889); it was also during these three years that the Japanese side had faced that anti-Japanese capital with a definite aim of "strategic-political bombings." So it would be appropriate to set that period of "strategic bombings" to those three years. Still it was something unheard of in the history of aerial wars that such persistent attacks as this had been given upon a single city, and even if the history of city-besieging by ground army was included, it will be impossible to find out many of such cases.

● The Chongqing Bombardments as a Missing Link
in the Indiscriminate Bombings upon Cities

The deaths of 11,889 residents in Chongqing caused by the Japanese air raids may not be taken as something so conspicuous to those who had seen the series of mass murders that were soon to occur in Hamburg, Dresden, Tokyo, Hiroshima and Nagasaki. This does mean: during the Second World War, the record of strategic bombings was kept broken in such a short period of time.

But if we came to know the fact that: the number of deaths—1,654—at Guernica in 1937 was surpassed more than doubly—4,091—by "5.3 - 5.4" air raids upon Chongqing, or even if compared with the U.S. strategic bombings upon the sixty-six cities in Japan toward the end of the Pacific War, the number of the deaths at Chongqing ranks fourth, following the atomic devastation upon Hiroshima and Nagasaki and the air raid upon Tokyo—or equal to the air raids upon Aichi, Hyogo and Osaka, each of which suffered deaths of 11,000 range. In fact, that was a new step or a great jump made after Guernica.

It was true that within several years after those air raids upon Chongqing, the damages caused by the city-bombings were remarkably increased. This led the ranking of the damages Chongqing had suffered to appear not so conspicuous among the many other cities that later came into the list, with the result that "Chongqing" rarely comes into the view of those investigating the history of strategic bombings. Still, just as no one underrates what Hiroshima and Nagasaki mean to us even when the following generations of nuclear weapons had turned "the Hiroshima-type atomic bomb" into "a sort of strategic nuclear warhead," what the air raids upon Chongqing means to us remains unchanged. That was one of the momentous turning points in the history of the evolution of wars—which might be called "a missing link"—thus it keeps asserting its existence as a starting point that proves the birth and growth of "the invasion from the sky."

Theodore White, who had experienced the air raids of "5.3 &.5.4," was a journalist—along with Edgar Snow—who had first pointed out the historical significance of the bombardments of Chongqing, and now I should like to review his way of thinking by what he wrote in his work, *In Search of History:*

> On May 3 and 4, 1939, Chungking was bombarded. Nowadays, these bombardments have become a sort of forgotten milestones in the history of aerial fear, but in those days, in the history of enhancing violence, they were the greatest massacres brought about from the sky upon those vulnerable people. That was carried out by the Japanese military. .... Such a large number of people as had never been heard of before were deprived of their lives by those might bombing. What is important concerning this massacre is the purpose of this terrorism the enemy has committed.

White's eye turned toward Japan had crossed Picasso's eye, which had firmly caught sight of the Nazis' view of human beings beyond those who had been killed at Guernica. Both Picasso and White warned with furious anger against the great massacres performed by disregarding the borderline between fighters and non-fighters, and an unusually large number of "massacres being performed without any appliance of human awareness," which was infuriating to them, seen from the standpoint of human dignity.

But when those actions performed by the German and the Japanese began to be regarded with indignation common to the Allied Nations, the war leaders and generals of the U.S. and the U.K. began to make use of them as "a reason for retaliation," thus justifying their carpet bombings performed day and night upon Hamburg, Dresden and other German cities—on the pretext of punishments upon the Nazism.

On the other hand, the graphic sights of misery in Chinese cities, including Chongqing, led them to approve of the order of attacking the whole islands of Japan with napalm bombs, thus forming "a just cause for retaliation." In this point, Theodore White was not an exception. Later, when he came to Japan immediately after it was defeated, he walked around "Yokohama which had turned into mere piles of cinders," and wrote in his work, *In Search of History:* "In those days, I never thought it shameful to massacre the Japanese either by bombs or by nuclear fission" This was how Japan's bombardments upon Chongqing had been creating "the chain of retaliations" that led to Hiroshima · Nagasaki.

● **Japan's Bombardments upon Chongqing and America's Bombardments upon Japanese Cities were of the Same Roots**

The tactics the Japanese military had adopted in making their bombing raids upon Chongqing were exactly the same as what the U.S. armed forces adopted during the Second World War and in the regional wars they engaged in after that. It was also of the same root with the conception that had been kept alive in the nuclear deterrence strategy in the latter half of the 20th century. What had differentiated the U.S. and Japan was: Japan failed in making China surrender, while America drove Japan into surrender, but it can be said: this was *not* by the conception of the strategic bombings *but* merely by the difference in the industrial power to turn that conception into air crafts and flame-throwing arms.

What could *it* be—"the evolution of war" which had been opened up by the bombardment upon Chongqing?

Firstly, both Japan and America did not hesitate to make "a city itself" an attack target. In making bombing raids on Germany, the U.S. Armed Forces put up an objection against "the regional bombing" or a British-style indiscriminate bombing and kept acting according to "the principle of attacking only on the military targets," but when they came to attack Japan, they never adopted any such reserved attitude. Japan, too, in the aerial operation against the U.S., they thought much of "the principle of attacking only on the military targets," according to the International Law in War Time, but toward China, they simply adopted the principle of what the Japanese military called "the attack on the strategic point" or a Japanese-style indiscriminate bombing. If the Japanese took any consideration, it was toward the Third Powers' rights and interests, not toward the Chinese civilians' living quarters. Both America and Japan had their own double standard, but after all, Japan, which had taken the initiative of the indiscriminate bombings toward China, was to suffer the greatest pain by the double standard adopted by America. Since the stages were "the cities themselves," the citizens were to suffer to the worst extent at the denouement.

Secondly, the bombings upon "the city itself" were planned and performed according to their own strategic purpose, independent of the ground troops' advancing operations. It was because of this characteristic of strategic bombings that Japan's Navy Air Force was always able to take the initiative in the bombardment upon Chongqing. In other words, "the intention to achieve some decisive results only by means of aerial capacity" was the essence of the bombardment upon Chongqing, and Inoue Shigeyoshi's declaration that "the bombardment upon Chongqing is comparable with the Battle of Tsushima"* meant that point. In Europe during the Second World War, this strategy became very common, and during the days of nuclear deterrence strategy after the War, this was to be expanded to the utmost by "an anti-city strategy," and it was in the bombardment upon Chongqing that its initial form had been established. Seen from this point, the bombardments upon such cities as Guernica and Madrid during the civil war in Spain having been performed in cooperation with the ground advancing operations of the Nationalist Army led by General Franco, they cannot be called strategic bombings in a strict sense of the words, even though they were massacres performed from the air. Thus the bombardments upon Chongqing performed by Japan's Navy Air Force—the strategy intended to subdue the enemy only by the attack from the air—became the first example in the world history of aerial battles. America's strategic bombings upon Japan, therefore, were none other than the enlarged version of what Japan had done upon Chongqing.

Thirdly, this strategy was characterized by the concentrated employment of men-slaughtering arms. The combination of the aircrafts and flame-throwing arms did remove the boundaries between the battlefield and the living quaters thus causing non-combatants to be thrown into the flame-hell. The bombs employed by the Navy—98-type No.7-6-1 & 2 and 1-type No.7-6-3—and the

ones employed by the Army—100-type 50kg incendiary bombs (*ka* 4 bombs)
—all these incendiary bombs were carried by the Navy's 96-type land-attack
planes or the Army's 97-type heavy bombers to be thrown upon the traditional-
style rows of houses made of wood and bamboo to drive the inhabitants
into such mortal fear as they had never experienced before. Theodore White
described its effect: "What I had witnessed then was the response or the total
panic shown by the medieval city when it received the first cruel blow from the
modern world."

The incendiary bombs, whose effect of spreading damage by dint of flaming
fire was such that it was soon made a symbol of fear in the city-bombardment.
In later years, the incendiary bombs employed by the U.S. Air Force—500
pound M 69, consisting of 48 incendiary bombs of 6 pounds—were so made
as to open at 300m above the target and turn themselves into "fire-rain" to pour
over the target, thus to easily burn up Japanese houses made of wood and paper.
This would be called a predecessor of the airdrop of defoliants in the Vietnam
War and of white phosphorus bombs in the Iraq War. Here, too, "the conception
applied to Chongqing" was to be adopted to torment those unfortunate citizens.

These three points—① making the city itself a target for bombardment ②
being performed independent of the land army's advancing operation ③ making
abundant use of antipersonnel weapons—and their systematic, repetitive and
continuous attacks upon the enemy—were none other than the essence of the
conception of strategic bombing, which had been developed by the Japanese
military (mainly by the Navy Air Corps) to be tried upon Chongqing as the
wartime capital of China for the purpose of "frustrating their fighting spirit."
These were the essence of the conception of strategic bombing.

This attempt made by the Japanese military turned out to be a failure
after having been carried out as long as three years, but the conception itself
remained alive to be handed down to the U.S., so that it could be employed in
performing the scorched-earth tactics upon Japan; then after World War II , it
was adopted in the military stratagem to be applied in such regional wars at
Korea, Vietnam, Persian Gulf and Iraq—and even in an imaginary fight to death
by employing ballistic missiles and nuclear bombs, while taking the enemy
nation as hostages, thus to build up the base of the conception of "the balance
of fears."

● **Japan has Shut up their Bombardments upon Chongqing**
                                          in the Dust Heap of History

On the other hand, the Japanese Government, which was defeated in the war without fulfilling the purpose of the strategic bombing of their own creation, had to prepare for their refutation against the criticism of their having performed indiscriminate bombings and having killed and injured so many Chinese people, because the Potsdam Declaration had given notice: "To all the war crimes, severe punishment shall be given."

In *The File of the Records on Verbal Evidences Concerning the China Incident, Prepared for The International Military Tribunal for the Far East,* which is included in *The Record of the Evidences of the Imperial Headquarters' Navy Department: The Details of the Greater East Asia War (1)* —included in Japan's Defense Agency's *Library of War History.* The following explanations had been made in preparation for the investigations into the war crimes:

1) According to the required circular notice, the standard concerning the air war, the bombardment rules and the like had thoroughly been notified to all the corps concerned. Thus the attacks were restricted only to the military targets with the result that: whether the city was defended or not, no city has ever been made a target of ours.

2) From the humanitarian viewpoint, some military targets were refrained from bombing, lest the attack upon them should cause serious damages, or when it was impossible to make sure whether or not something was a right target.

3) We paid the closest attention not to give any damage to the properties that belonged to the third powers or to those from the third powers. As for the International settlements and any other similar institutions, we paid the closest attention not to give any damage upon them.

4) According to the conventional laws, regulations and customs, there was no such system as to let the city declare itself to be an open city, while the armed forces and the military facilities within a city area were permitted to attack whether the city itself was defended or not. As it happened, we usually received fierce attacks from vacant lots in the city despite its declaration that it was an open city.

5) When our Imperial Navy attacked a military target at Nanking, the

then Consultative Committee of the International League gave us a strong protest according to their resolution: "Your having attacked that defenseless city was an unpardonable conduct," but our Navy Air Corps has never attacked a city itself. As for Chongqing, Chengdu and some other cities too, we shall say the same thing.

This official view Japan pronounced then still remains valid as the official view of the Japanese Government. But you need not go as far as the actual places in China to find out the rootlessness of this assertion, for it can easily be found if you visit a room for the historical materials of the Defense Agency in Tokyo and have a look at the materials I have often referred to in this book, such as *A Resume of the Actions,* in which all *the Orders to Attack* and *the Reports of the Missions* have been preserved. In this material, we can see even the map of the urban area which was divided into several sections to show which section they should drop their bombs on a certain date, thus belying the Government's efforts to destroy evidence. But the fact still remains to be faced as it should.

This is not just the matter of the Government's stance. In writing about the aerial battles in history, the Japanese are likely to mention the miseries brought about by the air raids in London or in Hamburg, but practically *not* the air raids in Chongqing. It might be said that Chongqing is mentioned only when "the Zero Fighters' first appearance" is talked about. To the Japanese people in general, "strategic bombings" simply remain as "something that has once inflicted damage upon themselves, and they have not yet brought themselves to know of what Japan had done during that period when the conception of "strategic bombings" was born and brought up into something that was to harm so many Chinese people.

Now let us come back once again to that memorable turning point in history.

The Start of the U.S.- Japanese War and Chongqing

● **At the News of the Start of the U.S.-Japanese War, Jiang Jieshi was**
Overjoyed, Keeping the Record of *Ave Maria* **Going**

On December 8, 1941, the Japanese military made a surprise attack on a group of U.S. warships anchoring at Pearl Harbor. At the same time, they exercised the landing operations, the aerial exterminating operations and the capturing operations on the Malay Peninsula, on the Philippines and at Hongkong. From this moment on, the Sino-Japanese War was to turn itself into a part of the World War between the Axis Powers and the Allied Powers.

The war fire that had risen on the Pacific—seen from the Chinese side— meant Japan's having set up "its second front," which also announced the end of the air raids that had kept annoying Chongqing and several other cities in the hinterland of Sichuan Province. To the people there, no news could be more welcome than this: there would be no more air raids; there would be no need to rush into the air-raid cave. Han Suyin has written down in her *Birdless Summer* that festive mood prevailing all over the downtown of Chongqing:

On the morning of December 8, we had the news about Pearl Harbor. All of a sudden, the street became noisy with the cries of those selling extras, the noises of those rushing out of the houses to buy them and the excited voices of men and women came piercing through the noises of the horses and vehicles on the street.

Her husband, Tang Baohuang, one of the officers close to Jiang Jieshi, also came home, clutching the newspaper and brought her the information.

Bao was brilliant with joy. The Military Committee was overflowing with delight; Jiang was also excited with the happy news, and hummed the melody of one old operatic song after another, while the record of *Ave Maria* was kept playing all day long. The government officials of the Nationalist Party were full of joy as if they had won a great victory, and walked around to exchange congratulations. According to their view, that was as good as their victory. The start of the war between Japan and the U.S. was what they had eagerly expected to occur. And now, the U.S. had finally opened hostilities with Japan! From now on, the strategic importance of China would become even greater than before. More and more U.S. dollars and materials would come flowing into China.

Both the military and the people in Chongqing, who had been enduring the heavy pressure inflicted by the Japanese military all by themselves, did celebrate the end of their hardship as if celebrating their victory.

But Jiang Jieshi himself could not remain in rapture in that recorded song. He now had to tackle with the military part China should take in the Sino-Japanese War which had now turned into part of the World War. Certainly, Ave Maria composed by Schubert was his favorite, as was mentioned to be "Jiang Jieshi's lullaby for his siesta" in *Inside the Asia* by John Gunther. But on that day, the Chief of the Military Committee ought to have been too busy to sing this song or to lay himself on the sofa beside his gramophone. No sooner had he been informed of the news of Japan's having attacked Pearl Harbor than Jiang summoned the Military Committee and the Nationalist Party's Central Executive Committee's Standing Committee so that they might investigate how they should make their attitude clear, corresponding to that new unfolding of the situations. He also demanded that: they should declare war on the Axis powers as the Japan's allies.

Owen Lattimore was there, too. Lattimore, as Theodore White was, was also an expert on Sinology as well as a journalist. He had been living in China till he was twelve since he arrived there as an infant with his parents. After having received an education in England, he returned to China as a journalist before he engaged himself in Sinology at the graduate school of Harvard University. His having edited *Pacific Affairs*—the bulletin of the Board of Investigation on the Pacific Matters—had led him to be invited to China to be a political adviser to Jiang Jieshi, and in July, 1941—in the midst of the period when Japan's Operation No. 102 were being performed—he flew to Chongqing by way of Hong Kong and got off at Shanhuba Air Port in Chongqing. Among his fellow passengers, there was Claire Chennault. Lattimore, being able to talk without any interpreter, immediately became deeply trusted by Jiang Jieshi.

What was taken up in that conference on December 8 was whether or not the start of war between the U.S. and Japan meant Japan's making a simultaneous start of a large-scaled strategy toward China, too. The answer was "No".

Lattimore wrote in his work, *China and I*, as follows:

> He (Jiang) was, however, definitely pleased in one respect. Pearl Harbor meant that the United States was not only officially but completely in the war. He thought that though the allies would suffer severe losses in the Pacific and South Asia, in the end they, principally the United States, would recover and defeat Japan.

According to Lattimore's observation, Jiang Jieshi's long-term view was: "We shall leave defeating Japan to America. What China should do will be to play a waiting game—to wait, anyhow, till the pressure to Japan applied by America will produce any fruit." In other words, he had intended to strengthen his power for the time being, so that, when the war was over, his Nationalist Government might be accepted anyhow in a form as he had intended. Lattimore regarded it as "the beginning of Jiang Jieshi's (Chang Kaishek's) destructive setback," as he wrote in his *China Memoir:*

> I might go on to say here that Chang Kaishek's analysis of the situation, which had proved to be correct so far, after Pearl Harbor, became the beginning of his disastrous defeat, because to take a passive attitude toward the war was in direct contradiction to the propaganda of courage, valiant resistance, fighting to the last, patriotism, and all the rest of it which the government was carrying on. If you supply that kind of propaganda and do not act on it, in the long run, the effect on the fighting troops will lead to demoralizing.

Zhou Enlai was not present at that conference, but soon after that, Lattimore met him and talked to him. Then Zhou Enlai said: "In my opinion, this is an opportunity to attack Japan from its Chinese flank, not only to diminish the amount of power the Japanese can divert toward East Asia, but also to restore Chinese morale, because the morale of the people who are on the attack is always likely to be higher than the people on the defensive. … Now is the time for China to take a policy of positive attack," as Lattimore wrote in *China and I*.

Anyway, things were undergoing a sudden change. A personal letter to the U.S. President F.D. Roosevelt was immediately drafted. One of the paragraphs in it went as follows:

> .... To this new warfare we are now taking part in, we, standing on the common ground with your nation, are ready to offer all that we possess until the Pacific Ocean and the world are liberated from the violence and infinite dangers.

It was not long before their being at war with Italy and Germany with which Japan had formed an alliance was pronounced and it was decided that a joint conference of the United Nations should be held at Chongqing within that same month. This was how the Sino-Japanese War was turned into "a new war against Japan to be performed by the union of China and America." Now the time was over when "Chongqing had to fight by herself in perseverance." Jiang Jieshi ought to have felt it more keenly than anyone else in China, as he wrote in his *Secret Memoir:*

> Now the achievement of our resistance strategy has reached its climax. When things reach their climax, its reaction is inevitable. Standing high and taking a broader view of things, I must see to it that I shall not lose a sense of danger and fear.

Just about this period of time, The U.K. Prime Minister Churchill, who had been fighting an isolated battle against Hitler for a couple of years, could not hide his pleasure and relief at the news of the outbreak of the war between the U.S. and Japan, or the U.S.' having joined in the War. But China's having been fighting single-handedly had surpassed the U.K.'s by a couple of years. So it was by no means amazing even if the song of Ave Maria had kept sounding in the heart of Jiang Jieshi as a Christian throughout the rest of the day—even after that recorded song was no longer heard in his room. An American who was seeing how joyful the people of Chongqing were is said to have given a comment: "For the People of Chungking (Chongqing), America's Pearl Harbor Day was their Anniversary for celebrating the End of the War." Certainly, he was right.

● **Zhou's Office in Exultation Received Emergency Directions**

At Zhou's Office at No.50, Zengjia-an, too, Zhou Enlai and his comrades had been happily excited at the dispatch of the U.S. and Japan having opened hostilities with each other. That was something they had already estimated, but now another World War had finally become a reality. That meant that: the U.S., too, along with the Soviet Union, had become a sworn friend of the Chinese Communist Party. How they should grasp that world war and what their relationship with the Nationalist Party should be—both of the issues obviously needed to be re-examined. The maneuvering of the National United Front was no longer merely the matter of domestic conditions but of an international battle against Fascism, and that was exactly what had been pointed out in the first secret telegram sent from the Chinese Communist Center in Yan-an to the Southern Bureau at Chongqing after the start of the World War.

On the other hand, Zhou Enlai had been facing even more urgent problems: All those telegrams that arrived one after another informed them of the Japanese military's rapid advance into those European colonies in various parts of Asia, keeping pace with their attack on Pearl Harbor: Early on the morning of December 8, there came one message after another, informing that: there appeared Japanese military planes in the skies of the Jiulong Peninsula at Hong Kong and dropped bombs on Qide Airport and part of the urban area, and that: there seemed to be landing operations as impending dangers.

At Hong Kong as a British territory, there stayed many political figures and intellectuals of the Chinese Communist factions or of the leftist wing of the United Front, who could not naturally stay not only in the areas occupied by Japan but also in such places as Chongqing under the control of the Nationalist Party; and now the Japanese military units were approaching there. Then these helpless Chinese must be kept safe from those Japanese military! The Southern Bureau under the control of Zhou Enlai had kept—not only in the capital Chongqing but also in such cities as Guilin and Changsha, Hong Kong, Guiyang and so on—such open institutions as the office of the Eighth Route Army, the branch office of *Xin Hua Ri Bao* (New China Daily News) and the like, and saving these comrades out of the danger approaching Hong Kong had now depended on Zhou Enlai.

In order to keep safe the essence of the revolutionary cultural sphere in our country, you shall rescue all those staying in Hongkong, while engaging in Anti-Japanese cultural maneuvering.

Zhou Enlai, having received this emergency direction from the Center of the Communist Party dispatched on December 8, started a rescue plan by directing Liao Chengzhi and Liu Xiaowen, the members of the Southern Bureau who were then resident at Hong Kong (the former had graduated from Waseda University in Japan and after the war, he was to be the president of the China-Japan Friendship Association). As for the working corps, the Tongjiang Company that had been engaged in guerrilla warfare in Southern China was appointed. Since then, the Chinese Communist underground maneuvering was to be unfolded, rescuing two thousand youths and eight hundred renowned people out of Hong Kong and the Jiulong Peninsula which had strictly been sealed off by the Japanese Army that had landed to occupy them. Through this project, many Nationalist leading figures, including He Xiangning and Chen Rutang and Song Qingling (Sun Wen's wife), and the staff of Hong Kong University, and Mao Dun, the writer, who had recently arrived there with his wife, and Zou Taofen, a man of the press, also escaping from the anti-Communist oppression at Chongqing, were rescued and received into the liberated areas of the Eighth Route Army and the New Fourth Army, which had been kept safe either from the Japanese Army or from the Nationalist Party.

Because of all these things, both Jiang Jieshi and Zhou Enlai were to be kept simply too busy to appreciate the arrival of this memorable day—December 8, 1941. There was an immense difference between them in understanding the present situation and the prospect into the future, but at least in one point, they must have been sharing the same idea—"Now, America and China have come to share the same aims, the same ideas and the same attitudes. America will do *it* thoroughly. Then, it will be Japan that has to be crashed to pieces...."

They were right in their prediction. And the turning of Fortune's wheel was to prepare Sichuan Province—where Chongqing is—as a base for the U.S. Air Force to perform a strategic bombings—by the formation of B29 bombers known as "Super Fortress"—upon Japanese cities. The initial report on "the bombing upon Yawata Iron-Manufacturing Company" which occurred three years later was informed of to the whole world from the broadcasting tower of

Chongqing. Then, it could be said that "December 8, 1941" was the day when "the conception of strategic bombing"—which started at Guernica to be passed over to Chongqing—was further brought over to the air raids upon the Japanese Islands.

● **The Start of the U.S.-Japanese War Brought about a Complete Change in the War in China.**

The start of the war between Japan and the U.S. was to bring about a complete change in the war that had been made in China so far. The changes were brought into view promptly and clearly to each country concerned.

For Japan, since December 8, what they had called "China Incident" so far was incorporated into a part of "the Greater East Asia War." According to the decision made by the Cabinet on December 12, it was decided that "the War we are to make against the U.S. and the U.K.—including the China Incident in it—shall be called the Greater East Asia War," and it was incorporated into one of the aims of the war to "construct a new order of the Greater East Asia." No longer could they solve the problem only by overthrowing "the Chongqing Administration." The Sino-Japanese War had been absorbed into that expanded purpose of war and the war zone.

For America, that state of things was accepted as something rather simplified and summed up, instead of being expanded: Now the world was divided into two—the Fascist camp and the Democratic camp; the Axis Powers and the Allied Powers; "the nations of invasion and foul play" and "the nations of liberation and justice." The enormous industrial power and military power of the United States, now discarding their political neutrality, were to be openly released in order to establish their control not only over the East-West Battle Line of the Eurasian Continent but also over both of the Atlantic Ocean and the Pacific Ocean. Now was the time for them to win or to lose. For them, China was a sworn friend in Asia to fight together against the atrocities of the Japanese military, while Jiang Jieshi was an irreplaceable leader to have kept attracting most of the Japanese Army to the Chinese mainland.

On the other hand, the Chinese Communist Party had also accepted the situation as clearly as the U.S.: Japan's having attacked upon the U.S. had led the world to be divided into two camps of fascism and anti-fascism; and it was stipulated that the China's resistance against Japan was not only for the fight for liberating their own races but also having entered the stage for demanding the formation of "the united front against Japan by rallying all the nations facing the Pacific." Those slogans raised by the Allied Powers—"Restoration of Democracy" and "Self-Determination of Peoples"—were quite free from any sense of discomfort of rather in concert with the Chinese Communists' anti-Japanese strategy, and this led them even to feel as if the National United Front Against Japan they had once proposed to the Nationalists was now given a stamp of approval from the standpoint of the world history. Thus it was accepted that the situation had developed into what it should be.

For Jiang Jieshi as the supreme leader of China, such a development of things as these was certainly in the direction he had desired, but he could not accept things in such a simple frame of mind as Mao Zedong and Zhou Enlai had done. The Sino-Japanese War having now become a part of the World War, Jiang Jieshi's status as the leader of "Free China" had been made solid and secure, and his having obtained such a grand title as "the Supreme Commander of the Chinese Theater of Operations" was welcome to him, but the Allied Nations' emphasis upon their unity and their growing amount of military aid which would benefit the Chinese Communist Party, as well, had led Jiang Jieshi to take additional worries upon himself. Jiang's situation was rather similar to Churchill's in the U.K.. Both of them had been well aware that they could not carry out the war without the assistance from the U.S.; On the other hand, they had kept an irresistible idea that their ultimate aim was to preserve "the British Empire" or "the Republic of China" rather than "anti-Fascism" or "protection of democracy," and this had kept them feel rather unable to concert with what the Americans were pursuing: "Down with the Axis Powers!" and "Winning the War shall come first and foremost!" For them, waging war ought to be something more complicated, and "pursuing the victory" is as important as "how the victory should be achieved" and "what should be done after the victory is achieved," but the American way of thinking seemed to be too straight forward, to their growing dissatisfaction. Thus, as the time went on, Jiang Jieshi no longer came to hide his irritation at the American way of directing the war, even though it did not come up till much later.

At Chongqing on the day of the outbreak of the Pacific War, all the people were happy and excited at the prospect that: there would no longer be any air raid and that: the tables would be turned.

- **The Three Nations Concerned Held a Military Council at Chongqing**

America's participation into the war had suddenly changed the atmosphere of Chongqing completely. In each administrative organ of the Nationalist Government, the advisory groups of Americans often came to be seen, while military conferences were also held frequently. Aid goods and commodities also having been arriving, the mountain-castle capital in the hinterland of Sichuan Province had suddenly been turning into an international metropolis.

In March, 1941, when the law of lend-lease came into being, President Roosevelt had already expressed his intention to strengthen the U.S. aid not only to the U.K. but also to China, and he sent his special envoy, Lauclean Kali, to Jiang Jieshi so that they could deliberate on the scheme of the economic aid; the President had sent to Jiang Jieshi's Administration, even before the start of the war, such advisory groups as concerning military affairs (Brigadier General John McGruder), concerning transportation & Burma Railroad Control (John Baker) and concerning Finances (Arthur Young). The main pillar of the assistance was the offer of the arms and materiel enough for the thirty Chinese divisions to arm themselves, and making these advisory groups' activities its core, "America in Chongqing"—including "Chinese-American Cooperative Workshop" under the Supervision of Milton Miles—was to rapidly expand after Japan's attack on the Pearl Harbor.

On the other hand, Captain Claire Chennault, who had been invited by Song Meiling—the consort of Jiang Jieshi—to be the head of China's Air Force Officers' School, and to organize the U.S. Volunteer Flying Corps, "the Flying Tiger," was now restored to active service after the start of the war as an officer in command in the U.S. Army Air Force and began to lead the regular flying corps.

In March, 1942, Lieutenant General Joseph Stilwell started the headquarters in Chongqing as the chief of the staff of Jiang Jieshi or "the Supreme Commander of the Chinese Theater of the Allied Nations," and as Commander of the U.S. Army in China.

This was how the significance of Chongqing underwent a great shift from "the Chinese people's stronghold of resistance against the Japanese military" to "the counteroffensive base" of the Allied Powers or CBI (China, Berma and India) War Zone.

On the day that followed the Pearl Harbor attack, Roosevelt sent a reply telegram to Jiang Jieshi's personal letter to him, and proposed setting up the military conference of the Anti-Axis powers:

> To my mind, the most important thing for us to do now will be to start prompt preparations so that we may be able to take common actions. So I sincerely propose that you should summon a joint military council at Chungking before December 17, so that we may exchange informations and investigate the most effective actions for our armies and navies to take in order to defeat Japan and its allied powers.

According to this proposal made by Roosevelt, the Allied Forces' United Military Conference concerning the Asian issues was held at Chongqing on December 23 with Jiang Jieshi presiding over it. The Soviet Union had not sent any representative for the reason of their having not yet prepared for taking part in the Pacific War, while Holland had not sent anyone there, either. On the other hand, the U.S. Government had sent Major General George Bret as their representative and Brigadier John Macgluder, resident in Chongqing, as his assistant; the U.K. had sent Admiral Sir Archibold Wavell, who had been fighting until that summer against Rommel's Army at the North African Battle Line, before he was appointed as the Commander of the Federation Army of the U.S., the U.K., Holland and Australia, according as the Japanese Army's advance to the Malay Peninsula. Thus all those representatives elaborated a strategy of their united front in "the CBI Theater."

Along with this United Military Conference, another military conference (whose password was "Arcadia") was being held at Washington between the U.K. Prime Minister Churchill and the U.S. President Roosevelt. "The Basic Principles of the Joint Strategy" confirmed here having formed the base of the supreme war plan of the Allied Nations, they naturally exerted a direct influence upon the conference at Chongqing. The principle in performing the war, as was agreed upon at the Arcadia Conference, was the confirmation of the principle of "Europe shall be the First"—that was, if Germany was defeated, Italy would collapse and Japan would fall, too, and upon this fundamental cognition, the Asia-Pacific theater was to be "of the secondary importance." On the other hand, however, the Chinese Army's war efforts, which had kept absorbing Japanese forces as many as one million upon their wide territory having been evaluated, while the importance of keeping China on their side by supplying arms and other commodities having been well aware of by the top leaders of the U.S. and the U.K., the assistance to be offered to China was placed—though within the limited sphere of some subsidiary strategy—on sending aerial power and opening new routes for supporting Jiang Jieshi. In other words, they had expected China to take such a part as the Soviet Union had taken in Europe—by keeping Germany's main ground forces to the Eastern Front. The joint military committee held at Chongqing had a long argument between Jiang who stressed the importance of establishing a long-term comprehensive schedule and the U.S. and the U.K., who, staying within the Arcadia Conference, wanted to restrict their action to defending Burma for the time being, finally adopted the following resolution to advise Roosevelt. That was far from the direction Jiang Jieshi had expected.

1) By taking a cooperative action with China, Berma, especially Rangoon, shall be kept safe from the enemy's attack. At the same time, within the limits of the present resources, Japanese Army's bases and facilities shall be attacked by air.
2) In order to train the Chinese Army for the final attack upon the Japanese Army, the commodities shall be kept supplying so that the Chinese may keep fighting.
3) The military action by the Chinese Army shall be kept on in order to keep the Japanese Army at *that* front line.

The outbreak of the U.S.-Japanese War did change the forms and the significance of the Anti-Japanese War that had been fought by the Chinese. What had made the citizens of Chongqing realize *this* was by the fact that: more and more Americans had come to live there and the end of the foggy season in 1942 had brought about the spring and summer free from any air raid for the first time in four years. The stages for the strategic bombings had now been brought over to Europe. By and by, that conception of mass murder and indiscriminate carnage, which had been enlarged over there, was to be brought back to Chongqing once again, and from the U.S. Headquarters *there*, the very same strategic bombings were ordered to be performed upon the Japanese cities this time, even though, at this point, no one could tell anything like that.

"The Retaliation Bombings" between Britain and Germany

● **Churchill had Suddenly Turned into a Supporter of Indiscriminate**
Bombings

The indiscriminate bombings from the sky—which had kept growing larger in scale since the bombing upon Guernica in 1937 and the bombings upon Chongqing from 1938 to 41—were to intensify their degree of cruelty and misery in World War Ⅱ which broke out in 1939—especially in "the aerial battles in Europe" which started in the years that followed.

The largest number of deaths brought about by a single air raid was 1,645 in Guernica and 3,318 in the bombing of "5.4." in Chongqing. And now in the cities of Germany and Britain during World War Ⅱ, that number came to be mentioned in ten thousands. Such rapid progress made in such a short period of time would not be found even in the long history of warfare on the earth. The conception of strategic bombing that moved from that hinterland in China to Europe where the air battle was to develop in a terrifying speed during the short period of time, causing the 550,000 deaths only in Britain and Germany, and upon the extension of that conception, there occurred the air raids in Tokyo in March, 1945, and the atomic bombings in Hiroshima and Nagasaki in August in the same year.

The first person to be placed on a list of those who had lent their power in enlarging the scale and intensity of the strategic bombings in Europe would be Winston Churchill, the prime minister of Britain during the wartime. In the European theater of operations, the leadership of the indiscriminate bombings upon cities had always been maintained by the U.K., not by Germany. As for the U.S. Air Force, they had been hesitating to discard their principle of "bombing only on the military facilities" till the final stage of the war—as far as the bombings upon the European cities were concerned.

Those large-scaled air raids which were expressed in such figures of speech as "bomber streams" or "a bombardment by one thousand bombers" had been registered—along with such terms as "regional bombing" and "saturation bombing"—into the dictionary of military terms by the British Air Force's bombers' group. And the person who had decided upon all those things was Churchill.

This does not mean Churchill had originally been an advocator of the indiscriminate bombings. The campaigns he took part in when young at Egypt, Afghanistan or South Africa were the 19th century-type of war in which light cavalrymen were able to take pride in their honorable tradition at the battlefield. As he mentioned with endearing nostalgia in *My Early life* published in 1930, the war meant: "a small number of well-trained professionals championing their country's cause with ancient weapons and a beautiful intricacy of archaic manoeuvre, sustained at every moment by the applause of their nation." Then he deplored the present situation: "It is a shame that war should have fling all this aside in its greedy base, opportunist march, and should turn instead to chemists in spectacles, and chauffeurs pulling the levers of aeroplanes or machine guns."

Churchill, who had engaged himself in World War I, had expressed his own view obviously different from Douhet's and Mitchell's. The following was what he wrote on October 21, 1917 in his *Memorandum*:

It is not reasonable to speak of an air offensive as if it were going to finish the war by itself. It is improbable that any terrorization of the civil population which could be achieved by air attack could compel the Government of a great nation to surrender. Familiarity with bombardment, a good system of dug-outs and shelters, a strong control by police and military authorities, should be sufficient to preserve the national fighting power unimpaired. In our case we have seen the combative spirit of the people aroused, and not quelled, by the German raids. Nothing we have learned of the capacity of the German population to endure sufferings justifies us in assuming that they could be cowed into submission by such methods , or, indeed, that they would not be rendered more desperately resolved by them. Therefore our air offensive should consistently be directed at striking at the bases and communications upon whose structure the fighting power of his armies and his fleets of the sea and of the air depends. Any injury which comes to the civil population from the process of attack must be regarded as incidental and inevitable.

——*The Conduct of War: 1789-1961* by J.F.C. Fuller

This same person who wrote this—as soon as he came to form his cabinet supported by the whole nation in May, 1940—suddenly began to pronounce: "The general public's morale is our military aim" and began to seek "all the methods to burn or bleed our enemies to death." (*The Times: 2/2, 1943*)

In his memorandum (dated September 3), issued immediately after he took office as Prime Minister, his transformation could clearly be seen:

> The Fighters are our salvation, but the Bombers alone provide the means of victory. We must therefore develop the power to carry an ever-increasing volume of explosives to Germany, so as to pulverize the entire industry and scientific structure on which the war effort and economic life of the enemy depend....

The military historiographer, John Fuller, points out: "the Bomber Command, which came directly under the Ministry of Defense, became Churchill's private army." (*The Conduct of War: 1789-1961*) His predecessor as the Prime Minister, Neville Chamberlain, had declared at the House of Commons (on February 15, 1940): "Whatever be the length to which others might go, the Government will never resort to blackguardly attacks on women and other civilians for the purposes of mere terrorism," but Churchill simply gave up succeeding that policy, and on the day that followed his having taken office as Prime Minister, he gave his approval of giving an air raid on Freiburg, an old university city in the southwestern part of Germany, thus clarifying his direction of deviating from the custom of the law of nations that prohibited employing flame-throwing arms and performing air raid upon anything but military targets.

At this same period, Japan's Operation No. 101 had been exercised upon Chongqing, causing it to suffer "another summer of air-raid," so the United Kingdom presided over by Churchill was not the first to violate that international law. But contrary to the Chinese Continent where things were of extensive nature, European Continent had already been congested; while the aerial capability and industrial productivity of both U.K. and Germany were such that it was not long before they surpassed Japan in their unfolding of strategic bombings.

● At First, Germany had Refrained from Bombing upon the Cities of the U.K.

Comparing with Churchill, Hitler could be said to have retained a more cautious attitude at first toward the bombardment upon the city of his enemy.

On August 1, 1940, Hitler issued an order of the strategy of advancing into the British mainland—"the Order No. 17"—and on August 13, he put a total confrontation with the British Air Force or "Adler Tag (Eagle Day)," but this was fought for an aerial extermination and did not include the aerial bombardment upon the city, as was also written clearly in the Fuhrer's order for the operations: "As for the horror bombing that aims at the city itself shall be withheld only as a means of retaliation." (*Fear, War and The bomb* by P. Blackett)

For prosecuting air and sea war against England, I have decided to carry on and intensify air and naval warfare against England in order to bring about her final defeat. For this purpose, I am issuing the following orders:

1) The German Air Force with all available forces will destroy the English Air Force as soon as possible. The attacks will be directed against airborne aircraft, then ground and supply organizations and then against industry, including the manufacture of air-craft equipment.

2) After gaining temporary or local air superiority, air attack will be continued on harbors, paying special attention to food storage depots in London.

3) Attacks on warships and on merchant shipping will be of secondary importance to those against enemy air power, except when specially favorable targets present themselves....

4) The intensified air war will be so planned that adequate forces may be diverted at any time to opportunity targets. Moreover fighting strength must be maintained at disposal for Operation Seelowe (Sea Lion).

5) I am reserving terror attack as reprisals.

Hitler had underlined on the final clause of his direction.

As is known by this fact, "the Battle of Britain" that had started with "*Adler Tag (Eagle Day)*" (the aerial battle performed in the skies of the British Isles) had been planned in order to remove all the aerial power there—as the preceding stage of their landing operations on the British Isles by the land force—so it had not intended to seek for the enemy's submission by destroying a city to a thorough extent. That could be called a transoceanic version of what the German Air Force had done as a herald of the ground forces about to advance into Warszawa or into Rotterdam. What the German Air Force had aimed at so far was aerial power (air bases), production factory (factories for producing air planes) and entry of food (supply route), but Hitler had remained prudent in making a British city itself a target of their aerial attack.

Recalling the fact that: in attacking Guernica, he performed a thorough destruction and massacre without showing any sign of self-restraint, what seems to be the dictator's motto—different tactics should be adopted for different nations—gives us a strange impression. This does remind us of the double standard adopted by the Japanese Navy Air Force—the limitless usage of their aerial power toward China and the limited usage of it toward the U.S..

Hitler as he was, he might not make himself so bold as to give such a reckless attack upon London as he had done upon Guernica,—as we may presume. But what Hitler aimed at then was to reduce the power of the British Air Force in preparation for his "Operation Seelowe (Sea Lion)"—the landing operation upon the British Isles—instead of the air raid upon a particular city.

On the other hand, Churchill, who had once regarded what happened at Guernica as "an experimental atrocity performed upon the vulnerable city," had turned himself into "a believer in aerial bombings" since he took office as Prime Minister, and if he could not find any other means of attacking the German mainland, he was not going to restrain himself or pay any calculative consideration in performing strategic bombings upon somewhere in German proper, as Japan was doing in Chongqing in China, thus betraying what John Fuller called "his cruel desire to burn his enemies to death or to make them bleed."

● The U.K. and Germany Started to Exchange their Indiscriminate Bombings upon Cities

Germany's Adler Tag (Eagles' Day) Operations as the preceding stage of Seelowe (Sea Lion) Operations for Landing on the British Mainland, and "the Battle of Britain" as the British effort to do her best in defending her sky and land were to get into full gear on August 13, 1940. And it was during this first couple of months and a half that the indiscriminate bombings upon the cities performed by both Britain and Germany began to be adopted as an ordinary practice in carrying out modern warfare.

It was the British side that had taken the initiative in the indiscriminate bombings upon cities. As was seen in "the Order No.17", Hitler at that point had reserved the right to decide upon "terror bombing." Jhon Lukacs also wrote in his work *Hitler versus Churchill:* "It would be wrong if you think that what had led Hitler to give a distinct order that they must not drop bombs upon any densely-populated area on the British Isles was because he had still retained any respect for the British people," but he made it clear what had made Churchill the first to adopt the indiscriminate bombings.

That was an accidental bombing brought about by a German bomber. On August 24, when one of the one hundred and seventy German bombers of Heinkel He 111—which were to give a night attack upon the air force base in the suburbs of London—failed to find out their target and dropped their bombs upon the City of London—without taking aim at anything specific, even though they had received a special order not to drop their bombs at random. Those who had come out of the pubs at the closing time or on their way home from movie theaters were to fall on an evil fate.

Churchill took advantage of this opportunity. The British Prime Minister, who had already permitted the group of bombers' activities upon the cities in Ruhr for more than a year, regarded this night attack upon the City as a signal for their start of indiscriminate bombings upon the German capital. The Chief of the General Staff of the Army, Field Marshal Alainburg, wrote as follows in his biography, *The Diary of The Chief of The General Staff,* as is recorded in *The Turn of the Tide (1939-1940)* by Arthor Bryant:

> The Fighter Command was still in being. And, though its numbers were dwindling fast, in the course of the day a remarkable change came over the air war. It was due primarily to Churchill. A fortnight earlier, on August 24th, the first bombs had fallen in the central London area. Though the maximum force available for bombing, Germany was scarcely a tenth of what the Luftwaffe could send over England and the distance from its airfields to the German capital six times greater than that between the French coast and London, the Prime Minister had without hesitation proposed the bombing of Berlin. On the night of 25th eighty-one British air craft set out, twenty-nine of which reached their objective. Other night raids followed and, though the damage was small, their effect on Hitler's temper was extensive. On

September 4th he announced his intention of wiping out London.

Obviously, Churchill's overreaction touched off, but on the side of Hitler, too, it came to work as something so disgraceful as to allow the enemy planes to perform the air raid upon the capital in the midst of his having led a successful war. As the Chief of the General Staff, Alainburg, had been aware of it, if the British bombers were to enter Berlin, they had to fly six times as long as the distance from London to the northern coast of France, while the British bombers' capability was no more than one tenth of the German Air Force's. These facts had led Hitler and Goring, the Commander-in-Chief of the Air Force, to declare the enemy's incapability of performing any air raid upon their capital, Berlin, to the relief of the German people. This infuriated Hitler. Naturally, this led Germany, stronger in military potential, to compete with the U.K. by enlarging its area for bombardment.

Hitler ordered Goring to change their aim of aerial strategy from devastating the air bases to performing the air raids upon London. This was how the serial bombings upon Berlin—six times during a couple of weeks—was followed by German Air Force's relentless, indiscriminate bombings upon London. Liddell Hart also came to discover, as he wrote in *History of The Second World War*, what Churchill was—through that series of overreactions he had shown on that occasion:

> All these cases were, actually, products of misinterpretation—if quite natural ones—as the Luftwaffe was still operating under orders to conform to the old, and longstanding, rules of bombardment, and exceptions hitherto arose from navigational mistakes. But they created a growing desire to hit back at German cities, and indiscriminately. Awareness that Bomber Command now constituted Britain's only offensive weapon in the near future, deepened both the instinct and the desire. Both were particularly evident in Mr. Churchill's attitude.

If spoken genuinely from what had actually occurred, it would be able to assert that: Churchill's having dared to perform the indiscriminate bombings upon German cities had rescued the U.K.. Because the shock of the air raid upon Berlin brought about a fatal failure upon Hitler's pursuit of the aim of his strategy against the U.K., thus causing him to change the aim of "the aerial strategy against the U.K." from "exterminating the enemy's aerial power in order to help his Army's landing operation" to "performing the air raids upon the City of London" by letting his personal anger dictate it. This gave the U.K. being engaged in "the Battle of Britain" a once-and-for-all opportunity to take a breath and recover herself. Hitler's change in policy resulted in the abandonment of his "Seelowe (Sea Lion) Operations," directly causing influence in the progress of the war situation thereafter. But at that point, one of the brakes on the warfare having been lifted, the mutual enlargement of the bombardments upon the cities in Europe were to lead to the endless runaway, causing the general citizens to suffer from extreme miseries, while the influence brought about by the generalization of such tactics was even greater to make the mankind suffer for a long period of time to come.

During the early period of the U.K.'s strategic bombings upon Germany— from August in 1940 to May in 1941—the British bombers dropped about 20,000 tons of bombs upon Germany, when the tonnage brought about to Chongqing so far was 2,000 tons. That was ten times larger. The damages brought about to the industrial production remained insignificant, but the citizens' deaths had reached about 3,000. One tonnage of bombs had brought about 0.15 human death; the number of deaths of each month was about 300.

On the other hand, the casualties among the British citizens were incomparable. The retaliatory attack by Germany, which started in September, 1940, to last till May the following year, was to bring 40,000 citizens to death by 50,000 tons of bombs dropped on the British Isles during the nine months. This meant one ton of bombs killed a 0.8 citizen, or five times more effective than those attacks given by the British upon the German, causing 4,500 deaths every month, or fifteen times as many deaths as those in Germany. The main reason for this was the difference in their aerial power. (*The Turn of the Tide* by Arthur Bryant)

London was exposed to the air raids for 57 days on end—from September 7 to November 2. Guarded by fighters of Messerschmidt Bf 109 & Me 110, more than three hundred Dornier & Heinkel middle-sized bombers in formation came into the skies of London day after day. They flew along the Thames to London, disregarding the airbases on their way and dropped incendiary bombs and high-efficiency bombs in the City and the living quarters of laborers. The citizens called these attacks directed toward their daily life "blitz." The average number of the planes that arrived at night was 165, and London was burnt to ashes in 57 days by 13,600 tons of bombs.

The air raids were performed not only on London but also on such provincial cities as Coventry, Birmingham, Southampton, Bristol, Liverpool and so on. Above all, the "blitz" given to Coventry, an industrial city in the middle of Warwickshire, was a re-advent of Guernica—a bombardment aiming at annihilating the whole city. The 437 bombers had been mobilized, as was reported in *LIFE: The History of The Second World War:*

On a moonlit night in mid-November 14, it was the turn of the medieval cathedral city of Coventry—also one of the biggest concentrations of armaments factories in the United Kingdom. Pathfinder aircraft blanketed Coventry with incendiaries, transforming the hapless city into a mammoth beacon on which 437 Heinkel-111s dropped 450 tons of high-explosive and incendiary bombs. By dawn the heart of Coventry had been all but wiped out. The Cathedral was devastated. More than 50,000 structures were damaged or destroyed, 380 people killed, 865 citizens seriously hurt.

The city life in Coventry had completely lost its function and remained still for quite a while. Churchill wrote in his autobiography: "This was the most destructive attack we had ever had." Goring declared over the radio: "The same thing will happen to every other city in the U.K.." Those reserved attitudes Hitler used to assume toward "the horror bombardment" had long been discarded.

● **Shigemitsu Mamoru's Note on the Air Raids in London**

About this period of time when a magazine published in Chongqing was featuring *A Tale of Two Cities—Chongqing & London*—describing their situations: "Encountering the Similar Adversities; Suffering the Same Kind of Hardship," a Japanese ambassador to the U.K. staying in London—Shigemitsu Mamoru—was writing down what he had witnessed and experienced in London at that time (1940). His embassy also had often been exposed to near hits, as he wrote in *Shigemitsu Mamoru's Note:*

The air raids occur day and night. Since Hitler declared his retaliatory attacks against the B.K.'s night attacks, their night attacks have grown especially intense. From East End to West End in London, from the urban area to the residential area, not a single spot has remained intact. It is gruesome, indeed. (Several paragraphs omitted)

On October 14: We were at supper. The air raid had already started. We remained at table, and when pudding—jam roll—was placed before us, *that* terrible whistling was heard, and the whole house shook hard and the chandelier above us rattled, when we heard windowpanes fall and crash on the ground. Another bomb and the following one, too, fell in the neighborhood. We looked at one another. Then Taira Osamu, saying "Excuse me!" jumped out of the room. He wanted to climb up to the roof so he might create a painting of London under the air raid. Jam rolls remained as they were on the table.

"It's too dangerous to remain here," we said to each other, and trying to hide ourselves under the table, we put our knees on the floor, when another bomb came. Leaving the jam rolls as they were, we decided to take refuge in the cellar. Since then, we have shared a password: "Beware when you have jam roll served." The bomb had fallen on the house one or two houses away.

Then Shigemitsu made up his mind, writing as follows:

I am prepared to die at this battlefield of mine. Even if I were to be bombed to death here and today, I shall be quite satisfied as long as I am staying at this diplomatic frontline. This is especially so, if I—someone so humble as myself—were able to put any soul into the future diplomacy of our Empire. My colleagues worry about me and recommend me to move somewhere safer, but I have not listened to them.

In the years to come, he was to experience in Tokyo the air raids so fierce as he had never experienced even in London, and then as the Foreign Minister, he was to sign the surrender. Shigemitsu in London may have been feeling a premonition of what would become of his own country.

Churchill's Theory on Bombardment

● The Theory on "the Regional Bombardment"

The full-scale strategic bombings by the U.K. Air Force upon German cities started in March, 1942. In Chongqing, they were in the fourth year of the air raids—by way of "5.3 & 5.4" and Japan's Operations No.1 and No.2—about the time when Guo Moruo's *Qu Yuan* was being premiered.

For Churchill, who had provoked Hitler into the exchanges of city-bombardments, there was no reason for hesitating to perform indiscriminate bombings against Germany. At that time—until 1944 when the Allied Nations' ground army started an operation for advancing into German territory—giving an offensive attack by bombers was the only means for the U.K. to be able to give direct attacks on Germany; it was also an effective way to raise the national morale under the banner of "retaliation," as Churchill, a man of politics, had been well aware of and calculated upon. Europe had been trampled down by the caterpillars of the German Armored Division, while in Asia, the Union Jacks raised abobe the battleships of the Oriental Fleet—*The Repulse* and *The Prince of Wales*—had sunken in vain together with a great deal of expectation placed upon them. Hong Kong had fallen into the hands of the Japanese military, while Singapore also had fallen.

On February 14, 1942, a new order was given to the U.K. Air Force's Bombers' Group. By then, the attack from the air had clearly been written down, as follows: "Focus on the morale of general public and industrial workers of the enemy nation." (From what Liddell Hart quoted from Vol. 1 of *The War History* published by the U.K. Government) That was an official recognition of the tactics called "regional bombardment," and none other than the tactical expression of the conception held by Churchill who had declared: "The morale of the general public shall be our military target." This led Liddell-Hart to criticize the new tactics, saying: "Thus in the questions and answers in the Parliament, he (Churchill) still kept up appearance, but the undisguised terror tactics had already become the definite tactics for the British Government to take."

Another military historian, John Fuller, also criticized the regional bombardment, saying: "This is closely related with Churchill's cruel desire to kill the German people." Certainly the U.K. Prime Minister's desire to "burn and bleed the enemies to death by all the means available" had been brought into being in a form of strategy.

That new theory on bombardment called "regional bombardment" was brought into being by the personality and the volition of the three persons: the Prime Minister Churchill and his counselor in the field of science, Lord Frederic Cherwell, a professor of physics of Oxford University, and Air Marshal, Sir Arthur Harris, who had been appointed Commander of the Bombers' Group. Cherwell was the planner; Churchill the arbiter; Harris the executor. Their regional bombardment was a larger-scaled and more-precisely-constructed version of what had once been attempted at Chongqing under the dictatorship of Inoue Shigeyoshi and Onishi Takijiro, and it could be called "a systematization of the indiscriminate bombings." Now the conclusion they had reached was: "The only target for their night attack to be performed effectively is a single town as a whole."

Professor Cherwell, by making use of the method of statistics, demonstrated the fact that: in carrying out the war, the attack upon the people's morale is more effective than the attack upon the industrial base. This demonstration of his was based on the air raids experienced by the British people. (*The Air War in Europe* by Ronald H. Bailey)

Charwell bolstered his case with statistics. He figured that for every ton of bombs the Germans had dropped in the cities in the survey, between 100 and 200 people had been made homeless. By this measure, a British bomber, assuming it lasted long enough to make 14 sorties, could "dehouse" 4,000 to 8,000 Germans. Cherwell noted that much of the German population—22 million people—was concentrated in 58 cities. He estimated that if these cities were subjected area bombing over a period of 18 months, the RAF could "dehouse" at least a third of the entire German population and thus "break the spirit of the people."

Here we can see the original form of what was to be performed in Vietnam in later years by the American strategists—blighting the jangles and burning up the farmhouses in the countryside. Also in the same 1960s, what the U.S. Secretary of Defense, Robert McNamara had added to the strategic terminology—"confirmed destructive potentiality"—though that concept parades a slogan of "staving off war," since it stresses the point in "frustrating the enemy nation's combative spirit" by dint of nuclear weapons "which are capable of destroying one third or one fourth of the population of the enemy nation and one third of the industrial power," it does correspond to Cherwell's theory of regional bombardment. McNamara's theory could be called a globalization of the regional bombardment. The conclusion presented by Cherwell—just like "the Northern Bombing" in Vietnam—soon came to be proved obviously wrong, but that objective method he adopted and the precise analysis and the clear conclusion he brought about was to bring the conception of strategic bombing from the period of "prediction and trial" to the period of "calculation and strength of material," to be handed down to the nuclear age.

Prime Minister Churchill had anxiously been waiting for Sir Cherwell's memorandum to be handed to him, and as soon as he received it, he appointed Air-Marshal Arthur Harris to be the person in charge of that Regional Bombing upon the German cities. This was how Harris, who was soon to be called "Butcher" or "Bomber," presented himself in the history of the strategic bombings. In February, 1942. Air Marshal Sir Arthur Harris was appointed Commander of the Bombers Fleet.

● Lubeck, the First City to Suffer a Regional Bombing

The first German city that had been burnt up according to that theory of the regional bombing created by that trio was Lubeck facing the Baltic, a storied city with its own history as "a Hanseatic town." The town that dated back to the medieval period had been checkered with its complicated narrow streets and most of the houses lining them were built of wood. Situated at the mouth of the Trave, it could easily be found and approached; its antiaircraft defense was not so strong; its structure was highly inflammable. These conditions had led Commander Harris to select that town as the first aim for the regional bombing. On March 28, 1942, the bombardment upon Lubeck was performed. The four-engined bombers "Lancaster," which had recently joined the B. K. Air Force, made their first appearance. Half of the 300 tons of bombs on board the 234 bombers were incendiary bombs. It was since this time when *the* tactics to be performed "at night, on a densely-populated area, with incendiary bombs"— which had long been adopted in attacking Chongqing—began to be adopted in Europe.

Taking advantage of the incomplete equipment of anti-aircraft fire, the swarms of the British bombers came flying down to the altitude of 600m to drop their incendiary bombs, which caused about half of the city of Lubeck to burn up, depriving more than fifteen thousand citizens of their houses. Lubeck Cathedral, which had been brought into being in the 12th century, was also destroyed. Both God and people had been made "homeless," according to Sir Cherwell. Goebbels, the Publicity Minister of Nazi Germany, having seen the news movie of Lubeck being burst into flames, wrote in his diary (on March 30 and 31, 1942) about how shocking it was to him:

> This Sunday was made to turn into a terrible day by the British Air Force's unusually powerful air raid. …. The eighty percent of the old part of the town must be considered to have been reduced to ashes. …. I was made to see the news film of how horribly the town had been brought into ruins. …. We cannot disregard the fact that the British air raids have been increasing its range and importance. If they were to keep going along this line for several weeks, it would become effective in destroying the people's morale.

Goebbel's having been shocked like this meant the growing confidence on the side of Harris and the British Bombers' fleet under him. By and by, a newly-coined word—"making another Lubeck"—began to be employed, meaning "exterminating an urban area." Harris, who had got a growing confidence in "regional bombing," began to turn his eyes upon another aim. By and by, two other Hanseatic towns—Koln and Bremen—were selected.

In attacking Koln from the air, Harris devised a new form of it. That was a plan of campaign performed by one thousand bombers, which was called "bomber stream" or "saturation bombing." In fact, an action of one thousand bombers was something unheard of. So far the greatest number of the planes mobilized for a single sortie was 234 for the air raid upon Lubeck, and that was considered to be a ceiling. Considering that the largest number of the planes the German Air Force had sent for their air raid upon London was 487, the number Haris was going to send to Koln was more than twice of it. In the Japanese Air Force's strategy upon Chongqing, they had never sent more than 200 planes for a single sortie.

Now Harris calculated that: employing 1,000 bombers, making two thirds of the bombs incendiary ones, to perform an overwhelming flame-attack to send the whole city to a total destruction, thus to cause the enemy's abilities in defense and fire-fighting and relief activities to reach their saturation point, it would surely succeed in frustrating the morale of the German people. Making the 1,000 bombers perform concentrated bombings upon the urban area within ninety minutes—this was the conception of what he called "the bomber stream" and "saturation bombardment."

Churchill, having been easily fascinated with this horrible tactics, made himself a powerful prompter of it. Having beaten off the objection presented by some members of the wartime cabinet, the cabinet meeting approved that strategy to be performed by one thousand bombers. Harris took time in giving Churchill a detailed explanation of this strategy, and it was at 3 in the morning when he left for home in good form.

The pressing need then was to collect such a large number of planes as that. Since four-engined bombers of Halifax and Lancaster had come up to the period of starting their mass production, if twin-engined bombers for training flight were added, they could manage to prepare even more than one thousand planes. What was even more difficult was to collect crew members. One plane needed a crew of seven on the average. How could they collect as many as seven thousand crew members? All the teaching staff and trainees were mobilized, and still it remained undermanned. Thus applicants were collected even from among the ground crew members, until at last scratch crews were formed. Such advancing operations from the sky—with seven thousand crew on board the one thousand airplanes—were naturally unprecedented in the war history.

● **From "the Bomber Stream" to "the Aerial Attack"**

On May 30, 1942, in the skies of Koln bathing in the light of the full moon, the onrush of "the Bomber Stream" did arrive. The bombers of all types, old and new, advanced in a huge belt as long as 110km in order to arrive at the third largest city in Germany, with a population of 800,000, an industrial strongpoint looking out on the Rhine.

At 0:47 a.m. the first incendiary bomb was released to cause the fire to indicate the planes behind where they should drop their bombs. At 2:25 a.m., the final bomb was dropped by the third wave—1,455 tons in all. Ninety-eight minutes had passed. The citizens of Koln had been thrown into a crucial horror and chaos caused by the new type of bombardment developed by the U.K. Air Force. The number of fires caused by it reached 12,000, and 18,432 houses were completely destroyed or burnt down. Koln had already been bombed, but the bombardment that night was by far greater than any other they had experienced so far, and it did deserved the name of "a saturation bombing." The following is what R. Bailey described it in his work, *The Air War in Europe:*

> In Cologne (Koln) the glare of the burning city outshone even the sun. Some 600 acres (about 2.4km squares) lay in flaming ruins. More than 250 factories—including metal and rubber and chemical works, and plants that manufactured machine tools and submarine engines—were either destroyed or badly damaged. The dead numbered 474. More than 45,000 people were made homeless, and the roads leading out of Cologne were clogged; officials fretted about the demoralizing effect on the rest of Germany and made a futile attempt to hush up eyewitness accounts of the horror.

Prime Minister Churchill gave a warning: "Cologne is nothing but the first stage of what would go on happening. Every city in Germany will be exposed to the same fate as Cologne was." In fact, in June or the month that followed, Essen and Bremen were to receive the bombardment of the same scale as Cologne. Goebbels, Publicity Minister of Nazi Germany, pledged himself to perform their retaliatory attacks against "the indiscriminate bombings to exterminate all those non-combatants and civilians, even though they were what we had kept avoiding so far," and that was to escalate into the development and adoption of their new weapons for strategic bombings—"Revenge Bombs" (Vergeltungswaffe) V1 and V2. A flow from the attacks by the aircraft to the jet-propelled guided missile (V1) and rocket propulsion unmanned aircraft (V2)—or the flow to "the attack by missiles"—came to the fore from the exchanges of bombardments between the U.K. and Germany with the Strait of Dover between them.

The following was what was mentioned on June 2 by a writer, George Orwell, who, at that time, had been engaged in radio broadcasting toward India once a week as a news commentator of BBC:[*]

> This week a couple of air raids—whose scales were unheard of even in

the world history—were performed upon Germany. On the night of May 30, more than one thousand bombers assaulted Cologne, and on the night of June 1, too, more than one thousand bombers made an attack on Essen in Ruhr. Then, two more raids were given, though not so large-scaled as before…. What was remarkable about these was that: all these planes engaged in them were produced in the U.K. and the assaults were made exclusively by the B.K. Air Force. …. But, these attacks were not unjustified ones, because even if some non-combatants might be unavoidably killed, those bombardments had not been aimed at ordinary citizens there. Koln is a seat of the liaison station for all the trunk lines in Germany and is also the center of essential industries in Germany. That was why it was assaulted.

*Partly because of economic reason, he was engaged in this job. Soon after he left BBC in 1943, he began to write *The Animal Farm* (1945) and *1984* (1949).

At this stage, those concerned with the U.S. Army Air Force, still having retained their "Puritanical" sensibility, were giving a cold stare at those British-style regional bombardments and would not allow themselves to join them.

● **The Night Attacks Performed by the U.K.; The Day Attacks by the U.S.**
During the same hour when one plane after another was taking off from the U.K. Air Base to join "the bomber stream," at Checkers or the Prime Minister's villa in the suburbs of London, a dinner party under the auspices of Churchill was at its height. Those who were invited there were the high-ranking officers of the U.S. Army Air Force, including General Henry Arnold of U.S.A.A.F. (United States' Army Air Force) and Brigadier General Ira Eaker as Commander of the Eighth Bombers' Group of the Eighth Air Force. Eaker's Eighth Bombers' Group at that time had been at its preparatory stage in deploying the then new and powerful bombers B17 from the U.S. to the U.K.. Beside Churchill, "Bomber Harris" was seated. At this significant night, the fact that the Commander himself of that strategy of sending one thousand bombers to Koln was being absent from the commanding office tacitly told that: that dinner party meant something more important than a mere ceremony. Churchill that evening had aimed at persuading the U.S. side relevant to the aviation that:

the night time bombing would be a short cut in subduing Germany, thus trying to invite the U.S. Aviation capability into the U.K. strategy.

As for the air-raiding, however, those from the U.S. had kept a conception clearly different from the one retained by Churchill and Harris. The reason was that: the U.S. bombers had been designed as daytime bombers equipped with powerful defensive firearm and effective power of a Norden sighting device, and it had been believed that: after approaching the sky above their aim, they were able to attack any specified small aim by their pinpoint bombing. With that basic conception behind their design, B17 "flying fortresses" and B24 "liberators" were being produced in rapid succession from their production line; and upon that same basic belief, the development of B29s or the first stratospheric bombers had already come to the final stage of their production. This precise technique of daytime pinpoint bombing from high altitudes by dint of dauntless courage to approach their objective was none other than the ideology of bombardment that had been kept retaining by the U.S. Army Air Force since Billy Mitchell advocated it. Indiscriminate bombing and incendiary bombing were believed to be astray from the beaten track of warfare, and President Roosevelt himself (even if he had his staff consider performing indiscriminate bombings upon Japanese cities) had been appealing to the other nations, saying: the aerial bombings should be restricted only to the military targets. Then such a regional attack as was being advocated by Churchill was out of question.

This difference of view had come up to the surface since the U.S. joined in the war, and in February, 1942, when Harris took office as Commander of the Bombers' Group, Brigadier General Eaker who arrived at London to take up a new position was often persuaded by Churchill that he should stop preparing for the daytime bombing and join the night bombing the U.K. Air Force was being engaged in, but Eaker, who had been an out-and-out believer in daytime pinpoint bombing, kept observing the basics of the U.S.' strategy and would not make any concession.

So it was quite natural that they were talking about this matter at the dinner party that evening when Koln was about to be assaulted by the one thousand British bombers, keeping Harris busy trying to convert the U.S. guests to the B.K.'s principle by making use of the information kept reported from the very spot. But both Arnold and Eaker, even though admiring their successful bombardments, managed to keep avoiding the situation in which they might be converted.

It was not until January, 1943, when this serious discordance in views between the U.K. and the U.S. was brought to an end, though provisionally, at the Casablanca Conference held between President Roosevelt and Prime Minister Churchill. In order to make Churchill change his mind when he proposed to Roosevelt that he should stop daytime attack but cooperate in U.K.'s night attack in order to bring Germany into annihilation, Eaker, according to Arnold's order, finished writing a memorandum to defend their "daytime pinpoint bombing." The conclusion he gave was: The U.K. should keep on the nighttime bombing; the U.S. should concentrate on the daytime bombing. Eaker, in order to satisfy the pride of Churchill, an epigrammatist, had adopted such an expression as "If we keep chasing the devils about for 24 hours on end, we shall be able to deprive the setup of German Army's Air Defense of their rest."

The Casablanca Conference summarized the aim of the strategic bombing as follows:

"Destroying and paralyzing Germany's military, industrial and economic organizations, thus to demoralize their fighting spirit and to lower their fighting capacity to a decisive extent."

This was how their united plan of attacks upon Germany was established: The B.K. Air Force's night attack should be aimed mainly at the industrial areas and densely built-up areas; the U.S. Air Force's daylight attack should be upon factories and other industrial facilities.

German Cities being Annihilated by the Air Raids

● **B17s and B24s were Sent over to the European Aerial Battles**

The U.S. Air Raid Unit's entry into the European Air Battles could not help completely changing what the air raiding used to be, because of its overwhelmingly large amount of materials brought into them. Those artillerymen who had rushed into the European aerial battles by their giant bomber B17s and B24s were brimming with confident that: if such bombers as theirs, whose armoring and armaments had been strengthened, were to perform an ultra-high altitude flight in a close order, they would be able to perform pinpoint bombings without suffering any serious damage. All those Americans were youthful and active, and more than anything else, they were brimming with a sense of mission of "saving Europe." To the Nazis' top leaders, this reinforcement from "the New World" could be an incident that made them anticipate the worst situation. Goebbels, the Publicity Minister of Nazi Germany, trembling with fury, wrote in his diary (dated March 3, 1942):

> I feel as if I were going mad to think that: the Canadian peasants—even unable to point where Europe is on the globe—have come flying from the land whose natural resources were such that they simply cannot tell what they should do to develop them—only to drop bombs upon us living in this over-populated continent.

But however much those living in the Old World might cry or scream, it was they themselves or their Nazism that had set fire on the fury of those living in the New World. The mechanism of the war had already been running with might and main. Under the command of the U.S. Eighth Army Air Forth, a heavy bomber unit—whose commission was to perform strategic bombing— was brought into being at Bushpark in the suburbs of London, and under the U.S. Army's European Theater of Operations led by General Dwight Eisenhower, the preparations for the strategic bombings against Germany were rapidly being made. Since the transport ships alone were not enough, the large expeditionary forces crossed the Occident on board the Queen Elizabeth.

At this period (June, 1941), the U.S. Air Force was reorganized from U.S.A.A.C. (U.S.A. Air Corps) to U.S.A.A.F. (U.S.A. Air Force), thus it was on its way to enlargement and independence, but seen from a personnel viewpoint, it had largely remained what it used to be at its early period. Still the time had come when all those who had been brought up by Colonel Mitchell— one of the founders of Army Air Force and one of the advocates of the theory of strategic bombings, but suffered demotion (from Brigadier General to Colonel) on a charge of having criticized the military authorities until at last he was purged from the Army—were to rise to the posts of the top leaders of the U.S. Air Force and command the European aerial battle.

All those young generals—Arnold, Sparts and Eaker—who had been brought up at what used to be called "Mitchel School" had kept an intense self-confidence in their master's conception, and had shared an unshakable faith in the aerial capability as the essential element to win the Great War. They had been backed up by the Wright Brothers and Mitchell, while being equipped with B17 bombers and Norden sighting devices. With old-fashioned Europe before them, they had not had anything that might dishearten them.

● General Arnold and Colonel LeMay were made Commanders

General Henry Arnold (the first General of the U.S. Air Force in the years to come), who was to direct the Army Air Force at every war zone throughout the whole period of World War II, had carefully been brought up by Mitchel since he was still a company officer, and when Mitchell was subjected to trial by court-martial, he took upon himself to an attendant of him, and this caused him to be demoted to a member of a reconnoitering party in Kansas from being an information officer in Washington. He himself was an airman, who, in 1934, led ten bombers—B10 bombers—to perform a successful nonstop flight from Alaska to Seattle thus to prove the potentiality of a long-range bombing. Later these B10 bombers were sent to China to be known as the planes employed in May, 1938, to fly and scatter the leaflets from the sky of Kyushu, Japan, for advocating stopping its invasion into China, as mentioned toward the end of Chapter V. Arnold, who had made himself a successor to Mitchell both nominally and virtually, was to make himself a central figure—by actually putting his theory on strategic bombing into practice—in raising the U.S. Air Force to an independent force.

Under Arnold, there were Major General Karl Spaatz, who was appointed Commander of the Eighth Bombers' Group which was sent to Europe, and Brigadier general Ira Eaker, who also became Commander of the 8th group of bombers under Karl Spaatz, had both been known as enthusiastic supporters of Mitchell, and in "the Inquisition," as was called by his supporters, Spaatz made himself a defense witness, while Eaker brought himself as an aide of the defense team, thus both had a period in which they had to endure the cold treatment from the mainstream of the military.

Anyway, both of them were out-and-out airmen, and in January, 1929, they made an unprecedented flight endurance record of more than 150 hours by making use of a newly-developed technique of aerial refueling—Major Colonel

Spaatz as a director, and Captain Eaker as a pilot. In this way, Arnold, Spaatz and Eaker had made themselves pioneers in the U.S. Army Air Force, and for more than twenty years from its establishment to World War Ⅱ, they had been keeping themselves united so much so that not a single year had passed without their getting together at some unit or other. And now, each of them— with the titles of Supreme Commander of the Army Air Force, Commander of the European Theater of War, and Commander of the Strategic Bombing Unit respectively—was blessed with the opportunity to prove the theory on the superiority of the air force they had kept advocating so far. So, they now had every reason for bracing themselves up.

There was one more American who had made himself unforgettable in this "aerial battle in Europe." A short-tempered one from Ohaio—Colonel Curtis LeMay—a 36-year-old commander of a bomber fleet, who was also made general in the years to come. LeMay, always having a cigar between his lips, while driving his subordinates hard, had been offered a nickname "Iron Bottom." But no sooner had he been appointed as Commander of No. 305 aerial bombing corps under Eaker than he began to distinguish himself to a remarkable extent. LeMay—who had grasped from his own experience that: in order to perform a daytime precision bombing upon a certain aim, not only the effective use of a Norden bombsight but also the strict preservation of a compact formation of bombers is indispensable—invented a battle formation of "a combat box," which enabled them to achieve both excellent defensive power and concentration power in bombing at the same time. Unlike the B.K. Air Force's "bomber stream" method, in the U.S.' method, whose principle was to enter the sky of the enemy during the day time without any fighter planes to protect their bombers, defending their bombers in their formation from the enemy fighter planes was an urgent task of great importance, and mastering how to constitute such a formation as not to have any blind spot in it and how to preserve it strictly became an important element to decide the result of their attack and the rate of their damage. Thus LeMay's reformation was adopted as a standard mode by the U.S. Bomber Unit. It was since this period of time that Colonel LeMay began to be known for his fighting spirit and severe training. By and by, he became known not only in Europe but also in the hinterland of China and then on the Mariana Islands. Even after World War Ⅱ, he was to be remembered, along with a term of "strategic air force," as a planner of strategic bombings in the nuclear age.

● The Defects of Bomb Sights Caused a Gradual Rise in the Damage Rate of the U.S. Bombers

The U.S. Air Force led by these commanders flew the first mission on July 4, 1942. Eight months had passed since they participated in the War. The first bombing action was performed by the six B17 bombers, which had joined the Royal Air Force's assault upon a Dutch airport. On August 17, the first independent mission was performed by twelve B17 bombers and dropped 18.5 tons of bombs upon Rouen 320km northwest of Paris. Two planes were shot by antiaircraft fire, but it was propitious enough that all were able to return to their base. Commander Ira Eaker himself accompanied the operation and gave an example of how the commander should take the lead in the air.

During that year (1942), Eaker's Eighth Air Force sent a total of 1,547 planes for sorties and lost 32 of them. The loss ratio was 2 percent. Comparing it with 4 percent in the BK Air Force, it was about half. This appeared to be a powerful evidence against the U.K.'s criticism that the daytime bombing of the large formation of B17s without any guard could not help suffering a great damage. The U.S. Air Force had not yet entered the skies of Germany where a large number of interceptor fighters were waiting for them, but Eaker and others from the U.S. confirmed their faith in what they had achieved in Europe so far.

But it was about this time that their brimming confidence began to be reduced by such unexpected miscalculation as would dampen their brimming confidence. The Norden bombsight which could be called the brain to realize their pinpoint bombing—a top-secret new weapon developed by the U.S. technology camp, which had made a sighting telescope and a calculator (an early computer) work together—did work as perfectly as was expected in good weather, but in Europe where the weather is usually far from good, that same device did not work as was expected. If the Norden bombsight was not available here, they had to turn to a raider even if the accuracy rate was inevitably lowered. To make the matter worse, as they brought their bombing aims into the territory of Germany, the U.S. bomber fleet which lacked escort fighters had to get more and more damages, making them realize the necessity of having their long-distance escort fighters. This was exactly the same problem as the Japanese middle-sized bombers had to face in their bombing flight to

Chongqing.

These two adversities—the defect of their sighting device and the rise of their damage rate—did press the revision of the U.S.' policy in achieving their strategic purpose, but the top leaders of the U.S. Air Force had not yet formally decided whether to revise or to abandon their line. Therefore, what was agreed upon at the Casablanca Conference—that the Allied Forces' strategic bombings upon Germany should be performed upon the principle: during the daytime, the U.S. would perform according to their principle of attacking only on the military target; during the nighttime, the U.K. would perform an indiscriminate bombing upon the city—was officially retained. But the U.S. bombers—under the weather in which they could not turn on their Norden bombsight—turned on the H2S bombsight radar, while they began to fly a night mission, too, thus rapidly turning their action more and more similar to "the regional bombing" retained by the U.K. Air Force. Ira Eaker, who had been an out-and-out retainer of "the attacking only on the military targets," was relocated, regardless of his own intention, to the Mediterranean District as a result of a change in personnel in December, 1943, and as a successor to him, there arrived Lieutenant General James Dolittle, who was to be known for the first air raid upon Tokyo. Curtis LeMay, who had been able to apply his ability whichever situation he was placed in, was remarkably promoted to General. These had reflected virtual changes in policy according to the situations even if the principle was kept as it was. But it was not in the skies of Europe but in the skies of Asia that their changes of lines—their conformity to the indiscriminate bombings under the name of "regional bombings"—presented themselves in a distinctive form.

● **The U.S. Air Force also Performed the Indiscriminate Bombings**
                                          upon Hamburg and Dresden

Still we cannot forget the two air raids—the one performed upon Hamburg in July and August, 1943, the other upon Dresden in February, 1945—which had occurred while the U.K. and the U.S. were approaching in their policies on air raids. Either of them was performed under the leadership of the U.K. Air Force, but the U.S. Air Force also having partially joined them. In the case of Hamburg, the U.S. Air Force was able to find an excuse of "having bombed only upon military facilities." But when it came to Dresden where there was not any such particular military target, it was impossible to find out any such excuse. And the new mode of the U.S. bombardment policy which had been tried toward the end of the European aerial war was to be immediately adopted in their tactics upon Japan until it became their ordinary way in air-raiding Japanese cities.

The air raids upon Hamburg were performed for nine successive days from late July to early August. That was literally a series of "round-the-clock bombings." The B.K.'s Lancaster bombers, adopting the tactics of "the bomber stream," dropped the bombs upon the urban area during the night; on the day that followed, the U.S.' B17 bombers performed bombings upon the shipyards and their port installations. Because of the aluminum pieces scattered to fly into the eyes of citizens, the German Army's air search radars were turned chalk white and their aerial defense function had been paralyzed. Both fire-fighting functions and relief systems were cut into pieces and it was impossible to take any action. Still huge bursts of flames created an ascending air current and caused an intense fire storm. The typhoon-like strong wind dug up trees and hurled up automobiles. Those who were fortunate enough to be able to enter the air raid shelters, unable to get away from the blasts of heated air were choked and burnt to death.

"Terror! Terror! Terror! Pure, plain, bloody terror!"

After the fourth air raid, Dr. Karl Hoffmann, a news commentator, exclaimed like this. The 26.5km squares of the urban area were destroyed, half of the buildings were leveled to the ground, and more than 50,000 people were presumed to have died.

During the nine-day bombardments, the U.S. bombers performed day-time bombardment three times. Their aims were shipyards, docks, power plants, arsenals and the like, and nominally it was possible to assert that what they did had not deviated from the line of pinpoint bombings. But the air raid upon Hamburg, as had accidentally been revealed in its secret nickname "Gomorrah strategy," had been performed, expecting to reenact the cursed city which had been destroyed by fire and sulfa, as was mentioned in the Book of Genesis, and so, having joined in it alone could be pointed out as a serious deviation from their bombing policy. Furthermore, by "Thunder Clap" or the air raid upon Dresden, which was performed three months before the surrender of Germany, the U.S. also was to be counted among the nations that had joined the indiscriminate bombings performed in Europe.

"Thunder Clap" had not originally been planned specifically for Dresden. After the Allied Powers landed on Normandy in June, 1944, Germany was obviously in an adverse situation, and in order to accelerate it, the Allied Powers had intended to perform large-scaled air raid upon any densely-inhabited district, thus to press Germany into an unconditional surrender, and this led them to choose several cities, including Berlin. Dresden had been among the lowest in rank. What had made the name of Dresden come up was the U.K.'s Prime Minister Churchill's idea: Churchill at that time was expecting to visit Yalta to have a conference with Roosevelt, the U.S. President, and Stalin, the Prime Minister of the Soviet Union. The Red Army's great offensive attacks in the Eastern Front had steadily been strengthening their position, while in the Western Front or the Allied Forces' advancing line, the battle situation had been at a standstill because of the German Army's strong resistance. It was quite probable that Stalin would point out the fact that the U.K. and the U.S. had not made so much war effort so far. This led Churchill to calculate that: if they were to give a fierce attack somewhere in eastern Germany while the Soviet Union's Army still kept their strength, the U.K. and the U.S. would be able to give Stalin a clear impression that they were unfolding a close united operation for the benefit of the Soviet Union. Another purpose would have been to show off their mighty air force to Stalin. This was how Dresden upon the Elbe, one of the main cities in the eastern part of Germany—with a population of 630,000, known as "a Firenze on the Elbe"—was to be mentioned "to please the Russians," as was pointed out by Riddell Hart in *History of The Second World War*. He also went on saying in the same book: "As a consequence, the distant city of Dresden was subjected to a devastating attack in mid-February— with deliberate intention of wreaking havoc among the civil population and refugees—striking at the city centre, not the factories or railways."

- **Germany Surrendered, and the U.K. & U.S. Type of Regional Bombings was to be Applied to Japan**

As Hamburg had been, Dresden was also attacked mainly by the B.K. Air Force, assisted by the U.S. Air Force. On the night of February 13, B.K. fleets consisting of 773 Lancaster bombers made a couple of waves of assault upon Dresden. The seventy percent of the dropped bombs were incendiary ones. By this period, the U.K. Air Force's regional bombing had been turned into that of a sort of conveyer-belt system. A couple of squadrons that had arrived first played the part of "primary markers" to illuminate the location of the city by dropping flare bombs and green-colored landmark bombers to show where the town was. Then by the eight mosquito bombers that entered its sky, red-colored landmark bombers were dropped so that they might enclose the area to be attacked from then on. Then there came the main force unit to start bombing "to cover that scheduled area at the scheduled time with the scheduled amount of bombs."

The scheduled amount of bombs for Dresden was 2,656 tons of incendiary bombs and destruction bombs. During the daytime on the following day, three hundred and eleven B17 bombers of the U.S.' 8th Air Force poured 771 tons of bombs in and around that blazing city. The U.S. airmen performed it not through visual inspection by employing Norden bombsights, but by radar.

Because Dresden was smaller in scale than Hamburg, the destruction they suffered was more thorough and more miserable. During a couple of days, the citizens were attacked by a larger amount of bombs dropped on Chongqing throughout the No. 101 Operations. The 15km squares that included the whole of the inner city of Dresden—an area slightly larger than that of Chongqing—had been turned into a totally uninhabited area. At the very least, 35,000 people were killed, and 35 schools, 40 hospitals and 114 public buildings were reduced to ashes. Such a firestorm as had ravaged Hamburg did occur at Dresden, too, and burnt everything, and even those who had managed to take refuge at the underground shelters could not escape danger. The fires kept burning as long as a week.

The air raid Dresden had suffered turned out the final large-scaled regional bombing in Europe. On April 30, 1945, the B.K.'s and the U.S.' military authorities announced the end of the offensive by strategic bombings. A week later, they were to celebrate a victory over Germany or "VE Day." Thus the wartime fire in Europe, which had lasted for five years and a half, finally ceased.

On the other hand, Japan was still at war—what they called "the Greater East Asia War" which had started at northern China on July 7, 1937—both at the Asian Continent and at the Pacific Ocean. Thus the tactics of strategic bombing, which had been tried in Europe so far, were to be applied to Japan. Spaatz and LeMay had been appointed to be commanders of the aerial battle against Japan, even before the European aerial battle was over. In Europe, they had been hesitating to put that British-style regional bombing into practice; but now they never hesitated to apply it to Japan. It is easy to find a shadow of racial discrimination here. But if we trace this stream, we shall find a fact that: what the Japanese Navy Air Force had been performing under the name of "an attack on the strategic point" was made to develope into "a regional bombing" in Europe. So it could be said that: "the conception of strategic bombing" was now brought back to those who had started it—as if by a boomerang effect.

The B29s Departed from China to Attack Japan

● **Major General Curtis LeMay was Transferred to the Far East Battle Line**

In August, 1944, Curtis LeMay, who had been commanding the bombers' unit of the U.S. Air Force in Europe, was ordered to move to the Far East Front. His new place of work was in Sichuan Province, China. His duty there was to command the unit that was to attack the Japanese mainland by the newly-produced airplanes B29 in place of Brigadier Kenneth Wolfe of the 20th Bombers' Group in the 20th Air Force. For LeMay, who had established his fame as a brilliant ace in the European aerial battle, it was with a sort of sentimentality to part with the Flying Fortress B17s, but his new mission had brought him all the forces of the Super-Fortress B29s and had directed him to lead Japan to surrender. So far not a single soldier of the U.S. Army had ever landed in Japan proper, and his mission was to perform strategic bombings literally as a genuine experiment. By way of India, LeMay in high spirits entered Chengdu in Sichuan Province—where the base for B29 bombers to take off had already been brought into being. His predecessor, Brigadier General Wolfe having been removed by General Arnold because of his half-heartedness in performing his duty, LeMay reached his new place of work with even more readiness to perform his mission. LeMay had been smart enough to perceive the change of the air concerning the bombardment policy in Washington.

At that time, the U.S. military force in China had its headquarters at Chongqing, and under Lieutenant General Joseph Stilwell with the concurrent post of the chief of staff under Jiang Jieshi (under Lieutenant General Albert Wedemeyer since October, 1944), had China Region U.S. Army Headquarters with its Army Air Force (under Lieutenant General G. Stratmeir at Chongqing), the 10th Flying Corps (under Major General H. Davidson at Liuzhou) and the 14th Flying Corps (under Major General C. Chennault at Kunming). But the 20th Bombers' Group, which was to be placed under the command of LeMay, even if their sortie base was in the suburbs of Chengdu quite close to Chongqing, did not belong either to Stilwell or to Stratmeir, but directly to General Henry Arnold or Commander-in-chief of U.S.A.A.F. (U.S. Army Air Force) in Washington.

According to the decision made by the Chief of the General Staff George Marshall, the management of the new type of bombers, instead of being subordinate to any of the theater commanders in China or in the Pacific Ocean, should be controlled at Washington as the Air Force under the direct control of the Joint Chief of Staff, while the whole strategy of B29s should be controlled by a single commander. Virtually, this amounted to an independence of the Air Force. Thus in April, 1944, the 20th Air Force started under the command of Arnold in Washington, and Arnold, who had grasped the war-making capacity of B29s in a form of the task force for the strategic bombings toward Japan, dismissed the first commander, Brigadier General Wolfe who had failed to achieve what was expected of him and adopted LeMay, the hero of the European aerial warfare. The following was what LeMay wrote in his autobiography:

> Thus I, instead of belonging to any other person, came to belong directly to the Joint Chiefs of Staff, under Arnold as the headman of the Army Air Force. This was why the 20th Air Force was called the first strategic corps in our country.

From this time onward, LeMay became a trump held by Arnold, and kept distinguishing himself as an active and brave promoter of the incendiary bombings upon the cities of Japan proper. The tactics Arnold and LeMay adopted in Asia were the succession of the regional bombings applied upon Germany by "a bomber Harris" of the U.K. and of the indiscriminate bombings upon the cities of Germany, which the U.S. Air Force had ostensibly been hesitating to perform till the final stage of the warfare, though it was to turn out even an enlarged reenactment in Japan.

The U.S. leaders of the war, while being engaged in the European aerial battle, had made the wording of "indiscriminate bombing upon the city" a taboo and hesitated to conform to "the regional bombing" adopted by Churchill and Harris; but toward Japan, they had long been trying to find out some movement to bring about any other standard to be applied to Japan. As for the conception itself of sending bombs across the ocean to the cities of Japan, it had already been mentioned by President Roosevelt and all sorts of Americans even before the U.S.-Japanese War broke out—since those days when Japan was engaged in indiscriminate bombings upon Chongqing and several other cities in the hinterland of China, making them the objects of its indiscriminate bombings. The following was what Carl Berger wrote in his book, *B 29, the Superfortress:*

> The decision to use them (B29s) in the Far East was President Roosevelt's. As early as December in 1940, a year before Pearl Harbor, he had expressed the hope to see the Japanese bombed.
>
> For more than three years, they had been assailing China on land and in the air. Japanese bombers had struck repeatedly at Chungking, the western refuge of the Nationalist government of President Chiang Kai-shek. The US ambassador in Chungking, Nelson T Johnson, by the summer of 1939 had personally undergone sixty-six of the aerial attacks. To Washington's protests about the indiscriminate raids, the Japanese responded that their forces were directed only against enemy military targets.
>
> The exasperated US government in late 1939 decided to retaliate by embargoing the sale of aviation products to Japan and further it announced it would not renew the Treaty of Commerce and Navigation signed with Tokyo in 1911, which would expire on 26th January 1940.
>
> The day after the expiration, Secretary of State Cordell Hull handed the Japanese Ambassador in Washington a letter listing more than thirty-five Chinese cities which had been bombed by Japanese aircraft and the specific dates of certain ones. He further cited approximately 200 instances in China 'of damage by aerial bombs to American properties, the location of the majority of which were previously notified to the Japanese authorities and nearly all of which were marked by American flags.

According to the same book, when the Japanese side denied those facts mentioned there, the Secretary of State, Hull, declared, as follows:

Detailed reports have come to this country, some official and some by way of private sources and the public press, which indicate that in their military operations in China the Japanese forces have in a large number of instances resorted to bombing and machine-gunning of civilians from the air at places near which there were no military establishments or organizations. Furthermore, the use of incendiary bombs (which inevitably and ruthlessly jeopardize non-military persons and properties) has inflicted appalling losses on civilian populations. Japanese air attacks in many instances have been of a nature and apparent plan which can be comprehended only as constituting deliberate attempts to terrorize unarmed populations.

As is guessed by what has been mentioned above, one of the reasons why the principle, apparently different from what was adopted in Europe, was adopted in performing strategic bombings upon Japan is as clear as clear can be. In 1940, General Arnold had received an opinion that: the incendiary bombings upon Japan should be included in the plan of actions of the U.S. Army Air Force—submitted from Shennault, the then aerial consultant on Jiang Jieshi whose wartime capital Chongqing had recently been seriously damaged by the No.101 Operations performed by Inoue Shigeyoshi and Onishi Takijiro. Arnold at that time, considering where he stood, simply played his role, saying: "Applying incendiary bombs upon a city goes against the line of our policy: our attack shall be restricted only on the military targets." But now that the U.S. was at war with Japan, he no longer said anything like that. On the other hand, Chennault, who had made a comeback to the Army Air Force, was no longer a volunteer but the commander of the 14th Air Force active in the skies of China. He was now waiting for an opportunity to put his "eye for eye" strategy into practice.

● A Project of Sending Bombers from the Chinese Continent
to the Japanese Islands

General Arnold, who had been at the Casablanca Conference in January, 1943, as an attendant of President Roosevelt, thus to put an end to the dispute between the U.S. and the U.K. on the strategic bombings upon Germany, visited Chongqing on February 6 and stayed there for four days and had a series of conferences with Jiang Jieshi. After returning home, he made it public that at

Chongqing he had held talks with Jiang Jieshi and Tell, Marshall of the Royal Air Force, who had accompanied him, concerning the probability of making an attack upon Japan from a base somewhere in China. At the end of that month, Arnold, who attended a welcome reception held by the city of New York for Song Meiling, the wife of Jiang Jieshi, who had come round there during her visit to the U.S., said in his speech: "We have already obtained a base from which we are able to attack the heart of Japan, and now we are at the final stage of that preparation." As it was, that was still far from "the final stage," but it was true that a project for attacking the heart of Japan from a base in China had been making a steady progress. In August, 1943, at the U.S. and the U.K. Military Conference held at Quebec, the plan of performing the air raids upon the Japanese Islands was talked about as part of "a long-term strategic program to counter Japan" and it was to be brought forward as strategic bombardments upon Japan, whose cord name was "Matterhorn," with Chengdu in Sichuan Province as its base. Then it was immediately approved of by Roosevelt, Churchill and Jiang Jieshi.

Before this plan was realized, a couple of problems had to be solved as soon as possible: One was to build a flight base wide enough to let the B29s take off; the other was to bring into being a supply line over the Himalayas so that bombs and fuel could be carried over and accumulated at that base. Above all, bringing the air bases into being was its prerequisite. Thus Roosevelt requested Jiang Jieshi to bring into being four airbases around Chongqing by the end of March, 1944, saying: "I firmly believe that: those surprise attacks by B29s would surely bring about destructive blows upon Japan." It had been decided that the first group of B29s or 175 bombers should be delivered to their bases in March, 1944, from Wichita Factory of Boeing Company.

In the month that followed that request made by Roosevelt—in December, 1943—Zhang Qun, the Chairman of Sichuan Province, ordered the main responsible persons in the Province and all the chiefs of all Prefectures in the Province to attend an emergency conference. That was the voice of authority given by the Chairman of the Province, who had been the Director of Foreign Affairs and the Vice Chief of the Executive Council under the Jiang's Regime. To those who had come up to the conference, Zhang Qun explained that: what made him invite them there was their Province having been appointed to receive the orders by the Chief of the Military Committee, Jiang Jieshi, to perform "a specific construction work." Then he went on saying: in order to counterattack Japan's invasion which now appeared to have reached its climax, the United States of America was going to support us with their large amount of aerial strength and was planning to perform bombing raids upon the mainland of Japan by their bombers that would take off from the air bases to be built *here* in the district of Chengdu.

"In order to perform this project," Zhang Qun went on saying, pouring his encouragement into his voice: "America is calling upon us to build several Air Force Bases as soon as possible. So far Sichuan Province have contributed a great deal in carrying out this Anti-Japanese War in such field as conscription and food supply, and now we are again expected to carry out "this special kind of construction work." In order to achieve this mission of ours within the prescribed time, thus to achieve this great cause of resistance to save our country, I implore you all to do your utmost!"

After this impassioned speech by Zhang Qun, the chief of the Public Welfare Bureau, Hu Ciwei, explained the general outlines of the plan and the allocation was given, to the amazement of the chiefs of the twenty-nine prefectures present there, who were suddenly caught by the weight of the huge projects and inescapable duty given to them. Following was the Plan made by the Committee to Perform the Special Construction Works in Sichuan Province:

1) The four bases for the U.S. bombers are to be built in the suburbs of Chengdu: Xinjin, Qiongxia, Pengshan and Guanghan (the first two are the expansion of what they are). Five places, including Chengdu, Wenjiang and Deyang, are to provide a sortie base for the fighter planes.

2) The people of Sichuan Province shall engage in construction works. 320,000 people shall be enlisted from 29 prefectures. Considering those who will fall ill or get injured, those engaged in the work will reach 550,000.

3) As for the food for the workers, 1.4 *sho* of rice a day for each will be supplied to each. Each prefecture shall prepare more than one million *hu* of rice to feed those 320,000 workers. The statute labor of a total of 20,000 people who would carry the rice to the construction site shall be borne by each prefecture.

4) Each prefecture shall have a new committee for dealing with these

compulsory labors in order to manage all those matters of recruiting, supplying goods needed in the construction sites, seizing the land, making compensation for the loss, and so on. Whatever reasons might be given, no delay in starting the construction works shall be pardoned.

● The Largest Airfields in the World were brought into Being at Chengdu

That was the world's largest construction work for building of the world's largest-scaled airfields suitable for the largest and the newest type of airplanes in the world. For the airplanes which had been so made as to fly mainly through the stratosphere, those whose ancestors had built the Great Walls of China were to lend their power in carrying the stones and harden the earth by employing the tools not so much different from those of the ancient times. Certainly the method of construction was the same, but unlike the works before Christ, those in the Twentieth Century, and that those during the wartime, never allowed them to spend several dozens of years but obliged them to finish it only in five months. So the density and speed of the construction works were incomparably modernistic. And, the Chinese did perform *them*.

In the case of the airbase for the B29s, the standards of the runway given by the U.S. side were: 2,600m long, 60m wide and 1m thick. As for the air base for fighter planes, they were: 2,200m, 40m and 40cm respectively. The Chinese people now were expected to produce nine runways for bombers and for fighters within five months. In addition, there were several other annexes at each of the air bases; three storehouses for aerial fuel, six powder magazines, two radio communication stations, evacuation magazines for thirty-five B29 bombers, a couple of engine-maintenance workshops, the command office and barracks were indispensable, too. In building a single runway and its taxiway, 100,000 cubic meters of ballast was estimated necessary. Especially in the construction of the runway, strict instructions had been given: several layers of mixed cobblestones and sands poured with adhesive ocher water must be made before they were trampled down. The amount of the gravel supplied for a single base at Penshan alone was equivalent to all of the round stones quarried from the both banks of the Min Jiang from Xinjin to Meishan (50km). Because of this quarrying, the Day for Releasing Water from Dujiang-yan Dam—whose building has been known as a large-scaled irrigation engineering work performed during the era of Qin (226BC-221BC), and whose merit has caused Chengdu Plain to win such a euphemism as "the Land of Heavenly Blessings"—was delayed for ten days (from April 1 to 10) so that the released water might not widen the river and prevent the quarrying.

A huge amount of round-shaped stones—even though only a part of it was carried on two-wheeled handcarts or wheelbarrows—was mostly carried on a shouldering pole all the way from the riverbed to the construction site. Those who offered such labor were the men and women of the neighboring farm villages. At first, they were able to get there and back ten times a day, but as the distance grew greater, the number of times to bring in stones grew smaller until at last those who left the worksite in the morning reached their destination the following morning. Seen from afar, it would have looked like columns of ants. It was not uncommon to have the flesh of their shoulders broken to bleed. Those who failed to work properly were relentlessly whipped, because Chairman Zhang Qun had declared: "Delay is inexcusable. Those who have done it well will receive a prize; those who are to blame will be punished."

● **Day and Night, the Construction of the Airfield Went on**
The air base building went on literally day and night. The gaslights were burning bright and people kept working even at night. In order to pull a heavy roller, hundreds of people squeezed their power. There was even a period when ninety thousand people were estimated to be engaged in a building single runway. By giving exclamations of self-encouragement or singing songs, statute laborers conquered their fatigue and sleepiness. The following was among the songs brought into being in those days:

> Carrying a shouldering pole in our hands,
> Keeping a cigarette between our lips,
> Some work hard; Others do not.
> However hard we may work,
> We've to receive the whipping all the same!
> Let's make effort, effort, one more effort!
> Let's make up the air base and go home!

Whatever the people were working for, their situation remained miserable. The peasants were gathered up, driven hard and injured to death. In case of the statute laborers from Jiangyang Prefecture alone, several hundred of deaths were recorded. So they could be called the first victims brought about by the B29s. On the other hand, on the side of these supervising this construction work, they could not do without making use of this golden opportunity for taking rake-offs and selling goods through illegal channels, and this caused the areas around the construction sites to be filled not only with the smell of blood and sweat but also with the hearsay of illegal money-grubbing and undue profit. The idleness in labor was readily blamed, but under the administration in those days, such despicable deeds as these were rarely exposed and this naturally led to the fact that all those complaints made by the laborers were also buried into the ground of those air bases. A total of more than 500,000 people from the farming villages could not do anything but keep working as they were told to.

Strange as it may sound, while such huge construction works were being performed in such a short period of time and that in such high-handed manners, there was not even a single opportunity for the people to let their complaints and dissatisfactions reveal themselves in any violent manner. They did keep those injustices they saw and heard in their mind and memory, but instead of running away from their daily labor, they kept working until everything was completed. What had led them to do so was unmistakably their patriotism, but it would be more appropriate and satisfying to them if that was termed "their spirit of resistance to Japan." Until 1941, the Chengdu district, too, though not so frequently as Chongqing, had been bombed as one of the aims of "the bombardment in the hinterland of China," and the people had known very well what terror and misery the air raid would bring to them. The anger against the unjustified attack from the sky had been shared by all those engaged in that compulsory labor. That was by no means mere volunteer labor. While enduring the hard labor, they might have been recalling the names of those places of historic fame of Chengdu brought to ashes by the Japanese air raiders—the marketplace of Yanshikou, which had lasted since the time of *Sanguo-zhi* (*A History of the Three Kingdoms*: 220-280), and the walls of the Imperial Castle resided by Liu Bei Xuande (161-223).

From that runway of their own building, the B29 Super Fortresses were expected to take off to make bombing raids upon the Japanese Islands. That would become the first opportunity for them to make the Japanese realize what the air raids were like. That would have been the very thing all the people working on those construction sites were repeating to themselves as if they were their magic words.

In April, 1944, "*those* special construction works" were completed literally by their physical labor alone, and that exactly within the prearranged construction period. On the day when the first group of B29s arrived at Xinjin Air base, Chairman of the Sichuan Province, Zhang Qun, the dignitaries of the Nationalist Government and the Chiefs of the Prefectures were seen there. While they were waiting in a tense atmosphere, a whirring was heard from afar in the sky and in due time their slender figures, glittering in silver, were beginning to make their appearance before their eyes. They were of the first group from the 20th bombers' group in the 20th Air Force, directed by the Brigadier General Wolfe. That formation of B29s had taken off from the air base in the suburbs of Calcutta, which had also been brought into being by many Indian laborers, and after having flown over "humps" or the high peaks of the mountain mass of the Himalayas that stretched as long as 800km from Assam in northeast India to Kunmin in China, they arrived in Chengdu to make their first landing there. Curtis LeMay wrote in his autobiography about what it was like, when seen from the sky—as an impression received by Captain William O'Murry:

> The landing of our planes was a great event. Both sides of the runway were lined with several thousands of Chinese laborers. After landing, we stood in a line and had our photographs taken for movies and gravures. Along with the Chinese officials from the Government and American engineers, General Chennault and his staff had come to meet us. All the Chinese people smiled upon us and cried: "Hao!"—meaning "the best!"

Zhang Qun, the Chairman of the Sichuan Province, having read aloud to the *kulis* (the laborers) the telegram from Jiang Jieshi and admired their great contribution of painful labor before he offered them a grand banquet.

● **From Chengdu, the First Air Raiders were Sent to Japan Proper**
It was from June 15 to 16, 1944, when the first mission of "Super Fortresses (B29s)" was sent to Japan from Chengdu. That was also the very same day when Japan had the U.S. Army land on Saipan Island of the Mariana Islands—

a part of what Japan had called "the range of absolute national defense." This meant that: Japan that day had allowed a couple of routes for its enemies to enter it to perform their bombings upon it—one from the east; the other from the west.

At the news of Yawata Ironworks in Kyushu (the southernmost main island of Japan) having been air-raided, those of the Imperial Headquarters were shocked. The following was what Captain Matsumura Hidehaya had recollected, as was recorded in *A History of the Facts in the Announcements of the Imperial Headquarters* authored by Tominaga Kengo:

> At 4 a.m., the first report on the air raid on Yawata Ironworks was sent to us at Ichigaya. "They did it!" we said. That was the first air raid by B29s from the Continent, about which we had been concerned.
>
> A variety of information came in from northern Kyushu—from the Western Army, the Flying Corps, the Military-Police Unit, the Prefectural Office, the police stations, the newspaper companies, the broadcasting stations and so on—saying: Yawata has got annihilated; Kokura is on fire, too; it's only a couple of melting furnaces that are burning; a certain number of enemy planes were shot down; no, it's ours that have fallen, and so on. All those reports were contradictory to each other; it was totally impossible to tell which was true.
>
> Saipan Island was being occupied, while Japan proper was suffering the first air raid; these sent us into a total confusion in the flood of false information.

Prime Minister Tojo appeared to remain calm. What he said at suppertime at the Official Residence remains in *The Record of the Prime Minister Tojo's Top Secrets:*

> You need not fly into such a panic. We are engaging in war; we must naturally be prepared for such things as those. They can be compared to such trifles as having had mosquitoes bite us or having got a splash from a muddy road. But you will be wrong if you think *that* is an air raid.

If we recall what happened to us one after another in the years to come, such a figure he used in his speech as "having got a splash from a muddy road" proved to be true.

As a matter of fact, the oncoming of B29s had not been unanticipated. According to *The Strategy for the Air Defense of the Mainland* in *A Series of the War History Edited by the Defense Agency*, the central organization of the Army—through a telegram from abroad—had held a definite evidence that the latest model of Boeing bombers was B29 from the information that Boeing's new-type of bomber had crashed during its test flight on February 18 in the suburbs of Seattle. About the same period, a telegram from abroad had also conveyed the information on the U.S.' project of bombardment on Japan proper:

◎ From Buenos Aires on February 21: *Domei**

The U.S. Navy's assistant secretary, Ralph Pearl boastfully talked of the U.S. air raid upon Japan in the speech he made on 20th at Baltimore:

Upon the Japanese mainland, we must give a large-scaled air raid regularly so we may thoroughly destroy its munitions factories; as for the people's will to fight, too, a fatal blow must be given.

Considering this speech along with what was uttered by Arnold and Nimitz, it could be judged that Japan would suffer the U.S. air raids before long. Now the Headquarters of the Army Air Force started an investigation team so that they could grasp the U.S.' capability in this direction.

B29: The type: a middle-sized monoplane with four engines, the whole weight is 40tons. The number of machine guns is unknown. The number of 20mm engine guns is four (or six).

The bomb: regular ones 4,500 tons

The largest horsepower: 2,500 horsepower; 4 in number

As for their radius of action, they had heard of the evaluation given by Genda Minoru as a member of the Naval General Staff: "The capacity of B29 of the U.S. is unknown but it would be probable that they would come over from "Midway" to the Japanese mainland to perform the air raids." Since it is 4,000km from Midway to Tokyo, that outlook was fairly correct.

By and by, the contingents in China also began to send some reports. The following was what was reported by the Chief of the General Staff Office of the Expeditionary Army in China on April 2, 1943: (by telegram No.676)

Putting all pieces of information together, our enemy has been taking the offensive for a considerably long period of time. Surely, they are planning to perform air raids upon the Japanese Islands if they take any opportunity to do so, So we need to keep guarding our mainland and Taiwan.

While all these pieces of information were confusing the Japanese side, the field headquarters also remained unable to identify B29, giving it a variety of code numbers—B24, B25 or B28—thus revealing the tense atmosphere of their homeland soon to be air-raided.

The 20th Bomber Command of 63 bombers carried out the raid upon Yawata Ironworks in northern Kyushu 2,600km east of Chengdu. That was the second air raid upon the mainland Japan; the first one had been performed on Tokyo in April, 1942, by the sixteen B25 bombers led by Lieutenant Colonel Dolittle, after having taken off the aircraft carrier Hornet on the Pacific.

Now the 47 bombers arrived at the sky over their aim, and 15 of them performed bombing by visual inspection while 32 performed pinpoint bombing by making use of their radar. Each bomber had been equipped with eight 500 pound AN-M64 bombs. All were destructive bombs; no incendiary bombs had been loaded. That decision had been judged proper in destroying the coke ovens of Yawata Iron Mill. But by the photographs taken after the bombings, it was judged that their bombings were not successful and the damages they had inflicted were insignificant. The fighter planes' interception was far from fierce, but six planes were lost for some other reasons but the air battle (failure in taking off or crash because of the engine trouble) and six planes were shot by antiaircraft fire. One of the captains on the bombers, Colonel Alan Clerk, wrote his sentiments in *B29 The Super Fortress:*

The result of our strategy turned out a miserable one. Among the bombs dropped on the Yawata district, only a small number of them hit the mark. Some even fell 20 miles (a little over 30km) away from their targets. The reason was because the radar-men had not yet got accustomed to radar-bombings.

It seemed that their first air raid upon Japan from the Chinese Continent was as good as Japan's Army Air Force's first air raid upon Chongqing.

Still it was reported on a large scale. One of the eight war correspondents who had accompanied the airmen reported to the Chinese people from the radio station in Chongqing as to how their first air raid upon Japan was performed:

On the afternoon of the 16th, the U.S. airplanes took off from certain base 5 in China. Both airplanes and war materials had been made ready there. These air planes are called B29 the super-fortress, and each of them takes eleven crew members, and the capacity tonnage of bombs is also great.

Those planes took off from different air bases but their target was the same—Yawata.

Yawata is a center of the steel industry. The steel produced there amounts to one fifth of all the steel produced in Japan. The number of steel-making furnaces there reaches 76 percent of all that exist in Japan. This was why the air raid upon Yawata was significant. Our air raid was something our enemy had never anticipated. When our first wave invaded their sky, we saw neither interceptor fighters nor anti-aircraft shells aiming at us. When the third wave in which I had joined arrived in their sky, their anti-aircraft guns and searchlight finally began to work. We turned off all the lights in the plane and looked out in darkness. The enemy's searchlights had lighted up our planes and there came their night fighters to do their job. But neither their searchlight nor their fighters nor their anti-aircraft guns could check the systematic bombardments we gave them according to our schedule. Our bombs hit the marks. I cannot tell precisely how much damage we have given to the Japanese side, because I cannot return there to check all that happened then and there.

Still, the bombardment we have performed this time remains extremely significant. Firstly, that was the first sortie we had ever made from the base of China. Secondly, that was the longest-distance bombing flight in history. Thanks to all those Chinese people who had dedicated their blood and sweat in bringing about these air bases, we were able to perform such a grand scheme as this. ....

From the sky of Chongqing, the first report on the bombardment upon Japan was thus broadcast to all over China. From the same broadcasting tower, which had exclusively been employed in reporting the approach of Japanese air-raiders after having taken off at Wuhan, they were now able to inform the people of what sort of air-raid had been performed upon that industrial city in Japan. The newspaper companies put out their extra; at teahouses and drinking places, the customers were eagerly arguing the air raid they had performed upon Japan. Now their positions of offenders and defenders had been changed, as everyone was keenly aware of it.

In his diary, Jiang Jieshi wrote about what had happened the day before:

Last night (June 15), the U.S.' superfortresses (B29s) took off at Chengdu and made a bombing raid upon the coke ovens of Yawara Ironworks in northern Kyushu, Japan. Two of the forty-seven planes got missing, but the rest returned safe. On the other hand, the U.S. Navy landed on Saipan Island—the island that has been placed under the mandate of Japan—in the Central Pacific. The U.S. Armed Forces are now making headway toward the heart of Japan.

Brigadier General Walfe also published an informal opinion to the reporters of *Zhong Yang* (Central) News Agency, admiring the efforts made by those 500,000 people from Chengdu area, who had left their farming in order to bring all those air bases into being, also saying that: without those patriotic Chinese people, they would not have been able to make any such sortie as they did this time, and that: from then on, the sortie from Sichuan Province would be kept on making. As it turned out, the bombardment under the direction of Wolfe was to last only for less than two months, because on July 4, he was relieved of his post by Arnold. The toothed wheels of war had demanded to go more quickly, and Wolfe could not keep pace with it. Considering the fact that: in order to bring in the aerial fuel from Calcutta in India to the airheads in the suburbs of Chengdu, eight B29s had to make a flight of 1,930km over the Himalayas, consuming the fuel they were carrying, Brigadier General Walfe, who was naturally sound and secure, had thought it essential to train the radar-men to improve their accuracy of bombing, and this had led him to conclude that: the sortie of fifty bombers should be performed once a week—*not* more than that, to the dissatisfaction of

General Arnold.

The U.S.' Concentration Attacks by Incendiary Bombs

● **LeMay's Scorched-Earth Tactics by means of Napalm Bombs**

On August 30, 1944, Major General Curtis LeMay who succeeded to the command of the 20th Bombing Group with its base in the hinterland of China, at once started their advancing operations from the sky: a series of air raids which started on September 18 upon Anshan (the Japanese invaders called it Anzan) which was the center of the steel industry in Manzhou*, followed by frequent attacks upon Yawata Iron Works in northern Kyushu, and the Naval Arsenal in Omura in western Kyushu.

Omura, now oppressed under the wings of B29s, used to be one of the bases from which the Japanese Navy airplanes took off to perform the first transoceanic bombing upon Nanjing (1937). Now together with its runway, its aerial arsenal was to receive a fatal blow by the bombardments repeated four times.

Washington had desired to give Japan even more vehement and thoroughgoing air raids. Their landing operation still being farther ahead, their only means available now in reaching Japan was the sortie of the bombers. Until they completed their sortie base at Mariana Island, Guam Island and Tinian Island after having occupied them, they had no other base but the one in Sichuan Province in China. To General Arnold who had placed the greatest importance on the aerial power, not even a single day should be wasted in vain. This led him to keep lighting a fire under his subordinates.

LeMay had been well aware of what his mission was. His predecessor, Brigadier General Volfe, because of his consideration of supply balance of aerial fuel, had failed to realize what General Arnold at Washington had encouraged him to do: by dint of B29s, to destroy the main spots of Japan proper and the main spots of Manshu (Chinese: Manzhou*). LeMay, who had made himself known as an able person in performing things in practical manners and in conducting warfare by means of bombers, was easily able to tell what would happen to him if he were to adopt that traditional tactics of daytime, high-altitude flight to perform pinpoint bombing. What was needed then was not a traditional way of thinking but the adaptability to what was actually happening or an insight into what Washington had desired to perform. General Arnold had wanted to have such a plan of operations as "to immediately burst the heart of Japan," and Volfe's strategy appeared to him "too amateurish" to let him remain where he was. LeMay had had no intention to share the fate of his predecessor. On September 8, he had accompanied the bomber fleet to Anshan and found the Japanese fighters' interceptive ability was extremely of low level, and this led him to judge that even more positive strategy should be adopted. Thus in place of the rhombic formation of four planes, a ladder-like formation of twelve planes, which had proved to be successful in Europe, was adopted at once. Then he had B29s converted into flying tankers, and had them transport more oil more frequently, thus to increase the storage of fuel.

● **An Attack on Japan's W Base at Hankou**

It was at the air raid upon Hankou on December 18, when the first flare of "earth-scorching tactics by napalm bombs," which LeMay had developed, was put into practice. That large base had strenuously been built up by the Japanese Navy Air Force in order to realize a brilliant performance of what they called "strategic & political bombings" that lasted from 1939 to 41 upon the cities of the Great Hinterland of China, such as Chongqing, Chengdu, Lanzhou and so on. It had also made itself a large supply base at the mid-basin of the Yangzi for the Japanese Army and Navy staying in China.

Now Hankou was given the first full-scale incendiary bombing in Asia, and after having kept burning for three days and nights, everything was crumbled down in flames. LeMay and Major General Chennault, who had now become Commander of the 14th Air Force with his commanding office at Kunming— who, as a retired captain or a director of a volunteer corps of "Flying Tigers," was standing in the street of Chongqing in the midst of the air raids of "5·3 & 5·4" in 1937, helplessly looking up at the Japanese planes of the Navy Air Force dropping incendiary bombs—had now turned into the hero of flame-throwing attack upon Hankou.

This bombardment upon Hankou had unmistakably been performed in retaliation for the air raids upon Chongqing, and the one who had proposed it was not LeMay but Chennault. After the start of the Japan-U.S. War, Chennault was restored to active service, and according to the U.S.' expansion policy of building up of war potential in China, he was quickly raised in rank—from Captain he used to be at his retirement to Colonel, Brigadier General and Major General—had been fighting against the Japanese Air Force, leading the 14th Air Force in the skies of China, while sending frequent letters to offer his opinion to Washington, asserting that: if he was allowed to have a necessary amount of bombs, he would be able to burn down the three major cities in Japan— Tokyo, Nagoya and Osaka-Kobe. But the 14th Air Force under him, consisting of tactical aircraft, could not fly so far; to make the matter worse, Chennault, a fighter pilot, had not been able to get along with Arnold who had regarded bombers as supreme. Thus there was little or no possibility for Chennault being appointed to perform anything in Japan. But LeMay having taken the place of Wolfe as a believer in pinpoint bombing, Chennault would have felt as if he had obtained "both bombs and bombers." Thus what he did first was to recommend LeMay to attack Hankou or Japan's central airbase in China.

At first, LeMay did not show much interest in it. He thought: if he were to have joint operations with the 14th air corps, that would mean degrading his B29s to the level of tactic capacity, thus to invite them to deviate from the strategic bombing to make an attack on "the enemy's heart." LeMay, who believed that the B29s belonged directly to General Arnold and the Joint Chiefs of Staff, hardly felt interested in that united operation under Wedemeyer, the new Commander of the U.S. Army in the China Region. But Chennault persistently worked out the plan, intending to realize his idea, and after having obtained a support from General Wedemeyer, requested LeMay to ask for the direction from the Joint Chiefs of Staff in Washington as to whether Wedemeyer's right of command would go as far as the 20th bombers group. When LeMay received the answer of "yes", LeMay started to deliberate on the matter with Chennault in Kunming. Their aim was the Japanese base at Hankou (Wuhan District). While they were giving shape that plan, LeMay received a strong impression by what Chennault called "concentration bombing of incendiaries," and this led him to take more positive attitude toward that plan, and this was to lead him to establish his conviction: "As for bombardment, the incendiary one is the most effective," as was recorded in *B29, the Superfortress:*

(The attack on Hankou) turned out to bring about an epoch-making proof in making us innovate our plan of performing the strategic bombings upon Japan.

The strategy we put into action on December 18 was the first large-scaled incendiary-bombing upon the Japanese Army's occupation zone, and this led us to learn that: the houses in the Far East, being mainly made of wood and paper, easily catch fire by the flames from the incendiary bombs we have dropped, thus causing a great effect of our aerial bombardment. Having obtained this knowledge was a great fruit we gained through performing this bombardment. Unlike European objects to aim at, which are made of stone and brick, these flammable aims go well with the incendiary bombs.

None other than Chennault, who were burning with the passion of retaliation against Japan that had kept bombing upon Chongqing, was the very person who had brought about "LeMay's tactics."

● **Japan's Military Institution and Concession at Hankou were**

Drowned in Fire

On December 18, the eighty-four B29s from Chengdu, in cooperation with the fighters of the 14th Air Force from Kunming, made an air raid on the military base and the urban area in Hankou. Comparing the number alone of eighty-four, it was not so different from that of the Japanese Navy Air Force's middle-sized bombers that used to take off from that same city of Hankou to attack Chongqing or Chengdu. But there was a remarkable difference in their offensive capability: The middle-sized bomber's carrying capacity was less than 1ton, while B29's was 10tons at the maximum (three times larger than B17 bombers). As for the incendiary bombs, too, the same thing could be said: The M69 incendiary bomb, which had come into use since this mission, was of a new type called napalm bomb, whose main ingredient was grease incendiary produced from jellified gasoline, and the heat and flames it produced was totally incomparable with those magnesium or electron incendiary bombs used by the Japanese Air Force. The M69-500 pound convergent incendiary bomb consisted of forty-eight 6-pound bullets, and one B29 was able to carry eighty of them. During the past four years, the U.S.' ability to create a blazing hell had greatly been developed, while Japan's had been left far behind. And now, that new power had come down from Chongqing of all places upon the district of Hankou 780km down the Yangzi.

The Chinese side had already been informed of what would happen before long—along with the advice to evacuate somewhere safe—by the U.S. Army as well as by the Chongqing Government. Since the day before the air raid, all the roads and streets in and around the city had unusually been crowded with the Chinese men and women and children—carrying their belongings—trying to run away from "the indiscriminate bombings to be performed by the U.S. Air Force."

At noon, on December 18, a formation of B29s made their appearance and performed low-altitude bombings, dropping a new type of incendiary bombs more than 500tons in weight upon the military facilities, the rows of warehouses, the dock area and the Japanese concession adjacent to it. On the 17th or the day before, the three crew members of the U.S. fighter plane, who had been captivated at Xianggui, were made to parade through the street of Wuhan before being executed by the Japanese corps under the command of the 34th troop guarding Wuhan. This might have made the U.S. attack even more fierce and relentless. Following the B29s, the 14th Air Force led by Chennault—about seventy of fighters and bombers united into one—arrived to give more incendiary-bombings and machine-gun attacks. These drowned the area—five kilometers along the shore of the Yangzi—into huge fires that had destroyed almost all of the Japanese Concessions. The air raiding lasted for three hours. In his autobiography, LeMay wrote: "Everything burnt like mad."

A Japanese news reporter, Masui Yasuichi, at the Branch Office of the *Mainichi* Newspaper Company, also could easily tell the changes in their way of attacks, as he wrote in his diary:

Those B29s had dropped a large amount of incendiary bombs, which turned the urban area of Hankou into a sea of fire covered up with black smoke. They dropped many other bombs and performed strafing, too, thus bringing about a hell on earth. The Chinese restaurant next door on the northern side also came to be wrapped in a raging fire, and as it came spreading to our office, I ran out to find a refuge here and there till I reached our branch office in the Japanese concession, but here, too, I found the third floor gone and the rest badly burnt, excepting one room on the first floor. The damage was serious. The whole city was drowned in fire. Many bodies lay in heaps. Certainly, the enemy's tactics have changed. We have had the first carpet bombing by incendiaries this time. The Chinese people are talking among themselves: that was the U.S.' retaliation against the Japanese having disgraced the U.S. airmen captives by making them parade through the street before being executed.

Certainly that airmen's execution might have enhanced the fighting spirit of the crew of the B29s, but the plan of action to give Hankou a carpet bombing raid had been decided upon by LeMay and Chennault even if it had not been for that parading the day before. That could be called a joint manifestation of Chennault's intense desire to retaliate against Japan's persistent attacks upon Chongqing and of LeMay's excellent adaptability to the reality which enabled him to realize the will of General Arnold.

LeMay, no sooner had he learned that Washington had wanted him to perform a joint operation with the 14th Air Force than he simply gave up his principle that B29s should not be employed for a tactical purpose, and at his discussion with Chennault too, he agreed to lower the B29's bombing height, according to Chennault's opinion, from more than 7,500m to 6,500m or even 5,500m. He also accepted Chennault's proposal that: 80 percent of the bombs to be loaded should be incendiary bombs and that: their main type of bombardment should be regional one by means of flames instead of pinpoint bombing. Such ample flexibility LeMay had shown on that occasion, even to an unprincipled extent, was to turn the B29s, which had been designed and developed as heavy bombers for the daytime precise bombing from high altitude, into the strategic bombers to be exclusively employed in full-time, low-altitude, indiscriminate bombings.

The one who stood at the front was Curtis LeMay with "an iron bottom," but behind him General Arnold at Washington and Chennault at Kunming were pulling the strings. Arnold had made it a rule to give directions from the aims to be bombed upon to the quantity of bombs to be put on board; while Chennault had retained those indelible scenes he had witnessed at Chongqing as something unbearably humiliating. For these two persons, LeMay was to be a successor to "Bomber Harris" in the bombardments upon Japan.

The sorties of B29s with Chengdu as their advance base occurred forty-nine times in all—including fifteen times upon cities—during the ten months from June, 1944. Yawata, Omura and Nagasaki in northwestern Kyushu in Japan and

Anshan (Anzan in Japanese) and Fengtian (Hoten in Japanese) or the largest city in Manchoukuo* in Northeastern China were repeatedly made the targets of their bombing flight. LeMay had made effort in improving both strategy and efficiency in bombardment, but still remained unable to satisfy General Arnold—Commander-in-Chief of the Army Air Force. But this was not because of his commanding ability but rather because of the geographical problem. Certainly the B29's flying range was great, and still it did surpass the limits of its ability to come from the hinterland of China to make a successful sortie to most of the main regions of Japan proper, including "the heart of Japan." Solving this problem had naturally surpassed the ability of the commander on the scene.

To make the matter worse, maintaining war supplies was also a serious matter. In order to bring fuel and bombs into the Chengdu region—because a large part of the Chinese territory and Burma having been seized by the Japanese military—they could not help crossing the skies over the Himalayas by employing C46 transport planes or B29s built for flying a mission. It was by such logistics, not only expensive but also dangerous even to sacrificial extent, that the U.S.' strategic bombings upon Japan had narrowly been kept performing. Those two adverse conditions having decided upon the extent and frequency of their strategic bombings upon Japan, it seemed far from reaching the level expected by General Arnold.

● The U.S. Air Force Built the Bases for B29s at the Marianas

General Arnold—wishing to break through such an adverse situation, so that the swift aerial invasion into Japan might be realized—decided that the base for making sorties to Japan should be moved to the Marianas, taking the opportunity of Saipan, Tenian and Guam Islands of the Mariana Islands having fallen into the hands of the U.S. armed forces.

From there, the heart of Japanese Islands could be taken directly into the attack range of their B29s; As for their logistics, unlike that difficult maintenance by crossing over "the roof of the world," their supply route being on the sea, they could easily get as much as they liked whenever they needed. Both the range and frequency of their sorties were sure to increase to a remarkable extent. General Arnold now, while keeping LeMay going on his strategy with the 20th bombers' group at Chengdu, started the 21st bombers' group under the 20th Air Force directly under himself, and appointed Brigadier General Haywood Hansell—who had been the chief of staff under himself—to be Commander. On October 12, Hansell reached his new post by the first B29 that had landed at Islay Airbase. This was how the second strategic bombers' group came into being here at Saipan Island after Chengdu.

Curtis LeMay wrote in *B29 The Super Fortress:*

> From the beginning, when the 20th Air Force's plan of formation was presented, it had been decided that each corps staying in different places should head for the hub of the Empire of Japan: The 20th Bombers' Group from the Chinese Continent; the 21st from Mariana Islands; the 22nd from Philippines or from Taiwan; the 23rd from Shemuya Island in Aleutian Islands, and so on. As it happened in the final stage of our attacks against Japan, the Mariana Islands proved to be quite fit for the bases of B29s. This led Arnold to cancel the 22nd and 23rd bombing corps to join the actual fighting and to incorporate all those aerial corps and their B29s into the 21st bombing corps.

The bases built in Mariana Islands were five: One at Saipan Island, two at Tinian Island, and two at Guam Island. The construction work had started as early as the time when the Japanese soldiers remaining there were still keeping resistance against the mopping-up operations by the U.S.. In August, the advance troops of the Headquarters arrived; in October 12, General Haywood Hansell, Commanding General of the 21st Bomber Command, arrived to take up the new position; in the month that followed, 119 B29s had finished their assembling.

The construction of the air bases on the Mariana Islands was also a magnificent one in a sense different from that of Chengdu. In place of human resources and shouldering poles, here the main forces were steam-rollers and bulldozers. The Seabees, making free use of cutting-edge technology, had built up the world's largest air base before you knew it. The North Field in Tinian Island had two couples of 2,800m-runways with the taxiways that produced a fine checkered pattern upon it. It was not long before one B29 took off in 45 seconds, or sixteen B29s took off from four runways in three minutes. At the southern edge of the island, an artificial port was brought into being after having broken a huge coral reef, and the North Field was directly connected with the marine supply line by means of "the Broad Way" with a couple of lines in each direction with the total length of 20km. It might have been called a great industrial complex or *kombinat* in performing the war.

● **Brigadier General Hansell, a Supporter of Pinpoint Bombing,**
had his Post Changed

Heywood Hansell, who had been appointed Commanding General of the 21st Bomber Command, could be called a product brought about by strategic bombing and B29. Hansell, who had been brought up under Mitchel's theory through General Arnold, after World War II broke out and the Army Air Force was reorganized into the numbered Air Force, was received by a new organization where they were allowed to produce a plan of operations independent of the Army's General Staff Office, and became a member of "the group for planning an aerial war" to fight against the aerial forces of the Axis Powers. The Commander, Lieutenant General Arnold, the Chief of the Aerial Staff Office, Brigadier General Carl Spaatz, and Major Colonel Hansell were the leading figures to have developed and established the American-style strategic aerial battle. The three, released from the bureaucracy that had kept irritating the airmen, devoted themselves to creating the program of defeating their enemies—Germany and Japan. The principal aims of their aerial bombing were decided to be the destruction of the electric power and transportation systems, and the required military potential to nullify them was probed into, and the number of the necessary planes and the time required for putting those projects into practice were calculated.

Thus in August, 1941, "the team for planning the aerial battles" presented their plan to the chief of the General Staff, General George Marshall. The main points of this project were: the scale of the Air Force should be made 42 times larger than it had been so far; all the planes existing now should be disposed of and ten times as many as the latest model planes should be produced, including ten thousand bombers with four and six discharge holes. The Staff of the Army made an objection to it, but General Marshall, who had heard of that plan, plainly said: "Why, everyone here, this project sounds great to me. I should like Stimson, the Secretary of the Army, to listen to those who have brought this project into being." LeMay, recalling that moment, later wrote in his Biography:

"At that moment, we have overcome the greatest difficulty lying before the Army Air Force."

This was how the U.S. Strategic Air Corps was brought into being. This also realized the dream dreamt by Billy Mitchell and Henry Arnold. The representative of the new war potentials brought into being by this project was the B29 or the long-distance bomber with two couples of engines that enabled them to fly through the stratosphere. While "the aerial battles in Europe" were being fought, a plan for mass production of B29s was made by aircraft producing companies, led by Boeing, followed by Douglas and Lockheed competing with each other, while all the factories in the U.S. were mobilized to produce tens of thousands of parts of great varieties, and these were to be put into orders according to the flows of designs and manufacturing processes, thus employing a large number of personnel for controlling all those processes, and that was why even such a scholar as Robert McNamara, who was to be the Secretary of Defense in the years to come, was being mobilized at the job site as a personnel required for production control. By the time the Mariana Islands came to the hands of the U.S. Armed Forces, a large number of B29s had been coming out of their assembly line. (The number of them produced throughout this period was to reach 3,628.) In the meantime, Hansell, having been promoted to the chief of staff of General Arnold, was participating in planning the program of the daytime high-altitude pinpoint bombing, and when the B29s were decided to be the main force in attacking Japan, he was to leave deskwork and move to the command of actual fighting.

Hansell, who had founded his headquarters at Guam, was swift enough to send to Arnold a plan of operations named "San Antonio I " for the air raid upon Tokyo. According to this plan, the air raid was to be performed by one hundred to one hundred and twenty B29s during the daytime from the altitude of 9,000m through visual inspection by means of Norden sights; each bomber's standard number of bombs to carry was: 30% of incendiary bombs and 70% of destructive ones. That was a daytime high-altitude pinpoint bombing, aimed at the military targets. After having performed some experimental bombings upon Truk Islands as the base for the Japanese Navy and upon Iwo Islands where the Japanese Army were holding up, the first aim in Japan proper was decided upon the Musashi Factory of Nakajima Air Plane Manufacturing Company in the suburbs of Tokyo. On November 24, the first air raid upon Tokyo was performed by 111 B29s, but the result was not recognized as satisfying enough. Judging from the photographic reconnaissance, only sixteen bombs had hit the factory. One plane had been lost (presumably because of having flown into a fighter plane). Commander Arnold proudly announced to the world that the U.S. Air Force had again performed their attack upon Tokyo, and though he declared that: that was not a hit-and-run as Dolittle had once done, he had kept at heart a strong wish to perform even a more positive attack upon the urban area by dint of incendiary bombs. Still, Hansell would not give up his pride on his pinpoint bombing. Even after the sortie from the Mariana Islands got started along the right lines, he had clung to the tactics to deliver a mortal blow upon an important military aim from a high altitude on a fine day. Certainly, in Europe, that used to be a principle held by the U.S. Air Force, but Hansell had not noticed that: that was no longer up to date. On the other hand, Roosevelt and Arnold at Washington had long been turned into believers in the regional bombing or the line Churchill and Harris had adopted toward Germany.

On December 18—on the same day when LeMay and Chennault had performed "the concentration attack on Hankou by incendiary bombs"— Hansell's bombers' group had sent eighty-nine B29s to Nagoya, Japan, and performed the precision bombings on the airplane factory of Mitsubishi Heavy Industry there. It was judged that they "had given serious damages upon it," but what had caught the eyes of Arnold and his staff was the scenes sent from Hankou which had turned into the hell of fire. On the day that followed, Arnold's Headquarters issued "an urgent demand" to perform a wholesale incendiary attack on the urban area of Nagoya. Hansell, having found it far from acceptable, wrote a letter to protest against Arnold:

"Our mission is to give continuous and decisive attacks on the enemy's main military or industrial institutions by visual inspection and radars," thus expressing his inability to accept Arnold's direction to drop incendiary bombs upon the residential area in the city. For this aviator officer, it could not be called a successful job unless he could drop his bomb exactly upon the object he had aimed at. But Arnold could no longer listen to him. (*B29 the Superfortress*) The following is Hansell's recollection:

I think the major element that had made General LeMay move to the Mariana Islands lay in General Arnold's dissatisfaction toward the effect of my strategy. I myself was dissatisfied with this step. I was saying to myself: as time went on, the effect would present itself. But he was too impatient to wait. General Arnold asked me if I might be Vice-Commander under General LeMay. But I asked Arnold to dismiss me.

Thus after Wolfe, Hansell was dismissed. The one who came to take his place was LeMay again. *The Published History of the U.S, Army Air Force* gives the reason for his dismissal: "General Arnold had directed him to perform a regional bombing by means of incendiary bombs, but Brigadier General Hansell would rather like to perform precision bombing according to his own faith." LeMay came flying from Chengdu to Guam on January 20, 1945, to command the 21st Bombers' Group. LeMay knew what Washington had wanted him to do. He had already given it a try at Hankou. He had not felt any hesitation in changing his strategy from daytime high-altitude precision bombing upon military targets to nighttime low-altitude incendiary bombing.

Then There Came the Atomic Bombing upon Hiroshima

● **The Denouement of the Ideology & the Technology of Strategic Bombings**
The strategic bombings performed by the B29s that flew from the five bases on Guam, Saipan and Tinian Islands of the Mariana Islands could be divided into three stages

>The 1st stage: November in 1944—February in 1945
>The 2nd stage: March in 1945—July in 1945
>The 3rd stage: August 6 and 9 in 1945

The first stage was the daytime precision bombings from high altitude, aiming at the airplane-producing factories. The second stage was the nighttime indiscriminate incendiary bombings upon the cities. The final stage was the daytime nuclear attacks to liquidate the cities.

The commander in the first stage, Brigadier General Hansell, unable to grow out of the traditional principle of bombing only on the military targets, was dismissed; The bombardments in the second stage and the third stage were performed under the command of Curtis LeMay, the Commander of the 21st Bombers' group, who had been moved from the hinterland of China to Guam Island on the Pacific.

"The six months under the command of LeMay" could be called the denouement of the conception and technique of the strategic bombing that had kept developing throughout the period of the Second World War. The accumulation of the destructions and cruelties recorded during this short period of time was a condensed re-advent of aerial war miseries that started at Guernica to be followed by Chongqing, London, Hamburg and Dresden, while bringing about numberless new epitaphs, until at last it added the dates and the significance of having released an unknown power called "nucleus" over the human beings and every living beings on the earth.

Between the air raids upon Tokyo (March 9-10, 1945) performed by 334 B29s with 1,665 tons of napalm incendiary bombs (the same type of air raid performed upon Hamburg and Dresden) and the appalling tragedies of Hiroshima and Nagasaki—each of which was brought about by a single atomic bomb carried over by a single B29 to carry out a single sortie—we can clearly see the traces of the continued conception and the jumped technique in the history of the strategic bombings. So, the calamities in Hiroshima and Nagasaki were certainly tragedies that have soared in the history of "war miseries," but it has also been true that: the sufferings of the two cities can be placed in the chain of the conception of strategic bombings that "can be traced back to Chongqing," so it was certain that: Japan could *not* remain only in the standpoint of the outsider·victim in the history of *the* conception and *the* practice of the strategic bombings.

Theodore White, having witnessed the first large-scaled air raid upon Chongqing (On May 3 & 4, 1939), compared it to a cruel blow inflicted upon the medieval city by the modern world. And now the U.S. Army Air Force's strategic bombings upon the six largest cities in Japan, even if their scales of bombardment had been enlarged, they fundamentally remained none other than "the mass murders in the war of the industrial age," just as Japan's "strategic-political bombings" upon Chinese cities were.

Seen in a broader perspective, the difference between "Chongqing" and "Hiroshima" could not be so decisive in their strategic conception, and if there were any difference, it would be only in the technique employed for destruction and in the amount of resources spent in performing it.

● The Command to Intensify the Incendiary Bombings upon the Cities

On February 19, 1945, Arnold's Headquarters issued a new order to the 21st Bombers' Group that: they should strengthen their attack on the major cities in Japan with incendiary bombs. LeMay, unlike Hansell, did not express his unwillingness to accept such order as to attack the residential areas with incendiary bombs. This decided the fate of Tokyo, Osaka, Nagoya, Kobe, Yokohama and so on.

In the publicized version of *A History on U.S. Army Air Force*, this was curtly recorded as follows: "Major General LeMay decided to perform a series of incendiary bombings of the largest scale." The reason was because "it was generally believed that the Japanese cities are quite fit for the incendiary attack." Another literature, *A Report on the Pacific War* (issued by the U.S. Inquiry Group on the Strategic Bombings)* gives a little more detailed explanation, as follows:

This was because Japan's industry had largely depended on the cooperative production of essential parts at thousands of petty industries and small factories. These subcontractors' workshops had been thickly packed in the urban areas all over Japan, and if we wanted to clear them away, all we could do was to destroy them by incendiary bombs. .... The problem was how we could perform a concentrated attack by dropping a necessary amount of bombs within a certain period of time.

The one who could solve that problem was LeMay. In his autobiography,* he wrote, as follows:

It had become clear that the high-altitude precision bombings would be of no use in defeating Japan. We were forced to start doing something new or totally different from what we had been doing so far. In other words, we had to change our way of employing our arms.

While looking at the photographs of reconnoitering the enemy, I noticed they had not possessed any low-altitude antiaircraft fire we used to be attacked in the skies of Europe. (In Japan, the antiaircraft guns were small in number, and antiaircraft machine guns were much smaller in number.) This led me to find out a reasonable strategy: In Japan, we can fly low, consuming a smaller amount of fuel, thus enabling us to carry a larger amount of bombs, and this would suit better for the night attack. Thus, judging the situation, and after recognizing the need of reforming our tactics, I reached my decision to perform the low-altitude incendiary bombings upon the industrial areas in the Japanese cities.

A series of night attacks upon the Japanese cities—starting with Tokyo on the night of March 9—had come from such a policy switching he had made. Here the principle applied to Japan was different from what had been applied to Germany, but the logic they adopted to justify themselves then was amazingly similar to the excuse the Japanese military had once given while performing their indiscriminate bombings upon the cities in China. LeMay asserted without hesitation, as follows:

I had not been killing the Japanese civilians; I had been destroying Japan's munitions works. All the Japanese houses were none other than munitions works: The Suzukis were producing bolts; the Kondos next door were producing nuts; the Tanakas across the street were producing washers. .... Each of those houses—made of wood and paper—in Tokyo and in Nagoya had turned into manufactories to produce weapons to attack us. What would be wrong if we attacked those workshops?

Thinking of the civilians being killed or injured, he could not be happy, but it did not worry him so much, because he knew how the Japanese had treated the captive Americans. LeMay, thus justifying the indiscriminate bombings being performed under his directions, raised the B29s' sortie hours a month to 120 hours—four times longer than the hours when they were engaged in the air raids on German cities.

● **The Project for the Atomic Bombings was Going on**

At that same period when the large number of groups of B29s released from the base under the control of LeMay at Guam Island were sending one city after another into the flames of bombs, General Arnold at Washington was making preparations for another strategy that would mark a new dimension in the strategic bombings—or dropping the nuclear bombs expected to be completed before long. In the spring, 1944, Arnold had already received a detailed explanation on that advanced type of bomb from Major General Leslie Groves, the chief executive on the military side in the Manhattan Project. They had already made such agreements as follows: the aircraft to carry the atomic bomb should be of the converted type of B29; a completely independent corps with high degree of ability should be formed; ample training should be given to be able to hit the mark without fail. Thus the plan of atomic bombings was gradually moving toward Arnold's sphere.

For Arnold who believed in the supremacy of the Air Force, the atomic bomb must have appeared "a dream new weapon" in several points. Only a single explosion of it was to burst the heart of the enemy nation. That potentiality had also given him an actuality of being able to produce a condition to make Japan surrender not only by MacArthur's landing operations on the Japanese Mainland and by Nimitz's naval blockade but also by "Arnold's Air Force's strategic bombardment." When the Air Force was about to be made into an independent force, if they were able to demonstrate the fact that their strategic bombings had brought the war to an end, that would make a golden opportunity for demonstrating their strength to the Army and the Navy. Furthermore, the occurrence of the U.S.' discord with the Soviet Union also should not be ignored, considering that: it had meant something appealing to Arnold's ambition from the phase of the U.S.' strategy for dealing with the Soviet Union after the War. General Henry Arnold—the last commander-in-chief of the U.S. Army Air Force—and also the first General of the U.S. Air Force to be brought into being before long—was energetically promoting the way to Hiroshima and Nagasaki, trying to provide that new-generation Air Force with an unparalleled power.

By and by, the order was issued that: the fifteen B29s should be improved into the ones suited to carry the atomic bombs; the formation of No. 509 Mixed Troop was over under the command of LeMay on Guam Island; then 225 commissioned officers and 1,542 noncommissioned officers to form the first unit to drop the atomic bomb—the group of those who were to perform the greatest massacre by the smallest personnel—advanced onto Tinian Island of the Mariana Islands. The person singled out as Commander was Colonel Paul

Tibbets, who, until immediately before that, had been on the strategy staff in the 97th Bombers' Group in the European war zone.

Curtis LeMay accepted the fact that he had been made the person in charge of a strategy of dropping the atomic bomb without feeling any special rush of emotion. As for the reason for that, he said later in retrospection: "What I had learned at physics class at school was such that I could not understand everything," and "what I had in my mind then was that: if it helps Jap surrender sooner, using it will be better than not using it." Even after Captain William Parsons, who was to join the attack on Hiroshima as an officer in command of arms, arrived at Guam on July 25 and showed LeMay and others the films of the enormous pillar of fire rising in the first A-bomb test performed at the desert of Alamogordo, LeMay did not change his mind. According to LeMay's belief, the men of fighting service always wish to make their own damage as little as possible while giving their enemies much damage, and "if such arms as would straightforwardly realize this wish of ours were to be given to us, *not* employing it would not occur to us as long as we were servicemen of common sense." When he received an explanation from Major General Leslie Groves concerning the delivering of the atomic bomb, he presented an unexpected proposition that: he would do *it* in a single bomber without employing any escort fighters, thus to give Groves a strong impression. The explanation given by LeMay then was: "The Japanese side will not pay much attention to a single plane flying in high altitude, simply taking it as a mere scout plane or a plane for weather-observation." LeMay's ability to grasp the situation proved to be outstanding in such a direction as this, too.

● **"Our First Aim is Hiroshima."**

On July 25, 1945, General Carl Spaatz, Commander of Strategic Air Force in the Pacific Theater, received the directive of Releasing an Atomic Bomb, signed by George Marshall, the Chief of the General Staff of the Army. The place of dispatch was Potsdam in Germany. From the very place which had been burnt up by the strategic air force below Spaatz's knee—and also from the place of the Potsdam Conference, where the ultimatum toward Japan was being discussed—the order to perform the strategic atomic bombing had been issued. The opening of "The Centerboard Plan of Operations" read as follows:

The 20th Air Force's No.509 Combined Troop, on or after August 3, 1945, as soon as possible if weather permits, shall drop the first special bomb upon one of the following aims: Hiroshima, Kokura, Niigata and Nagasaki.

President Truman, who had also been at Potsdam, wrote as follows, after having been reported that Marshall's order had already been conveyed to the very unit to perform it, as he wrote in his *Memoir:*

> According to this order, the preparation for the first atomic bombing was being made toward that single military aim. In other words, I had made a decision. I had also issued an official directive to Stimson (Director of the Army) that the order would remain valid till Japan gave us its answer of having accepted the Potsdam Declaration.

On the day that followed—on the 26th—at the artificial port of Tinian Island, the heavy cruiser *Indianapolis* sailed in with what corresponded to "the gun barrel and the bullet," followed by a couple of transport planes bringing in the triggering devices to make uranium cause nuclear reaction, and they were carried to North Field (Airport) through "the Broadway" that crossed the central part of the island. No. 509 mixed troop that had been trained day after day had already been judged to have attained the desired level. Tibbets had intended to perform that first attack under his command. He had named the B29 he was to take Enola Gay after his own mother.

On August 2, LeMay at his headquarters on Guam gave his instructions to Tibbets as to their attack target:

"Paul, our first aim is Hiroshima."

Tibbets gave a ready answer:

"I myself have always held Hiroshima as our aim."

LeMay had chosen Hiroshima, because it had been left almost untouched by B29s, and still the effect of the bombardment would be great. In *The Order for the Special Duties to Perform the Bombardment (No.13)* drafted by LeMay, the first aim was given as "Hiroshima: its urban area & industrial area," followed by "the urban area of Kokura as the second aim" and "the urban area of Nagasaki as the third aim." It seemed as if "the urban area" and "the atomic bombing" had been inseparably connected with each other in the conception of strategic bombing from the very beginning without any doubt being held by anyone.

The toothed wheels of their fate mechanically started going along. Before or after the order of the atomic attack was issued from Potsdam, the Potsdam Declaration was notified as a joint statement made by Truman, Churchill and Jiang Jieshi, but Japan's Prime Minister, Suzuki Kantaro, simply "ignored it"* and declared to "keep fighting," thus to finally lose any opportunity to cut off the linkage of Hiroshima and Enola Gay and the atomic bomb. That turned out the "critical reaction" of the atomic bomb in the international politics. Thus, Truman's instruction—"the order will remain valid till Japan gives us its answer of having accepted the Potsdam Declaration"—became the only manual for LeMay, and this led him to do his best in realizing what was written at the closing paragraph of the Potsdam Declaration: "Any choice Japan will make, excepting making the unconditional surrender, shall lead to its swift and complete destruction." Now he adopted the same businesslike attitude as he had done in attacking Hamburg, Hankou and Tokyo. On the other hand, the Japanese Government, even though they had held the means by which they could immediately check what LeMay and Tibbets were about to perform—by accepting the Potsdam Declaration—would not employ *it* until August 10.

*Prime Minister Suzuki had employed the word, 黙殺 (*mokusatsu*), intending to mean *"let it pass in silence"*—in giving his comment on the Potsdam Declaration he had received, but when it was translated into English by a reporter of his, *"mokusatsu"* was translated as *"ignore it."*

Before dawn on August 6, Enola Gay took off at North Air Base at Tinian Island. At once, Captain Persons (whose code name was "Judge") went down to the magazine room to control the triggering device of the atomic bomb. Captain Tibbets sent a short telegram to the control tower at Tinian Island: "Judge has gone to do his job." Six hours later, Enola Gay was over Hiroshima.

The spectacle brought into being in Hiroshima at that moment was something to be called "a negative denouement" in the conception of strategic bombardment.

As to what these airmen were doing on that moment when "the Conception of Strategic Bombings" disclosed itself in the sky of Hiroshima that day, the U.S. Smithsonian Institute made a plan to display it in 1995 at the Aerospace

Museum as the Special Event in Commemoration of the 50th Anniversary of the End of World War Ⅱ, but it was not realized because of the opposition presented by the Air Force Society and others. The following is the explanation given in *The Bombing of Hiroshima & Nagasaki. Judgment at the Smithonian* Edited by Philip Nobile; Afterword by Barton Bernstein.

Arming the Bomb

At 7:15 a.m. (6:15 a.m. in Hiroshima) the weather scout plane over the city of Hiroshima reported to Tibbets that the cloud cover was favorable for a visual bombing of the city. Tibbets announced to his crew: "It's Hiroshima." At 7:30 a.m., an hour and forty-five minutes before"bombs away,"assistant weaponeer Morris Jepson once again entered the bomb bay. Throughout the flight, three green plugs inserted into the forward part of the bomb had inactivated the electronic firing circuitry. Jepson's final task was to replace the green plugs with the red plugs that would open the firing circuit.

Hiroshima on August 6, 1945

Bombs Away

Tibbets handed over control of the plane to bombardier Ferebee and navigator van Kirk. Ferrebi trained the plane's Norden bombsight on the target. Then van Kirk fed Ferrebi updated calculations on wind speed and altitude, which Ferrebi, in turn entered into the bombsight's computer. Using the target as a base point, it automatically corrected the course of the airplane. At 17 seconds after 9:14 a.m. (8:14 a.m. Hiroshima time), Ferrebi flipped a switch which turned over control of the plane and the bomb to the bombsight's computer. One minute later, it automatically dropped the bomb.

The lightened plane lurched upward, Tibets took back the controls and turned the Enola Gay in the practiced violent escape turn. Eleven miles from the blast, a flash of light filled the cockpit and the first of the two chock waves hit the plane. Tibbets announced,"Fellows, you have just dropped the first atomic bomb in History."

——BANNED HISTORY, The Uncensored Script of the Smithonian's 50ʰ Anniversary Exhibit of The Enola Gay

The sight below them was none other than the atrocity of light and heat that would have been unimaginable even to Picasso who had produced *Guernica* or to Guo Moruo who had turned the misery of Chongqing into poetry. Certainly that was an enormous scale of carnage, but the underlying conception remained totally unchanged from what they used to be in the days of Guernica and Chongqing. Such a conception of mass-murder as was actualized in Hiroshima had been brought into being with the advent of the aircraft to be tempered thoroughly throughout the periods of the two World Wars, and it could be regarded as a consummation of the periods of the World Wars. Hiroshima was a summit but not an independent phenomenon. "Hiroshima as a conception" had already been trod down hard. That was, therefore, the final stage of the tragedy or "the negative denouement."

● **Japan is not Qualified to Denounce "the Conception of Dropping a Nuclear Bomb"**

Looking over the chronology of the birth and growth of the strategic bombings, the Japanese will certainly be able to assert that they had nothing to do with "the conception of creating nucleus." Even if they had held any such conception, they had not had any such technology nor industrial power as to produce such bombs. Still, even if we did not have any such bombs as material objects, we shall never be able to plead *not* guilty of the crime of having had "any such conception of dropping nuclear bombs." No Japanese—excepting those who were exposed to the radiation from the atomic bombs—are not qualified to make themselves "a judge" of those atomic bombings. The reason was: if we inspect the history of Asia from the viewpoint of strategic bombings or indiscriminate mass murders, we shall surely come to face the facts of atrocities the Japanese military had committed here and there in China and in South-East Asia—before we are led to Hiroshima and Nagasaki. In many places in China and in Southeast Asia, "the Hiroshimas before Hiroshima" brought about by the Japanese military still remain in agony, suffering from irrecoverable injuries.

"Hiroshima" as "a terminal point" in the history of strategic bombings having had such significance as this, it remains not only the place name that denounces the conception of performing a mass murder from high in the sky by simply pressing a button—but also an eternal piercer through Japan as an offender.

Receiving the news of Hiroshima having been attacked by an atomic bomb, *Xin Hua Ri Bao* (New China Daily News) or the Communist Party's bulletin for August 9 carried three articles concerning it. One of them or the editorial comments entitled "On the Atomic Bombing" was unsigned, but later Xia Yan, a writer, made it clear in his autobiography, *The Pen and the War,"* that he had written *it:*

> The invention of the atomic bomb and its having been dropped for the first time in history were literally earthshaking events to the whole world. The revolution in science and the revolution in war-making did occur on the same day. As for the practical potentiality of the atomic bomb, we have not yet had any sufficient materials to start any investigation. But judging from all those pieces of information we have received so far from the newspapers, there is no room for doubt about the fierceness of its destructive power and the monstrosity of its effectiveness. It was a natural punishment for the Japanese fascist invaders to have been attacked by this most powerful weapon in human history, and we, the Chinese, who have been suffering from all these barbarous carnages for these eight years, cannot feel any

pity for the Japanese militarists—excepting the innocent Japanese people who have been simply fooled by them. On the other hand, science, which primarily ought to contribute to the happiness of human life, has now been applied in producing such a cruel weapon with so much destructive power and lethality as that. This, we believe, has led all the people in the world, especially the scientists, to feel worried to a serious extent.

—*The Pen and The War*

The article was closed, as follows: Science must belong to the people; the fruit of science must be applied to the maintenance of peace and happiness of the people.

On the day that followed—August 10—the people in Chongqing heard the news of Japan's having accepted the Potsdam Declaration. At that welcome news, all the people in Chongqing jumped out into the streets and left themselves wild with joy. After the eight-years' resistance, and after the ferocious air raids that lasted throughout the three summers, they had finally won a victory over Japan. All the streets were filled with people, and that mountain castle city was being frenzied with joy, setting off fierce crackers worth as much as three hundred thousand *yuan* in a single day. In contrast to the worry expressed in *Xin Hua Ri Bao* (New China Daily), in which the significance of the appearance of nuclear weapons was sharply seen through, the people in Chongqing were letting their joy burst all day long at the news of Japan's surrender that followed the news of Hiroshima and Nagasaki which had also been devastated on August 9 by a different type of atomic bomb.

Xia Yan recalls what it was like in the same autobiography—*The Pen and The War:*

On hearing the news of Japan's surrender, all the staff of *Xin Hua Ri Bao* went mad. In fact, all the people in Chongqing and all the people in this country had gone mad. If "gone mad" did not sound decent, I shall describe it with the character of 狂 which means "so joyful as if one's joy has been enhanced to madness." Some were dancing with joy; others were silent in flowing tears. I myself, being too excited to go to sleep, spent all night in reading the press proof, and then decided to go out into the town to see the sight of cheers—the cheers shared by all the people in this country—which I thought would never be seen again in my life.

At five, I came to the foot the mountain, and found all the streets of Hualong-quiao were overcrowded with men, women and children; I took a bus to find it filled with shouts of joy—all the people exchanging words, totally indifferent to their differences in sex, age and where they were from, simply sharing the happy news they had already been well-informed of. All were simply happy to talk and share their pleasure with others. The Sichuan people are fond of talking or what they call "the Battle at Longmen (Dragons' Gate)," and the thickly-crowded bus was reverberating with shouts of joy. A white-bearded old man was also giving his sentiment in a loud voice: "I have seen *this* day with my own eyes. I shall be very, very happy even if I were pegged out tomorrow morning."

But the battle of Chongqing had not yet been over completely. Japan's surrender was also a sign of the resumption of the civil war to be made for liberating China.

As for the fact that Japan's defeat was brought about by the atomic bombings upon their islands, it was accepted with profound feelings by Jiang Jieshi, too, as was recorded in the entry on August 31 in *The Reflection of This Month, 1945*, in *Jiang Jieshi's Secret Memoir:*

These atomic bombings were not only the one and only force to put an end to this World War but also the element to bring about a solution to all these global war disasters that had lasted for these ten years. The capability of science is as great as this. But, if the Heaven's Emperor had not endowed us human beings with such divine wisdom as this, such an invention as this would have remained impossible.

On the day when they won a victory over Japan, the ruins and heaps of rubbles left all over this anti-Japanese capital would not have been different at all from what was seen in Tokyo, Berlin, London and so on, which had also been badly stricken by the air raids. But anyone who happened to arrive at Chongqing that day ought to have sensed in the atmosphere and in the people's expressions a faint tension that could not be explained only as a shadow of despondency or as an explosion of great joy. In the midst of the situation moving from the victory of the anti-Japanese war toward the breakdown of the Nationalist-Communist collaboration and even toward the outbreak of the civil war—Chongqing was again destined to be the focal point. Having been deprived of any opportunity to have a doze for a rest or to think over what the Japanese military's bombardments had meant to them, this mountain castle city on the bank of the Yangzi was to expose herself in the coming phase of storm and stress of the Chinese Revolution.

● **The Negotiation between Jiang Jieshi and Mao Zedong was Held at Chongqing**

On August 28, 1945—two weeks after the *Tenno* Hirohito, the Emperor of Japan, announced his having accepted the Potsdam Declaration to the Japanese people—there arrived at Chongqing Air Port a transport plane from Yan-an with Mao Zedong and other top leaders of the Chinese Communist Party on board, and the following day saw the start of "the Chongqing Negotiation."

Jiang and Mao were seated, facing each other, in order to struggle for the assumption of ruling power, at the hall for the negotiation near Guiyuan (Laurel Garden) near Zenjia-an in Shizhong Word; behind each of them stood the elite troop of each side—the corps of He Yingquin, the commander of the Chinese Army, and the elite corps of Zhu De, the Commander-in-Chief of the Eighth Route Army—each letting out the sounds of demonstration and fierce competition. Chongqing this time was to play the role of the listener to the movement of the fetus of a new China. The citizens of Chongqing were looking at Mao Zedong with great curiosity, and wherever he went, they were eager to have a look at him, the top leader of the Communist Party, who had recently entered the capital as the seat of Jiang Jieshi. The people's minds had already been moving toward the Communist Party.

After the Chongqing Negotiation that had lasted more than a month, "*Shuang Shi Xie Ding* (the Double Ten Agreements)" was finally signed on October 10. But immediately after that, a civil war broke out between the Nationalist and the Communist; in order to put an end to it, "a political entente conference" was held toward the end of the same year again at Chongqing; then the U.S. President Truman sent General of the Army, George Marshall as his special envoy, who brought into being "Three Persons' Conference" with Zhou Enlai, Zhang Qun and Marshall himself, but no progress was seen.... The citizens of

Chongqing, while watching over the struggling between the Nationalists and the Communists, and between the U.S. and China, were gradually recovering themselves from the piles of rubbish. On April 30, 1946, the Nationalist Government announced the transfer of their capital to Nanjing, and on the same day, Jiang Jieshi left for Xian. On May 5, the ceremony for the relocation of the capital was held at Nanjing, thus putting an end to the status of Chongqing as the interim capital which had lasted for eight years and a half. From May 3 to 18, Zhou Enlai, Dong Biwu and other members of the Communist delegation in Chongqing left their seat at Zengjia-an and Hong-an, and "their Central Headquarters of their revolutionary struggles in the regions under the Nationalist rule finished moving to Nanjing." (*The Comprehensive Record of the Southern Bureau*)

Thus the political center of China left Chongqing, and after a brief period of time, Jiang Jieshi, who had declared that *the* place should be "the Capital of Free China," failed to keep his fate flourishing in the Chinese mainland.

In October, 1949, the People's Republic of China was founded and its capital was decided upon Beijing, and the sacred place of that revolution was decided upon Yan-an where Mao Zedong had spent several years. Chongqing, which used to be "the White District," having doubly been deviated from the direction the New China adopted, came to be looked upon as "somewhere out of place and out of date." For a long time since then, therefore, in the history of the anti-Japanese War, the record of the sufferings and resistance of this city has never been treated as something important.

The authority of the Japanese side, too, who had boastfully kept announcing their having made "their rain of giant bombs" fall on the seat of "the Chongqing Administration," simply stopped talking anything about it after the war was over. Thus Chongqing was to remain no more than a place name only mentioned by the Japanese when talking of "the sky in which the Zero fighters made their first appearance." On the other hand, the U.S. that had sent in such an enormous amount of materials and a large number of personnel into the hinterland of Sichuan Province in China had their interest retreat from the mainland China— along with Jiang Jieshi who had retreated from the Chinese mainland—and those who were able to talk about their experiences in the anti-Japanese Capital, such as Theodore White, Edgar Snow, Agnes Smedley, and such diplomats as John Service and others who were well-informed of China, were obliged to fall on hard times, withdrawn from society, for many years—from the opening of the cold war between the U.S. and the U.S.S.R. through the long period of McCarthyism, when the Chinese Government remained unrecognized. In short, what Chongqing meant—in the Sino-Japanese War and in the history of aerial battles in the world—was destined to remain sealed and driven to the limbo of oblivion for a long period of time.

● The Changes of the Inscriptions on the Monuments Symbolize the Vicissitudes and Anguishes Chongqing has Gone Through

Today, however, Chongqing has grown into one of the leading industrial cities in China, and when I look up at the dignified *Monument of Liberation* from where *Minzu-lu* (the Peoples' Road) meets *Minquan-lu* (the Peoples' Rights' Road)—the area that used to be coded as "Section B" for the bombardment of Japan's No.101 Operations—I feel as if I could visualize how it was like when its predecessor—*The Monument of the Victory of Our Resistance (to Japan)*—was brought into being here. In December, 1946, the people from all walks of life in Chongqing assembled here to start the construction work for the monument to memorialize the days when they were living in perfect perseverance even though they had to helplessly run away from the air raids, until they finally won their victory. For Chongqing then, whose status had been returned to a mere provincial city again, that was the first large event they had performed. That tower, which looked like an arm with its fist thrusting toward the sky which used to be controlled by the middle-sized bombers of the Japanese Navy Air Force, was completed in August in the year that followed—in time for the second anniversary of their victory over Japan.

When I let the time go further back, I can see a huge crowd of people make their appearance in "the large assembly for declaring the general mobilization of the national spirit" sponsored by the Center of the Nationalist Party. On May 1, 1939, Jiang Jieshi called out to the people who had been mobilized there: "Let us build our *Spiritual Stronghold* in our determination to win the Anti-Japanese War!" Three days later, the citizens of Chongqing were to suffer the air raids of "5.3 & 5.4"—so devastating as had never been experienced in the world history of aerial wars. After that, however, a single pole was erected at the place where *the Spiritual Stronghold* was to be erected, and it did keep standing there throughout the war period, as if guarding that spot.

The Spiritual Stronghold, The Monument of the Victory of Our Resistance war and *The Monument of Liberation*—the changes of the names given to that same tower standing at the central part of Chongqing do narrate the history of changes and pains this city has suffered, and in the depth of each of these names, there have always been the buzzing sounds and explosions that frightened the night sky, the air-splitting sounds of incendiary bombs coming falling, the smell of clotted blood and the expressions of beloved ones' last moment have firmly been enveloped along with the thoughts and sentiments of those who have kept retaining those memories. Even though ignored or forgotten by the offenders or outsiders, their memories of the air raids upon Chongqing still keep standing firm—like that *Monument of Liberation* soaring in the center of the city—in the bosom of many people and in the scenes shared by every citizen of Chongqing. That tower also recounts the fact that: "*Hiroshima as the conception of strategic bombing*" has started at this very spot in China.

At the entrance to the Exhibition Hall for The Anti-Japanese War at the Chinese People's Museum of the Revolution and Military Affairs in Beijing, we see the following numerals given on the bulletin board:

$$1937 \cdot 7 \sim 1945 \cdot 8$$

The Deaths	9,325,000
The Injured	9,470,000
The Missing	2,890,000
The Total	21,685,000

In such large numbers of victims and casualties, the toll of victims of the Chongqing Air Raids might not be so large, but to the citizens of Chongqing then, that was an experience totally out of the ordinary, and the form of carnage committed then and there was to bring about a turning point to what war had been so far. This fact must be taken seriously especially by the Japanese who were responsible for that history. It is not until this is recognized by the Japanese that what Hiroshima and Nagasaki meant will be generalized and turned into a part of the spiritual history of human beings.

German Bomber, HE111, flying over the Thames in London (see P.537)

Coventry Cathedral in Coventry in West-Midland, England after having suffered the air-raid by the German Air Force (see P.539)

The four-engined bombers, Lancaster and Halifax (see P.545)

The B24s attacking the military facilities in Germany (see P.556)

atop Dresden's town hall, a sandstone gure gestuers toward the ruins of the ity's old quarter (see P.555)

The Chinese people were mobilizaed to construct the airport in Chengdu (see P.565)

The B29, the super-fortress (see P.558)

One of the B29s attacking the Iron and Steel Works at Yawata, Japan (see P.571)

The B29s at the airport on Saipan Island (see P.579)

The B-29 "Enola Gay"piloted by Colonel Paul Tibbets (see P.591)

① Tokyo after the airraid on
March 10, 1945, and other
major cities immediately after
the end of the war.

② Kobe ③ Yokohama
④ Osaka ⑤ Nagoya

THE FINAL CHAPTER

THE MASSACRES
FROM THE AIR STILL GO ON

● **"Killing One Man makes a Rascal; Killing One Million makes a Hero"**
Guernica led to Chongqing, and then to Hiroshima. What sort of influences and traces did that conception of strategic bombing—which had gone so far as employing the nuclear bombs in such a short period of time—give to the world after the World War Ⅱ?

Just as Goya, the artist, handed down to the posterity *The Horrors of War* in the days of Napoleon, and Picaso, also a Spanish, painted *Guernica,* while Guo Moruo, a Chinese poet, wrote *I Groan on seeing the Misery,* in order to carve in history the terrors from the sky, several movies released in the 1940s when the embers brought about by the World War Ⅱ were still smoldering also groped and found what sort of devastation the wars in the 20th Century had brought to human mind, thus to reveal the essence of the new violence. Considering the fact that the movie as a new mode of expression was also brought into being in the 20th century—just like the air planes which enabled us to perform the strategic bombings—it would be an appropriate means of expression in denouncing the miseries of war performed in the same age so that it could be sent over to the posterity.

Roberto Rossellini presented in *Germania Anno Zero* (produced in 1948) what miseries the people in Berlin had to face when their city was reduced to ashes—with an innocent boy as the hero, who had to make himself a minion of a black marketer, then a thief, until at last he had to kill his own father who was badly suffering from illness. Rossellini presented all the process of it "neither to accuse nor to vindicate anyone but to introduce *the* fact." In the comment he gave at the opening, Rossellini mentions: "When all kinds of ideas and the moral sense and faith that had lain at the base of human existence so far crumbled away, the ideological prejudice creates crimes and insanity. That cannot do without contaminating even the pure heart of children." That was a verification of what traces the indiscriminate bombings had inflicted upon the human mind.

The Third Man, a British movie, released in 1949—written and dramatized by Graham Greene, and directed by Carol Reed—clearly depicted the absurdity of the era when one was able to come high up in the sky, holding the power of life and death over other people—under the pretext of the world taken by and the impression received by the criminal Harry Lime. The melody of a zither that flows throughout the movie sounds like the *biwa* (a Japanese lute) that used to accompany the narration of *The Tale of the Heikes*—a war romance that actually occurred in Japan (1180-1185)—describing the downfall of the ancient nobility and the rise of the warrior class.

To Harry, who has made himself an illicit dealer of smuggled penicillin, an old friend of his, Martins, demands an explanation for what has led him to engage in such a job as that. They are in the Ferris wheel in a pleasure park which alone has miraculously remained intact in Wien. The two men are facing each other in the car rising slowly. Martins asks: "Have you ever visited the children's hospital? Have you seen any of your victims?" To this accusation given by his friend, Harry answers bluntly. The Ferris wheel has reached its top. The people below appear as tiny as ants.

"Victims? Don't be melodramatic, Rollo. Look down there. Would you really feel any pity if one of those dots stopped moving—forever? If I said you can have twenty thousand pounds for every dot that stops, would you really, old man, tell me to keep my money—without hesitation?"

In this movie, Harry Lime is not acting as a former crew member of the Lancaster bombers of the U.K. Air Force which had brought about a flame hell upon Hamburg and Dresden. Neither does he seem to be talking of his own experience. But his speech is unmistakably that of the generation that has known "the bomber stream" and "the saturation bombing," and that incomparably fiercest paradox in which "the wartime justice" is thrown back to the peacetime society never fails to shrink us back.

"In these days, old man, nobody thinks in terms of human beings. Governments don't, so why should we? They talk of the people and the proletariat, and I talk of the mugs. It's the same thing. They have their five-year plans and so have I."

Thus by the impudent presence of Harry Lime acted by Orson Welles, the audience are forced to realize the meaning of the indiscriminate murders performed by the body politic. Through this speech given to what was being looked down upon from the Ferris wheel, Carol Reed generalized "the conception of strategic bombing" through the screen images he had created.

Another movie producer, Charlie Chaplin, showed in his work of *Monsieur Verdoux*—released in 1948, with its historical background taken in 1937, the year the horror of Guernica occurred—how the indiscriminate mass murder performed by the name of the Government was based upon the dangerous plot—through the caricatured actions of a mania for killing one wealthy widow after another for money. This movie would not have come into being, either, if it had not been for the horrors of Dresden and of Hiroshima. For Chaplin, who had already appealed to the public for the protest of love and humanism against Hitler's Nazism by his former work *The Dictator* (produced in 1940, immediately after the outbreak of World War Ⅱ), those eight years with World War Ⅱ in between must have been of profound frustration and indignation. While the efforts were being made to destroy the evil of fascism, another type of violence was invited to settle down. The speech made by an evil murderer Verdoux: "Killing one man makes a baddy; killing a million makes a hero. Quantity makes *it* sacred." does resound to the words given by Harry Lime in *The Third Man:* "A hero? A hero is someone living in a world totally different from ours," and it sharply points out the trend of the new age which has jumped to a world totally different from the world where war could be explained by one's personal moral sense or by the justice of a body politic. The headline of the newspaper Verdoux was reading on the screen—"The Nazis made a bombing raid upon the Republicans in Spain, killing several thousand citizens"—does suggest the tragedy of Guernica and Chaplin's message about it.

For Henri Verdoux as the defendant of serial murders, his public prosecutor demands a death penalty, saying:

"Gentlemen in the jury boxes. What you are seeing before your eyes is a monster, cruel and sardonic...."

Verdoux, who has received a death sentence, makes a statement:

"As for being a mass killer, does not the world encourage it? Is it not building weapons of destruction for the sole purpose of mass killing? Has it not blown unsuspecting women and little children to pieces? And done it very scientifically? As a mass killer, I am an amateur by comparison. However, I do not wish to lose my temper, because very shortly, I shall lose my head. Nevertheless, upon leaving this spark of earthly existence, I have this to say: I shall see you all... very sonn... very soon."

According to the law, Monsieur Verdoux was guillotined, but the guillotine of the law could not do so far as to check "the prediction of his survival." How true his prediction was can be verified by a variety of events in the regional conflicts that occurred since the Cold War period in the latter half of the 20th century. That union of "indiscriminate bombing" and "a nuclear bomb" which, after having been loaded on the B29 at a corner of the North Air Port of Tinian Island, was dropped on Hiroshima—or that extreme power of strategic bombing was to wrap up the human species after World War II for the plausible reason of "the deterrent by nuclear," and to control the international society in peacetime in the state of "a stay of execution of a war that would lead human beings to extinction."

On the other hand, under the East-West confrontation, in not a few local wars that broke out in the Third World, napalm bombs and antipersonnel arms for indiscriminate carnage were recklessly employed to deliver cruelties and indiscretions. Under the strategy of nuclear deterrence where "the quantity consecrates," the balance of fears and the extermination strategy from the sky to "blast innocent women and children to pieces" remained immortal—as Chaplin had foretold in *Monsieur Verdoux*.

The Korean War → the Vietnam War → the Persian Gulf War → the air raids upon the Autonomous Province of Kosovo → the attack on Afghanistan → the Iraq War.... The scenes brought into being by those wars were none other than the enlarged extension of what *The Third Man* in the car of the Great Wheel had caught with his cold eyes. The same thing can be said about "the 9.11 Incident" that shocked us at the start of this century and about the form of carnages that followed it.

● What had the 20ᵗʰ Century Brought to Warfare?

In closing this documentary of the merciless bombardments upon the cities that started at Guernica and at Chongqing to spread to Dresden, to Tokyo, and to Hiroshima, while intensifying the degree of their monstrosity, let us consider "what the 20ᵗʰ century brought to warfare," and "what the 20ᵗʰ century meant in the history of wars."

In order to find out what sort of base "the conception of strategic bombing" was built upon, I should like to bring the trace of the development of the aerial war potential—as was mentioned in Chapter I: How the Strategic Bombing was Brought into Being—further to the historical survey of death and destruction brought about by the wars and modern technology. Then we shall be able to understand that: the 21ˢᵗ century that started with "the 9.11 incident" is still upon the extension of "the 20ᵗʰ century of prolonged warfare." Our sense of aloofness toward warfare—because of the long distance to the actual murder, because of the great efficiency in performing the murder, because of the apathetic method of murder—keeps increasing until we need not feel any physical impact in the man-slaughter we are performing. In other words, between the killer and the killed, there is "a region of invisibility" and "vanishing of physicality," or rather "War thus becomes *virtual* from the technological point of view and *bodiless* from the military point of view," as Antonio Negri pointed out in *Multitude* (2004).

If we were to define "war" as "a systematic fight fought between different groups of people by means of arms, whatever their aims might be" (Samuel Lily), its origin must be traced as far back as the prehistoric age. According to Lily, our making a war has been closely connected with the agriculture we began to engage in:

Duelo a Garrotazos

War rarely occurred or never occurred until agriculture was brought into being. Because they could not engage in hunting while they were making war, and if they stopped hunting, they could not survive under such a lowly condition of life.

——*A History of Human Beings and Machines*

If so, in prehistoric times, war could not occur excepting as an accidental struggle concerning a hunting ground or the distribution of the game. Increase in agricultural productivity and settled habitation brought about the storage of food, the concentration of wealth and power, and, above all, the time needed in making a war. Since then, there ought to have been innumerable wars. But one common phenomenon in all those wars made during the prehistoric times, the ancient times and the early modern times was that: all the wars were made on the land, only between individuals, and by thrusting themselves against each other. This reminds us of the scene of *Two Men Exchanging Blows* (*Duelo a garrotazos*) created by Goya toward the end of his life. They had neither tactics nor formation. They were simply trying to knock the other person down by means of sticks and stones. By and by, they came to employ arms of bronze or iron. Group tactics were worked out; horses were brought in as a new element of mobility. Then, bows and arrows of all sizes were brought in, followed by explosives and matchlock muskets. The employment of these arms led to "the extension of hands" and "the extension of eye-sight," thus widening their battlefields and developing their mobility. Still the warriors, because of their limited strength of legs, had been kept remaining on the ground all the same.

Arthur Ferrell, in his study of the progress of human beings and their arms—from the stone age when slow but steady progress in arms and a mode of war was being made to the age of Alexandros (356BC-323BC)—reached a conclusion: "Alexandros, as early as 2,000 years before Napoleon (1769-1821), had already raised his battle technique almost to the level of the modern times." Or the form of battles that had been adopted till the 19th century had already been established by 300B.C. and this led Ferrell to give a daring hypothesis: if Alexandros had appeared with his Macedonian-style solid square with all their equipment, strategy and supply ability at the battlefield of Waterloo in 1815 to fight against the British infantry under General Wellington—in place of Napoleon's Army—"they ought to have engaged in a very close combat, even though he cannot say they did expel the British."

According to Ferrell, Alexandros' bows and his ballasters (to discharge stones and his catapults to shoot arrows and spears) were favorably comparable with Wellington Army's small guns and cannons in shooting range, in loading speed and in on-target rate, too, and if they were to fight close combat, the combat power of the Macedonians in a solid square ought to have overwhelmed the British infantry corps. Such an intellectual assumption as this reveals the fact that: the progress of the warfare from the ancient times to early modern times had been made so slowly as to allow us to enjoy playing such an intellectual game as this. Upon this fact, Ferrell points out the shift brought into the history of warfare in the 20th century:

> The combat method adopted by Alexandros in founding his Macedonian Army did remain as it used to be until the age of Napoleon, even though some changes might have been made in military technique and organization. It was not until the 20th century—when there came into being incomparably large-scaled armies, airplanes, submarines, machine guns, rapid-fire guns and even nuclear weapons—that the fundamental changes in combats came to take place.

This view would have something in common with what Andre Malraux said, during the Vietnam War, criticizing the U.S. President Johnson, who had ordered to perform "the bombing of North Vietnam" by sending a large number of B52 bombers: "Caesar was able to talk with Napoleon, but Napoleon would not be able to find any word to say to President Johnson."

Certainly, in such strategy and manners in the battlefield as is seen in Julius Caesar's *Commentaries on the Gallic War,* we cannot find any fundamental difference from the Napoleonic Wars in the 19ᵗʰ century. The slaughters they performed did remain with them as something graphic; there were physical limitations, too. Because that was a physical crash between the fighters, the danger of death was always with them, and for this very reason, there still remained some sphere that had let in the chivalry or the virtue in the battlefield.

But as Ferrell pointed out, after the Napoleonic Wars, the aspect of the battlefield came to assume dramatic changes. According to *A Sociological Study on Wars LE DÉFI DE LA GUERRE (1740-1974)*—for which the two scholars at the French Research Institute of Wars analyzed 366 main armed conflicts that had occurred from 1740 to 1974—"the three major mutations" which occurred during this period brought forth the archetype of modern warfare, as follows:

1775: People and ideologies rushed into politics and warfare, causing the monarchism to begin to decline.

1914: People and industrial power rushed into warfare, distinctly causing both the aggravation of inflation rate of currency and the rise of the death rate of servicemen and civilians. This means the start of a relative decline of the European society.

1945: The atomic bombs exploded, while population explosion occurred. The traditional society began to subside, while the third world began to make their appearance into the international politics and industrial society.

It goes without saying that: the mutation in 1775 meant "the War of Independence" in America (to be followed by the years to lead to the French Revolution from1789 to 99), and that: "1914" meant the outbreak of World War I and "1945" meant the denouement of World War II. After "these three mutations," according to the authors of *A Sociological Study on Wars,* the traditional type of wars had evolved into a new type of wars. In that background, we should not overlook the fact that: the changes in capitalistic production or the industrial revolution had been going on. The industrial revolution was none other than the very base of the military revolution. Werner Sombart had pointed out this relationship in his work, *Capitalism and Wars:*

"If it had not been for war, capitalism would not have come into being. War accelerated the growth of capitalism. The modern nations have been brought into being solely by the military preparations." This also comes in contact with the aphorism by John Fuller: "The muskets brought about the infantry, and the infantry brought about democracy." Warfare—while keeping pace with the formation of nation-states, their industrial revolution and the globalization of capitalism—had tremendously strengthened the intensity of carnage till it sent the chivalry to extinction. *A Sociological Study on Wars* gives that process in numerals, as follows:

The French Revolution (1789-99) and the Napoleonic Wars (1792-1815)
The population involved in them was about one hundred million. The number of combatants from 1813 to 1815 was more than one million; those killed during the years from 1792 to 1815 were more than two millions.
The two World Wars in the 20th Century:
The population involved from 1914 to18 was more than one billion. The combatants were 11,000,000 (65,000,000 mobilized), and 8,500,000 were killed.
The population involved in war during the period from 1939 to 45 was about 2,000,000,000, including 16,000,000 combatants (92,000,000 mobilized ones), and 38,000,000 were killed (including a great many who were slaughtered).

As is shown by these numerals, an unexpected phenomenon in warfare is shown in the fact that: the number of deaths of those who had been involved in war (non-combatants) sharply increased, when compared with that of the combatants.

● From the Eras of Cannonades to the Centuries of Bombardments

Above all, the primary factors of "military revolution" brought about by engines and motors were remarkable. Engines brought about the propellers of the planes, the screws of the steel ships and the caterpillars of the tanks. These arms, whose power could be converted into "horsepower" in place of horses, did widen the battlefield, while mechanizing the battles, limitlessly enlarging the scale and the strength in performing the massacre—from the combatants in the combat area to the general public in unarmed areas.

In 1934, Charles De Gaulle as a colonel wrote in his *Memoir of the Second World War*, as follows:

> The skill of those who operate the military machines has become an important factor of the arms' capability. This was especially true in the new type of arms such as tanks, air planes and warships, which were brought into being by motors and changed our strategy completely.
>
> The motors quickly carry things necessary to wherever we want. The motors, when properly armed, display amazing power against fire and attack, and the rhythm of the battle comes to correspond to the rhythm of machines.

About this time (1933), Trotsky also said: "All the characteristics that tell one race from another have vanished now that all those internal-combustion engines are brought into being," and this same comment was quoted by Paul Virilio in an essay he wrote after "the 9.11,"—*The World Moves Towards Suicide**—putting emphasis on the great influence the engines had brought to warfare

Then, the impact which the industrial revolution and the appearance of the engine have brought to the warfare will be able to put in order, as follows:

The industrialization of war
The mass production of standardized goods and the close relationship between science and government → the military-industrial complex
The three-dimensional battlefield
The enlargement of operations from land into the air and into the sea → a three-dimensional war in the world war.
The massacre performed without awareness
Long-distance murder and invisible invasion to perform massacre →
The relationship between the battle front and the home front vanishes, while the relationship between the combatants and the noncombatants also vanishes

This is how what we call war, which used to be performed with a single gun to shoot a single person to death with a single bullet, enlarged itself to the sphere of activities of "wholly-armored tanks," "steel-gilled submarines" and "duralumin-winged aircraft"—all combined with "steel whips" called machine guns, rockets and missiles—the soldiers have come to engage in battles anywhere—on the earth, in the water or in the air—without even having a glimpse of those they are going to kill. Not men but machines have become masters in battle. Modris Eksteins wrote in his *Rites of Spring:*

> Now the chivalry has vanished forever. Like all the noble feelings possessed by human beings, it has given way to the new tempo and to the new rules of arms.

In *A Social History of Machine Gun,* John Ellis also pointed out the new era of war brought about by the revolution of motive power in firearms:

> The machine gun represented the very antithesis of this desperate faith in individual endeavor and courage. One had only to see the thing being demonstrated to realize that the force of such a deluge of fire, directed by just one man, could sweep away whole units with nonchalant ease. Neither the resolution of the opposing gunner nor of the troops in his sights would count for anything. The weapon itself, a mere machine, completely dominated the situation. As long as it did not jam or run out of ammunition the men themselves were helpless before it. Cavalry or infantry, officer or soldier, coward or hero, all could be bowled over like rats before a hosepipe.

Ōoka Shohei, a Japanese novelist, who wrote *A Record on the Battles on Leyte Island* also quoted in it a poem written by Wilfred Owen:

> What passing-bells for those who die as cattle?
> Only the monstrous anger of the guns
> Only the stuttering riffles' rapid rattle
> Can patter out their hasty orisons.

It is incontestable that the termination of human relationship comes from the lack of seeing each other, and what had shown this fact most of all was the

Mode de Volar

appearance of the aircraft and the evolution of warfare prompted by it. As soon as the Wright Brothers—Wilbur and Orville—succeeded in their first power flight in 1903, the era of "air power" arrived in no time, as was mentioned in Chapter 1. Artillerymen began to fly high—thus "the age of bombardment" moved on to "the century of aerial bombardment." Since then, the cities have been made to turn into "the aims to be looked down at" or "the roofless fortresses," and the urban residents have been turned into "objects to be looked down at" under what Michel Foucault called "panopticon." In other words, the people there have been turned into "the mere dots called human beings," as was regarded as such by Harry Lime in *The Third Man*.

● **"A Good Father" Pushes the Button for a Massacre**

Goya—about the same period when he created *Duelo a Garrotazos* (*The Two Men Exchanging Blows*)—produced *Modo de Volar* (*The Mode of Flight*), one of the block prints for his *Disparates* (*Fantasies*), by carving the five weird-looking men, each in an eagle-hat, flying across the night sky, while maneuvering the wings of a huge bat with their arms and legs. Those winged men flying across the night sky, maneuvering the glider-like wings, could also be taken as if suggesting that: the heaven has changed from the sphere of the angels into that of the devils. Looking at this work, Michel Foucault read in it the profound solitude Goya had been feeling in those days and wrote:

The *Disparates* are without landscape, without walls, without setting—and this is still a further difference from the *Caprichos;* there is not a star in the night sky of the great human bats we see in the *Mode of Flight.* The branch on which these witches jabber—out of what tree does it grow? Does it fly? Toward what sabbath, and what clearing? Nothing in all this deals with a world, neither this one nor any other.

—*Madness & Civilization*

If Goya, while creating this work, had seen through what the future war would be like, the scene below the wings of these huge bats did reveal itself in the 20th century—taking the forms of the burning hells of *Guernica* in the broad daylight and of *the Miseries* in Chongqing as were witnessed by Guo Moruo. Goya, who had firmly grasped what Napoleonic War was by depicting the scene of the execution on the hill on *May 3rd, 1808,* might have been feeling a premonition of the coming era in which "massacres come falling from the sky." In fact, it did not take even a century before such an era arrived.

Konrad Lorenz, a scholar on animal behavior, who was born in Wien in 1903 when the Wright brothers' plane flew high up in the sky of Kitty Hawk in North Carolina, wrote in one of his works *On Aggression:*

My childhood dream of flying is realized: I am floating weightlessly in an invisible medium, gliding without effort over sunlit fields.

Come to think of it, however, what terrible things are happening on the earth! We human beings must not put the gods to the test. We must never wish to see what the gods had thoughtfully hidden from us by covering it with the darkness at night and the fear we naturally feel toward darkness.

Konrad Lorenz, while commenting on the aggressiveness possessed by human beings, gives his opinion as to the relative indifference to the murder they are committing if only it was done from a sky they had sent themselves to:

The distance at which all shooting weapons take effect screens the killer against the stimulus situation which would otherwise activate his killing inhibitions. The deep, emotional layers of our personality simply do not register the fact that the crooking of the forefinger to release a shot tears the entrails of another man. .... The same principle applies, to an even greater degree, to the use of modern remote-control weapons. The man, who presses the releasing button is so completely screened against seeing, hearing, or otherwise emotionally realizing the consequences of his action, that he can commit it with impunity—even if he is burdened with the power of imagination. Only thus can it be explained that perfectly good-natured men, who would not even smack a naughty child, proved to be perfectly able to release rockets or to lay carpets of incendiary bombs on sleeping cities, thereby committing hundreds and thousands of children to a horrible death in the flames. The fact that it is good, normal men who did this, is as eerie as any fiendish atrocity of war!

—On Aggression

Thus the evolution of war was to cause the 20th century to be remembered as "the century for the air raids." What the poet Apollinaire once wrote in his poem—*The Victory*—has been actualized high in the air:

Victory means, above all,
Seeing things afar clearly;
Seeing everything
Near at hand,
Seeing everything
Possess a new name.

The formula of victory—"seeing everything possess a new name"—is none other than "the conception of strategic bombing." Guernica and Chongqing were the first cities sacrificed.

Following is a chronicle to show how the strategic bombings were brought into being to be developed decade after decade:

The 1910s: The tentative use of the air planes in World War I was made firstly in scouting & observing, then in air battles & aerial bombings. Pistol-shooting to each other in the air developed into air battles and then aerial bombings upon the city firstly by Zeppelin airship and then by bombing craft. Germany performed air raids on London and BK on

Paris.

The 1920s: The predictors made their appearance—J. Douhet, B. Mitchell and others brought forth their theories in which the air force was regarded as omnipotent.

The 1930s: "The terrors from the air" started: the air raid on Guernica in 1937; the series of air raids on Chongqing lasted from 1938 to 41.

The 1940s: The aerial battles in Europe lasted from 1939 to 45:

- The B.K.'s aerial strategy—"the bomber stream" by Churchill & Harris
- Germany's aerial strategy—The Nazi Air Force's retaliatory bombardments. The appearance of Vergeltungswaffe 1 & 2 (V1 & V2).
- The U.S.' aerial strategy—From "precision bombing" to "strategic bombing." The atomic attacks on Japan.

The 1940s: Japan's aerial strategy—The attack on Pearl Harbor (the union of sea power and air power). *Kamikaze* attack (the appearance of a manned missile loaded with bombs)

The 1950s: The Korean War and the U.S.' employment of napalm bombs.

The 1960s: The Vietnam War and the U.S. Army's "bombing on North Vietnam" and "defoliant attack"

The 1970s: The Soviet Union's invasion into Afghanistan and "the vertical envelopment" from the air toward the guerrillas.

The 1980s: The Iran-Iraq War saw the union of missiles and chemical weapons.

The 1990s: The Persian Gulf War—Kosovo Air Raids. "Damage-free" remote-controlled air raids upon a remote aim by means of precision-guided missiles (PGM).

This chronology of the air raids, having been carried over to the 21st century without any break, has not yet been over; the land and the people in Iraq have still—as of 2006—been kept trampled upon. "The 20th century of the prolonged wars" has not yet been over.

And in 2001, there occurred "the 9.11 Incident." Those huge bats painted by Goya did transmigrate to the new century—as was mentioned by Jean Baudrillard in *Power Inferno**:

This time, a *kamikaze* air corps, consisting of eighteen members—by making use of their high-performance technology which would make their suicide bombing several times more effective—has put the process of a global-scaled catastrophe in motion.

● The War has been Made Virtual and Non-Physical

From the Persian Gulf War to the Iraq War, the U.S. had introduced into the battlefield the RMA (the Revolution in Military Affairs) adopted by the Bush (Father & Son) Administrations. That was the communication-information technology incorporated into the bombs. In addition to the engines, "unmanned scout planes," "bombs equipped with eyesight" and "missiles with the artificial intelligence" were brought into being. This saved soldiers even entering the sky of the battlefield. Antonio Negri wrote in *MULTITUDE:*

> According to the ideology of the RMA, war no longer needs masses of soldiers who are massacred in the trenches. The humans on the battlefield, in the air, and at sea have become prostheses of the machines or, better, internal elements of the complex mechanical and electronic apparatus. ....
>
> There have been many indications that within the highest circles of military leadership the technologists have tended to have the upper hand in the debate with traditionalists and that the plan is going forward—from the first Gulf War to Kosovo, Afghanistan, and back to Iraq—for war gradually to be "decorporalized." Increasingly, U.S. leaders seem to believe that the vast superiority of its firepower, the sophistication of its technology, and the precision of its weapons allow the U.S. military to attack its enemies from a safe distance in a precise and definitive way, surgically removing them like so many cancerous tumors from the global social body, with minimal side effects. War thus becomes *virtual* from the technological point of view and *bodyless* from the military point of view.

This is what "the conception of strategic bombing" has finally arrived at— or what "a *bodiless* war" actually is. A battlefield with no boundary; a massacre performed without any physical action....

Be that as it may, a high-technology war and a virtual war would be none other than a unilateral assumption held by the U.S. strategists. However much the forms of battles may be affected by "the highly-developed military technology and the precision of arms," the war will not lose its true nature of ambiguity of the chameleon and the situation will remain unable to tell. As Karl Von Clausewitz (1780-1831), a Prussian general and military thinker, had already stipulated in his *Theory on War*, the true nature of war lies only in "likeliness to be sure" and "nothing in human activities makes more constant contact and general contact with fortuitous circumstance than war. Of all human activities, card games and war-making resemble each other most of all." Then he went on: "It goes without saying that: war has its own *grammar*. But war is not equipped with its own *logic*."

If so, is it not possible to say that: that weird work—*Modo de Volar* (*A Mode of Flight*) created by Goya in his declining year—did present itself in the sky of New York in September, 2001, as an incarnation of "the Conception of Strategic Bombing" that had been retained by the weak against the America's RMA (the Revolution in Military Affairs)? This also will be able to be regarded as a subspecies of "logics on war" in "the century of aerial bombing." Such a suicide bombing as might also be called a transmigration of Goya's prediction into the 21st century had already been attempted by the Japanese airmen as a *kamikaze attack*—a manned missile loaded with bombs—around the mid-20th century. It was by no means accidental, therefore, that the Japanese word, "*kamikaze* (*divine wind*)," was immediately called back after that incident.

According to George Friedman, "the 9.11 attack" was none other than an extension of "the conception of *kamikaze attack*":

> Al Qaeda looked at commercial aircraft in a totally novel way— not as prepackaged hostages but as enormous explosive devices. A large commercial jet, carrying fuel for long distances, is a flying bomb, guaranteed to explode on impact. Moreover, it can cause extraordinary secondary damage as the remaining fuel burns at extremely high temperatures until consumed.
>
> —*AMERICA'S SECRET WAR*

"The 9.11 attack" was a desperate resistance performed by those underprivileged ones who had been kept down and deprived of their place to stay at by the American globalism. Those who called themselves Al Qaeda were then driving *the* huge bat to perform their counterattack—and as long as this point is considered, this incident has assumed a certain universality, as Baudrillard said: "It was *they* who had performed *it*, but it was *we* who had wanted *it*." That was not a groundless attack upon the innocent America.

On the other hand, the Japanese would be required *not* to forget the fact that: *that* has told of "a recurrence of *the* history" which would fall upon the Japanese, too. Just as *"Kamikaze"* had been recalled by that terror from the sky, the site where the high-rise buildings used to be soaring was called "ground zero" ("hypocenter"). The Americans must have been made to recall what they had once done—according to their depth psychology. Here, too, we can see how "the conception of strategic bombings" has underlain our modern existence.

● "The 9.11 Incident"—Has Another War Broken Out?

On September 20, 2001, at "the site of the World Trade Center" at Manhattan, New York, the recovering of corpses was still going on, when President Bush gave a speech at Congress in an assertive tone of voice:

> On September 11th, enemies of freedom committed an act of war against our country. .... American have known surprise attacks, but never before on thousands of civilians. .... All of this was brought upon us in a single day, and night fell on a different world, a world where freedom itself is under attack. .... Every nation in every region now has a decision to make: Either you are with us or you are with the terrorists. ....

Since this speech was made, declaring the All-Out War Against Terrorism or Bush Doctrine that justified the endless battle against terrorism, it began to be told as a political signal that justifies an endless fighting against international terrorism.

This does not mean, however, "the 9.11 Incident" has completely changed what war used to be.

Even if we were to admit, according to George Friedman, that hijacking air craft to turn it into a manned missile was "the ultimate form of terrorism," it should be regarded as a mutation of war-making which was brought about in the 20th century, or "a sudden fall of fear from the sky" or "a mechanized massacre performed without any awareness".

Ironically, it was none other than the U.S. Government itself that had first warned "aerial terrorism" after World War Ⅱ was over. In 1947 and in 1948, a couple of reports were published from the U.S. President's Consultative Committees:

> *A Program for National Security: Report of the President's Advisory*
> *Committee on Universal Training: Washington 1947*
> *Survival in the Air Age: A Report by the President's Air Policy Committee:*
> *Washington 1948*

Following was part of the former report:

Such "stealing-in attacks," as we suffered at Pearl Harbor, has conspicuously increased its possibility, because the airplane increased its flying range and the nuclear weapons have strengthened their destructive power. (omission) The activities of the Fifth Line, in the program of the invaders, would increase their importance than when they were placed under the dictatorship of Hitler. The enemy, as a preparation for their attack, will try to turn over the people's trust placed upon the U.S.' Governmental Organization. They will also put their efforts in checking our defensive preparations by means of fractionalization and slowdown; they will also propagate defeatism so they may win our surrender by their first large-scaled attack.

While succeeding to this recognition, Chalmers Johnson had foretold the inevitable occurrence of "the 9.11 attack" in his works, *BLOWBACK: The Costs & Consequences of American Empire.*

In light of these experiences, in the late 1990s, I devoted myself to writing a book about American foreign policy, which I entitled *Blowback,* using the CIA's term for the unanticipated consequences of unacknowledged actions in other people's countries. My intention was to warn my fellow Americans about the conduct of our foreign policy over the previous half century, focusing particularly on the decade after the demise of the Soviet Union and on the evolving political situation in East Asia. The book appeared in the early spring of 2000. In it I argued that many aspects of what the American government had done abroad virtually invited retaliatory attacks from nations and peoples who had been victimized. .... In a sense, blowback is simply another way of saying that a nation reaps what it sows. ....

Given its wealth and power, the United States will be a prime recipient in the foreseeable future of all of the more expectable forms of blowback, particularly terrorist attacks against Americans in and out of the armed forces anywhere on earth, including the United States.

The author of this book—*The Conception of Strategic Bombing*—has once made the same kind of indication in a comment on the U.S.' missile attacks on Sudan and Afghan—in a cultural column of the evening edition of the *Asahi* (a newspaper in Japan) on August 26, 1998:

The U.S. .... has ventured into enlarging the conception of what war is.

They have brought into being such an automatic weapon as would hit the mark from the ocean more than 1,000km away. Thus they have achieved great results without exposing even a single soldier on its side to any danger. But such confidence and preponderance as they feel on the U.S. side also predict what will happen in the near future: the extinction of the relationship between the offenders and the casualties, or the carnage to be performed in an extreme stupor. There is no guarantee that such a sort of attack will not be given to America.

A German jurist, Carl Schmitt, who, in the 1960s, while analyzing the partisans' strategy during the Napoleonic Wars, had come to see through the mutual infiltration of combat skills between the intruders and the intruded, saying: "The power and significance of the non-regular can be stipulated conversely by the power and significance of the regular which have been considered questionable by the partisans." In *The Partisans' Theory*,[*] he wrote:

The partisans in the Spain-Guerrilla War in 1808 were the first to dare to perform an atypical fight against the first modern regular army. .... A plan of operations against the partisans often turned out to be a mere returning of what they had received. Thus that old familiar proposition that: one must fight as a partisan when fighting against partisans—often quoted as an order

Napoleon had given to General Lefebvre on September 12, 1813—was proved to be true.

Having reviewed this fact, Schmitt foretold, as follows:

After all, everything comes down to the working area called technical-industrial development. The more mechanized the partisans were, the more land they had to lose, and the more they came to rely on the technical-industrial means necessary for keeping their fighting. The modern partisans fight with automatic rifles, hand grenades and plastic bombs, and in due time, they will presumably come to fight with tactical nuclear weapons. Both the modern partisans themselves and those trying to subjugate them are keeping pace with the rapid progress of modern technology and science of that sort.

These comments will be applied to the tactical relevancy between the U.S. Armed Forces and Al Qaeda. Against the U.S. precision-guided missile, the terrorists' side, too, had made a counterattack by employing their own precision-guided missile. In the essence of partisans' struggle of attack and resistance, Al Qaeda's tactics has not been so much different from that of the Spanish peasants who employed their hoes and rakes in fighting against the regulars of Napoleon's Army.

● The New Stage of the Terrors from the Air

As he had declared, President Bush set "the new war" going. In twenty-one days since the start of the Iraq War on March 20, 2003, Baghdad fell; on the 26th day, the whole land of Iraq was seized; on May 1, "the end of the main plans of operations" was declared. As were the cases with "the Persian Gulf War" and "the attack on Afghanistan" prior to the Iraq War, a huge number of guided bombs—more than ten thousand "cluster bombs (double bombs)," "daisy-cutters (fuel air explosives)," "bunker-busters (precision-guided bombs through the earth)" and more than eight hundred "Tomahawk" cruise missiles—had been dropped or discharged.

What was more, a large amount of information that reported "the Shock and Awe" of the aerial bombardments was sent and spread by reporting live from the scene of the battle, thus bringing in the ambience that had never existed so far. By this U.S. Army's media strategy that had started at the opening of their attack, more than eight hundred war correspondents from abroad kept reporting their announcement as if from "the Imperial Headquarters," mentioning "the sharp needles of shock and awe," "the fruits of RMA (Revolution in Military Affairs)" and the like, admiring their having achieved the greatest results with the minimum sacrifices, like a sort of exhibition of "rewarding good & punishing evil," through television and colored photographs on the newspapers. These reports from the battlefield—along with such headlines as: "The War has Evolved into a Higher Form," "The Precision-Guided Munitions (PGM) that has changed what war used to be," "In Attacking, Quality comes before Quantity," and the like—had been so made as to give the general public such impression as if another Clausewitz had appeared in the sphere of the theory of war.

But true was that maxim: "When information floods, it will lead to mal-distribution and omission." Even before only several months passed after May 1, when President Bush declared "the Termination of the Main Battles," "the new tactics" in "the new war" began to reveal their weak points. After the flood of information subsided, the same media was revealing another fact—the continuity of the will to keep on fighting a resistance war on the side of those on the earth, which remained unconquerable (the number of the deaths and injuries of the U.S. soldiers in the occupied areas had kept increasing in a speed greater than that in their advancing period); the growing criticism both from the international society and from among the U.S. citizens themselves against the Bush Administration's "preemptive strike" and "a preventive war," (including the United Nations Secretary-General Annan's having pointed its having violated the law of nations), and the proliferation of the serious damages brought about by the cruelties of the modern ordnance (successive occurrences of citizens' sufferings from discarded unexploded shells or cluster bombs, and the spread of radioactive contamination among the citizens by depleted-uranium shells).... These pieces of information given after the facts had occurred exhaustively showed where the information had been overflowing, and where it had been lacking.

Summing up those situations, it was a generalization of massacres in which the relationship between "the killing and the killed" was being made more and more distant because of its mechanical and nonsensical manner of performing massacres, while what differentiated the effects of the Precision-Guided Munitions (PGM) from the traditional manner of air-raiding was: "the former is a computerized indiscriminate bombing" or "the precisely-guided arms are precise in accidental bombing."[*]

[*] According to NGO Iraq Body Count (http://www.iraqbodycount.net/), the death toll of the citizens of Iraq was 38,475 at the least estimate and 42,889 at the largest.

After all, the essential realities of "the Iraq War" that have revealed themselves from its history so far can be concluded that: it was not at all deviated from the stream of "that conception of aerial massacres"—which had started with "an aerial bombardment upon Guernica" by the Nazis' Air Force (1937), followed by the series of "Chongqing Air Raids" by the Japanese military (1939/40/41), which were to lead to "the atomic bombings upon Hiroshima and Nagasaki" (1945) by the U.S.' strategic bombers—and what the sharp needles of those guided missiles had done at Iraq was no more than "the digitalization of those indiscriminate bombings."

Then, the deceptiveness in all those empty headlines like "A New-Type of War" or "a War in which Quality Comes Before Quantity"—scattered by the media—will need to be corrected and opposed to by means of "the memories retained in the history." In order to achieve that task, too, the conception and the genealogy of the indiscriminate bombings performed during the 20th century must be confirmed. That was why Guernica and Chongqing must be recalled.

● **The Process from Guernica & Chongqing to Iraq**

About the time the Iraq War broke out, Christian Barros, a writer of Chile, made a statement as follows:

> In February this year (2003), when the U.S. Secretary of State, Powell, was expected to arrive at the Conference Hall to attend at the United Nations Security Council, the painting of Picaso's *Guernica* (a reproduction) that had been hanged there was covered with a cloth. If that was done from the consideration that they might not recall the misery of the war in the hall where the (Iraq) War was to be discussed, it would be a considerable

paradox.... The action of covering the painting of *Guernica* does symbolize what this age is. .... Between what happened to *Guernica* from then on and what happened to Iraq after it was defeated, there were too many things in common. Those who see *Guernica* before their eyes do awake their soul. No one can take it as something that happened long ago.

—*The World's Eye* in *The Mainichi* (a daily paper in Japan

for June 28, 2003)

Overthrowing the enemy nation's Administration by performing the aerial bombing. That was exactly what the U.S. Government and its Secretary of State, Powell, were about to perform upon Iraq. Then their having covered *Guernica*—just as the German military authorities at that time (1937) were trying hard to hide what they had done at Guernica—did symbolize the guilty feelings of those concerned with the U.S. Government at that time.

As is known very well, neither bombers nor bombs could be seen in *Guernica* by Picasso. All we see on the canvas are people and animals painted in an abstract manner; it hardly reveals whether or not the creator intended to denounce the tragedies caused by war. Still those who have known what happened in Guernica are able to see the white phosphorescence from the incendiary bombs, a horse madly romping about because of the splinters of bombs it had received, a woman crying over her dead child in her arms, and those new forms of carnages brought about with the appearance of the aircraft do come to rise from those figures depicted in black and gray and white in an abstract manner. To those U.S. leaders who had made up their mind to start a series of air raids upon Baghdad, those scenes would have naturally been the last things they would like to see then. In the ears of the Secretary of State Powel, too, the reverberation of that historical frenzy must have been lingering.

Then, it would *not* be useless to place the bombardments in Iraq in the historical axis of "the conception of massacre performed from the sky," which can be traced back to "the bombardment upon "Guernica" in April, 1937, and "the bombardments upon Chongqing" that started in 1938, and "the bombardments upon London, Hamburg, Dresden, Tokyo, and Hiroshima · Nagasaki during the Second World War, (1939-45), and even after the World War was over, the regional wars occurred one after another: Korea → Vietnam → the Persian Gulf → Kosovo. What could be found in "those new wars" was the fact that: the "bombardment" itself was strengthened by dint of the sensors and digitalization, but in their intention and technique, they have kept following the process of growing dehumanization until it reaches "an ultimate form of warfare."

What is more, this historical verification calls back another fact that: Japan has once put a new strategy into practice. In the history of city bombardments, Japan has occupied the place that never allows it to remain an outsider. The bombing upon Guernica was a single-day occurrence, while Japan's "strategic and political bombings" upon Chongqing lasted as long as more than three years.

In this book, I have examined what sort of war Japan made in China, with the priority placed on the wars after the emergence of the aircraft and the new attack technique brought about since then. And now, when I see what the world has been after "9.11," I find it incorrect to put them all in a simple category of "a new type of wars." All we can see *there* are the miseries of wars which have remained unchanged both in nature and in reality since those bombardments upon Chongqing. If I were forced to give any change brought about since then, all I could say would be that: the more rarified the relationship between the killing and the killed has become, the more light-heartedly the killers would be lured into warfare by simply pulling the trigger—thus the irresponsible sense of "happy triggering" has unusually been developed. What has taken the lead of such a war while escalating that tendency was mainly on the side of the U.S.—the interests of the military-industrial complex with petroleum and high-technology as their medium—and the mutual relationship of "terrorism and counter-terrorism," as is well revealed in the Israel's assassination strategy applied to Palestine, and it would not reach any solution even if all the responsibilities were to be pressed upon Saddam Hussein's regime and Osama Bin Laden.

There would be some counterarguments. In a sense, it is easy to find out some differences between "Chongqing and Iraq." In the technical method in bombardment, there lies a distinct difference between them—not to mention the difference between a vacuum tube and LSI (Large-Scale Integration). The difference between precision bombing and indiscriminate bombing; whether or not they are able to perform what is called a surgical operational bombing performed only after the process of the choice of aim and its pin-pointing. ....
These will immediately be pointed out.

But such still remains a superficial viewpoint. As mentioned before, even the Japanese military that performed the Chongqing bombardments had asserted that: theirs were precision bombing, saying "The bombers of the Japanese Navy Air Force aim precisely at the military facilities only, keeping the private houses safe, thus enabling the general public to be safely engaged in their occupation," or "The Japanese airmen are incomparably brave; as for their quality, it's the highest in the world." And today, the same kind of assertion was being made by the spokesmen of the U.S. Armed Forces in Iraq or in Afghanistan in denying their accidental bombings. But, even if we were to admit a remarkable accuracy in the U.S.' Precision-Guided Munitions (PGM), it does not necessarily mean that: their new technique had overcome their indiscriminate bombings. Such wordings as "accidental bombing" and "incidental damage"—even though often employed by the military party concerned—are none other than the replacement of "indiscriminate bombing."

Firstly, even if the word "precision bombing (pinpoint bombing)" was employed, since free-falling bombs had occupied most part (the rate in the Iraq War was unknown, but in the aerial bombardments in the Persian Gulf War, the 90 percent of them was of carpet bombing style), the high rate of accidental bombings brought about by technical error (reportedly more than 30 percent) will not deserve "pinpoint bombing." Probably theirs would have been a little more precise than the Japanese bombardments upon Chongqing.

Secondly, in the case of precisely-guided missiles, even if their technical precision might be secured, if such places as express highways, broadcasting stations, railways or oil factories were appointed to be "their military targets," it must not be overlooked that, at that very point, they had already been engaged in "an indiscriminate bombing in their intention." If the decision on the target was made arbitrarily, "unintentional bombing" performed with "incomparable precision" necessarily occurs. As a matter of fact, both in the Persian Gulf War and in the Air Raids on Kosovo, such an attack occurred frequently. In one of the air raids in Kosovo, the Chinese Embassy in Beograd was made the target of a cruise missile "because of an input mistake of the computer."

According to The *Sankei Shimbun* (a Japanese daily paper) dated May 9, 1999, "It was the seventh time that the NATO had made an accidental bombing, causing deaths and injuries, and the number of deaths had come to exceed two hundred. Even in the case of the cruise missiles equipped with the guidance system created by bringing high technology together, "it is around 90% that hits the aimed mark (according to the U.S.' Department of Defense)."

Thirdly, the wreckage of the cluster bombs and depleted uranium shells abandoned in the urban areas are also likely to cause "prolonged indiscriminate bombings" and to threaten the citizens' life even after the war is over. The rate of missing fire of cluster bombs reportedly being 5% to 30%, the indiscriminate casualties can be said to have regarded as something anticipated. On the other hand, in the case of radioactive particulates that come from depleted-uranium shells, they conceal themselves in the land or spread in the air and keep demonstrating their effectiveness even after the war is over. This also must be investigated as the prolonged damage brought about by what is called precision bombing. The residual effect of depleted-uranium shells can be regarded as "an indiscriminate bombing directed toward genes." Another problem is oil refining facilities. Even though they themselves are military facilities, if they were damaged, it would lead to their secondary damage by polluting the rivers and the seas. These reveal the fact that: the development of the bombing skill does not give any effect in limiting the damages given by war. Considering these points, the history of "the political and strategic bombings" opened up by the Japanese military has not yet been brought to an end.

● **The Bombardments upon Chongqing will Never be Canceled**
by the Statute of Limitations

Like "the 9.11 incident," "Hiroshima" and "Nagasaki" were something far removed from other human experiences in the history of aerial bombardments, but they were by no means isolated phenomena. Even if those atomic bombings were the climax of "the warfare of the 20th century," they still remain merely a couple of rings in the chains of "the miseries of war." Because of the exceptionally huge destructive power the atomic bombs had demonstrated, and because of their having attracted much attention from all over the world as the evidences of "the horror of the atomic age," many of the Japanese have half justified the situation in which they can do without thinking about the aerial terrors they have inflicted upon the Chinese people. But, Japan's having had "Hiroshima" and "Nagasaki" does not nullify what Japan had done *before* "Hiroshima and Nagasaki" were brought about.

The former mayor of Nagasaki City, Motojima Hitoshi, had once asked what

Nagasaki meant by following "the path that led *to Nagasaki*" and wrote it out in the message he sent to the *Asahi* (one of the leading papers in Japan) for January 1, 1995:—"When they heard of the atomic bombs having been dropped on the cities of Japan, those Asian peoples whose territories had been invaded by the Japanese said: "we have had divine salvation," and more than half of the world's population were pleased with *the* news. The tragedy of Japan has lain *there*." Thus the memories of what the Japanese military have done upon Chongqing are still alive to be called back whenever the opportunity arises.

On March 30, 2006, a petition—in which the then Japan's Minister of Justice, Matsuura Masatake, was made a defendant—was presented to the Civil Affairs Department of Tokyo District Court. The plaintiff group consisted of forty Chinese people represented by Wang Zixiong, resident at Shapingba, Chongqing in the People's Republic of China. Most of them were elderly persons over seventy. The purport of their request was: "To each plaintiff, a written apology shall be delivered and *that* piece of news shall be published in the official gazette of Japan," and "To each plaintiff, ¥ 10,000,000 shall be paid."

The petition, while describing the details of damages and casualties they have suffered, summarizes what has led them to present that petition, as follows:

- Japan was the first nation in the world to have performed its systematic and continuous air raids under the official name of "the strategic bombing."
- Since more than five years before Japan's sixty-six cities began to be exposed to the napalm bombardments, Japan had performed ceaseless air raids upon the citizens of Chongqing more than two hundred times, sending more than twenty thousand people to death or casualties, thus forcing us to suffer poignant experiences.
- The Japanese, without considering what sort of historical responsibilities they should bear, have spent many decades after the war, calling themselves victims of the air raids, simply impressing themselves with "only the ways *from* Tokyo air raid and *from* Hiroshima," while disregarding "*what* had led them *to* those sufferings."

Pointing out these facts, those people from Chongqing demanded "an apology and compensation from the Japanese Government, saying that: Japan must not forget the fact that: at the onset of "the aerial warfare," Japan committed "those series of bombardments upon Chongqing," and that: they must face "what sort of injuries they had inflicted upon the other nation before they themselves came to suffer casualties."

The following is among the passages in *The Reasons for Requesting the Japanese Government to Take the Responsibility for What They have Done:*

It goes without saying that: those series of great bombardments upon Chongqing have forced the inhabitants to suffer large-scaled and serious damages: many were injured; many had their family members killed, or lost their property or had their heart and mind injured, but *we* have managed to live on for more than sixty years. Most of those who suffered the series of large bombardments upon Chongqing—remaining unable to pick themselves up either economically or physically or mentally—have grown old or no more or about to die before long.

All of us, who have managed to survive those series of large-scaled air-raids upon Chongqing, heartily wish to have the Japanese Government and the people who have damaged our course of life realize the fact that: they have not yet fulfilled their responsibility to amend what they have done upon us. In other words, we should like the Japanese Government to fulfill their legal responsibility by "apologizing to us for what they have done, while compensating us for what they have done." These are all of those who have suffered from those fierce air raids upon Chongqing have sincerely wished.

It is unknown what sort of development the case will make.* But what is apparent is that: "the prolonged 20th century of war" has not yet been over, even though we are already in the 21st century. It must be re-examined what the 20th century meant in the war history. Those scenes in the photographs—the sudden falls of terrors from the sky, the charred bodies of the citizens having been burnt to death by incendiary bombs—as were seen in Tokyo, Dresden, Hiroshima·Nagasaki and so on—do show us what the new type of war meant. Indeed, the 20th century was "the century of the aerial bombardments."

It is apparent where such a new type of war came from. What happened at

Guernica in Spain in April, 1937, and the Japanese air force's indiscriminate bombings upon Chongqing as a provisional capital of China, which lasted as long as five years since 1938.—These did bring about a new type of *Desastres de la Guerre* (*Disasters of War*), or such barbarities as to infringe not only on the Law of War but also on the International Law of Humanity. Because they have not yet been brought to terms, and because it has still been reproduced—by way of Korean War, Vietnam War and Kosovo conflict—in Iran-Iraq War still going on, to the fear of the Iraq people, the 20th century has not yet been over as long as warfare is concerned. Considering these facts, Japan's having committed itself in "the bombardments upon Chongqing" on the first page of "the aerial warfare" has not yet been canceled by the statute of limitations.

*On February 25, 2015, the judgment was delivered. The Presiding Judge, Hitoshi Murata, did acknowledge the fact of their having suffered the bombardments inflicted by the Japanese military, but as for their demand of indemnity based on the international law and the State Redress Law, he turned it down, mentioning: "It is undue," and "unreasonable."

(The End)

THE ANNOTATIONS

Nisshin Sensō 日清戦争 (the Sino-Japanese War of 1894-1895). The war of 1894-1895 between Japan and China. It left a decisive mark on the capitalist expansion of both countries. Since the Kanghwa-do (in Japanese, Kōkatō) incident of 1875, Japan had made many inroads into Korea. But China contended that Korea was within the Chinese sphere of influence. This situation resulted in a scramble for power, not only in the political field but mainly in the economic field. The cotton-cloth market in Korea, which from about 1892 had been favoring Japan, began to favor China. This was a setback keenly felt by Japanese industrial circles, which had started upon larger-scale industrial production. The efforts of Li Hung-chang (in Japanese, Ri Kō-shō) to modernize China were partially successful, as Korean diplomatic circles as well as foreign countries recognized China's supremacy over Japan. It was Li's aim that Korea should follow the Chinese, not the Japanese, example. Subject to pressure, Japan wanted to protect her cotton industry. Antigovernment uprisings in Korea provided the occasion for the Japanese invasion. Taking advantage of the Tōgaku Party rebellion in 1894 (TŌGAKU-TŌ NO RAN), Japan sent an army to Korea. The Japanese forces clashed with Chinese troops also sent to Korea. The clash developed into a war. The Japanese forces were victorious in P'yongyang (in Japanese, Heijō), the Yellow Sea, Dairen, Port Arthur, and Weihaiwei (in Japanese, Ikaiei). China surrendered. A peace treaty was signed at Shimonoseki by the Japanese plenipotentiary, Itō Hirobumi, and the Chinese plenipotentiary, Li Hung-chang. China recognized Korea's independence, ceded the Liaotung Peninsula and Formosa to Japan, and paid an indemnity of 200 million taels or 38 million pounds (360 million yen). Russia, Germany, and France, pretending that Japanese possession of Liaotung menaced China's integrity, forced Japan to relinquish this territory. Being unable to combat this intervention, Japan complied. China's weakness had become obvious, and Western powers acquired leaseholds and military bases in China.

Nichi-Ro Sensō 日露戦争 (Russo-Japanese War, 1904-1905). The war with Russia during the Meiji era. Struggle for supremacy between the two powers led to the war. After the Sino-Japanese War (1894-1895), Russia persuaded France and Germany to join her in inducing Japan to return the Liaotung Peninsula to China. In return for this "favor" to China, Russia was granted a lease on Port Arthur (in Japanese, Ryojun) and Dairen, where she made strongholds for her southward expansion. She extended her influence as far as Korea. Japan, which had established a market in Korea, came into conflict with Russia. When the Russian plans were clear, Japan hurriedly concluded the Anglo-Japanese Alliance (1902). Then she attempted to settle the issues with Russia. However, Russia continued to reinforce her military potential and planned to invade Manchuria. This caused the war, the issue of which was in favor of Japan. The main battlefields were P'yongyang (in Japanese, Heijō), Liaoyang, Port Arthur, and Mukden. The sea battles took place in the Yellow Sea, Ulsan (in Japanese, Urusan) on the coast of Korea, and the Japan Sea. Before Russia intended to conclude hostilities, the revolutionary movement in Russia intensified. In late summer, 1905, through the good offices of the United States, and in compliance with the request of the American president Theodore Roosevelt, the plenipotentiary Komura Jutarō and the Russian prime minister Sergei Witte met in Portsmouth, New Hampshire, and concluded a peace treaty. Russia recognized Japan's supremacy in Korea, and Japan replaced Russia in Manchuria. Southern Sakhalin became an integral part of the Japanese empire. After the war, Japan's industry greatly expanded, and the exploitation of Korea and Manchuria established Japan's capitalistic economy on firm ground.

Manshū jihen 満州事変 (the Manchurian incident). An aggressive war during the Shōwa era. Following the world crisis of 1929, the great powers strengthened their bloc economy. The Japanese overseas market collapsed, and only China was left as the last potential market. At the same time China tried hard to recover her sovereign rights, and a conflict, due to the stiffening Japanese attitude toward Manchuria, was inevitable. The anti-Japanese movement grew in violence, and the Japanese militarists planned a settlement by force. On September 18, 1931, on the pretext that the Chinese had blown up the Manchurian railway at Liut'iaokou, the Japanese began military operations. The following year, the Shanghai incident (SHANGHAI JIHEN) took place. Japan occupied the whole of Manchuria and established it as the state of MANSHU-KOKU. Owing to economic antagonism between the United States and Great

Britain and Soviet Russia's being in the process of building up her economy, the Western powers confined themselves to launching a protest based on moral justice. The temporary success of the Manchurian incident worsened Japanese difficulties at home, for the war spirit was waning and internationally Japan stood alone. Furthermore, anti-Japanese feeling was at its peak. All this led to the strengthening of Japanese fascism and to the Sino-Japanese and Pacific wars.

Manshūkoku 満州国 (Manchoukuo). A so-called independent state created out of Manchuria by the Japanese militarists during the Shōwa era. When the Manchurian incident (MANSHŪ JIHEN) took place, Japanese army circles established under their own control an independent government for the northeastern provinces. In 1932, they summoned the provincial governors of these four provinces and declared the establishment of an independent state. They set up the last emperor of the Ch'ing dynasty, P'u-i (in Japanese, Fugi), as ruler of the so-called Manchurian empire. Japan had affixed her seal to the Manchuria-Japan protocol, recognizing the independence of Manchoukuo, but the general in command of the Kwantung army was also ambassador to Manchuria and controlled all matters. The entire administrative work was carried out by Japanese nationals, and independence existed only in name. It was decided that the Japanese army should be stationed permanently in Manchuria and that the country should become a war plant of the Japanese military clique. The main interests were the development of the Manchurian railway, the Central Bank of Manchuria, and Manchurian heavy industry. Furthermore, to help solve home problems, one million Japanese nationals were persuaded to emigrate to Manchuria. Japanese monopoly of rice, cotton, etc. resulted in the destitution of Chinese farmers. The Concordia Association, known as Kyōwa-kai (in Chinese, Hsieh-ho Hui), controlled the life of the people. All newspapers and information were controlled by the Association for Public Information (Kōhō Kyōkai). Manchoukuo was a product of the aggressive policy of the Japanese militarists. It ceased to exist with the surrender of Japan in 1945.

Shanghai jihen 上海事変 (the Shanghai incident). The incident in which Japanese troops clashed with Chinese troops in the vicinity of Shanghai. Since the Manchu incident, the anti-Japanese movement of the Chinese people had become more intense. Taking advantage of the assassination of a Japanese Buddhist priest in Shanghai, the Japanese government in 1931, in spite of its declared nonaggression policy, dispatched troops to Shanghai. Landing forces clashed with the Chinese Nineteenth Route Army. When the Japanese sent reinforcements, American-Japanese relations worsened. A cease-fire agreement was reached, but anti-Japanese sentiment among the Chinese people had reached its peak. The incident eventually led to the Sino-Japanese war.

go-ichigo jiken 五・一五事件 (the incident of May 15, 1932). Fascist terrorism of May 15, 1932. Ōkawa Shūmei, Tachibana Kōzaburō, Homma Ken'ichirō, and other ultranationalists, with the help of forty-two young military officers, planned a military reform. They attacked the privileged classes, the big concerns (ZAIBATSU), and the political parties. They also attacked the offices of the prime minister, the minister of home affairs, the metropolitan police, the Nippon Bank, the Mitsubishi Bank, and the headquarters of the SEIYŪ-KAI political association and assassinated Prime Minister Inukai Tsuyoshi (1855-1932). Trying to black out Tōkyō, some attacked the electric transformer station. This incident was preceded by the assassination in February of Inoue Junnosuke (1866-1932), who was finance minister in 1923, and the assassination in March of the businessman Dan Takuma (1858-1932) by ultranationalists. The rebellion, which aimed at strengthening fascism, resulted in the defeat of the political parties and the formation of a coalition government.

ni-niroku jiken 二・二六事件 (the incident of February 26, 1936). The army rebellion of February 26-29, 1936, in Tokyo. Young unit officers of Konoe's first division, leading a squad, occupied the prime minister's official residence and the War Office, assassinated ex-Finance Minister Takahashi Korekiyo (1854-1936), ex-Premier Saitō Makoto (1858-1936), who was lord keeper of the privy seal, and General Watanabe Jōtarō (1874-1936), who was inspector general of military education. They also seriously wounded Suzuki Kantarō (1867-1948), the grand chamberlain. The army executives tried to give an explanation but failed, and it was decided to quell the military revolt by military means. In response to appeals broadcast by radio, the rebels surrendered, and the riot was subdued. Fifteen officers and several civilian accomplices were executed. Like the revolt of May 15, 1932 (GO-ICHIGO JIKEN), it was an attempt to rebuild the nation by direct action, to reform society, and to actualize the so-called Shōwa restoration. The upper-class politicians and the political parties were already intimidated by militarist fascism. They were no longer able to prevent politics from becoming fascist and Japan from becoming still more militaristic. The incident marked the establishment of a despotic control system.

Rokōkyō 芦溝橋 (Lukouch'iao). Name of a place in China. On July 7, 1937, a clash occurred at Lukouch'iao, on the edge of Peking, between Chinese troops and Japanese soldiers. This minor incident was utilized by the Japanese army to rush reinforcements into Hopei Province. The incident led to the Sino-Japanese conflict.

From
A DICTIONARY OF JAPANESE HISTORY
by
Joseph M. Goedertier, C.I.C.M.

BIBLIOGRAPHY

In Search of History   Theodore White   Harper & Row Publishers   New York Hagers town, San Francisco, London（1978）

THE SECOND WORLD WAR   Winston Churchill   PIMLICO（2002）

On Aggression   KONRAD LORENZ   MJF Books（1966）

MULTITUDE   Michael Hardt & Antonio Negri   Penguin Books（2005）

THE SORROWS OF EMPIRE   Chalmers Johnson   Henry Holt and Company（2004）

AMERICA'S SECRET WAR   George Friedman   Abacus（2004）

Madness & Civilization   Michel Foucault   Vintage Books（1988）

HISTORY of THE SECOND WORLD WAR   B. H. Liddell Hart   PAN BOOKS（1970）

HISTORT of THE FIRST WORLD WAR   B. H. Liddell Hart   CASSELL & COMPANY（1930, 34）

B29, the Superfortress   Carl Berger   Purnell's Weapon Book, No.17   Macdonald（1970）

The Conduct of War: 1789-1961   J. F. C. Fuller   DA CAPO PRESS（1992）

The Third Man   Graham Greene   PENGUIN BOOKS（1999）

FEAR, WAR AND THE BOMB: MILITARY AND POLITICAL CONSEQUENCES OF ATOMIC ENERGY   *Compton Report* & *Finletter Report* included, Patrick Maynard Stuart Blackett   Whittlesey House・McGraw-Hill Book Company, Inc. New York and Toronto（1948）

BLOWBACK   Chalmers Johnson   Holt Paperbacks & Company, LLC（2001）

RITES of SPRING   Modris Eksteins   ANCHOR BOOKS DOUBLEDAY（1990）

THE AIR WAR IN EUROPE: 1940-1945   Ronald H. Bailey & the Editors of TIME-LIFE BOOKS（1981）

WW Ⅱ *Time-Life Books History of the Second World War*   By the Editors of *Time-Life Books*（1989）

Inside Asia - 1942 WAR EDITION   John Gunther   HARPER & BROTHERS NEW YORK AND LONDON（1942）

TEN YEARS IN JAPAN   *A Contemporary Record drawn from the Diaries and Private and Official Papers of* Joseph C. Grew   UNITED STATES AMBASSADOR TO JAPAN 1932-1942   CPSIA information can be obtained at www.ICGtesting.com, Printed in USA

REMINISCENCES   General Douglas MacArthur   A DA CAPO PAPERBACK（1964）

The Social History of the MACHINE GUN   John Ellis   The Johns Hopkins University Press
(1986)

THE WORLD ALMANAC OF WORLD WAR   II Edited by Brigadier Peter Young   World
Almanac /An Imprint of Pharos Books, New York (1992)

STRATEGY OF DECEPTION   Paul Virilio   Editions Galilee (1999)

WINGED DEFENSE   William Mitchell   Dover Publications, INC (2006)

WW II *Time-Life Books: History of the Second World War*   Prentice Hall Press (1989)

THE YANGTZE VALLEY AND BEYOND   Isabella Bird   Cambridge University Press (2010)

Daughter of Earth   Agnes Smedley   Dover Publishing, INC. (2011)

Destination Chungking   Han Suyin   Reprints from the Collection of the University of Michigan
Library (*An Atlantic Monthly Press Book, Little Brown & Company*, (1942)

A MANY-SPLENDOURED THING   Han Suyin   TRIAD GRAFTON BOOKS (1986)

Birdless Summer   Han Suyin   G. P. Putnam's Sons   New York (1968)

The Goebbels Diaries 1942-1943   Edited, Translated and with an introduction   By Louis P.
Lochner   Doubleday & Company, Inc. (1948)

President Bush Address the Nation   September 20, 2001   *Washington Post Archives*

EDGER SNOW's CHINA   Lois Wheeler Snow   Random House New York (1981)

The Turn of the Tide (1939-1943)   Arthur Bryant   Collins (1957)

China Memoirs   Owen Lattimore   University of Tokyo Press (1990)

Yangtze Patrol, The U.S. Navy in China   Kemp Tolley   Naval Institute Press (1944)

A DICTIONARY OF JAPANESE HISTORY   Joseph Goedertier, C.I.C.M. Research Fellow,
Orient Institute for Religious Research, Tokyo   WALKER / WEATHERHILL (1968)

1945 Year of Decisions, Memoirs by Harry S. Truman   A SIGNET BOOK Published by THE
NEW AMERICAN LIBRARY   Copyright 1955, by TIME, Inc. (1955)

FOREIGN RELATIONS, 1939, VOLUME III UNDECLARED WAR

Hiroshima   John Hersey   Alfred A. Knopf Inc. (1946)

Far Eastern Front   Edgar Snow   JARROLDS Publishers, LONDON (1934)

My Early Life   Winston S. Churchill (1874-1908)   Collins (1959)

Judgment at the Smithsonian: Edited & Introduced by Philip Nobile, Smithsonian script by the
curators at the National Air and Space Museum (Afterword by Barton J. Bernstein)   Marlowe
& Company, New York, (1955)

Survival in the air age, a report - United States. President's Air Policy Commission   Reprints from the collection of the University of Michigan Library   Washington January 1, 1948

Monsieur Verdoux   CHAPLIN Memorial Edition   *DVD* Roy Export SAS （2003）

The Battle for Asia   Edgar Snow   Random House （1941）

The Journals of David E. Lilienthal （1897-1981） The TVA YEARS （1939-1945）   Harper & Row Publishers   N.Y. EVANSTON & LONDON （1964）

What War Means: Japanese Terror in China H.J.Timperley, China Correspondent, Manchester Guardian, London, Victor Gollancz L.T.D. （1938）

The RAGGED, RUGGED WARRIORS   Martin Caidin E,P. Dutton & Company   E.P. Dutton & Company   21 Park Ave. South, NY （2003）

The Library of War History published by Japan's Defense Agency's Defense Research Institute （ Asagumo News Paper Company）

China Fights Back   Agnes Smedley   Left Book Club Edition （1938） Not for sale to the public

Battle Hymn of China   Agnes Smedley   London Victor Gollancz LTD （1944）

Red Star Over China   Edgar Snow   New York: Grove Press （1968）

Far Eastern Front   Edgar Snow   New York: H. Smith & R. Haas （1933）

An Introduction of the Author

Tetsuo Maeda（1938-　）

Tetsuo Maeda started his career as a news reporter at Nagasaki Broadcasting Station. Then he made himself a freelance reporter to investigate firstly what was happening at Bikini Atoll, secondly at Chongqing, thirdly at Japan's self-defense force and what has been happening under the Japan-U.S. security Treaty.

From 1995 to 2005, he was invited to teach as a professor of international relationship at Tōkyō International University.

*　　*　　*

This book was brought into being step by step: Firstly what the author had collected appeared as a serial in *Asahi Journal* from the Asahi Newspaper Company. The first edition of this book appeared from the same company in August, 1988. The paperback edition was published in 1997 from Shakai-Shisō-sha Company. In 2006, Gaifu-sha Company completed the original version of this book by collecting all the studies, investigations and informations available so far.

To the Readers of *The Conception of Strategic Bombing*

From the Author, Tetsuo Maeda

Seventy years have passed since the end of the Second World War (1945). The memories of the War have naturally been called back to be talked about or discussed all over the world. The air raids upon the urban areas are also brought back to our mind. Memorial events are being held at many places in the various parts of the world — including London, Berlin, Dresden, Tokyo, Hiroshima, and so on.

Now in that very year, *The Conception of Strategic Bombings: Guernica, Chongqing & Hiroshima* — an English version of 戦略爆撃の思想 — has been published to reach the new readers all over the world, to the great relief of the author and all those concerned both in China and in Japan.

The author, born in 1938, naturally retains no memory of those indiscriminate bombings the Japanese military started in the very same year upon Chongqing or the then interim capital of China. Nevertheless, I feel as if those strange sounds — "*Jū-kei-baku-geki* (the bombardments on Chongqing)" — had already been made familiar to me even in my infancy. Probably, those scraps of sounds in the conversations being exchanged among the grownups around me might have happened to pop into my ears to remain stuck at the depth of my brain.

In later years when I came to study *the* war history, those faint sounds that had been left in my ears began to bring about a great resonance to my brain. By and by, I began to realize that: a grave turning point in *the* war history had started *then* and *there*, and still, the Japanese simply remained totally ignorant of what they had done during what they called "China Incident," — thus depriving themselves of any opportunities to learn even fundamental facts about *it* or to make any investigation into what they had done, to say nothing of offering the casualties any sincere repentance for the crimes they had committed *then* and *there*, to my great compunction as a Japanese researcher into *that* warfare. About forty years have passed since then.

In the meantime, I visited Chongqing five times to meet those who had suffered *the* air raids and those who had been investigating the matter. I walked around the historical remains of the air raids and the memorial places of resistance to Japan in "the mountain castle city of Chongqing." Even though I was amazed at the great development the city had been making every time I visited there, I could not help feeling — when listening to what had remained in the piles of the memories kept buried beneath that great earth of *hongan (scarlet rock)* as the very base of those high-rising modern buildings and the high-spirited activities of the local people — as if I could hear the distant voices of those who had to die a lonely death, even if they had wished to appeal anything they had kept in their mind.

On the other hand, I kept myself busy at home, too, making frequent visits to the Defense Agency's Research Library to read through the huge volumes of *The Battle Records (The General Version & The Detailed Version)*, trying to obtain a wide-scopic viewpoint to grasp how the murderous intent from the sky and the resistant spirit on the earth came to meet. In other words, I had intended to find out the true nature of modern warfare in which the offenders in the sky and the casualties on the earth remain aloof or lacking in any relationship with each other because of their total inability to *see* each other. It can be called "a form of slaughter peculiar to the war in the industrial period" or "*the Massacre in Nanjing*, deprived of its physical nature."

After having had all these experiences, if I am asked what it was that had characterized the warfare in the 20th century, I shall give an immediate answer without any hesitation: "The aerial bombardments." The airplanes were the products of the 20th century, and their working altitude was so high that it deprived both attackers and defenders of their sense of (physical) reality in the massacre. Undoubtedly, on the first page of the history of the aerial massacres, what the Japanese military had inflicted upon the citizens of Chongqing would be mentioned and regarded as the first case to have taken the initiative in adopting such a new method of massacre in warfare. In fact, it was *then* and *there* that "the city was looked down at" and "the people were helplessly exposed to the danger" for the first time in the history of wars. And that pattern of the air raiding that started *there* still remains existent somewhere on the earth even to this day in the 21st century. The global significance of the bombardments upon Chongqing, therefore, lies in this point, I believe.

This, therefore, means that we are still living in "the prolonged 20th century," instead of having grown out of it. I think the readers of this book will also agree with me, if only you picture in your mind those bloody and firy bird's-eye views of the Korean War, the Vietnam War, the Persian Gulf War, the Iraq War.... What I had intended to do in writing this book was: to dig out what the air-raidings upon Chongqing as "the first victims" of the modern warfare in the 20th century were really like, to record them, to inspect their historical significance and the whereabouts of their responsibility so that I may throw them back to the present situation we live in. Then it goes without saying that Japan will be blamed as "the very nation to have thrown *the first stone*." Japan's crime will lie not only in what it has once done but also in the ignorance and apathy it has kept assuming even to this day.

More than seventy years have passed since *then*, and those who have remembered what was happening *then* and *there* are growing smaller in number. And still, I think all those things happening in Chongqing *then* must be kept remembered and denounced generation after generation for the reasons as follows:

1) The intention to attack the city itself was cruel and inhuman.
2) The massacres were performed mechanically and apathetically, both of "the killers and the killed" having been deprived of any possibility to *see* each other.
3) The new technology brought about in the 20th century has enabled us to commit "the terrorism from the sky."

These are the apparent labels to distinguish the wars in the 20th century from all the wars in the previous centuries. The aerial attack brought about "a great leap" in the history of making wars — no less than the appearance of the bow and arrows or the invention of the rifle had done. It is impossible for us to know how it was like when a bow and arrow or a rifle made the first appearance in the battlefield. As for the aerial bombardment, however, we are able to follow all the processes of its development minutely, including "the mutations it has brought about in the history of wars," as I have done in writing this book, beginning with what happened in Chongqing as its starting point. And still, this method of war-making, despite of its incomparably cruel nature, has not yet been treated in history as properly as it should, even though it has repeatedly been employed in those regional conflicts after World War II, thus demanding "the actualization and generalization of the bombardments upon Chongqing."

Let me emphasize again: the bombardments upon Chongqing have not yet been shut up in the closed past. That conception has been turned into the model of "the new type of war." At the final stage when the Sino-Japanese War was turned into World War Ⅱ, "the Conception of Strategic Bombing" was taken over by the U.S.A. to be developed and escalated into the bombardments upon many cities in Japan until it reached its climax of the atomic bombings upon Hiroshima and Nagasaki. This was how Chongqing and Hiroshima·Nagasaki got connected with each other by the same-rooted conception of strategic bombing — even though separate in timing: the former occurred *before* the outbreak of the Pacific War, the latter *toward* the end of it.

Certainly, the latter turned out to have brought about "a boomerang effect of punishment" to the militarist Japan, but this did not mean the end of "the new-type of war." In the regional conflicts that followed World War Ⅱ, the same sort of nightmares as had once been experienced by the citizens of Chongqing did come round to fall upon the citizens of the Third World. This is something we must not forget. The bombardments upon the urban areas have turned into a new type of cancer cells in war-making, and spread far and wide all over the world. Thus "the lesson offered by the example of Chongqing" still remains to be shared by us all. Even though the reality of the U.S. bombardments is hidden under such a false name as "a precision-guided bombardment," the actual scenes one may see with one's own eyes or through mass media never fail to reveal the fact that: Kosovo, Baghdad, and Kabul are now suffering the same kind of tragedies as Chongqing suffered in "5.3 & 5.4." or in "the tragic incident in the air-raid tunnel."

Thus following the flow of history, while facing the present reality, we shall have to check "the history of the terrorism from the sky," which had started in Chongqing to reach the climax at Hiroshima. Without the knowledge of what occurred in Chongqing, we shall never be able to grasp "what Hiroshima·Nagasaki meant" nor be qualified to inquire into the criminal nature of "the urban bombardments" being performed by the U.S. Air Force in such a light-hearted manner as if being engaged in a daily chore. What has kept me concerned in "the bombardments upon Chongqing" by the Japanese military has come from such awareness of the matter as mentioned above.

As I have offered detailed explanations in this book, Japan's bombardments upon Chongqing were performed with the intention to win the war by discouraging the people's intention to go on fighting, thus making the city itself a target, by employing the air force only, and mainly by the Navy Air Corps.

According to *The History on Chongqing's Resistance To Japan*, published in 1985, 11,885 residents were brought to death by the 218 air raids performed during the two years and a half. (According to the latest research conducted at Xinan University by Professors Pan Xun and Peng Xinghua — the authors of *The Losses We Suffered by the Great Bombardments upon Chongqing during the War Against Japan: Along with the Problems Left Behind* — the number of the deaths was 14,652.) The victory Japan had intended to win was *not* by annihilating the enemy troops at the battlefield *but* by "crushing the enemy nation's intention to go on fighting." Such a kind of attack had been attempted in the year before (in April, 1937) at Guernica in Spain by Nazi's Air Force, but it was a single-day attack that caused 1,654 deaths, while what the citizens of Chongqing suffered was incomparably greater in degree and longer in period.

Nevertheless, what actually occurred in Chongqing still remains almost unknown.

Why ?

Firstly because "the International Military Tribunal held in Tokyo" did judge such wartime crimes as "barbaric slaughters inflicted upon the locals in Nanjing, Guangdong, Haikou, Changsha, Liuzhou, Guilin and so on," and they were all indicted. But, as for "the bombardments upon Chongqing," they were excluded (obviously intentionally) from the causes of the legal actions. The U.S., having intended to hide and justify the urban bombardments they had inflicted upon Japanese cities, averted their eyes from Japan's bombardments upon Chongqing, thus acquitting Japan of the crimes it had committed in Chongqing. The same thing occurred at the International Military Tribunal at Nuremberg. That was, the air raids upon London by the Nazi Germany were not questioned so that the inhuman air raids upon Berlin and Dresden might not be offered as the counterevidences. These also prevented the Japanese from facing the fact honestly, as they should. Here lies one of the roots of the sin of ignorance.

Secondly, what had started at Guernica and Chongqing were to lead to the air-raid on Tokyo and finally to the atomic bombings upon Hiroshima and Nagasaki, thus revealing the ultimate form of air-raiding. Since the impact of the atomic bombings was such that the Japanese, instead of grasping the process from Chongqing to Hiroshima·Nagasaki as something that had occurred according to the law of cause and effect, took it as a mutation or something first and last of its kind in the course of human history. The mayor of Nagasaki, Motojima Hitoshi, pointed out in the *Asahi*, one of the leading newspapers in Japan, dated January 1st, 1995: "When the atomic bombings on the cities of Japan were reported, the Asian peoples, who had been suffering the invasion of the militarist Japan, were pleased with *it*, calling *it* a divine salvation, while more than half of the world population were pleased with *it*, too. *There*, in that point, another tragedy Japan must face was lying." Considering the fact that they were the first to have suffered the atomic bombardment, it would be natural for them to have taken it as a mutation. But that was to cause the Japanese to remain lacking in the consciousness of their having committed a variety of atrocities in China. This also shows how ignorance is likely to lead to a wrong recognition of things.

Because of such an intentional and unconscious discontinuation of relationship between the offenders and the victims, the tragedy Chongqing had suffered became shut up and hidden behind "the thick fog of history" for many years to come. Upon the extension of such historical facts, there have come such frequent bombardments upon cities as are being performed by the U.S..

Another new situation — the 9.11 incident in 2001 — must also be recognized as something that has risen from the same conception as has once supported the bombardments upon Chongqing. The indiscriminate bombings, which used to be adopted only by the powerful, have now become something to be employed by anyone, anywhere, anytime — offering even another mutation "to perform an international terrorism," and that, "by the union of terrorism and nuclear energy." This is the third problem we are facing now.

I believe: these detailed facts I have offered in this book will help you learn the true nature of the modern world we live in. I hope all these facts I have presented here will work as the stepping stones for Japan to approach the better relationship with China as well as the world peace we must achieve in the future.

Last but not least, I offer my heart-felt thanks to Akiko Takemoto, who had kindly offered herself as the translator of this book.

June 23, 2015

Tetsuo Maeda

前 田 哲 男

*　*　*

The translator, Akiko Takemoto（1937-　）, started her career in 1959 as a teacher of English at a senior high school in Japan. In 1967, she attended the annual assembly of all Japan English Teachers' Association, held in Tokyo. It was then and there that the English poet, James Kirkup（1918-2009）, gave an enchanting recital of poetry-reading as the guest speaker at the grand hall known as "the Ōtsuma Auditorium." This led her to keep writing to him for more than forty years to come until he passed away.

About a few years before his decease in Andorra, those hundreds of letters and cards we had exchanged so far happened to come to the knowledge of THE BEINECKE RARE BOOK AND MANUSCRIPT LIBRARY of YALE UNIVERSITY LIBRARY in New Haven, Connecticut, U.S.A., and we were politely invited to send them all the letters and cards we had exchanged so far. For a moment, I felt rather reluctant to part with all those papers that seemed immensely precious to me. But now that he is no more, and I myself am growing older, I feel quite relieved by the fact that: all those papers are now safely resting at the right place for them all.

During World War Ⅱ, the poet, James Kirkup — a lifelong pacifist — chose to be sent to a labour camp as a conscientious objector. After the War was over, he usually stayed away from home, as if he had determined to enjoy the freedom in the true sense of the word.

Last but not least, I must say that: we, the Japanese people themselves, were very fortunate to have had this book, 戦略爆撃の思想 (*The Conception of Strategic Bombing*), because it does awaken us to look back and learn the true nature of the crimes we have once committed in China, as if we had totally forgotten the fact how much we had been indebted to the Chinese people for almost all kinds of civilization and culture we have kept enjoying so far throughout our history — as I realized, while being engaged in another work of my translation: *KUKAI, THE UNIVERSAL*, authored by Ryōtaro Shiba, (1923-1996), edited by James Kirkup (mentioned above) — first published in 2001.

June 26, 2015

Akiko Takemoto